Frommer's

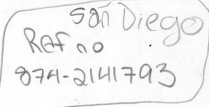
W9-CHS-574

San Francisco

2005

by Erika Lenkert

(handwritten) Ref no San Diego 874-2141793

(handwritten) Ref no 1823-2141822

Here's what the critics say about Frommer's:

"Amazingly easy to use. Very portable, very complete."

—*Booklist*

"Detailed, accurate, and easy-to-read information for all price ranges."
—*Glamour Magazine*

"Hotel information is close to encyclopedic."

—*Des Moines Sunday Register*

"Frommer's Guides have a way of giving you a real feel for a place."
—*Knight Ridder Newspapers*

WILEY

Wiley Publishing, Inc.

About the Author

A native San Franciscan, **Erika Lenkert** resides in Napa Valley when she's not traipsing through San Francisco and across the globe in search of adventure and great food. She frequently writes *InStyle* magazine's entertaining guide and has contributed to *Travel + Leisure, Food & Wine, Bride's, Wine Country Living, San Francisco Magazine, Los Angeles Magazine,* and *Time Out*. Her latest achievement, an entertaining and cooking book called *The Last-Minute Party Girl: Fashionable, Fearless, Foolishly Simple Entertaining,* mixes fun, humor, and San Francisco dining experiences and recipes into one tasty and useful guide to living large, Bay Area style.

Published by:

Wiley Publishing, Inc.

111 River St.
Hoboken, NJ 07030-5774

ISBN 0-7645-7185-0

Editor: Kendra L. Falkenstein
Production Editor: M. Faunette Johnston
Cartographer: Elizabeth Puhl
Photo Editor: Richard Fox
Production by Wiley Indianapolis Composition Services

Front cover photo: Man jogging near Golden Gate Bridge
Back cover photo: Roast chicken and duck display in the window of a Chinatown barbeque restaurant

For information on our other products and services or to obtain technical support, please contact our Customer Care Department within the U.S. at 800/762-2974, outside the U.S. at 317/572-3993 or fax 317/572-4002.

Wiley also publishes its books in a variety of electronic formats. Some content that appears in print may not be available in electronic formats.

Manufactured in the United States of America

5 4 3 2 1

Contents

List of Maps   vi

What's New in San Francisco   1

1 The Best of San Francisco   3

1 Frommer's Favorite San Francisco
  Experiences 3
2 Best Hotel Bets 5

Politics of the City Today 6
3 Best Dining Bets 9

2 Planning Your Trip to San Francisco   11

1 Visitor Information 11
2 Money 11
3 When to Go 12
  *Destination San Francisco:
  Red Alert Checklist* 13
  *San Francisco Calendar
  of Events* 14
4 Travel Insurance 18
5 Health & Safety 19
6 Specialized Travel Resources 20

7 Planning Your Trip Online 23
  *Frommers.com: The Complete
  Travel Resource* 24
  Online Traveler's Toolbox 25
8 Getting There 26
  Flying with Film & Video 30
9 Packages for the Independent
  Traveler 31
10 Recommended Books 32

3 For International Visitors   34

1 Preparing for Your Trip 34
2 Getting to the U.S. 40
3 Getting Around the U.S. 41

*Fast Facts: For the International
Traveler* 42

4 Getting to Know San Francisco   48

1 Orientation 48
  Neighborhoods in Brief 49

2 Getting Around 54
  Fast Facts: San Francisco 61

5 Where to Stay   64

1 Union Square 65
2 Nob Hill 83
  *Free Parking in the City
  by the Bay* 87
3 SoMa .87
  *The Best Family-Friendly
  Hotels* 93

4 The Financial District 94
  Sleeping Seaside 94
5 North Beach/Fisherman's
  Wharf .95
6 The Marina/Pacific Heights/
  Cow Hollow 98
7 Japantown & Environs 100

8 Civic Center 102

9 The Castro 103

10 Haight-Ashbury 104

11 Near San Francisco
International Airport 105

6 Where to Dine   106

1 Restaurants by Cuisine 107

2 Union Square 111

3 Financial District 117

    *The Sun on Your Face at
Belden Place* 119

4 SoMa 121

5 Nob Hill/Russian Hill 127

6 Chinatown 129

    *The Best of San Francisco's
Family-Friendly Restaurants* . . .130

7 North Beach/Telegraph Hill 132

8 Fisherman's Wharf 137

9 The Marina/Pacific Heights/
Cow Hollow 140

10 Civic Center 146

    Hidden Treasures 148

11 Mission District 149

12 The Castro 151

13 Haight-Ashbury 152

14 Richmond/Sunset Districts 154

7 Exploring San Francisco   157

1 Famous San Francisco Sights . . .157

    *Funky Favorites at
Fisherman's Wharf* 163

2 Museums 165

3 Neighborhoods
Worth a Visit 171

4 Golden Gate Park 176

5 The Presidio & Golden Gate
National Recreation Area 179

6 Religious Buildings Worth
Checking Out 182

7 Architectural Highlights 183

    Especially for Kids 186

8 Self-Guided &
Organized Tours 186

9 Getting Outside 189

10 Spectator Sports 193

8 City Strolls   195

    *Walking Tour 1: Chinatown:
History, Culture, Dim Sum &
Then Some* 195

    *Walking Tour 2: Getting to
Know North Beach* 202

9 Shopping   208

1 The Shopping Scene 208

2 Shopping A to Z 209

10 San Francisco After Dark   224

1 The Performing Arts 225

2 Comedy & Cabaret 229

3 The Club & Music Scene 230

4 The Bar Scene 235

    *Midnight (or Midday)
Mochas* 239

5 Gay & Lesbian Bars & Clubs . . .240

6 Film .242

11 Side Trips from San Francisco   243

1 Berkeley 243
  *People's Park/
  People's Power* 246
2 Oakland 250
3 Angel Island & Tiburon 256
4 Sausalito 260
5 Muir Woods &
  Mount Tamalpais 263
6 Point Reyes National
  Seashore 264
  Johnson's Oyster Farm 266

12 The Wine Country   269

1 Napa Valley 269
  *The Ins & Outs of
  Shipping Wine Home* 280
  Enjoying Art & Nature 283
  *Where to Stock Up for
  a Gourmet Picnic* 298
2 Sonoma Valley 303
  *Touring the Sonoma Valley
  by Bike* 306
  The Super Spa 312

Appendix: San Francisco in Depth   320

  Dateline 320

Index   330

General Index 330
Accommodations Index 337
Restaurant Index 339

List of Maps

San Francisco Neighborhoods   50

San Francisco Mass Transit   56

Accommodations near
Union Square & Nob Hill   67

Accommodations Around Town   88

Dining in Union Square &
the Financial District   113

Dining Around Town   122

Dining near Chinatown &
North Beach   131

Major San Francisco
Attractions   158

Fisherman's Wharf & Vicinity   161

Yerba Buena Gardens &
Environs   167

Haight-Ashbury & the Castro   173

Golden Gate Park   177

Golden Gate National
Recreation Area   180

The Civic Center   185

Walking Tour 1: Chinatown   197

Walking Tour 2: North Beach   203

San Francisco Shopping   210

San Francisco After Dark   226

The Bay Area   245

Berkeley   247

Oakland   252

Marin County   257

The Wine Country   271

An Invitation to the Reader

In researching this book, we discovered many wonderful places—hotels, restaurants, shops, and more. We're sure you'll find others. Please tell us about them, so we can share the information with your fellow travelers in upcoming editions. If you were disappointed with a recommendation, we'd love to know that, too. Please write to:

Frommer's San Francisco 2005
Wiley Publishing, Inc. • 111 River St. • Hoboken, NJ 07030-5774

An Additional Note

Please be advised that travel information is subject to change at any time—and this is especially true of prices. We therefore suggest that you write or call ahead for confirmation when making your travel plans. The authors, editors, and publisher cannot be held responsible for the experiences of readers while traveling. Your safety is important to us, however, so we encourage you to stay alert and be aware of your surroundings. Keep a close eye on cameras, purses, and wallets, all favorite targets of thieves and pickpockets.

Acknowledgments

Huge thanks to expert researcher Michele Addey, who tirelessly helped ensure the most up-to-date accuracy of this book and also happens to be an excellent friend.

Other Great Guides for Your Trip:

Frommer's Irreverent Guide to San Francisco
Frommer's Memorable Walks in San Francisco
Frommer's Portable Wine Country
Frommer's Portable San Francisco
The Unofficial Guide to San Francisco
Frommer's San Francisco from $70 a Day
Frommer's San Francisco with Kids
Frommer's California
Frommer's California from $70 a Day
The Unofficial Guide to California with Kids
San Francisco For Dummies
California For Dummies

Frommer's Star Ratings, Icons & Abbreviations

Every hotel, restaurant, and attraction listing in this guide has been ranked for quality, value, service, amenities, and special features using a **star-rating system.** In country, state, and regional guides, we also rate towns and regions to help you narrow down your choices and budget your time accordingly. Hotels and restaurants are rated on a scale of zero (recommended) to three stars (exceptional). Attractions, shopping, nightlife, towns, and regions are rated according to the following scale: zero stars (recommended), one star (highly recommended), two stars (very highly recommended), and three stars (must-see).

In addition to the star-rating system, we also use **seven feature icons** that point you to the great deals, in-the-know advice, and unique experiences that separate travelers from tourists. Throughout the book, look for:

Finds	Special finds—those places only insiders know about
Fun Fact	Fun facts—details that make travelers more informed and their trips more fun
Kids	Best bets for kids, and advice for the whole family
Moments	Special moments—those experiences that memories are made of
Overrated	Places or experiences not worth your time or money
Tips	Insider tips—great ways to save time and money
Value	Great values—where to get the best deals

The following **abbreviations** are used for credit cards:

AE	American Express	DISC	Discover	V	Visa
DC	Diners Club	MC	MasterCard		

Frommers.com

Now that you have the guidebook to a great trip, visit our website at **www.frommers.com** for travel information on more than 3,000 destinations. With features updated regularly, we give you instant access to the most current trip-planning information available. At Frommers.com, you'll also find the best prices on airfares, accommodations, and car rentals—and you can even book travel online through our travel booking partners. At Frommers.com, you'll also find the following:

- Online updates to our most popular guidebooks
- Vacation sweepstakes and contest giveaways
- Newsletter highlighting the hottest travel trends
- Online travel message boards with featured travel discussions

What's New in San Francisco

Much is ado in the City by the Bay—especially in the new restaurant department. And, surprisingly, many hotels listed in this guide dropped their published rates a bit, giving you a few extra bucks to throw toward that fancy dinner. Yes, the city's on an upswing, and evidence is listed below.

WHERE TO STAY Hotel rates in San Francisco are still substantially discounted from their late '90s highs. Shop the Internet or call hotels directly and inquire about their best bargains or promotions.

Many hotels renovated rooms over the past year, which means if you book a stay at any of the following hotels, you're guaranteed a brand-spanking new crash pad. The **Pan Pacific San Francisco** hotel underwent room remodeling in 2004, replacing the already dignified digs with more modern flare (think Herman Miller chairs and white on white). **The Cartwright Hotel, Hotel Beresford, The Monticello Inn,** and **Cow Hollow Motor Inn & Suites** also gussied up rooms with new paint and textiles. Along with a face-lift on each room, the contemporary Italian-style **Villa Florence** added luxury amenities such as flatscreen TVs and DVD and CD players. The **San Francisco Marriott** forked over $34 million for complete room renovations, including new paint, textiles, and furnishings.

New on the scene is the Kimpton Group's new reason to shack up in Fisherman's Wharf: Its nautically influenced **Argonaut Hotel** boasts flatscreen TVs and DVD and CD players.

WHERE TO DINE San Francisco's restaurants are booming again—and there are plenty of new must-visits to consider adding to your itinerary. For fancy affairs, **Michael Mina,** in the Westin St. Francis, 335 Powell St. (© 415/397-7000), opened in August of 2004, promises a decadent contemporary California menu and swank surroundings. **Town Hall,** run by the brother chefs Mitchell and Steven Rosenthal and smooth frontman Doug Washington, is one of the hottest new spots to gather and nosh on large portions of American cuisine. Comfy and tightly packed **Tablespoon** ladles out tasty "New American" cuisine on a bustling section of Russian Hill. With only 15 tables, tiny **Quince** restaurant is having a hard time accommodating the throngs of diners who have rightfully heard that the house-made pasta served here is the best in town. The hottest thing going in the Marina is **A16,** which serves delicious and affordable Neapolitan cuisine and has great boutique Italian wine selections in smart surroundings.

Ever-popular Vietnamese restaurant **The Slanted Door** relocated its clay pot dishes and green papaya salad to a new custom-built home at the bayfront Ferry Building Marketplace. **Pane e Vino** also moved, relocating its classic Italian cuisine and casual attitude to a nearby Cow Hollow location.

Foodie alert: Many San Francisco chefs have projects in the works as this book goes to press—all are slated for completion by late 2004. If you're set on seeking out the newest and the latest, find out if any of the following upcoming restaurants have come to fruition yet and check culinary sites such as www.sfgate.com (the dining section), www.zagat.com, and www.citysearch.com to learn if the new restaurant's buzz is good.

Traci des Jardins of **Jardinière** is opening a taco stand called **Mijita** at the Ferry Building Marketplace. Luke Sung spins off the popularity of his small-plate sensation **Isa** with a more casual option called **Lüx,** which will be located near Isa and serve Asian- and European-inspired small plates. Deft chef Craig Stoll, of the Italian favorite **Delfina,** will lend his magic touch to a new and ultracasual pizza joint (yet to be named) also in the Mission District.

Masa's excellent chef Ron Siegel moved to the **Dining Room** at the Ritz-Carlton, where he will add a little Asian flare and a surefire dining buzz to the formal, French, and very white-glove establishment. His replacement at Masa's is Richard Reddington, who arrived from Napa's Auberge du Soleil in July 2004.

ATTRACTIONS   There's good news in the attractions area. The **Ferry Building Marketplace** continues to add new restaurants and food-related shops to its cadre of edible delights. Spending a few hours here is a favorite local pastime and will be one of yours, too. Trust me on this one.

The **California Academy of Sciences** moved from Golden Gate Park to temporary downtown digs, at 875 Howard St. (© **415/750-7145**), providing yet another reason to head to the attractions surrounding SoMa's Yerba Buena Gardens. On the other side of town, the **San Francisco Zoo** is enticing animal lovers of all ages with its new exhibit, African Savanna, which features giraffes, zebras, antelope, and birds mingling in a 3-acre habitat.

SAUSALITO   Italian and elegant dining made its way to the North Bay with new **Poggio,** where killer pastas and gorgeous surroundings give new reason to stay in town after the shops close.

THE WINE COUNTRY   Fab food is still a big draw in Wine Country, and the following new additions definitely up the culinary ante.

The French Laundry owner, Thomas Keller, extended his edible empire with **Bouchon Bakery,** in Yountville. It's the area's premier place to go for authentic French pastries, bread, sweets, sandwiches, and coffee.

Sonoma's doing its darnedest to add more world-class spots to its bucolic backdrop. New on the downtown Sonoma scene are **Harmony Club,** which provides an elegant environment for savoring sophisticated small plates of Continental food and Ledson wines, and **Sonoma Saveurs,** an incredibly appetizing place to stop for outstanding charcuterie, pâté, foie gras, and duck specialties.

Pastoral Glen Ellen also has new drive-worthy dining destinations. **Wolf House** serves up sophisticated updated American fare in its warm and polished dining room and on its riverfront patio and **the fig café & wine bar** offers a more casual taste of country cuisine with French-influenced preparations.

Rutherford's **Auberge du Soleil** restaurant lost its talented chef, Richard Reddington, to San Francisco's Masa's. There's no word yet on who his replacement will be.

The Best of San Francisco

Finally! After having to start this book the past few years with the announcement that San Francisco is still recovering from the repercussions of the dot.com crash, the terrorist attacks of September 11, 2001, a dramatic influx of new residents (up 13% since the '90s), and the general economic strains of 2002 and 2003, there's great news to report: San Francisco is definitely on an upswing!

No indicator better defines the city's mood than the beloved local restaurant scene, and after a rather boring couple of years, during which our dining rooms played it safe, closed, or cut back while awaiting more freewheeling times, it is smooth sailing once again. Eateries all over town are now abuzz with chatter and the clinking of wineglasses, and new and exciting restaurants are popping up faster than you can say "Exactly *how* long do I have to wait for a reservation?"

Sure, even during harder times, the City by the Bay was still a fantastic place to visit with all the classic offerings: stunning bay vistas, Victorian architecture, swank boutiques, killer restaurants, walkable beaches, those oh-so-charming cable cars, the trademark dash of liberalism, and only-in-San Francisco style (remember the gay marriages of 2004?)—all tightly tucked into about 7 miles squared. But for us locals, the change is obvious and very welcome. The city feels exciting again.

So, what can you expect from the country's most romantic European-style city, which was founded on—and still revels in—the pioneers' boom-or-bust lifestyle? Whatever your heart desires! Like an eternal world's fair, it's all happening in San Francisco, and everyone's invited.

1 Frommer's Favorite San Francisco Experiences

- **An Early Morning Cable-Car Ride:** Skip the less-scenic California line and take the Powell-Hyde cable car down to Fisherman's Wharf—the ride is worth the wait. When you reach the top of Nob Hill, grab the rail with one hand and hold your camera with the other, because you're about to see a view of the bay that'll make you a believer. Oh, and don't call it a trolley. See p. 54.

- **An Adventure at Alcatraz:** Even if you loathe tourist spots, you'll like Alcatraz. The rangers have done a fantastic job of preserving The Rock—just looking at it is enough to give you the heebie-jeebies—and they give excellent guided tours (highly recommended). Heck, even the boat ride across the bay is worth the price, so don't miss this attraction. See p. 157.

- **A Walk Across the Golden Gate Bridge:** Don your windbreaker and walking shoes and prepare for a wind-blasted, exhilarating journey across San Francisco's most famous landmark. It's simply one of those things you have to do at least once in your life. See p. 164.

- **A Meander Along the Marina's Golden Gate Promenade and**

Crissy Field: Join the joggers, windsurfers, dog-walkers, and frolickers in one of the city's favorite pastimes—strolling the bayfront Marina. You won't find more fabulous views of the Golden Gate, Marin Headlands, beach, bay, and native flora and fauna anywhere else. See p. 192.

- **A Cruise through the Castro:** The most populated and festive street in the city is not just for gays and lesbians (although the best cruising in town *is* right here). While there are some great shops and cafes, it's the people-watching that makes the trip a must. If you have time, catch a flick at the beautiful 1930s Spanish colonial movie palace, the Castro Theatre (p. 242). See "Neighborhoods Worth a Visit," beginning on p. 171, for more on the Castro.

- **Feasting at the Ferry Building:** During Farmers Market days, this bayfront alfresco market is packed with shoppers vying for the freshest in local produce, breads, and flowers. But the building itself has become a mecca for food lovers who daily browse the outstanding artisan food shops and restaurants and linger over glasses of wine at the festive wine bar. See p. 162.

- **A Walk along the Coastal Trail:** Stroll the forested Coastal Trail from Cliff House to the Golden Gate Bridge, and you'll see why San Franciscans put up with living on a fault line. Start at the parking lot just above Cliff House and head north. On a clear day, you'll have incredible views of the Marin Headlands, but even on foggy days, it's worth the trek to scamper over old bunkers and relish the crisp, cool air (dress warmly). See "The Presidio & Golden Gate National Recreation Area," beginning on p. 179, for more on this area.

- **A Stroll through Chinatown:** Chinatown is a trip. I've been through it at least 100 times, and it has never failed to entertain me. Skip the crummy camera and luggage stores and head straight for the markets, where a cornucopia of sights you just don't see that often in America sits in boxes for you to scrutinize (one day we saw an armadillo for sale, and it wasn't meant to be a pet). Better yet, take one of Shirley Fong-Torres's Wok Wiz tours of Chinatown (p. 188). See "Walking Tour 1: Chinatown," beginning on p. 195, for our walking tour of Chinatown.

- **Cafe Hopping in North Beach:** One of the most pleasurable smells of San Francisco is the aroma of roasted coffee beans wafting down Columbus Avenue. Start the day with a cup of Viennese at Caffè Trieste (a haven for true San Francisco characters), and follow it with a walk in and around Washington Square. Continue with lunch at Mario's Bohemian Cigar Store (à la focaccia sandwiches), book browsing at City Lights, more coffee at Caffè Greco, and dinner at L'Osteria del Forno or Moose's. Finish the day with a nightcap as Enrico Caruso plays on the jukebox at Tosca. See "Walking Tour 2: Getting to Know North Beach," beginning on p. 202, for our walking tour of the area.

- **A Day in Golden Gate Park:** Golden Gate Park is a crucial—and relaxing—part of the San Francisco experience. Its arboreal paths stretch from the Haight all the way to Ocean Beach, offering dozens of fun things to do along the way. Top sights are the Conservatory of Flowers, Japanese Tea Garden, and Steinhart Aquarium. The best time to go is Sunday, when portions of the park are closed to traffic (rent skates or a bike for the full effect). Toward the end of the day, head west to the beach and watch the sunset. See p. 176.

- **A Soul-Stirring Sunday Morning Service at Glide Memorial United Methodist Church:** Preacher Douglas Fitch turns churchgoing into a spiritual party that leaves you feeling elated, hopeful, and unified with the world. All walks of life attend the service here, which focuses not on any particular religion, but on what we have in common as people. It's great fun, with plenty of singing and hand clapping. See p. 182.

- **A Visit to MOMA and Yerba Buena:** Ever since the new Museum of Modern Art opened in 1995, this area has been the best place to go for a quick dose of culture. Start by touring the museum, then head straight for the gift shop (oftentimes more entertaining than the rotating exhibits). Have a light lunch at Caffé Museo, where the food is a vast improvement over most museums' mush. Finish the trip with a stroll through the Yerba Buena Gardens and its slew of new attractions across from the museum. See p. 169 for the museum and p. 171 for the gardens.

- **A Shopping Spree:** Up your credit card limit and bring an extra suitcase, because you're sure to find hundreds of must-haves in the department stores and boutiques surrounding San Francisco's retail epicenter, Union Square. Boutique hounds should head to North Beach's Grant Avenue and upper Fillmore for the best selections of chic women's wear. See chapter 9 for more on San Francisco's shopping.

- **A Drive to Muir Woods, Stinson Beach, and Point Reyes:** If you have wheels, reserve a day for a trip across the Golden Gate Bridge. Take the Stinson Beach exit off Highway 101 and spend a few hours gawking at the monolithic redwoods at Muir Woods (people, I'm telling you, this place is amazing). Continue to Stinson Beach for lunch at the Parkside Café, then head up the coast to the spectacular Point Reyes National Seashore. Rain or shine, it's a day trip you'll never forget. See "Muir Woods & Mount Tamalpais" and "Point Reyes National Seashore," on p. 263 and 264, respectively.

- **A Cocktail in the Clouds:** Some of the greatest ways to view the city are from top-floor lounges in fine hotels such as the Sir Francis Drake (p. 72), the Grand Hyatt San Francisco (p. 68), and The InterContinental Mark Hopkins (p. 84).

2 Best Hotel Bets

- **Best for Families:** Kids like the **Westin St. Francis,** 335 Powell St. (© **800/WESTIN-1** or 415/397-7000), because upon arrival, children under 12 get a Kids Club hat and a special sport bottle that includes complimentary refills in the restaurants. Those ages 3 to 7 also get coloring books and dinosaur soaps and sponges. See p. 69.

- **Best for Romance:** Check out the whimsical and affordable **The Archbishop's Mansion,** 1000 Fulton St. (© **800/543-5820** or 415/563-7872); boutique spot **The Hotel Bohème,** 444 Columbus Ave. (© **415/433-9111**); and old-world elegant **The Hotel Majestic,** 1500 Sutter St. (© **800/869-8966** or 415/441-1100). See p. 100, 96, and 102 respectively.

Politics of the City Today

Shaken but not stirred by the Loma Prieta earthquake in 1989, San Francisco witnessed a spectacular rebound during the 1990s. The seaside Embarcadero, once plagued by a horrendously ugly freeway overpass, was revitalized by a multimillion-dollar face-lift, complete with palm trees, a cable-car line, wide cobblestone walkways, new restaurants, and a skating, biking, and walking promenade. SoMa, the once-shady neighborhood south of Market Street, exploded with new development and became home to the Museum of Modern Art; the beautiful and attraction-packed Yerba Buena Gardens; the überluxurious Four Seasons and W hotels (and allegedly the St. Regis in 2005); a slew of hip clubs, cafes, and condos; a new baseball stadium; and, most influential, dot.com companies. And the tourist and shopping mecca Union Square got a gussied-up central plaza.

But what comes up must come down. And in San Francisco, it came down harder than Marina District homes on landfill during an earthquake.

When the Internet industry bubble burst, which was evident by spring 2000, it left serious damage to San Francisco in its wake. Contrary to the previous years' soar in population, rental and housing prices, and salaries, it was unemployment, commercial space availability, and dismal economic forecasts that were hitting new highs.

San Francisco definitely bore the brunt of the recent economic hiccup, but, not surprisingly, the city founded on the boom-and-bust mentality of gold seekers survived the experience just fine. New businesses slowly filled the dot.com office spaces, the Ferry Building Marketplace and its Farmers Market became the city's gastronomic Disneyland, and waiters who fled the restaurant industry for high-tech jobs returned to the dining rooms and resurrected the recognized importance of excellent service with them.

- **Best Public Space in a Historic Hotel: The Palace Hotel,** 2 New Montgomery St. (© **800/325-3535** or 415/512-1111), the extravagant creation of banker "Bonanza King" Will Ralston in 1875, has one of the grandest rooms in the city: the Garden Court. See p. 91. Running a close second is the magnificent lobby at Nob Hill's **The Fairmont Hotel & Tower,** 950 Mason St. (© **800/441-1414** or 415/772-5000). See p. 83.
- **Best Old-World Hotel:** Those who appreciate comfort, beautiful surroundings, absolute privacy, and unobtrusive service choose **The Huntington Hotel,** 1075 California St. (© **800/227-4683** or 415/474-5400). See p. 84.
- **Best Luxury Hotel: The Ritz-Carlton,** 600 Stockton St. (© **800/241-3333** or 415/296-7465), is the granddaddy of luxury, with all the traditional bells and whistles and every possible amenity. See p. 85. **Four Seasons Hotel San Francisco,** 757 Market St. (© **800/332-3442** or 415/633-3000), opened in 2001 after being built from the ground up. A perfect

Of course, San Francisco still has typical big-city problems—and then some. Homelessness and panhandling have gone largely ignored. Visitors new to the city will be surprised by it's dirtiness in some areas. Those with enough funds to buy a spacious home in most parts of the U.S. can't afford a one-bedroom condo here. Rental units are still expensive enough to have changed the city's demographics: Artists, young transplants, and others seeking an alternative lifestyle can no longer afford to move here and sustain their lifestyle. Parking is beyond a nightmare, even in the outer neighborhoods. Public transportation is embarrassingly inefficient. Congestion and impatient drivers make cruising the town an anxiety-ridden and very slow ride.

But the city's in good spirits—especially since electing Mayor Gavin Newsome in 2003. After barely settling into office, the young (and media savvy) mayor created international controversy and heightened Bay Area pride by allowing gay marriages in San Francisco. It didn't take long to be overruled by the higher-ups. But not before Mayor Newsome won the respect of locals, many of whom see alternative lifestyles and equal rights as trademark San Francisco, at least in theory if not in practice.

As a whole, San Francisco is doing just fine. Its symphony is in the black, restaurants' cheaper prices (lowered during harder times) and new exciting destination haunts woo locals to dine out, and though many of the once instantly rich residents lost it all in the stock market, many argue it's been a good thing for the city. We needed a little reality, not to mention elbowroom for those making under six figures.

Anyone who remembers the old, liberal, truly progressive, and funky San Francisco knows those days are long behind us. But even without the hard-core alternative edge, San Francisco rightfully retains its title as Americans' favorite city destination.

combination of opulence, hipness, and class, this is one of my favorite modern luxury hotels. But it doesn't share the grandeur or sheer number of perks found at the Ritz. See p. 87.

- **Best for Your Budget:** Sure, the rooms at **The San Remo Hotel,** 2237 Mason St. (© **800/352-REMO** or 415/776-8688), are small, but the North Beach location, friendly staff, and low prices can't be beat. Besides, you're here to see the city, not your hotel room. See p. 97. For overall extra perks, my vote is for the adorable and supercheap **Marina Inn,** 3110 Octavia St. (© **800/274-1420** or 415/928-1000). See p. 100.

- **Best Moderately Priced Hotel: Laurel Inn,** 444 Presidio Ave. (© **800/552-8735** or 415/567-8467), may be off the beaten track, but it's one of the best affordable, fashionable hotels in the city—and it has free parking. See p. 99. If you prefer more classically San Francisco surroundings, try the quaint **White Swan Inn,** 845 Bush St. (© **800/999-9570** or 415/775-1755). See

p. 73. Closer to downtown are two great boutique hotels, **The Warwick Regis,** 490 Geary St. (© **800/827-3447** or 415/928-7900), which is extremely quaint and cozy, and **The Savoy Hotel,** 580 Geary St. (© **800/227-4223** or 415/441-2700), a boutique European-style oasis. See p. 77 and 83 respectively.

- **Best Bed-and-Breakfast:** Attention to detail, cute rooms, and a location along a prime stretch of Union Street make the **Union Street Inn,** 2229 Union St. (© **415/346-0424**), an excellent way to experience true San Francisco–style living. See p. 98.

- **Best Funky Hotel: The Phoenix Hotel,** 601 Eddy St. (© **800/248-9466** or 415/776-1380), wouldn't look out of place in Palm Springs. A favorite with the rock and movie set, including Sinéad O'Connor, k.d. lang, and the Red Hot Chili Peppers, in May 2003 it debuted its hip new restaurant/lounge the Bambuddha Lounge. It's also one of the only moderate hotels in San Francisco with an outdoor pool. See p. 102.

- **Best Trendy Chic Hotel:** The **W San Francisco Hotel,** 181 Third St. (© **800/877-WHOTEL** or 415/777-5300), is less than a block from the Museum of Modern Art and has a swank, fresh vibe. See p. 92. However, the W's star power has been overshadowed by Ian Schrager's **Clift Hotel,** 495 Geary St. (© **800/652-5438** or 415/775-4700), the only choice for the tragically hip. See p. 66.

- **Best Views:** From the rooms in **The Mandarin Oriental,** 222 Sansome St. (© **800/622-0404** or 415/276-9888), all of which are on the 38th to the 48th floors, you'll have a great view of the city and the entire Bay Area, although you'll pay dearly for the vista. See p. 94.

- **Best Service:** The historic, eager-to-please **Ritz-Carlton,** 600 Stockton St. (© **800/241-3333** or 415/296-7465), wins in all ultraluxury categories, including their trademark white-glove service—from the servers at teatime to the formal restaurant staff. You'll find the **Mandarin Oriental,** 222 Sansome St. (© **800/622-0404** or 415/276-9888), to be lovely and modern, with a pampering staff that jumps when you beckon whether it's during their Japanese afternoon tea or helping secure reservations at heavily booked restaurants. Kudos also goes to the **Four Seasons Hotel San Francisco,** 757 Market St. (© **800/332-3442**), which offers superfluous hospitality from staff that consistently refills yummy bottomless snack bowls in the sexy lounge to a concierge who helps guests buy their own Four Seasons mattress. Other best bets include the small, luxurious **Campton Place Hotel,** 340 Stockton St. (© **800/235-4300** or 415/781-5555). See p. 85, 94, 87, and 65 respectively.

- **Best Hotel Dining Room:** Ron Siegel's contemporary French cooking at **Masa's,** 648 Bush St. (© **415/989-7154**)—located in a sleek-chic room adjoining boutique best-bet Hotel Vintage Court—is one of the city's best overall dining experiences (p. 75). On the other side of Market Street, Laurent Gras whips up superb postmodern French fare at **Fifth Floor Restaurant** in the swank **Hotel Palomar,** 12 Fourth St. (© **877/294-9711** or 415/348-1555). See p. 91. The **Dining Room at the Ritz-Carlton,** 600 Stockton St. (© **800/241-3333** or 415/296-7465), serves up good and seriously formal French cuisine and surroundings. See p. 85.

3 Best Dining Bets

- **Best for a Formal Affair:** Flawless and quiet best describes an evening at boutique restaurant **Charles Nob Hill,** 1250 Jones St. (© **415/771-5400**). Swoon over your companions and the exquisite California-French cuisine by executive chef Melissa Perello, who was nominated in 2004 for a James Beard Award for Best Rising Star. See p. 127.

- **Best for Impressing Clients:** Show your business associates you've got class—and deep pockets—by reserving a table at the Financial District's **Aqua,** 252 California St. (© **415/956-9662**). It pairs rather noisy power lunching with excellent seafood and wine. See p. 117.

- **Best Romantic Spot:** Anyone who loves classic French cooking will be seduced at **Fleur de Lys,** 777 Sutter St. (© **415/673-7779**), under the rich burgundy-tented canopy that swathes the elegant room in romance. Lots of question-popping here, too. See p. 111.

- **Best for a Celebration:** Great food, a full bar, and a lively atmosphere are the key ingredients that make **Boulevard,** 1 Mission St. (© **415/543-6084**), the place to celebrate. See p. 124. For more grandiose surroundings and more elbow room, gather your pals around a table at downtown's **Grand Café,** 501 Geary St. (© **415/292-0101**). See p. 112. Care less about fancy food and more about an affordable bill, festive surroundings, and awesome grub? Head straight to the Haight's **Cha Cha Cha,** 1801 Haight St. (© **415/386-7670**). See p. 153.

- **Best Decor:** Celeb restaurant designer Pat Kuleto spent a week sketching sea life at the Monterey Bay Aquarium before applying his Midas touch to whimsical **Farallon,** 450 Post St. (© **415/956-6969**). The result is an orgy of oceanic artwork, from jellyfish lamps to sea urchin chandeliers. It's truly a spectacular achievement in restaurant design, although some argue that its underwater antics are over the top p. 111.

- **Best Wine List:** Thanks to renowned master sommelier Larry Stone, **Rubicon,** 558 Sacramento St. (© **415/434-4100**), is known to have one of the best lists in the country. See p. 117.

- **Best Pizza:** Gourmands and everyday diners squeeze into North Beach's **Tommaso's,** 1042 Kearny St. (© **415/398-9696**), for killer pizza and a no-frills Italian cafe atmosphere. See p. 137.

- **Best Desserts:** What a decision! Your sweet tooth can be satisfied in a number of spots around town, including my all-around favorite newcomer **Piperade,** 1015 Battery St. (© **415/391-2555**), which woos with astoundingly tasty orange-essence beignets and chocolate tortes; and **Absinthe,** 398 Hayes St. (© **415/551-1590**), a glamorously casual and festive restaurant serving seasonal southern French cuisine and sensationally sweet finales by French pastry chef Murielle Roux. See p. 135 and 147 respectively.

- **Best Value:** No other place in town serves up heaping plates of fresh pasta at penny-pinching prices the way **Pasta Pomodoro,** 655 Union St. (© **415/399-0300**), does. See p. 136. It has other locations at 2304 Market St. (© **415/558-8123**), 3611 California St. (© **415/831-0900**), and 816 Irving St. (© **415/566-0900**). Want a little more atmosphere and more sophisticated cooking with your value? Then head to **Delfina,** 3621 18th St. (© **415/552-4055**). See p. 149.

- **Best Brunch:** The Sunday spread at the **Terrace Restaurant** (p. 85) in the **Ritz-Carlton,** 600 Stockton St. (© **800/241-3333** or 415/ 773-6198), will set your eyes popping and your feet tapping. Strut around the lavish buffet featuring sushi, caviar, freshly made blinis, and traditional egg dishes. A jazz trio brings even more joy to it all. Book well in advance. Each weekend sells out. Want something a little more low key? Then head to **Ella's** (p. 142), 500 Presidio Ave. (© **415/441-5669**), for some revered breakfast food.

- **Best Dim Sum:** Downtown and Chinatown dim sum restaurants may be more centrally located, but that's all they've got on **Ton Kiang,** 5821 Geary Blvd. (© **415/387-8273**), where carts bring the freshest and most delicious Chinese

dumplings and other dim sum delicacies to your table. See p. 156.

- **Best Vegetarian Food:** For the food, the view of the Golden Gate, and the redwood booths, go to **Greens Restaurant,** Building A, Fort Mason Center (© **415/ 771-6222**). If you want to experience how rich and varied vegetables can taste, sample the extraordinary five-course tasting menu. See p. 143.

- **Best Coffee Shop or Cafe:** With all the wonderful coffee shops throughout this cafe town, there can be no one winner. We do, however, love the authentic atmosphere at **Mario's Bohemian Cigar Store,** 566 Columbus Ave. (© **415/362-0536**), and **Caffè Trieste,** 601 Vallejo St. (© **415/ 392-6739**). See p. 135 and 206 respectively. If you see another cafe you like, pull up a chair and enjoy. Just do San Francisco the favor of supporting our unique coffee culture.

2

Planning Your Trip to San Francisco

1 Visitor Information

Visitors from outside the United States should also see chapter 3, "For International Visitors," for entry requirements and other pertinent information.

The **San Francisco Convention and Visitors Bureau,** 900 Market St. (at Powell St.), Hallidie Plaza, Lower Level, San Francisco, CA 94102 (© **415/391-2000;** www.sfvisitor.org), is the best source of specialized information about the city. Even if you don't have a specific question, you might want to request the free *Visitors Planning Guide* and the *San Francisco Visitors* kit. The kit includes a 6-month calendar of events, a city history, shopping and dining information, and several good, clear maps, plus lodging information. If you need specific information faxed to you, you can call © **800/220-5747;** follow the prompts to receive information by fax only. The bureau highlights only its members' establishments, so if it doesn't have what you're looking for, that doesn't mean it's nonexistent.

You can also get the latest on San Francisco at the following online addresses:

- The *Bay Guardian,* the city's free weekly paper: **www.sfbg.com**
- Hotel reservations: **www.hotelres.com**
- *SF Gate,* the city's *Chronicle* newspaper: **www.sfgate.com**
- CitySearch: **www.citysearch.com**.

2 Money

See chapter 3, "For International Visitors," for more information.

ATMS

All over San Francisco, you'll find ATMs (automated teller machines) linked to a national network that most likely includes your bank at home. Withdrawing cash as you need it is the easiest way to deal with money while you're on the road. **Cirrus** (© **800/424-7787;** www.mastercard.com) and **PLUS** (© **800/843-7587;** www.visa.com) are the two most popular networks. Look at the back of your bank card to see which network you're on, then call or check online for ATM locations at your destination. Be sure you know your personal identification number (PIN) before you leave home, and be sure to find out your daily withdrawal limit before you depart. Also keep in mind that many banks impose a fee (approximately $3) every time a card is used at a different bank's ATM. On top of this, the bank from which you withdraw cash may charge its own fee. To compare banks' ATM fees within the U.S., use www.bankrate.com.

TRAVELER'S CHECKS

Traveler's checks are something of an anachronism from the days before the

> **Tips Dear Visa: I'm Off to San Francisco!**
>
> Some credit card companies recommend that you notify them of any impending trip, so that they don't become suspicious when the card is used numerous times in a foreign destination and they block your charges. Even if you don't call your credit card company in advance, you can always use the card's toll-free emergency number if a charge is refused—a good reason to carry the phone number with you. But perhaps the most important lesson here is to carry more than one card with you on your trip; a card might not work for any number of reasons, so having a backup is the smart way to go.

ATM made cash accessible at any time. Traveler's checks used to be the only sound alternative to traveling with dangerously large amounts of cash. They were as reliable as currency, but, unlike cash, could be replaced if lost or stolen.

These days, traveler's checks are less necessary because most cities have 24-hour ATMs that allow you to withdraw small amounts of cash as needed. However, keep in mind that you will likely be charged an ATM withdrawal fee if the bank is not your own, so if you're withdrawing money every day, you might be better off with traveler's checks—provided that you don't mind showing identification every time you want to cash one.

You can get traveler's checks at almost any bank. **American Express** offers denominations of $20, $50, $100, $500, and (for cardholders only) $1,000. You'll pay a service charge ranging from 1% to 4%. You can also get American Express traveler's checks over the phone by calling ℂ **800/221-7282;** Amex gold and platinum cardholders who use this number are exempt from the 1% fee.

Visa offers traveler's checks at Citibank locations nationwide, as well as at several other banks. The service charge ranges between 1.5% and 2%; checks come in denominations of $20, $50, $100, $500, and $1,000. Call ℂ **800/732-1322** for information. AAA members can obtain Visa checks without a fee at most AAA offices or by calling ℂ **866/339-3378. MasterCard** also offers traveler's checks. Call ℂ **800/223-9920** for a location near you.

If you choose to carry traveler's checks, be sure to keep a record of their serial numbers separate from your checks in the event that they are stolen or lost. You'll get a refund faster if you know the numbers.

CREDIT CARDS

Credit cards are a safe way to carry money: They also provide a convenient record of all your expenses, and they generally offer relatively good exchange rates. You can also withdraw cash advances from your credit cards at banks or ATMs, provided you know your PIN. If you've forgotten yours, or didn't even know you had one, call the number on the back of your credit card and ask the bank to send it to you. It usually takes 5 to 7 business days, though some banks will provide the number over the phone if you tell them your mother's maiden name or some other personal information.

3 When to Go

If you're dreaming of convertibles, Frisbee on the beach, and tank-topped evenings, change your reservations and head to Los Angeles. Contrary to California's sunshine-and-bikini image, San Francisc's weather is "mild" (to put it nicely) and can often be downright bone-chilling because of the common wet, foggy air and cool winds—it's nothing like that of Southern California. Summer, the most popular time to visit, is often characterized by damp, foggy days; cold, windy nights; and crowded tourist destinations. A good bet is to visit in spring or, better yet, autumn. Every September, right about the time San Franciscans mourn being cheated (or fogged) out of another summer, something wonderful happens: The thermometer rises, the skies clear, and the locals call in sick to work and head for the beach. It's what residents call "Indian summer." The city is also delightful during winter, when the opera and ballet seasons are in full swing; there are fewer tourists, many hotel prices are lower, and downtown bustles with holiday cheer.

CLIMATE

San Francisco's temperate, marine climate usually means relatively mild weather year-round. In summer, chilling fog rolls in most mornings and evenings, and if temperatures top 70°F (21°C), the city is ready to throw a celebration. Even when autumn's heat occasionally stretches into the 80s (upper 20s Celsius) and 90s (lower 30s Celsius), you should still dress in layers, or by early evening you'll learn firsthand why sweatshirt sales are a great business at Fisherman's Wharf.

Destination San Francisco: Red Alert Checklist

- Have you packed a warm jacket or coat? When the fog's in and the wind picks up, San Francisco will feel like winter regardless of the time of year. And don't forget walking shoes.
- Have you made all critical restaurant reservations well in advance? (Ditto for theater or any other live performances.)
- If you purchased traveler's checks, have you recorded the check numbers and stored the documentation separately from the checks?
- Did you make sure your favorite attraction is open? Call ahead to double-check opening and closing times: Museums vary in days and hours they are open, and restaurants sometimes change service times.
- Did you stop the newspaper and mail delivery, and leave a set of keys with someone reliable?
- Did you pack your camera and an extra set of camera batteries, and purchase enough film?
- Do you have a safe, accessible place to store money?
- If you're flying, are you carrying a current, government-issued ID, such as a driver's license or passport?
- Did you bring your ID cards that could entitle you to discounts such as AAA and AARP cards, student IDs, and so on?
- Did you bring emergency drug prescriptions and extra glasses and/or contact lenses?
- Did you find out your daily ATM withdrawal limit?
- Do you have your credit card personal identification numbers (PINs)? Is there a daily withdrawal limit on credit card cash advances?
- If you have an e-ticket, do you have documentation?
- Did you leave a copy of your itinerary with someone at home?

Tips **Travel Attire**

Even if it's sunny out, don't forget to bring a jacket; the weather can change almost instantly from sunny and warm to windy and cold in San Francisco.

In winter, the mercury seldom falls below freezing and snow is almost unheard of, but that doesn't mean you won't be whimpering if you forget your coat. Still, compared to most of the states' weather conditions, San Francisco's is consistently pleasant.

It's that beautifully fluffy, chilly, wet, heavy, sweeping fog that makes the city's weather so precarious. A rare combination of water, wind, and topography creates Northern California's summer fog bank. It lies off the coast, and rising air currents pull it in when the land heats up. Held back by coastal mountains along a 600-mile front, the low clouds seek out any passage they can find. The easiest access is the slot where the Pacific Ocean penetrates the continental wall—the Golden Gate.

San Francisco's Average Temperatures & Rainfall

	Jan	Feb	Mar	Apr	May	June	July	Aug	Sept	Oct	Nov	Dec
High °F	56	59	61	64	67	70	71	72	73	70	62	56
Low °F	43	46	47	48	51	53	55	56	55	52	48	43
High °C	13	15	16	18	19	21	22	22	23	21	17	13
Low °C	6	8	8	9	11	12	13	13	13	11	9	6
Rain (in.)	4.5	4.0	3.3	1.2	0.4	0.1	0.1	0.1	0.2	1.0	2.5	2.9
Rain (mm)	113.0	101.9	82.8	30.0	9.7	2.8	0.8	1.8	5.1	26.4	63.2	73.4

SAN FRANCISCO CALENDAR OF EVENTS

For more information, visit www.sfvisitor.org for an annual calendar of local events.

February

Chinese New Year, Chinatown. In 2005, public celebrations will again spill onto every street in Chinatown. Festivities begin with the "Miss Chinatown USA" pageant parade, and climax a week later with a celebratory parade of marching bands, rolling floats, barrages of fireworks, and a block-long dragon writhing in and out of the crowds. The revelry runs for several weeks and wraps up with a memorable parade through Chinatown that starts at Market and Second streets and ends at Kearny Street. Arrive early for a good viewing spot on Grant Avenue. Make your hotel reservations early. For dates and information, call ☎ **415/982-3000** or visit www.chineseparade.com.

March

St. Patrick's Day Parade, Union Square and Civic Center. Everyone's an honorary Irish person at this festive affair, which starts at 12:45pm at Market and Second streets and continues to City Hall. But the party doesn't stop there. Head down to the Civic Center for the post-party, or venture to The Embarcadero's Harrington's bar (245 Front St.) and celebrate with hundreds of the Irish-for-a-day yuppies as they gallivant around the closed-off streets and numerous pubs. No contact information. Sunday before March 17.

April

Cherry Blossom Festival, Japantown. Meander through the arts-and-crafts and food booths lining the blocked-off streets around Japan Center and watch traditional drumming, flower arranging, origami making, or a parade celebrating the cherry blossom and Japanese culture. Call © **415/563-2313** for information. Mid- to late April.

San Francisco International Film Festival, around San Francisco with screenings at the AMC Kabuki 8 Cinemas (Fillmore and Post sts.), and at many other locations. Begun in 1957, this is America's oldest film festival. It features more than 200 films and videos from more than 50 countries, as well as awards ceremonies in which renowned honorees join the festivities. Tickets are relatively inexpensive, and screenings are accessible to the public. Entries include new films by beginning and established directors. For a schedule or information, call © **415/931-FILM** or visit www.sffs.org. Mid-April to early May.

May

Cinco de Mayo Celebration, Mission District. This is when the Latino community celebrates the victory of the Mexicans over the French at Puebla in 1862; mariachi bands, dancers, food, and a parade fill the streets of the Mission. The parade starts at 10am at 24th and Bryant streets and ends at the Civic Center. No contact information. The Sunday before May 5.

Bay to Breakers Foot Race, The Embarcadero through Golden Gate Park to Ocean Beach. Even if you don't participate, you can't avoid this run from downtown to Ocean Beach, which stops morning traffic throughout the city. More than 60,000 entrants gather—many dressed in wacky, innovative, and sometimes X-rated costumes—for the approximately 7½-mile run. If you don't want to run, join the throng of spectators who line the route. Sidewalk parties, bands, and cheerleaders of all ages provide a good dose of true San Francisco fun. The *San Francisco Examiner* (© **415/359-2800;** www.examiner. com) sponsors the event. Third Sunday of May.

Carnival, Mission District, Mission Street between 14th and 24th streets, and Harrison Street between 16th and 21st streets. The Mission District's largest annual event is a day of festivities that culminates in a parade on Mission Street. For one of San Franciscans' favorite events, more than half a million spectators line the route, and samba musicians and dancers continue to entertain on 14th Street, near Harrison, at the end of the march. Call the hot line at © **415/920-0125** for information. The Sunday of Memorial Day weekend.

June

Union Street Art Festival, Pacific Heights, along Union Street from Steiner to Gough streets. This outdoor fair celebrates San Francisco with themes, gourmet food booths, music, entertainment, and a juried art show featuring works by more than 350 artists. Call the **Union Street Association** (© **415/441-7055**) for more information or see www.unionstreetfestival.com. First weekend of June.

Haight Street Fair, Haight-Ashbury. A far cry from the froufrou Union Street Fair, this grittier fair features alternative crafts, ethnic foods, rock bands, and a healthy number of hippies and street kids whooping it up and slamming beers in front of the blaring rock-'n'-roll stage. The fair usually extends along Haight between Stanyan and

Ashbury streets. For details and the exact date, call © **415/661-8025.**

North Beach Festival, Grant Avenue, North Beach. In 2004, this party celebrated its 50th anniversary; organizers claim it's the oldest urban street fair in the country. Close to 100,000 city folk meander along Grant Avenue, between Vallejo and Union streets, to eat, drink, and browse the arts-and-crafts booths, poetry readings, swing-dancing venue, and *arte di gesso* (sidewalk chalk art). But the most enjoyable part of the event is listening to music and people-watching. Call © **415/989-2220** for details. Usually Father's Day weekend, but call to confirm.

Stern Grove Midsummer Music Festival, Sunset District. Pack a picnic and head out early to join the thousands who come here to lie in the grass and enjoy classical, jazz, and ethnic music and dance in the grove, at 19th Avenue and Sloat Boulevard. The free concerts take place every Sunday at 2pm between mid-June and August. Show up with a lawn chair or blanket. There are food booths if you forget snacks, but you'll be dying to leave if you don't bring warm clothes—the Sunset District can be one of the coldest parts of the city. Call © **415/ 252-6252** for listings. Sundays, mid-June through August.

San Francisco Lesbian, Gay, Bisexual, Transgender Pride Parade & Celebration, downtown's Market Street. This prideful event draws up to half a million participants who celebrate all of the above—and then some. The parade proceeds west on Market Street until it gets to Market and Eighth Street, where hundreds of food, art, and information booths are set up around several soundstages. Call © **415/864-3733** or visit www.sfpride.org for information. Usually the third or last weekend of June.

July

Fillmore Street Jazz Festival, Pacific Heights. July starts with a bang, when the upscale portion of Fillmore closes to traffic and several blocks of arts and crafts, gourmet food, and live jazz fill the street. (The blocked-off section is changing, so call for details.) Call © **510/ 970-3217** for more information. First weekend in July.

Fourth of July Celebration & Fireworks, Fisherman's Wharf. This event can be something of a joke—more often than not, fog, like everyone else, comes into the city to join in the festivities. Sometimes it's almost impossible to view the million-dollar pyrotechnics from PIER 39 on the northern waterfront. Still, it's a party, and if the skies are clear, it's a darn good show. No contact information.

San Francisco Marathon, San Francisco and beyond. This is one of the largest marathons in the world. For entry information, contact West End Management, the event organizer (© **800/698-8699;** www.chroniclemarathon.com). Usually the second or third weekend in July.

September

A La Carte, A La Park, Sharon Meadow, Golden Gate Park. You probably won't get to go to all the restaurants you'd like while you're visiting the city, but you can get a good sampling at this annual event. More than 40 of the town's favorite restaurants, accompanied by 20 microbreweries and 20 wineries, offer tastings in San Francisco's favorite park. There's entertainment as well, and proceeds benefit the Friends of Recreation & Parks.

Admission is around $10 adults in advance and $12 on-site, $8 seniors in advance and $10 on-site, free for children under 12. Call ℂ **415/458-1988** for 2005 prices. Labor Day weekend.

Renaissance Pleasure Faire, Gilroy (south of San Francisco). This is an expensive, but enjoyable, festival held south of San Francisco that takes you back to Renaissance times—with games, plays, and arts-and-crafts and food booths. Previously held north of the city, it's now in a location to the south at Casa del Fruita in Hollister, near Gilroy. For more information, call ℂ **800/52-FAIRE.** Six to eight weekends in September and October.

Sausalito Art Festival, Sausalito. A juried exhibit of more than 180 artists, this festival includes music—provided by Bay Area jazz, rock, and blues performers—and international cuisine, enhanced by wines from some 50 Napa and Sonoma producers. Parking is impossible; take the **Blue & Gold Fleet ferry** (ℂ **415/705-5555**) from Fisherman's Wharf to the festival site. For more information, call ℂ **415/332-3555** or log on to www.sausalitoartfestival.org. Labor Day weekend.

Opera in the Park, usually in Sharon Meadow, Golden Gate Park. Each year the San Francisco Opera launches its season with a free concert featuring a selection of arias. Call ℂ **415/861-4008** to confirm the location and date. Usually the Sunday after Labor Day.

San Francisco Blues Festival, on the grounds of Fort Mason, The Marina. The largest outdoor blues music event on the West Coast was 30 years old in 2002 and continues to feature local and national musicians performing back-to-back during the 3-day extravaganza. You can charge tickets by phone at ℂ **415/421-8497** or online at www.ticketmaster.com. For schedule information, call ℂ **415/826-6837;** for recorded information, call ℂ **415/979-5588** or visit www.sfblues.com. Usually in late September.

Folsom Street Fair, along Folsom Street between 7th and 12th streets, SoMa. This is a local favorite for its kinky, outrageous, leather-and-skin gay-centric blowout celebration. It's hard-core, so only open-minded and adventurous types need head this way. Call ℂ **415/861-3247** or visit www.folsomstreetfair.com for the date, which is usually at the end of September.

October

Fleet Week, Marina and Fisherman's Wharf. Residents gather along the Marina Green, The Embarcadero, Fisherman's Wharf, and other great vantage points to watch incredible aerial performances by the Blue Angels, flown in tribute to our nation's marines. Call ℂ **415/705-5500** or visit www.fleetweek.com for details and dates.

Artspan Open Studios, various San Francisco locations. Find an original piece of art to commemorate your trip, or just see what local artists are up to by grabbing a map to over 700 artists' studios that are open to the public during weekends in October. Call ℂ **415/861-9838** for more information.

Castro Street Fair, The Castro. Celebrate life in the city's most famous gay neighborhood. Call ℂ **415/841-1824** or visit www.castrostreetfair.org for information. First Sunday in October.

Reggae in the Park, Sharon Meadow, Golden Gate Park. This event draws thousands to the park to dance and celebrate the soulful sounds of reggae. Big-name reggae and world-beat bands play all weekend, and ethnic arts-and-crafts and food booths line the stage's periphery. Tickets are about $20 in advance, $25 on-site. Two-day discounted passes are available for $35. Free for children under 12. Call ✆ **415/458-1988** for more details. First weekend in October.

Italian Heritage Parade, North Beach and Fisherman's Wharf. The city's Italian community leads the festivities around Fisherman's Wharf, celebrating Columbus's landing in America. The festival includes a parade along Columbus Avenue and sporting events, but for the most part, it's a great excuse to hang out in North Beach and people-watch. For information and the exact date, call ✆ **415/434-1492** or visit www.sfcolumbusday.org. Sunday near October 12.

Exotic Erotic Halloween Ball, The Cow Palace, on the southern outskirts of San Francisco. Thousands come here dressed in costume, lingerie, and sometimes even less than that. It's a wild fantasy affair with bands, dancing, and costume contests. *Beware:* It can be somewhat cheesy. Tickets cost approximately $35 per person. For information, call ✆ **415/567-BALL** or visit www.exoticeroticball.com.

Friday or Saturday night before Halloween.

Halloween, The Castro. This is a huge night in San Francisco. A fantastical parade is organized at Market and Castro streets, and a mixed gay/straight crowd revels in costumes of extraordinary imagination. No contact information. October 31.

San Francisco Jazz Festival, various San Francisco locations. This festival presents eclectic programming in an array of fabulous jazz venues throughout the city. With close to 2 weeks of nightly entertainment and dozens of performers, the jazz festival is a hot ticket. Past events have featured Herbie Hancock, Dave Brubeck, the Modern Jazz Quartet, Wayne Shorter, and Bill Frisell. For information, call ✆ **800/850-SFJF** or 415/788-7353; or visit www.sfjazz.org. Also check the website for other events throughout the year. Late October and early November.

December

The Nutcracker, War Memorial Opera House, Civic Center. The **San Francisco Ballet** (✆ **415/865-2000**) performs this holiday classic annually. Order tickets to this Tchaikovsky tradition well in advance.

4 Travel Insurance

Check your existing insurance policies and credit card coverage before you buy travel insurance. You may already be covered for lost luggage, canceled tickets or medical expenses.

The cost of travel insurance varies widely, depending on the cost and length of your trip, your age and health, and the type of trip you're taking, but expect to pay between 5% and 8% of the vacation itself.

TRIP-CANCELLATION INSURANCE Trip-cancellation insurance helps you get your money back if you have to back out of a trip, if you have to go home early, or if your travel supplier goes bankrupt. Allowed reasons for cancellation can range from sickness to natural disasters to the State Department declaring your destination unsafe for travel. (Insurers usually won't cover vague fears, though, as many travelers discovered who tried to cancel their trips in Oct 2001 because they were wary of flying.) In this unstable world, trip-cancellation insurance is a good buy if you're getting tickets well in advance—who knows what the state of the world, or of your airline, will be in 9 months? Insurance policy details vary, so read the fine print—and make sure that your airline or cruise line is on the list of carriers covered in case of bankruptcy. A good resource is **"Travel Guard Alerts,"** a list of companies considered high-risk by Travel Guard International (see website below). Protect yourself further by paying for the insurance with a credit card—by law, consumers can get their money back on goods and services not received if they report the loss within 60 days after the charge is listed on their credit card statement.

For more information, contact one of the following recommended insurers: **Access America** (© 866/807-3982; www.accessamerica.com); **Travel Guard International** (© 800/826-4919; www.travelguard.com); **Travel Insured International** (© 800/243-3174; www.travelinsured.com); and **Travelex Insurance Services** (© 888/457-4602; www.travelex-insurance.com).

MEDICAL INSURANCE Most health insurance policies cover you if you get sick away from home—but check, particularly if you're insured by an HMO.

LOST-LUGGAGE INSURANCE On domestic flights, checked baggage is covered up to $2,500 per ticketed passenger. On international flights (including U.S. portions of international trips), baggage coverage is limited to approximately $9.07 per pound, up to approximately $635 per checked bag. If you plan to check items more valuable than the standard liability, see if your valuables are covered by your homeowner's policy, get baggage insurance as part of your comprehensive travel-insurance package or buy Travel Guard's "BagTrak" product. Don't buy insurance at the airport, as it's usually overpriced. Be sure to take any valuables or irreplaceable items with you in your carry-on luggage, as many valuables (including books, money and electronics) aren't covered by airline policies.

If your luggage is lost, immediately file a lost-luggage claim at the airport, detailing the luggage contents. For most airlines, you must report delayed, damaged, or lost baggage within 4 hours of arrival. The airlines are required to deliver luggage, once found, directly to your house or destination free of charge.

5 Health & Safety

STAYING HEALTHY
No worries about staying healthy in San Francisco. The water's A-OK to drink, food's fresh—and tasty—and we tend to be a fit bunch. That said, you can spend your vacation in your hotel room if you wear shoes impractical for hiking the city's hills, or if you catch a cold because you don't dress for winter, spring, and summer—which often occur all in 1 day. Also, consider bringing pants with expandable waistbands,

because you'll probably overindulge in San Francisco's restaurants.

WHAT TO DO IF YOU GET SICK AWAY FROM HOME
In most cases, your existing health plan will provide the coverage you need. But double-check; you may want to buy **travel medical insurance** instead. (See the section on insurance, above.) Bring your insurance ID card with you when you travel.

If you suffer from a chronic illness, consult your doctor before your departure. For conditions like epilepsy, diabetes, or heart problems, wear a **MedicAlert identification tag** (✆ **888/633-4298;** www.medicalert.org), which will immediately alert doctors to your condition and give them access to your records through MedicAlert's 24-hour hot line.

Pack **prescription medications** in your carry-on luggage, and keep them in their original containers, with pharmacy labels—otherwise, they won't make it through airport security. Also bring along copies of your prescriptions

in case you lose your pills or run out. Don't forget an extra pair of contact lenses or prescription glasses.

STAYING SAFE

San Francisco is as safe as any big city, and requires only that you use common sense (for example, don't leave the new video camera on the seat of your parked car). However, in neighborhoods such as Lower Haight, the Mission, the Tenderloin (a few blocks west of Union Square), and Fisherman's Wharf (at night especially), it's a good idea to pay attention to yourself and your surroundings.

6 Specialized Travel Resources

TRAVELERS WITH DISABILITIES

Most disabilities shouldn't stop anyone from traveling. There are more options and resources out there than ever before.

Most of San Francisco's major museums and tourist attractions have wheelchair ramps. Many hotels offer special accommodations and services for wheelchair users and other visitors with disabilities. As well as the ramps, they include extra large bathrooms and telecommunication devices for hearing-impaired travelers. The San Francisco Convention and Visitors Bureau (p. 11) should have the most up-to-date information.

Travelers in wheelchairs can request special ramped taxis by calling **Yellow Cab** (✆ **415/626-2345**), which charges regular rates for the service. Travelers with disabilities can also get a free copy of the *Muni Access Guide,* published by the San Francisco Municipal Railway, Accessible Services Program, 949 Presidio Ave. (✆ **415/923-6142**), which is staffed weekdays from 8am to 5pm. Many of the major car-rental companies offer hand-controlled cars for drivers with disabilities. **Alamo** (✆ **800/651-1223**), **Avis**

(✆ **800/331-1212,** ext. 7305), and **Budget** (✆ **800/314-3932**) have special hot lines that help provide such a vehicle at any of its U.S. locations with 48 hours' advance notice; **Hertz** (✆ **800/654-3131**) requires between 24 and 72 hours' advance notice at most locations.

Many travel agencies offer customized tours and itineraries for travelers with disabilities. **Flying Wheels Travel** (✆ **507/451-5005;** www.flyingwheelstravel.com) offers escorted tours and cruises that emphasize sports, as well as private tours in minivans with lifts. **Accessible Journeys** (✆ **800/846-4537** or 610/521-0339; www.accessiblejourneys.com) caters specifically to slow walkers and wheelchair travelers and their families and friends.

Organizations that offer assistance to travelers with disabilities include **MossRehab** (www.mossresourcenet.org), which provides a library of accessible-travel resources online; **SATH** (Society for Accessible Travel & Hospitality) (✆ **212/447-7284;** www.sath.org; annual membership fees: $45 adults, $30 seniors and students), which offers a wealth of travel resources for all types of disabilities and informed recommendations on destinations, access guides, travel agents, tour operators, vehicle rentals, and companion services; and the **American Foundation for the Blind (AFB;** ✆ **800/232-5463;** www.afb. org), a referral resource for the blind or visually impaired that includes information on traveling with Seeing Eye dogs.

For more information specifically targeted to travelers with disabilities, the community website **iCan** (www. icanonline.net/channels/travel/index. cfm) has destination guides and several regular columns on accessible travel. Also check out the quarterly magazine **Emerging Horizons** ($14.95 per year, $19.95 outside the U.S.; www. emerginghorizons.com)*;* and *Open World* magazine, published by SATH (see above; subscription $13 per year, $21 outside the U.S.).

GAY & LESBIAN TRAVELERS

If you head down to the Castro—an area surrounding Castro Street near Market Street—you'll understand why the city is a mecca for gay and lesbian travelers. Since the 1970s, this unique part of town has remained a colorfully festive neighborhood, teeming with "outed" city folk who meander the streets shopping, eating, partying, or cruising. If anyone feels like an outsider in this part of town, it's heterosexuals, who, although warmly welcomed in the community, may feel uncomfortable or downright threatened if they harbor any homophobia or aversion to being "cruised." For many San Franciscans, it's just a fun area (especially on Halloween) with some wonderful shops.

Gays and lesbians make up a good deal of San Francisco's population, so it's no surprise that clubs and bars all over town cater to them. Although lesbian interests are concentrated primarily in the East Bay (especially Oakland), a significant community resides

in the Mission District, around 16th and Valencia streets.

Several local publications concentrate on in-depth coverage of news, information, and listings of goings-on around town for gays and lesbians. The *Bay Area Reporter* has the most comprehensive listings, including a weekly calendar of events. Distributed free on Thursday, it can be found stacked at the corner of 18th and Castro streets and at Ninth and Harrison streets, as well as in bars, bookshops, and stores around town. It may also be available in gay and lesbian bookstores elsewhere in the country.

GUIDES & PUBLICATIONS For a good book selection, contact **Giovanni's Room,** 345 S. 12th St., Philadelphia, PA 19107 (✆ **215/923-2960;** www.giovannisroom.com), and **A Different Light Bookstore,** 489 Castro St., San Francisco, CA 94114 (✆ **415/431-0891;** www.adlbooks. com). There's another Different Light location in Los Angeles (✆ **310/854-6601**).

For other guides, try the *Spartacus International Gay Guide* and *Odysseus,* both good, annual English-language guidebooks focused on gay men; the *Damron* guides (www. damron.com), with separate, annual books for gay men and lesbians; and *Gay Travel A to Z: The World of Gay & Lesbian Travel Options at Your Fingertips* by Marianne Ferrari (Ferrari International; Box 35575, Phoenix, AZ 85069; ✆ **602/863-2408**), a very good gay and lesbian guidebook series.

Our World, 1104 N. Nova Rd., Suite 251, Daytona Beach, FL 32117 (✆ **386/441-5367;** www.ourworld mag.com), is a magazine devoted to gay and lesbian travel worldwide. An annual international subscription costs $50, and a U.S. subscription costs $25. *Out & About,* P.O. Box 500, San Francisco, CA 94104 (✆ **800/929-2268;** www.outandabout.com), has been hailed for its "straight" reporting about gay travel. It profiles the best gay or gay-friendly hotels, restaurants, clubs, and other places, with coverage of destinations throughout the world. It costs $20 a year for 10 issues. Both of these publications are available at most gay and lesbian bookstores.

ORGANIZATIONS The International Gay and Lesbian Travel Association (IGLTA; © 800/448-8550 or 954/776-2626; www.iglta.org) is the trade association for the gay and lesbian travel industry, and offers an online directory of gay- and lesbian-friendly travel businesses; go to their website and click on "Members."

TRAVEL AGENCIES Many agencies offer tours and travel itineraries specifically for gay and lesbian travelers. **Above and Beyond Tours** (© 800/397-2681; www.above beyondtours.com) is the exclusive gay and lesbian tour operator for United Airlines. **Now, Voyager** (© 800/255-6951; www.nowvoyager.com) is a well-known San Francisco–based gay-owned and operated travel service. You might also want to try **Skylink Women's Travel,** 1455 N. Dutton Ave, Suite A, Santa Rosa, CA 95401 (© 800/225-5759 or 707/546-1212).

SENIOR TRAVEL

Mention the fact that you're a senior when you make your travel reservations. Although all of the major U.S. airlines except America West have canceled their senior discount and coupon book programs, many hotels still offer discounts for seniors. If you're a senior, don't be shy about asking for discounts; in most cities, people over the age of 60 qualify for reduced admission to theaters, museums, and other attractions, as well as discounted fares on public transportation. Always carry some kind of identification, such as a driver's license, that shows your date of birth.

The **Senior Citizen Information Line** (© 415/626-1033) offers advice, referrals, and information on city services. The **Friendship Line for the Elderly** (© 415/752-3778) is a support, referral, and crisis-intervention service.

Members of **AARP** (formerly known as the American Association of Retired Persons), 601 E St. NW, Washington, DC 20049 (© 888/687-2277; www.aarp.org), get discounts on hotels, airfares, and car rentals. AARP offers members a wide range of benefits, including *AARP: The Magazine* and a monthly newsletter. Anyone over 50 can join.

Many reliable agencies and organizations target the 50-plus market. **Elderhostel** (© 877/426-8056; www.elderhostel.org) arranges study programs for those ages 55 and over (and a spouse or companion of any age) in the U.S. and in more than 80 countries around the world. Most courses last 5 to 7 days in the U.S. (2–4 weeks abroad), and many include airfare, accommodations in university dormitories or modest inns, meals, and tuition.

Recommended publications offering travel resources and discounts for seniors include: the quarterly magazine *Travel 50 & Beyond* (www.travel 50andbeyond.com); *Travel Unlimited: Uncommon Adventures for the Mature Traveler* (Avalon); *101 Tips for Mature Travelers,* available from Grand Circle Travel (© 800/221-2610 or 617/350-7500; www.gct.com); and *Unbelievably Good Deals and Great Adventures That You Absolutely Can't Get Unless You're Over 50* (McGraw-Hill), by Joann Rattner Heilman.

FAMILY TRAVEL

If you have enough trouble getting your kids out of the house in the morning, dragging them thousands of miles away may seem like an insurmountable challenge. But family travel can be immensely rewarding, giving you new ways of seeing the world through smaller pairs of eyes.

San Francisco is full of sightseeing opportunities and special activities geared toward children. See "Especially for Kids," in chapter 7, beginning on p. 186 for information and ideas for families.

Recommended family travel Internet sites include **Family Travel Forum** (www.familytravelforum.com), a comprehensive site that offers customized trip planning; **Family Travel Network** (www.familytravelnetwork.com), an award-winning site that offers travel features, deals, and tips; **Traveling Internationally with Your Kids** (www. travelwithyourkids.com), a comprehensive site offering sound advice for long-distance and international travel with children; and **Family Travel Files** (www.thefamilytravelfiles.com), which offers an online magazine and a directory of off-the-beaten-path tours and tour operators for families.

PUBLICATIONS *Frommer's San Francisco with Kids* (Wiley Publishing, Inc.) is a good source of kid-specific information for your trip.

7 Planning Your Trip Online

SURFING FOR AIRFARES

The "big three" online travel agencies—**Expedia.com, Travelocity,** and **Orbitz**—sell most of the air tickets bought on the Internet. (Canadian travelers should try expedia.ca and Travelocity.ca; U.K. residents can go for expedia.co.uk and opodo.co.uk.). Each has different business deals with the airlines and may offer different fares on the same flights, so it's wise to shop around. Expedia and Travelocity will also send you **e-mail notification** when a cheap fare becomes available to your favorite destination. Of the smaller travel agency websites, **Side-Step** (www.sidestep.com) has gotten the best reviews from Frommer's authors. It's a browser add-on that purports to "search 140 sites at once," but in reality only beats competitors' fares as often as other sites do.

Also remember to check **airline websites,** especially those for low-fare carriers such as Southwest, JetBlue, Air-Tran, WestJet, or Ryanair, whose fares are often misreported or simply missing from travel agency websites. Even with major airlines, you can often shave a few bucks from a fare by booking directly through the airline and avoiding a travel agency's transaction fee. But you'll get these discounts only by **booking online:** Most airlines now offer online-only fares that even their phone agents know nothing about. For the websites of airlines that fly to and from your destination, go to "Getting There," p. 26.

Great **last-minute deals** are available through free weekly e-mail services provided directly by the airlines. Most of these are announced on Tuesday or Wednesday and must be purchased online. Most are only valid for travel that weekend, but some (such as Southwest's) can be booked weeks or months in advance. Sign up for weekly e-mail alerts at airline websites or check megasites that compile comprehensive lists of last-minute specials, such as **Smarter Living** (smarterliving. com). For last-minute trips, **site59. com** and **lastminutetravel.com** in the U.S. and **lastminute.com** in Europe often have better air-and-hotel package deals than the major-label sites. A website listing numerous bargain sites and airlines around the world is **www. itravelnet.com**.

If you're willing to give up some control over your flight details, use what is called an "**opaque" fare service** like **Priceline** (www.priceline.com;

www.priceline.co.uk for Europeans) or its smaller competitor **Hotwire** (www.hotwire.com). Both offer rock-bottom prices in exchange for travel on a "mystery airline" at a mysterious time of day, often with a mysterious change of planes en route. The mystery airlines are all major, well-known carriers—and the possibility of being sent from Philadelphia to Chicago via Tampa is remote; the airlines' routing computers have gotten a lot better than they used to be. But your chances of getting a 6am or 11pm flight are pretty high. Hotwire tells you flight prices before you buy; Priceline usually has better deals than Hotwire, but you have to play their "name our price" game. If you're new at this, the helpful folks at **BiddingForTravel** (www.biddingfortravel.com) do a good job of demystifying Priceline's prices and strategies. Priceline and Hotwire are great for flights within North America and between the U.S. and Europe. But for flights to other parts of the world, consolidators will almost always beat their fares. *Note:* In 2004 Priceline added nonopaque

service to its roster. You now have the option to pick exact flights, times, and airlines from a list of offers—or opt to bid on opaque fares as before.

For much more about airfares and savvy air-travel tips and advice, pick up a copy of *Frommer's Fly Safe, Fly Smart* (Wiley Publishing, Inc.).

SURFING FOR HOTELS

Shopping online for hotels is generally done one of two ways: by booking through the hotel's own website or through an independent booking agency (or a fare-service agency like Priceline; see below). These Internet hotel agencies have multiplied in mind-boggling numbers of late, competing for the business of millions of consumers surfing for accommodations around the world. This competitiveness can be a boon to consumers who have the patience and time to shop and compare the online sites for good deals—but shop they must, for prices can vary considerably from site to site. And keep in mind that hotels at the top of a site's listing may be there for no other

---

Frommers.com: The Complete Travel Resource

For an excellent travel-planning resource, we highly recommend **Frommers.com** (www.frommers.com), voted Best Travel Site by *PC Magazine*. We're a little biased, of course, but we guarantee that you'll find the travel tips, reviews, monthly vacation giveaways, bookstore, and online-booking capabilities thoroughly indispensable. Among the special features are our popular **Destinations** section, where you'll get expert travel tips, hotel and dining recommendations, and advice on the sights to see for more than 3,500 destinations around the globe; the **Frommers.com Newsletter,** with the latest deals, travel trends, and money-saving secrets; our **Community** area featuring **Message Boards,** where Frommer's readers post queries and share advice (sometimes even our authors show up to answer questions); and our **Photo Center,** where you can post and share vacation tips. When your research is done, the **Online Reservations System** (www.frommers.com/book_a_trip) takes you to Frommer's preferred online partners for booking your vacation at affordable prices.

Online Traveler's Toolbox

Veteran travelers usually carry some essential items to make their trips easier. Following is a selection of online tools to bookmark and use.

- **Visa ATM Locator** (www.visa.com), for locations of PLUS ATMs worldwide; or **MasterCard ATM Locator** (www.mastercard.com), for locations of Cirrus ATMs worldwide.
- **Intellicast** (www.intellicast.com) and **Weather.com** (www.weather.com). Both give weather forecasts for all 50 states and for cities around the world.
- **Mapquest** (www.mapquest.com). This best of the mapping sites lets you choose a specific address or destination and, in seconds, it will return a map and detailed directions.
- **Airplane Seating and Food.** Find out which seats to reserve and which to avoid (and more) on all major domestic airlines at www.seatguru.com. And check out the type of meal (with photos) you'll likely be served on airlines around the world at www.airlinemeals.com.
- **Universal Currency Converter** (www.xe.com/ucc). See what your dollar or pound is worth in more than 100 other countries.
- **Subway Navigator** (www.subwaynavigator.com). Download subway maps and get savvy advice on using subway systems in dozens of major cities around the world.
- **OpenTable.com** (www.opentable.com). Book San Francisco restaurant reservations without being put on hold!
- **SF Gate** (www.sfgate.com). The *San Francisco Chronicle* posts all the latest news and happenings, along with a food section that includes The Inside Scoop, a weekly column that includes in-depth restaurant reviews.
- **City Search** (www.citysearch.com). Get the dirt on everything city-specific from hotel and restaurant reviews to movie showings, spas, bars, and nightclubs.
- **San Francisco Convention and Visitors Bureau** (www.sfvisitor.org). Cruise the pages for a calendar of events, dining and attractions discounts, and basic travel information on San Francisco.
- **Chowhound** (www.chowhound.com). Food fiends peruse this site for insider info on the latest restaurants. Its message board makes for tasty restaurant-related chats.

reason than that they paid money to get the placement.

Of the "big three" sites, **Expedia** offers a long list of special deals and "virtual tours" or photos of available rooms so you can see what you're paying for (a feature that helps counter the claims that the best rooms are often held back from bargain booking websites). **Travelocity** posts unvarnished customer reviews and ranks its properties according to the AAA rating system. Also reliable are **Hotels. com** and **Quikbook.com**. An excellent free program, **TravelAxe** (www.travelaxe.net), can help you search multiple hotel sites at once, even ones you may never have heard of—and conveniently lists the total price of the room, including the taxes and service charges. Another booking site, **Travelweb** (www.travelweb), is partly owned by the hotels it represents (including the Hilton, Hyatt, and Starwood chains) and is therefore plugged directly into the hotels' reservations systems—unlike independent online agencies, which have to fax or e-mail reservation requests to the hotel, a good portion of which get misplaced in the shuffle. More than once, travelers have arrived at the hotel, only to be told that they have no reservation. To be fair, many of the major sites are undergoing improvements in service and ease of use, and Expedia will soon be able to plug directly into the reservations systems of many hotel chains— none of which can be bad news for consumers. In the meantime, it's a good idea to **get a confirmation number** and **make a printout** of any online booking transaction.

In the opaque website category, **Priceline** and **Hotwire** are even better for hotels than for airfares; with both, you're allowed to pick the neighborhood and quality level of your hotel before offering up your money. Priceline's hotel product even covers Europe and Asia, though it's much better at getting five-star lodging for three-star prices than at finding anything at the bottom of the scale. On the downside, many hotels stick Priceline guests in their least desirable rooms. Be sure to go to the BiddingForTravel website (see above) before bidding on a hotel room on Priceline; it features a fairly up-to-date list of hotels that Priceline uses in major cities. For both Priceline and Hotwire, you pay upfront, and the fee is nonrefundable. *Note:* Some hotels do not provide loyalty program credits or points or other frequent-stay amenities when you book a room through opaque online services.

8 Getting There

BY PLANE

The Bay Area has two major airports: San Francisco International and Oakland International.

SAN FRANCISCO INTERNATIONAL AIRPORT Almost four dozen major scheduled carriers serve **San Francisco International Airport** (© 650/821-8211; www.flysfo.com), 14 miles directly south of downtown on U.S. 101. Travel time to downtown during commuter rush hour is about 40 minutes; at other times, it's about 20 to 25 minutes.

The airport offers a **hot line** (© 415/817-1717) for information on ground transportation. It gives you a rundown of all your options for getting into the city from the airport (also see below for this information). Each of the three main terminals has a desk where you can get the same information.

GETTING INTO TOWN FROM SAN FRANCISCO INTERNATIONAL AIRPORT

Great news for the budget traveler! **BART** (Bay Area Rapid Transit; © 510/464-6000 or 415/989-2278; www.bart.gov) began running from SFO to numerous stops within downtown San Francisco in June 2003. This new route, which takes about 35 minutes, avoids gnarly traffic on the way and costs a heck of a lot less (around $6 each way, depending on exactly where you're going) than taxis or shuttles. Just jump on the airport's free shuttle bus to the International terminal, enter the BART station there, and you're on your way to San Francisco. Trains leave approximately every 15 minutes.

A **cab** from the airport to downtown costs $30 to $35, plus tip, and takes about 20 to 25 minutes, traffic permitting.

SFO Airporter buses (☎ **650/246-8942;** www.sfoairporter.com) depart from outside the lower-level baggage-claim area for downtown San Francisco every 30 minutes from 5:35am to 9:05pm. Shuttles on the 30-minute circuit stop at several Union Square–area hotels, including the Westin St. Francis, Hilton, Nikko, Renaissance Parc 55, and downtown Marriott. A shuttle running every 60 minutes stops at the Palace Hotel, Crowne Plaza, Hyatt Regency, and Grand Hyatt. No reservations are needed. For the return trip, SFO Airporter picks up at hotels as early as 5:30am; make a reservation 24 hours in advance if possible. The cost per person is $14 one-way, $22 round-trip; children under 3 ride free.

Other private shuttle companies offer door-to-door airport service, in which you share a van with a few other passengers. **SuperShuttle** (☎ **415/558-8500;** www.supershuttle.com) takes you anywhere in the city, charging $14 to a residence or business. Add $8 for each additional person. It costs $65 plus $1 per each passenger to charter an entire van for up to seven people. The shuttle stops every 20 minutes or so and picks up passengers from the marked areas outside the terminals' upper levels. Reservations are required for the return trip to the airport only and should be made 1 day before departure. These shuttles often demand they pick you up 2 hours before your domestic flight and 3 hours before international flights and during holidays. Keep in mind that you could be the first one on and the last one off, so this trip could take a while; you might want to ask before getting in.

The San Mateo County Transit system, **SamTrans** (☎ **800/660-4287** in Northern California, or 650/508-6200; www.samtrans.com), runs two buses between the San Francisco Airport and the Transbay Terminal at First and Mission streets. Bus no. 292 costs $1.25 and makes the trip in about 55 minutes. The KX bus costs $3.50 and takes just 35 minutes but permits only one carry-on bag. Both buses run daily. The 292 starts at 5:27am and the KX starts at 6:03am. Both run frequently until 8pm, and then hourly until about midnight.

OAKLAND INTERNATIONAL AIRPORT About 5 miles south of downtown Oakland, at the Hegenberger Road exit of Calif. 17 (U.S. 880), **Oakland International Airport** (☎ **510/563-3300;** www.oaklandairport.com) primarily serves passengers with East Bay destinations. Some San Franciscans prefer this less crowded, accessible airport during busy periods—especially because by car it takes around half an hour to get there from downtown San Francisco (traffic permitting). Also, the airport is accessible by BART, which is not influenced by traffic because it travels on its own tracks (see below for more information).

GETTING INTO TOWN FROM OAKLAND INTERNATIONAL AIRPORT

Taxis from the Oakland Airport to downtown San Francisco are expensive—approximately $50, plus tip.

Bayporter Express (☎ **877/467-1800** in the Bay Area, or 415/467-1800 elsewhere; www.bayporter.com) is a shuttle service that charges $26 for the first person and $12 for each additional person for the ride from the Oakland Airport to downtown San Francisco. Children under 12 pay $7. The fare for outer areas of San Francisco is higher. The service accepts advance reservations. To the right of the Oakland Airport exit, there are usually shuttles that take you to San Francisco for around $20 per person. The shuttles in this fleet are independently owned, and prices vary.

The cheapest way to reach downtown San Francisco is to take the shuttle bus from the Oakland Airport to **BART** (Bay Area Rapid Transit; ℭ 510/464-6000; www.bart.gov). The AirBART shuttle bus runs about every 15 minutes Monday through Saturday from 6am to 11:30pm and Sunday from 8:30am to 11:30pm. It makes pickups in front of terminals 1 and 2 near the ground transportation signs. Tickets must be purchased at the Oakland Airport's vending machines prior to boarding. The cost is $2 for the 10-minute ride to BART's Coliseum station in Oakland. BART fares vary, depending on your destination; the trip to downtown San Francisco costs $2.75 and takes 20 minutes once you're on board. The entire excursion should take around 45 minutes.

AIRLINES

Dozens of carriers serve San Francisco International Airport and Oakland International Airport, including the following major domestic airlines: **Alaska Airlines** (ℭ 800/252-7522; www.alaskaair.com), **America West Airlines** (ℭ 800/327-7810; www.americawest.com), **American Airlines** (ℭ 800/433-7300; www.aa.com), **Continental Airlines** (ℭ 800/523-3273; www.continental.com), **Delta Air Lines** (ℭ 800/221-1212; www.delta.com), **Hawaiian Airlines** (ℭ 800/367-5320; www.hawaiianair.com), **JetBlue** (ℭ 800/538-2583; www.jetblue.com), **Northwest Airlines** (ℭ 800/225-2525; www.nwa.com); **Southwest Airlines** (ℭ 800/I-FLY-SWA; www.southwest.com), **United Airlines** (ℭ 800/864-8331; www.ual.com), and **US Airways** (ℭ 800/428-4322; www.usairways.com).

If you're coming from outside the United States, refer to chapter 3, which lists the major international carriers.

GETTING THROUGH THE AIRPORT

With the federalization of airport security, security procedures at U.S. airports are more stable and consistent than ever. Generally, you'll be fine if you arrive at the airport **1 hour** before a domestic flight and **2 hours** before an international flight; if you show up late, tell an airline employee and she'll probably whisk you to the front of the line.

Bring a **current, government-issued photo ID** such as a driver's license or passport. Keep your ID at the ready to show at check-in, the security checkpoint, and sometimes even the gate. (Children under 18 do not need government-issued photo IDs for domestic flights, but they do for international flights to most countries.)

In 2003, the Transportation Security Administration (TSA) phased out **gate check-in** at all U.S. airports. And **e-tickets** have made paper tickets nearly obsolete. Passengers with e-tickets can beat the ticket-counter lines by using airport **electronic kiosks** or even **online check-in** from your home computer. Online check-in involves logging on to your airlines' website, accessing your reservation, and printing out your boarding pass—and the airline may even offer you bonus miles to do so! If you're using a kiosk at the airport, bring a credit card or your frequent-flier card. Print out your boarding pass from the kiosk and simply proceed to the security checkpoint with your pass and a photo ID. If you're checking bags or looking to snag an exit-row seat, you will be able to do so using most airline kiosks. Even the smaller airlines are employing the kiosk system, but always call your airline to make sure these alternatives are available. **Curbside check-in** is also a good way to avoid lines, although a few airlines still ban curbside check-in; call before you go.

Security checkpoint lines are getting shorter than they were during 2001 and 2002, but some doozies remain. If you have trouble standing for long periods of time, tell an airline employee; the airline will provide a wheelchair. Speed up security by **not wearing metal objects** such as big belt buckles. If you've got metallic body parts, a note from your doctor can prevent a long chat with the security screeners. Keep in mind that only **ticketed passengers** are allowed past security, except for folks escorting passengers with disabilities or children.

Federalization has stabilized **what you can carry on** and **what you can't.** The general rule is that sharp things are out, nail clippers are okay, and food and beverages must be passed through the X-ray machine—but that security screeners can't make you drink from your coffee cup. Bring food in your carry-on rather than checking it, as explosive-detection machines used on checked luggage have been known to mistake food (especially chocolate, for some reason) for bombs. Travelers in the U.S. are allowed one carry-on bag, plus a "personal item" such as a purse, briefcase, or laptop bag. Carry-on hoarders can stuff all sorts of things into a laptop bag; as long as it has a laptop in it, it's still considered a personal item. The TSA has issued a list of restricted items; check its website (www.tsa.gov/public/index.jsp) for details.

Airport screeners may decide that your checked luggage needs to be searched by hand. You can now purchase luggage locks that allow screeners to open and relock a checked bag if hand-searching is necessary. Look for Travel Sentry certified locks at luggage or travel shops and Brookstone stores (you can buy them online at www.brookstone.com). These locks, approved by the TSA, can be opened by luggage inspectors with a special code or key. For more information on the locks, visit www.travelsentry.org.

If you use something other than TSA-approved locks, your lock will be cut off your suitcase if a TSA agent needs to hand-search your luggage.

FLYING FOR LESS: TIPS FOR GETTING THE BEST AIRFARE

Passengers sharing the same airplane cabin rarely pay the same fare. Travelers who need to purchase tickets at the last minute, change your itinerary at a moment's notice, or fly one-way often get stuck paying the premium rate. Here are some ways to keep your airfare costs down.

- Passengers who can book your ticket **long in advance,** who can **stay over Saturday night,** or who **fly midweek** or **at less-trafficked hours** may pay a fraction of the full fare. If your schedule is flexible, say so, and ask if you can secure a cheaper fare by changing your flight plans.

- You can also save on airfares by keeping an eye out in local newspapers for **promotional specials** or **fare wars,** when airlines lower prices on their most popular routes. You rarely see fare wars offered for peak travel times, but if you can travel in the off months, you may snag a bargain.

- Search the **Internet** for cheap fares (see "Planning Your Trip Online," earlier in this chapter).

- **Consolidators,** also known as bucket shops, are great sources for international tickets, although they usually can't beat the Internet on fares within North America. Start by looking in Sunday newspaper travel sections; U.S. travelers should focus on the *New York Times, Los Angeles Times,* and *Miami Herald.* For less-developed destinations, small travel agents who cater to immigrant communities in large cities often have the best deals. ***Beware:*** Bucket shop

Flying with Film & Video

Never pack film—developed or undeveloped—in checked bags, as the new, more powerful scanners in U.S. airports can fog film. The film you carry with you can be damaged by scanners as well. X-ray damage is cumulative; the faster the film, and the more times you put it through a scanner, the more likely the damage. Film under 800 ASA is usually safe for up to five scans. If you're taking your film through additional scans, U.S. regulations permit you to demand hand inspections. In international airports, you're at the mercy of airport officials. On international flights, store your film in transparent baggies, so you can remove it easily before you go through scanners. Keep in mind that airports are not the only places where your camera may be scanned: Highly trafficked attractions are X-raying visitors' bags with increasing frequency.

Most photo supply stores sell protective pouches designed to block damaging X-rays. The pouches fit both film and loaded cameras. They should protect your film in checked baggage, but they also may raise alarms and result in a hand inspection.

You'll have little to worry about if you are traveling with **digital cameras.** Unlike film, which is sensitive to light, the digital camera and storage cards are not affected by airport X-rays, according to Nikon. Still, if you plan to travel extensively, you may want to play it safe and hand-carry your digital equipment or ask that it be inspected by hand.

An organization called **Film Safety for Traveling on Planes (FSTOP;** 🕿 888/301-2665; www.f-stop.org), can provide additional tips for traveling with film and equipment.

Carry-on scanners will not damage **videotape** in video cameras, but the magnetic fields emitted by the walk-through security gateways and handheld inspection wands will. Always place your loaded camcorder on the screening conveyor belt or have it hand-inspected. Be sure your batteries are charged, as you will probably be required to turn the device on to ensure that it's what it appears to be.

tickets are usually nonrefundable or rigged with stiff cancellation penalties, often as high as 50% to 75% of the ticket price, and some put you on charter airlines, which may leave at inconvenient times and experience delays. Several reliable consolidators are worldwide and available on the Net. **STA Travel** is now the world's leader in student travel, thanks to their purchase of Council Travel. It also offers good fares for travelers of all ages. **ELTExpress** (**Flights.com;** 🕿 800/TRAV-800; www.elt express.com) started in Europe and has excellent fares worldwide, but particularly to that continent. It also has "local" websites in 12 countries. **FlyCheap** (🕿 800/ FLY-CHEAP; www.1800flycheap. com) is owned by package-holiday megalith MyTravel and so has especially good access to fares for sunny destinations. **Air Tickets Direct** (🕿 800/778-3447; www. airticketsdirect.com) is based in Montreal and leverages the currently weak Canadian dollar for low fares; it'll also book trips to places that U.S. travel agents won't touch, such as Cuba.

- Join **frequent-flier clubs.** Accrue enough miles, and you'll be rewarded with free flights and elite status. It's free, and you'll get the best choice of seats, faster response to phone inquiries, and prompter service if your luggage is stolen, your flight is canceled or delayed, or if you want to change your seat. You don't need to fly to build frequent-flier miles—**frequent-flier credit cards** can provide thousands of miles for doing your everyday shopping.
- For many more tips about air travel, including a rundown of the major frequent-flier credit cards, pick up a copy of *Frommer's Fly Safe, Fly Smart* (Wiley Publishing, Inc.).

BY CAR

San Francisco is easily accessible by major highways: **Interstate 5,** from the north, and **U.S. 101,** which cuts south-north through the peninsula from San Jose and across the Golden Gate Bridge to points north. If you drive from Los Angeles, you can take the longer coastal route (437 miles and 11 hr.) or the inland route (389 miles and 8 hr.). From Mendocino, it's 156 miles and 4 hours; from Sacramento, 88 miles and 1½ hours; from Yosemite, 210 miles and 4 hours.

If you are driving and aren't already a member, it's worth joining

the **American Automobile Association** (AAA; © 800/922-8228). It charges $49 to $79 per year (with an additional one-time joining fee), depending on where you join, and provides roadside and other services to motorists. **Amoco Motor Club** (© 800/334-3300) is another recommended choice.

For information about renting a car, see the "Car Rentals" section (beginning on p. 58) of chapter 4, "Getting to Know San Francisco."

BY TRAIN

Traveling by train takes a long time and usually costs as much as, or more than, flying. Still, if you want to take a leisurely ride across America, rail may be a good option.

San Francisco–bound **Amtrak** (© 800/872-7245 or 800/USA-RAIL; www.amtrak.com) trains leave from New York and cross the country via Chicago. The journey takes about 3½ days, and seats sell quickly. At this writing, the lowest round-trip fare costs $266 from New York and $244 from Chicago. Round-trip tickets from Los Angeles can cost as little as $100 or as much as $150. Trains arrive in Emeryville, just north of Oakland, and connect with regularly scheduled buses to San Francisco's Ferry Building and CalTrain station in downtown San Francisco.

CalTrain (© 800/660-4287 or 415/546-4461) operates train service between San Francisco and the towns of the peninsula. The city depot is at 700 Fourth St., at Townsend Street.

9 Packages for the Independent Traveler

Before you start your search for the lowest airfare, you may want to consider booking your flight as part of a travel package. Package tours are not the same thing as escorted tours. Package tours are simply a way to buy the airfare, accommodations, and other elements of your trip (such as car

rentals, airport transfers, and sometimes even activities) at the same time and often at discounted prices—kind of like one-stop shopping. Packages are sold in bulk to tour operators—who resell them to the public at a cost that usually undercuts standard rates.

One good source of package deals is the airlines themselves. Most major airlines offer air/land packages, including **American Airlines Vacations** (© 800/321-2121; www.aavacations.com), **Delta Vacations** (© 800/221-6666; www.deltavacations.com), **Continental Airlines Vacations** (© 800/301-3800; www.covacations.com), and **United Vacations** (© 888/854-3899; www.unitedvacations.com). Several big **online travel agencies**—Expedia, Travelocity, Orbitz, Site59, and Lastminute.com—also do a brisk business in packages. If you're unsure about the pedigree of a smaller packager, check with the Better Business Bureau in the city where the company is based, or go online at www.bbb.org. If a packager won't tell you where they're based, don't fly with them.

Travel packages are also listed in the travel section of your local Sunday newspaper. Or check ads in the national travel magazines such as *Arthur Frommer's Budget Travel Magazine, Travel + Leisure, National Geographic Traveler,* and *Condé Nast Traveler.*

Package tours can vary by leaps and bounds. Some offer a better class of hotels than others. Some offer the same hotels for lower prices. Some offer flights on scheduled airlines, while others book charters. Some limit your choice of accommodations and travel days. You are often required to make a large payment up front. On the plus side, packages can save you money, offering group prices but allowing for independent travel. Some even let you to add on a few guided excursions or escorted day trips (also at prices lower than if you booked them yourself) without booking an entirely escorted tour.

Before you invest in a package tour, get some answers. Ask about the **accommodations choices** and prices for each. Then look up the hotels' reviews in a Frommer's guide and check their rates online for your specific dates of travel online. You'll also want to find out what **type of room** you get. If you need a certain type of room, ask for it; don't take whatever is thrown your way. Request a nonsmoking room, a quiet room, a room with a view, or whatever you fancy.

Finally, look for **hidden expenses.** Ask whether airport departure fees and taxes, for example, are included in the total cost.

10 Recommended Books

San Francisco was a popular setting for many early literary works, including Mark Twain's *San Francisco,* a collection of articles that glorified "the liveliest, heartiest community on our continent." It was also the birthplace of Jack London, who wrote several short stories of his younger days as an oyster pirate on the San Francisco Bay, as well as *Martin Eden,* his semiautobiographical account of life along the Oakland shores.

For all you mystery buffs, two must-reads are Frank Norris's *McTeague: A Story of San Francisco,* a violent tale of love and greed set at the turn of the 20th century; and Dashiell Hammett's *The Maltese Falcon,* a steamy detective novel that captures the seedier side of San Francisco in the 1920s (you can even take a walking tour of Hammett's famous haunts).

California has always been a hotbed of alternative—and, more often than not, controversial—literary styles. Joan Didion, in her novel *Slouching Toward Bethlehem,* and Hunter S. Thompson, in his columns for the *San Francisco Examiner* (brought together in the collection *Generation of Swine*), both used a "new journalistic" approach in their studies of San

Francisco in the 1960s. Tom Wolfe's early work *The Electric Kool-Aid Acid Test* follows the Hell's Angels, the Grateful Dead, and Ken Kesey's Merry Pranksters as they ride through the hallucinogenic 1960s. Meanwhile, Beat writers Allen Ginsberg and Jack Kerouac were penning protests against political conservatism—and promoting their bohemian lifestyle—in the former's controversial poem "Howl" (daringly published by Lawrence Ferlinghetti, poet and owner of City Lights in San Francisco's North Beach District) and the latter's famous tale of American adventure, *On the Road.*

Among Wallace Stegner's many works of contemporary fiction and nonfiction about the West is his novel *All the Little Live Things,* which explores the conflicts faced by retired literary agent Joe Allston; the book is set in the San Francisco Bay Area of the 1960s. *The Spectator Bird* (winner of the 1976 National Book Award) revisits Allston's character as he reflects on his life and his memories of a search for his roots.

3

For International Visitors

Whether it's your 1st visit or your 10th, a trip to the United States may require an additional degree of planning. This chapter will provide you with essential information, helpful tips, and advice for the more common problems that some visitors encounter.

1 Preparing for Your Trip

ENTRY REQUIREMENTS
Check at any U.S. embassy or consulate for current information and requirements. You can also obtain a visa application and other information online at the **U.S. State Department**'s website, at **www.travel.state.gov**.

VISAS The U.S. State Department has a **Visa Waiver Program** allowing citizens of certain countries to enter the United States without a visa for stays of up to 90 days. At press time these included Andorra, Australia, Austria, Belgium, Brunei, Denmark, Finland, France, Germany, Iceland, Ireland, Italy, Japan, Liechtenstein, Luxembourg, Monaco, the Netherlands, New Zealand, Norway, Portugal, San Marino, Singapore, Slovenia, Spain, Sweden, Switzerland, and the United Kingdom. Citizens of these countries need only a valid passport and a round-trip air or cruise ticket in their possession upon arrival. If they first enter the United States, they may also visit Mexico, Canada, Bermuda, and/or the Caribbean islands and return to the United States without a visa. Further information is available from any U.S. embassy or consulate. Canadian citizens may enter the United States without visas; they need only proof of residence.

Citizens of all other countries must have (1) a valid passport that expires at least 6 months later than the scheduled end of their visit to the United States, and (2) a tourist visa, which may be obtained without charge from any U.S. consulate.

To obtain a visa, the traveler must submit a completed application form (either in person or by mail) with a 1½-inch-square photo, and must demonstrate binding ties to a residence abroad. Usually you can obtain a visa at once or within 24 hours, but it may take longer during the summer rush from June through August. If you cannot go in person, contact the nearest U.S. embassy or consulate for directions on applying by mail. Your travel agent or airline office may also be able to provide you with visa applications and instructions. The U.S. consulate or embassy that issues your visa will determine whether you will be issued a multiple- or single-entry visa and any restrictions regarding the length of your stay.

British subjects can obtain up-to-date visa information by calling the **U.S. Embassy Visa Information Line** (© 0891/200-290) or by visiting the "Consular Services" section of the American Embassy London's website at www.usembassy.org.uk.

Irish citizens can obtain up-to-date visa information through the **Embassy of the USA Dublin,** 42 Elgin Rd.,

Dublin 4, Ireland (℗ **353/1-668-8777**), or by checking the "Consular Services" section of the website at www.usembassy.ie.

Australian citizens can obtain up-to-date visa information by contacting the **U.S. Embassy Canberra,** Moonah Place, Yarralumla, ACT 2600 (℗ **02/6214-5600**), or by checking the U.S. Diplomatic Mission's website at http://usembassy-australia.state.gov/consular.

Citizens of **New Zealand** can obtain up-to-date visa information by contacting the **U.S. Embassy New Zealand,** 29 Fitzherbert Terrace, Thorndon, Wellington (℗ **644/472-2068**), or get the information directly from the "Services to New Zealanders" section of the website at http://usembassy.org.nz.

MEDICAL REQUIREMENTS

Unless you're arriving from an area known to be suffering from an epidemic (particularly cholera or yellow fever), inoculations or vaccinations are not required for entry into the United States. If you have a medical condition that requires **syringe-administered medications,** carry a valid signed prescription from your physician—the Federal Aviation Administration (FAA) no longer allows airline passengers to pack syringes in their carry-on baggage without documented proof of medical need. If you have a disease that requires treatment with **narcotics,** you should also carry documented proof with you—smuggling narcotics aboard a plane is a serious offense that carries severe penalties in the U.S.

For **HIV-positive visitors,** requirements for entering the United States are somewhat vague and change frequently. According to the latest publication of *HIV and Immigrants: A Manual for AIDS Service Providers,* the Immigration and Naturalization Service (INS) doesn't require a medical exam for entry into the United States,

but INS officials may stop individuals because they look sick or because they are carrying AIDS/HIV medicine.

If an HIV-positive noncitizen applies for a nonimmigrant visa, the question on the application regarding communicable diseases is tricky no matter which way it's answered. If the applicant checks "no," INS may deny the visa on the grounds that the applicant committed fraud. If the applicant checks "yes" or if INS suspects the person is HIV-positive, it will deny the visa unless the applicant asks for a special waiver for visitors. This waiver is for people visiting the United States for a short time, to attend a conference, for instance, to visit close relatives, or to receive medical treatment. It can be a confusing situation. For up-to-the-minute information, contact **AIDSinfo** (℗ **800/448-0440,** or 301/519-6616 outside the U.S.; www.aidsinfo.nih.gov) or the **Gay Men's Health Crisis** (℗ **212/367-1000;** www.gmhc.org).

DRIVER'S LICENSES Foreign driver's licenses are mostly recognized in the U.S., although you may want to get an international driver's license if your home license is not written in English.

PASSPORT INFORMATION

Safeguard your passport in an inconspicuous, inaccessible place like a money belt. Make a copy of the critical pages, including the passport number, and store it in a safe place, separate from the passport itself. If you lose your passport, visit the nearest consulate of your native country as soon as possible for a replacement. Passport applications are downloadable from the websites listed below.

Note: The International Civil Aviation Organization has recommended a policy requiring that *every* individual who travels by air have a passport. In response, many countries are now requiring that children must be issued their own passport to travel internationally, where before those under 16 or so may have been allowed to travel on a parent or guardian's passport.

FOR RESIDENTS OF CANADA

You can pick up a passport application at one of 28 regional passport offices or most travel agencies. Canadian children who travel must have their own passport. However, if you hold a valid Canadian passport issued before December 11, 2001, that bears the name of your child, the passport remains valid for you and your child until it expires. Passports cost C$85 for those 16 years and older (valid 5 years), C$35 children 3 to 15 (valid 5 years), and C$20, children under 3 (valid 3 years). Applications, which must be accompanied by two identical passport-size photographs and proof of Canadian citizenship, are available at travel agencies throughout Canada or from the central **Passport Office,** Department of Foreign Affairs and International Trade, Ottawa, ON K1A 0G3 (② **800/567-6868;** www.dfait-maeci.gc.ca/passport). Processing takes 5 to 10 days if you apply in person, or about 3 weeks by mail.

FOR RESIDENTS OF THE UNITED KINGDOM

As a member of the European Union, you need only an identity card, not a passport, to travel to other E.U. countries. However, if you already possess a passport, it's always useful to carry it. To pick up an application for a standard 10-year passport (5-year passport for children under 16), visit the nearest Passport Office, major post office, or travel agency. You can also contact the **United Kingdom Passport Service** at ② **0870/571-0410** or visit its website at www.passport.gov.uk. Passports are £33 for adults and £19 for children under 16, with another £30 fee if you apply in person at a Passport Office. Processing takes about 2 weeks

(1 week if you apply at the Passport Office).

FOR RESIDENTS OF IRELAND

You can apply for a 10-year passport, costing €57, at the **Passport Office,** Setanta Centre, Molesworth Street, Dublin 2 (② **01/671-1633;** www.irlgov.ie/iveagh). Those under 18 and over 65 must apply for a €12 3-year passport. You can also apply at 1A South Mall, Cork (② **021/272-525**) or over the counter at most main post offices.

FOR RESIDENTS OF AUSTRALIA

You can get an application from your local post office or any branch of Passports Australia, but you must schedule an interview at the passport office to present your application materials. Call the **Australian Passport Information Service** at ② **131-232,** or visit the government website at www.passports.gov.au. Passports for adults are A$144 and for those under 18 are A$72.

FOR RESIDENTS OF NEW ZEALAND

You can pick up a passport application at any New Zealand Passports Office or download it from their website. Contact the **Passports Office** at ② **0800/225-050** in New Zealand, or 04/474-8100, or log on to www.passports.govt.nz. Passports for adults are NZ$80 and for children under 16 NZ$40.

CUSTOMS
WHAT YOU CAN BRING IN

Every visitor more than 21 years of age may bring in, free of duty, the following: (1) 1 liter of wine or hard liquor; (2) 200 cigarettes, 100 cigars (but not from Cuba), or 3 pounds of smoking tobacco; and (3) $100 worth of gifts. These exemptions are offered to travelers who spend at least 72 hours in the United States and who have not claimed them within the preceding 6 months. It is altogether forbidden to bring into the country foodstuffs (particularly fruit, cooked meats, and canned goods) and plants (vegetables, seeds, tropical plants, and the like). Foreign tourists may bring in or take out up to $10,000 in U.S. or foreign currency with no formalities; larger sums must be declared to U.S. Customs on entering or leaving, which includes filing form CM 4790. For more specific information regarding U.S. Customs and Border Protection, contact your nearest U.S. embassy or consulate, or the **U.S. Customs** office (✆ **202/927-1770;** www.customs.us treas.gov).

WHAT YOU CAN TAKE HOME

U.K. citizens returning from a non-E.U. country have a customs allowance of: 200 cigarettes; 50 cigars; 250 grams of smoking tobacco; 2 liters of still table wine; 1 liter of spirits or strong liqueurs (over 22% volume); 2 liters of fortified wine, sparkling wine or other liqueurs; 60cc (ml) perfume; 250cc (ml) of toilet water; and £145 worth of all other goods, including gifts and souvenirs. People under 17 cannot have the tobacco or alcohol allowance. For more information, contact HM Customs & Excise at ✆ **0845/010-9000** (from outside the U.K., 020/8929-0152), or consult their website at www.hmce.gov.uk.

For a clear summary of **Canadian** rules, request the booklet *I Declare,* issued by the **Canada Customs and Revenue Agency** (✆ **800/461-9999** in Canada, or 204/983-3500; www. ccra-adrc.gc.ca). Canada allows its citizens a C$750 exemption, and you're allowed to bring back duty-free 1 carton of cigarettes, 1 can of tobacco, 40 imperial ounces of liquor, and 50 cigars. In addition, you're allowed to mail gifts to Canada valued at less than C$60 a day, provided they're unsolicited and don't contain alcohol or tobacco (write on the package "Unsolicited gift, under $60 value"). All valuables should be declared on the Y-38 form before departure from Canada, including serial numbers of valuables you already own, such as expensive foreign cameras. *Note:* The $750 exemption can only be used once a year and only after an absence of 7 days.

The duty-free allowance in **Australia** is A$400 or, for those under 18, A$200. Citizens age 18 and over can bring in 250 cigarettes or 250 grams of loose tobacco, and 1,125 milliliters of alcohol. If you're returning with valuables you already own, such as foreign-made cameras, you should file form B263. A helpful brochure available from Australian consulates or Customs offices is *Know Before You Go.* For more information, call the **Australian Customs Service** at ✆ **1300/363-263,** or log on to www. customs.gov.au.

The duty-free allowance for **New Zealand** is NZ$700. Citizens over 17 can bring in 200 cigarettes, 50 cigars, or 250 grams of tobacco (or a mixture of all three if their combined weight doesn't exceed 250g); plus 4.5 liters of wine and beer, or 1.125 liters of liquor. New Zealand currency does not carry import or export restrictions. Fill out a certificate of export, listing the valuables you are taking out of the country; that way, you can bring them back without paying duty. Most questions are answered in a free pamphlet available at New Zealand consulates and Customs offices: *New Zealand Customs Guide for Travellers, Notice no. 4.* For more information, contact **New Zealand Customs,** The Customhouse, 17–21 Whitmore St., Box 2218, Wellington (✆ **0800/428-786** or 04/473-6099; www.customs. govt.nz).

HEALTH INSURANCE

Although it's not required of travelers, health insurance is highly recommended. Unlike many European countries, the United States does not usually offer free or low-cost medical care to its citizens or visitors. Doctors and hospitals are expensive, and in most cases will require advance payment or proof of coverage before they render their services. Policies can cover everything from the loss or theft of your baggage and trip cancellation to the guarantee of bail in case you're arrested. Good policies will also cover the costs of an accident, repatriation, or death. Packages such as **Europ Assistance's "Worldwide Healthcare Plan"** are sold by European automobile clubs and travel agencies at attractive rates. **Worldwide Assistance Services, Inc.** (© 800/821-2828; www.worldwideassistance.com) is the agent for Europ Assistance in the United States.

Though lack of health insurance may prevent you from being admitted to a hospital in nonemergencies, don't worry about being left on a street corner to die: The American way is to fix you now and bill the living daylights out of you later.

INSURANCE FOR BRITISH TRAVELERS

Most big travel agents offer their own insurance and will probably try to sell you their package when you book a holiday. Think before you sign. **Britain's Consumers' Association** recommends that you insist on seeing the policy and reading the fine print before buying travel insurance. **The Association of British Insurers** (© 020/7600-3333; www.abi.org.uk) gives advice by phone and publishes *Holiday Insurance,* a free guide to policy provisions and prices. You might also shop around for better deals: Try **Columbus Direct** (© 020/7375-0011; www.columbusdirect.net).

INSURANCE FOR CANADIAN TRAVELERS

Canadians should check with their provincial health plan offices or call **Health Canada** (© 613/957-2991; www.hc-sc.gc.ca) to find out the extent of their coverage and what documentation and receipts they must take home in case they are treated in the United States.

MONEY

CURRENCY The U.S. monetary system is very simple: The most common **bills** are the $1 (colloquially, a "buck"), $5, $10, and $20 denominations. There are also $2 bills (seldom encountered), $50 bills, and $100 bills (the last two are usually not welcome as payment for small purchases). All the paper money was recently redesigned, making the famous faces adorning them disproportionately large. The old-style bills are still legal tender.

There are seven denominations of coins: 1¢ (1 cent, or a penny); 5¢ (5 cents, or a nickel); 10¢ (10 cents, or a dime); 25¢ (25 cents, or a quarter); 50¢ (50 cents, or a half dollar); the new gold-colored "Sacagawea" coin worth $1; and, prized by collectors, the rare, older silver dollar.

Note: The "foreign-exchange bureaus" so common in Europe are rare even at airports in the United States, and nonexistent outside major cities. It's best not to change foreign money (or traveler's checks denominated in a currency other than U.S. dollars) at a small-town bank, or even a branch in a big city; in fact, leave any currency other than U.S. dollars at home—it may prove a greater nuisance to you than it's worth.

TRAVELER'S CHECKS Though traveler's checks are widely accepted, make sure that they're denominated in U.S. dollars, as foreign-currency checks are often difficult to exchange. The three traveler's checks that are most widely recognized—and least likely to be denied—are **Visa, American Express,** and **Thomas Cook.** Be sure to record the numbers of the checks, and keep that information in a separate place in case they get lost or stolen. Most businesses are pretty good about taking traveler's checks, but you're better off cashing them in at a bank (in small amounts, of course) and paying in cash. Remember: You'll need identification, such as a driver's license or passport, to change a traveler's check.

CREDIT CARDS & ATMS Credit cards are the most widely used form of payment in the United States: **Visa** (Barclaycard in Britain), **MasterCard** (EuroCard in Europe, Access in Britain, Chargex in Canada), **American Express, Diners Club, Discover,** and **Carte Blanche.** There are, however, a handful of stores and restaurants that do not take credit cards, so be sure to ask in advance. Most businesses display a sticker near their entrance to let you know which cards they accept. (*Note:* Businesses may require a minimum purchase, usually around $10, to use a credit card.)

It is strongly recommended that you bring at least one major credit card. You must have a credit or charge card to rent a car. Hotels and airlines usually require a credit card imprint as a deposit against expenses, and in an emergency a credit card can be priceless.

You'll find **automated teller machines (ATMs)** on just about every block—at least in almost every town—across the country. Some ATMs will allow you to draw U.S. currency against your bank and credit cards. Check with your bank before leaving home, and remember that you will need your personal identification number (PIN) to do so. Most accept Visa,

MasterCard, and American Express, as well as ATM cards from other U.S. banks. Expect to be charged up to $3 per transaction, however, if you're not using your own bank's ATM.

One way around these fees is to ask for cash back at grocery stores that accept ATM cards and don't charge usage fees. Of course, you'll have to purchase something first.

ATM cards with major credit card backing, known as "debit cards," are now a commonly acceptable form of payment in most stores and restaurants. Debit cards draw money directly from your checking account. Some stores enable you to receive "cash back" on your debit card purchases as well.

SAFETY
GENERAL   SUGGESTIONS
Although tourist areas are generally safe, U.S. urban areas tend to be less safe than those in Europe or Japan. You should always stay alert. This is particularly true of large American cities. If you're in doubt about which neighborhoods are safe, don't hesitate to make inquiries with the hotel front desk staff or the local tourist office.

Avoid deserted areas, especially at night, and don't go into public parks after dark unless there's a concert or similar occasion that will attract a crowd.

Avoid carrying valuables with you on the street, and keep expensive cameras or electronic equipment bagged up or covered when not in use. If you're using a map, try to consult it inconspicuously—or better yet, study it before you leave your room. Hold onto your pocketbook, and place your

---

Tips **Travel Tip**

Be sure to keep a copy of all your travel papers separate from your wallet or purse, and leave a copy with someone at home should you need it faxed in an emergency.

billfold in an inside pocket. In theaters, restaurants, and other public places, keep your possessions in sight.

Always lock your room door—don't assume that once you're inside the hotel you are automatically safe and no longer need to be aware of your surroundings. Hotels are open to the public, and in a large hotel, security may not be able to screen everyone who enters. Yes, this advice is a little paranoid. San Francisco tends to be a very safe city. But it never hurts to be careful—especially if you're wandering through areas of the Mission, Tenderloin (a few blocks west of Union Square), Hunter's Point, SoMa, and Lower Haight.

DRIVING SAFETY Driving safety is important too, and carjacking is not unprecedented. Question your rental agency about personal safety and ask for a traveler-safety brochure when you pick up your car. Obtain written directions—or a map with the route clearly marked—from the agency showing how to get to your destination. (Many agencies now offer the option of renting a cellphone for the duration of your car rental; check with the rental agent when you pick up the car. Otherwise, contact **InTouch USA** at © **800/872-7626** or www.intouch usa.com for short-term cellphone rental.) And, if possible, arrive and depart during daylight hours.

If you drive off a highway and end up in a dodgy-looking neighborhood, leave the area as quickly as possible. If you have an accident, even on the highway, stay in your car with the doors locked until you assess the situation or until the police arrive. If you're bumped from behind on the street or are involved in a minor accident with no injuries, and the situation appears to be suspicious, motion to the other driver to follow you. Never get out of your car in such situations. Go directly to the nearest police precinct, well-lit service station, or 24-hour store.

Park in well-lit and well-traveled areas whenever possible. Always keep your car doors locked, whether the vehicle is attended or unattended. Never leave any packages or valuables in sight. If someone attempts to rob you or steal your car, don't try to resist the thief/carjacker. Report the incident to the police department immediately by calling © **911.**

2 Getting to the U.S.

AIRLINE DISCOUNTS The smart traveler can find innumerable ways to reduce the price of a plane ticket simply by taking time to shop around. For example, overseas visitors can take advantage of the APEX (advance purchase excursion) reductions offered by all major U.S. and European carriers. For more money-saving airline advice, see "Getting There," in chapter 2. For the best rates, compare fares and be flexible with the dates and times of travel.

A number of international carriers serve the Bay Area airports. They include **Aer Lingus** (© **01/0818/ 365000** in Dublin; www.aerlingus.ie),

Air Canada (© **888-247-2262;** www.aircanada.ca), **British Airways** (© **0845/773-3377** in the U.K.; www.british-airways.com), **Japan Airlines** (© **0120-25-5971** in Tokyo; www.jal.co.jp), **Qantas** (© **13-13-13** in Australia; www.qantas.com.au), and **Virgin Atlantic** (© **870/380-2007** in the U.K.; www.virgin-atlantic.com). British Airways and Virgin Atlantic offer direct flights to San Francisco from London. **Air New Zealand** (© **0800/352-266** in New Zealand; www.airnewzealand.co.nz) flies to Los Angeles and will book you through to San Francisco on a partner airline.

Tips   **Prepare to Be Fingerprinted**

Starting in January 2004, many international visitors traveling on visas to the United States will be photographed and fingerprinted at Customs in a new program created by the Department of Homeland Security called **US-VISIT.** Non–U.S. citizens arriving at airports and on cruise ships must undergo an instant background check as part of the government's ongoing efforts to deter terrorism by verifying the identity of incoming and outgoing visitors. Exempt from the extra scrutiny are visitors entering by land or those from 28 countries (mostly in Europe) that don't require a visa for short-term visits. For more information, go to the Homeland Security website at **www.dhs.gov/dhspublic**.

Major U.S. carriers, such as **Continental** (② **01293/776-464** in the U.K.; www.continental.com), **United** (② **084/584-44777** in the U.K.; www.ual.com), **American** (② **207-365-0777** in London, or 8457-789-789 outside London in the U.K.; www.aa.com), and **Delta** (② **0800/414-767** in the U.K.; www.delta.com), have service from Europe to the United States. **United** (② **61/2/9251-3211** in Australia) flies from Sydney to San Francisco.

IMMIGRATION & CUSTOMS CLEARANCE Visitors arriving by air, no matter what the port of entry, should cultivate patience and resignation before setting foot on U.S. soil. Getting through immigration control can take as long as 2 hours on some days, especially on summer weekends, so be sure to carry this guidebook or something else to read. This is especially true in the aftermath of the World Trade Center attacks, when security clearances have been considerably beefed up at U.S. airports.

People traveling by air from Canada, Bermuda, and certain countries in the Caribbean can sometimes clear Customs and Immigration at the point of departure, which is much quicker.

3 Getting Around the U.S.

BY PLANE Some large airlines (for example, Northwest and Delta) offer travelers on their transatlantic or transpacific flights special discount tickets under the name **Visit USA,** allowing mostly one-way travel from one U.S. destination to another at very low prices. These discount tickets are not on sale in the United States and must be purchased abroad in conjunction with your international ticket. This system is the best, easiest, and fastest way to see the United States at low cost. You should obtain information well in advance from your travel agent or the office of the airline concerned, since the conditions attached to these discount tickets can be changed without advance notice.

BY TRAIN International visitors (excluding Canada) can also buy a **USA Rail Pass,** good for 15 or 30 days of unlimited travel on Amtrak (② **800/USA-RAIL;** www.amtrak.com). The pass is available through many overseas travel agents. Prices in 2004 for a 15-day pass were $295 off-peak, $440 peak; a 30-day pass costs $385 off-peak, $550 peak; children ages 2 to 15 are half price. With a foreign passport, you can also buy passes at some Amtrak offices in the United States, including locations in San Francisco, Los Angeles, Chicago, New

York, Miami, Boston, and Washington, D.C. Reservations are generally required and should be made for each part of your trip as early as possible. Regional rail passes are also available.

BY BUS   Although bus travel is often the most economical form of public transit for short hops between U.S. cities, it can also be slow and uncomfortable—certainly not an option for everyone (particularly when Amtrak, which is far more luxurious, offers similar rates). **Greyhound/Trailways** (© **800/231-2222;** www.greyhound. com), the sole nationwide bus line, offers an **International Ameripass** that must be purchased before coming to the United States, or by phone through the Greyhound International Office at the Port Authority Bus Terminal in New York City (© **888/454-7277** or 212/971-0492). The pass can be obtained from foreign travel agents or through Greyhound's website (order at least 21 days before your departure to the U.S.) and costs less than the domestic version. Passes for 2005 cost as follows: 7 days ($209), 10 days ($259), 15 days ($309), 21 days ($359), 30 days ($399), 45 days ($459), or 60 days ($569). You can get more info on the pass at the Greyhound website. In addition, special rates are available for seniors and students.

BY CAR   Unless you plan to spend the bulk of your vacation time in San Francisco where walking, taxis, or public transportation are the best and easiest ways to get around, the most cost-effective, convenient, and comfortable way to travel around the United States is by car. The interstate highway system connects cities and towns all over the country; in addition to these high-speed, limited-access roadways, there's an extensive network of federal, state, and local highways and roads. Some of the national car-rental companies include **Alamo** (© 800/462-5266; www.alamo.com), **Avis** (© 800/230-4898; www.avis. com), **Budget** (© 800/527-0700; www.budget.com), **Dollar** (© 800/800-3665; www.dollar.com), **Hertz** (© 800/654-3131; www.hertz.com), **National** (© 800/227-7368; www. nationalcar.com), and **Thrifty** (© 800/847-4389; www.thrifty.com).

If you plan to rent a car in the United States, you probably won't need the services of an additional automobile organization. If you're planning to buy or borrow a car, automobile-association membership is recommended. **AAA, the American Automobile Association** (© **800/222-4357**), is the country's largest auto club and supplies its members with maps, insurance, and, most important, emergency road service. The cost of joining runs from $66 for singles to $96 for two members, but if you're a member of a foreign auto club with reciprocal arrangements, you can enjoy free AAA service in America. See "Getting There," in chapter 2, for more information.

FAST FACTS: **For the International Traveler**

Automobile Organizations Auto clubs will supply maps, suggested routes, guidebooks, accident and bail-bond insurance, and emergency road service. The **American Automobile Association (AAA)** is the major auto club in the United States. If you belong to an auto club in your home country, inquire about AAA reciprocity before you leave. You may be able to join AAA even if you're not a member of a reciprocal club; to inquire, call AAA (© **800/222-4357**). AAA is actually an organization of regional auto clubs; so look under "AAA Automobile Club" in the White Pages of the telephone directory. AAA has a nationwide emergency road service telephone number (© 800/AAA-HELP). The **AAA** office in San Francisco is located at 150 Van Ness Ave.

Business Hours See "Fast Facts: San Francisco," on p. 61.

Currency & Currency Exchange Foreign-exchange bureaus are rare in the United States, and most banks are not equipped to handle currency exchange. San Francisco's money-changing offices include **Bank of America,** 345 Montgomery St. (© **415/622-2451**), open Monday through Friday from 9am to 6pm; and **Thomas Cook,** 75 Geary St. (© **415/362-3452;** www.us.thomascook.com), open Monday through Friday from 9am to 5pm and Saturday from 10am to 4pm. Also, see "Entry Requirements" and "Money" under "Preparing for Your Trip," earlier in this chapter.

Drinking Laws The legal age for purchase and consumption of alcoholic beverages is 21; proof of age is required and often requested at bars, nightclubs, and restaurants, so it's always a good idea to bring ID when you go out. In San Francisco, supermarkets and grocery and liquor stores sell liquor daily from 6am to 2am. Licensed restaurants are permitted to sell alcohol during the same hours. Note that many restaurants are licensed only for beer and wine.

Do not carry open containers of alcohol in your car or any public area that isn't zoned for alcohol consumption. The police can fine you on the spot. And nothing will ruin your trip faster than getting a citation for DUI (driving under the influence), so don't even think about driving while intoxicated.

Electricity Like Canada, the United States uses 110–120 volts AC (60 cycles), compared to 220–240 volts AC (50 cycles) in most of Europe, Australia, and New Zealand. If your small appliances use 220–240 volts, you'll need a 110-volt transformer and a plug adapter with two flat parallel pins to operate them here. Downward converters that change 220–240 volts to 110–120 volts are difficult to find in the United States, so bring one with you.

Embassies & Consulates All embassies are located in the nation's capital, Washington, D.C. Some consulates are located in major U.S. cities, and most nations have a mission to the United Nations in New York City. If your country isn't listed below, call for directory information in Washington, D.C. (© **202/555-1212**) or log on to **www.embassy.org/embassies**.

The embassy of **Australia** is at 1601 Massachusetts Ave. NW, Washington, DC 20036 (© **202/797-3000;** www.austemb.org). There are consulates in New York, Honolulu, Houston, Los Angeles, and San Francisco.

The embassy of **Canada** is at 501 Pennsylvania Ave. NW, Washington, DC 20001 (© **202/682-1740;** www.canadianembassy.org). Other Canadian consulates are in Buffalo (New York), Detroit, Los Angeles, New York, and Seattle.

The embassy of **Ireland** is at 2234 Massachusetts Ave. NW, Washington, DC 20008 (© **202/462-3939;** www.irelandemb.org). Irish consulates are in Boston, Chicago, New York, and San Francisco.

The embassy of **Japan** is at 2520 Massachusetts Ave. NW, Washington, DC 20008 (© **202/238-6700;** www.embjapan.org). Japanese consulates are located in many cities including Atlanta, Boston, Detroit, New York, San Francisco, and Seattle.

The embassy of **New Zealand** is at 37 Observatory Circle NW, Washington, DC 20008 (© **202/328-4800**; www.nzemb.org). New Zealand consulates are in Los Angeles, Salt Lake City, San Francisco, and Seattle.

The embassy of the **United Kingdom** is at 3100 Massachusetts Ave. NW, Washington, DC 20008 (© **202/462-1340**; www.britainusa.com). Other British consulates are in Atlanta, Boston, Chicago, Cleveland, Houston, Los Angeles, New York, San Francisco, and Seattle.

Emergencies Call © **911** to report a fire, call the police, or get an ambulance anywhere in the United States. This is a toll-free call. (No coins are required at public telephones.)

If you encounter serious problems, contact the **Traveler's Aid International** (© **202/546-1127**; www.travelersaid.org) to help direct you to a local branch. This nationwide, nonprofit, social-service organization geared to helping travelers in difficult straits offers services that might include reuniting families separated while traveling, providing food and/or shelter to people stranded without cash, or even emotional counseling. If you're in trouble, seek them out.

Gasoline (Petrol) Petrol is known as gasoline (or simply "gas") in the United States, and petrol stations are known as both gas stations and service stations. Gasoline costs about half as much here as it does in Europe (though lately prices have been skyrocketing, fluctuating between about $2.30 and $2.50 per gallon at press time), and taxes are already included in the printed price. One U.S. gallon equals 3.8 liters or .85 imperial gallons.

Holidays Banks, government offices, post offices, and many stores, restaurants, and museums are closed on the following legal national holidays: January 1 (New Year's Day), the third Monday in January (Martin Luther King, Jr., Day), the third Monday in February (Presidents' Day, Washington's Birthday), the last Monday in May (Memorial Day), July 4 (Independence Day), the first Monday in September (Labor Day), the second Monday in October (Columbus Day), November 11 (Veterans' Day/Armistice Day), the fourth Thursday in November (Thanksgiving Day), and December 25 (Christmas). Also, the Tuesday following the first Monday in November is Election Day and is a federal government holiday in presidential-election years (held every 4 years, and most recently in 2004).

Legal Aid If you are "pulled over" for a minor infraction (such as speeding), never attempt to pay the fine directly to a police officer; this could be construed as attempted bribery, a much more serious crime. Pay fines by mail, or directly into the hands of the clerk of the court. If accused of a more serious offense, say and do nothing before consulting a lawyer. Here the burden is on the state to prove a person's guilt beyond a reasonable doubt, and everyone has the right to remain silent, whether he or she is suspected of a crime or actually arrested. Once arrested, a person can make one telephone call to a party of his or her choice. Call your embassy or consulate.

Mail If you aren't sure what your address will be in the United States, mail can be sent to you, in your name, c/o General Delivery at the main post office of the city or region where you expect to be. (Call © **800/275-8777** for information on the nearest post office.) The addressee must pick up mail in person and must produce proof of identity (driver's license, passport, or something similar). Most post offices will hold your mail for up to 1 month, and are open Monday to Friday from 8am to 6pm, and Saturday from 9am to 3pm.

Generally found at intersections, mailboxes are blue with a red-and-white stripe and carry the inscription U.S. MAIL. If your mail is addressed to a U.S. destination, don't forget to add the five-digit postal code (or zip code), after the two-letter abbreviation of the state to which the mail is addressed. This is essential to prompt delivery.

At press time, domestic postage rates were 23¢ for a postcard and 37¢ for a letter. For international mail, a first-class letter of up to ½ ounce costs 80¢ (60¢ to Canada and Mexico); a first-class postcard costs 70¢ (50¢ to Canada and Mexico); and a preprinted postal aerogramme costs 70¢.

Measurements See the chart on the inside front cover of this book for details on converting metric measurements to U.S. equivalents.

Taxes The United States has no value-added tax (VAT) or other indirect tax at the national level. Every state, county, and city has the right to levy its own local tax on all purchases, including hotel and restaurant checks, airline tickets, and so on. For information on sales and room taxes in San Francisco, see "Fast Facts: San Francisco," in chapter 4.

Telephone, Telegraph, Telex & Fax The telephone system in the United States is run by private corporations, so rates, especially for long-distance service and operator-assisted calls, can vary widely. Generally, hotel surcharges on long-distance and local calls are astronomical, so you're usually better off using a **public pay telephone,** which you'll find clearly marked in most public buildings and private establishments as well as on the street. Convenience grocery stores and gas stations always have them. Many convenience groceries and packaging services sell **prepaid calling cards** in denominations up to $50; these can be the least expensive way to call home. Many public phones at airports now accept American Express, MasterCard, and Visa credit cards.

You may want to look into leasing a cellphone for the duration of your trip.

In San Francisco, **local calls** made from public pay phones cost 50¢. To make a local call, dial the seven-digit local number. For domestic long-distance calls or international calls, stock up with a supply of quarters; after you dial the number, a recorded voice instructs you when and in what quantity you should put the coins into the slot. Pay phones do not accept pennies, and few will take anything larger than a quarter.

Most long-distance and international calls can be dialed directly from any phone. **For calls within the United States and to Canada,** dial 1 followed by the area code and the seven-digit number. **For other international calls,** dial 011 followed by the country code, city code, and the telephone number of the person you are calling.

Calls to area codes 800, 888, 877, and 866 are toll-free. However, calls to numbers in area codes 700 and 900 (chat lines, bulletin boards, "dating" services, and so on) can be very expensive—usually a charge of 95¢

to $3 or more per minute, and they sometimes have minimum charges that can run as high as $15 or more.

For **reversed-charge or collect calls,** and for person-to-person calls, dial 0 (zero, not the letter O) followed by the area code and number you want; an operator will then come on the line, and you should specify that you are calling collect, or person-to-person, or both. If your operator-assisted call is international, ask for the overseas operator.

For **local directory assistance** ("information"), dial 411; for long-distance information, dial 1, then the appropriate area code and 555-1212.

Telegraph and telex services are provided primarily by Western Union. You can bring your telegram into the nearest Western Union office (there are hundreds across the country) or dictate it over the phone (© **800/ 325-6000**). You can also telegraph money, or have it telegraphed to you, very quickly over the Western Union system, but this service can cost as much as 15% to 20% of the amount sent.

Most hotels have **fax machines** available for guest use (be sure to ask about the charge to use it). Many hotel rooms are even wired for guests' fax machines. A less expensive way to send and receive faxes may be at stores such as **The UPS Store** (formerly Mail Boxes Etc.), a national chain of retail packing service shops. (Look in the Yellow Pages directory under "Packing Services.")

There are two kinds of telephone directories in the United States. The so-called **White Pages** list private households and business subscribers in alphabetical order. The inside front cover lists emergency numbers for police, fire, ambulance, the Coast Guard, poison-control center, crime-victims hot line, and so on. The first few pages will tell you how to make long-distance and international calls, complete with country codes and area codes. Government numbers are usually printed on blue paper within the White Pages. Printed on yellow paper, the so-called **Yellow Pages** list all local services, businesses, industries, and houses of worship according to activity with an index at the front or back. (Drugstores/pharmacies and restaurants are also listed by geographic location.) The Yellow Pages also include city plans or detailed area maps, postal zip codes, and public transportation routes.

Time The continental United States is divided into **four time zones:** Eastern Standard Time (EST), Central Standard Time (CST), Mountain Standard Time (MST), and Pacific Standard Time (PST). Alaska and Hawaii have their own zones. For example, noon in New York City (EST) is 11am in Chicago (CST), 10am in Denver (MST), 9am in San Francisco (PST), 8am in Anchorage (AST), and 7am in Honolulu (HST).

Daylight saving time is in effect from 1am on the first Sunday in April to 1am on the last Sunday in October, except in Arizona, Hawaii, most of Indiana, and Puerto Rico. Daylight saving time moves the clock 1 hour ahead of standard time.

Tipping Tips are a very important part of certain workers' salaries, so it's necessary to leave appropriate gratuities. In hotels, tip **bellhops** at least $1 per bag ($2–$3 if you have a lot of luggage) and tip the **chamber staff** $2 to $3 per day (more if you've left a disaster area for him or her to clean up). Tip the **doorman** or **concierge** only if he or she has provided you with some specific service (for example, calling a cab for you or obtaining difficult-to-get theater tickets).

In restaurants, bars, and nightclubs, tip **service staff** 15% to 20% of the check, tip **bartenders** 10% to 15%, tip **checkroom attendants** $1 per garment, and tip **valet-parking attendants** $1 every time you get your car.

As for other service personnel, tip **cab drivers** 15% of the fare; tip **skycaps** at airports at least $1 per bag ($2–$3 if you have a lot of luggage); and tip **hairdressers, barbers, manicurists, masseuses, etc.,** 15% to 20%.

Toilets Public toilets can be hard to find in San Francisco. A handful of fancy French stalls are strategically placed on high-volume streets, and a few small stores may allow you access to their facilities. You can almost always find a toilet in museums, department stores, railway and bus stations, service stations, and restaurants and bars; note, however, a growing practice in some restaurants and bars of displaying a notice that toilets are for the use of patrons only. You can ignore this sign or, better yet, avoid arguments by paying for a cup of coffee or soft drink, which qualifies you as a patron. Large hotels and fast-food restaurants are probably the best bet for good, clean facilities. Museums, department stores, shopping malls, and, in a pinch, gas stations all have public toilets. If possible, avoid the toilets at parks and beaches, which tend to be dirty and may even be unsafe.

4

Getting to Know San Francisco

This chapter offers useful information on how to become better acquainted with the city, even though half the fun of becoming familiar with San Francisco is wandering around and haphazardly stumbling upon great shops, restaurants, and vistas that even locals might not know about. You'll find that, although it's metropolitan, San Francisco is a small town, and you won't feel like a stranger for long.

If you get disoriented, just remember that downtown is east and the Golden Gate Bridge is north—and even if you do get lost, you probably won't go too far, since water surrounds three sides of the city. The most difficult challenge you'll have, if you're traveling by car (which I suggest you avoid), is mastering the maze of one-way streets.

1 Orientation

VISITOR INFORMATION

The **San Francisco Visitor Information Center,** on the lower level of Hallidie Plaza, 900 Market St., at Powell Street (© **415/283-0177;** fax 415/362-7323), has information, brochures, discount coupons, and advice on restaurants, sights, and events in the city. The staff can provide answers in German, Japanese, French, Italian, and Spanish (as well as English, of course). To find the office, descend the escalator at the cable car turnaround. The office is open Monday through Friday from 8:30am to 5pm, Saturday and Sunday from 9am to 3pm. It's closed on January 1, Thanksgiving Day, and December 25.

Dial © **415/283-0177** any time, day or night, for a recorded message about current cultural events, theater, music, sports, and other special happenings. This information is also available in German, French, Japanese, and Spanish. Keep in mind that this service only recommends businesses that are members of the Convention and Visitors Bureau and is very tourist oriented. While there's tons of information, it's not representative of all that the city has to offer. You can get a fax with information anytime from the bureau's automated service if you call © **800/220-5747** and follow the prompts.

Pick up a copy of the *Bay Guardian* or the *S.F. Weekly,* the city's free alternative papers, to get listings of all city happenings. You'll find them in kiosks throughout the city and in most coffee shops.

For specialized information on Chinatown's shops and services, and on the city's Chinese community in general, contact the **Chinese Chamber of Commerce,** 730 Sacramento St. (© **415/982-3000**), open daily from 9am to 5pm.

CITY LAYOUT

San Francisco occupies the tip of a 32-mile peninsula between San Francisco Bay and the Pacific Ocean. Its land area measures about 46 square miles, although the city is often referred to as being 7 square miles. At more than 900 feet high, the towering Twin Peaks marks the geographic center of the city and is a killer place to take in a vista of San Francisco.

With lots of one-way streets and plenty of nooks and crannies, San Francisco might seem confusing at first, but it will quickly become easy to negotiate. The city's downtown streets are arranged in a simple grid pattern, with the exceptions of Market Street and Columbus Avenue, which cut across the grid at right angles to each other. Hills appear to distort this pattern, however, and can disorient you. As you learn your way around, the hills will become your landmarks and reference points. But even if you get lost, it's no big deal: San Francisco's a small town—so much so, in fact that I've run from one end to the other (during the Bay to Breakers Foot Race) in an hour flat.

MAIN ARTERIES & STREETS   **Market Street** is San Francisco's main thoroughfare. Most of the city's buses travel this route on their way to the Financial District from the outer neighborhoods to the west and south. The tall office buildings clustered downtown are at the northeast end of Market; 1 block beyond lies The Embarcadero and the bay.

The Embarcadero ✯—an excellent strolling, skating, and biking route (thanks to recent renovations)—curves along San Francisco Bay from south of the Bay Bridge to the northeast perimeter of the city. It terminates at Fisherman's Wharf, the famous tourist-oriented pier. Aquatic Park, Fort Mason, and the Golden Gate National Recreation Area are on the northernmost point of the peninsula.

From the eastern perimeter of Fort Mason, **Van Ness Avenue** runs due south, back to Market Street. The area just described forms a rough triangle, with Market Street as its southeastern boundary, the waterfront as its northern boundary, and Van Ness Avenue as its western boundary. Within this triangle lie most of the city's main tourist sights.

FINDING AN ADDRESS   Since most of the city's streets are laid out in a grid pattern, finding an address is easy when you know the nearest cross street. Numbers start with 1 at the beginning of the street and proceed at the rate of 100 per block. When asking for directions, find out the nearest cross street and the neighborhood where your destination is located, but be careful not to confuse numerical avenues with numerical streets. Numerical avenues (Third Ave. and so on) are in the Richmond and Sunset Districts in the western part of the city. Numerical streets (Third St. and so on) are south of Market Street in the east and south parts of town.

NEIGHBORHOODS IN BRIEF

For further discussion of some of the below neighborhoods, see the "Neighborhoods Worth a Visit" section of chapter 7, beginning on p. 171.

Union Square   Union Square is the commercial hub of the city. Most major hotels and department stores are crammed into the area surrounding the actual square, which was named for a series of violent pro-union mass demonstrations staged here on the eve of the Civil War. A plethora of upscale boutiques, restaurants, and galleries occupy the spaces tucked between the larger buildings. A few blocks west is the **Tenderloin,** a patch of poverty and blight where you should keep your wits about you. The **Theater District** is 3 blocks west of Union Square.

The Financial District   East of Union Square, this area, bordered by The Embarcadero and by Market,

San Francisco Neighborhoods

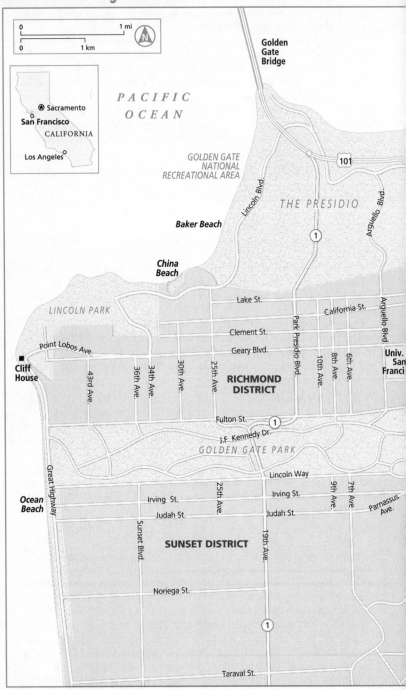

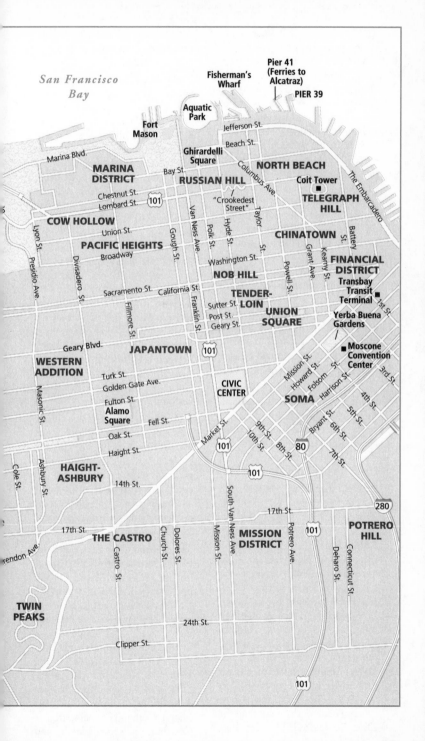

San Francisco Bay

Fisherman's Wharf

Pier 41 (Ferries to Alcatraz)

PIER 39

Fort Mason

Aquatic Park

Jefferson St.

Ghirardelli Square

Beach St.

NORTH BEACH

Marina Blvd.

MARINA DISTRICT

Bay St.

Columbus Ave.

RUSSIAN HILL

Coit Tower

The Embarcadero

Chestnut St.

101

"Crookedest Street"

TELEGRAPH HILL

Lombard St.

Taylor St.

COW HOLLOW

Union St.

Van Ness Ave.

Gough St.

Hyde St.

Polk St.

CHINATOWN

Battery St.

PACIFIC HEIGHTS

Broadway

Washington St.

Grant Ave.

Kearny St.

Powell St.

FINANCIAL DISTRICT

Lyon St.

Presidio Ave.

Divisadero St.

Fillmore St.

NOB HILL

Transbay Transit Terminal

1st St.

Sacramento St.

California St.

TENDER-LOIN

Sutter St.

UNION SQUARE

Yerba Buena Gardens

Franklin St.

Post St.

Geary St.

Geary Blvd.

JAPANTOWN

101

Moscone Convention Center

WESTERN ADDITION

CIVIC CENTER

Mission St.

Howard St.

Folsom St.

Harrison St.

3rd St.

Masonic St.

Turk St.

Golden Gate Ave.

SOMA

Fulton St.

Alamo Square

Fell St.

4th St.

5th St.

6th St.

Bryant St.

Oak St.

Market St.

9th St.

10th St.

8th St.

80

7th St.

Haight St.

101

Cole St.

Ashbury St.

HAIGHT-ASHBURY

14th St.

101

280

17th St.

South Van Ness Ave.

Potrero Ave.

POTRERO HILL

rendon Ave.

17th St.

THE CASTRO

Castro St.

Church St.

Dolores St.

Mission St.

MISSION DISTRICT

101

Deharo St.

Connecticut St.

TWIN PEAKS

24th St.

Clipper St.

101

Third, Kearny, and Washington streets, is the city's business district and the stomping grounds for many major corporations. The pointy TransAmerica Pyramid, at Montgomery and Clay streets, is one of the district's most conspicuous architectural features. To its east sprawls the Embarcadero Center, an 8½-acre complex housing offices, shops, and restaurants. Farther east still is the old Ferry Building, the city's pre-bridge transportation hub. Ferries to Sausalito and Larkspur still leave from this point. However, in 2003, the building became an attraction in itself when it was completely renovated, jampacked with outstanding restaurant and gourmet food- and wine-related shops, and surrounded by a farmers market a few days a week, making it one of San Francisco's residents' favorite places to grace and gossip.

Nob Hill & Russian Hill Bounded by Bush, Larkin, Pacific, and Stockton streets, Nob Hill is a genteel, well-heeled district, still occupied by the major power brokers and the neighborhood businesses they frequent. Russian Hill extends from Pacific to Bay and from Polk to Mason. It contains steep streets, lush gardens, and high-rises occupied by both the moneyed and the more bohemian.

Chinatown A large red-and-green gate on Grant Avenue at Bush Street marks the official entrance to Chinatown. Beyond lies a 24-block labyrinth, bordered by Broadway, Bush, Kearny, and Stockton streets, filled with restaurants, markets, temples, shops—and, of course, a substantial percentage of San Francisco's Chinese residents. Chinatown is a great place for exploration all along Stockton and Grant streets, Portsmouth Square, and the alleys that lead off them, like Ross

and Waverly. This area is jampacked, so don't even think about driving here.

North Beach The Italian quarter, which stretches from Montgomery and Jackson to Bay Street, is one of the best places in the city to grab a coffee, pull up a cafe chair, and do some serious people-watching. Nightlife is equally happening; restaurants, bars, and clubs along Columbus and Grant avenues attract folks from all over the Bay Area, who fight for a parking place and romp through the festive neighborhood. Down Columbus toward the Financial District are the remains of the city's Beat Generation landmarks, including Ferlinghetti's City Lights Bookstore and Vesuvio's Bar. Broadway—a short strip of sex joints—cuts through the heart of the district. **Telegraph Hill** looms over the east side of North Beach, topped by Coit Tower, one of San Francisco's best vantage points.

Fisherman's Wharf North Beach runs into Fisherman's Wharf, which was once the busy heart of the city's great harbor and waterfront industries. Today, it is a tacky but interesting tourist area with little, if any, authentic waterfront life, except for recreational boating and some friendly sea lions.

The Marina District Created on landfill for the Pan Pacific Exposition of 1915, the Marina District boasts some of the best views of the Golden Gate, as well as plenty of grassy fields alongside San Francisco Bay. Elegant Mediterranean-style homes and apartments, inhabited by the city's well-to-do singles and wealthy families, line the streets. Here, too, are the Palace of Fine Arts, the Exploratorium, and Fort Mason Center. The main street is Chestnut, between Franklin and

Lyon, which abounds with shops, cafes, and boutiques. Because of its landfill foundation, the Marina was one of the hardest-hit districts in the 1989 quake.

Cow Hollow Located west of Van Ness Avenue, between Russian Hill and the Presidio, this flat, grazable area supported 30 dairy farms in 1861. Today, Cow Hollow is largely residential and largely yuppie. Its two primary commercial thoroughfares are Lombard Street, known for its many relatively inexpensive motels, and Union Street, a flourishing shopping sector filled with restaurants, pubs, cafes, and shops.

Pacific Heights The ultra-elite, such as the Gettys and Danielle Steel—and those lucky enough to buy before the real-estate boom—reside in the mansions and homes here. When the rich meander out of their fortresses, they wander down to Union Street and join the yuppies and the young who frequent the street's long stretch of chic boutiques and lively neighborhood restaurants, cafes, and bars.

Japantown Bounded by Octavia, Fillmore, California, and Geary, Japantown shelters only a small percentage of the city's Japanese population, but exploring these few square blocks and the shops and restaurants within them is still a cultural experience.

Civic Center Although millions of dollars have gone toward brick sidewalks, ornate lampposts, and elaborate street plantings, the southwestern section of Market Street remains somewhat dilapidated. The Civic Center, at the "bottom" of Market Street, is an exception. This large complex of buildings includes the domed and dapper City Hall, the Opera House, Davies Symphony Hall, and the Asian Art Museum. The landscaped plaza connecting the buildings is the staging area for San Francisco's frequent demonstrations for or against just about everything.

SoMa No part of San Francisco has been more affected by recent development than the area south of Market Street (dubbed "SoMa"). The area—until recently, a district of old warehouses and industrial spaces, with a few scattered underground nightclubs, restaurants, and shoddy residential areas—was the hub of dot-commercialization and half-million-dollar-plus lofts. Today, it's still alive with loft residents and surviving businesses. It also houses urban entertainment a la the Museum of Modern Art, Yerba Buena Gardens, Sony Metreon, and a slew of big-bucks hotels that make tons of money from businesspeople. The official boundaries are The Embarcadero, Highway 101, and Market Street, with the greatest concentrations of interest around Yerba Buena Center, along Folsom and Harrison streets between Steuart and Sixth, and at Brannan and Market. Along the waterfront are an array of restaurants and the absolutely fab SBC Park. Farther west, around Folsom, between 7th and 11th streets, much of the city's nightclubbing occurs.

Mission District This is another area that was greatly affected by the city's new wealth. The Mexican and Latin American populations here, with their cuisine, traditions, and art, make the Mission District a vibrant area to visit. Some parts of the neighborhood are still poor and sprinkled with the homeless, gangs, and drug addicts, but young urbanites have settled in the area, attracted by its "reasonably" (a relative term) priced rentals and endless oh-so-hot restaurants and bars that stretch from 16th and Valencia streets to 25th and Mission streets.

Less adventurous tourists may just want to duck into Mission Dolores, cruise by a few of the 200-plus amazing murals, and head back downtown. But anyone who's interested in hanging with the hipsters and experiencing the hottest restaurant and bar nightlife should definitely beeline it here. Don't be afraid to visit this area, but do use caution at night.

The Castro One of the liveliest streets in town, the Castro is practically synonymous with San Francisco's gay community (even though it is technically a street in the Noe Valley District). Located at the very end of Market Street, between 17th and 18th streets, the Castro has dozens of shops, restaurants, and bars catering to the gay community. Open-minded straight people are welcome, too.

Haight-Ashbury Part trendy, part nostalgic, part funky, the Haight, as it's most commonly known, was the soul of the psychedelic, free-loving 1960s and the center of the counterculture movement. Today, the neighborhood straddling upper Haight Street on the eastern border of Golden Gate Park is more gentrified, but the commercial area still harbors all walks of life. Leftover aging hippies mingle with grungy, begging street kids outside Ben & Jerry's Ice Cream Store (where they might still be talking about Jerry Garcia), nondescript marijuana dealers whisper "Buds" as shoppers pass, and many people walking down the street have Day-Glo hair. But you don't need to be a freak or wear tie-dye to enjoy the Haight—the food, shops, and bars cover all tastes. From Haight Street, walk south on Cole Street for a more peaceful and quaint neighborhood experience.

Richmond & Sunset Districts San Francisco's suburbs of sorts, these are the city's largest and most populous neighborhoods, consisting mainly of small (but expensive) homes, shops, and neighborhood restaurants. Although they border Golden Gate Park and Ocean Beach, few tourists venture into "The Avenues," as these areas are referred to locally.

2 Getting Around

BY PUBLIC TRANSPORTATION

The **San Francisco Municipal Railway,** 401 Van Ness Ave., better known as "Muni" (© **415/673-6864;** www.sfmuni.com), operates the city's cable cars, buses, and streetcars. Together, these three services crisscross the entire city. Fares for buses and streetcars are $1.25 for adults, 35¢ for seniors over 65 and children 5 to 17. Cable cars, which run from 6:30am to 1:30am, cost a whopping $3 for all people over 5 ($1 for seniors 6:30–7am and 9pm–midnight). Needless to say, they're packed primarily with tourists. Exact change is required on all vehicles except cable cars. Fares are subject to change.

For detailed route information, phone Muni or consult the bus map at the front of the San Francisco Yellow Pages. If you plan to use public transportation extensively, you might want to invest in a comprehensive transit and city map ($2), sold at the San Francisco Visitor Information Center (p. 11), Powell/Market cable car booth, and many downtown retail outlets. Also, see the "Muni Discounts" box for more information.

CABLE CAR San Francisco's cable cars might not be the most practical means of transport, but the rolling historic landmarks are a fun ride. The three lines are concentrated in the downtown area. The most scenic, and exciting, is the

Powell-Hyde line, which follows a zigzag route from the corner of Powell and Market streets, over both Nob Hill and Russian Hill, to a turntable at gaslit Victorian Square in front of Aquatic Park. The **Powell-Mason line** starts at the same intersection and climbs Nob Hill before descending to Bay Street, just 3 blocks from Fisherman's Wharf. The least scenic is the **California Street line,** which begins at the foot of Market Street and runs a straight course through Chinatown and over Nob Hill to Van Ness Avenue. All riders must exit at the last stop and wait in line for the return trip. The cable car system operates from approximately 6:30am to 1:30am, and each ride costs $3.

BUS   Buses reach almost every corner of San Francisco and beyond—they even travel over the bridges to Marin County and Oakland. Overhead electric cables power some buses; others use conventional gas engines. All are numbered and display their destinations on the front. Signs, curb markings, and yellow bands on adjacent utility poles designate stops, and most bus shelters exhibit Muni's transportation map and schedule. Many buses travel along Market Street or pass near Union Square and run from about 6am to midnight. After midnight, there is infrequent all-night "Owl" service. For safety, avoid taking buses late at night.

Popular tourist routes include bus nos. 5, 7, and 71, all of which run to Golden Gate Park; 41 and 45, which travel along Union Street; and 30, which runs between Union Square and Ghirardelli Square. A bus ride costs $1.25 for adults and 35¢ for seniors over 65 and children 5 to 17.

STREETCAR   Five of Muni's six streetcar lines, designated J, K, L, M, and N, run underground downtown and on the streets in the outer neighborhoods. The sleek rail cars make the same stops as BART (see below) along Market Street, including Embarcadero Station (in the Financial District), Montgomery and Powell streets (both near Union Square), and the Civic Center (near City Hall). Past the Civic Center, the routes branch off: The J line takes you to Mission Dolores; the K, L, and M lines run to Castro Street; and the N line parallels Golden Gate Park and extends all the way to The Embarcadero and SBC Park. Streetcars run about every 15 minutes, more frequently during rush hours. They operate Monday through Friday from 5am to 12:45am, Saturday from 6am to 12:45am, and Sunday from 8am to 12:20am. The L and N lines operate 24 hours

---

(*Value* **Muni Discounts**

Muni discount passes, called **Passports,** entitle holders to unlimited rides on buses, streetcars, and cable cars. A Passport costs $9 for 1 day, $15 for 3 days, and $20 for 7 consecutive days. Muni's **City Pass,** which costs $40 for adults, $31 for seniors 65 and older, and $24 for kids 5 to 17, entitles you to unlimited rides for 7 days, plus admission to the California Academy of Sciences, Palace of the Legion of Honor, Steinhart Aquarium, Museum of Modern Art, Exploratorium, and Blue & Gold Fleet Bay or Alcatraz cruises for 9 days. You can buy a Passport or City Pass at the San Francisco Visitor Information Center, Powell/Market cable car booth, Holiday Inn Civic Center, and TIX Bay Area booth at Union Square, among other outlets. But to include the Blue & Gold Fleet tour, you must purchase tickets through them by calling Blue & Gold Fleet at © 415/705-5555. A $2.25 fee applies when you get your tickets through this phone service.

San Francisco Mass Transit

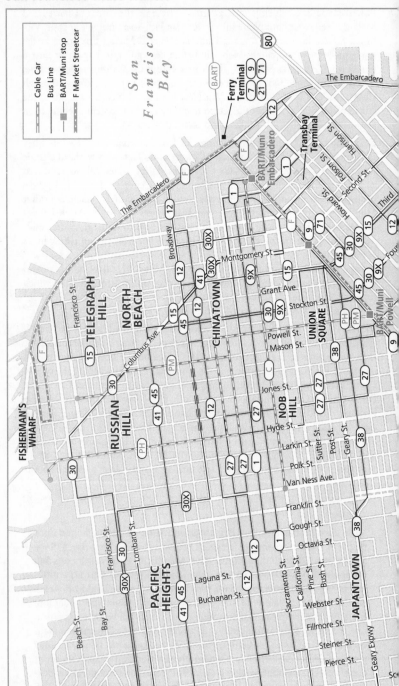

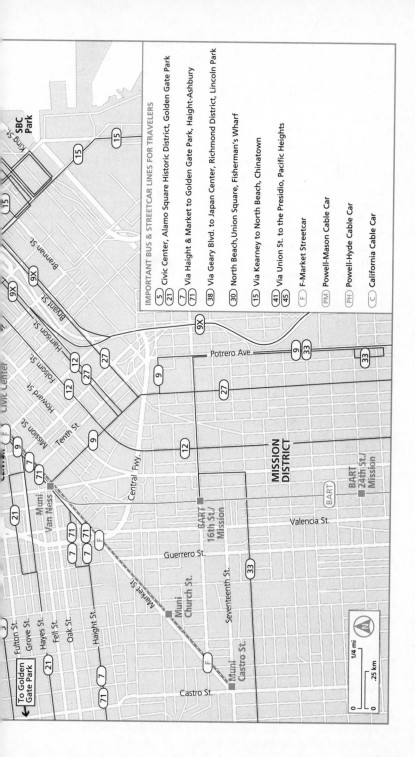

IMPORTANT BUS & STREETCAR LINES FOR TRAVELERS

- 5 Civic Center, Alamo Square Historic District, Golden Gate Park
- 21 Via Haight & Market to Golden Gate Park, Haight-Ashbury
- 7 71
- 38 Via Geary Blvd. to Japan Center, Richmond District, Lincoln Park
- 30 North Beach, Union Square, Fisherman's Wharf
- 15 Via Kearney to North Beach, Chinatown
- 41 Via Union St. to the Presidio, Pacific Heights
- 45
- F F-Market Streetcar
- PM Powell-Mason Cable Car
- PH Powell-Hyde Cable Car
- C California Cable Car

MISSION DISTRICT

a day, 7 days a week, but late at night, regular buses trace the L and N routes, which are normally underground, from atop the city streets. Because the operation is part of Muni, the fares are the same as for buses, and passes are accepted.

A recent addition to this system is not a newcomer at all, but is, in fact, San Francisco's beloved rejuvenated 1930s streetcar. The beautiful multicolored F-Market line runs from 17th and Castro streets to Beach and Jones streets; every other streetcar continues to Jones and Beach streets in Fisherman's Wharf. This is a quick and charming way to get up- and downtown without any hassle.

BART BART, an acronym for **Bay Area Rapid Transit** (© **415/989-2278;** www.bart.gov), is a futuristic-looking, high-speed rail network that connects San Francisco with the East Bay—Oakland, Richmond, Concord, and Fremont. Four stations are on Market Street (see "Streetcar," above). Fares range from $1.25 to $7.10, depending on how far you go. Machines in the stations dispense tickets that are magnetically encoded with a dollar amount. Computerized exits automatically deduct the correct fare. Children 4 and under ride free. Trains run every 15 to 20 minutes, Monday through Friday from 4am to midnight, Saturday from 6am to midnight, and Sunday from 8am to midnight.

The 33-mile BART extension, which extends all the way to San Francisco International Airport, opened in June 2003.

BY TAXI

This isn't New York, so don't expect a taxi to appear whenever you need one—if at all. If you're downtown during rush hour or leaving a major hotel, it won't be hard to hail a cab; just look for the lighted sign on the roof that indicates the vehicle is free. Otherwise, it's a good idea to call one of the following companies to arrange a ride; even then, there's been more than one time when the cab never came for me. What to do? Call back if your cab is late and insist on attention, but don't expect prompt results on weekends, no matter how nicely you ask. The companies: **Veteran's Cab** (© **415/552-1300**), **Luxor Cabs** (© **415/282-4141**), and **Yellow Cab** (© **415/626-2345**). Rates are approximately $2.85 for the first mile and $2.25 for each mile thereafter.

BY CAR

You don't need a car to explore downtown San Francisco. In fact, with the city becoming more crowded by the minute, a car can be your worst nightmare—you're likely to end up stuck in traffic with lots of aggressive and frustrated drivers, pay upward of $30 a day to park, and spend a good portion of your vacation looking for a parking space. Don't bother. However, if you want to venture outside the city, driving is the best way to go.

Before heading outside the city, especially in winter, call © **800/427-7623** for California **road conditions.**

CAR RENTALS All the major rental companies operate in the city and have desks at the airports. When we last checked, you could get a compact car for a week for about $200, including all taxes and other charges, but prices change dramatically on a daily basis and depend on which company you rent from.

Some of the national car-rental companies operating in San Francisco include **Alamo** (© 800/327-9633; www.goalamo.com), **Avis** (© 800/331-1212; www.avis.com), **Budget** (© 800/527-0700; www.budget.com), **Dollar** (© 800/800-4000; www.dollar.com), **Enterprise** (© 800/325-8007; www.enterprise.com), **Hertz** (© 800/654-3131; www.hertz.com), **National** (© 800/227-7368; www.nationalcar.com), and **Thrifty** (© 800/367-2277; www.thrifty.com).

Tips Safe Driving

Keep in mind the following handy driving tips:

- California law requires that both drivers and passengers wear seat belts.
- You can turn right at a red light (unless otherwise indicated), after yielding to traffic and pedestrians, and after coming to a complete stop. Reservations agents won't volunteer this information, so don't be shy about asking.
- Cable cars always have the right-of-way, as do pedestrians at intersections and crosswalks.
- Pay attention to signs and arrows on the streets and roadways, or you might suddenly find yourself in a lane that requires exiting or turning when you want to go straight. What's more, San Francisco's many one-way streets can drive you in circles, but most road maps of the city indicate which way traffic flows.

Car-rental rates vary even more than airline fares. Prices depend on the size of the car, where and when you pick it up and drop it off, the length of the rental period, where and how far you drive it, whether you buy insurance, and a host of other factors. A few key questions can save you hundreds of dollars, but you have to ask—reservations agents don't often volunteer money-saving information:

- Are weekend rates lower than weekday rates? Ask if the rate is the same for pickup Friday morning, for instance, as it is for Thursday night. Reservations agents won't volunteer this information, so don't be shy about asking.
- Does the agency assess a drop-off charge if you don't return the car to the same location where you picked it up?
- Are special promotional rates available? If you see an advertised price in your local newspaper, be sure to ask for that specific rate; otherwise you could be charged the standard rate. Terms change constantly.
- Are discounts available for members of AARP, AAA, frequent-flier programs, or trade unions? If you belong to any of these organizations, you may be entitled to discounts of up to 30%.
- How much tax will be added to the rental bill? Will there be local tax and state tax?
- How much does the rental company charge to refill your gas tank if you return with the tank less than full? Most rental companies claim their prices are "competitive," but fuel is almost always cheaper in town, so you should try to allow enough time to refuel the car before returning it.

Some companies offer "refueling packages," in which you pay for an entire tank of gas upfront. The cost is usually fairly competitive with local prices, but you don't get credit for any gas remaining in the tank. If a stop at a gas station on the way to the airport will make you miss your plane, then by all means take advantage of the fuel purchase option. Otherwise, skip it.

Most agencies enforce a minimum-age requirement—usually 25. Some also have a maximum-age limit. If you're concerned that these limits might affect you, ask about rental requirements at the time of booking to avoid problems later.

Make sure you're insured. Hasty assumptions about your personal auto insurance or a rental agency's additional coverage could end up costing you tens of thousands of dollars, even if you are involved in an accident that is clearly the fault of another driver.

If you already have your own car insurance, you are most likely covered in the United States for loss of or damage to a rental car and liability in case of injury to any other party involved in an accident. Be sure to check your policy before you spend extra money (usually $10 per day) on the **collision damage waiver (CDW),** offered by all agencies.

Most major credit cards (especially gold and platinum cards) provide some degree of coverage as well—if they were used to pay for the rental. Terms vary widely, however, so be sure to call your credit card company directly before you rent and rely on the card for coverage. If you are uninsured, your credit card may provide primary coverage as long as you decline the rental agency's insurance. If you already have insurance, your credit card may provide secondary coverage, which basically covers your deductible. However, note that *credit cards will not cover liability,* which is the cost of injury to an outside party and/or damage to an outside party's vehicle. If you do not hold an insurance policy, you should seriously consider buying additional liability insurance from your rental company, even if you decline the CDW.

PARKING   If you want to have a relaxing vacation, don't even attempt to find street parking on Nob Hill, in North Beach, in Chinatown, by Fisherman's Wharf, or on Telegraph Hill. Park in a garage or take a cab or a bus. If you do find street parking, pay attention to street signs that explain when you can park and for how long. Be especially careful not to park in zones that are tow areas during rush hours.

Curb colors also indicate parking regulations. *Red* means no stopping or parking; *blue* is reserved for drivers with disabilities who have a California-issued disabled plate or placard; *white* means there's a 5-minute limit; *green* indicates a 10-minute limit; and *yellow* and *yellow-and-black* curbs are for commercial vehicles only. Also, don't park at a bus stop or in front of a fire hydrant, and watch out for street-cleaning signs. If you violate the law, you might get a hefty ticket or your car might be towed; to get your car back, you'll have to get a release from the nearest district police department and then go to the towing company to pick up the vehicle.

When parking on a hill, apply the hand brake, put the car in gear, and *curb your wheels*—toward the curb when facing downhill, away from the curb when facing uphill. Curbing your wheels not only prevents a possible "runaway" but also keeps you from getting a ticket—an expensive fine that is aggressively enforced.

BY FERRY

TO/FROM SAUSALITO OR LARKSPUR   The **Golden Gate Ferry Service** fleet (© 415/923-2000) shuttles passengers daily between the San Francisco Ferry Building, at the foot of Market Street, and downtown Sausalito and Larkspur. Service is frequent, departing at reasonable intervals every day of the year except January 1, Thanksgiving Day, and December 25. Phone for an exact schedule. The ride takes half an hour, and one-way fares are $5.60 for adults and $4.20 for kids 6 to 12. Seniors and passengers with disabilities ride for $2.80. Up to two children under 6 with paying adults ride free on weekdays; on weekends, up to two children under 12 ride free with paying adults. Family rates are available on weekends.

Ferries of the **Blue & Gold Fleet** (© 415/773-1188 for recorded info, or 415/705-5555 for tickets) also provide round-trip service to downtown Sausalito and Larkspur, leaving from Fisherman's Wharf at Pier 41. The one-way cost is $7.25 for adults, $4 for kids 5 to 11. Boats run on a seasonal schedule; phone for departure information. Expect to pay an extra $3.50 per ticket for phone orders or skip the fee by buying in person at Pier 41.

FAST FACTS: **San Francisco**

Airports See the "Getting There" section, in chapter 2, beginning on p. 26.

American Express For travel arrangements, traveler's checks, currency exchange, and other member services, an office is at 455 Market St., at First Street (✆ **415/536-2600**), in the Financial District, open Monday through Friday from 9am to 5:30pm and Saturday from 10am to 2pm. To report lost or stolen traveler's checks, call ✆ **800/221-7282.** For American Express Global Assist, call ✆ **800/554-2639.**

Area Code The area code for San Francisco is **415;** for Oakland, Berkeley, and much of the East Bay, **510;** for the peninsula, generally **650.** Most phone numbers in this book are in San Francisco's 415 area code, but there's no need to dial it if you're within city limits.

Business Hours Most banks are open Monday through Friday from 9am to 5pm. Many banks also have ATMs for 24-hour banking (see the "Money" section, in chapter 2, beginning on p. 11).

Most stores are open Monday through Saturday from 10 or 11am to at least 6pm, with shorter hours on Sunday. But there are exceptions: Stores in Chinatown, Ghirardelli Square, and PIER 39 stay open much later during the tourist season, and large department stores, including Macy's and Nordstrom, keep late hours.

Most restaurants serve lunch from about 11:30am to 2:30pm and dinner from about 5:30 to 10pm. They sometimes serve later on weekends. Nightclubs and bars are usually open daily until 2am, when they are legally bound to stop serving alcohol.

Car Rentals See "Getting Around," earlier in this chapter.

Climate See the "When to Go" section in chapter 2, beginning on p. 12.

Dentists In the event of a dental emergency, see your hotel concierge or contact the **San Francisco Dental Office,** 131 Steuart St. (✆ **415/777-5115**), between Mission and Howard streets, which offers emergency service and comprehensive dental care Monday and Tuesday from 8am to 4:30pm, Wednesday and Thursday from 10:30am to 6:30pm, and Friday 8am to 2pm.

Doctors **Saint Francis Memorial Hospital,** 900 Hyde St., between Bush and Pine streets on Nob Hill (✆ **415/353-6000**), provides emergency service 24 hours a day; no appointment is necessary. The hospital also operates a **physician-referral service** (✆ **800/333-1355** or 415/353-6566).

Drugstores **Walgreens** pharmacies are all over town, including one at 135 Powell St. (✆ **415/391-4433**). The store is open Monday through Friday from 7am to midnight and Saturday and Sunday from 8am to midnight; the pharmacy is open Monday through Friday from 8am to 9pm, Saturday from 9am to 5pm; it's closed on Sunday. The branch on Divisadero Street at Lombard (✆ **415/931-6415**) has a 24-hour pharmacy. **Merrill's** pharmacy and store, 1091 Market St. (© **415/431-5466**), smack in the middle of downtown tourist action, is open Monday through Friday from 9am to 6pm and is closed on weekends.

Earthquakes There will always be earthquakes in California, most of which you'll never notice. However, in case of a significant shaker, there are a few basic precautionary measures you should know. When you are inside a building, seek cover; do not run outside. Stand under a doorway or against a wall, and stay away from windows. If you exit a building after a substantial quake, use stairwells, not elevators. If you are in your car, pull over to the side of the road and stop—but not until you are away from bridges, overpasses, telephone poles, and power lines. Stay in your car. If you're out walking, stay outside and away from trees, power lines, and the sides of buildings. If you're in an area with tall buildings, find a doorway in which to stand.

Emergencies Dial © **911** for police, an ambulance, or the fire department; no coins are needed from a public phone.

Internet Access Surprisingly, San Francisco has very few Internet cafes. However, there are locations around town where you can get online access, perhaps with a sandwich and a cup o' joe. You can do your laundry, listen to music, dine, and check your stocks online at SoMa's **Brainwash,** 1122 Folsom St., between Seventh and Eighth streets (© **415/861-FOOD**). It's open Monday through Saturday from 7am to 11pm and Sunday from 8am to 11pm; rates are $1 per 5 minutes. For access without the ambience, try **Copy Central,** 110 Sutter St., at Montgomery Street (© **415/392-6470**), which provides access cards costing $3 for 20 minutes, $5 for 40 minutes, and $7 for 60 minutes. Ditto **Kinko's,** 1967 Market St., near Gough Street (© **415/252-0864**), which charges 20¢ per minute. Both of these companies have numerous locations around town.

Liquor Laws Liquor stores and grocery stores, as well as some drugstores, can sell packaged alcoholic beverages between 6am and 2am daily. Most restaurants, nightclubs, and bars are licensed to serve alcoholic beverages during the same hours. The legal age for purchase and consumption of alcohol is 21; proof of age is required.

Newspapers & Magazines The city's two main dailies are the *San Francisco Chronicle* and the *San Francisco Examiner;* both are distributed throughout the city. Check out the *Chronicle's* massive Sunday edition that includes a pink "Datebook" section—an excellent preview of the week's upcoming events. The free weekly *San Francisco Bay Guardian* and *San Francisco Weekly,* tabloids of news and listings, are indispensable for nightlife information; they're widely distributed through street-corner kiosks and at city cafes and restaurants.

Of the many free tourist-oriented publications, the most widely read are *Key, San Francisco Guide,* and *Where San Francisco.* The first two are handbook-size weeklies contain maps and information on current events. The latter is a glossy regular format monthly magazine. You can find them in most hotels, shops, and restaurants in the major tourist areas.

Police For emergencies, dial © **911** from any phone; no coins are needed. For other matters, call © **415/553-0123.**

Post Office Dozens of post offices are located around the city. The closest to Union Square is inside the Macy's department store at 170 O'Farrell St. (© **800/275-8777**). You can pick up mail addressed to you and marked "General Delivery" (Poste Restante) at the **Civic Center Post Office Box Unit,** P.O. Box 429991, San Francisco, CA 94142-9991 (© **800/275-8777**). The street address is 101 Hyde St.

Safety San Francisco, like any other large city, has its fair share of crime, but most folks luckily don't have firsthand horror stories. In some areas, you need to exercise extra caution, particularly at night—notably the Tenderloin, the Western Addition (south of Japantown), the Mission District (especially around 16th and Mission sts.), the lower Fillmore area (also south of Japantown), around lower Haight Street, and around the Civic Center. In addition, there are a substantial number of homeless people throughout the city, with concentrations in and around Union Square, the Theater District (3 blocks west of Union Square), the Tenderloin, and Haight Street, so don't be alarmed if you're approached for spare change. Just use common sense.

For additional crime-prevention information, phone **San Francisco SAFE** (© **415/553-1984**).

Smoking If San Francisco is California's most European city in looks and style, the comparison stops when it comes to smoking in public. Each year, smoking laws in the city become stricter. Since 1998, smoking has been prohibited in restaurants and bars. Hotels are also offering more non-smoking rooms, which often leaves those who like to puff out in the cold—sometimes literally.

Taxes An 8.5% sales tax is added at the register for all goods and services purchased in San Francisco. The city hotel tax is a whopping 14%. There is no airport tax.

Taxis See "Getting Around," earlier in this chapter.

Time Zone San Francisco is in the Pacific Standard Time zone, which is 8 hours behind Greenwich Mean Time and 3 hours behind Eastern Standard Time. To find out what time it is, call © **415/767-8900**.

Transit Information The San Francisco Municipal Railway, better known as **Muni,** operates the city's cable cars, buses, and streetcars. For customer service, call © **415/673-6864** weekdays from 7am to 5pm, weekends from 9am to 5pm. At other times, you can call this number to get recorded information.

5

Where to Stay

Whether you want a room with a view or just a room, San Francisco is more than accommodating to its 14 million annual guests. Most of the city's 200-plus hotels cluster near Union Square, but some smaller independent gems are scattered around town.

When reading over your options, keep in mind that prices listed are "rack" (published) rates. At big, upscale hotels, almost no one actually pays them—and with the dramatic travel downturn over the past few years, there are still deals to be had. Therefore, you should always ask for special discounts or, even better, vacation packages. It's often possible to get the room you want for $100 less than what is quoted here, except when the hotels are packed (usually during summer and due to conventions) and bargaining is close to impossible. Use the rates listed here for the big hotels as guidelines for comparison only; prices for inexpensive choices and smaller B&Bs are closer to reality, though.

Hunting for hotels in San Francisco can be a tricky business, particularly if you're not a seasoned traveler. What you don't know—and the reservations agent may not tell you—could very well ruin your vacation, so keep the following pointers in mind when it comes time to book a room:

- Prices listed below do not include state and city taxes, which total 14%. Other hidden extras include parking fees, which can be up to $40 per day, and hefty surcharges—up to $1 per local call—for telephone use.

- San Francisco is Convention City, so if you want a room at a particular hotel during high season (summer, for example), book well in advance.

- Be sure to have a credit card in hand when making a reservation, and know that you may be asked to pay for at least 1 night in advance (this doesn't happen often, though).

- Hotels usually hold reservations until 6pm. If you don't tell the staff you're arriving late, you might lose your room.

- Almost every hotel in San Francisco requires a credit card imprint for "incidentals" (and to prevent walkouts). If you don't have a credit card, be sure to make special arrangements with the management before you hang up the

---

Pricing Categories

The accommodations listed below are classified first by area, then by price, using the following categories: **Very Expensive,** more than $250 per night; **Expensive,** $200 to $250 per night; **Moderate,** $150 to $200 per night; and **Inexpensive,** less than $150 per night. These categories reflect the rack rates for an average double room during the high season, which runs approximately from April to September.

Value **Dial Direct**

When booking a room in a chain hotel, call the hotel's local line and the toll-free number and see where you get the best deal. A hotel makes nothing on a room that stays empty. The clerk who runs the place is more likely to know about vacancies than someone from the toll-free number is and will often grant deep discounts in order to fill up rooms.

---

phone, and make a note of the name of the person you spoke with.

• When you check in, if your room isn't up to snuff, politely inform the front desk of your dissatisfaction and ask for another. If the hotel can accommodate you, they almost always will—and sometimes will even upgrade you!

Read the below entries carefully: Many hotels also offer rooms at rates above and below the price category that applies to most of the units. If you like the sound of a place that's a bit over your budget, it never hurts to call and ask a few questions. Also note that we do not list single rates. Some hotels, particularly more affordable choices, do charge lower rates for singles, so inquire about them if you are traveling alone.

Other than the exceptional circumstances of the past few years, hotel rates in San Francisco don't vary much because the city is so popular year-round. Still, you should always ask about weekend discounts, corporate rates, and family plans; most larger hotels, and many smaller ones, offer them, but many reservations agents don't mention them unless you ask about them specifically.

You'll find nonsmoking rooms available in all larger hotels and many smaller hotels; reviews indicate establishments that are entirely nonsmoking. Nowadays, the best advice for smokers is to confirm a smoking-permitted room in advance.

While you'll find that most accommodations have an abundance of amenities (including phones, unless otherwise noted), don't be alarmed by the lack of air-conditioned guest rooms. San Francisco weather is so mild, you'll never miss them.

Most larger hotels can accommodate guests who use wheelchairs and those who have other special needs. Ask when you make a reservation to ensure that your hotel can accommodate your needs, especially if you are interested in a bed-and-breakfast.

HELPING HANDS   Having reservations about your reservations? Leave it up to the pros:

San Francisco Reservations, 360 22nd St., Suite 300, Oakland, CA 94612 (© **800/677-1500** or 510/628-4450; www.hotelres.com), arranges reservations for more than 200 of San Francisco's hotels and often offers discounted rates. Their nifty website allows Internet users to make reservations online.

Other good online sites with discounted rates include **www.hotels. com** and **www.placestostay.com**.

---

1 Union Square

VERY EXPENSIVE

Campton Place Hotel ★★★   With a $15-million room renovation completed at the end of 2001, this already fabulous luxury boutique hotel offers some of the best accommodations in town—not to mention the most expensive.

Rooms were completely gutted, old furnishings were replaced with limestone, pearwood, and more Italian-modern decor. The two executive suites and one luxury suite push the haute envelope to even more luxurious heights. Discriminating returning guests will still find superlative service, extralarge beds, exquisite bathrooms, bathrobes, top-notch toiletries, slippers, and every other necessity and extra that's made Campton Place a favored temporary address. Chef Daniel Humm delights diners with delicately prepared and very sculpted cuisine at the excellent Campton Place Restaurant, which underwent a glamorous face-lift in 2002.

340 Stockton St. (between Post and Sutter sts.), San Francisco, CA 94108. ✆ **800/235-4300** or 415/781-5555. Fax 415/955-5536. www.camptonplace.com. 110 units. $345–$475 double; from $550–$2,000 suite. American breakfast $17. AE, DC, MC, V. Valet parking $35. Cable car: Powell-Hyde and Powell-Mason lines (1 block west). Bus: 2, 3, 4, 30, or 45. **Amenities:** Restaurant; health club; concierge; courtesy car; secretarial services; 24-hr. room service; laundry service; same-day dry cleaning. *In room:* A/C, TV w/pay movies, T1 line, dataport, minibar, hair dryer, iron, safe.

Clift Hotel ★★   Ian Schrager, king of such ultrahip hotels as New York's Royalton and Paramount, L.A.'s Mondrian, and Miami's Delano, renovated this classic old luxury property in 2001, erasing virtually every trace of its original integrity and replacing it with trendy hipness. No longer the spot for the older clientele, now it's all about young trendsetters who flock here for monochrome pale-purple streamlined rooms with often-miniscule bathrooms, glamorous atmosphere, and a heavy dose of attitude. Situated in the city's Theater District, 2 blocks from Union Square, the hotel's location is still key. The Redwood Room bar underwent renovation and is noticeably different, with its original sexy redwood walls and light fixtures accompanying Philippe Starck's whimsically luxurious and rather uncomfortable interior. Equally trend and expensive Asia de Cuba restaurant adjoins the swank lounge. Guest-room extras include individual climate control, two-line telephones, and windows that open—a nice touch for guests who appreciate fresh air, but in my mind, the only reason to pay the high prices here is if you're interested in being surrounded by the young and hip. Otherwise, there are far better rooms about town at a similar or less-expensive price.

495 Geary St. (at Taylor St.), San Francisco, CA 94102. ✆ **800/652-5438** or 415/775-4700. Fax 415/441-4621. www.ianschragerhotels.com. 363 units. $325–$460 double; from $425 studio suite; from $950 deluxe suite. AE, DC, MC, V. Valet parking $40. Cable car: Powell-Hyde and Powell-Mason lines (2 blocks east). Bus: 2, 3, 4, 30, 38, or 45. **Amenities:** Restaurant; bar; exercise room; concierge; limited room service; same-day laundry service/dry cleaning. *In room:* TV/DVD, minibar, hair dryer, iron.

The Donatello ★ *Value*   If you're not looking for trendy lodgings or an anonymous business hotel but want old-world elegance, book a room here. The Donatello is, in a word, dignified. The lobby is classy, with Italian marble and a serious staff. The rooms, which are some of the largest in the city (an average of 425 sq. ft.!), are airy, updated classic European and even better than before, since they were completely redecorated in 2000 with contemporary French antiques, stripes, tapestries, original art, king-size mattresses, and textiles. Thankfully, the face-lift didn't include going the trendy bold-and-colorful route, which seems to be infectious among downtown hotels. Unfortunately, most of the extralarge

---

⟨ **Fun Fact** Inflation at the Clift

The Clift Hotel charged a mere $2 per night when it first opened in 1915. The price for a room now? More than $350.

Accommodations near Union Square & Nob Hill

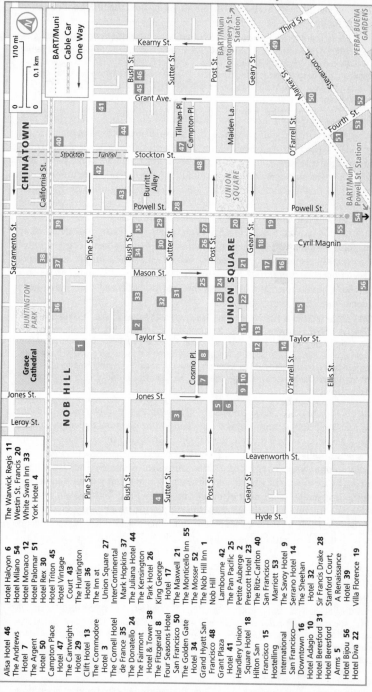

Alisa Hotel **46**
The Andrews Hotel **7**
The Argent Hotel **50**
Campton Place Hotel **47**
The Cartwright Hotel **29**
Cliff Hotel **13**
The Commodore Hotel **3**
The Cornell Hotel de France **35**
The Donatello **24**
The Fairmont Hotel & Tower **38**
The Fitzgerald **8**
Four Seasons Hotel San Francisco **50**
The Golden Gate Hotel **34**
Grand Hyatt San Francisco **48**
Grant Plaza Hotel **41**
Handlery Union Square Hotel **18**
Hilton San Francisco **15**
Hostelling International San Francisco—Downtown **16**
Hotel Adagio **10**
Hotel Beresford **31**
Hotel Beresford Arms **5**
Hotel Bijou **56**
Hotel Diva **22**

Hotel Halcyon **6**
Hotel Milano **54**
Hotel Monaco **12**
Hotel Palomar **51**
Hotel Rex **30**
Hotel Triton **45**
Hotel Vintage Court **43**
The Huntington Hotel **36**
The Inn at Union Square **27**
InterContinental Mark Hopkins **37**
The Juliana Hotel **44**
The Kensington Park Hotel **26**
King George Hotel **17**
The Maxwell **21**
The Monticello Inn **55**
The Mosser **52**
The Nob Hill Inn **1**
The Pan Pacific **25**
Petite Auberge **23**
Prescott Hotel **40**
The Ritz-Carlton San Francisco Marriott **53**
The Savoy Hotel **9**
Serrano Hotel **14**
The Sheehan Hotel **32**
Sir Francis Drake **28**
Stanford Court, A Renaissance Hotel **39**
Villa Florence **19**

The Warwick Regis **11**
Westin St. Francis **20**
White Swan Inn **33**
York Hotel **4**

windows lack great views, but if it's fresh air you're after, the fifth floor has seven terrace rooms.

501 Post St. (at Mason St.), San Francisco, CA 94102. © **800/227-3184** or 415/441-7100. Fax 415/885-8842. 94 units. $179–$295 double. Children under 12 stay free in parent's room. AE, DC, DISC, MC, V. Valet parking $28. Cable car: Powell-Hyde and Powell-Mason lines (1 block west). Bus: 2, 3, 4, 30, 38, or 45. **Amenities:** Restaurant; bar; exercise room; concierge; limited room service; same-day laundry service/dry cleaning; 2 meeting spaces. *In room:* A/C, TV w/pay movies, dataport, fridge, coffeemaker, hair dryer, iron, CD player, toaster, microwave.

Grand Hyatt San Francisco ⊛ If the thought of a 10-second walk to Saks Fifth Avenue makes your pulse race, this high-rise luxury hotel is the place for you. The Grand Hyatt sits amid all the downtown shopping while also boasting some of the best views in the area. The lobby is indeed grand, with Chinese artifacts and enormous ceramic vases. Thankfully, the well-kept rooms were recently renovated; they're swankier than they used to be, but they still have an upscale corporate vibe. Each room has a lounge chair as well as a small desk and sitting area. Views from most of the 36 floors are truly spectacular.

Rates for concierge-level Regency Club rooms ($45 extra) include access to the lounge, honor bar, continental breakfast, and evening hors d'oeuvres. Three floors hold business-plan guest rooms, each of which has a private fax and special services; for the extra $20 cost of the room, you get 24-hour access to a printer, a photocopier, and office supplies; free local calls and credit card phone access; and a daily newspaper.

345 Stockton St. (between Post and Sutter sts.), San Francisco, CA 94108. © **800/233-1234** or 415/398-1234. Fax 415/391-1780. www.sanfrancisco.grand.hyatt.com. 685 units. $159–$319 double; Regency Club $45 additional. AE, DC, DISC, MC, V. Valet parking $39. Cable car: Powell-Hyde and Powell-Mason lines (2 blocks west). Bus: 2, 3, 4, 30, 38, or 45. **Amenities:** Restaurant; bar; health club; concierge; business center; secretarial services; limited room service; laundry service; same-day dry cleaning. *In room:* A/C, TV w/pay movies, dataport, minibar, coffeemaker, hair dryer, iron, safe, high-speed Internet access, 2 phone lines with speaker capability.

Hotel Monaco ⊛ This remodeled 1910 Beaux Arts building made its debut in June 1995 and instantly claimed title as one of the divas among Union Square's luxury hotels. For $24 million, the Kimpton Group did this place right—from the whimsically ethereal lobby with a two-story French inglenook fireplace to the guest rooms with canopy beds, Chinese-inspired armoires, bamboo writing desks, bold stripes, and vibrant color. Everything is bold but tasteful, and as playful as it is serious, with nifty extras like flatscreen TVs, Web TV, and two-line phones. The decor, combined with the truly grand neighboring Grand Café restaurant that's ideal for cocktails and mingling, would put this place on my top-10 list if it weren't for rooms that tend to be way too small (especially for the price), the lack of a sizable gym, and the 2001 arrival of the Four Seasons Hotel San Francisco (p. 87). That said, this place has great character—especially in the common areas. If you stay here, take advantage of their nightly complimentary wine service accompanied by shoulder and neck massages.

501 Geary St. (at Taylor St.), San Francisco, CA 94102. © **800/214-4220** or 415/292-0100. Fax 415/292-0111. www.monaco-sf.com. 201 units. $229–$399 double; $269–$599 suite. Rates include evening wine hour. Call for discounted rates. AE, DC, DISC, MC, V. Valet parking $35. Bus: 2, 3, 4, 27, or 38. Pets accepted. **Amenities:** Restaurant; exercise room; spa; Jacuzzi; sauna; concierge; courtesy car; business center; 24-hr. room service; in-room massage; laundry service; dry cleaning. *In room:* A/C, TV, dataport, minibar, coffeemaker with Starbucks coffee, hair dryer, iron, safe, high-speed Internet access, CD player, copier/printer/fax.

Pan Pacific San Francisco ⊛⊛ The Pan Pacific—located conveniently close to Union Square—is artistically glitzy, enormous, and somehow romantic, all at the same time. If this were a Hollywood set, James Bond might hoodwink a villain here, magically drop down from the sky-rise's atrium, and disappear into the night. But all is quiet and intimate in the third-floor lobby, even though the skylight ceiling is another 18 floors up. The lobby's marble fountain with four dancing figures and its player piano set the mood for guests relaxing in front of the fireplace. Major room updating in 2004 means each rather large abode is now swathed in chic white-on-white decor and adorned with flatscreen TVs and Herman Miller chairs. The bathrooms remain regal and lavishly marble-clad with a mini-TV at the sink and cozy bathrobes.

500 Post St. (at Mason St.), San Francisco, CA 94102. © **800/533-6465** or 415/771-8600. Fax 415/398-0267. www.panpacific.com. 329 units. $340–$465 double; from $480 suite. AE, DC, DISC, MC, V. Valet parking $39. Cable car: Powell-Hyde and Powell-Mason lines. Bus: 2, 3, 4, 30, 38, or 45. Dogs under 25 lb. welcome for an additional $75 fee. **Amenities:** Restaurant; bar; exercise room; concierge; business center; 24-hr. room service; in-room massage; laundry service; same-day dry cleaning; butler service. *In room:* A/C, TV, fax, dataport, minibar, hair dryer, iron, safe.

Prescott Hotel ★★   It may be small and lack common areas, but the boutique Prescott Hotel has some big things going for it. The staff treats you like royalty, rooms are attractively unfrilly and masculine, the location (just a block from Union Square) is perfect, and limited room service is provided by one of the most popular downtown restaurants, Postrio (p. 112). Ralph Lauren fabrics in dark tones of green, plum, and burgundy blend well with the cherrywood furnishings in each of the soundproof rooms; the view, alas, isn't so pleasant. The very small bathrooms contain terry robes and Aveda products, and the suites have Jacuzzi bathtubs. Concierge-level guests are pampered with a free continental breakfast, evening cocktails and hors d'oeuvres, and even 3 days per week head-and-shoulders massages.

545 Post St. (between Mason and Taylor sts.), San Francisco, CA 94102. © **800/283-7322** or 415/563-0303. Fax 415/563-6831. www.prescotthotel.com. 164 units. $275–$340 double; $300 concierge-level double (including breakfast and evening cocktail reception); from $365 suite. AE, DC, DISC, MC, V. Valet parking $35. Cable car: Powell-Hyde and Powell-Mason lines (1 block east). Bus: 2, 3, 4, 30, 38, or 45. **Amenities:** Restaurant; bar; small exercise room; concierge; limited courtesy car; limited room service. *In room:* TV w/pay movies, fax/printer, dataport, minibar, hair dryer, iron, safe, high-speed Internet access, video games.

Westin St. Francis ★★ *Kids*   At the turn of the 20th century, Charles T. Crocker and a few of his wealthy buddies decided that San Francisco needed a world-class hotel, and up went the St. Francis. Since then, hordes of VIPs have hung their hats and hosiery here, including Emperor Hirohito of Japan, Queen Elizabeth II of England, Mother Teresa, King Juan Carlos of Spain, the shah of Iran, and all the U.S. presidents since Taft. In 1972, the hotel gained the 32-story Tower, doubling its capacity and adding banquet and conference centers. The older rooms of the main building vary in size and have more old-world charm than the newer rooms, but the Tower is remarkable for its great views of the city from above the 18th floor.

Although the St. Francis is too massive to offer the personal service you get at the smaller deluxe hotels on Nob Hill, few other hotels in San Francisco can

---

Fun Fact **Hotel Rendezvous**

For nearly a century, the most popular place for visitors to rendezvous in San Francisco has been under the magnificent hand-carved grandfather clock in the lobby of the Westin St. Francis hotel.

match its majestic aura. Stroll through the vast, ornate lobby, and you can feel 100 years of history oozing from its hand-carved redwood paneling. The hotel has done massive renovations costing $185 million over the past decade, replacing the carpeting, furniture, and bedding in every main-building guest room; gussying up the lobby; and restoring the facade.

The Westin makes kids feel right at home, too, with a goody bag upon check-in. The tower's Grandview Rooms, which were renovated in 2001, today evoke a contemporary design along the lines of the W Hotel. The historic main building accentuates its history with traditional, more elegant ambience, high ceilings, and crown molding. Alas, the venerable Compass Rose tearoom is no longer, but in its place is a new (debuted in August of 2004) fancy restaurant, Michael Mina, by the famed chef of Aqua.

335 Powell St. (between Geary and Post sts.), San Francisco, CA 94102. ✆ **800/WESTIN-1** or 415/397-7000. Fax 415/774-0124. www.westin.com. 1,195 units. Main building: $199–$499 double; Tower (Grand View): $219–$549 double; from $550 suite (in either building). Extra person $30. Continental breakfast $15–$18. AE, DC, DISC, MC, V. Valet parking $42. Cable car: Powell-Hyde and Powell-Mason lines (direct stop). Bus: 2, 3, 4, 30, 38, 45, or 76. Pets under 40 lb. accepted (dog beds available on request). **Amenities:** 2 restaurants; bar with pianist nightly; elaborate health club and spa; concierge; car-rental desk; business center; 24-hr. room service. *In room:* A/C, TV, dataport, minibar, fridge, hair dryer, iron, high-speed Internet access, cordless phones.

EXPENSIVE

Handlery Union Square Hotel ★ *Kids* A mere half block from Union Square, the Handlery was already a good deal frequented by European travelers before the 1908 building underwent a complete overhaul in 2002. Now you'll find every amenity you could possibly need, plus lots of extras, in the extremely tasteful and modern (although sedate and a little dark) rooms. Rooms range from coral and gray in the historic building to taupe and tan in the newer club-level building. In between is a clean heated outdoor pool. Literally everything was replaced here: mattresses, alarm radios, refrigerators, light fixtures, paint, carpets, and furnishings. Perks include adjoining L.A.-based chain restaurant The Daily Grill (which is unfortunately not as tasty as its sister restaurants down south) and club-level options (all in the newer building) that include larger rooms, a complimentary morning newspaper, a bathroom scale, robes, two two-line phones, and adjoining doors that make the units great choices for families. Downsides? Not a lot of direct light, no grand feeling in the lobby, and lots of trekking if you want to go to and from the adjoining buildings that make up the hotel. All in all, it's a good value for downtown. Personally, this would be a choice second to the less expensive The Warwick Regis or Savoy.

351 Geary St. (between Mason and Powell sts.), San Francisco, CA 94102. ✆ **800/843-4343** or 415/781-7800. Fax 415/781-0269. www.handlery.com. 377 units. $189 double. Club section from $289 double, from $280 suite. Extra person $10. AE, DC, DISC, MC, V. Parking $28. Cable car: Powell-Hyde and Powell-Mason lines (direct stop). Bus: 2, 3, 4, 30, 38, or 45. **Amenities:** Restaurant; heated outdoor swimming pool; access to nearby health club ($10 per day); sauna; barber shop; room service (7am–10pm); babysitting; same-day laundry. *In room:* A/C, TV w/Nintendo and pay movies, dataport, fridge, complimentary coffee/tea-making facilities, hair dryer, iron, safe, wireless Internet access, voice mail.

Hilton San Francisco ★ Complete with bustling conventioneers and a line to register that resembles airport check-in, the Hilton's lobby is so enormous and busy that it feels more like a convention hall than a hotel. The three connecting buildings (the original 19-story main structure, a 46-story tower topped by a panoramic restaurant, and a 23-story landmark with 386 luxurious rooms and suites) bring swarms of visitors. Even during quieter times, the sheer enormity of the place makes the Hilton somewhat overwhelming.

After you get past the sweeping grand lobby, jump on an elevator, and wind through endless corridors to your room, you're likely to find the mystique ends with clean but run-of-the-mill standard-size corporate accommodations. That said, some of the views from the floor-to-ceiling windows in the main tower's rooms are memorable, and since the hotel continues with ongoing renovations, you're likely to sleep in newish quarters.

Unless you're staying in one of the more luxurious units, the feel and decor are impersonal and plain—perfect for conventioneers, but not for a romantic weekend. One bonus: A 13,000-square-foot health club and day spa was added in 2003. The Hilton has four restaurants: Cityscape, on the 46th floor, offers classic California cuisine and a breathtaking 360-degree view; Intermezzo serves Mediterranean-style food; The Café offers a buffet; and Kiku's of Japan offers—you guessed it—Japanese food.

333 O'Farrell St. (between Mason and Taylor sts.), San Francisco, CA 94102. © 800/HILTONS or 415/771-1400. Fax 415/771-6807. www.sanfrancisco.hilton.com. 1,908 units. $159–$309 double; from $465 suite. Children stay free in parent's room. AE, DC, DISC, MC, V. Parking $33 (some oversize vehicles cannot be accommodated, depending on height). Cable car: Powell-Hyde and Powell-Mason lines (1 block east). Bus: 2, 3, 4, 7, 9, 21, 27, 30, 38, 45, or 71. **Amenities:** 4 restaurants; outdoor pool; health club; spa; sauna; concierge; tour desk; car-rental desk; business center; secretarial services; room service (6am–midnight); laundry service; dry cleaning; wireless Internet access in public spaces. *In room:* A/C, TV, dataport, minibar, coffeemaker, hair dryer, iron, high-speed Internet access.

Hotel Milano ⭐   Neoclassical Italian design, elegantly streamlined rooms (with double-paned soundproof windows), moderate prices, and a central location next to the San Francisco Centre make Hotel Milano a popular choice for tourists and businesspeople alike. The hotel also has a film-production facility and private screening room to entice media types. Corporate travelers come for the spacious guest rooms, which feature everything an executive could want, from fax/computer modem hookups to Nintendo game systems. Some rooms have spa tubs, bidets, and two bathrooms.

55 Fifth St. (between Market and Mission sts.), San Francisco, CA 94103. © 800/398-7555 or 415/543-8555. Fax 415/543-5885. 108 units. $109–$239 double. Extra person $20. AE, DC, DISC, MC, V. Valet parking $28 (no oversize vehicles or SUVs). Bus: All Market St. buses. **Amenities:** Restaurant; health club; spa; steam room and sauna; concierge; room service; laundry; valet. *In room:* A/C, TV w/Nintendo, fax, dataport, minibar, hair dryer, iron, safe.

Hotel Rex ⭐   Joie de Vivre, the most creative hotel group in the city, is the brilliance behind this restored historic building, which is near several fine galleries, theaters, and restaurants. The group kept some of the imported furnishings and the European boutique hotel ambience, but gave the lobby and rooms a $2-million face-lift, adding the decorative flair that makes its hotels among the most popular in town. The clublike lobby lounge is modeled after a 1920s literary salon and is, like all the group's properties, cleverly stylish. The renovated rooms are above average in size. If you have one of the rooms in the back, you'll look out over a shady, peaceful courtyard.

562 Sutter St. (between Powell and Mason sts.), San Francisco, CA 94102. © 800/433-4434 or 415/433-4434. Fax 415/433-3695. www.thehotelrex.com. 94 units. $199–$239 double; $275–$575 suite. AE, DC, MC, V. Valet parking $30; self-parking $22. Cable car: Powell-Hyde and Powell-Mason lines (1 block east). Bus: 2, 3, 4, 30, 38, or 45. **Amenities:** Access to nearby health club; concierge; business center; limited room service; same-day laundry service/dry cleaning. *In room:* TV w/pay movies, dataport, minibar, hair dryer, iron, high-speed Internet access, CD player.

The Maxwell Hotel ⭐⭐ *Value* *Kids*   Its location, 1 block from Union Square, and chic-boutique surroundings make this 13-story 1908 hotel a favorite with business travelers, families, die-hard shoppers, and even Eminem (who stayed here in 2003). Rooms show their age, but rather than wrinkles, you're more likely to look at the imperfections as laugh lines thanks to the rooms' surprising spaciousness (though bathrooms are small) and "Theatre Deco" meets Victorian decor (a sort of smoking club/study atmosphere). Expect velvets, brocades, stripes, plaids, rich color, handcrafted artistic accents, upholstered chairs, hand-painted bedside lamps, luxurious pillows, writing desks, and boldly tiled vanities. The hotel's roomy junior suites offer excellent value, but best of all are the pair of one-bedroom suites on the 13th floor, both of which offer separate living rooms and exceptional views of the city (one has a private rooftop deck and kitchenette). Perks at The Maxwell include a foot masseuse on request for weary shoppers, discount coupons for the local department stores, and a "Kids are VIPs" program that lets parents rent an adjoining room for their kids at half the regular rate and tosses in some kid-friendly extras.

386 Geary St. (at Mason St.), San Francisco, CA 94102. ⓒ **888/734-6299** or 415/986-2000. Fax 415/986-2193. www.maxwellhotel.com. 153 units. $169–$215 double; $199–$349 suite. Extra person $15. Corporate discounts available. AE, DC, DISC, MC, V. Valet parking $32, self-parking $24. Cable car: Powell-Hyde and Powell-Mason lines (1 block east). Bus: 2, 3, 4, 30, 38, or 45. **Amenities:** Restaurant; concierge; meeting facilities; limited room service; dry cleaning; free wireless Internet in lobby. *In room:* A/C, TV w/pay movies, high-speed Internet access, hair dryer, iron, safe, bathrobes, CD players in executive rooms and suites.

Sir Francis Drake ★★ It took a change of ownership and a multimillion-dollar restoration to revive the Sir Francis Drake, but the stately old queen is again housing guests with old–San Francisco aplomb. Granted, the venerable septuagenarian is still showing signs of age despite the fact that the owners continue to throw millions toward renovations. But the price of imperfection certainly shows in the room rate: a good $100 less per night than its Nob Hill cousins. The hotel is perfect for people who are willing to trade a chipped bathroom tile or oddly matched furniture for the opportunity to vacation in pseudo-grand fashion. Allow Tom Sweeny, the ebullient (and legendary) Beefeater doorman, to handle your bags as you enter the elegant, captivating lobby and live like the king or queen of Union Square without all the pomp, circumstance, and credit card bills.

Scala's Bistro (p. 115), one of the most festive restaurants downtown, serves good Italian cuisine in a stylish setting; the Parisian-style Café Expresso does an equally commendable job serving coffees, pastries, and sandwiches daily. The superchic Starlight Room, on the 21st floor, offers cocktails, entertainment, and dancing nightly with a panoramic view of the city.

450 Powell St. (at Sutter St.), San Francisco, CA 94102. ⓒ **800/227-5480** or 415/392-7755. Fax 415/391-8719. www.sirfrancisdrake.com. 417 units. $219–$259 double; $500–$700 suite. AE, DC, DISC, MC, V. Valet parking $35. Cable car: Powell-Hyde and Powell-Mason lines (direct stop). Bus: 2, 3, 4, 45, or 76. **Amenities:** 2 restaurants; bar; exercise room; concierge; limited room service; same-day laundry service/dry cleaning. *In room:* A/C, TV w/pay movies, dataport, minibar, hair dryer, iron, Nintendo.

⎛ *Fun Fact* **A Living Legend**

Tom Sweeny, the head doorman at the Sir Francis Drake hotel, is San Francisco's living historical monument. Dressed in traditional Beefeaters attire (you can't miss those $1,400 duds), he's been the subject of countless snapshots—an average 200 per day for the past 20 years—and has shaken hands with every president since Jerry Ford.

White Swan Inn ★★ *Value* From the moment you're buzzed into this well-secured great-value inn, you'll know you're not in a generic bed-and-breakfast. If the nearly 50 teddy bears gracing the lobby don't cure homesickness, then the homemade cookies, tea, and coffee will. The romantically homey rooms are warm and cozy—the perfect place to snuggle up with a good book. They're also quite big, with hardwood entryways, rich dark-wood furniture, working fireplaces, and an assortment of books tucked in nooks. The decor is English elegance at its best, if not to excess, with floral prints almost everywhere. The luxury king suites are not much better than regular rooms, just a little bigger, and feature perks like chocolates, champagne, and a VCR. Each morning, a generous breakfast is served in a common room just off a tiny garden. Afternoon tea, consisting of hors d'oeuvres, sherry, wine, and home-baked pastries, can be enjoyed in front of the fireplace while you browse through the books in the library.

The inn's location—2½ blocks from Union Square—makes this nonsmoking 1900s building a charming and serene choice, with service and style that will please even the most discriminating traveler.

845 Bush St. (between Taylor and Mason sts.), San Francisco, CA 94108. ℂ 800/999-9570 or 415/775-1755. Fax 415/775-5717. www.whiteswaninnsf.com. 26 units. $219–$309 double; $259 luxury king suite; $309 2-room suite. Extra person $20. Rates include breakfast and afternoon wine and hors d'oeuvres. AE, DC, DISC, MC, V. Valet parking (7:30am–10:30pm) $30. Cable car: Powell St. line (1 block north). Bus: 1, 2, 3, 4, 27, or 45. **Amenities:** Small exercise room; concierge; laundry service. *In room:* Dataport, fridge with complimentary beverages, coffeemaker, hair dryer, iron.

MODERATE

A few worthy hotel companies operate many properties throughout the city. **Holiday Inn** (ℂ 800/465-4329; www.holiday-inn.com) has several strategic locations, including pretty properties in Fisherman's Wharf and Cow Hollow. **Personality Hotels** (ℂ 800/553-1900; www.personalityhotels.com) spiffs up older buildings in central locales, and **Joie de Vivre** (ℂ 800/SF-TRIPS; www.jdvhospitality.com) has lots of festive options scattered around town.

The Commodore Hotel ★ If you're looking to pump a little fun and fantasy into your vacation, this six-story downtown Art Deco building is the place to go. San Francisco hotelier Chip Conley of Joie de Vivre Hospitality is behind this groovy revamped hotel frequented by an eclectic mix of 20-somethings and everyday folks in search of reasonably priced accommodations. Stealing the show is the Red Room, a small New York–slick bar and lounge that reflects no other color of the spectrum but ruby red (you gotta see this one). The stylish lobby, which was renovated in 2000, comes in a close second, followed by the adjoining Titanic Café, a cute little diner that serves American fare for breakfast and lunch. The "Neo-Deco" rooms, all of which underwent upgrades through 2001, are simple but lively with bright colors, whimsical furnishings, pretty artwork, and small bathrooms refurbished in 1998.

825 Sutter St. (at Jones St.), San Francisco, CA 94109. ℂ 800/338-6848 or 415/923-6800. Fax 415/923-6804. www.thecommodorehotel.com. 110 units. $125–$169 double. AE, DC, DISC, MC, V. Parking $25. Bus: 2, 3, 4, 27, 19, 47, 49. **Amenities:** Diner; bar; access to nearby health club ($15 per day); concierge; Internet access in lobby. *In room:* TV w/pay movies, dataport, coffeemaker, fridge, hair dryer, iron.

Hotel Adagio ★★ *Value* Now under new management and after an $11-million renovation, this 1929 Spanish Revival hotel has a new name and a gorgeous modern style—and usually costs about half the price of other hotels in the area. Local hip hoteliers Joie de Vivre revamped its 171 large, bright guest rooms, and though there's no fixing the dark and gloomy hallways, once inside your abode you'll find plenty to cheer about, like the chocolate brown and mocha color palette, dark wood, firm mattresses, double-paned windows that open, quiet surroundings, all-around cleanliness, voice mail, lots and lots of elbowroom, and corporate floors (12 and 16) with irons, robes, and free continental breakfast. Bathrooms are old but clean, and most have tubs. Feel like splurging? Go for one of the five penthouse-level suites, which have lovely terraces with a New York vibe. Or simply step into the restaurant bar at night which has funky glowing ball lamps, a youngish crowd, "small plates," and a full bar. *Tip:* Rooms above the ninth floor have good, but not great, southern views of the city.

550 Geary St., San Francisco, CA 94102. © 800/228-8830 or 415/775-5000. www.thehoteladagio.com. 173 units. $209 double. AE, DISC, MC, V. Valet parking $29. **Amenities:** Restaurant; bar; fitness center; concierge; room service; business center w/free wireless Internet; laundry service; dry cleaning; luggage storage room. *In room:* TV w/pay movies and Nintendo, dataport, minibar, fridge, hair dryer, iron, safe, complimentary high-speed Internet access, CD player.

Hotel Diva ★   The Diva is the prima donna of San Francisco's affordable modern hotels. A showbiz darling when it opened in 1985, the sleek, ultra-modern Diva won "Best Hotel Design" from *Interiors* magazine. A profusion of curvaceous glass, marble, and steel marks the Euro-tech lobby; the minimalist rooms, spotless and neat, are softened with utterly fashionable "Italian modern" furnishings of monochromatic colors, silver, and wood. Enormous headboards are made of polished stainless steel meant to evoke the bow of a ship. Personally, I find the hotel a little on the cold side (figuratively speaking). But toys and services abound, and fitness and business centers complete the package. *Insider tip:* Reserve one of the rooms ending in 09 because they have extralarge bathrooms with vanity mirrors and makeup tables. The downside is that these rooms have views that make you want to keep the chic curtains closed.

440 Geary St. (between Mason and Taylor sts.), San Francisco, CA 94102. © 800/553-1900 or 415/885-0200. Fax 415/346-6613. www.hoteldiva.com. 115 units. $175 double; $215 junior suite; $550 suite. Extra person $10. AE, DC, DISC, MC, V. Valet parking $30. Cable car: Powell-Mason line. Bus: 38 or 38L. **Amenities:** 24-hr. coffee/tea service; exercise room; concierge; secretarial services; laundry service; dry cleaning; complimentary Internet access. *In room:* A/C, TV/VCR, fax, dataport, minibar, hair dryer, iron, safe, CD player.

Hotel Triton ★   Described as vogue, chic, retrofuturistic, and even neo-baroque, this Kimpton Group property is whimsy at its boutique-hotel best, from the Dalí-esque lobby to the funky-fun if not a wee bit too small designer suites a la Jerry Garcia, Wyland (the ocean artist), and Santana. Two dozen environmentally sensitive "EcoRooms"—with biodegradable soaps, filtered water and air, and all-natural linens—please the tree-hugger in all of us. All the rooms were completely redone in 2002, also the year the hotel welcomed a brand-new and equally whimsical lobby. One bummer: When I stayed in a south-facing suite, I could hear the garbage truck way too early in the morning!

The hotel serves coffee each morning, and wine, beer, and tarot readings each evening (included in the room rate) in the lobby. The bustling and casual Café de la Presse, a European-style newsstand and outdoor cafe, serves breakfast, lunch, and dinner.

342 Grant Ave. (at Bush St.), San Francisco, CA 94108. © 800/433-6611 or 415/394-0500. Fax 415/394-0555. www.hoteltriton.com. 140 units. $199 double; $329 suite. AE, DC, DISC, MC, V. Parking $33, no over-size vehicles. Cable car: Powell-Hyde and Powell-Mason lines (2 blocks west). Pets stay free with conditional agreement. **Amenities:** Cafe; exercise room; business center; room service (7am–11pm); same-day laundry service/dry cleaning; high-speed Internet access. *In room:* A/C, TV w/pay movies, fax, dataport, minibar, coffeemaker, hair dryer, iron, Web TV.

Hotel Vintage Court ★★ *Value*   Consistent personal service and great value attract a loyal clientele at this European-style hotel 2 blocks north of Union Square. The chocolate brown lobby, accented with comfy couches, is welcoming enough to actually spend a little time in, especially when California wines are being poured each evening from 5 to 6pm free of charge.

But the varietals don't stop at ground level. Each tidy, quiet, and comfortable room, renovated in 2000, is named after a winery. While the decor used to suggest an old-fashioned Wine-Country excursion, today it has a more modern country look (think Pottery Barn meets Napa Valley), where greens and earth tones reign supreme, with cream duvets and lovely mahogany-slat blinds. Niebaum-Coppola (named after the winery owned by the movie maverick), the deluxe two-room penthouse suite, has an original 1912 stained-glass skylight, wood-burning fireplace, whirlpool tub, complete entertainment center, and panoramic views of the city. Smokers, book a room elsewhere, as puffing is prohibited in all rooms here.

Masa's, one of the city's top restaurants (p. 112), serves fantastic—and very expensive—contemporary French dinners here.

650 Bush St. (between Powell and Stockton sts.), San Francisco, CA 94108. © **800/654-1100** or 415/392-4666. Fax 415/433-4065. www.vintagecourt.com. 107 units. $150–$199 double; $325–$350 penthouse suite. Rates include continental breakfast and evening wine service. AE, DC, DISC, MC, V. Valet parking $34; self-parking $24. Cable car: Powell-Hyde and Powell-Mason lines (direct stop). Bus: 2, 3, 4, 30, 45, or 76. **Amenities:** Restaurant; access to off-premises health club ($12 per day); concierge; in-room massage; same-day laundry service/dry cleaning. *In room:* A/C, TV, dataport, minibar, coffeemaker, hair dryer, iron, video games.

The Inn at Union Square ★★   As narrow as an Amsterdam canal house, the Inn at Union Square is the antithesis of the big, impersonal hotels that surround Union Square. If you need plenty of elbowroom, skip this one. But if you're looking for an inn whose staff knows each guest's name, read on. One-half block west of the square, this seven-story inn makes up for its small stature by spoiling guests with a pile of perks. Mornings start with breakfast served in lounges stocked with the *New York Times,* and evening hors d'oeuvres are served in sweet little fireplace lounges at the end of each hall. The handsome rooms, which were renovated in 2003, are individually decorated with Georgian reproductions and floral fabrics, and they are smaller than average but infinitely more appreciated than the cookie-cutter rooms of most larger hotels. Smoking is not allowed in the rooms.

440 Post St. (between Mason and Powell sts.), San Francisco, CA 94102. © **800/288-4346** or 415/397-3510. Fax 415/989-0529. www.unionsquare.com. 30 units. $139–$209 double; $350 suite. Rates include continental breakfast, afternoon wine and hors d'oeuvres, and evening tea and cookies. AE, DC, DISC, MC, V. Valet parking $28. Cable car: Powell-Hyde and Powell-Mason lines. Bus: 2, 3, 4, 30, 38, or 45; all Market St. buses. **Amenities:** Free access to nearby health club; concierge; secretarial services; limited room service; laundry service; dry cleaning. *In room:* TV, dataport, hair dryer, iron, high-speed Internet access.

The Juliana Hotel ★★ *Value*   A European-style boutique hotel in the best possible way, the Juliana is hard not to like. Completely renovated in 1996 and again in 2001, rooms are trendy-French, with yellow and pale-blue-striped wallpaper, and candy-striped yellow-and-red upholstered chairs. It's vibrant and cheery, for sure, but not the kind of place where you'd want to nurse a wicked hangover. With coffee available in the lobby in the morning and wine at night (included in the room rate), there's no real reason to leave. Guest rooms and bathrooms can be on the small side, but the junior suites have plenty of space and lovely homey touches.

590 Bush St. (at Stockton St.), San Francisco, CA 94108. © **800/328-3880** or 415/392-2540. Fax 415/391-8447. www.julianahotel.com. 107 units. $129–$205 double; $159–$235 junior suite; $189–$265 executive suite. Special winter packages available. AE, DC, MC, V. Valet parking $32; self-parking $24. Cable car: Powell-Hyde and Powell-Mason lines (1 block west). Bus: 2, 3, 4, 30, 38, or 45. **Amenities:** Exercise room; high-speed Internet access in lobby; same-day laundry service/dry cleaning. *In room:* A/C, TV, dataport, minibar, coffeemaker, hair dryer, iron.

The Kensington Park Hotel 👶👶   The Kensington is a spiffed-up fairly old hotel with a cheery, eager-to-please (albeit sometimes short-handed) staff, tasteful accommodations, and extra efforts—like afternoon tea and sherry—that show the hotel cares about its guests. Large rooms on the 5th through 12th floors have handsome furnishings, and the bathrooms, though small, are sweetly appointed in brass and marble. As for the views, ask for an upper corner room, and you'll get far more than your money's worth. If you want the full treatment, book the Royal Suite, which contains a canopy bed, fireplace, Jacuzzi, and wet bar. The hotel adjoins popular fantasy—and fancy—seafood restaurant Farallon (p. 111).

450 Post St. (between Powell and Mason sts.), San Francisco, CA 94102. © **800/553-1900** or 415/788-6400. Fax 415/399-9484. www.kensingtonparkhotel.com. 96 units. $169–$205 double; $550 suite. Extra person $10. Rates include afternoon tea and sherry. AE, DC, DISC, MC, V. Valet parking $30. Cable car: Powell-Hyde and Powell-Mason lines (½ block east). **Amenities:** Restaurant (Farallon); 24-hr. coffee/tea service; concierge; business center; limited room service; same-day dry cleaning. *In room:* TV w/pay movies, fax, dataport, hair dryer, iron.

The Monticello Inn 👶   Federal-style decor, Chippendale furnishings, grandfather clocks, Revolutionary War paintings, a brass-mantled fireplace, and other old stuff scattered around the lobby (renovated in 2002) attempt to create a colonial milieu. Although it makes for a pleasant entrance, the period effect doesn't follow through to the comfortable, spacious rooms, which were completely renovated in 2004 with new textiles, carpet, striped white and light blue wallpaper, and mattresses. Despite the homely air conditioners in the walls, you'll be quite content here, especially considering the extras—umbrellas, voice mail, and a morning ride to the Financial District. The service is wonderful and the downtown location is *primo*. The adjoining Puccini & Pinetti restaurant features modern Italian cuisine.

127 Ellis St. (at Powell St.), San Francisco, CA 94102. © **800/669-7777** or 415/392-8800. Fax 415/398-2650. www.monticelloinn.com. 91 units. $129–$219 double; $179–$229 suite. Extra person $20. Rates include coffee and tea in the lobby and evening wine. AE, DC, DISC, MC, V. Valet parking $29. Pets accepted with $25 cleaning deposit. Cable car: Powell-Hyde and Powell-Mason lines (direct stop). Streetcar: All Market St. streetcars. Bus: All Market St. buses. **Amenities:** Access to great nearby health club ($15 per day); continental breakfast $6; concierge; limited room service; laundry service; dry cleaning. *In room:* A/C, TV w/pay movies and Nintendo, dataport, minibar, fridge, hair dryer, iron.

Petite Auberge 👶👶   The Petite Auberge is so pathetically cute I can't stand it. I want to say it's overdone, that any hotel that's filled with teddy bears is absurd, but I can't. Bribed each year with fresh-baked cookies from the never-empty platter, I make rounds through the rooms and ruefully admit that I'm just going to have to use that word I loathe: adorable.

Nobody does French country like the Petite Auberge. Handcrafted armoires, delicate lace curtains, cozy little fireplaces, adorable (there's that word again) little antiques and knickknacks—no hotel in Provence ever had it this good. Honeymooners should splurge on the petite suite, which has a private entrance, deck, and spa tub. The breakfast room, with its mural of a country market scene, terra-cotta tile floors, and gold-yellow tablecloths, opens onto a small garden.

California wines, tea, and hors d'oeuvres (included in the room rates) are served each afternoon, and guests have free rein of the fridge stocked with soft drinks. Bathers take note: Eight rooms have showers only.

863 Bush St. (between Taylor and Mason sts.), San Francisco, CA 94108. © 415/928-6000. Fax 415/775-5717. www.petiteaubergesf.com. 26 units. $179–$269 double; $269 petite suite. Rates include full breakfast and afternoon tea. AE, DC, DISC, MC, V. Parking $30. Cable car: Powell-Hyde and Powell-Mason lines. Bus: 2, 3, 4, 30, 38, or 45. **Amenities:** Access to small exercise room next door; concierge; babysitting; same-day laundry service/dry cleaning. *In room:* TV, dataport, hair dryer, robes.

Serrano Hotel ★★ Los Angeles designer Cheryl Rowley (who also designed the Hotel Monaco; p. 68) swathed this 17-story 1920s Kimpton Group property in her trademark vibrant color and added a playful dash of Moroccan flair while preserving the building's Spanish Revival integrity. Original architectural elements dot the colorful lobby, with its whimsically painted beams, high ceilings, large ornate fireplace, and dramatic colonnade. Equally vibrant guest rooms have oversize windows and high ceilings, cherrywood headboards, terry robes, and theater-themed artwork. The hotel is in the heart of the Theater District, right off Union Square.

405 Taylor St. (at O'Farrell St.), San Francisco, CA 94102. © **877/294-9709** or 415/885-2500. Fax 415/474-4879. www.serranohotel.com. 236 units. From $179 double; from $299 suite. Rates include morning coffee and tea service and afternoon beverages. AE, DC, DISC, MC, V. Valet parking $35. Cable car: Powell and Market. Bus: 2, 3, 4, 27, or 38. **Amenities:** Restaurant/bar; exercise room; sauna; concierge; courtesy car; business center; limited room service; babysitting; same-day laundry service/dry cleaning. *In room:* A/C, TV w/pay movies, fax, dataport, minibar, hair dryer, iron, safe in most rooms.

Villa Florence ★★ Located ½ block south of Union Square, fronting the Powell Street cable car line, the seven-story Villa Florence is in one of the liveliest sections of the city (no need to drive, 'cause you're already here). In 2004, a renovation brightened up the reasonably affordable rooms considerably. In its newest reincarnation, Villa Florence provides guests a taste of contemporary Italian flare with all new cherrywood furniture and luxury perks such as 27-inch flatscreen TVs with DVD players (with DVDs upon request) and CD players. You'll like the large, comfortable beds draped in down comforters with Frette duvets, as well as such frivolities as Aveda bath products, Frette bathrobes, and umbrellas. The hotel's ground-floor restaurant helps make it a worthy contender among Union Square's medium-priced inns—as if the location alone weren't reason enough to book a room. Adjacent to the hotel is Kuleto's (p. 114), one of downtown's most bustling and stylish Italian restaurants.

225 Powell St. (between Geary and O'Farrell sts.), San Francisco, CA 94102. © **800/553-4411** or 415/397-7700. Fax 415/397-1006. www.villaflorence.com. 183 units. $199–$239 double; $239–$269 executive kings. Rates include evening wine. AE, DC, DISC, MC, V. Valet parking $33, plus an extra $10–$15 per day for oversize vehicles and SUVs. Cable car: Powell-Hyde and Powell-Mason lines (direct stop). Bus: 2, 3, 4, 30, 38, or 45. **Amenities:** Access to nearby health club ($15 per day); concierge; courtesy car; business center; secretarial services; babysitting; same-day laundry service/dry cleaning. *In room:* A/C, TV w/pay movies, dataport, minibar, fridge, coffeemaker, hair dryer, iron, CD player.

The Warwick Regis ★★ *Value* Louis XVI might have been a rotten monarch, but he certainly had taste. Fashioned in the style of pre-Revolutionary France, the Warwick is awash with pristine French and English antiques, Italian marble, chandeliers, four-poster beds, hand-carved headboards, and the like. The result is an expensive-looking hotel that, for all its pleasantries and perks, is surprisingly affordable when compared to its Union Square contemporaries—especially considering that all rooms underwent a renovation in 2002. Rooms can be on the small side; nonetheless, they're some of the city's most charming. Honeymooners should splurge on the fireplace rooms with canopy beds—ooh la la! Adjoining the lobby is La Scene Café, a beautiful place to start your day with a latte and end it with a nightcap.

490 Geary St. (between Mason and Taylor sts.), San Francisco, CA 94102. © **800/827-3447** or 415/928-7900. Fax 415/441-8788. www.warwicksf.com. 80 units. $119–$159 double; $159–$269 suite. AE, DC, DISC, MC, V. Parking $28. Cable car: Powell-Hyde and Powell-Mason lines. Bus: 2, 3, 4, 27, or 38. **Amenities:** Restaurant; access to nearby health club ($15 per day); concierge; business center; secretarial services; 24-hr. room service; babysitting; laundry service; dry cleaning. *In room:* TV, dataport, minibar, hair dryer, iron, safe, wireless Internet access.

INEXPENSIVE

Alisa Hotel ⭐⭐ *Value* The five-story Alisa Hotel is definitely a budget gem. While it has standard characteristics of discount European-style hotels—small lobby, narrow hallways, cramped rooms—the owners here have distanced themselves from the competition by including a very pleasing dose of artistry. The lobby, for example, hosts rotating art exhibits and contains groovy furnishings, while the guest rooms are soothingly outfitted with quality Pan-Asian furnishings and tasteful accouterments such as Japanese fans, framed prints, and your very own personal "Moon Frog," the Chinese symbol of peace and harmony. You'll love the lively location as well: right across the street from the entrance to Chinatown and 2 blocks from Union Square. Considering the price (rooms with a very clean shared bathroom start at $49), quality, and location, it's quite possibly the best budget hotel in the city. Don't sweat it if they're booked: Their sister property, The Olympic Hotel (call the 800 number or see www.olympic hotelsf.com), acquired in December 2003, is nearby and equally priced and hospitable.

447 Bush St. (at Grant St.), San Francisco, CA 94108. © **800/956-4322** or 415/956-3232. Fax 415/956-0399. www.alisahotel.com. 51 units, 26 with private bathroom. $69–$119 double with bathroom; $49–$69 double without bathroom. Rates include continental breakfast. AE, DC, MC, V. Nearby parking $20. Bus: All Market St. buses. Cable car: Powell-Hyde and Powell-Mason lines. **Amenities:** 24-hour concierge; fax and copy services. *In room:* TV, 2-line direct dial telephone w/dataport and voice mail, hair dryer, iron/ironing board, wireless Internet, small fridge and microwave in some rooms.

The Andrews Hotel ⭐ For the location and price, the Andrews is a safe bet for an enjoyable stay. Two blocks west of Union Square, the Andrews was a Turkish bath before its conversion in 1981. As is typical in Euro-style hotels, the rooms are small but well maintained and comfortable, with nice touches like white lace curtains and fresh flowers. Upgrades in 2002 included new mattresses and carpets. And even though the bathrooms were painted in 2003, they will remain tiny no matter how lovely the face-lift may be. A bonus is the adjoining Fino Bar and Ristorante, which offers respectable Italian fare and free wine to hotel guests in the evening.

624 Post St. (between Jones and Taylor sts.), San Francisco, CA 94109. © **800/926-3739** or 415/563-6877. Fax 415/928-6919. www.andrewshotel.com. 48 units (some with shower only). $99–$145 double; $149–$159 superior rooms. Rates include continental breakfast and evening wine. AE, DC, MC, V. Valet parking $28. Cable car: Powell-Hyde and Powell-Mason lines (3 blocks east). Bus: 2, 3, 4, 30, 38, or 45. **Amenities:** Restaurant; access to nearby health club; concierge; room service (5:30–10pm); babysitting; coffee in lobby; nearby self-service laundromat; laundry service; dry cleaning. *In room:* TV/VCR w/video library, dataport, fridge in suites only, hair dryer on request, iron, high-speed Internet access ($10 per day).

The Cartwright Hotel ⭐⭐ Diametrically opposed to the hip-hop, happenin' Hotel Triton down the street, the Cartwright Hotel is geared toward the more mature traveler. Management takes pride in its reputation for offering comfortable rooms at fair prices, which explains why most guests have been repeat customers for a long time. Remarkably quiet, despite its convenient location near one of the busiest downtown corners, the eight-story hotel looks not unlike it did when it opened some 80 years ago. High-quality antiques collected during its decades of faithful service furnish the lobby and the individually decorated rooms, all of which were blessed with new carpets, mattresses, wallpaper, phones, and window treatments in 2001 and underwent a complete restoration in 2004 (think new paint and new furniture finishes). A nice perk usually reserved for fancier hotels is the fully equipped bathrooms, all of which have tubs, massaging showers, terry robes, and thick fluffy towels. *Tip:* Request a room with a view of the backyard; they're the quietest. Complimentary wine is served in the small library each night, and afternoon tea and cookies are a daily treat, as are the apples and hot beverages in the lobby. A breakfast room added in 2004 serves a complimentary expanded continental breakfast.

524 Sutter St. (at Powell St.), San Francisco, CA 94102. (℃) **800/227-3844** or 415/421-2865. Fax 415/398-6345. www.cartwrighthotel.com. 114 units. $89–$159 double; $139–$189 family/business suite (sleeps 4). Rates include 24-hr. tea, coffee, and apples in the lobby, continental breakfast, nightly wine hour, weekday newspapers, and afternoon cookies. AE, DC, DISC, MC, V. Valet parking $30; self-parking $22. Cable car: Powell-Hyde and Powell-Mason lines (direct stop). Bus: 2, 3, 4, 30, or 45. **Amenities:** Access to nearby health club; concierge; pay-for-use Internet access. *In room:* TV, dataport, minibar, fridge, hair dryer, iron.

The Cornell Hotel de France ★   Its quirks make this old hotel more charming than many others in its price range. Resident pooch, Noel, greets you when you enter the small French-style hotel. Pass the office, where a few faces will glance in your direction and smile, and embark on a ride in the old-fashioned elevator (we're talking seriously old-school here) to get to your very basic room. Each floor is dedicated to a French painter and decorated with reproductions. Rooms are all plain and comfortable, with desks and chairs, and are individually and simply decorated. Smoking is not allowed. Breakfast, which is included in the rate, is served in the very cool cavernlike provincial basement restaurant, Jeanne d'Arc. Union Square is just a few blocks away.

715 Bush St. (between Powell and Mason sts.), San Francisco, CA 94108. (℃) **800/232-9698** or 415/421-3154. Fax 415/399-1442. www.cornellhotel.com. 58 units. $85–$130 double. Rates include full American breakfast. Package including 7 breakfasts and 5 dinners: $1,085 double per week. AE, DC, DISC, MC, V. Parking across the street $16. Cable car: Powell-Hyde and Powell-Mason lines. Bus: 2, 3, 4, 30, or 45. **Amenities:** Restaurant. *In room:* TV w/cable, dataport, hair dryer.

The Fitzgerald ★   The Fitzgerald's guest accommodations may be outfitted with newish furniture and sweet striped wallpaper, and accented with bright bedspreads and patterned carpeting, but some of the rooms are really small. (One that I saw had a dresser less than a foot from the bed.) Of course, at $80 per night, there's no room for complaining. But do ask for a larger room. If you can live without a sizable closet, you'll find that the price, breakfast (home-baked breads, scones, muffins, juice, tea, and coffee), and cleanliness of this hotel make it a good value. Take heed: The view of the Golden Gate that's printed on the brochure is not actually visible from the hotel—or the area for that matter.

620 Post St. (between Jones and Taylor sts.), San Francisco, CA 94109. (℃) **800/334-6835** or 415/775-8100. Fax 415/775-1278. www.fitzgeraldhotel.com. 47 units. $65–$125 double. Extra person $10. Rates include continental breakfast. Lower rates in winter. AE, DC, DISC, MC, V. Self-parking $22. Cable car: Powell-Hyde and Powell-Mason lines. Bus: 2, 3, 4, or 27. **Amenities:** Access to a nearby indoor pool and exercise room; dry cleaning. *In room:* TV, dataport, hair dryer.

The Golden Gate Hotel ★★ *Value*   San Francisco's stock of small hotels in historic turn-of-the-20th-century buildings includes some real gems, and the Golden Gate Hotel is one of them. It's 2 blocks north of Union Square and

2 blocks down (literally) from the crest of Nob Hill, with cable car stops at the corner for easy access to Fisherman's Wharf and Chinatown. The city's theaters and best restaurants are also within walking distance. But the best thing about the 1913 Edwardian hotel is that it's family run: John and Renate Kenaston and daughter Gabriele are hospitable innkeepers who take obvious pleasure in making their guests comfortable. Each individually decorated room has handsome antique furnishings (plenty of wicker) from the early 1900s, quilted bedspreads, fresh flowers, and recently updated carpeting. Request a room with a claw-foot tub if you enjoy a good, hot soak. Afternoon tea is served daily from 4 to 7pm, and guests are welcome to use the house fax and computer with wireless DSL free of charge.

775 Bush St. (between Powell and Mason sts.), San Francisco, CA 94108. ✆ **800/835-1118** or 415/392-3702. Fax 415/392-6202. www.goldengatehotel.com. 25 units, 14 with bathroom. $85 double without bathroom; $130 double with bathroom. Rates include continental breakfast and afternoon tea. AE, DC, MC, V. Self-parking $15. Cable car: Powell-Hyde and Powell-Mason lines (1 block east). Bus: 2, 4, 30, 38, or 45. BART: Powell and Market. **Amenities:** Access to health club 1 block away; activities desk; office equipment available; laundry service/dry cleaning next door. *In room:* TV, dataport, hair dryer and iron upon request, wireless Internet access.

Grant Plaza Hotel   You won't find any free little bottles of shampoo here. What you will find are cheap rates and basic—and I mean basic—rooms right in the middle of the Union Square–Chinatown action. Many of the small and stark but well-kept abodes—with little more than a clean bed and desk—in the six-story building overlook Chinatown's main street. The downsides are minuscule bathrooms with small showers. Corner rooms on higher floors are both larger and brighter. Ask for a room on the top floor—they're the newest, and they are substantially nicer than the older rooms.

465 Grant Ave. (at Pine St.), San Francisco, CA 94108. ✆ **800/472-6899** or 415/434-3883. Fax 415/434-3886. www.grantplaza.com. 72 units, most with shower only. $59–$89 double. AE, DC, DISC, MC, V. Nearby parking $18. Cable car: Powell-Hyde, Powell-Mason, and California–Van Ness lines. **Amenities:** Access to nearby health club ($8 per day); concierge; Internet stations in lobby. *In room:* Dataport, hair dryer.

Hostelling International San Francisco–Downtown   For just over $20 per night (with a notarized ID), you can relive college-dorm life in an old San Francisco–style building right in the heart of Union Square. Occupying five sparsely decorated floors—each with its own pay phone—rooms here are simple and clean. Each has two or three bunk beds with linens, its own sink, a closet, and lockers (bring your own lock or buy one at the front desk). Although most private rooms share hallway bathrooms, a few have private facilities. Laminated posters adorn the hallways, and there are several common rooms, including a reading room and a large kitchen with lots of tables, chairs, and refrigerator space. There are laundry facilities in the building and a helpful information desk where you can book tours and sightseeing trips. The hostel is open 24 hours, and reservations are essential, especially during the summer. Persons under 18 must be accompanied by an adult.

312 Mason St. (between Geary and O'Farrell sts.), San Francisco, CA 94102. ✆ **800/909-4776** or 415/788-5604. Fax 415/788-3023. www.sfdowntownhostel.org. 98 units (40 private and 58 dorm [285 dorm beds]). Hostelling members $22–$25 per person in dorm; nonmembers $25–$29 per person in dorm; $60 per private room. Children under 12 $12 when accompanied by a parent. Maximum stay 21 nights per month. MC, V. Cable car: Powell-Mason line. Bus: 7 or 38; 292 or KX from SFO. **Amenities:** Tour desk; TV lounge; kitchen; Internet access; laundry facilities. *In room:* Lockers, no phone.

Hotel Beresford ✦   The small and friendly sister property of the Hotel Beresford Arms (see below), the seven-floor Hotel Beresford is another good, moderately priced choice near Union Square. Perks are the same: $5 video rentals for the VCR, clock radios, a mishmash of furniture, and stocked fridges. To block out street noise, management recently installed soundproof windows. Everything's well kept and modest renovations over the last year—paint, wallpaper, and the like—promise fresh-looking, but very modest surroundings. The on-site White Horse Tavern, an attractive and quaint replica of an old English pub, serves breakfast, lunch, and dinner and is a favorite for folks who like less trendy hullabaloo with their meal.

635 Sutter St. (near Mason St.), San Francisco, CA 94102. ℂ 800/533-6533 or 415/673-9900. Fax 415/474-0449. www.beresford.com. 114 units. $89–$165 double. Extra person $10. Rates include continental breakfast. Children under 12 stay free in parent's room. AE, DC, DISC, MC, V. Self-parking $20. Cable car: Powell-Hyde line (1 block east). Bus: 2, 3, 4, 30, 38, or 45. **Amenities:** Restaurant/bar; access to nearby health club ($10 per day); laundry service; free Internet access. *In room:* TV/VCR, dataport, minibar, hair dryer, iron.

Hotel Beresford Arms ★★ *Value*   The bargain prices are the main reason I recommend this dependable, though slightly unfashionable, hotel. On the plus side, many rooms have bidets and Jacuzzi bathtubs. You also have the choice of a wet bar or fully equipped kitchen—an advantage for families—and continental breakfast is included in the rock-bottom price. All accommodations include plenty of in-room perks, including clock radios and $5 video rentals for the VCR, and there's a "Manager's Social Hour" (included in the room rates) with wine, tea, and snacks. The downsides are minimal: a few funky furnishings, small bathrooms, and the occasional old mattress. The location, between the Theater District and Union Square, in a quieter section of San Francisco, is ideal for visitors without cars, and the price for what you get is hard to beat. *Tip:* Rooms that face Post Street might be a bit noisier than others, but they're also larger and sunnier, and some have window seats.

701 Post St. (at Jones St.), San Francisco, CA 94109. ℂ 800/533-6533 or 415/673-2600. Fax 415/929-1535. www.beresford.com. 95 units. $99 double; $129 Jacuzzi suite; $169 parlor suite. Extra person $10. Rates include continental breakfast and afternoon wine and tea. Children under 12 stay free in parent's room. Senior and AAA discounts available. AE, DC, DISC, MC, V. Valet parking $20. Cable car: Powell-Hyde line (3 blocks east). Bus: 2, 3, 4, 27, or 38. **Amenities:** Access to nearby health club ($10 per day); laundry service; free Internet access in lobby. *In room:* TV/VCR, dataport, minibar, hair dryer, iron.

Hotel Bijou ★ *Value*   Three words sum up this hotel: clean, colorful, and cheap. Although it's on the periphery of the gritty Tenderloin (just 3 blocks off Union Square), once inside this gussied-up 1911 hotel, all's cheery, bright, and perfect for the budget traveler who wants a little style with your savings. Joie de Vivre hotel group disguised the hotel's age with lively decor, a Deco theater theme, and a heck of a lot of vibrant paint. To the left of the small lobby is a "theater" where guests can watch San Francisco–based movies nightly (cute old-fashioned theater seating, though it's just a basic TV showing videos). Upstairs, rooms named after locally made films are small, clean, and colorful (think buttercup, burgundy, and purple), and have all the basics from clock radios, dressers, and small desks to tiny bathrooms (one of which is so small you have to close the door to access the toilet). Alas, a few mattresses could be firmer, and there's only one small and slow elevator. But considering the price, and perks like the continental breakfast and friendly service, you can't go wrong here.

111 Mason St., San Francisco, CA 94102. ℂ 800/771-1022 or 415/771-1200. www.hotelbijou.com. 65 units. $95–$139 double. Rates include continental breakfast. AE, DC, DISC, MC, V. Valet parking $21. Streetcar: Powell St. station. Bus: All Market St. buses. **Amenities:** Concierge; limited room service, same-day laundry service/dry cleaning. *In room:* TV, dataport, hair dryer, iron.

Hotel Halcyon ★ *Value*   Inside this small, four-story brick building is a penny pincher's dream come true, the kind of place where you'll find everything you need yet won't have to pay through the nose to get it. The small but very clean studio guest rooms are equipped with microwave ovens, refrigerators, flatware and utensils, toasters, alarm clocks, phones with free local calls, and voice mail—all the comforts of home in the heart of Union Square. A coin-operated washer and dryer are located in the basement, along with free laundry soap and irons. You also get your own individual doorbell and mailbox. The owners are usually on hand to offer friendly, personal service, making this option all in all an unbeatable deal. Heck, they even throw in a basket of fresh seasonal fruit. Be sure to ask about special rates for weekly stays.

649 Jones St. (between Geary and Post sts.), San Francisco, CA 94102. © **800/627-2396** or 415/929-8033. Fax 415/441-8033. www.halcyonsf.com. 25 units. $79–$129 double year-round; $510–$590 weekly. Minimum length of stay Oct–Apr is 7 days. AE, DC, DISC, MC, V. Parking garage nearby $14–$16 per day. Bus: 2, 3, 4, 9, 27, or 38. **Amenities:** Access to nearby health club; concierge; tour desk; car-rental desk; laundry facilities. *In room:* Fax, dataport, kitchen, fridge, coffeemaker, hair dryer, iron, safe, voice mail.

King George Hotel ★★ *Value*   Built in 1914 for the Panama-Pacific Exhibition (when rooms went for $1 per night), the delightful boutique King George has fared well over the years with its mostly European clientele. The location—surrounded by cable car lines, the Theater District, Union Square, and dozens of restaurants—is superb, and the rooms, all of which were renovated in 1999 and received new textiles in 2002, are surprisingly quiet for such a busy spot. Although rooms can be small, the hotel makes the most of the space; and truth be told, with affordable prices, spiffy bathrooms, firm mattresses, desks, and a handsome studylike ambience, the smaller quarters come off pretty darned well. A big hit since it started a few years back is the hotel's English afternoon tea, served in the Windsor Tea Room Saturday, Sunday, and holidays from 2 to 5 pm. Recent additions include a pub and 24-hour business center.

334 Mason St. (between Geary and O'Farrell sts.), San Francisco, CA 94102. © **800/288-6005** or 415/781-5050. Fax 415/835-5991. www.kinggeorge.com. 153 units. $140 double; $240 suite. Breakfast $6.50–$8. Special-value packages available seasonally. AE, DC, DISC, MC, V. Valet parking $25; self-parking $22. Cable car: Powell-Hyde and Powell-Mason lines (1 block west). Bus: 1, 2, 3, 4, 5, 7, 30, 38, 45, 70, or 71. **Amenities:** Tearoom; evening lounge/bar; access to health club ½ block away; concierge; 24-hr. business center; secretarial services; 24-hr. room service; same-day laundry service/dry cleaning; wireless Internet access in lobby. *In room:* TV w/pay movies and Nintendo, dataport, hair dryer, iron, safe, complimentary high-speed Internet access.

Renoir Hotel ★   Housed in a majestic 1909 Flatiron-style brick building, the Renoir is one of the few low-priced hotels in the downtown area whose guest rooms actually have pleasing views and direct sunlight. Located within walking distance to most of the city's main attractions, this privately owned and family-run hotel was completely renovated in 2001 with a pseudo European turn-of-the-20th-century theme—the high-ceiling lobby is replete with ornate columns, gilded elevators doors, large chandeliers, antique furnishings, and spiffily dressed staff. Ostentation comes to a screeching halt once you enter your guest room, however, each of which is simply furnished with modern dark-wood furnishings, flower-patterned bedspreads and matching drapes, and those ubiquitous awful prints screwed into the wall above the bed. No matter: The hotel is in such a great location that you'll probably spend very little time supine. The hotel's restaurant, Café do Brasil, is San Francisco's first (and only) Brazilian "Churrasco Rodizio," the classic eat-until-you-say-uncle Brazilian style of barbecue. *Tip:* Request a room overlooking Market Street, since they receive the morning sun.

45 McAllister St. (at Market St.), San Francisco, CA 94102. ℭ **800/576-3388** or 415/626-5200. Fax 415/626-5581. www.renoirhotel.com. 135 units. $119–$189 double; $175–$250 suite. Children 12 and under stay free in their parent's room. AE, DC, MC, V. Valet parking $25. Streetcar: F, and all underground Muni and BART. **Amenities:** Restaurant; lounge; fax and copy services; laundry service; dry cleaning. *In room:* TV, hair dryer, safe, iron/ironing board upon request, direct-dial phone with voice mail.

The Savoy Hotel ★★ *Value*   A European-style hotel through and through, the Savoy is one of my favorite moderately priced downtown hotels (The Warwick Regis, see below, is my other top pick). With a nice cozy apartment-like feel to each guest room, old well-cleaned bathrooms with original tiles, 18th-century period furnishings, fluffy featherbeds, and goose-down pillows, it's easy to relax here. Not all rooms are alike—they can be small, but each has beautiful white wood shutters, full-length mirrors, and two-line telephones. Guests also enjoy access to the newly relocated Millennium (p. 114), San Francisco's only gourmet vegan restaurant, which moved here from the Civic Center in 2003.

580 Geary St. (between Taylor and Jones sts.), San Francisco, CA 94102. ℭ **800/227-4223** or 415/441-2700. Fax 415/441-0124. www.thesavoyhotel.com. 83 units. $119–$139 double; $149–$169 junior suite. Complimentary wine and cheese 4:30–6pm daily. Ask about package (like an extra $30 for parking and continental breakfast), government, senior, and corporate rates. AE, DC, DISC, MC, V. Parking $26. Bus: 2, 3, 4, 27, or 38. **Amenities:** Restaurant; bar; concierge; laundry service; dry cleaning. *In room:* TV, dataport, hair dryer, iron, safe.

The Sheehan Hotel ★   Formerly a YWCA hotel, the Sheehan is dirt cheap, considering its location 2 blocks from Union Square. Of course, this isn't the Ritz—but the basic rooms (think a step up from a generic motel) have large, springy beds, and nice touches like gilded mirrors, newish textiles in purples and plums, and original art along with the simple furnishings and clean but plain bathrooms. Ask for one of the remodeled rooms and you'll do just fine.

620 Sutter St. (near Mason St.), San Francisco, CA 94102. ℭ **800/848-1529** or 415/775-6500. Fax 415/775-3271. www.sheehanhotel.com. 65 units, 62 with bathroom. $69 double without bathroom; $89–$109 double with bathroom. Rates include continental breakfast. DC, DISC, MC, V. Cable car: Powell-Hyde and Powell-Mason lines (2 blocks east). Bus: 2, 3, 4, 30, 38, or 45. **Amenities:** Indoor heated pool; exercise room; dry cleaning. *In room:* TV, hair dryer.

York Hotel ★★   Even as a local, I drop by the York frequently because it's home to the Empire Plush Room (p. 231), the city's best jazz and cabaret club that also features Va Va Voom, a cheesy-fun burlesque show. But for the visitor, the hotel, built in 1922 and boasting a role in Hitchcock's *Vertigo,* is a boon because it's a hell of a deal. Awarded three diamonds by AAA, the hotel has ridiculously helpful staff, a workout room, and promotional rates, which include a continental breakfast served in the spacious lobby. Rooms swathed in terra cotta and green are abundantly cheery and come loaded with nice touches like dark-wood writing desks, newly upholstered and comfy chairs, alarm clocks, tub/showers, and walk-in closets.

940 Sutter St. (between Leavenworth and Hyde sts.), San Francisco, CA 94109. ℭ **800/808-9675** or 415/885-6800. Fax 415/885-2115. www.yorkhotel.com. 96 units. $119–$149 double. Rates include continental breakfast. AE, DC, DISC, MC, V. Valet parking $35, self parking $25. Bus: 4. **Amenities:** Jazz club; bar; workout room; valet or self-serve laundry. *In room:* TV w/pay movies, coffeemaker, hair dryer, iron on request, safe, Internet access.

2 Nob Hill

VERY EXPENSIVE

The Fairmont Hotel & Tower ★★   The granddaddy of Nob Hill's elite cadre of ritzy hotels, the Fairmont wins high honors for an incredibly jaw-dropping lobby. Even if you're not a guest, it's worth a side trip to gape at its massive marble Corinthian columns, vaulted ceilings, velvet chairs, gilded mirrors, and spectacular wraparound staircase. In previous years, we've warned that the rooms fell short, but thanks to an $85-million renovation completed in 2001, the glamour carries to guest rooms where everything is new and in good taste. In addition to the expected luxuries, guests will appreciate such details as goose-down pillows, electric shoe buffers, bathroom scales, and large walk-in closets. Spectacular views from the top floors remain the showstoppers, but nuances such as a 24-hour on-call dentist and doctor, high-speed Internet access, a notary public, a travel agency, and in-room PlayStations and dual phone lines enhance every guest's stay. Whatever you do, make a point of getting to the Tonga Room, a fantastically kitsch Disneyland-like tropical bar and restaurant where happy hour hops and "rain" falls every 20 minutes.

950 Mason St. (at California St.), San Francisco, CA 94108. © 800/441-1414 or 415/772-5000. Fax 415/391-4833. www.fairmont.com. 591 units. Main building $289–$409 double; from $500 suite. Tower $269–$359 double; from $800 suite. Extra person $30. AE, DC, DISC, MC, V. Parking $39. Cable car: California St. line (direct stop). **Amenities:** 3 restaurants; bar; health club ($15 daily); concierge; tour desk; car-rental desk; wireless Internet in lobby; business center; shopping arcade; salon; 24-hr. room service; massage; babysitting; same-day laundry service/dry cleaning. *In room:* A/C, TV w/pay movies and PlayStation, fax, dataport, kitchenette in some units, minibar, coffeemaker, hair dryer, iron, safe, high-speed Internet access.

The Huntington Hotel ★★★   One of the kings of Nob Hill, the stately Huntington Hotel has long been a favorite retreat for Hollywood stars and political VIPs who desire privacy and security. Family owned since 1924—an extreme rarity among large hotels—the Huntington eschews pomp and circumstance; absolute privacy and unobtrusive service are its mainstays. Although the lobby, decorated in grand 19th-century style, is rather petite, the guest rooms are quite large; they feature Brunschwig and Fils fabrics and bed coverings, antique French furnishings, and views of the city. The lavish suites, so opulent that they've been featured in *Architectural Digest*, are individually decorated with custom-made and antique furnishings. Prices are steep, as you would expect, but special offers such as a Romance Package, which includes champagne, sherry, and limousine service, make the Huntington worth considering for a special occasion.

The Big Four restaurant offers expensive contemporary American cuisine. Live piano music is played nightly in the lounge.

1075 California St. (between Mason and Taylor sts.), San Francisco, CA 94108. © 800/227-4683 or 415/474-5400. Fax 415/474-6227. www.huntingtonhotel.com. 135 units. $315–$460 double; $490–$1,120 suite. Continental breakfast $14. Special packages available. AE, DC, DISC, MC, V. Valet parking $29. Cable car: California St. line (direct stop). Bus: 1. **Amenities:** Restaurant; lounge; indoor heated pool (ages 16 and up); health club; spa; steam room; sauna; concierge; massage; babysitting; same-day laundry service/dry cleaning. *In room:* A/C, TV w/pay movies, fax, dataport, kitchenettes in some units, minibar, fridges in some units, hair dryer, iron, safe.

InterContinental Mark Hopkins ★★★   Built in 1926 on the spot where railroad millionaire Mark Hopkins's turreted mansion once stood, the 19-story Mark Hopkins gained global fame during World War II when it was de rigueur for Pacific-bound servicemen to toast their good-bye to the States in the Top of the Mark cocktail lounge. Nowadays, this great hotel, which renovated its rooms in 2000, caters mostly to convention-bound corporate executives, since its prices often require corporate charge accounts. Each neoclassical room is exceedingly comfortable and comes with all the fancy amenities you'd expect from a world-class hotel, including custom furniture, plush fabrics, sumptuous bathrooms, Frette bathrobes, and extraordinary views of the city. Luxury suites, renovated in

---

Fun Fact I'll Have a Scotch

The Ritz-Carlton's bar holds claim to one of the country's largest collection of single-malt scotches. Prices range from $7.25 to $66 per glass.

---

early 2001, are twice the size of most San Francisco apartments and cost close to a month's rent per night. A minor caveat: The hotel has only three guest elevators, making a quick trip to your room difficult during busy periods.

The Top of the Mark (p. 239), a fantastic bar/lounge, offers dancing to live jazz or swing, Sunday brunch, and cocktails in swank, old-fashioned style. (Romantics, this place is for you, but keep in mind that there's a $10 cover fee on Fri and Sat after 8:30pm for the live nightly entertainment.) The Top of the Mark serves cocktails Monday through Saturday. The formal Nob Hill Restaurant offers California cuisine on Sundays only.

1 Nob Hill (at California and Mason sts.), San Francisco, CA 94108. ℂ 800/327-0200 or 415/392-3434. Fax 415/421-3302. www.markhopkins.net. 380 units. $395–$525 double; from $650 suite; from $3,000 luxury suite. Continental breakfast $20; breakfast buffet $35. AE, DC, DISC, MC, V. Valet parking $35, some oversize vehicles prohibited. Cable car: California St. and Powell lines (direct stop). Bus: 1. **Amenities:** 2 restaurants; bar; exercise room; concierge; car-rental desk; business center; secretarial services; 24-hr. room service; massage; babysitting; laundry service/dry cleaning; concierge-level floors. *In room:* A/C, TV w/pay movies, VCR in suites only, dataport, minibar, coffeemaker, hair dryer, iron, safe.

The Ritz-Carlton ✮✮✮   Ranked among the top hotels in the world, the Ritz-Carlton has been the benchmark for San Francisco's luxury hotels since it opened in 1991. A Nob Hill landmark, the former Metropolitan Insurance headquarters stood vacant for years until the Ritz-Carlton company acquired it and embarked on a $100-million, 4-year renovation. The interior was completely gutted and restored with fine furnishings, fabrics, and artwork, including a pair of Louis XVI blue marble urns with gilt mountings, and 19th-century Waterford candelabras. The Italian marble bathrooms offer every possible amenity: double sinks, telephone, name-brand toiletries, and plush terry robes. The more expensive rooms take advantage of the hotel's location—the south slope of Nob Hill—and have good views of the city. Club rooms, on the top floors, have a dedicated concierge, separate elevator-key access, and complimentary meals throughout the day. No restaurant in town has more formal service than this hotel's Dining Room, which is a fine place but is not included in this book's dining chapter, because, while excellent, others in its price range are more exciting. The less formal Terrace Restaurant offers contemporary Mediterranean cuisine and the city's best Sunday brunch. The lobby lounge serves afternoon tea and cocktails, daily, and sushi twice a week, with low-key live entertainment from 3pm to 1am.

600 Stockton St. (between Pine and California sts.), San Francisco, CA 94108. ℂ 800/241-3333 or 415/296-7465. Fax 415/986-1268. www.ritzcarlton.com. 336 units. $395–$695 double; $475–$695 club-level double; from $695 suite. Buffet breakfast $27; Sun champagne brunch $65. Weekend discounts and packages available. AE, DC, DISC, MC, V. Parking $45. Cable car: Powell-Hyde and Powell-Mason lines (direct stop). **Amenities:** 2 restaurants; bar; indoor heated pool; outstanding health club; Jacuzzi; sauna; concierge; courtesy car; business center; secretarial services; 24-hr. room service; in-room massage and manicure; babysitting; same-day laundry service/dry cleaning. *In room:* A/C, TV w/pay movies, dataport, minibar, hair dryer, iron, safe, Internet access.

Stanford Court, A Renaissance Hotel ✮✮   The Stanford Court has maintained a long and discreet reputation as one of San Francisco's most exclusive hotels. Keeping company with the Ritz, Fairmont, Mark Hopkins, and Huntington hotels atop Nob Hill, it's frequented mostly by corporate execs. The foundation was originally the mansion of Leland Stanford, whose legacy lives on in the many portraits and biographies that adorn the rooms. At first, the guest rooms come across as austere and antiquated compared to those at most other top-dollar business hotels, but the quality and comfort of the furnishings are so superior that you're forced to admit there's simply no room for improvement. The Stanford Court also prides itself on its impeccable service. The lobby, furnished in 19th-century style with Baccarat chandeliers, French antiques, and a gorgeous stained-glass dome, makes for a grand entrance.

Many of the guest rooms have partially canopied beds; all have writing desks, extremely comfortable beds, and oak armoires that conceal new television sets. Bathrooms contain mini-TVs, telephones, and heated towel racks. A thoughtful perk: There is no charge for toll-free or credit card calls made from your room.

905 California St. (at Powell St.), San Francisco, CA 94108. ⓒ 800/HOTELS-1 or 415/989-3500. Fax 415/391-0513. www.renaissancehotels.com/sfosc. 393 units. $329 double; from $775 suite. Continental breakfast $18; American breakfast $23. AE, DC, DISC, MC, V. Valet parking $38. Cable car: Powell-Hyde, Powell-Mason, and California—Van Ness lines (direct stop). Bus: 1. **Amenities:** Restaurant; lounge; fitness center; concierge; complimentary car to downtown destinations; business center; 24-hr. room service; babysitting; same-day laundry service/dry cleaning. *In room:* A/C, TV w/pay movies and Web TV, dataport, hair dryer, iron, high-speed Internet access, bathrobes.

MODERATE

The Nob Hill Inn ★★ (Value) Although most of the rooms at the luxurious Nob Hill Inn are well out of budget range, the three Gramercy rooms are among the most opulent you will find in the city for $125. Built in 1907 as a private home, the four-story inn has been masterfully refurbished with Louis XV antiques, expensive fabrics, reproduction artwork, and a magnificent etched-glass European-style lift. Even the lowest-priced rooms receive equal attention: large bathrooms with marble sinks and claw-foot tubs, antique furnishings, faux-antique phones and discreetly placed televisions, and a comfortable full-size bed. Granted, the Gramercy rooms are small. But they're so utterly charming that it's tough to complain, especially when you consider that rates include continental breakfast, afternoon tea and sherry, and the distinction of staying at one of the city's most prestigious hotels.

1000 Pine St. (at Taylor St.), San Francisco, CA 94109. ⓒ 415/673-6080. Fax 415/673-6098. www.nobhill inn.com. 21 units. $125–$195 double; $245–$275 suite. Rates include continental breakfast, afternoon tea, and sherry. AE, DC, DISC, MC, V. Valet parking $30 per day (7:30am–10:30pm); self-parking 2 blocks away $20 per day. Cable car: California St. line. Bus: 1. **Amenities:** Concierge. *In room:* TV, kitchenette in some, hair dryer, iron.

Nob Hill Lambourne ★★ One of San Francisco's top "business boutique" hotels, the Nob Hill Lambourne bills itself as an urban health spa, offering massages, aromatherapy, and yoga tapes to ease corporate-level stress. Even without this hook, the Lambourne deserves a top-of-the-class rating. Sporting one of San Francisco's most stylish interiors, the hotel flaunts the comfort and quality of its contemporary French design, made even better with its renovation in early 2003. Top-quality, hand-sewn mattresses and goose-down comforters complement a host of thoughtful in-room accouterments that include umbrellas and CD player/stereos. Bathrooms have oversize tubs. Suites include an additional sitting room. The wine hour starts at 6pm. Smokers should seek a room elsewhere: This place prohibits puffing.

725 Pine St. (between Powell and Stockton sts.), San Francisco, CA 94108. © **800/274-8466** or 415/433-2287. Fax 415/433-0975. www.nobhilllambourne.com. 20 units. From $175 double; $299 suite. Rates include continental breakfast and evening wine hour. AE, DC, DISC, MC, V. Valet parking $30. Cable car: Powell-Mason, Powell-Hyde, and California St. lines (1 block north). **Amenities:** Access to nearby health club; spa treatments; concierge; in-room massage; laundry service; same-day dry cleaning. *In room:* TV/VCR, dataport, kitchenette, minibar, coffeemaker, hair dryer, iron, free high-speed Internet access, CD player.

3 SoMa
VERY EXPENSIVE

The Argent Hotel ★★   The large number of rooms and fine location—just a block south of Market Street, and a block from the Moscone Convention Center—make the Argent attractive to both groups and business travelers. Rooms, which are decorated with warm, modern, and surprisingly attractive furnishings (surprising considering what a corporate hotel it is) and textiles, have floor-to-ceiling windows and are well outfitted with three telephones (with voice mail). Corner suites look across the Bay Bridge and to SBC (formerly Candlestick) Park. But then again, so long as you're on an upper story, you're bound to get a good view of the city. Rooms are available for visitors with disabilities.

50 Third St. (between Market and Mission sts.), San Francisco, CA 94103. © **800/505-9039** or 415/974-6400. Fax 415/495-6152. www.argenthotel.com. 667 units. $245–$265 double; from $449 suite. $40 extra for executive-level rooms. AE, DC, DISC, MC, V. Valet parking $37. Streetcar: All Market St. streetcars. Bus: All Market St. buses. **Amenities:** Restaurant; bar; fitness center; concierge; business center; secretarial services; limited room service; in-room massage; babysitting; same-day laundry service/dry cleaning. *In room:* A/C, TV w/pay movies, dataport, kitchenettes in some rooms, minibar, coffeemaker, hair dryer, iron, safe, high-speed Internet access (deluxe rooms).

Four Seasons Hotel San Francisco ★★★   What makes this überluxury hotel that opened in late 2001 one of my favorites in the city is its perfect combination

Accommodations Around Town

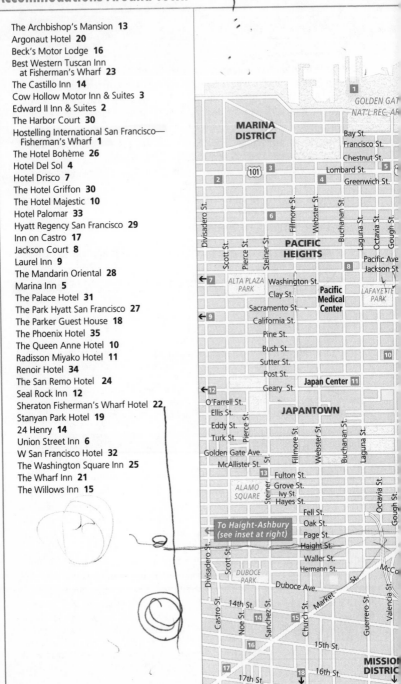

The Archbishop's Mansion **13**
Argonaut Hotel **20**
Beck's Motor Lodge **16**
Best Western Tuscan Inn
  at Fisherman's Wharf **23**
The Castillo Inn **14**
Cow Hollow Motor Inn & Suites **3**
Edward II Inn & Suites **2**
The Harbor Court **30**
Hostelling International San Francisco—
  Fisherman's Wharf **1**
The Hotel Bohème **26**
Hotel Del Sol **4**
Hotel Drisco **7**
The Hotel Griffon **30**
The Hotel Majestic **10**
Hotel Palomar **33**
Hyatt Regency San Francisco **29**
Inn on Castro **17**
Jackson Court **8**
Laurel Inn **9**
The Mandarin Oriental **28**
Marina Inn **5**
The Palace Hotel **31**
The Park Hyatt San Francisco **27**
The Parker Guest House **18**
The Phoenix Hotel **35**
The Queen Anne Hotel **10**
Radisson Miyako Hotel **11**
Renoir Hotel **34**
The San Remo Hotel **24**
Seal Rock Inn **12**
Sheraton Fisherman's Wharf Hotel **22**
Stanyan Park Hotel **19**
24 Henry **14**
Union Street Inn **6**
W San Francisco Hotel **32**
The Washington Square Inn **25**
The Wharf Inn **21**
The Willows Inn **15**

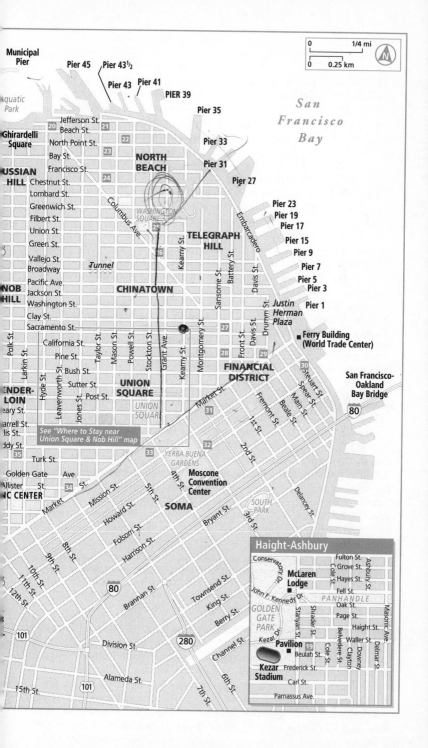

Municipal
Pier

Pier 45   Pier 43½
Pier 43   Pier 41
PIER 39
Pier 35

*Aquatic
Park*

Ghirardelli
Square

**USSIAN
HILL**

**NOB
HILL**

Jefferson St.
Beach St.
North Point St.
Bay St.
Francisco St.
Chestnut St.
Lombard St.
Greenwich St.
Filbert St.
Union St.
Green St.
Vallejo St.
Broadway
Pacific Ave.
Jackson St.
Washington St.
Clay St.
Sacramento St.

20   21
22
23
24

Columbus Ave.

*WASHINGTON
SQUARE*

25

26

Tunnel

**NORTH
BEACH**

**TELEGRAPH
HILL**

CHINATOWN

Kearny St.

Pier 33

Pier 31

Pier 27

Pier 23
Pier 19
Pier 17

Pier 15

Pier 9

Pier 7

Pier 5
Pier 3

*San
Francisco
Bay*

Embarcadero

*Justin
Herman
Plaza*

Pier 1

■ **Ferry Building
(World Trade Center)**

**FINANCIAL
DISTRICT**

California St.
Pine St.
Bush St.
Sutter St.
Post St.

**ENDER-
LOIN**

ary St.
arrell St.
lis St.

ddy St.

35

Polk St.
Larkin St.
Hyde St.
Leavenworth St.
Jones St.

**UNION
SQUARE**

*UNION
SQUARE*

Taylor St.
Mason St.
Powell St.
Stockton St.
Grant Ave.
Kearny St.
Montgomery St.
Sansome St.
Battery St.
Front St.
Davis St.
Drumm St.

27

28   29

30

Steuart St.
Spear St.
Main St.
Beale St.
1st St.
Fremont St.

**San Francisco-
Oakland
Bay Bridge**

80

Market St.

31

*See "Where to Stay near
Union Square & Nob Hill" map*

Turk St.
Golden Gate   Ave.
Allister   St.   34
IC CENTER

33

32

Market

Mission St.
Howard St.
Folsom St.
Harrison St.

5th St.
4th St.

*YERBA BUENA
GARDENS*

**Moscone
Convention
Center**

SOMA

2nd St.

*SOUTH
PARK*

Delancey St.

8th St.
9th St.
10th St.
11th St.
12th St.

80

Brannan St.

Townsend St.

King St.

Berry St.

Bryant St.

3rd St.

101

Division St.

280

Channel St.

Alameda St.

15th St.

101

6th St.
7th St.

Haight-Ashbury

Conservatory Dr.

John F. Kennedy Dr.

*GOLDEN
GATE
PARK*

Kezar Dr.

Pavilion ■

**Kezar
Stadium**

■ **McLaren
Lodge**

PANHANDLE

Stanyan St.
Shrader St.

Fulton St.
Grove St.
Hayes St.

Cole St.
Ashbury St.

Fell St.
Oak St.
Page St.

Haight St.

Belvedere St.
Cole St.

Waller St.

Downey
Clayton

Masonic Ave.

Delmar St.

Beulah
Frederick St.

Carl St.

Parnassus Ave.

19

0   1/4 mi
0   0.25 km

of elegance, trendiness, and modern luxury. The entrance, either off Market or through a narrow alley off Third Street, is deceptively underwhelming, although it does tip you off to the hotel's overall discreetness. Take the elevators up to the lobby and you're instantly surrounded by calm, cool, and collected hotel perfection. I have yet to get familiar with the confusing lobby-level elevators, some of which go to luxury apartments and others to hotel guest quarters. But I quickly adopted the sexy cocktail lounge as my second home. After all, what's not to love about dark mood lighting, comfy leather chairs, bottomless bowls of olives and spicy wasabi-covered peanuts, a great wine and cocktail list, and a pianist playing jazz standards intermingled with Pink Floyd and No Doubt? Many of the oversize rooms (starting at 460 sq. ft. and including 46 suites) overlook Yerba Buena Gardens. Not too trendy, not too traditional, they're just right, with custom-made mattresses and pillows that guarantee the all-time best night's sleep, beautiful works of art, and huge luxury marble bathrooms with deep tubs and L'Occitane toiletries. Hues of taupe, beige, and green are almost as soothing as the superfluous service. Adding to the perks are free access to the building's huge Sports Club L.A., round-the-clock business services, a 2-block walk to Union Square and the Moscone Convention Center, and a vibe that combines sophistication with a hipness far more refined than the W or the Clift.

757 Market St. (between Third and Fourth sts.), San Francisco, CA 94103. ℂ 800/332-3442 or 415/633-3000. Fax 415/633-3001. www.fourseasons.com. 277 units. $469–$600 double; $800 executive suite. AE, DC, DISC, MC, V. Parking $39. Streetcar: F, and all underground streetcars. BART: All trains. Bus: All Market St. buses. **Amenities:** Restaurant; bar; huge fitness center; spa; 24-hr. multilingual concierge; high-tech business center; secretarial services; salon; 24-hr. room service; in-room massage; overnight dry-cleaning and laundry service. *In room:* AC, TV w/pay movies, fax, minibar, hair dryer, safe.

The Harbor Court ★★★   When the Embarcadero Freeway was torn down after the Big One in 1989, one of the major benefactors was the Harbor Court hotel: The 1926 landmark building's backyard view went from a wall of cement to a dazzling vista of the Bay Bridge (be sure to request a bay-view room, for an extra fee). Located just off The Embarcadero at the edge of the Financial District, this former YMCA books a lot of corporate travelers, but anyone who seeks stylish, high-quality accommodations—half-canopy beds, large armoires, writing desks, soundproof windows—with a superb view and lively scene will be perfectly content here. A major bonus for health nuts is the free use of the adjoining fitness club, a top-quality facility with an indoor Olympic-size swimming pool. And for the lounger in all of us, there's an evening wine reception and morning coffee, tea, and apples.

165 Steuart St. (between Mission and Howard sts.), San Francisco, CA 94105. ℂ 800/346-0555 or 415/882-1300. Fax 415/882-1313. www.harborcourthotel.com. 131 units. $165–$399 double. Continental breakfast $15. AE, DC, MC, V. Parking $32. Streetcar: Embarcadero. Bus: 14 or 80X. Pets accepted. **Amenities:** Access to adjoining health club and large, heated indoor pool; courtesy car; room service (breakfast only); same-day laundry service/dry cleaning. *In room:* A/C, TV, fax, dataport, minibar, hair dryer, iron, safe.

The Hotel Griffon ★★   After pumping a cool $10 million into a complete rehab in 1989, the Hotel Griffon emerged as a top contender among San Francisco's small hotels. Ideally situated on the historic waterfront and steps from the heart of the Financial District, the Griffon is impeccably outfitted with a masculine design sensibility. It boasts contemporary features such as whitewashed brick walls, lofty ceilings, marble vanities, window seats, cherrywood furniture, and Art Deco–style lamps (really, this place is smooth). Be sure to request a bay-view room overlooking the Bay Bridge—the added perks and view make it well worth the extra cost. Smokers, book a room elsewhere—there's no puffing here.

155 Steuart St. (between Mission and Howard sts.), San Francisco, CA 94105. © 800/321-2201 or 415/495-2100. Fax 415/495-3522. www.hotelgriffon.com. 62 units. $220–$285 double; $375–$435 suite. Rates include extended continental breakfast and newspaper. AE, DC, DISC, MC, V. Parking $24. All Market St. buses and streetcars, BART, and ferries. **Amenities:** Restaurant; free access to large health club and pool next door; concierge; morning car service to downtown; secretarial services; wireless Internet access; limited room service; in-room massage; babysitting; laundry service; dry cleaning. *In room:* TV, dataport, minibar, coffeemaker, hair dryer, iron, free high-speed Internet access.

Hotel Palomar ★★   The Kimpton Boutique Hotels' most luxurious downtown property occupies the top five floors of a refurbished 1907 landmark office building. As the group's most refined boutique property, the French-inspired interior designed by Cheryl Rowley features rooms with an updated twist on 1930s modern design, with artful, understated textural elements such as emerald-tone velvets, fine woods, and raffia. Tailored lines and rich textures throughout lend a sophisticated, fresh aspect to the overall air of elegance. Rooms, however, can range from very cozy (read: small) to ultracool and spacious (try for a corner room overlooking Market St.). There's not much in the way of public spaces, but the hotel makes up for it with its rooms' fab-factor, homey luxuries like CD players and 27-inch televisions, and its dining room, the Fifth Floor Restaurant (p. 124), which is one of the hottest (and most expensive) restaurants in town. That said, if you want the full-blown luxury hotel experience, you're better off with one of the Nob Hill or Union Square big boys.

12 Fourth St. (at Market St.), San Francisco, CA 94103. © 877/294-9711 or 415/348-1111. Fax 415/348-0302. www.hotelpalomar.com. 198 units. From $349 double; from $449 suite. Continental breakfast $18. AE, DC, DISC, MC, V. Parking $36. Streetcar: F, and all underground streetcars. BART: All trains. Dogs welcome. **Amenities:** Restaurant; fitness center; concierge; courtesy car; business center; secretarial services; room service; in-room massage; babysitting; same-day laundry service/dry cleaning. *In room:* A/C, TV, fax/copier, dataport, minibar, fridge, hair dryer, iron, safe, complimentary high-speed Internet, CD player.

The Palace Hotel ★   The original 1875 Palace was one of the world's largest and most luxurious hotels, and every time you walk through the doors, you'll be reminded how incredibly majestic old luxury really is. Rebuilt after the 1906 quake, and most recently renovated in 2002 (guest rooms only), its most spectacular attributes remain the regal lobby and the Garden Court, a San Francisco landmark restaurant that was restored to its original 1909 grandeur. A double row of massive Italian-marble Ionic columns flank the court, and 10 huge chandeliers dangle above. The real heart-stopper, however, is the 80,000-pane stained-glass ceiling (good special effects made Mike Douglas look like he fell through it in the movie *The Game*). Regrettably, the rooms aren't *quite* as grand. But they're vastly improved and emulate yesteryear's refinement with mahogany four-poster beds, warm gold paint and upholstery, and tasteful artwork.

The Garden Court is famous for its $75 brunch on special holidays and a scaled-down version on regular weekends. Maxfield's Restaurant, a traditional San Francisco grill, serves lunch and dinner. Kyo-ya, an authentic Japanese restaurant, is highly regarded; and The Pied Piper Bar is named after the $2.5-million Maxfield Parrish mural that dominates the room.

2 New Montgomery St. (at Market St.), San Francisco, CA 94105. © 800/325-3589 or 415/512-1111. Fax 415/543-0671. www.sfpalace.com. 552 units. $550–$650 double; from $775 suite. Extra person $40. Children under 18 sharing existing bedding stay free in parent's room. Weekend rates and packages available. AE, DC, DISC, MC, V. Parking $40. Streetcar: All Market St. streetcars. Bus: All Market St. buses. **Amenities:** 4 restaurants; bar; health club with skylight-covered heated lap pool; spa; Jacuzzi; sauna; concierge; business center; conference rooms with wireless Internet access; 24-hr. room service; laundry service; dry cleaning. *In room:* A/C, TV w/pay movies, dataport, minibar, hair dryer, iron, safe.

W San Francisco Hotel ★★   Starwood Hotels & Resorts' 31-story property is as modern and hip as its fashionable clientele. Sophisticated, slick, and stylish, it suits its neighbors, which include the Museum of Modern Art, the Moscone Center, and the Metreon Sony entertainment center. The striking gray granite facade, piped with polished black stone, complements the octagonal three-story glass entrance and lobby. The hip, urban style extends to the guest rooms, which have a residential feel. Each contains a "luxury" feather bed with a goose-down comforter and pillows, Waterworks linens, an oversize dark-wood desk, an uphol-stered chaise longue, and louvered blinds that open to (usually) great city views. Each room also contains a compact media wall complete with a Sony CD and videocassette player, an extensive CD library, and a 27-inch color TV with Inter-net service (and an infrared keyboard). Bathrooms are supersleek and stocked with Aveda products. Furthering the supercool vibe is a bi-level bar and XYZ restaurant, which serves fresh and bold American fare within a zippy white-on-white interior. All in all, since 2000, this has been one of the top places to be.

181 Third St. (between Mission and Howard sts.), San Francisco, CA 94103. ✆ **800/877-WHOTEL** or 415/777-5300. Fax 415/817-7823. www.whotels.com/sanfrancisco. 423 units. From $469 double; from $1,000 suite. AE, DC, DISC, MC, V. Valet parking $40. Streetcar: J, K, L, or M to Montgomery. Bus: 15, 30, or 45. **Amenities:** Restaurant; 2 bars; heated atrium pool and Jacuzzi; fitness center; spa; concierge; business center; Wi-Fi in public spaces; secretarial services; 24-hr. room service; same-day laundry service/dry cleaning. *In room:* A/C, TV/VCR w/pay movies and Internet access, fax, dataport, minibar, coffeemaker, hair dryer, iron, safe, CD player.

EXPENSIVE

San Francisco Marriott ★★   Some call it a masterpiece; others liken it to the world's biggest parking meter. In either case, the Marriott is one of the largest buildings in the city, making it a popular stop for convention-goers and those looking for a room with a view. Fortunately, the controversy does not extend to the rooms, which were renovated to the tune of $34 million in 2003; expect a pleasant place to crash with large bathrooms and exceptional city vistas. *Tip:* Upon arrival, enter from Fourth Street, between Market and Mission, to avoid a long trek to the registration area.

55 Fourth St. (between Market and Mission sts.), San Francisco, CA 94103. ✆ **800/228-9290** or 415/896-1600. Fax 415/486-8101. www.sfmarriott.com. 1,500 units. $199–$349 double; $499–$3,250 suite. AE, DC, DISC, MC, V. Parking $38. Cable car: Powell-Hyde and Powell-Mason lines (3 blocks west). Streetcar: All Market St. streetcars. Bus: All Market St. buses. **Amenities:** 2 restaurants; 2 bars; indoor pool; health club; tour desk; car rental; business center; laundry service; dry cleaning. *In room:* A/C, TV w/pay movies, dataport, hair dryer, iron.

MODERATE

The Mosser ★★ *Value*   "Hip on the Cheap" might best sum up The Mosser, a highly atypical budget hotel that incorporates Victorian architecture with modern interior design. It originally opened in 1913 as a luxury hotel only to be dwarfed by far more modern sky rise hotels that surround it. But a major mul-timillion-dollar renovation in the fall of 2001 transformed this aging charmer into a sophisticated, stylish, and surprisingly affordable SOMA lodging. Guest rooms are replete with original Victorian flourishes—bay windows, high ceil-ings, hand-carved moldings—that juxtapose well with the contemporary cus-tom-designed furnishings, granite showers, stainless steel fixtures, ceiling fans, Frette linens, and modern electronics. The least expensive rooms share a bath-room but are an incredible deal with rates starting at $60. The hotel's restaurant, Annabelle's Bar and Bistro, serves lunch and dinner, and The Mosser even houses Studio Paradiso, a state-of-the-art recording studio. The location is excel-lent as well—3 blocks from Union Square, 2 blocks from the MOMA and Moscone Convention Center, and half a block from the cable car turnaround.

(Kids) The Best Family-Friendly Hotels

Argonaut Hotel (p. 96)   Not only is it near all the funky kid fun of Fisherman's Wharf and the National Maritime Museum, but this bay-side hotel, a winner for the whole family, also has kid-friendly perks like the opportunity for each child to grab a gift from the hotel's "treasure chest."

Comfort Suites (p. 105)   A Nintendo in each room, enough pay cable channels to keep you and your kids glued to the TV set for an entire day, and a pull-out sleeper sofa in addition to a king-size bed make this an attractive option for families.

Cow Hollow Motor Inn & Suites (p. 99)   Two-bedroom suites allow kids to shack up in style instead of camping on the pull-out couch.

Handlery Union Square Hotel (p. 70)   Never mind that it's been completely renovated. The real kid-friendly kickers here are the adjoining rooms in the "newer" addition; a heated, clean, outdoor pool; and the adjoining restaurant, The Daily Grill, which offers the gamut of American favorites.

Hotel Del Sol (p. 98)   It's colorful enough to represent a Crayola selection, but tots are more likely to be impressed by the in-room CD player and VCR and the toys available at the courtyard pool.

The Maxwell Hotel (p. 71)   The colorful environs of this "theater Deco meets Victorian" style hotel are only half the reason kids will get a kick out of a stay here. Added bonuses are a VIP kids program, which includes a second, adjoining room at half the regular price.

The Phoenix Hotel (p. 102)   If you want to up your cool factor with the little ones, check them into this ultra-hip hotel. So long as you don't mind the hipsters who frequent this place and its popular nightspot, the Bambuddha Lounge, kids will love the funky retro vibe and the courtyard pool.

San Francisco Airport North Travelodge (p. 105)   It's nothing fancy, but if you've got an early flight out, want to stay near the airport, and don't want to rent an extra room to accommodate the little ones, this place (with pull-out couches in every room) is a good bet.

Stanyan Park Hotel (p. 104)   Plenty of elbow room and a half-block walk to Golden Gate Park's Children's Playground make this a prime spot for crashing family style. But the biggest bonuses are the suites, which come with one or two bedrooms, a full kitchen, and a dining area.

Westin St. Francis (p. 69)   A classic San Francisco hotel down to its hospitality, the Westin welcomes the little ones with fun gifts and free drink refills at their restaurants.

---

54 Fourth St. (at Market St.), San Francisco, CA 94103. ℂ **800/227-3804** or 415/986-4400. Fax 415/495-4091. www.themosser.com. 166 units, 112 with bathroom. $109–$179 double with bathroom; $59–$89 double without bathroom. Rates include safe deposit boxes, fax, and mail services. AE, DC, MC, V. Parking $27. Streetcar: F, and all underground Muni and BART. **Amenities:** Restaurant; bar; 24-hr. concierge; same-day

laundry service/dry cleaning. *In room:* TV, dataport, hair dryer, iron/ironing board, ceiling fan, AM/FM stereo with CD player, voice mail.

4 The Financial District

VERY EXPENSIVE

The Mandarin Oriental ★★★ *Finds* No hotel boasts better ultraluxury digs with incredible views than this gem. The only reason to pause in the lobby or mezzanine is for the recommended Asian tea service (complete with bento box of incredible bite-size delicacies) or cocktails. Otherwise, heaven begins after a rocketing ride on the elevators to the rooms, all of which are located between the 38th and 48th floors of a high-rise. Each of the very roomy accommodations offers extraordinary panoramic views of the bay and city. Not all rooms have tub-side views (incredible and standard with the signature rooms!), but every one does have a luxurious marble bathroom stocked with a natural loofah, a large selection of name-brand toiletries, terry and cotton cloth robes, a makeup mirror, and silk slippers. Guest rooms are equally opulent, with beautiful Asian-influenced decor, handsome furnishings, and all-around comfort and accouterments that make it difficult to leave your room.

222 Sansome St. (between Pine and California sts.), San Francisco, CA 94104. (*C*) **800/622-0404** or 415/276-9888. Fax 415/433-0289. www.mandarinoriental.com. 158 units. $470–$655 double; $675–$725 signature rooms; from $1,400 suite. Continental breakfast $21; American breakfast $32. AE, DC, DISC, MC, V. Valet parking $36. Streetcar: J, K, L, or M to Montgomery. Bus: All Market St. buses. **Amenities:** Restaurant; bar; fitness center; concierge; car rental; business center; 24-hr. room service; in-room massage; laundry service; same-day dry cleaning. *In room:* A/C, TV w/pay movies, fax, dataport, minibar, hair dryer, iron, safe, high-speed Internet access, CD player.

The Park Hyatt San Francisco ★★ If you're looking for a small luxury business hotel in the heart of the Financial District—especially if you're billing it to

---

Finds **Sleeping Seaside**

You would think that a city surrounded on three sides by water would have a slew of seaside hotels. Oddly enough, it has very few, one of which is the **Seal Rock Inn.** It's about as far from Union Square and Fisherman's Wharf as you can place a hotel in San Francisco, but that just makes it all the more unique. The motel fronts Sutro Heights Park, which faces Ocean Beach. Most rooms in the four-story structure have at least partial views of the ocean; at night, the sounds of the surf and distant foghorns lull guests to sleep. The rooms, although large and spotless, are basic, with rose and teal floral accents. While only some rooms have kitchenettes, phones, TVs, fridges, covered parking, and use of the enclosed patio and pool area are standard. On the ground floor of the inn is a small old-fashioned restaurant serving breakfast and lunch. Golden Gate Park and the Presidio are both nearby, and the Geary bus—which snails its way to Union Square and Market Street—stops right out front.

The Seal Rock Inn ((*C*) **888/732-5762** or 415/752-8000; fax 415/752-6034; www.sealrockinn.com) is at 545 Point Lobos Ave. (at 48th Ave.), San Francisco, CA 94121. Double rooms range from $105 to $155.

the boss—stay at The Park Hyatt San Francisco. About half the size of Hyatt's typical mega-hotels, the 24-story Park Hyatt has a rather plain exterior, but it is a pleasure to behold from within. The lobby is lavishly appointed with Australian lacewood paneling, polished Italian granite, handmade custom carpets from China, and opalescent Spanish alabaster chandeliers. A magnificent spiral staircase leads to the upper-level restaurant, The Park Grill. Guest rooms are more understated, with Italian wood furnishings, large bathrooms, and exceedingly comfortable beds. They also have extraordinary views of the city, particularly from the corner suites on the upper floors, which also come with outdoor balconies or a Jacuzzi tub (a tough choice).

333 Battery St. (at Clay St.), San Francisco, CA 94111. *©* **800/778-7477** or 415/392-1234. Fax 415/421-2433. www.parkhyatt.com. 360 units. $295–$370 double; $375–$4,200 suite. AE, DC, DISC, MC, V. Valet parking $38. Cable car: California line. Bus: 12, 15, 41, or 83. **Amenities:** Restaurant; 2 lounges; fitness center; concierge; courtesy car; business center; secretarial services; 24-hr. room service; in-room massage; babysitting; laundry service; same-day dry cleaning. *In room:* A/C, TV w/pay movies, dataport, minibar, hair dryer, iron, safe, high-speed Internet access, CD player.

EXPENSIVE

Hyatt Regency San Francisco ⭐

The Hyatt Regency, a convention favorite, rises from the edge of the Embarcadero Center at the foot of Market Street. The gray concrete structure, with a 1970s, bunkerlike facade, is shaped like a vertical triangle, serrated with long rows of jutting balconies. The 17-story atrium lobby, illuminated by museum-quality theater lighting, features flowing water and a simulated environment of California grasslands and wildflowers.

Rooms, most of which were part of an $50-million renovation in 2000, are comfortably furnished in "contemporary decor" a la corporate hotel fashion. Bonuses include new ergonomic workstation chairs, and all new textiles in shades of gold, charcoal gray, and celadon. Upgraded digs for Gold Passport members, which, along with the suites, underwent a textiles renovation in 1999, have extra perks like tea- and coffeemaking facilities and private fax machines on request. The hotel's 16th and 17th floors house the Regency Club, with 102 larger guest rooms, complimentary continental breakfast, and after-dinner cordials.

The Eclipse Café serves breakfast and lunch daily; during evenings it becomes A Cut Above steakhouse. Thirteen-Views Bar serves cocktails and bar food for dinner. The Equinox, a revolving rooftop restaurant and bar that's open for dinner and Sunday brunch, has 360-degree city views.

5 Embarcadero Center, San Francisco, CA 94111. *©* **800/233-1234** or 415/788-1234. Fax 415/398-2567. www.hyatt.com. 805 units. $159–$315 double; extra $50 for executive suite. Continental breakfast $15. AE, DC, DISC, MC, V. Valet parking $38. Streetcar: All Market St. streetcars. Bus: All Market St. buses. **Amenities:** Restaurant; cafe; bar; access to health club; concierge; business center; laundry; dry cleaning. *In room:* A/C, TV, dataport, minibar, high-speed Internet access.

5 North Beach/Fisherman's Wharf

EXPENSIVE

Best Western Tuscan Inn at Fisherman's Wharf ⭐⭐

The Best Western Tuscan Inn is one of the best midrange hotels at Fisherman's Wharf. Like an island of respectability in a sea of touristy schlock, it exudes a level of style and comfort far beyond those of its neighboring competitors. Splurge on hotel parking—which is actually cheaper than the wharf's outrageously priced garages—and then saunter toward the plush lobby, warmed by a grand fireplace. Even the rooms are a definite cut above competing Fisherman's Wharf hotels. Most have writing desks and armchairs. The only caveat is the lack of scenic views—a small price to pay for a good hotel in a great location. This hotel also offers seven wheelchair-accessible rooms.

425 North Point St. (at Mason St.), San Francisco, CA 94133. (© **800/648-4626** or 415/561-1100. Fax 415/561-1199. www.tuscaninn.com. 221 units. $189–$269 double; $229–$369 suite. Rates include coffee, tea, and evening fireside wine reception. AE, DC, DISC, MC, V. Parking $26. Cable car: Powell-Mason line. Bus: 10, 15, or 47. Pets welcome for $50 fee. **Amenities:** Access to nearby gym; concierge; courtesy car; secretarial services; limited room service; same-day laundry service/dry cleaning. *In room:* A/C, TV w/pay movies, dataport, minibar, coffeemaker, hair dryer, iron, Nintendo.

Sheraton Fisherman's Wharf Hotel ⭐   Built in the mid-1970s, this contemporary, four-story hotel offers the reliable comforts of a Sheraton in San Francisco's most popular tourist area. In other words, the clean, modern rooms are comfortable and well equipped but nothing unique to the city. A corporate floor caters exclusively to business travelers.

2500 Mason St. (between Beach and North Point sts.), San Francisco, CA 94133. (© **800/325-3535** or 415/362-5500. Fax 415/956-5275. www.sheratonatthewharf.com. 529 units. $239–$274 double; $550–$1,000 suite. Extra person $20. Continental breakfast $11. AE, DC, DISC, MC, V. Valet parking $30. Cable car: Powell-Mason line (1 block east, 2 blocks south). Streetcar: F. Bus: 10 or 49. **Amenities:** Restaurant; bar; outdoor heated pool; exercise room; concierge; car-rental desk; business center; limited room service; laundry; dry cleaning. *In room:* A/C, TV, fax (in suites only), dataport, coffeemaker, hair dryer, high-speed Internet access.

MODERATE

Argonaut Hotel ⭐⭐ *Kids*   The Kimpton Hotel Group gives visitors a new reason to stay at Fisherman's Wharf with this boutique gem, which opened in 2003 at the very cool San Francisco Maritime National Historic Park (p. 169). Half a block from the bay (though miraculously quiet), the four-story timber and brick landmark building, originally built in 1909 as a warehouse for the California Fruit Canners Association (and later used by William Randolph Hearst to store items that eventually ended up inside his Hearst Castle in San Simeon), is your best choice in this category at the wharf. Its 239 rooms and 13 suites are whimsically decorated to emulate a luxury cruise ship in cheerful nautical colors of blue, white, red, and yellow (though evidence of its modest past appears in original brick walls, large timbers, and steel warehouse doors). Luxurious touches include flat-screen TVs, DVD and CD players, Aveda toiletries, and—get this—leopard-spotted bathrobes along with all the standard hotel amenities. All guests are welcome at nightly weekday wine receptions and can use the lobby's two very popular (and free) Internet terminals. Suites have killer views and come fully loaded with telescopes and spa tubs. Get a "view" room, which peers onto the wharf or bay (some rooms offer fabulous views of Alcatraz). If you're bringing the kids, know that the Argonaut's friendly staff goes out of their way to make little ones feel at home and allows each pint-size guest to pick a new plaything from the hotel's "treasure chest." *Tip:* The concierge seems to be able to work wonders when you need tickets to Alcatraz—even when the trips are officially sold out.

495 Jefferson St (at Hyde St.), San Francisco, CA 94109. (© **866/415-0704** or 415/563-0800. Fax 415/345-5513. www.argonauthotel.com. 252 units. $159–$339 double; $249–$599 suite. Rates include evening wine in the lobby, daily newspaper, and kid-friendly perks like cribs and strollers. AE, DC, DISC, MC, V. Parking $32. Bus: 10, 30, or 47. Streetcar: F. Cable car: Powell-Hyde line. **Amenities:** Restaurant; bar; fitness center; concierge; laundry service; dry cleaning; yoga video and mats. *In room:* TV w/pay movies, minibar, coffeemaker, hair dryer, iron, safe, high-speed Internet access, DVD player, Nintendo, Web TV.

The Hotel Bohème ⭐⭐ *Finds*   Romance awaits at the intimate Bohème. Although it's located on the busiest strip in the neighborhood, once you climb the staircase to this narrow second-floor boutique hotel, you'll discover a style and demeanor reminiscent of a home in upscale Nob Hill. Alas, there are no common areas other than a little booth for check-in and concierge, but rooms, lining a skinny corridor, though small, are truly sweet, with gauze-draped canopies, stylish decor such as ornate parasols shading ceiling lights, and walls dramatically colored with lavender, sage green, black, and pumpkin. The staff is ultrahospitable, and bonuses include sherry in the lobby each afternoon. Some fabulous cafes, restaurants, bars, and shops are just a few steps away, and Chinatown and Union Square are within walking distance. *Note:* While the bathrooms are spiffy, they're also absolutely tiny and have showers only. *Tip:* Request a room off the street side; these rooms are quieter.

444 Columbus Ave. (between Vallejo and Green sts.), San Francisco, CA 94133. © 415/433-9111. Fax 415/362-6292. www.hotelboheme.com. 15 units. $149–$169 double. Rates include afternoon sherry. AE, DC, DISC, MC, V. Parking $31 at nearby public garage. Cable car: Powell-Mason line. Bus: 12, 15, 30, 41, 45, or 83. **Amenities:** Concierge. *In room:* TV, dataport, hair dryer.

The Washington Square Inn ★ Reminiscent of a traditional European inn—right down to the afternoon tea, wine, and cheese hour—this small, comely bed-and-breakfast is ideal for older couples who prefer a quieter, more subdued environment than the commotion of downtown San Francisco. It's across from Washington Square in North Beach—a coffee-craver's haven—and within walking distance of Fisherman's Wharf and Chinatown. Each room is decorated in English floral fabrics with quality European antique furnishings and plenty of fresh flowers.

1660 Stockton St. (between Filbert and Union sts.), San Francisco, CA 94133. © 800/388-0220 or 415/981-4220. Fax 415/397-7242. www.washingtonsquareinnsf.com. 15 units, 2 with bathroom across the hall. $145–$245 double. Rates include continental breakfast and afternoon tea, wine, and hors d'oeuvres. AE, DC, DISC, MC, V. Valet parking $25. Bus: 15, 30, 41, or 45. **Amenities:** Limited room service. *In room:* TV/VCR, fax, dataport, hair dryer, iron on request.

The Wharf Inn ★★ *Value* My top choice for good-value lodging at Fisherman's Wharf, the Wharf Inn offers above-average accommodations at one of the most popular tourist attractions in the world. The recently refurbished rooms, done in handsome tones of forest green, burgundy, and pale yellow, come well stocked. But more important, they are well situated smack-dab in the middle of the wharf, 2 blocks from PIER 39 and the cable car turnaround, and they're within walking distance of The Embarcadero and North Beach. The inn is ideal for carbound families because parking is free (that saves $25 a day right off the bat).

2601 Mason St. (at Beach St.), San Francisco, CA 94133. © 800/548-9918 or 415/673-7411. Fax 415/776-2181. www.wharfinn.com. 51 units. $95–$199 double; $299–$425 penthouse. AE, DC, DISC, MC, V. Free parking. Cable car: Powell-Mason line. Streetcar: F. Bus: 10, 15, 39, or 47. **Amenities:** Access to nearby health club ($10 per day); concierge; tour desk; car-rental desk; complimentary coffee/tea and newspapers. *In room:* TV, dataport, coffeemaker, hair dryer, iron on request.

INEXPENSIVE

The San Remo Hotel ★★ *Value* This small, European-style *pensione* is one of the best budget hotels in San Francisco. In a quiet North Beach neighborhood, within walking distance of Fisherman's Wharf, the Italianate Victorian structure originally served as a boardinghouse for dockworkers displaced by the great fire of 1906. As a result, the rooms are small and bathrooms are shared, but all is forgiven when it comes time to pay the bill. Rooms are decorated in cozy country style, with brass and iron beds; oak, maple, or pine armoires; and wicker furnishings. The immaculate shared bathrooms feature tubs and brass pull-chain toilets with oak tanks and brass fixtures. If the penthouse is available, book it:

You won't find a more romantic place to stay in San Francisco for so little money. It has its own bathroom, TV, fridge, and patio.

2237 Mason St. (at Chestnut St.), San Francisco, CA 94133. ⓒ **800/352-REMO** or 415/776-8688. Fax 415/776-2811. www.sanremohotel.com. 62 units, 61 with shared bathroom. $55–$95 double; $155–$175 penthouse suite. AE, DC, MC, V. Self-parking $10–$14. Cable car: Powell-Mason line. Streetcar: F. Bus: 10, 15, 30, or 47. **Amenities:** Access to nearby health club; self-service laundry; TV room. *In room:* Ceiling fan.

6 The Marina/Pacific Heights/Cow Hollow

EXPENSIVE

Hotel Drisco ⭐⭐ *(Finds)*   Located on one of the most sought-after blocks of residential property in all of San Francisco, the Drisco, built in 1903, is one of the city's best small hotels. Refinements by interior designer Glenn Texeira (who also did the Ritz-Carlton in Manila) are evident from the very small lobby and sitting areas to the calming atmosphere of the cream, yellow, and green guest rooms. As with the neighboring mansions, traditional antique furnishings and thick, luxurious fabrics abound here. The hotel's comfy beds will make you want to loll late into the morning before primping in the large marble bathrooms, complete with robes and slippers. Each suite has a couch that unfolds into a bed (although you would never guess from the looks of it), an additional phone and TV, and superior views. There is 24-hour coffee and tea service available on the ground floor, in the same comfy rooms where breakfast is served. The only things here that prevent a top ranking are the service, which is nowhere near the level of that at the Ritz-Carlton, and the lack of parking.

2901 Pacific Ave. (at Broderick St.), San Francisco, CA 94115. ⓒ **800/634-7277** or 415/346-2880. Fax 415/567-5537. www.hoteldrisco.com. 48 units. $235 double; $345–$475 suite. Rates include buffet breakfast and evening wine hour. AE, DC, DISC, MC, V. No parking available. Bus: 3 or 24. **Amenities:** Exercise room and free pass to YMCA; concierge; business center; limited room service; same-day laundry service/dry cleaning. *In room:* TV/VCR, dataport, minibar, fridge, hair dryer, iron, safe, CD player.

Union Street Inn ⭐⭐   Who would have guessed that one of the most delightful B&Bs in California would be in San Francisco? This two-story 1903 Edwardian fronts perpetually busy (and trendy shopping and bar-hopping stop) Union Street, but it's quiet as a church on the inside. The individually decorated rooms are comfortably furnished with down comforters, fresh flowers, and bay windows (beg for one with a view of the garden). A few even have Jacuzzi tubs. An extended full breakfast is served in the parlor, in your room, or on an outdoor terrace overlooking a lovely English garden. The ultimate honeymoon retreat is the private carriage house behind the inn, but any room at this warm, friendly inn is guaranteed to please.

2229 Union St. (between Fillmore and Steiner sts.), San Francisco, CA 94123. ⓒ **415/346-0424.** Fax 415/922-8046. www.unionstreetinn.com. 5 units, 1 cottage. $169–$279 standard double; $269 cottage. Rates include breakfast, hors d'oeuvres, and evening beverages. AE, MC, V. Nearby parking $15. Bus: 22, 28, 41, or 45. *In room:* TV.

MODERATE

Hotel Del Sol ⭐⭐ *(Kids)(Value)*   The cheeriest motel in town is located just 2 blocks off the Marina District's bustling section of Lombard. Three-level Hotel del Sol is all about festive flair and luxury touches. The sunshine theme extends from the Miami Beach–style use of vibrant color, as in the yellow, red, orange, and blue exterior, to the heated courtyard pool, which beckons the youngish clientele as they head for their cars parked (for free!) in cabana-like spaces. (The great pool with pool toys can keep the tots busy all day.) Fair-weather fun doesn't stop at the front door of the hotel, which boasts 57 spacious rooms with equally cheery interior decor (read: loud and very colorful) as well as unexpected extras like CD players, Aveda products, and tips on the town's happenings and shopping meccas. Sorry, smokers: You'll have to step outside to puff.

3100 Webster St. (at Greenwich St.), San Francisco, CA 94123. © **877/433-5765** or 415/921-5520. Fax 415/931-4137. www.thehoteldelsol.com. 57 units. $119–$165 double; $160–$235 suite. Rates include continental breakfast. AE, DC, DISC, MC, V. Free parking. Bus: 22, 28, 41, 43, 45, or 76. **Amenities:** Heated outdoor pool; dry cleaning. *In room:* TV/VCR, dataport, kitchenettes in some units, iron, wireless high-speed Internet access ($10 per day), CD player.

Jackson Court ★★   The Jackson Court, a stately three-story brownstone Victorian mansion, is in one of San Francisco's most exclusive neighborhoods, Pacific Heights. Its only fault—that it's far from the action—is also its blessing: If you crave a blissfully quiet vacation in elegant surroundings, this is the place. Each recently renovated room is individually furnished with superior-quality antique furnishings; two have wood-burning fireplaces (whose use is de rigueur in the winter) and two have gas fireplaces. The Blue Room features an inviting window seat; the Garden Suite has handcrafted wood paneling and a large picture window looking onto the private garden patio. After a continental breakfast of muffins, scones, croissants, oatmeal, juice, and fruit, spend the day browsing the shops along nearby Union and Fillmore streets, and return in time for afternoon tea.

2198 Jackson St. (at Buchanan St.), San Francisco, CA 94115. © **415/929-7670.** Fax 415/929-1405. www. jacksoncourt.com. 10 units. $150–$225 double. Rates include continental breakfast and afternoon tea. AE, MC, V. Parking on street only. Bus: 1, 3, 12, or 22. **Amenities:** Concierge; dry cleaning. *In room:* TV, dataport, hair dryer, iron.

Laurel Inn ★★ *Value*   If you don't mind being out of the downtown area, this lovely hotel, renovated in 1999, is one of the most tranquil, affordable places to rest your head. Tucked just beyond the southernmost tip of the Presidio and Pacific Heights, the outside is nothing impressive—just another motor inn. And that's what it was until the hotel group Joie de Vivre breathed new life into the place. Now decor is *très* chic and modern, with Zen-like influences (think W Hotel at half the price). Some rooms have excellent city views; all have spiffy bathrooms. The continental breakfast is fine, but why bother when you're across the street from Ella's (p. 142), which serves San Francisco's best breakfast? Other thoughtful touches: 24-hour coffee and tea service, pet-friendly rooms, and free parking! Add the great shopping 1 block away at Sacramento Street and the new and very hip bar, G, which serves libations and a surprisingly active slice of glamorous young Pacific Heights–style revelry, and there are plenty of reasons to stay here.

444 Presidio Ave. (at California Ave.), San Francisco, CA 94115. © **800/552-8735** or 415/567-8467. Fax 415/928-1866. www.thelaurelinn.com. 49 units. $155–$190 double. Rates include continental breakfast and afternoon lemonade and cookies. AE, DC, DISC, MC, V. Free parking. Bus: 1, 3, 4, or 43. Pets accepted. **Amenities:** Adjoining bar; concierge; valet service; access to great new JCC gym across the street at $10 per day. *In room:* TV/VCR, dataport, kitchenette in some units, hair dryer, iron, CD player.

INEXPENSIVE

Cow Hollow Motor Inn & Suites ★ *Kids*   If you're less interested in being downtown than in playing in and around the beautiful bayfront Marina, check out this modest brick hotel on busy Lombard Street. There's no fancy theme, but each room, which was completely renovated in 2004, has cable TV, free local phone calls, free covered parking, and a coffeemaker. Families will appreciate the one- and two-bedroom suites, which have full kitchens and dining areas as well as antique furnishings and surprisingly tasteful decor.

2190 Lombard St. (between Steiner and Fillmore sts.), San Francisco, CA 94123. ℂ **415/921-5800.** Fax 415/922-8515. www.cowhollowmotorinn.com. 129 units. $86–$125 double; from $225 suite. Extra person $10. AE, DC, MC, V. Free parking. Bus: 28, 30, 43, or 76. **Amenities:** Car-rental desk; laundry and dry cleaning within a block. *In room:* A/C, TV, dataport, kitchenettes in suites only, coffeemaker, hair dryer.

Edward II Inn & Suites 🖈🖈 This three-story "English country" inn has a room for almost anyone's budget, ranging from *pensione* units with shared bathrooms to luxuriously appointed suites and cottages with living rooms, kitchens, and whirlpool bathtubs. Originally built to house guests who attended the 1915 Pan-Pacific Exposition, it's still a good place to shack up in spotless and comfortably appointed rooms with cozy antique furnishings. Room prices even include a standard continental breakfast. Nearby Chestnut and Union streets offer some of the best shopping and dining in the city. The adjoining pub serves evening drinks on Fridays and Saturdays. The only caveat is that the hotel's Lombard Street location is usually congested with traffic.

3155 Scott St. (at Lombard St.), San Francisco, CA 94123. ℂ **800/473-2846** or 415/922-3000. Fax 415/931-5784. www.edwardii.com. 32 units, 21 with bathroom. $83–$88 double with shared bathroom; $115 double with private bathroom; $185–$235 suite. Extra person $25. Rates include continental breakfast and evening sherry. AE, MC, V. Self-parking $12 1 block away. Bus: 28, 30, 43, or 76. **Amenities:** Pub (Fri–Sat). *In room:* TV, hair dryer and iron available on request.

Hostelling International San Francisco—Fisherman's Wharf 🖈 *(Finds)* Unbelievable but true—you can get front-row bay views for a mere $22 nightly. This hostel, on national park property, provides dorm-style accommodations and offers easy access to the Marina's shops and restaurants. Rooms sleep 2 to 12 people; communal space includes a fireplace, kitchen, dining room, coffee bar, and foosball. The breakfast alone practically makes it worth the price. Make reservations well in advance.

Fort Mason, Building 240, San Francisco, CA 94123. ℂ **800/909-4776** or 415/771-7277. Fax 415/771-1468. www.sfhostel.org. 170 beds. $22–$29 per person per night; kids $15–$17 per night. Rates include breakfast. MC, V. Free limited parking. Bus: 28, 30, 47, or 49. **Amenities:** Self-service laundry and kitchen; meeting room; baggage storage; secure lockers; Internet access.

Marina Inn 🖈🖈 *(Value)* Marina Inn is one of the best low-priced hotels in San Francisco. How it offers so much for so little is mystifying. Each guest room in the 1924 four-story Victorian looks like something from a country furnishings catalog, complete with rustic pinewood furniture, a four-poster bed with silky-soft comforter, pretty wallpaper, and soothing tones of rose, hunter green, and pale yellow. You also get remote-control televisions discreetly hidden in pine cabinetry—all for as little as *$65 a night!* Combine that with continental breakfast, friendly service, and an armada of shops and restaurants within easy walking distance, and there you have it: the top choice for best overall value. (*Note:* Traffic can be a bit noisy here, so the hotel added double panes on windows facing the street.)

3110 Octavia St. (at Lombard St.), San Francisco, CA 94123. ℂ **800/274-1420** or 415/928-1000. Fax 415/928-5909. www.marinainn.com. 40 units. Nov–Feb $65–$105 double; Mar–May $75–$125 double; June–Oct $85–$135 double. Rates include continental breakfast. AE, DC, MC, V. Bus: 28, 30, 43, or 76. *In room:* TV, hair dryer and iron on request.

7 Japantown & Environs

EXPENSIVE

The Archbishop's Mansion 🖈🖈 *(Finds)* One thing is certain, the archbishop who built this 1904 Belle Epoque beauty was no Puritan. Though the hotel isn't world-class, it is drippingly romantic, tucked away in a very residential but central neighborhood, and likely to be the most opulently decorated B&B you could possibly imagine. Here, within the uniquely adorned rooms, it's all about whimsy and drama. The Don Giovanni suite—larger than many San Francisco houses—holds a huge, French four-poster bed with cherubs carved into it, a grand fireplace, elaborate linens, and a shower with seven heads that you'll never want to leave. Slightly closer to Earth is the Carmen suite, which has a deadly romantic combination of a claw-foot bathtub fronting a wood-burning fireplace. In the morning, breakfast is delivered to the guest rooms, and in the evening, wine is served in the elegant parlor. With a CD player in every room and a video and CD library accessible to every guest, this is one hotel that is enticing enough to make you linger in your room.

1000 Fulton St. (at Steiner St.), San Francisco, CA 94117. © **800/543-5820** or 415/563-7872. Fax 415/885-3193. www.thearchbishopsmansion.com. 15 units. $145–$495 double. Rates include continental breakfast and evening wine. AE, DC, MC, V. Limited free parking. Bus: 5 or 22. **Amenities:** Access to nearby gym ($20 daily); concierge; room service; same-day laundry service/dry cleaning. *In room:* TV/VCR, dataport, hair dryer, iron, CD player.

Radisson Miyako Hotel ✦ Japantown's Miyako is a tranquil alternative to staying downtown, which is only about 12 blocks away. The 16-story tower and five-story Garden Wing overlook the Japan Center, the city's largest complex of Japanese shops and restaurants (as well as a huge movie complex). The hotel, which underwent a $3-million renovation in 2002, manages to maintain a feeling of peace and quiet you'd expect somewhere much more remote. Rooms are Zen-like with East-meets-West decor. The Western-style (don't think cowboy) rooms are fine, but romantics and adventurers should opt for the traditional-style Japanese rooms with tatami mats and futons, a *tokonoma* (alcove for displaying art), and shoji screens that slide away to frame views of the city. Two futon luxury suites have Japanese rock gardens and deep-tub Japanese bathrooms. A bonus: Fillmore Street's upscale boutiques are just a few blocks away.

1625 Post St. (at Laguna St.), San Francisco, CA 94115. © **800/333-3333** or 415/922-3200. Fax 415/921-0417. www.miyakohotel.com. 218 units. $149–$229 double; from $2,69 suite. Children under 18 stay free in parent's room. AE, DC, DISC, MC, V. Valet parking $20; self-parking $13. Bus: 2, 3, 4, or 38. **Amenities:** Limited exercise room; business center; limited room service; in-room massage; same-day laundry service/dry cleaning. *In room:* TV w/pay movies, dataport, coffeemaker, hair dryer, iron.

MODERATE

The Queen Anne Hotel ✦✦ Value This majestic 1890 Victorian building, which was once a grooming school for upper-class young women, is today a stunning hotel. Restored in 1980 and most recently renovated in 2003, the four-story building recalls San Francisco's golden days. Walk under rich red draperies to the lavish "grand salon" lobby, complete with English oak paneling and period antiques. Guest rooms also contain antiques—armoires, marble-top dressers, and other Victorian pieces. Some have corner turret bay windows that look out on tree-lined streets, as well as separate parlor areas and wet bars; others have cozy reading nooks and fireplaces. All rooms have a telephone in the bathroom. Guests can relax in the parlor, with an impressive floor-to-ceiling fireplace, or in the hotel library. If you don't mind staying outside the downtown area, this hotel is highly recommended and very San Francisco.

1590 Sutter St. (between Gough and Octavia sts.), San Francisco, CA 94109. © **800/227-3970** or 415/441-2828. Fax 415/775-5212. www.queenanne.com. 48 units. $99–$199 double; $185–$205 suite. Extra person

$10. Rates include continental breakfast, afternoon tea and sherry, and morning newspaper. AE, DC, DISC, MC, V. Parking $14. Bus: 2, 3, or 4. **Amenities:** Access to nearby health club; 24-hr. concierge; business center; same-day dry cleaning; front desk safe. *In room:* TV, dataport, hair dryer, iron.

INEXPENSIVE

The Hotel Majestic ★★ *Value*   Both tourists and business travelers adore the all-nonsmoking Majestic because it covers every professional need while retaining the ambience of a luxurious old-world hotel. It was built in 1902, and the lobby alone sweeps guests into another era, with an overabundance of tapestries, tasseled brocades, Corinthian columns, and intricate, lavish detail. Guest rooms are just as opulent, with French and English antiques; the centerpiece of many rooms is a large four-poster canopy bed. You'll also find custom-made, mirrored armoires and antique reproductions. All drapes, fabrics, and carpets were replaced in 1997. Beds got new spreads in 2002, and half the bathrooms and guest rooms underwent a $2-million renovation in 1999.

Perks go beyond the usual. As well as bathrobes, two phones (one of which is portable), and umbrellas, the hotel offers complimentary faxes sent and received by the office (a nice touch!), fresh-baked cookies with turndown service, and well-lit desks. Some rooms have fireplaces. Their intimate and very atmospheric Avalon cocktail lounge has a beautiful French mahogany bar topped with marble and a collection of African butterflies.

1500 Sutter St. (between Octavia and Gough sts.), San Francisco, CA 94109. © **800/869-8966** or 415/441-1100. Fax 415/673-7331. www.thehotelmajestic.com. 58 units. $135–$150 double; from $250 suite. Rates include complimentary continental breakfast in lobby 7–10am, and wine and appetizers 4–6pm. Group, government, corporate, and relocation rates available. AE, DC, DISC, MC, V. Valet parking $19. Bus: 2, 4, 47, or 49. **Amenities:** Bar; access to nearby health club ($10 per day); concierge; 24-hr. room service; in-room massage; babysitting; same-day laundry/dry-cleaning service. *In room:* TV, dataport, fridge in some rooms, hair dryer, iron, wireless Internet access.

8 Civic Center

MODERATE

The Phoenix Hotel ★★ *Kids*   If you'd like to tell your friends back home that you stayed in the same hotel as Linda Ronstadt, Arlo Guthrie, Moby, and the Red Hot Chili Peppers, this is the place. On the fringes of San Francisco's less-than-pleasant Tenderloin District, this retro 1950s-style hotel is a gathering place for visiting rock musicians, writers, and filmmakers who crave a dose of Southern California—hence the palm trees and pastel colors. The focal point of the Palm Springs–style hotel is a small, heated outdoor pool adorned with a mural by artist Francis Forlenza and ensconced in a modern-sculpture garden.

The rooms, while more pop than plush, were upgraded in 1998 with more updates in the works for late 2004, and are comfortably equipped with bright festive furnishings, potted plants, and original local art. In addition to the usual amenities, the hotel offers VCRs and movies on request and a party vibe that's not part of the package at most city hotels. Some big bonuses: free parking and the hotel's hot new restaurant and club, the very groovy and very hip Bambuddha Lounge (© 415/885-5088), which serves Southeast Asian cuisine with cocktail-lounge flair.

601 Eddy St. (at Larkin St.), San Francisco, CA 94109. © **800/248-9466** or 415/776-1380. Fax 415/885-3109. www.thephoenixhotel.com. 44 units. $149–$169 double; $185–$205 suite. Rates include continental breakfast. AE, DC, MC, V. Free parking. Bus: 19, 31, 38, or 47. **Amenities:** Bar; heated outdoor pool; concierge; tour desk; in-room massage; same-day laundry service/dry cleaning. *In room:* TV, VCR on request, dataport, fridge and microwave in some rooms, hair dryer, iron on request.

9 The Castro

Though most accommodations (mostly converted homes) in the Castro cater to a gay and lesbian clientele, everyone is welcome. Unfortunately, there are few choices, and their amenities don't really compare to those at most of the better (and much larger) hotels throughout San Francisco.

MODERATE

The Parker Guest House ★★   This is the best B&B option in the Castro, and one of the best in the entire city. In fact, even some of the better hotels could learn a thing or two from this fashionable, gay-friendly, 5,000-square-foot, 1909 beautifully restored Edwardian home and new adjacent annex a few blocks from the heart of the Castro's action. Within the bright, cheery urban compound, period antiques abound. But thankfully, the spacious guest rooms are wonderfully updated with smart patterned furnishings, voice mail, robes, and spotless private bathrooms (plus amenities) en suite or, in two cases, across the hall. A fire burns nightly in the cozy living room, and guests are also welcome to make themselves at home in the wood-paneled common library (with fireplace and piano), sunny breakfast room overlooking the garden, and spacious garden with fountains and a steam room. Animal lovers will appreciate the companionship of the house pug named Parker.

520 Church St. (between 17th and 18th sts.), San Francisco, CA 94114. © **888/520-7275** or 415/621-3222. Fax 415/621-4139. www.parkerguesthouse.com. 21 units. $119–$200 double; $200 junior suite. Rates include extended continental breakfast and evening wine and cheese. AE, DISC, MC, V. Self-parking $15. Streetcar: J Church. Bus: 22 or 33. **Amenities:** Access to nearby health club; steam room; concierge; wireless Internet access. *In room:* TV, dataport, hair dryer, iron.

INEXPENSIVE

Beck's Motor Lodge ★   In a town where DINK (double income, no kids) tourists happily spend fistfuls of money, you'd think someone would create a gay luxury hotel—or even a moderate hotel, for that matter. But absurdly, the most commercial and modern accommodations in the touristy Castro is this run-of-the-mill motel. Standard but contemporary, the ultratidy rooms include motel furnishings, a sun deck overlooking upper Market Street's action, and free parking. Unless you're into homey B&Bs, this is really your only choice in the area—fortunately, it's very well maintained.

2222 Market St. (at 15th St.), San Francisco, CA 94114. © **800/227-4360** in the U.S., except Calif., or 415/621-8212 (within Calif., call collect to make reservations). Fax 415/241-0435. 58 units. $119–$145 double. AE, DC, DISC, MC, V. Free parking. Streetcar: F. Bus: 8 or 37. **Amenities:** Coin-operated washing machines. *In room:* TV, dataport, fridge, coffeemaker, free Internet access in some rooms.

The Castillo Inn ★   Just 2 minutes from the heart of the Castro, this charming little house provides a safe, quiet environment. Catering mostly to gay men (although anyone is welcome), the Castillo makes its clientele feel at home. Hardwood floors decorated with throw rugs aid in the warmth. Rooms are small yet cozy, and the front desk uses voice mail to collect phone messages. The Castillo also offers the shared use of a large refrigerator and microwave oven in the kitchen.

48 Henry St., San Francisco, CA 94114. © **800/865-5112** or 415/864-5111. Fax 415/641-1321. 4 units, none with bathroom. $80 double. Rates include continental breakfast. AE, MC, V. Streetcar: F, K, L, or M. Bus: 8, 22, 24, or 37.

Inn on Castro ★   One of the better choices in the Castro, half a block from all the action, is this Edwardian-style inn decorated with contemporary furnishings, original modern art, and fresh flowers throughout. It definitely feels more like a home than an inn, so if you like less commercial abodes, this place is for you. Most rooms share a small back patio, and the suite has a private entrance and outdoor sitting area. The inn also offers access to four individual nearby apartments ($85–$200, with discounts on stays of more than 4 nights) with complete kitchens.

321 Castro St. (at Market St.), San Francisco, CA 94114. © 415/861-0321. Fax 415/861-0321. www.innon castro.com. 8 units (2 with bathroom across the hall), 4 apts. $95–$160 double; $135–$175 suite. Rates include full breakfast and evening brandy. AE, DC, MC, V. Streetcar: F, K, L, M. *In room:* TV, dataport, hair dryer.

24 Henry Its Castro location is not the only thing that makes 24 Henry a good choice for gay travelers. The building, an 1870s Victorian on a serene side street, is quite charming. The 10 guest rooms have high ceilings, period furniture, and voice mail. Guests tired of tromping around the neighborhood can watch TV or read in the double parlor (where breakfast is served). All rooms are nonsmoking.

24 Henry St. (near Sanchez Sts.), San Francisco, CA 94114. © 800/900-5686 or 415/864-5686. Fax 415/864-0406. www.24henry.com. 10 units, 3 with bathroom. $65–$90 double with shared bath; $109–$139 double with private bathroom. Extra person $20. Rates include continental breakfast. AE, MC, V. Streetcar: F, J, K, L, M, or N. Bus: 8, 22, 24, or 37.

The Willows Inn ⭐ Right in the heart of the Castro, the all-nonsmoking Willows Inn employs a staff eager to greet and attend to visitors. The country and antique willow furnishings don't strictly suit a 1903 Edwardian home, but everything's quite comfortable—especially considering the extras, which include an expanded continental breakfast (fresh fruit, yogurt, baked goods, gourmet coffee, assorted teas, and fresh orange juice), the morning paper, nightly cocktails, a sitting room, and a pantry with limited kitchen facilities. The homey rooms vary in size from large (queen-size bed) to smaller (double bed) and are priced accordingly. Each room has a vanity sink, and all the rooms share eight water closets and shower rooms.

710 14th St. (near Church and Market sts.), San Francisco, CA 94114. © 800/431-0277 or 415/431-4770. Fax 415/431-5295. www.willowssf.com. 12 units, none with bathroom. $99–$109 double; $139–$159 suite. Rates include continental breakfast. AE, DISC, MC, V. Limited off-street parking $15. Streetcar: Church St. station (across the street) or F. Bus: 22 or 37. *In room:* TV, fridge, free wireless Internet.

10 Haight-Ashbury

MODERATE

Stanyan Park Hotel ⭐⭐ (Kids) (Value) The only real hotel on the east end of Golden Gate Park and the west end of funky-chic Haight Street, this small inn offers classic San Francisco–style living at a very affordable price. The Victorian structure, which has operated as a hotel under a variety of names since 1904 and is on the National Register of Historic Places, offers good-size rooms all done in period decor. Its three stories are decorated with antique furnishings, Victorian wallpaper, and pastel quilts, curtains, and carpets, much of which—including mattresses—was updated in 2001. Families will appreciate the six one- and two-bedroom suites, each of which has a full kitchen and formal dining and living rooms and can sleep up to six comfortably. Tea is served each afternoon and evening. Continental breakfast is served in a pleasant room off the lobby. All rooms are nonsmoking.

750 Stanyan St. (at Waller St.), San Francisco, CA 94117. © 415/751-1000. Fax 415/668-5454. www. stanyanpark.com. 36 units. $130–$185 double; $265–$315 suite. Rates include continental breakfast and afternoon and evening tea service. Rollaway $20; cribs free. AE, DISC, MC, V. Off-site parking $12. Streetcar: N. Bus: 7, 33, 43, 66, or 71. *In room:* TV, dataport, kitchen (in suites only), hair dryer.

11 Near San Francisco International Airport

MODERATE

Embassy Suites ★ If you've stayed at an Embassy Suites before, you know the drill. But this hotel is one of the best airport options, if only for the fact that every room is a suite. But there is more: The property has an indoor pool, whirlpool, courtyard with fountain, palmtrees, and a bar/restaurant. Plus, each tastefully decorated two-room suite has nice additions such as two TVs. Additionally, a complimentary breakfast of your choice is available before you're whisked to the airport on the free shuttle—all that and the price is still right.

250 Gateway Blvd., South San Francisco, CA 94080. © 800/362-2779 or 650/589-3400. Fax 650/589-1183. www.embassysf.com. 312 units. $109–$199 double. Rates include breakfast and complimentary evening beverages. AE, DC, MC, V. **Amenities:** Restaurant; bar; indoor pool; Jacuzzi; airport shuttle. *In room:* A/C, TV, fridge, coffeemaker, hair dryer, iron, wireless high-speed Internet access, microwave.

INEXPENSIVE

Comfort Suites *(Kids)* Two miles north of the airport, well outside the heart of the city, Comfort Suites is a well-appointed option for travelers on the way into or out of town. Each studio-suite has a king-size bed, queen-size sleeper sofa (great for the kids), and all the basic amenities for weary travelers. There are enough pay cable channels to keep you glued to your TV set for an entire day, although kids will also enjoy the Nintendo in each room. Rooms are fine, but the freebies are the most attractive part of this hotel: continental breakfast, an airport shuttle, and use of the outdoor hot tub.

121 E. Grand Ave., South San Francisco, CA 94080. © 800/293-1794 or 650/589-7100. Fax 650/589-7796. www.csusfo.com. 168 units. $109 double. Rates include continental breakfast. AE, DC, DISC, MC, V. **Amenities:** Outdoor Jacuzzi; airport shuttle. *In room:* A/C, TV w/Nintendo, fridge, coffeemaker, hair dryer, iron, microwave, high-speed Internet access in some rooms.

San Francisco Airport North Travelodge *(Kids)* The Travelodge is a good choice for families, mainly because of the hotel's large heated pool. Although new carpets and bedspreads were added in 2001, the rooms are as ordinary as you'd expect from a Travelodge. Still they're comfortable and come with plenty of perks like Showtime and free toll-free and credit card calls. Each junior suite has a microwave and refrigerator. The clincher is the 24-hour complimentary shuttle, which makes the 2-mile trip to the airport in 5 minutes.

326 S. Airport Blvd. (off Hwy. 101), South San Francisco, CA 94080. © 800/578-7878 or 650/583-9600. Fax 650/873-9392. www.sfotravelodge.com. 199 units. $79–$129 double. AE, DC, DISC, MC, V. Free parking. **Amenities:** Restaurant; heated outdoor pool; courtesy shuttle to airport; fax and copier services; dry cleaning. *In room:* A/C, TV w/pay movies, coffeemaker, hair dryer, iron, safe, microwaves available.

Where to Dine

San Francisco's restaurants are so renowned that many people visit the city just to eat—and with good reason. The city's brilliant chefs, combined with California's abundance of organic produce, seafood, free-range meats, and Northern California wine, guarantee some of the world's finest dining, and fierce competition means slackers need not apply to any local kitchen.

Unfortunately, over the past few years, kitchen talent and quality ingredients have cost more and more (and higher gas prices aren't helping, since delivery expenses are also on the rise). Add to that the new San Francisco $8.50 minimum wage, which is threatening the already struggling livelihood of strapped restaurants (especially since it applies even to waiters, who don't need a raise as much as kitchen staff).

But on the bright side, "small plate" menus—or snacking through a meal on cheaper, smaller dishes—are more popular than ever, as are cheaper, more affordable, and casual newcomer destinations. Thus, though there are plenty of bargains to be found, the costlier spots included in this book can be so good, you might not mind spending $25 to $35 per entree.

Though trendy, much of San Francisco dining is *not only* about trendy fare. As one of the world's cultural crossroads, the city is blessed with a cornucopia of cuisines. Afghan, Cajun, Burmese, Jewish, Moroccan, Persian, Cambodian, vegan—whatever you're in the mood for, this town has it covered. So book your reservations and break out the credit cards, because half the fun of visiting San Francisco is the rare opportunity to sample most of the flavors of the world in one fell swoop.

As you join the locals in their most beloved pastime, there are a few things you should keep in mind:

- If you want a table at the restaurants with the best reputations, you probably need to book 6 to 8 weeks in advance for weekends, and a couple of weeks ahead for weekdays.
- If there's a long wait for a table, ask if you can order at the bar, which is often faster and more fun.
- Don't leave *anything* valuable in your car while dining, particularly in or near high-crime areas such as the Mission, downtown, or—believe it or not—Fisherman's Wharf (thieves know tourists with nice cameras and a trunkful of

Pricing Categories

The restaurants listed below are classified first by area, then by price, using the following categories: **Very Expensive,** dinner from $75 per person; **Expensive,** dinner from $50 per person; **Moderate,** dinner from $35 per person; and **Inexpensive,** dinner less than $35 per person. These categories reflect prices for an appetizer, main course, dessert, and glass of wine.

---

mementos are headed there). Also, it's best to give the parking valet only the key to your car, *not* your hotel room or house key.

- *Remember:* It is against the law to smoke in any restaurant in San Francisco, even if it has a separate bar or lounge area. You're welcome to smoke outside, however.

- This ain't New York: Plan on dining early. Most restaurants close their kitchens around 10pm.

1 Restaurants by Cuisine

AMERICAN

Beach Chalet Brewery & Restaurant ✹ (Richmond District, $$, p. 154)

Bix ✹✹ (North Beach, $$$, p. 132)

Boulevard ✹✹ (SoMa, $$$$, p. 124)

Chow ✹✹ (The Castro, $, p. 151)

Dottie's True Blue Café ✹ (Union Square, $, p. 115)

Ella's ✹✹ (Pacific Heights, $$, p. 142)

Firewood Café ✹ (The Castro, $, p. 152)

Fog City Diner ✹ (Telegraph Hill, $$, p. 133)

Hard Rock Cafe (Fisherman's Wharf, $, p. 140)

Mecca ✹ (The Castro, $$$, p. 151)

Mel's Diner ✹ (The Marina, $, p. 145)

MoMo's (SoMa, $$$, p. 125)

Moose's ✹ (North Beach, $$$, p. 132)

Mo's Gourmet Burgers ✹✹ (North Beach, $, p. 136)

Postrio ✹ (Union Square, $$$$, p. 112)

The Ramp ✹ (China Basin, $, p. 148)

RNM ✹✹ (Haight-Ashbury, $$, p. 153)

San Francisco Art Institute Café ✹ (North Beach, $, p. 136)

Tablespoon ✹✹ (Russian Hill, $$$, p. 128)

Town Hall ✹ (SoMa, $$$, p. 125)

Universal Café ✹✹ (Mission District, $$, p. 149)

The Waterfront Restaurant (Financial District, $$$, p. 120)

AMERICAN BRASSERIE

bacar ✹✹ (SoMa, $$$$, p. 121)

ARGENTINEAN

Il Pollaio ✹ (North Beach, $, p. 135)

ASIAN

AsiaSF ✹ (SoMa, $, p. 126)

BASQUE

Piperade ✹✹ (Telegraph Hill, $$, p. 133)

BELGIAN

Frjtz Fries ✹ (Fisherman's Wharf, $, p. 140)

BREAKFAST

Dottie's True Blue Café ✹ (Union Square, $, p. 115)

Ella's ✹✹ (Pacific Heights, $$, p. 142)

CAJUN/CREOLE

The Elite Café ✦ (Pacific Heights, $$, p. 142)

CALIFORNIA

AsiaSF ✦ (SoMa, $, p. 126)

Bix ✦✦ (North Beach, $$$, p. 132)

Cafe Kati ✦✦ (Pacific Heights, $$$, p. 141)

Caffé Luna Piena ✦ (The Castro, $$, p. 151)

Cliff House ✦ (Richmond District, $$, p. 155)

Enrico's ✦ (North Beach, $$, p. 133)

Gordon Biersch Brewery Restaurant (SoMa, $$, p. 125)

Jardinière ✦✦ (Civic Center, $$$$, p. 146)

One Market ✦✦ (Financial District, $$$, p. 118)

PlumpJack Café ✦✦ (The Marina, $$, p. 144)

Pluto's ✦ (The Marina, $, p. 146)

2223 Restaurant & Bar ✦✦ (The Castro, $$, p. 151)

The Waterfront Restaurant (Financial District, $$$, p. 120)

CALIFORNIA-FRENCH

Charles Nob Hill ✦✦✦ (Nob Hill/Russian Hill, $$$$, p. 127)

Rubicon ✦✦ (Financial District, $$$$, p. 117)

CALIFORNIA-ITALIAN

Quince ✦✦ (Pacific Heights, $$$, p. 141)

CARIBBEAN

Cha Cha Cha ✦✦ (Haight-Ashbury, $, p. 153)

CHINESE

Brandy Ho's Hunan Food ✦ (Chinatown, $, p. 129)

Eliza's ✦✦ (Pacific Heights, $, p. 145)

House of Nanking ✦ (Chinatown, $, p. 129)

The Mandarin ✦ (Fisherman's Wharf, $$$, p. 139)

R&G Lounge ✦✦ (Chinatown, $, p. 129)

Tommy Toy's ✦✦ (Financial District, $$$, p. 119)

CHINESE/DIM SUM

Harbor Village ✦ (Financial District, $$$, p. 117)

Ton Kiang ✦✦ (Richmond District, $, p. 156)

Yank Sing ✦✦ (Financial District, $$, p. 121)

CREPES

Ti Couz ✦ (Mission District, $, p. 150)

EAST-WEST FUSION

Cafe Kati ✦✦ (Pacific Heights, $$$, p. 141)

Eos Restaurant & Wine Bar ✦ (Haight-Ashbury, $$, p. 152)

FRENCH

Absinthe ✦ (Civic Center, $$, p. 147)

Cafe Bastille (Financial District, $$, p. 119)

Café Claude ✦✦ (Union Square, $, p. 115)

Chez Nous ✦✦ (Pacific Heights, $, p. 144)

Fifth Floor Restaurant ✦✦✦ (SoMa, $$$$, p. 124)

Fleur de Lys ✦ (Union Square, $$$$, p. 111)

Florio ✦✦ (Pacific Heights, $$, p. 142)

Forbes Island ✦ (Fisherman's Wharf, $$$$, p. 137)

Grand Café ✦ (Union Square, $$$, p. 112)

Isa ✦✦ (The Marina, $$, p. 143)

Jardinière ✦✦ (Civic Center, $$$$, p. 146)

La Folie ✦✦ (Russian Hill, $$$$, p. 127)

Masa's ✦✦✦ (Union Square, $$$$, p. 112)

PlumpJack Café ★★ (The Marina,
$$, p. 144)

Restaurant Gary Danko ★★★
(Fisherman's Wharf, $$$$,
p. 138)

Scala's Bistro ★ (Union Square,
$$, p. 115)

Universal Café ★★ (Mission
District, $$, p. 149)

GREEK

Kokkari ★★★ (Financial District,
$$, p. 120)

ITALIAN

A16 ★★ (The Marina, $$, p. 141)

Cafe Pescatore ★ (Fisherman's
Wharf, $$, p. 139)

Cafe Tiramisu (Financial District,
$$, p. 119)

Caffè Macaroni ★★ (North Beach,
$, p. 134)

Caffè Sport ★ (North Beach, $$$,
p. 132)

Capp's Corner ★ (North Beach, $,
p. 134)

Delfina ★★ (Mission District, $,
p. 149)

E'Angelo Restaurant ★
(The Marina, $, p. 145)

Emporio Armani Cafe ★
(Union Square, $, p. 116)

Firewood Café ★ (The Castro, $,
p. 152)

Florio ★★ (Pacific Heights, $$,
p. 142)

The Gold Spike (North Beach, $,
p. 135)

Il Pollaio ★ (North Beach, $,
p. 135)

Kuleto's ★ (Union Square, $$,
p. 114)

L'Osteria del Forno ★★
(North Beach, $, p. 135)

Mario's Bohemian Cigar Store ★
(North Beach, $, p. 135)

Mocca ★ (Union Square, $,
p. 116)

Pane e Vino ★ (Pacific Heights,
$$, p. 143)

Pasta Pomodoro ★★
(North Beach, $, p. 136)

Scala's Bistro ★ (Union Square,
$$, p. 115)

The Stinking Rose (North Beach,
$$, p. 134)

Tommaso's ★★ (North Beach, $,
p. 137)

JAPANESE

Ace Wasabi's Rock 'n' Roll
Sushi ★★ (The Marina, $$,
p. 142)

Ebisu (Sunset District, $$, p. 155)

Kabuto A&S ★★ (Richmond
District, $$, p. 155)

Kyo-Ya ★ (Financial District, $$$,
p. 118)

Sanraku Japanese Restaurant ★
(Union Square, $, p. 116)

MEDITERRANEAN

Caffè Luna Piena ★ (The Castro,
$$, p. 151)

Foreign Cinema ★★ (Mission
District, $$, p. 149)

Kokkari ★★★ (Financial District,
$$, p. 120)

La Méditerranée ★ (Pacific
Heights, $, p. 145)

PlumpJack Café ★★ (The Marina,
$$, p. 144)

Zuni Café ★★★ (Civic Center,
$$, p. 147)

MEXICAN

Andalé Taqueria ★★ (The Marina,
$, p. 144)

Sweet Heat ★ (Haight-Ashbury, $,
p. 153)

Taquerias La Cumbre ★ (Mission
District, $, p. 150)

MOROCCAN

Aziza ★★ (Richmond District, $$,
p. 154)

NOODLES

Long Life Noodle Company
& Jook Joint ★ (SoMa, $,
p. 126)

PERSIAN/MIDDLE EASTERN
Maykedah ✹ (North Beach, $$, p. 133)

PIZZA
Pauline's ✹✹ (Mission District, $, p. 150)

SEAFOOD
A. Sabella's ✹✹ (Fisherman's Wharf, $$$$, p. 137)

Alioto's (Fisherman's Wharf, $$$, p. 138)

Aqua ✹✹ (Financial District, $$$$, p. 117)

Cliff House ✹ (Richmond District, $$, p. 155)

Farallon ✹ (Union Square, $$$$, p. 111)

Hayes Street Grill ✹ (Civic Center, $$, p. 147)

Plouf (Financial District, $$, p. 119)

Sam's Grill & Seafood Restaurant ✹ (Financial District, $$, p. 120)

Scoma's ✹ (Fisherman's Wharf, $$$$, p. 138)

Swan Oyster Depot ✹✹ (Russian Hill, $$, p. 128)

Tadich Grill ✹✹ (Financial District, $$, p. 121)

SINGAPOREAN
Straits Café ✹ (Richmond District, $$, p. 156)

SPANISH
B44 (Financial District, $$, p. 119)

STEAKHOUSE
Harris' ✹✹ (Pacific Heights, $$$$, p. 140)

House of Prime Rib ✹✹ (Russian Hill, $$$, p. 128)

SUSHI
Ace Wasabi's Rock 'n' Roll Sushi ✹✹ (The Marina, $$, p. 142)

Ebisu (Sunset District, $$, p. 155)

Kabuto A&S ✹✹ (Richmond District, $$, p. 155)

Kyo-Ya ✹ (Financial District, $$$, p. #118)

Sanraku Japanese Restaurant ✹ (Union Square, $, p. 116)

THAI
Khan Toke Thai House ✹✹ (Richmond District, $$, p. 156)

Manora's ✹ (SoMa, $, p. 126)

Thep Phanom ✹✹ (Haight-Ashbury, $, p. 154)

VEGAN
Millennium ✹ (Union Square, $$, p. 114)

VEGETARIAN
Greens Restaurant ✹✹ (The Marina, $$, p. 143)

VIETNAMESE
Ana Mandara ✹✹ (Fisherman's Wharf, $$$, p. 139)

The Golden Turtle ✹ (Russian Hill, $, p. 128)

Pho Hoa ✹ (Union Square, $, p. 116)

Le Colonial ✹ (Union Square, $$$, p. 114)

The Slanted Door ✹✹ (Financial District, $$$, p. 118)

Tú Lan ✹ (SoMa, $, p. 126)

Tips Multicourse Dining

Ordering a "fixed-price," "prix-fixe," or "tasting" menu can be a good bargain as well as a great way to sample lots of dishes at one sitting. Many dining rooms in town offer these multicourse menus, which tend to cost around $75 for four courses, including dessert.

---

2 Union Square

VERY EXPENSIVE

Farallon ⭐ SEAFOOD   While this seafood restaurant is hands-down the most whimsical in its stunning oceanic decor, the high price tag and fine, but not mind-blowing, food make it a better cocktail-and-appetizer or lunch stop than dinner choice. The multimillion-dollar attraction's outrageous decor follows the "coastal" cuisine theme; hand-blown jellyfish lamps, kelp bedlike backlit columns, glass clamshells, sea-urchin light fixtures, a sea-life mosaic floor, and a tentacle-encircled bar set the scene. (Thankfully, designer Pat Kuleto's impressive renovation of the 1924 building left the original Gothic arches intact.)

Executive chef Mark Franz, who opened the once-famous restaurant Stars with Jeremiah Tower, orchestrates the cuisine. He offers starters ranging from the expected (a variety of very expensive oysters) to the more ambitious (seared breast of squab with roasted foie gras, leg confit raviolo, and rhubarb chutney). While most main courses (the menu changes daily and seasonally) stick with the seaside theme, meat and game eaters will still have a few decadent options. The whimsy-meets-sophistication extends only as far as the food—the service and wine lists (more than 400 by the bottle; 30 by the glass) are seriously professional. Personally, I suggest stopping by for lunch or cocktails. The scene may be swank, but for seafood, Aqua is worlds better.

450 Post St. (between Mason and Powell sts., adjoining the Kensington Park Hotel). ⓒ **415/956-6969**. www.farallonrestaurant.com. Reservations recommended. 3-course prix-fixe lunch menu $25. Main courses $17–$19 lunch, $27–$35 dinner. AE, DC, DISC, MC, V. Tues–Sat 11:30am–2:30pm; Tues–Sat 2:30–5pm (bistro menu); Mon 5:30–10pm; Tues–Wed 5:30–10:30pm; Fri–Sat 5:30–11pm; Sun 5–10pm. Valet parking (dinner only) $12. Bus: 2, 3, 4, or 38.

Fleur de Lys ⭐ FRENCH   Fleur de Lys is the city's most traditional and formal classic French affair. Draped in 700 yards of rich patterned fabric mood-lit with dim French candelabras, and accented with an extraordinary sculptural floral centerpiece, this restaurant is a romantic spot, so long as your way of wooing includes donning a dinner jacket. Equally formal is the cuisine of chef Hubert Keller (former President Clinton's first guest chef at the White House), who is usually in the kitchen preparing the menus (and watching a closed-circuit TV of the dining room to ensure all goes smoothly). Diners in favor of grazing should start with the "Symphony" appetizer, a culinary medley with bite-size samplings of foie gras terrine, sea scallop cake, and lobster gelée. Other sure things include radicchio-wrapped salmon with canellini beans and Banyuls vinegar and olive oil; and lamb loin with spiced honey, caramelized cumin-seed sauce, and mint oil. The selection of around 700 French and California wines is also impressive.

777 Sutter St. (at Jones St.). ⓒ **415/673-7779**. www.fleurdelyssf.com. Reservations required. 3-course menu $68, 4-course $76, 5-course $88; vegetarian and vegan options available. AE, DC, MC, V. Mon–Thurs 6–9:30pm; Fri–Sat 5:30–10:30pm. Valet parking $12. Bus: 2, 3, 4, 27, or 38.

Masa's ☆☆☆ FRENCH   One of the city's veteran contenders for best—and most expensive—French restaurant is now presided over by executive chef Richard Reddington, who arrived from Napa's Auberge du Soleil in July 2004. As this book goes to press Reddington has yet to redefine the menu, but no doubt his composed, fantastic fare will follow in the footsteps of previous chef Ron Siegel (who went to the Ritz-Carlton), with outstanding and beautifully presented three-, six-, and nine-course tasting menus within the mood-lit, minimalist-chic room. Fortunately, the space provides a rare opportunity to easily hear your dining companions, because there's lots to chat about: *Amuses-bouches* (French for "amuse the mouth" and equivalent to free little treats from the chef) abound the minute your attentive French waiter appears. Previous menu delights included seared scallops atop sun choke puree and lobster reduction; John Dory with golden Osetra caviar, caramelized salsify, braised romaine, beet reduction; and filet mignon with bone marrow, spinach, wild mushrooms, roasted potatoes, and bordelaise. It'll be exciting to see what Reddington does here, but if you want to try it, hurry up: Rumor is he's only onboard until he opens his own restaurant in Napa within a year or so. After dinner, look forward to the cheese cart and candy cart, the latter of which wheels up a complimentary selection of house-made lollipops, chocolates, and mini cookies.

In the Hotel Vintage Court, 648 Bush St. (at Stockton St.). ✆ 415/989-7154. Reservations required and accepted up to 3 months in advance. Fixed-price dinner $65–$115; 6-course vegetarian dinner $85. AE, DC, DISC, MC, V. Tues–Sat 5:30–9:30pm. Closed 1st 2 weeks in Jan, 1st week in July. Valet parking $15. Cable car: Powell-Mason and Powell-Hyde lines. Bus: 2, 3, 4, 30, or 45.

Postrio ☆ AMERICAN   Eating is only part of the reason you come to this Wolfgang Puck–owned glamorous downtown restaurant. After squeezing through the perpetually swinging bar—which dishes out excellent pizzas from a wood-burning oven and is a great place to grab an affordable bite at lunch or dinner—guests are forced to make a grand entrance down the antebellum staircase to the cavernous dining room below (it's everyone's 15 seconds of fame, so make sure your fly is zipped). Pure Hollywood, for sure, but it's fun.

The menu, by brother executive chefs Mitchell and Steven Rosenthal, who also run SoMa's Town Hall (p. 125), combines Italian, Asian, French, and California styles with mixed results—sometimes the kitchen is on, other evenings it's way off. The nightly changing menu might include grilled chicken breast with potato sausage, onion purée, and walnut vinaigrette; or roasted salmon with potato eggplant ravioli, Thai basil mint salad, and orange coconut-milk cream. If you're up for a fancy dinner, there are better options around town, but for a bar bite or a scene with your seared rare tuna with shoestring potatoes, bacon lardons, salad Lyonnaise, and sauce au poivre, this is a prime pick. *Note:* Lunch is served in the bar only.

In the Prescott Hotel, 545 Post St. (between Mason and Taylor sts.). ✆ 415/776-7825. www.postrio.com. Reservations recommended. Main courses $12–$16 lunch, $24–$36 dinner. AE, DC, DISC, MC, V. Mon–Sat 11:30am–2pm; Sun–Wed 5:30–10pm; Thurs–Sat 5:30–10:30pm. Bar menu daily 11:30am–11:30pm. Valet parking $12 at lunch for 3 hr., $14 at dinner for 3 hr. Cable car: Powell-Mason and Powell-Hyde lines. Bus: 2, 3, 4, or 38.

EXPENSIVE

Grand Café ☆ FRENCH   If you aren't interested in exploring restaurants beyond those in Union Square and want a huge dose of atmosphere with your seared salmon, Grand Café is your best bet. Its claims to fame? The most *grand* dining room in San Francisco, an enormous turn-of-the-20th-century grand-ballroom–like dining oasis that's a magnificent combination of old Europe and

Dining in Union Square & Financial District

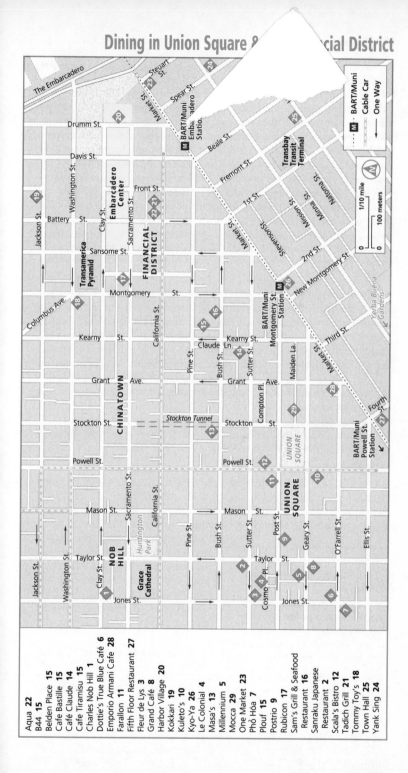

Aqua **22**
B44 **15**
Belden Place **15**
Cafe Bastille **15**
Café Claude **14**
Cafe Tiramisu **15**
Charles Nob Hill **1**
Dottie's True Blue Café **6**
Emporio Armani Cafe **28**
Farallon **11**
Fifth Floor Restaurant **27**
Fleur de Lys **3**
Grand Café **8**
Harbor Village **20**
Kokkari **19**
Kuleto's **10**
Kyo-Ya **26**
Le Colonial **4**
Masa's **13**
Millennium **5**
Mocca **29**
One Market **23**
Phô Hòa **7**
Plouf **15**
Postrio **9**
Rubicon **17**
Sam's Grill & Seafood
  Restaurant **16**
Sanraku Japanese
  Restaurant **2**
Scala's Bistro **12**
Tadich Grill **21**
Tommy Toy's **18**
Town Hall **25**
Yank Sing **24**

Art Nouveau; and a festive (read: crowded) cocktail area. No matter where you sit while dining on the French-inspired, California-based cuisine, you'll see playful sculptures, original murals, and a cadre of dazzling Deco chandeliers.

Chef Paul Arenstam serves up some sexy specialty dishes such as flaky-creamy wild mushroom tart with black truffle sabayon and indulgent sautéed skate wing with braised cabbage and bacon bathed in a browned-butter capers sauce. *Note:* The bar area—known as the Petit Café—has its own exhibition kitchen and menu, offering similar dishes for about half the price. Sit at the cherrywood bar or at a cocktail table for food from $3 to $12 (including stuffed piquillo peppers with feta cheese; steak tartare; pizzas; and a duck confit tart with grilled bread, mashed potatoes, and shredded duck confit). Libation lovers stop here for the great selection of small-batch American whiskies and single-malt Scotches.

501 Geary St. (at Taylor St., adjacent to the Hotel Monaco). (415/292-0101. Reservations recommended. Main courses $15–$25. AE, DC, DISC, MC, V. Mon–Fri 7–10:30am; Sat 8–11am; Sun 8am–2:30pm; Mon–Sat 11:30am–2:30pm; Sun–Thurs 5:30–10pm; Fri–Sat 5:30–11pm. Valet parking $10 for 3 hr., $3 each additional ½ hr. Bus: 2, 3, 4, 27, or 38.

Le Colonial ★ *Finds* VIETNAMESE   Sexy environs and decent—albeit pricey—French Vietnamese food make this an excellent choice for folks who enjoy bar snacking. I'm sorry to say that a chef change in 2002 knocked the food down a few notches since previous visits. But the vibrant flavors of tender wok-seared beef tenderloin with watercress onion salad still do the trick. The upstairs lounge (which opens at 4:30pm) is where romance reigns, with cozy couches, seductive surroundings, and a kicked-back cocktail crowd of swank professionals. My advice: Skip the dining room, head upstairs, and nosh your way through the appetizer menu.

20 Cosmo Place (off Taylor St., between Post and Sutter sts.). (415/931-3600. Reservations recommended. Main courses $18–$33. AE, DC, MC, V. Sun–Wed 5:30–10pm; Thurs–Sat 5:30–11pm. Valet parking $5 1st hr., $2 each additional ½ hr. Bus: 2, 3, 4, or 27.

MODERATE

Kuleto's ★ ITALIAN   After systematic retrofitting and a face-lift in spring 2002, Kuleto's is back in business as one of downtown's Italian darlings. Muscle a seat at the antipasto bar, and fill up on Italian specialties and selections from the wine list featuring 40 by-the-glass options. Or partake in the likes of penne pasta drenched in tangy lamb-sausage marinara sauce, clam linguine (generously overloaded with fresh clams), or any of the fresh-fish specials grilled over hardwoods in the casually refined dining room. If you don't arrive by 6pm, expect to wait—this place fills up fast.

Impressions

[San Francisco is] the city that knows how.

—Pres. William Howard Taft

[San Francisco is] the city that knows chow.

—Trader Vic, restaurateur

In the Villa Florence Hotel, 221 Powell St. (between Geary and O'Farrell sts.). (415/397-7720. Reservations recommended. Breakfast $5–$10; main courses $10–$20. AE, DC, MC, V. Mon–Fri 7–10:30am; Sat–Sun 8–10:30am; daily 11:30am–11pm. Cable car: Powell-Mason and Powell-Hyde lines. Streetcar: Powell. Bus: 2, 3, 4, or 38.

Millennium ★ VEGAN   Banking on the trend toward lighter, healthier cooking, chef Eric Tucker and his band of merry waiters set out to prove that a meatless menu doesn't mean you have to sacrifice taste. In a narrow, handsome, Parisian-style dining room with checkered tile flooring, French windows, and sponge-painted walls, Millennium has had nothing but favorable reviews for its egg-, butter-, and dairy-free creations since the day it opened. Favorites include sweet-and-spicy plantain torte served over a wonderful papaya and black-bean salsa appetizer, and main courses such as the phyllo purse stuffed with mushrooms, root vegetables, and almond-baked tofu with creamy garlic and corn pudding, or pan-seared black rice risotto cakes stuffed with black Himalayan truffle "butter" over a sherried parsnip and parsley root purée with roasted winter squash, sweet peppers, exotic mushrooms, and sorrel coulis. No need to divert from PC dining with your wine choice—all the selections here are organic.

In the Savoy Hotel, 580 Geary St. (between Taylor and Jones sts.). ✆ 415/487-9800. www.millennium restaurant.com. Reservations recommended. Main courses $13–$19. AE, DC, MC, V. Daily 5–10pm. Valet parking $11. Bus: 38.

Scala's Bistro ⭐ FRENCH/ITALIAN   Firmly entrenched at the base of the refurbished Sir Francis Drake hotel, this downtown favorite blends Parisian-bistro and old-world atmosphere with jovial and bustling results. With just the right balance of elegance and informality, it's a perfect place to have some fun (and apparently most people do).

Of the lovely array of Italian and French dishes, it's worth starting with the "Earth and Surf" calamari appetizer or grilled portobello mushrooms. Golden beet salad and Anchor Steam mussels are also good bets. Generous portions of moist, rich duck-leg confit will satisfy hungry appetites, but if you can order only one thing, make it Scala's signature dish: seared salmon. Resting on a bed of creamy buttermilk mashed potatoes and accented with a tomato, chive, and white-wine sauce, it's downright delicious. Finish with Bostini cream pie, a dreamy combo of vanilla custard and orange chiffon cake with a warm chocolate glaze.

In the Sir Francis Drake hotel, 432 Powell St. (at Sutter St.). ✆ 415/395-8555. Reservations recommended. Breakfast $7–$10; main courses $12–$24 lunch and dinner. AE, DC, DISC, MC, V. Mon–Sun 8am–midnight. Cable car: Powell-Hyde line. Bus: 2, 3, 4, 30, 45, or 76.

INEXPENSIVE

Café Claude ⭐⭐ FRENCH   Euro transplants love Café Claude, a crowded and lively restaurant tucked into a narrow (and very European feeling) side street near Union Square. Seemingly everything—every table, spoon, saltshaker, and waiter—is imported from France. With prices topping out at about $18 on the menu featuring classics like steak tartare, steamed mussels, duck confit salad, escargot, New York steak with spinach gratin and crisp potatoes, and lamb chops with braised baby fennel, leeks, and red-wine garlic jus, Café Claude offers an affordable slice of Paris without leaving the city. There is live jazz on Saturdays from 7:30 to 10:30pm, and atmospheric sidewalk seating is available when the weather permits.

7 Claude Lane (off Sutter St.). ✆ 415/392-3515. www.cafeclaude.com. Reservations recommended. Main courses $12–$18. AE, DC, DISC, MC, V. Mon 11:30am–5:30pm; Tues–Wed 11:30am–10:30pm; Thurs–Fri 11:30am–10:30pm; Sat 11:30am–10pm. Cable car: Powell-Mason and Powell-Hyde lines.

Dottie's True Blue Café ⭐ *Kids* AMERICAN/BREAKFAST   This family-owned breakfast restaurant is one of my favorite downtown diners. It's the kind of place you'd expect to see off Route 66, where most customers are on a first-name basis with the staff and everyone is welcomed with a hearty hello and steaming mug of coffee. Dottie's serves above-average American morning fare (big portions of French toast, pancakes, bacon and eggs, omelets, and the like), delivered to tables laminated with old movie star photos on rugged, diner-quality plates. Whatever you order arrives with delicious homemade bread, muffins, or scones, as well as homemade jelly. There are also daily specials and vegetarian dishes.

In the Pacific Bay Inn, 522 Jones St. (at O'Farrell St.). © **415/885-2767**. Reservations not accepted. Breakfast $5–$10. DISC, MC, V. Wed–Mon 7:30am–3pm. Cable car: Powell-Mason line. Bus: 2, 3, 4, 27, or 38.

Emporio Armani Cafe ✿ ITALIAN   All the hobnobbing of an elite luncheon comes at a moderate price at the Armani Cafe. It's nothing more than a circular counter in the middle of Armani's ever-fashionable (and expensive) clothing store, a few newer tables on a mezzanine, and some crowded sidewalk seats when the weather's right. But the fare and upscale casual atmosphere are enough to lure folks who have only lunch, not a new designer suit, on their minds. Local favorites include the homemade antipasto *misto,* panini, salads, and daily pizza specials. There's also a nice variety of pricey lunch entrees, such as pasta specials, and in case you need a stiff drink after swallowing the steep shopping prices, the bar stays open until 7pm.

1 Grant Ave. (at O'Farrell St., off Market St.). © **415/677-9010**. Reservations not accepted. Main courses $9–$17. AE, DC, DISC, MC, V. Mon–Sat 11:30am–4:30pm; Sun noon–4:30pm. Bus: All Union Square buses.

Mocca ✿ ITALIAN   If you're like me and can't be bothered with a long lunch when there's serious shopping to be done, head to this classic Italian deli on foottraffic-only Maiden Lane. Here it's counter service and cash only for sandwiches, caprese (Italian tomato and mozzarella salad), and big leafy salads. You can enjoy them at the few indoor tables or the pedestrian-only street-front tables shaded by umbrellas, which look onto Union Square.

175 Maiden Lane (at Stockton St.). © **415/956-1188**. Reservations not accepted. Main courses $7–$13. No credit cards. Pastry and coffee daily 9:30am–4:30pm; lunch daily 11am–4:30pm. Bus: All Union Square buses.

Pho Hoa ✿ *(Value* VIETNAMESE   Although it's only a few blocks off of Union Square, the walk to this simple Vietnamese restaurant in the downtrodden Tenderloin District is quite an adventure, often characterized by crack-smoking loiterers (literally) and plenty of people down on their luck. Thing is, the folks along the way are usually friendly enough and the arrival promises huge, killer bowls of Vietnamese soup with all the classic fixings (basil, bean sprouts, and so on) at absurdly low prices. Any of the dozens of selections is a meal in itself, be it my favorite—the seafood soup with rice noodles—or those with beef, chicken, shrimp, or flank steak. There are also plenty of rice dishes—with beef, vegetables, deep-fried egg rolls, or barbecued pork, and intensely strong iced coffee. For a cheap, hearty, but light meal, this is my favorite downtown option, and could be yours, too, provided you can overlook the fact that they use MSG and that the atmosphere is nothing more than clean cafeteria-style.

431 Jones St. (between O'Farrell and Ellis sts.). © **415/673-3163**. Reservations not accepted. Soups and main courses $5.50–$9. No credit cards. Daily 8am–7pm. Bus: 27 or 38.

Sanraku Japanese Restaurant ✿ *(Value* JAPANESE/SUSHI   A perfect combination of great cooked dishes and sushi at bargain prices makes this straightforward, bright, and busy restaurant the best choice for folks hankering for Japanese food. The friendly, hardworking staff does their best to keep up with diners' demands, but the restaurant gets quite busy during lunch when a special box lunch of the likes of a California roll, soup, seaweed salad, deep-fried salmon roll, and beef with noodles with steamed rice comes at a very digestible $8.50. The main menu, which is always available, features truly irresistible sesame chicken with teriyaki sauce and rice; tempura; a vast selection of *nigiri* (raw fish sushi) and rolls;

and delicious combination plates of sushi, sashimi, and teriyaki. Dinner sees brisk business, too, but magically, there always seems to be an available table.

704 Sutter St. (at Taylor St.). ℰ **415/771-0803.** www.sanraku.com. Main courses $6.25–$11 lunch, $10–$21 dinner. AE, DISC, MC, V. Mon–Sat lunch 11am–4pm, dinner 4–10pm; Sun 4–10pm. Cable car: Powell-Mason line. Bus: 2, 3, 4, 27, or 38.

3 Financial District
VERY EXPENSIVE

Aqua ✿✿ SEAFOOD   Without question, Aqua remains San Francisco's finest seafood restaurant, light years beyond the genre of shrimp cocktails and lemon-butter sauce. In 2003, heralded chef Laurent Manrique arrived from Campton Place to preside over the tasty traditions of previous chefs Michael Mina and George Marrone, and he continues to dazzle customers with a bewildering juxtaposition of earth and sea. The ahi tartare—my favorite all-time rendition, period—is mixed tableside with pears, pine nuts, quail egg, and spices. Sculptural grilled medallions of ahi tuna with foie gras in Pinot sauce are beyond decadent. Desserts are equally impressive. The large dining room with high ceilings, one big floral arrangement, and otherwise stark decor can be seriously loud, but that doesn't stop power-lunchers from powwowing by day and well-dressed gourmands from feasting in style at night. Steep prices prevent most people from making a regular appearance, but for special occasions or billable lunches, Aqua is on my top-10 list. Keep in mind that there's no valet or street parking at lunch, so you'll have to pull into one of The Embarcadero lots 2 blocks away.

252 California St. (near Battery). ℰ **415/956-9662.** Reservations recommended. Main courses $29–$39; 5-course tasting menu $90 or $100; vegetarian tasting menu $55. AE, DC, MC, V. Mon–Fri 11:30am–2pm; Mon–Sat 5:30–10:30pm; Sun 5:30–9:30pm. Bus: All Market St. buses.

Rubicon ✿✿ CALIFORNIA-FRENCH   Opened in 1994, Rubicon won instant publicity because of its celebrity backers, who include restaurateurs Drew Nieporent, Robin Williams, Francis Ford Coppola, and Robert De Niro. More than a decade later, the place named after one of Coppola's wines still deserves celebrity status, especially for its famous wine list, which is overseen by internationally renowned master sommelier Larry Stone. Masculine, contemporary, and a bit stark within the bi-level brick building, this is one of the top picks for a loyal clientele of big-business power-lunchers who opt for the three-course $25 lunch. At night, an upscale, middle-aged crowd converges to handpick from the menu or splurge on three- or six-course menus ranging from $45 to $85.

Executive chef Dennis Leary is departing at press time, but no doubt his successor Steuart Brioza will continue the tradition of edible excellence—think gratin of Dungeness crab and ricotta with cauliflower puree and crab-paprika jus; Liberty duck breast and confit with garlic sausage and dried plum-Armagnac sauce; and syrah-braised Kobe beef short ribs with celery root purée, wild mushrooms, and Brussels sprouts. *Hint:* Request a downstairs table if possible; the second floor has less character, although it is quieter.

558 Sacramento St. (between Sansome and Montgomery sts.). ℰ **415/434-4100.** www.sfrubicon.com. Reservations recommended. Main courses $14–$18 lunch, $22–$32 dinner. AE, DC, DISC, MC, V. Wed 11:30am–2:30pm; Mon–Sat 5:30–10:30pm. Valet parking (dinner only, from 6pm) $10. Bus: 1, 15, or 41.

EXPENSIVE

Harbor Village ✿ CHINESE/DIM SUM   This is one of the city's most upscale Chinese restaurants, serving primarily Cantonese dishes, and, during the lunch rush, great dim sum. The courteous staff will guide you through the extensive menu, which includes some 30 seafood dishes, such as striped bass steamed with ginger and scallions. Tasty appetizers include shredded spicy chicken and minced squab in lettuce cups. Stir-fried garlic prawns, beggar's chicken cooked in a clay pot, and sizzling beef in black-pepper sauce are excellent main-course choices. The dim sum lunch, served daily, is definitely worth trying. The waitstaff brings trays filled with steaming-hot appetizers (and will happily explain what they are), and you choose what you like. Try Shanghai-style steamed pork dumplings flavored with ginger and scallions; rice-paper dumplings filled with sweet shrimp; taro cake; or curried beef wonton.

The restaurant offers validated parking at all the Embarcadero Center garages (at the foot of Clay St.). It'll cost you a few dollars on weekdays, but it's free up to 4 hours after 5pm Monday through Friday and all day on weekends and holidays.

4 Embarcadero Center, lobby level (at Drumm St. between Sacramento and Clay sts.). © **415/781-8833.** Reservations recommended. Main courses $10–$35. AE, DC, DISC, MC, V. Mon–Fri 11am–2:30pm; Sat–Sun 10:30am–2:30pm; daily 5:30–9:30pm. Bus: 15, 45, or 76.

Kyo-Ya ✪ JAPANESE/SUSHI   It's anything but cheap, but this restaurant offers an authentic Japanese experience, from the decor to the service to (most assuredly) the tasty sushi (skip the less impressive box lunch). Specialties include the freshest sushi, sashimi, and their elegant fixed-price menu. To start, try any of the appetizers, and move on to the grilled butterfish with miso sauce. Complete dinners include *kobachi* (tiny appetizer of chef's choice), soup, rice, pickles, and dessert. Kyo-Ya gets extra points for serving fresh wasabi, which puts the powdered stuff to shame. Many consider this—along with Kabuto (p. 155)—among the top five sushi restaurants in the city. (Unfortunately—and surprisingly—San Francisco is dreadfully lacking in truly great sushi spots.)

In the Palace Hotel, 2 New Montgomery St. (at Market St.). © **415/546-5090.** www.kyo-ya-restaurant.com. Reservations recommended. Sushi $5–$20; main courses $25–$50 lunch and dinner; 7-course fixed-price menu $75. AE, DC, DISC, MC, V. Tues–Fri 11:30am–2pm; Tues–Sat 6–10pm. Streetcar: All Market St. streetcars. Bus: All Market St. buses.

One Market ✪✪ CALIFORNIA   If you don't mind enormous restaurants, this one, which features a farm-fresh menu, is outstanding thanks to executive chef Adrian Hoffman, who is undoubtedly one of the city's most talented and creative chefs. Amid the airy dining room of banquettes, mahogany, slate floors, seating for 220, and a bar that displays a prominent colorful mural of a market scene, a sea of diners feasts on delights from the ever-changing menu of fresh salads, fish, meat, and game, which manage to be fresh, far more inventive than most dishes around town, and outstanding in flavor. Go headfirst into decadence with the excellent shaved foie gras and hazelnut salad, in which cherries and duck liver brioche create an exciting combination of texture and flavor. Swoon over grilled Sonoma quail with bitter chicory glaze. Or take it over the top with osso buco for two with poached pears, apples, potatoes, and mustard greens. Arrive early to mingle with the corporate crowd that convenes from 4:30 to 7pm for happy hour.

1 Market St. (at Steuart St., across from Justin Herman Plaza). © **415/777-5577.** www.onemarket.com. Reservations recommended. Main courses $19–$31. AE, DC, MC, V. Mon–Fri 11:30am–2pm; Mon–Thurs 5:30–9pm; Fri–Sat 5:30–9pm. Valet parking $10. Bus: All Market St. buses, streetcar, and BART.

The Slanted Door ✪✪ *Finds* VIETNAMESE   This restaurant is so popular that Mick Jagger and former President Clinton made stopovers when they hit town. Why? Despite the sometimes can't-be-bothered staff, the restaurant serves incredibly fresh and flavorful (albeit relatively expensive) Vietnamese food. No doubt it's even more of a hot spot since its April 2004 relocation to its beautiful

---

Finds The Sun on Your Face at Belden Place

San Francisco has always been woefully lacking in the alfresco dining department. One exception is **Belden Place,** an adorable little brick alley in the heart of the Financial District that is open only to foot traffic. When the weather is agreeable, the restaurants that line the alley break out the big umbrellas, tables, and chairs, and voilà—a bit of Paris just off Pine Street.

A handful of adorable cafes line Belden Place and offer a variety of cuisines all at a moderate price. There's **Cafe Bastille,** 22 Belden Place (© **415/986-5673**), a classic French bistro and fun speakeasy basement serving excellent crepes, mussels, and French onion soup; it schedules live jazz on Fridays. **Cafe Tiramisu,** 28 Belden Place (© **415/421-7044**), is a stylish Italian hot spot serving addictive risottos and gnocchi. **Plouf,** 40 Belden Place (© **415/986-6491**), specializes in big bowls of mussels slathered in a choice of seven sauces, as well as fresh seafood. **B44,** 44 Belden Place (© **415/986-6287**), serves up a side order of Spain alongside its revered paella and other seriously zesty Spanish dishes.

Conversely, come at night for a Euro-speakeasy vibe with your dinner.

---

bay-inspired custom-designed space in the Ferry Building Marketplace. But no matter. This is the place to be. Pull up a chair and order anything from clay-pot catfish or amazing green papaya salad to one of the lunch rice dishes, which come in a large ceramic bowl and are topped with such options as grilled shrimp and stir-fried eggplant. Dinner items, which change seasonally, might include beef with garlic and organic onions, grapefruit, and jicama salad. Whatever you order, it's bound to be wholesome, flavorful, and outstanding. There's also an eclectic collection of teas, which come by the pot for $3 to $5.

1 Ferry Plaza (at The Embarcadero and Market). © **415/861-8032**. Reservations recommended. Lunch main courses $8.50–$16; most dinner dishes $9–$27. AE, MC, V. Mon–Sun 11:30am–2:30pm; Sun–Thurs 5:30–10pm; Fri–Sat 5:30–10:30pm. Bus: All Market Street buses. Streetcar: F, N-Judah line.

Tommy Toy's ★★ Finds CHINESE If you want romantic, extravagant Chinese, come to Tommy's: Lavish, dark, unmistakably Asian, and perhaps the only Chinese restaurant where dressing up is apropos, here the dining room is glamorized with mood-lit candelabras and antique paintings. Most days and evenings, the restaurant is crowded with tourists and some locals who come for the fixed-price meals. Not much changes on the French-influenced Chinese menu, but that's fine with the loyalists who return year after year for beautifully presented minced squab in leaves of lettuce; sautéed lobster with mushrooms, chives, and angel-hair crystal noodles; puff-pastry-topped creamy lobster bisque; Peking duck accompanied by lotus buns and sweet-and-tangy plum sauce; beef medallions; and a dessert of fluffy peach mousse. The a la carte menu flaunts vanilla prawns and other delicacies. I've been here twice; once the food was very good, and the next time it was fine. Both times, the portions were substantial and the environment memorable. In any case, their many-course fixed-price "business" lunch is a steal at $23.

655 Montgomery St. (at Clay. and Washington sts.). © **415/397-4888**. www.tommytoys.com. Reservations recommended. Main courses $17–$23; fixed-price dinner $58–$65. AE, DC, DISC, MC, V. Mon–Fri 11:30am–2:30pm; daily 5:30–9:30pm. Valet parking (dinner only) $5. Bus: 9AX, 9BX, 12, 15, or 41.

The Waterfront Restaurant CALIFORNIA   Bay Bridge views, a sunny patio, a sleek industrial-chic dining room, and great food made the Waterfront an instant hit after its renovation and reopening in late 1997. Unfortunately, the parade of chefs in and out of the kitchen has made a sure thing more of an interesting gamble. Still, the nautical atmosphere alone can induce idyllic San Francisco memories—especially when seated outdoors on a sunny day. Fortunately, the menu's now trying to stick with safe classics such as Dungeness crab cakes (yum); sautéed chicken breast with herbed polenta, spinach, and truffle rosemary pan sauce; and salads, pizzas, and wood-fired grill items. The wine list is fine and includes many selections starting at a very affordable $20. Brunch is served on Sundays.

Pier 7 (on The Embarcadero near Broadway). ℰ 415/391-2696. www.waterfrontsf.com. Reservations recommended. Main courses $18–$30. AE, DC, DISC, MC, V. Mon–Sat 11:30am–10pm; Sun 10:30am–10pm. Valet parking $5. Streetcar: F.

MODERATE

Kokkari ✦✦✦ *Finds* GREEK/MEDITERRANEAN   It figures that it would take a French chef to make Greek food fabulous, and executive chef Jean Alberti (the mastermind behind the moussaka) who departed in early 2004, did exactly that. Thankfully, he left his secret recipes behind, and at least for the meantime, Kokkari (Ko-*car*-ee) is still wonderful in fashion and flavor. The love affair starts with the setting: a beautifully rustic living room–like dining area with a commanding fireplace and oversize furnishings. Past the tiny bar, the other main room is pure rustic revelry with exposed wood beams, pretty standing lamps, and a view of the glass-enclosed private dining room. Then there are the traditional Aegean dishes. Start with *pikilia* (a sampling of traditional Greek spreads served with dolmades) or fabulous baby octopus salad. Try not to overindulge before the main courses, which include grilled whole striped bass with braised greens and lemon-oregano vinaigrette, to-die-for moussaka (eggplant, lamb, potato, and béchamel) and braised lamb shank over orzo. Take my advice and don't leave without sinking your fork into whichever chocolate dessert they're featuring; you'll thank me later.

200 Jackson St. (at Front St.). ℰ 415/981-0983. www.kokkari.com. Reservations recommended. Main courses $14–$23 lunch, $19–$35 dinner. AE, DC, DISC, MC, V. Lunch Mon–Fri 11:30am–2:30pm; bar menu 2:30–5:30pm; dinner Mon–Thurs 5:30–10pm, Fri 5:30–11pm, Sat 5–11pm. Valet parking (dinner only) $8. Bus: 12, 15, 41, or 83.

Sam's Grill & Seafood Restaurant ✦ *Finds* SEAFOOD   Power-lunching at Sam's is a San Francisco tradition, and Sam's has done a brisk business with Financial District suits since—get this—1867. Even if you're not carrying a briefcase, this is the place to come for time-capsule dining at its most classically San Francisco. Pass the crowded entrance and small bar to get to the main dining room—packed with virtually all men—kick back, and watch yesteryear happen today. (Or conversely, slither into a curtained booth and see nothing but your dining companion.) Tuxedo-clad waiters race around, doling out big crusty cuts of sourdough bread and distributing salads overflowing with fresh crab and Roquefort vinaigrette, towering plates of seafood pasta with marinara, charbroiled fish, roasted chicken, and old-school standbys like calves' liver with bacon and onions or Salisbury steak. Don't worry—they didn't forget classic creamed spinach. The restaurant's mildly salty service and good old-fashioned character make everything on the menu taste that much better.

374 Bush St. (between Montgomery and Kearny sts.). ℰ 415/421-0594. www.samsgrill.citysearch.com. Reservations recommended for dinner and for 6 or more at lunch. Main courses $9–$24. AE, DC, DISC, MC, V. Mon–Fri 11am–9pm. Bus: 15, 45, or 76.

Tadich Grill ⭑⭑ *Finds* SEAFOOD   Not that the veteran restaurant needed more reason to be beloved, but the city's ongoing loss of local institutions makes 156-year-old Tadich the last of a long-revered dying breed. This business began as a coffee stand during the 1849 gold rush and claims to be the very first to broil seafood over mesquite charcoal, in the early 1920s. An old-fashioned power-dining restaurant to the core, Tadich boasts its original mahogany bar, which extends the length of the restaurant, and seven curtained booths for private powwows. Big plates of sourdough bread top the tables.

You won't find fancy California cuisine here. The novella-like menu features a slew of classic salads, such as sliced tomato with Dungeness crab or prawn Louis; daily specials; meats and fish from the charcoal broiler; grilled items; and casseroles. Hot dishes include baked avocado with shrimp Diablo; baked casserole of stuffed turbot with crab and shrimp à la Newburg; charcoal-broiled steaks; and petrale sole with butter sauce, a local favorite. Plus, almost everyone orders a side of big, tasty french fries.

240 California St. (between Battery and Front sts.). (C) **415/391-1849.** Reservations not accepted. Main courses $14–$20. MC, V. Mon–Fri 11am–9:30pm; Sat 11:30am–9:30pm. Streetcar: All Market St. streetcars. BART: Embarcadero. Bus: All Market St. buses.

Yank Sing ⭑⭑ CHINESE/DIM SUM   Loosely translated as "a delight of the heart," cavernous Yank Sing is the best dim sum restaurant in the downtown area. Confident, experienced servers take the nervousness out of novices—they're good at guessing your gastric threshold as they wheel carts carrying small plates of exotic dishes past each table. Most dim sum dishes are dumplings, filled with tasty concoctions of pork, beef, fish, or vegetables. *Congees* (porridges), spare ribs, stuffed crab claws, scallion pancakes, shrimp balls, pork buns, and other palate-pleasers complete the menu. While the food is delicious, the location makes this the most popular tourist spot and weekday lunch spot; at other times, residents generally head to Ton Kiang (p. 156), the undisputed top choice for these Chinese delicacies. A second location, open during weekdays for lunch only, is at 49 Stevenson St., off First Street ((C) **415/541-4949**).

101 Spear St. (at Mission St. at Rincon Center). (C) **415/957-9300.** Dim sum $2.80–$4.50 for 2–4 pieces. AE, DC, MC, V. Mon–Fri 11am–3pm; Sat–Sun 10am–4pm. Free validated parking in Rincon Center Garage on weekends. Cable car: California St. line. Streetcar: F. Bus: 1, 12, 14, or 41; BART.

4 SoMa

For a map of restaurants in this section, see the "Dining Around Town" map on p. 122.

VERY EXPENSIVE

bacar ⭑⭑ AMERICAN BRASSERIE   No other dining room makes wine as integral to the meal as popular bacar. Up to 250 eclectic, fashionable diners pack into this warehouse-restaurant's three distinct areas—the casual (loud) downstairs salon, the bustling bar and loud mezzanine, or the more quiet upstairs, which looks down on the mezzanine's action—for chef Arnold Eric Wong's "American Brasserie" (that is, French bistro with a California twist) cuisine. I'm a fan of the creamy salt-cod and crab *brandade* (purée) and zesty roasted mussels with a chile-and-garlic sauce that begs to be soaked up by the accompanying grilled bread. Ditto the braised beef short ribs. Just as much fun is the wine selection, which gives you 1,300 choices. Around 100 come by the glass, 2-ounce pour, or 250- or 500-milliliter decanter, and wine director Debbie Zachareas is often available to introduce you to new and exciting options. (She

Dining Around Town

A. Sabella's **49**
A16 **6**
Absinthe **34**
Ace Wasabi's
  Rock 'n' Roll Sushi **3**
Alioto's **48**
Ana Mandara **45**
Andalé Mexican
  Restaurant **4**
AsiaSF **63**
Aziza **18**
bacar **61**
Beach Chalet Brewery
  & Restaurant **19**
Boulevard **57**
Cafe Kati **16**
Cafe Pescatore **50**
Caffè Luna Piena **25**
Cha Cha Cha **67**
Chez Nous **14**
Chow **27**
Cliff House **17**
Delfina **29**
E'Angelo Restaurant **5**
Ebisu **20**
The Elite Café **13**
Eliza's **11**
Ella's **11**
Eos **67**
Firewood Café **24**
Florio **14**
Fog City Diner **53**
Forbes Island **51**
Foreign Cinema **32**
Frjtz Fries **46**
The Golden Turtle **40**
Gordon Biersch Brewery
  Restaurant **59**
Greens Restaurant **1**
Hard Rock Cafe **52**
Harris' **39**
Hayes Street Grill **35**
House of Prime Rib **38**
Isa **2**
Jardinière **36**

Kabuto A&S **11**
Khan Toke Thai
  House **11**
La Folie **42**
La Méditerranée **12**
Long Life Noodle
  Company &
  Jook Joint **58**
The Mandarin **44**
Manora's **65**
Mecca **28**
Mel's Diner **9**
MoMo's **61**
Pane e Vino **10**
Park Chow **20**
Pauline's **26**
Piperade **54**
PlumpJack Café **8**
Pluto's **7**
Quince **15**
The Ramp **60**
Restaurant
  Gary Danko **46**
RNM **21**
San Francisco Art
  Institute Café **43**
Scoma's **47**
The Slanted Door **56**
Straits Café **18**
Swan Oyster Depot **37**
Sweet Heat **69**
Tablespoon **41**
Taquerias
  La Cumbre **31**
Thanh Long **23**
Thep Phanom **22**
Ti Couz **30**
Ton Kiang **18**
Tú Lan **63**
2223 Restaurant
  & Bar **26**
Universal Café **66**
The Waterfront
  Restaurant **55**
Zuni Café **33**

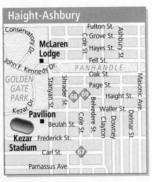

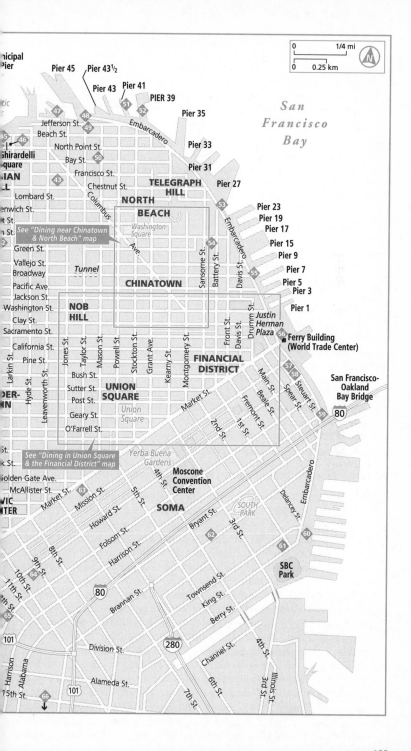

Municipal Pier

Pier 45 Pier 43½ Pier 41

Pier 43 PIER 39

Pier 35

Pier 33

Pier 31

Pier 27

Jefferson St.

Beach St.

North Point St.

Bay St.

Francisco St.

Chestnut St.

Lombard St.

Greenwich St.

Green St.

Vallejo St.

Broadway

Pacific Ave.

Jackson St.

Washington St.

Clay St.

Sacramento St.

California St.

Pine St.

Bush St.

Sutter St.

Post St.

Geary St.

O'Farrell St.

San Francisco Bay

Embarcadero

Ghirardelli Square

RUSSIAN HILL

TELEGRAPH HILL

NORTH BEACH

Washington Square

Columbus

Ave.

Tunnel

CHINATOWN

NOB HILL

FINANCIAL DISTRICT

UNION SQUARE

Union Square

Market St.

Pier 23
Pier 19
Pier 17
Pier 15
Pier 9
Pier 7
Pier 5
Pier 3
Pier 1

Sansome St.

Battery St.

Davis St.

Embarcadero

Front St.

Davis St.

Drumm St.

Justin Herman Plaza

Ferry Building (World Trade Center)

San Francisco-Oakland Bay Bridge

Main St.

Beale St.

Fremont St.

1st St.

2nd St.

Spear St.

Steuart St.

80

Jones St.

Taylor St.

Mason St.

Powell St.

Stockton St.

Grant Ave.

Kearny St.

Montgomery St.

Larkin St.

Hyde St.

Leavenworth St.

TENDER-LOIN

See "Dining near Chinatown & North Beach" map

See "Dining in Union Square & the Financial District" map

Golden Gate Ave.

McAllister St.

CIVIC CENTER

Market St.

Mission St.

Howard St.

Folsom St.

Harrison St.

9th St.

10th St.

11th St.

8th St.

80

Brannan St.

101

Harrison

Alabama

15th St.

101

Division St.

Alameda St.

Yerba Buena Gardens

Moscone Convention Center

SOMA

4th St.

5th St.

Bryant St.

3rd St.

Townsend St.

King St.

Berry St.

Channel St.

SOUTH PARK

SBC Park

Delancey St.

Embarcadero

280

7th St.

6th St.

4th St.

3rd St.

Illinois St.

0 ¼ mi

0 0.25 km

also periodically offers half off on every bottle on Mondays, during which restaurant staff from around the city converge to splurge.) If you want a festive night out, this is the place to come—especially when jazz is playing Monday through Saturday evenings.

448 Brannan St. (at Third St.). ℂ 415/904-4100. www.bacarsf.com. Reservations recommended. Main courses lunch $14–$17, dinner $22–$38. AE, DC, DISC, MC, V. Sun 5:30–11pm; Mon–Thurs and Sat 5:30pm–midnight; Fri 11:30am–2:30pm and 5:30pm–midnight. Valet parking (Mon–Sat beginning at 6pm) $10. Bus: 15, 30, 45, 76, or 81.

Boulevard ★★ *Finds* AMERICAN   Master restaurant designer Pat Kuleto and chef Nancy Oaks teamed up to create one of San Francisco's most revered restaurants, and although it made its debut in 1993, it's still one of my—and the city's—all-time favorites.

The dramatically artistic Belle Epoque interior, with vaulted brick ceilings, floral banquettes, a mosaic floor, and tulip-shaped lamps, is the setting for Oaks's equally impressive sculptural and mouthwatering dishes. Starters alone could make a perfect meal, especially if you indulge in sweetbreads wrapped in prosciutto on watercress and Lola Rose lettuce, with garlic croutons and whole-grain mustard vinaigrette; Sonoma foie gras with elderberry syrup, toast, and Bosc pear salad; or Maine sea scallops on garlic mashed potato croustade with truffle and portobello mushroom relish. The nine or so main courses are equally creative and might include pan-roasted miso-glazed sea bass with asparagus salad, Japanese rice, and shiitake mushroom broth; or spit-roasted cider-cured pork loin with sweet potato–swirled mashed potatoes and sautéed baby red chard. Vegetarian items, such as wild-mushroom risotto with fresh chanterelles and Parmesan, are also offered. Three levels of formality—bar, open kitchen, and main dining room—keep things from getting too snobby. Although steep prices prevent most from making Boulevard a regular gig, you'd be hard-pressed to find a better place for a special, fun-filled occasion. Cocktailers: Do ask the bartender about the special martinis—they're some of the best in town.

1 Mission St. (between The Embarcadero and Steuart sts.). ℂ 415/543-6084. Reservations recommended. Main courses $9–$17 lunch, $24–$32 dinner. AE, DC, DISC, MC, V. Mon–Fri 11:30am–2:15pm; Sun–Thurs 5:30–10pm; Fri–Sat 5:30–10:30pm. Valet parking $12 lunch, $10 dinner. Bus: 15, 30, 32, or 45.

Fifth Floor Restaurant ★★★ FRENCH   Executive chef Laurent Gras made his way through Michelin-star restaurants in France, spent 5 years as chef de cuisine at Restaurant Alain Ducasse, and forged his own ground at the Waldorf Astoria's Peacock Alley before wowing diners at this swank French spot. Like the decor—rich colors and fabrics, red leather and velvet banquettes, Frette linens, zebra-striped carpeting, and a clublike atmosphere—Gras's menu is luxurious. But it's his creativity and attention to detail that makes this place one of the city's top restaurants. Here nearly everything is original and incredibly well executed—from an avocado dome hiding a mound of crabmeat brought to life with jalapeño and basil to "Lobster cappuccino," a lobster broth emulsified with chestnuts, prawns, and sautéed lobster. Main courses, like veal tournedos caramelized with sweetbread, black-pepper *jus*, and braised potato; or slow-baked lamb with truffle, pistachio, and olives with steamed cabbage, are also precisely prepared. The wine program also reigns, with one of the most prestigious and expensive lists around and a professional team to serve it. To see where this restaurant falls on a map, see the "Dining in Union Square & the Financial District" map on p. 113.

In the Hotel Palomar, 12 Fourth St. (at Market St.). ℂ 415/348-1555. www.fifthfloor.citysearch.com. Reservations required. Main courses $31–$65; tasting menu $95. AE, DC, DISC, MC, V. Mon–Wed 5:30–9:30pm; Thurs–Sat 5:30–10pm. Valet parking $12. Bus: All Market St. buses.

EXPENSIVE

MoMo's AMERICAN   With an abundance of patio seating, a huge swank-yet-casual dining room, and proximity to SBC Park baseball stadium, festive MoMo's hits a home run if you're headed to a Giants game, but is not a destination in itself. On the patio and in the bar, snack foods, like greasy-good thin-sliced onion rings, refreshing seared ahi salad, good old french fries, a-okay thin-crust pizza, and awesome burgers, and crowds of sports enthusiasts, make this place fun, if not a little claustrophobic. Come sundown, there are dozens of other restaurants where I'd prefer to spend my money. But singles appreciate the bar after work, and the dining room welcomes an eclectic mix of sports fans (midseason) and white-collar workers, many of whom are likely to start their lunch or dinner with a martini before indulging in braised short ribs or New York steak. If you're headed here on game day, make a reservation or arrive early, because party people form a line around the block to get in and it's no fun trying to eat standing at the bar or wrestling for one of the coveted patio tables.

760 Second St. (at King St.). ✆ 415/227-8660. www.sfmomos.com. Reservations recommended. Main courses $10–$29. AE, MC, V. Daily 11:30am–10pm. Valet parking $8 lunch, $11 dinner, $20 game hours. Streetcar: F and N. Bus: 15, 30, 45, or 80x.

Town Hall ✰ AMERICAN   Mitchell and Steven Rosenthal (Postrio) and front man Doug Washington (One, Vertigo, Jardiniere, and Postrio) are behind this SoMa warehouse hot spot, which opened at the end of 2003, featuring an attractive and rustically glitzy interior (brick, windows, airy, communal tables) and huge portions of hearty American regional cuisine. The homey food's good, but during my visits the menu tended to play it safe (think cioppino; grilled chicken with caramelized shallot mashed potatoes, banger sausage, and mustard herb jus; wild mushroom lasagna with salsa verde; and grilled rib-eye with hash brown potatoes, creamed leeks, and brown-butter garlic sauce). That said, everything was well done and butterscotch and the chocolate pot de creme by Janet Rikala Dalton astounded. There's definitely a scene here, so if you want a side of schmoozing with your dinner, this is your place. *Note:* A light menu is served between lunch and dinner.

342 Howard St. (at Fremont St.). ✆ 415/908-3900. www.townhallsf.com. Reservations recommended. Main courses $10–$17 lunch, $16–$25 dinner. AE, MC, V. Mon–Thurs 11:30am–10pm; Fri 11:30am–11pm; Sat 5:30–11pm; Sun 5:30–10pm. Bus: 10 or 76.

MODERATE

Gordon Biersch Brewery Restaurant CALIFORNIA   Popular with the young Republican crowd (loose ties and tight skirts predominate), this modern, two-tiered brewery and restaurant eschews traditional brewpub fare—no spicy chicken wings on this menu—in an attempt to attract a more upscale clientele. And it works. Goat cheese ravioli is a bestseller, followed by the herb-roasted half-chicken with garlic mashed potatoes. Start with the delicate and crunchy calamari *fritti* appetizer or, if you're a garlic hound, the tangy Caesar salad. Most dishes can be paired with one of the brewery's lagers. Couples bent on a quiet, romantic dinner can skip this place; when the lower-level bar fills up, you practically have to shout to be heard. Beer-lovers who want to pair their suds with decent grub will be quite content.

2 Harrison St. (on The Embarcadero). ✆ 415/243-8246. www.gordonbiersch.com. Reservations recommended. Main courses $9.50–$20. AE, DC, DISC, MC, V. Sun–Tues 11:30am–11pm; Wed–Thurs 11:30am–midnight; Fri–Sat 11am–2am. Bus: 32.

INEXPENSIVE

AsiaSF ✮ ASIAN/CALIFORNIA Part restaurant, part gender-illusionist musical revue, AsiaSF manages to be completely entertaining and extremely high-quality. As you're entertained by Asian men—dressed as women—who lip-sync show tunes, you can nibble on excellent grilled shrimp and herb salad; baby-back pork ribs with honey tamarind glaze, pickled carrots, and sweet-potato crisps; or filet mignon with Korean dipping sauce, miso eggplant, and fried potato stars. The full bar, *Wine Spectator* award–winning wine list, and sake list add to the festivities. Fortunately, the food and the atmosphere are as colorful as the staff, which means a night here is more than a meal—it's a very happening event.

201 Ninth St. (at Howard St.). ℂ 415/255-2742. www.asiasf.com. Reservations recommended. Main courses $9–$19. AE, DISC, MC, V ($25 minimum). Sun–Thurs 6–10pm; Fri–Sat 5–10pm. Streetcar: Civic Center on underground streetcar. BART: Civic Center. Bus: 9, 12, or 47.

Long Life Noodle Company & Jook Joint ✮ NOODLES The concept at sleek Long Life is to offer a wide range of unfamiliar noodle dishes from China, Korea, Japan, and other Asian lands and serve them in a familiar Westernized setting (in this case, a supermodern space with lots of neon and Plexiglas). The problem is choosing from the 30 or so noodle dishes, all of which are wildly different. Do you go with Buddha's Bliss (ramen noodles in miso broth with smoked trout, tofu, and enoki mushrooms) or Enchanted Heat (a "Chinese hangover cure" composed of whole-wheat noodles, lily pods, tree ears, and secret healing ginseng herbs)? I recommend Ghengis' Buns, crisp sesame biscuits filled with Chinese roast beef, cucumber, cilantro, and hoisin sauce. Wash it all down with Cool Cucumber Juice or Ginseng Ginger Ale. Another branch is in the Metreon food court (101 Fourth St.; ℂ 415/369-6188).

139 Steuart St. (near Mission St.). ℂ 415/281-3818. Reservations recommended. Main courses $6.50–$8.50. MC, V. Mon–Fri 11:30am–9pm. Bus: 15, 30, 32, or 45.

Manora's ✮ THAI Manora's cranks out some of the best Thai food in town and is well worth a jaunt to SoMa. But this is no relaxed affair: It's perpetually packed (unless you come early), and you'll be seated sardinelike at one of the cramped but well-appointed tables. During the dinner rush, the noise level can make conversation among larger parties almost impossible, but the food is so darned good, you'll probably prefer to turn toward your plate and stuff your face. Start with a Thai iced tea or coffee and tangy soup or chicken satay, which comes with decadent peanut sauce. Follow these with any of the wonderful dinner dishes—which should be shared—and a side of rice. There are endless options, including a vast array of vegetarian plates. Every remarkably flavorful dish arrives seemingly seconds after you order it, which is great if you're hungry, a bummer if you were planning a long, leisurely dinner. *Tip:* Come before 7pm or after 9pm if you don't want a loud, rushed meal.

1600 Folsom St. (at 12th St.). ℂ 415/861-6224. Reservations recommended for 4 or more. Main courses $7–$12. MC, V. Mon–Fri 11:30am–2:30pm; Mon–Sat 5:30–10:30pm; Sun 5–10pm. Bus: 9, 12, or 47.

Tú Lan ✮ VIETNAMESE Only adventurous foodies interested in a cheap, midday snack need to read this review. You'll have to brave the winos, weirdos, and street stench to get to this total dive in an unsavory neighborhood bordering Union Square and SoMa, but I do it happily to get my hands on the best imperial rolls on the planet. Alas, the atmosphere inside isn't much better—it's about as greasy as greasy spoons get, and if you head to the upstairs bathroom you might even catch an unsavory glimpse of kitchen staff hovering over mounds of ground meat meant for tonight's dinner piled high on a banquet table. But once I get a bite of the crisp, thick imperial rolls, which are served over rice noodles and accompanied by lettuce, mint, peanuts, and a yummy dipping sauce, I could care less. There's also a good selection of stir-fried rice plates—including awesome barbecued pork, which can be washed down with intense iced coffee. In any case, you'll feel brave just eating here, where I have, on one occasion, shared my table with a cockroach.

8 Sixth St. (at Market St.). © 415/626-0927. Reservations not accepted. Main courses $4–$7.50. No credit cards. Mon–Sat 11am–9pm. Cable car: Powell-Mason and Powell-Hyde lines. Streetcar: F, J, K, L, M, or N. Bus: 6, 7, 27, 31, 66, or 71.

5 Nob Hill/Russian Hill

For a map of restaurants in this section, see the "Dining Around Town" map on p. 122.

VERY EXPENSIVE

Charles Nob Hill ★★★ CALIFORNIA-FRENCH Considering executive chef Melissa Perello's mind-blowing contemporary French cuisine, it's no surprise that the 28-year-old prodigy was nominated for the culinary equivalent of an Academy Award (the James Beard Award) in 2004. Everything at this formal spot is flawless—from the two small (and almost too intimate) old-world club-like dining rooms swathed in dark woods and mirrors and flanked by comfy banquettes to the daily changing menu, adventurous wine list, and friendly and well-informed staff. It's so unusually quiet here that it'd be easy to eavesdrop on diners across the room, but Perello's food is so divine it's impossible to focus on anything else. Roasted baby beet carpaccio redefines the elegance of simplicity with a crunch of toasted pistachio, bite of goat cheese, and surrounding drops of 100-year-old balsamic vinegar. A simple salad reaches celestial status with fresh winter greens, sautéed chicken liver, bacon, shallots, and banyuls vinegar. Entrees, too, command attention—from the medallion of veal with caramelized cauliflower, black trumpet mushrooms, and veal sweetbread ragout to braised lamb shank scented with orange and star anise with black mission fig and creamy polenta. For serious food lovers, this is a must-try.

1250 Jones St. (at Clay St.). © 415-771-5400. www.charlesnh.com. Reservations recommended. Main courses $28–39, fixed-price menus $58–$90. AE, DISC, DC, MV, V. Wed–Sun 5:30–9:30pm. Closed Mon–Tues. Valet parking: $8. Bus: 1. Cable car: California.

La Folie ★★ *Finds* FRENCH My mother and I call this unintimidating, cozy, intimate French restaurant "the house of foie gras." Why? Because on our first visit, virtually every dish overflowed with the ultrarich delicacy. But in truth, there's more to chef Roland Passot's fantastic three-, four-, and five-course menus. Like what? Melt-in-your-mouth starters such as roast quail and—drum roll, please—foie gras with salad, wild mushrooms, and roasted garlic. Generous main courses include rôti of quail and squab stuffed with wild mushrooms and wrapped in crispy potato strings; and roast venison with vegetables, quince, and huckleberry sauce. The country-French decor is undergoing a remodel as this book goes to press, but no doubt the room will remain tasteful but not too serious. The staff is friendly, knowledgeable, and accommodating, and the food is outstanding. Best of all, the environment is relaxed, comfortable, and very neighborhoody. Finish with any of the delectable desserts. If you're not into the tasting menu, don't be deterred; the restaurant tells me they'll happily price out individual items.

2316 Polk St. (between Green and Union sts.). ✆ 415/776-5577. www.lafolie.com. Reservations recommended. 3-course tasting menu $60; 4-course tasting menu $75; 5-course chef's tasting menu $85; vegetar-
ian tasting menu $60. AE, DC, DISC, MC, V. Mon–Sat 5:30–10pm. Bus: 19, 41, 45, 47, 49, or 76.

EXPENSIVE

House of Prime Rib ★★ STEAKHOUSE   Anyone who loves a huge slab of
meat and old-school–style dining will feel right at home at this shrine to prime
(rib). It's a fun and ever-packed affair within the men's clublike dining rooms
(fireplaces included), where drinks are stiff, waiters are loose, and all the beef is
roasted in rock salt, sliced tableside, and served with salad dramatically tossed
tableside, followed by creamed spinach and either a baked potato and Yorkshire
pudding, which accompany the entree. To placate the occasional non-meat
eater, they offer a fish-of-the-day special. Another bonus: kids prime rib dinners
are a paltry $8.95.

1906 Van Ness Ave. (near Washington St.). ✆ 415/885-4605. Reservations recommended. Complete dinners $24–$30. AE, DC, MC, V. Mon–Thurs 5:30–10pm; Fri–Sat 5–10pm; Sun 4–10pm. Valet parking: $6. Bus:
47 or 49.

Tablespoon ★★ AMERICAN   Barely wider than the stem of the utensil for
which it's named, this tightly packed neighborhood restaurant ladles out such
tasty and well-priced New American cuisine that no one seems to mind sitting
practically elbow-to-elbow in the narrow dining room, the rather loud acoustics,
or wait for a table—sometimes despite a reservation. The winning recipe is a
savvy mix of casually sophisticated food and semiswank surroundings by co-
owners chef Robert Riescher (previously of Central California's renowned Erna's
Elderberry House) and frontman John Jasso who worked the crowds at destination restaurants Gary Danko and Fifth Floor. Like most hot spots these days, the
menu highlights small plates (as well as entrees), but its selections are seasoned
with uncommon panache, such as winter items like creamy white-bean soup with
decadent duck croquettes, delicate ahi tuna carpaccio with fennel salad and
Meyer lemon vinaigrette, and hearty roast duck breast and confit leg with braised
red cabbage, root veggies, and spätzle. If you're looking to taste your way through
an affordable meal surrounded by locals, this is one of the best places to do it.

2209 Polk St. (between Vallejo and Green sts.). ✆ 415/268-0140. Reservations recommended. Main courses
$17–$23. Mon–Sat 6pm–midnight; Sun 5–10pm. Bus: 19, 36, 41, or 45.

MODERATE

Swan Oyster Depot ★★ *Finds* SEAFOOD   Turning 93 years old in 2005,
Swan Oyster Depot is a classic San Francisco dining experience you shouldn't
miss. Opened in 1912, this tiny hole-in-the-wall, run by the city's friendliest
servers, is little more than a narrow fish market that decided to slap down some
bar stools. There are only 20 or so seats here, jammed cheek-by-jowl along a
long marble bar. Most patrons come for a quick cup of chowder or a plate of
oysters on the half shell that arrive chilling on crushed ice. The menu is limited
to fresh crab, shrimp, oyster, clam cocktails, Maine lobster, and Boston-style
clam chowder, all of which are exceedingly fresh. *Note:* Don't let the lunchtime
line dissuade you—it moves fast.

1517 Polk St. (between California and Sacramento sts.). ✆ 415/673-1101. Reservations not accepted.
Seafood cocktails $7–$15; clams and oysters on the half shell $7–$7.50 per half-dozen. No credit cards.
Mon–Sat 8am–5:30pm. Bus: 19.

INEXPENSIVE

The Golden Turtle ★ VIETNAMESE   The unfussy and casual Golden Turtle is widely regarded as one of the city's best Vietnamese restaurants, a far cry

better than the typical *pho* noodle houses that have recently sprung up all over the place. In a converted Victorian home on a busy stretch of Van Ness, the restaurant's elaborate carved-wood paneling creates a romantic ambience. Recommended dishes are five-spice roasted chicken; clay-pot spare ribs; imperial rolls with minced pork, prawn, and crab; and any of the seasonal crab dishes. There are lots of vegetarian options, too.

2211 Van Ness Ave. (between Broadway and Vallejo St.). ℂ **415/441-4419**. www.goldenturtle.net. Reservations recommended. Most main courses $9–$14. AE, DISC, MC, V. Tues–Sun 5–11pm. Closed Dec 25–30. Free validated parking on weekends. Bus: 38 or 45.

6 Chinatown

For a map of restaurants in this section, see the "Dining near Chinatown & North Beach" map on p. 131.

INEXPENSIVE

Brandy Ho's Hunan Food ★ *Kids* CHINESE   Fancy black-and-white granite tabletops and a large, open kitchen give you the first clue that the food at this casual and fun restaurant is a cut above the usual Hunan fare. Take my advice and start immediately with fried dumplings (in sweet-and-sour sauce) or cold chicken salad and then move on to fish-ball soup with spinach, bamboo shoots, noodles, and other goodies. The best main course is Three Delicacies, a combination of scallops, shrimp, and chicken with onion, bell pepper, and bamboo shoots, seasoned with ginger, garlic, and wine, and served with black-bean sauce. Most dishes are quite hot and spicy, but the kitchen will adjust the level to meet your specifications. A full bar includes Asian-food–friendly libations like plum wine and sake from 11:30am to 11pm.

217 Columbus Ave. (at Pacific Ave.). ℂ **415/788-7527**. www.brandyhos.com. Reservations recommended. Main courses $8–$13. AE, DC, DISC, MC, V. Sun–Thurs 11:30am–11pm; Fri–Sat 11:30am–midnight. Bus: 15 or 41.

House of Nanking ★ CHINESE   This place would be strictly a tourist joint if it weren't for the die-hard fans who happily wait—sometimes up to an hour—for a coveted seat at this inconspicuous little restaurant serving Shanghai-style cuisine. Order the requisite pot stickers, green-onion-and-shrimp pancakes with peanut sauce, or any number of pork, rice, beef, seafood, chicken, or vegetable dishes from the menu, but I suggest you trust the waiter when he recommends a special. Even with an expansion that doubled the available space, seating is tight, so prepare to be bumped around a bit and don't expect perky or attentive service—it's all part of the Nanking experience.

919 Kearny St. (at Columbus Ave.). ℂ **415/421-1429**. Reservations accepted for groups of 8 or more. Main courses $6–$12. MC, V. Mon–Fri 11am–10pm; Sat–Sun noon–10pm. Bus: 9, 12, 15, or 30.

R&G Lounge ★★ CHINESE   It's tempting to take your chances and duck into any of the exotic restaurants in Chinatown, but if you want a sure thing, go directly to the two-story R&G Lounge. During lunch, both recently modernized floors are packed with hungry neighborhood workers who go straight for the $5 rice-plate specials. Even then, you can order from the dinner menu, which features legendary deep-fried salt-and-pepper crab (a little too greasy and rich for my taste); and delicious chicken with black-bean sauce. A personal favorite is melt-in-your-mouth R&G Special Beef, which explodes with the tangy flavor of the accompanying sauce. I was less excited by the tired chicken salad, house specialty noodles, and bland spring rolls. But that was just fine since I saved room for generous and savory seafood in a clay pot and delicious classic roast duck.

Kids The Best of San Francisco's Family-Friendly Restaurants

Andalé Taqueria (p. 144)   So casual, so inexpensive, and offering lots of options, you can feed the whole clan here—and fit them comfortably in the dining room or on the patio.

Beach Chalet Brewery & Restaurant (p. 154)   You can relax and enjoy house-made beers and snacks while the kids peer at the ocean through picture windows or check out the Beach Chalet historic displays downstairs.

Brandy Ho's Hunan Food (p. 129)   So long as the kids like Chinese food, they're welcome in this bustling, casual dining room.

Cliff House (p. 155)   The folks at this oceanfront multiplex of restaurants are used to churning out fast meals for tourists with kids in tow.

Dottie's True Blue Café (p. 115)   It's a cramped, casual breakfast spot with lots of items to tempt the tots.

Eliza's (p. 145)   Serving some of the most flavorful and vibrant California-influenced Chinese food in town, Eliza's is fun for the whole family. Parents will love the quality of the cuisine and the casual surroundings that make it okay for the kids to really get into their meal. Kids will also get a kick out of the whimsical art-glass around the dining room.

Ella's (p. 142)   Provided your kids are patient enough to wait in the ever-growing line for the best breakfast in town, they'll be thrilled with the offerings in this bright, cheery, and bustling Pacific Heights restaurant—especially when they get their huge stack of yummy pancakes.

Hard Rock Cafe (p. 140)   You know the drill: Loud music, pseudohip environs, and kid-friendly fare.

Mel's Diner (p. 145)   A 1950s-style diner with all the trappings (think shakes, burgers, fries, and 25¢ jukeboxes), this family-friendly spot gives tots Crayons and coloring-book pages.

Mo's Gourmet Burgers (p. 136)   Perfect for everyone, it's got killer burgers and a very low-key atmosphere.

Pane e Vino (p. 143)   It's the accommodating staff at this neighborhood Italian restaurant that makes it a good spot to take the kids. Plus their menu is classic Italian, which means there are plenty of inoffensive offerings for the tots in tow.

Pasta Pomodoro (p. 136)   Cheap, fast, and informal is the perfect recipe for a tasty Italian dining experience.

Tomasso's (p. 137)   You can satisfy the kids' (and your) pizza craving at this small North Beach joint, which is known to serve the best brick-oven baked pies in town in a very casual, cramped, and old-school authentic atmosphere.

Ton Kiang (p. 156)   Chinese families head here every weekend to gather around large round tables and indulge in dim sum small-plate feasts. Decor is minimal, which makes the folks feel that much better when the soy sauce hits the plate or a few bites of rice hit the floor.

Dining near Chinatown & North Beach

Bix **16**
Brandy Ho's Hunan Food **13**
Caffè Macaroni **15**
Caffè Sport **7**
Capp's Corner **5**
Enrico's **11**
Gold Spike **4**
House of Nanking **14**
Il Pollaio **4**
L'Osteria del Forno **6**

Mario's Bohemian Cigar Store **3**
Maykedeh **8**
Mo's Gourmet Burgers **9**
Moose's **1**
Pasta Pomodoro **2**
R & G Lounge **17**
The Stinking Rose **10**
Tommaso's **12**

631 Kearny St. (at Clay St.). ℂ **415/982-7877.** Reservations recommended. Main courses $9–$30. AE, DC, DISC, MC, V. Mon–Thurs 11am–9:30pm; Fri 11am–10pm; Sat 11:30am–10pm; Sun 11:30am–9:30pm. Parking validated across the street at Portsmouth Sq. garage 24 hr. or Holiday Inn after 5pm. Bus: 1, 9AX, 9BX, 12, or 15.

7 North Beach/Telegraph Hill

For a map of restaurants in this section, see the "Dining near Chinatown & North Beach" map on p. 131.

EXPENSIVE

Bix ★★ *Moments* AMERICAN/CALIFORNIA   The martini lifestyle may now be *en vogue,* but it was never out of style in this sexy and glamorous retro supper club. Bix is utterly stylish, with curving mahogany paneling, giant silver pillars, and dramatic lighting, all of which sets the stage for live music and plenty of hobnobbing. While the ultrasleek setting has overshadowed the food in the past, the legions of diners entranced by the Bix experience don't seem to care—and it seems as of late Bix is "on" again. Chicken hash has been a menu favorite for the past 17 years, but newer luxury comfort-food dishes—such as caviar service, marrow bones with toast and shallot confit, steak tartare, and panroasted seasonal fish dishes—are developing their own fan clubs. *Bargain tip:* At lunch there's a three-course prix-fixe menu for $20.

56 Gold St. (between Sansome and Montgomery sts.). ℂ **415/433-6300.** Reservations recommended. Main courses $12–$15 lunch, $16–$32 dinner. AE, DC, DISC, MC, V. Mon–Fri 11:30am–3:30pm; Mon–Thurs 5:30–11pm; Fri–Sat 5:30pm–midnight; Sun 5:30–10pm. Valet parking $10. Bus: 15, 30, 41, or 45.

Caffè Sport ★ ITALIAN   People either love or hate this stodgy Sicilian eatery. Cluttered with hanging hams, fishnets, decorative plates, dolls, mirrors, and about three decades worth of dust, Caffè Sport was once a culinary landmark. Now it's better known for its surly staff and eclectic ambience than for its good, but cream- and butter-heavy, and notably expensive, food. The southern Italian fare is served up with hearty portions of attitude along with huge garlic-laden pasta dishes. Lunch is tame in comparison to dinner, when the Sport is mobbed and lively, and strangers might be packed together family-style. Disregard the framed menu that sits on each table and accept the waiter's "suggestions." Whatever arrives—whether calamari, mussels, shrimp in tomato-garlic sauce, or pasta in pesto sauce—it's bound to be *bene.* Bring a huge appetite and check your bill for accuracy (I've found a few errors). Above all, don't be late for your reservation.

574 Green St. (between Grant and Columbus aves.). ℂ **415/981-1251.** Reservations recommended. Main courses $15–$30. No credit cards. Fri–Sat noon–2:30pm and 5–10:30pm. Bus: 15, 30, 41, or 45.

Moose's ★ *Value* AMERICAN   A big blue neon moose marks your arrival at North Beach's most schmoozy restaurant, where Nob Hill socialites and local politicians come to dine and be seen. But convivial Moose's is not just an image. On recent visits, the food—which highlights seasonal local ingredients—has been quite good. Appetizers are innovative, fresh, and well balanced (thank goodness for a truly good Caesar salad and chilled lobster salad). Main courses (especially meats) tend to be lovingly prepared. Try the cast iron–roasted halibut; wood oven–roasted game hen with leek smashed potatoes, baby carrots, and wild mushroom *jus;* or braised beef short ribs. Another reason to love Moose's: They make a darned good hamburger.

The bar, separated from the main dining room by a low, frosted-glass partition, remains busy long after the kitchen closes. There's excellent jazz piano nightly and during Sunday brunch.

1652 Stockton St. (between Filbert and Union sts.). © 800/28-MOOSE or 415/989-7800. www.mooses.com. Reservations recommended. Main courses $17–$30. AE, DC, DISC, MC, V. Mon–Wed 5:30–10:30pm; Thurs 11:30am–10:30pm; Fri 11:30am–11pm; Sat 5:30–11:30pm; Sun 10am–2:30pm and 5–10:30pm. Thurs–Sun bar menu 2:30–5:30pm. 3-hr. valet parking $6 lunch, $9 dinner. Bus: 15, 30, 41, or 45.

MODERATE

Enrico's 🎯 CALIFORNIA   Enrico's is the most fun sidewalk-restaurant/supper-club destination on North Beach's Broadway strip. Anyone with an appreciation for live jazz (featured nightly), late-night noshing, and people-watching from the outdoor patio will be quite content spending an alfresco evening under the heat lamps. (However, the best view of the band is from inside.) I tend to drop by and snack on wine and addictive deep-fried olives or pizza Margherita, and move on. But when I linger for dinner, entrees are usually satisfying and range from roasted chicken under a brick with mashed potatoes to flat-iron steak or butternut-squash ravioli. The best part? No cover charge.

504 Broadway (at Kearny St.). © 415/982-6223. www.enricossidewalkcafe.com. Reservations recommended. Main courses $7–$12 lunch, $11–$23 dinner. AE, MC, V. Sun–Thurs 11:30am–11pm; Fri–Sat 11:30am–midnight; bar daily 11:30am–1:30am or earlier depending on patronage. Valet parking (dinner only) $10. Bus: 9X, 12, or 15.

Fog City Diner 🎯 AMERICAN   More popular because of its Visa commercial than for its food, Fog City is a tourist destination, with locals straggling in for business lunches. The restaurant looks like a genuine American metallic diner—but only from the outside. Inside, dark polished woods, inspired lighting, and a well-stocked raw bar tell you this is no hash-slinger. Here dressed-up diner dishes include gourmet burgers, salads, "warm breads," soups, sandwiches, cioppino, macaroni with Gouda cheese, and pork chops. Fancier fish and meat meals include grilled catches of the day and thick-cut steaks. Light eaters can make a meal out of the long list of "small plates," which include crab-and-cheese-stuffed pequillo peppers and quesadillas with asparagus and leek. The food is fine, but if your heart is set on coming here, do so at lunch (and sit outside if the weather's agreeable)—you'll be better off elsewhere if you want a special dinner.

1300 Battery St. (at The Embarcadero.). © 415/982-2000. Reservations recommended. Main courses $11–$22. DC, DISC, MC, V. Mon–Thurs 11:30am–10:30pm; Fri 11:30am–11pm; Sat 10:30am–11pm; Sun 10:30am–10pm. Bus: 42.

Maykedah 🎯 PERSIAN/MIDDLE EASTERN   If you're looking to add a little exotic adventure to your dinner plans, this is the place. Surrounded by a sea of Italian bistros, Maykedah is one of San Francisco's best and most elegant Persian restaurants. The Middle East may no longer be the culinary capital of the world, but at Maykedah you can still sample the exotic flavors that characterize Persian cuisine. Of the dozen or so appetizers, some of the best are eggplant with mint garlic sauce; stuffed grape leaves; and lamb tongue with lime juice, sour cream, and saffron (c'mon, live a little). About eight mesquite-grilled items are on the menu, including filet of lamb marinated in lime, homemade yogurt, saffron, and onions. House specialties include half a dozen vegetarian dishes, among them eggplant braised with saffron, fresh tomato, and dried lime.

470 Green St. (between Kearny St. and Grant Ave.). © 415/362-8286. Reservations recommended. Main courses $10–$23. MC, V. Mon–Thurs 11:45am–10:30pm; Fri–Sat 11:45am–11pm; Sun 11:45am–10pm. Valet parking $6 lunch, $7 dinner. Bus: 15 or 41.

Piperade 🎯🎯 BASQUE   Chef Gerald Hirigoyen takes diners on a Basque adventure in this charming, small restaurant. Surrounded by a low wood-beamlined ceiling, oak floors, and soft sconce lighting, it's a casual affair where diners huddle around white tablecloth–topped tables and indulge in small and large plates of Hirigoyen's superbly flavorful West Coast Basque cuisine. Your edible odyssey starts with small plates—or plates to be shared—like my personal favorites: moist crab meat coddled in a paper-thin crepe accompanied by a sweet and sassy mango and red-pepper salsa; and a bright and simple salad of giant white beans, eggs, chives, and marinated anchovies. Share entrees, too. Indulge in flat-iron steak with braised shallots and french fries or sop up every drop of the sweet and savory red-pepper sauce with the braised seafood and shellfish stew. Save room for orange blossom beignets: Light and airy with a delicate and moist web of dough within and a kiss of orange essence, the beignet is dessert at its finest. There's a community table for drop-in diners and front patio seating during warmer weather.

1015 Battery St. (at Green St.). ✆ 415/391-2555. www.piperade.com. Reservations recommended. Main courses $15–$18. AE, DC, DISC, MC, V. Mon–Fri 11:30am–3pm and 5:30–10:30pm; Sat 5:30–10:30pm; closed Sun. Bus: 10, 12, 30, or 82x.

The Stinking Rose ITALIAN   Garlic is the "flower" from which this restaurant gets its name. From soup to ice cream, the supposedly healthful herb is a star ingredient in almost every dish. ("We season our garlic with food," exclaims the menu.) From a strictly gourmet point of view, the Stinking Rose is unremarkable. Pizzas, pastas, and meats smothered in simple, overpowering sauces are tasty, but they're memorable only for their singular garlicky intensity. That said, this is a fun place; the restaurant's lively atmosphere and odoriferous aroma combine for good entertainment. The best dishes include iron-skillet–roasted mussels with garlic sauce; smoked mozzarella, garlic, and tomato pizza; salt-roasted tiger prawns with garlic parsley glaze; and 40-clove garlic chicken (served with garlic mashed potatoes, of course).

325 Columbus Ave. (between Vallejo and Broadway). ✆ 415/781-7673. www.thestinkingrose.com. Reservations recommended. Main courses $13–$30. AE, DC, MC, V. Sun–Thurs 11am–11pm; Fri–Sat 11am–midnight. Bus: 15, 30, 41, or 45.

INEXPENSIVE

Caffè Macaroni ★★ ITALIAN   You wouldn't know it from the looks (or name) of it, but this tiny, funky restaurant on busy Columbus Avenue is one of the best southern Italian restaurants in the city. It looks as though it can hold only two customers at a time, and if you don't duck your head when entering the upstairs dining room, you might as well ask for one lump or two. Fortunately, the kitchen also packs a wallop, dishing out a large variety of antipasti and excellent pastas. The spinach-and-cheese ravioli with wild-mushroom sauce and the gnocchi are outstanding. The owners and staff are always vivacious and friendly, and young ladies in particular will enjoy the attentions of the charming Italian men manning the counter. If you're still pondering whether you should eat here, consider that most entrees are under $15.

59 Columbus Ave. (at Jackson St.). ✆ 415/956-9737. www.caffemacaroni.com. Reservations accepted on weekdays only. Main courses $9–$18. No credit cards. Mon–Sat 5:30–10pm. Closed last week of Dec–1st week of Jan. Bus: 15 or 41.

Capp's Corner ★ Value ITALIAN   Capp's is a place of givens: It's a given that high-spirited regulars are hunched over the bar and that you'll be served huge portions of straightforward Italian fare at low prices in a raucous atmosphere that prevails until closing. The waitresses are usually brusque and bossy, but always with a wink. Long tables are set up for family-style dining: bread, soup, salad, choice of around 20 classic main dishes (herb-roasted leg of lamb, spaghetti with meatballs, osso buco with polenta, fettuccine with prawns and white-wine sauce), and dessert—all for $15 to $17 or so per person, around $10 for kids. You might have to wait a while for a table, but if you want fun and authentic old-school dining without pomp or huge prices, you'll find the wait worthwhile.

1600 Powell St. (at Green St.). ✆ 415/989-2589. www.cappscorner.com. Complete dinners $15–$17. AE, DC, MC, V. Daily 11:30am–2:30pm; Sun–Thurs 4:30–10:30pm; Fri–Sat 4:30–11pm. Bus: 15, 30, or 41.

The Gold Spike ITALIAN   This dusty, dark, funky, cavelike restaurant has endured a love-hate relationship with San Francisco since 1920. (Food critics Don and Betty Martin hit the nail on the head when they described it as "a pioneer museum that exploded.") Thousands of yellowing business cards plaster the walls alongside war memorabilia, stuffed moose heads, and an endless array of knickknacks that have accumulated since the place opened. Dinner consists mainly of Italian-American standards such as osso buco and veal parmigiana, all served family style at small booths opposite the bar. Recommended dishes are the eggplant Parmesan, chicken Marsala, and Italian pot roast, served either a la carte or as part of a six-course dinner for a few extra dollars. A "Crab Cioppino Feed" is held every Friday night during crab season (winter). Is the food good? Not particularly, but it's filling and fairly inexpensive, and the ambience is undeniably unique.

527 Columbus Ave. (between Green and Union sts.). ✆ 415/421-4591. Reservations accepted for parties of 6 or more. Main courses $10–$17. AE, DISC, MC, V. Mon–Tues and Thurs 5–10:30pm; Fri 5–11pm; Sat 3–11pm; Sun 3–10pm. Bus: 15, 30, or 41.

Il Pollaio ✮ *Value* ITALIAN/ARGENTINEAN   Simple, affordable, and consistently delicious is a winning combination at superbasic Il Pollaio. Seat yourself in the tiny unfussy room, order, and wait for the fresh-from-the-grill chicken, which is so moist it practically falls off the bone. Each meal comes with a choice of salad or fries. If you're not in the mood for chicken, you can opt for rabbit, lamb, pork chop, or Italian sausage.

555 Columbus Ave. (between Green and Union sts.). ✆ 415/362-7727. Reservations not accepted. Main courses $7–$15. DISC, MC, V. Mon–Sat 11:30am–9pm. Cable car: Powell-Mason line. Bus: 15, 30, 39, or 41.

L'Osteria del Forno ✮✮ ITALIAN   L'Osteria del Forno might be only slightly larger than a walk-in closet, but it's one of the top three authentic Italian restaurants in North Beach. Peer in the window facing Columbus Avenue, and you'll probably see two Italian women with their hair up, sweating from the heat of the brick-lined oven, which cranks out the best focaccia (and focaccia sandwiches) in the city. There's no pomp or circumstance here: Locals come strictly to eat. The menu features a variety of superb pizzas, salads, soups, and fresh pastas, plus a good selection of daily specials (pray for the roast pork braised in milk), which includes a roast of the day, pasta, and ravioli. Small baskets of warm focaccia keep you going until the arrival of the entrees, which should always be accompanied by a glass of Italian red. Good news for folks on the go: You can get pizza by the slice.

519 Columbus Ave. (between Green and Union sts.). ✆ 415/982-1124. Reservations not accepted. Sandwiches $5.50–$6.50; pizzas $10–$17; main courses $6–$14. No credit cards. Sun–Mon and Wed–Thurs 11:30am–10pm; Fri–Sat 11:30am–10:30pm. Bus: 15 or 41.

Mario's Bohemian Cigar Store ✮ *Finds* ITALIAN   Across the street from Washington Square is one of North Beach's most popular neighborhood hangouts. The century-old bar—small, well worn, and perpetually busy—is best known for its focaccia sandwiches, including meatball and eggplant. Wash it down with an excellent cappuccino or a house Campari as you watch the tourists stroll by. And no, they do not sell cigars.

566 Columbus Ave. (at Union St.). © 415/362-0536. Sandwiches $6.75–$7.25. MC, V. Daily 10am–11pm. Closed Dec 24–Jan 1. Bus: 15, 30, 41, or 45.

Mo's Gourmet Burgers ★★ *Kids* AMERICAN   This simple diner offers a straightforward but winning combination: big, thick, grilled patties of fresh-ground, best-quality, center-cut chuck; fresh french fries; and choice of cabbage slaw, sautéed garlic mushrooms, or beans and rice. Voilà! You've got the city's burger of choice (Zuni Café's is a contender, but at almost twice the price— p. 147). The other food—spicy chicken sandwich; steak with veggies, garlic bread, and potatoes; and token veggie dishes—is also up to snuff, but it's that messy, memorable burger that keeps the carnivores captivated (the sinisterly sweet shakes are fantastic, too). Bargain-diners will appreciate prices, with burgers ranging from $5.50 for a classic to $8.75 for an "Alpine" burger with cheese, sautéed mushrooms, and fries. Entrees start at $9 for a roasted half-chicken with three sides and top out at $14 for New York steak. The classic breakfast menu is also a bargain. A second location at SoMa's Yerba Buena Gardens, 772 Folsom St., between Third and Fourth streets (© 415/957-3779), is open Tuesday through Saturday from 9am to 8pm, Sunday and Monday from 9am to 5pm. It features breakfast and burgers.

1322 Grant Ave. (between Vallejo and Green sts.). © 415/788-3779. Main courses $5–$14. MC, V. Sun–Thurs 11am–10:30pm; Fri–Sat 11am–11:30pm; breakfast daily 9am–2pm. Bus: 9X, 15, 30, 39, 41, or 45.

Pasta Pomodoro ★★ *Kids* *Value* ITALIAN   If you're looking for a good, cheap meal in North Beach—or anywhere else in town, for that matter—this San Francisco chain can't be beat. There can be a short wait for a table, but after you're seated, you'll be surprised at how promptly you're served. Every dish is fresh and sizable and, best of all, costs a third of what you'd pay elsewhere. Winners include spaghetti *frutti di mare* made with calamari, mussels, scallops, tomato, garlic, and wine; and *genelli pollo,* with roast chicken, sun-dried tomatoes, cream, mushrooms, and Parmesan—both under $8. When I don't feel like cooking, I often stop here for angel-hair pasta with tomato and basil and a decadent spinach salad with candied walnuts and bleu cheese. The tiramisu is huge, delicious, and cheap, too.

655 Union St. (at Columbus Ave.). © 415/399-0300. www.pastapomodoro.com. Reservations not accepted. Main courses $6–$11. AE, MC, V. Sun–Thurs 11am–10:30pm; Fri–Sat 11am–11pm. Cable car: Powell-Mason line. Bus: 15, 30, 41, or 45. There are 7 other locations, including 2304 Market St., at 16th St. (© 415/558-8123); 3611 California St. (© 415/831-0900); and 816 Irving St., between Ninth and 10th sts. (© 415/566-0900).

San Francisco Art Institute Café ★ *Finds* AMERICAN   Never in a million years would you stumble upon the Art Institute Café by accident (unless you happen to be wandering around the top floor of San Francisco's oldest and largest art school). One of the best-kept secrets in San Francisco, this cafe offers fresh, affordable cafe standards for in-the-know residents and visitors as well as Art Institute students: a wide array of hearty breakfast dishes, fresh salads, focaccia sandwiches, daily ethnically inspired specials, and anything with caffeine in it—all priced at or under $6. The view, which extends from Alcatraz Island to Coit Tower and beyond, is so phenomenal that the exterior served as the outside of Sigourney Weaver's ridiculously chic apartment in the movie *Copycat.* The cafe itself is rather blasé—a rectangular cement structure with an open kitchen, a dozen or so well-worn tables, and leftover artwork from various student showings. A large courtyard with cement tables (and the same Hollywood view) is the perfect spot for an alfresco lunch high above the tourist fray.

800 Chestnut St. (at Jones and Leavenworth sts.). © **415/749-4567**. Main courses $3–$6. No credit cards. Fall–spring Mon–Fri 9:15am–4:15pm. Closed Sat–Sun. Cable car: Powell-Hyde or Powell-Mason line. Bus: 30.

Tommaso's ★★ *Kids* ITALIAN From the street, Tommaso's looks wholly unappealing—a drab, windowless brown facade sandwiched between sex shops. Then why are people always waiting in line to get in? Because everyone knows that Tommaso's, which opened in 1935, bakes one of San Francisco's best traditional-style pizzas. The center of attention in the downstairs dining room is the chef, who continuously tosses huge hunks of garlic and mozzarella onto pizzas before sliding them into the oak-burning brick oven. Nineteen different toppings make pizza the dish of choice, even though Italian classics such as veal Marsala, chicken cacciatore, superb lasagna, and wonderful calzones are also available. Tommaso's also offers half-bottles of house wines, homemade manicotti, and good Italian coffee. If you can overlook the seedy surroundings, this fun, boisterous restaurant is a great place to take the family.

1042 Kearny St. (at Broadway). © **415/398-9696**. www.tommasosnorthbeach.com. Reservations not accepted. Pasta and pizza $14–$24; main courses $11–$18. AE, DC, DISC, MC, V. Tues–Sat 5–10:30pm; Sun 4–9:30pm. Closed Dec 15–Jan 15. Bus: 15 or 41.

8 Fisherman's Wharf

For a map of restaurants in this section, see the "Dining Around Town" map on p. 122.

VERY EXPENSIVE

A. Sabella's ★★ *Finds* SEAFOOD The Sabella family has been serving seafood in San Francisco since the turn of the 20th century and has operated A. Sabella's restaurant on the wharf continuously since 1920, catering heavily to the tourist trade. The menu offers something for everyone—steak, lamb, seafood, chicken, and pasta, all made from scratch with fresh local ingredients. Where A. Sabella's really shines, however, is in the shellfish department. Its 1,000-gallon saltwater tank allows for fresh crab, abalone, and lobster year-round, which means no restaurant in the city can touch A. Sabella's when it comes to feasting on fresh Dungeness crab and abalone out of season. Of course, such luxuries are anything but cheap. But on the bright side, with their kids' menu, you can fill up tots' tummies for a mere $7.50. Added bonuses: The third-floor restaurant overlooks the wharf, and the wine list offers many tasty choices.

Fisherman's Wharf, 2766 Taylor St. (at Jefferson St.), 3rd floor. © **415/771-6775**. www.asabellas.com. Reservations recommended. Most main courses $16–$28. AE, DC, DISC, MC, V. Daily 5–10pm. 2-hr. validated parking at the Wharf Garage, 350 Beach St. Cable car: Powell-Mason and Powell-Hyde lines. Streetcar: F.

Forbes Island ★ *Moments* FRENCH Been there and done that in every San Francisco dining room? Then it's time for Forbes Island, a wonderfully ridiculous floating restaurant disguised as an island (complete with lighthouse and real 40-ft. palm trees) and unknown to even most locals. The idea's kitschy, but the execution's actually quite wonderful. Here's how it works: Arrive at the dock next to PIER 39, call the restaurant via the courtesy phone, climb aboard their pontoon boat that takes you on a 2-minute journey to the "island" located 75 feet from the city's famed sea lions, and descend into the island's bowels to find a surprisingly classy, Tudor-like wood-paneled dining room. Warmed by a fireplace and amused by fish swimming past the portholes (yes, the dining room is a wee bit underwater), guests dine on surprisingly well-prepared classic French food such as decadent ragout of wild mushrooms, toasted brioche, and soft goat cheese or roasted half-rack of lamb with herb brioche crust and tomato lamb *jus*. **But be warned:** The menu is very limited, the wine list features basic big-name producers without listing the vintage, and the "island" does gently rock (landlubbers need not apply or should take Dramamine 2 hr. beforehand). **One annoyance:** There's a mandatory $3 shuttle fee since the only other way to get there is to swim.

Water shuttle is just left of PIER 39. ℂ 415/951-4900. www.forbesisland.com. Reservations recommended. Main courses $24–$34. AE, MC, V. Wed–Sun 5–10pm. Validated parking at PIER 39 garage $8 for up to 6 hr.

Restaurant Gary Danko ★★★ *Finds* FRENCH James Beard Award—winning chef Gary Danko presides over my top pick for fine dining. Eschewing the white-glove formality of yesteryear's fine dining, Danko offers impeccable cuisine and perfectly orchestrated service in an untraditionally unstuffy environment of wooden paneling and shutters and well-spaced tables. The three- to five-course fixed-price seasonal menu is freestyle, so whether you want a sampling of appetizers or a flight of meat courses, you need only ask. I am a devoted fan of his trademark buttery-smooth glazed oysters with leeks, salsify, and Osetra caviar; seared foie gras, which may be accompanied by peaches, caramelized onions, and *verjus* (a classic French sauce); and adventurous Moroccan spiced squab with *chermoula* (a Moroccan sauce made with cilantro) and orange-cumin carrots. Truthfully, I've never had a dish here that wasn't precious. And wine? The list is stellar, albeit expensive. If after dinner you have the will to pass on the glorious cheese cart or flambéed dessert of the day, a plate of petit fours reminds you that Gary Danko is one sweet and memorable meal. *Tip:* If you can't get a reservation and are set on dining here, slip in and grab a seat at the 10-stool first-come, first-served bar where you can also order a la carte.

800 North Point St. (at Hyde St.). ℂ 415/749-2060. www.garydanko.com. Reservations required. 3- to 5-course fixed-price menu $55–$78. AE, DC, MC, V. Sun–Wed 5:30–9:30pm; Thurs–Sat 5:30–10pm. Valet parking $10. Cable car: Hyde. Bus: 10. Streetcar: F.

Scoma's ★ SEAFOOD A throwback to the dining of yesteryear, Scoma's eschews trendier trout preparations and fancy digs for good old-fashioned seafood served in huge portions amidst a very casual windowed waterfront setting. Gourmands should skip this one. But if your idea of heaven is straightforward seafaring classics like fried calamari, raw oysters, pesto pasta with rock shrimp, and lobster Thermidor with old-time hospitality to match, this is about as good as it gets. Unfortunately, a taste of tradition will cost you big time. Prices are as steep as those at some of the finest restaurants in town. Personally, I'd rather splurge at Gary Danko, Masa's, or A. Sabellas. But many of my out-of-town guests insist we meet at Scoma's, which is fine by me since it's a change of pace from today's chic spots, and the parking's free.

Pier 47 (between Jefferson and Jones sts.). ℂ 415/771-4383. www.scomas.com. Reservations recommended. Most main courses $18–$38. AE, MC, V. Sun–Thurs noon–10pm; Fri–Sat 11:30am–10:30pm; hours change seasonally so call to confirm. Valet parking free. Streetcar: F. Bus: 10 or 47.

EXPENSIVE

Alioto's SEAFOOD One of San Francisco's oldest restaurants, run by one of the city's most prominent families, the Aliotos, this Fisherman's Wharf landmark has a long-standing reputation for great cioppino. The curbside crab stand, Café 8, the Steam Kettle Bar, and the newer Nonna Rose restaurant (all separate establishments in the same location) are great for quick, inexpensive doses of San

Francisco's finest; for more formal and fancy selections, continue up the carpeted stairs to the multilevel, harbor-view dining room here. Don't mess around with the menu: You're after Dungeness crab. Cracked, caked, stuffed, or stewed, it's impossible to get your fill, so bring plenty of money—particularly if you intend to order from Alioto's prodigious (and pricey) wine list. If you don't care for cracked crab (hard to imagine!), try the griddle-fried sand dabs or the rex sole served with tartar sauce.

Fisherman's Wharf (at Taylor St.). ☎ **415/673-0183**. Reservations recommended. Main courses $15–$30 lunch; most main courses $20–$35 dinner. AE, DC, DISC, MC, V. Daily 11am–11pm. Cable car: Powell-Hyde line. Streetcar: F. Bus: 10, 15, 39, or 47.

Ana Mandara ★★ VIETNAMESE   Yes, Don Johnson is part owner. But more important, this Fisherman's Wharf favorite serves fine Vietnamese food in an outstandingly beautiful setting. Amid a shuttered room with mood lighting, palm trees, and Vietnamese-inspired decor, diners (mostly tourists) splurge on crispy rolls; lobster with sweet-and-sour sauce and black sticky rice; and wok-charred tournedos of beef tenderloin with sweet onions and peppercress. There is no more expensive Vietnamese dining room in town, but, along with the enjoyable fare, diners pay for the atmosphere, which, if they're in the neighborhood and want something more exotic than the standby seafood dinner, is worth the price.

891 Beach St. (at Polk St.). ☎ **415/771-6800**. www.anamandara.com. Reservations recommended. Main courses $17–$29. AE, DISC, MC, V. Mon–Fri 11:30am–2pm; Sun–Thurs 5:30–9:30pm; Fri–Sat 5:30–10:30pm. Valet parking Tues–Sun $9. Bus: 19 or 32. Streetcar: F.

The Mandarin ★ CHINESE   Created by Madame Cecilia Chiang in 1968, the Mandarin is meant to feel like a cultured, northern Chinese home. Fine furnishings, silk-covered walls, and good-quality Asian art create one of the most elegant Chinese restaurants in the city. Tables are spaced comfortably apart, and the better of three softly lit dining rooms offers matchless views of the bay.

True to its name, The Mandarin offers solid northern Chinese cuisine. Start with sesame prawns or minced squab. Follow with smoked tea duck (the house version of Beijing duck, but smoked over burning tea leaves until crispy) or—if you have a party of two or more and call a day in advance—Beggar's Chicken stuffed with ham, mushrooms, bamboo shoots, and water chestnuts. The chicken is encased in clay and slowly cooked to perfection. A fixed-price four-course dinner costs $29 to $64. Yes, it's pricey for Chinese food, but if you want atmosphere with your pot stickers, this place is for you.

At Ghirardelli Sq., 900 North Point St. ☎ **415/673-8812**. www.themandarin.com. Reservations recommended. Main courses $16–$25. AE, DC, DISC, MC, V. Daily 11:30am–10pm. Parking in Ghirardelli Sq. lot (validation with purchase). Cable car: Powell-Hyde line. Bus: 19, 30, 47, or 49.

MODERATE

Cafe Pescatore ★ ITALIAN   This cozy trattoria is one of the better bets in Fisherman's Wharf. Two walls of sliding glass doors offer pseudo-sidewalk seating when the weather's warm, although heavy vehicular traffic can detract from the alfresco experience. All the classics are well represented here: crisp Caesar salad; fried calamari; bruschetta; cioppino; pastas; chicken Marsala; and veal medallions with mushrooms, caramelized onions, sage, and veal sauce. The consensus is to order anything that's cooked in the open kitchen's wood-fired oven, such as pizza (Margherita), roasts (sea bass with pine-nut crust, sun-dried tomato pesto, and roasted veggies), or panini (lunch only; grilled chicken or grilled eggplant). By the way, they serve darned good breakfasts, too.

2455 Mason St. (at North Point St., adjoining the Tuscan Inn). ℂ **415/561-1111.** Reservations recommended. Main courses $6–$12 breakfast, $8.50–$17 lunch and dinner. AE, DC, DISC, MC, V. Daily 7am–10pm. Cable car: Powell-Mason line. Bus: 15, 39, or 42.

INEXPENSIVE

Frjtz Fries ✦ BELGIAN   Deep-fried offerings are as abundant as sea lions in the Fisherman's Wharf area, but thankfully this funky-artsy "Belgian fries, crepes, and DJ/Art teahouse" features killer, fat french fries with a barrage of exotic dipping sauces that are head and flippers above the rest. Grab a bag of the addictively crisp and thick fried potatoes—perhaps with chipotle rémoulade or balsamic mayo—or swerve toward less lardy options such as a sweet or savory crepe—ranging from Nutella, banana, and whipped cream to grilled rosemary chicken and Swiss cheese—a big, leafy salad, or a chunky focaccia sandwich packed with roasted peppers, red onions, pesto mayo, grilled eggplant, and melted Gorgonzola. Wash it down with Belgian ale and rejoin the tourist trample. A second, equally groovy location is in Hayes Valley at 579 Hayes St. (at Laguna St.; ℂ **415/864-7654**).

Ghirardelli Square, 900 North Point St. (between Larkin and Polk sts). ℂ **415/928-3886.** www.frjtzfries.com. Reservations not accepted. Fries $3–$4.50; crepes $4.25–$7.50; sandwiches $5.95–$7.25. AE, MC, V. Sun–Thurs 10am–6pm. Fri–Sat 10am–7pm; open later during summer, so call for hours. Bus: 66. Streetcar: F line.

Hard Rock Cafe *Kids* AMERICAN   I hate to plug chains, and this loud, rock-nostalgia-laden place would be no exception if: 1) I knew tourists were no longer interested in it; and 2) it didn't serve a fine burger and overall decent heaping plates of food at such moderate prices. For many, the real draw—more than 20 years past the time when it was hip to wear the restaurant's logo—is the merchandise shop, but a shopper's gotta eat. The friendly menu offers burgers, fajitas, baby back ribs, grilled fish, chicken, salads, and sandwiches, the munching of which tend to be muffled by blaring music. Although it's nothing unique to San Francisco, the Hard Rock is a fine place to bring the kids and grab a bite.

PIER 39. ℂ **415/956-2013.** Reservations accepted for groups of 15 or more. Main courses $8–$20. AE, DC, DISC, MC, V. Sun–Thurs 11am–11pm; Fri–Sat 11am–midnight. Validated parking for 1 hr. free at PIER 39 lot. Streetcar: F.

9 The Marina/Pacific Heights/Cow Hollow

For a map of restaurants in this section, see the "Dining Around Town" map on p. 122.

VERY EXPENSIVE

Harris' ✦✦ STEAKHOUSE   Every big city has a great steak restaurant, and in San Francisco it's Harris'—a comfortably elegant establishment where the handsome wood-paneled dining room has curving banquettes and stately waiters. Here, the point, of course, is steak, which can be seen hanging in a glass-windowed aging room off Pacific Avenue. They are cut thick—New York–style or T-bone—and are served with a baked potato and seasonal vegetables. You'll also find classic spinach or Caesar salads, and sides of delicious creamed spinach, sautéed shiitake mushrooms, or caramelized onions. Harris' also offers lamb chops, fresh fish, and lobster, and occasionally venison, buffalo, and other seasonal game.

2100 Van Ness Ave. (at Pacific Ave.). ℂ **415/673-1888.** www.harrisrestaurant.com. Reservations recommended. Most main courses $17–$40. AE, DC, DISC, MC, V. Mon–Thurs 5:30–9:30pm; Fri 5:30–10pm; Sat 5–10pm; Sun 5–9:30pm. Valet parking $7. Bus: 12, 47, 49, or 83.

EXPENSIVE

Cafe Kati ★★ *Finds* CALIFORNIA/EAST-WEST FUSION   Chef Kirk Webber works small wonders in an even smaller kitchen at this diminutive yet distinctive and romantic restaurant off Fillmore Street. The menu highlights California-style dishes spiced with dashes of Asia and Italy and presented in high form, such as the signature Caesar salad sculpted into a towering monument of romaine; or the "dragon roll" of crispy prawns, *shiso* (Japanese basil), avocado, and cucumber wrapped with smoked salmon and seasoned with wasabi vinaigrette. The seasonally changing menu offers such cross-cultural creations as miso-glazed black bass in *dashi* (broth); *udon* (noodles); Shanghai bok choy; tempura kabocha squash and *tagarashi* (a Japanese spice blend); or marinated skirt steak with crème fraîche whipped potatoes, crispy Vidalia onion rings, and port-wine sauce. When making a reservation, request a table in the front room.

1963 Sutter St. (between Fillmore and Webster sts.). ℂ 415/775-7313. Reservations recommended. Main courses $19–$26. AE, MC, V. Tues–Sun 5:30–10pm. Bus: 2, 3, or 4.

Quince ★★ CALIFORNIA-ITALIAN   Its discrete location in a quiet residential neighborhood hasn't stopped this tiny and predominantly white-hued restaurant from becoming one of the city's hottest reservations since it opened in late 2003. With only 15 tables, diners are clamoring for a seat in order to savor the pristine nightly changing Italian-inspired menu by Michael Tusk, who mastered the art of pasta while working at the East Bay's famed Chez Panisse and Oliveto restaurants. Regardless, it's worth the effort—especially if you love simple food that honors a few high-quality ingredients. Dining divinity might start with a pillowy spring garlic soufflé or white asparagus with a lightly fried egg and brown butter, but it really hits heavenly notes with the pasta course, be it garganelli with English peas and proscuitto, tagliatelle with veal ragout and fava beans, or artichoke ravioli. Meat and fish selections don't fall short either, with delicately prepared mixed grill plates, tender Alaskan halibut with fava beans, and juicy lamb with fennel and olives. Desserts, though tasty, aren't as celestial, which is just fine since it may leave room for an extra pasta course.

1701 Octavia St. (at Bush St.). ℂ 415/775-8500. www.quincerestaurant.com. Reservations required. Main courses $16–$27. Thurs and Sun 5:30–10pm; Fri–Sat 5:30–10:30pm. Valet parking: $8. Bus: 1, 31, or 38.

MODERATE

A16 ★★ ITALIAN   This sleek spot featuring Neapolitan-style pizza and cuisine from the region of Campania has been so hot since its 2004 opening that on my first visit, tables were filled with reputed chefs and critics. Even without the fanfare, it feels exciting to be at A16, which is named after the motorway that traverses the region. The divided space boasts a full bar up front, a larger dining area and open kitchen in the back, and a wall of wines in between. But its secret weapon is chef Christophe Hille who whips up outstanding appetizers, pizza, and entrees with aplomb. Even if you must have the insanely good braised pork breast with olives, herbs, and caramelized chestnuts to yourself, start by sharing dried fava beans with fennel salad and tuna conserva with braised dandelion greens and crunchy bread crumbs. Shortly after opening, a few items were ho-hum (ricotta and chard involtini, desserts) and service was uneven. But even with its shortcomings, the restaurant still fell under the great category—especially factoring in Shelley Lindgren, who guides diners through the exciting wine list featuring 40 wines by the half-glass, glass, and carafe.

2355 Chestnut St. (between Divisadero and Scott sts.). ✆ 415/771-2216. www.a16sf.com. Reservations recommended. Main courses $8–$10 lunch, $14–$19 dinner. AE, MC, V. Wed–Mon 11:30am–2:30pm; Mon and Wed–Fri 5:30–10:30pm; Sat–Sun 5:30–11pm. Bus: 30 or 30X.

Ace Wasabi's Rock 'n' Roll Sushi ✶✶ JAPANESE/SUSHI   What differentiates this Marina hot spot from the usual sushi spots around town are the unique combinations, the varied menu, and the young, hip atmosphere. The innovative rolls are a nice change for those bored with traditional styles, but don't worry if someone in your party isn't a raw fish fan: There are also plenty of nonseafood and cooked items on the menu. Don't miss the rainbow "Three Amigos" roll, or the "Rock and Roll" with cooked eel, avocado, and cucumber. The service, like the surroundings, is jovial.

3339 Steiner St. (at Chestnut St.). ✆ 415/567-4903. Reservations not accepted. Sushi $4–$12. AE, MC, V. Mon–Thurs 5:30–10:30pm; Fri–Sat 5:30–11pm; Sun 5–10pm. Bus: 30.

The Elite Café ✶ CAJUN   Some habits do indeed die hard, and the Elite is one of them. This place—especially the bar—is always bustling with Pacific Heights's beautiful people, who come for flirtation and a festive environment in which to down fresh oysters, blackened beef filet with Cajun butter, jambalaya, Granddad's chicken and dumplings, and other well-spiced Cajun dishes. The high-backed booths provide more intimate dining than the crowded tables and bar. Brunch here is good, too, and includes all kinds of egg dishes—Benedict, Sardou, and many more—as well as such goodies as cornbread, bagels, and lox.

2049 Fillmore St. (between Pine and California sts.). ✆ 415/346-8668. Reservations accepted for parties of 4 or more. Main courses $17–$26. AE, DC, DISC, MC, V. Sun 10am–3pm and 5–10pm; Mon–Sat 5–10pm. Bus: 22, 41, or 45.

Ella's ✶✶ *Kids* AMERICAN/BREAKFAST   Well known throughout town as the undisputed king of breakfasts, this restaurant's acclaim means you're likely to wait to get in up to an hour on weekends. But midweek and in the wee hours of morning, it's possible to slide onto a counter or table seat in the colorful split dining room and lose yourself in outstanding and obscenely generous servings of chicken hash, crisped to perfection and served with eggs any way you like them, with fluffy buttermilk biscuits. Pancakes, omelets, and the short list of other breakfast essentials are equally revered. Alas, service can be woefully slow, but at least the buspersons are quick to fill coffee cups. Come lunchtime, solid entrees like salads, chicken potpie, and grilled salmon with mashed potatoes remind you what's great about good old American cooking.

500 Presidio Ave. (at California St.). ✆ 415/441-5669. www.ellassanfrancisco.com. Reservations accepted for lunch. Main courses $5.50–$11 breakfast, $6–$12 lunch. AE, MC, V. Mon–Fri 7am–4pm; Sat–Sun 8:30am–2pm. Bus: 1, 5, or 43.

Florio ✶✶ FRENCH/ITALIAN   When I'm in the mood for a good meal without hoopla, I head directly to bistrolike Florio. Not only because the staff is friendly; not only because it's almost always painless to get a table or dine at the bar; and not even because the place is accommodating enough to not force quick turnover. The real reason is that I'm addicted to the chicken liver pâté, roasted chicken, steak frites, and virtually every other comfort dish that makes its way to the table. The wines by the glass (and by the bottle) tend to disappoint, but I don't care. I pull up a chair, make myself at home, and enjoy casual and cozy surroundings and consistently satisfying food. I suggest you do the same.

1915 Fillmore St. (between Pine and Bush sts.). ✆ 415/775-4300. www.floriosf.com. Most main courses $13–$28. AE, MC, V. Sun–Wed 5:30–10pm; Thurs–Sat 5:30–11pm. Bus: 3, 22, 41, or 45.

Greens Restaurant ★★ *Finds* VEGETARIAN   In an old waterfront warehouse, with enormous windows overlooking the bridge, boats, and the bay, this vegetarian restaurant is a pioneer and a legend. Renowned vegetarian cook and executive chef Annie Somerville (author of *Fields of Greens*) cooks with the seasons, using produce from local organic farms. Within the quiet dining room, a weeknight dinner might feature such appetizers as mushroom soup with Asiago cheese and tarragon; or grilled portobello and endive salad. Entrees run the gamut from pizza with wilted escarole, red onions, lemon, Asiago, and Parmesan, to Vietnamese yellow curry or risotto with black trumpet mushrooms, leeks, savory spinach, white-truffle oil, Parmesan Reggiano, and thyme. Those interested in the whole shebang should make reservations for the $46 four-course dinner served on Saturday only. Lunch and brunch are equally fresh and tasty.

The adjacent Greens To Go sells homemade breads, sandwiches, soups, salads, and pastries.

Building A, Fort Mason Center (enter Fort Mason opposite the Safeway at Buchanan and Marina sts.). ℂ 415/771-6222. Reservations recommended. Main courses $9.50–$14 lunch, $15–$20 dinner; fixed-price dinner $46; Sun brunch $8–$14. DISC, MC, V. Tues–Sat noon–4pm; Sun 10:30am–2pm; Mon–Fri 5:30–9:30pm; Sat 5:30–9pm. Greens To Go Mon–Thurs 8am–8pm; Fri–Sat 8am–5pm; Sun 9am–4pm. Free parking. Bus: 28 or 30.

Isa ★★ FRENCH   Luke Sung, who trained with some of the best French chefs in the city, has captured my and many locals' hearts by creating the kind of menu us foodies dream of: a smattering of small dishes that allow you to try numerous items in one sitting. It's a good thing the menu, considered "French tapas," offers small portions at reasonable prices. After all, it's asking a lot to make a diner choose between sweetbreads and mushroom ragout, seared foie gras with caramelized apples, potato-wrapped sea bass in brown butter, and rack of lamb. Here, a party of two can choose all of these plus one or two more and not be rolled out the door afterward. Adding to the allure is the warm boutique dining environment—60 seats scattered amid a very small dining room in the front, and a tented heated patio out back that sets the mood with a warm yellow glow. Take a peek at the "kitchen," a shoebox of a cooking space, to appreciate Sung's accomplishments that much more. Cocktailers, have your predinner drink elsewhere: Isa serves beer and wine only.

3324 Steiner St. (between Lombard and Chestnut sts.). ℂ 415/567-9588. Reservations recommended. Main courses $9–$16. MC, V. Mon–Thurs 5:30–10pm; Fri–Sat 5:30–10:30pm. Bus: 22, 28, 30, 30X, 43, or 76.

Pane e Vino ★ *Kids* ITALIAN   Pane e Vino recently moved to a space with indoor and outdoor tented dining, and it remains one of San Francisco's favorite ultracasual Italian restaurants. While the rest of the city tries to modernize their manicotti, here food focuses on huge helpings of classics, which are fine for the traditional diner, but not fabulous for the gourmand. That said, prices are reasonable here and the mostly Italian-accented staff is always smooth and efficient under pressure (you'll see). The menu offers a wide selection of appetizers, including a fine carpaccio, *vitello tonnato* (sliced roasted veal and capers in lemony tuna sauce), and the hugely popular chilled artichoke stuffed with bread and tomatoes and served with vinaigrette. The antipasti of mixed grilled vegetables always spurs a fork fight. The broad selection of pastas includes flavorful *pennette alla boscaiola* with porcini mushrooms and pancetta in tomato cream sauce. Other specialties are grilled fish and meat dishes, including chicken breast marinated in lime juice and herbs. Top dessert picks are any of the Italian ice creams, crème caramel, and (but of course) creamy tiramisu.

1715 Union St. (between Gough and Octavia sts.). ℂ **415/346-2111.** Reservations highly recommended. Main courses $10–$24. AE, MC, V. Mon–Thurs 11:30am–2:30pm and 5–9:30pm; Fri–Sat 11:30am–10pm; Sun 11:30am–9:30pm. No parking. Bus: 41 or 45.

PlumpJack Café ★★ CALIFORNIA/FRENCH/MEDITERRANEAN Wildly popular among San Francisco's style-setters, this small, 55-seat Cow Hollow restaurant, with a hint of whimsical Shakespearian decor, is once again one of the neighborhood's most "in" places to dine. That's partly because it's affiliated with the Getty clan (as in J. Paul) and was founded by sweetheart Mayor Gavin Newsom, and partly because chef James Ormsby took over the kitchen a few years ago after the restaurant began losing its luster.

Ormsby is a local favorite who's hopscotched through the city's kitchens over the past few years. But with a three-and-a-half-star rating from the *Chronicle,* he's likely to stay put, which means diners can be treated to his beloved signature dishes such as mini-cones of ahi tartare enlivened with horseradish, lime, capers, and caviar; decadent wild mushroom risotto; and rich red-wine braised oxtail. The extraordinarily extensive California wine list—gleaned from the PlumpJack wine shop down the street—is sold at next to retail prices, with many wines available by the glass.

3127 Fillmore St. (between Filbert and Greenwich sts.). ℂ **415/563-4755.** www.plumpjack.com. Reservations recommended. Main courses $20–$28. AE, DC, DISC, MC, V. Mon–Fri 11:30am–2pm; Mon–Sun 5:30–10pm. Valet parking $14 for 3 hr. Mon–Sat after 6pm. Bus: 41 or 45.

INEXPENSIVE

Andalé Taqueria ★★ *Kids* *Value* MEXICAN Andalé (Spanish for "hurry up") offers incredible high-end fast food for the health-conscious and the just plain hungry. As the long menu explains, this small California chain prides itself on its fresh ingredients and low-cal options. Lard, preservatives, and canned items are eschewed; Andalé favors salad dressings made with double virgin olive oil, whole vegetarian beans (not refried), skinless chicken, salsas and *aguas frescas* made from fresh fruits and veggies, and mesquite-grilled meats. Add the location (on a sunny shopping stretch), sophisticated decor, full bar, and check-me-out patio seating (complete with corner fireplace), and it's no wonder the good-looking, fitness-fanatic Marina District considers this place home. Cafeteria-style service keeps prices low. ***Bargain tips:*** No one can complain about a quarter of a mesquite-roasted chicken with potatoes, salsa, and tortillas for $6.75. If you want to go traditional, stick with the giant burritos or the fantastic $2.95 tacos—a nibbler's dream.

2150 Chestnut St. (between Steiner and Pierce sts.). ℂ **415/749-0506.** Reservations not accepted. Most dishes $5.25–$9.50. MC, V. Mon 11am–9pm; Tues–Thurs and Sun 11am–10pm; Fri–Sat 11am–10:30pm. Bus: 22, 28, 30, 30X, 43, 76, or 82X.

Chez Nous ★★ FRENCH Diners get crammed into the 45-seat dining area of this bright, cheery, small, and bustling cafelike dining room, but the French tapas are so delicious and affordable, no one seems to care. Indeed, this friendly and fast-paced neighborhood haunt has become a blueprint for other restaurants that understand the allure of small plates. But Chez Nous stands out as more than a petite-portion trendsetter. The clincher is that most of its Mediterranean dishes taste so clean and fresh you can't wait to come back and dine here again. Start with the soup, whatever it is; don't skip tasty french fries with *harissa* (Tunisian hot sauce) aioli; savor the lamb chops with lavender sea salt; and save room for their famed dessert, the minicustard-cakelike *canneles de Bordeaux.*

1911 Fillmore St. (between Pine and Bush sts.). ℰ **415/441-8044.** Reservations recommended. Main courses $3.50–$12. MC, V. Daily 11:30am–3pm and 5:30–10pm (Fri–Sat until 11pm). Bus: 22, 41, or 45.

E'Angelo Restaurant ✦ ITALIAN   Back when I was barely making enough to cover my rent, I would often treat myself to a night out at E'Angelo. All the house specialties, pastas, and pizzas cost less than $15; the atmosphere is casual and fun; the gingham-covered tables are cozy-cramped; and the Italian staff is friendly. For me, the combination made not only for a hearty meal, but for an opportunity to mingle with San Francisco: to live a little, eavesdrop on neighbors' conversations, and perhaps even run into local celebrities such as Robin Williams with his family. While years have passed, not much has changed at this traditional Italian hot spot: The place still won't take reservations or credit cards. It still serves decent portions of pastas, veal, lamb, chicken, and fish; a carafe of red or white wine for about 16 bucks (thrifty by-the-bottle prices, too); and one heck of a rich eggplant parmigiana. And unlike those at most of the neighboring restaurants, desserts are dirt cheap.

2234 Chestnut St. (between Pierce and Scott sts.). ℰ **415/567-6164.** Reservations not accepted. Main courses $10–$15. No credit cards. Mon–Sat 5–11pm; Sun 5–10pm. Bus: 22, 28, 30, 30X, 43, or 76.

Eliza's ✦✦ *Value Kids* CHINESE   Despite the curiously colorful design of modern architecture, whimsy, and glass art, this perennially packed neighborhood haunt serves some of the freshest, best-tasting California-influenced Chinese food in town. Unlike comparable options, here the atmosphere (albeit unintentionally funky) and presentation parallel the food. The fantastically fresh soups, salads, seafood, pork, chicken, duck, and such specials as spicy eggplant are outstanding and are served on beautiful Italian plates. (Get the sea bass with black-bean sauce and go straight to heaven!) I often come at midday and order the wonderful kung pao chicken lunch special (available weekdays only): a mixture of tender chicken, peanuts, chile peppers, subtly hot sauce, and perfectly crunchy vegetables. It's one of 32 main-course choices that come with rice and soup for around $5. The place is also jumping at night, so prepare to stand in line.

2877 California St. (at Broderick St.). ℰ **415/621-4819.** Reservations not accepted. Main courses $4.95–$5.75 lunch, $6.50–$13 dinner. MC, V ($10 minimum). Mon–Fri 11am–3pm and 5–9:45pm; Sat–Sun 4:30–9:45pm. Bus: 6, 7, 21, 66, or 71.

La Méditerranée ✦ *Value* MEDITERRANEAN   With an upscale-cafe ambience and quality food, La Méditerranée has long warranted its reputation as one of the quainter inexpensive restaurants on upper Fillmore. Here you'll find freshly prepared traditional Mediterranean food that's worlds apart from the Euro-eclectic fare many restaurants now call "Mediterranean." Baba ghanouj, tabbouleh, dolmas, and hummus start out the menu. More important, the menu offers one very tasty chicken Cilicia, a phyllo-dough dish that's hand-rolled and baked with cinnamony spices, almonds, chickpeas, and raisins; also good is zesty chicken pomegranate drumsticks on a bed of rice. Both come with green salad, potato salad, or soup for around $9.25. Ground lamb dishes, quiches, and Middle Eastern combo plates round out the very affordable menu, and wine comes by the glass and in half- or full liters. A second location is at 288 Noe St., at Market Street (ℰ **415/431-7210**).

2210 Fillmore St. (at Sacramento St.). ℰ **415/921-2956.** www.cafelamed.com. Main courses $7–$10 lunch, $8–$10 dinner. AE, MC, V. Sun–Thurs 11am–10pm; Fri–Sat 11am–11pm. Bus: 1, 1BX, 22, or 24.

Mel's Diner ✦ *Kids* AMERICAN   Sure, it's contrived, touristy, and nowhere near healthy, but when you get that urge for a chocolate shake and banana cream pie at the stroke of midnight—or when you want to entertain the kids—no other place in the city comes through like Mel's Diner. Modeled after a classic 1950s diner, right down to the jukebox at each table, Mel's harkens back to the halcyon days when cholesterol and fried foods didn't jab your guilty conscience with every greasy, wonderful bite. Too bad the prices don't reflect the '50s; a burger with fries and a Coke costs about $9.50.

There's another Mel's at 3355 Geary St., at Stanyan Street (© **415/387-2244**); it's open from 6am to 3am Thursday through Saturday.

2165 Lombard St. (at Fillmore St.). © **415/921-3039**. Main courses $4–$6 breakfast, $6–$8 lunch, $8–$12 dinner. MC, V. Sun–Wed 6am–2am; Thurs 6am–3am; Fri–Sat 24 hr. Bus: 22, 30, or 43.

Pluto's ★ *Value* CALIFORNIA   Catering to the Marina District's DINK (double income, no kids) crowd, Pluto's combines assembly-line efficiency with high quality. The result is cheap, fresh fare: huge salads with a dozen choices of toppings; oven-roasted poultry and grilled meats (the flank steak is great); sandwiches; and a wide array of sides like crispy garlic potato rings, seasonal veggies, and barbecued chicken wings. Pluto's serves teas, sodas, bottled brews, and Napa wines, as well as homemade desserts. The ordering system is bewildering to newcomers; grab a checklist, then hand it to the servers who check off your order and relay it to the cashier. Seating is limited during the rush, but the turnover is fairly fast. A second location is at 627 Irving St., at Eighth Avenue (© **415/753-8867**).

3258 Scott St. (at Chestnut St.). © **415/7-PLUTOS**. Reservations not accepted. Main courses $3.50–$5.75. MC, V. Mon–Fri 11am–10pm; Sat–Sun 9:30am–10pm. Bus: 28, 30, or 76.

10 Civic Center

For a map of restaurants in this section, see the "Dining Around Town" map on p. 122.

VERY EXPENSIVE

Jardinière ★★ CALIFORNIA/FRENCH   Jardinière is a pre- and postsymphony favorite, and it also happens to be the perfect setting for a cocktail. A culinary dream team runs the sexy dining room: owner-chef Traci Des Jardins and owner-designer Pat Kuleto, who created the swank champagne-inspired decor. On most evenings, the two-story brick structure is abuzz with an older crowd (including ex-mayor Brown, a regular) that sips cocktails at the centerpiece mahogany bar or watches the scene discreetly from the circular balcony. The restaurant's champagne theme extends to twinkling lights and fun ice buckets built into the balcony railing, making the atmosphere conducive to throwing back a few in the best of style—especially when there's live jazz (at 7:30pm nightly).

The daily changing menu is lovely; it might include seared scallops with truffled potatoes and truffle reduction, sautéed petrale sole with Alsatian cabbage and Riesling sauce, or venison with celery root, red wine, braised cabbage, and juniper sauce. But the atmosphere just doesn't have enough warmth for me. Still, anyone in search of a quality meal will not be disappointed. I also have to give kudos to the outstanding cheese selection, great wine list—many by the glass, and over 300 bottles—and Traci and manager Larry Bain's commitment to leading the industry supporting sustainably farmed, wholesome ingredients and environmentally conscious business operations.

300 Grove St. (at Franklin St.). © **415/861-5555**. www.jardiniere.com. Reservations recommended. Main courses $24–$35; 6-course tasting menu $75. AE, DC, DISC, MC, V. Sun–Wed 5–10:30pm; Thurs–Sat 5–11:30pm. Valet parking $10. Bus: 19 or 21.

MODERATE

Absinthe ✮ FRENCH   This Hayes Valley hot spot is a sexy, fun, reasonably priced, and frequented by everyone from the theatergoing crowd to the young and chic. Decor is scrumptious brasserie, with French rattan cafe chairs, copper-topped tables, a pressed-tin ceiling, soft lighting, period art, and a rich use of color and fabric, including leather and mohair banquettes. The menu is hit and miss—from fun specialty cocktails (ever had a "Ginger Rogers," made with gin, mint, lemon juice, ginger ale, and a squeeze of lime?) and good wine list to the slew of bar snacks ranging from Caesar salad to chicken liver pâté to a respectable burger. In the divided dining room, main courses are equally satisfying, from coq au vin and steak fries to roasted whole Dungeness crab with poached leeks in mustard vinaigrette, salt roasted potatoes, and aioli. Interested in weekend brunch? Anticipate creamy polenta with mascarpone, maple syrup, bananas, and toasted walnuts; soft-boiled eggs with sage croutons; as well as the usual suspects.

398 Hayes St. (at Gough St.). ✆ **415/551-1590.** www.absinthe.com. Reservations recommended. Brunch $6–$14; most main courses $12–$28 lunch, $16–$28 dinner. AE, DC, DISC, MC, V. Tues–Fri 11:30am–midnight; Sat 10:30am–midnight; Sun 10:30am–10:30pm. Valet parking (Tues–Sat) $10. Bus: 21.

Hayes Street Grill ✮✮ SEAFOOD   For well over a decade, this small, no-nonsense seafood restaurant (owned and operated by revered food writer and chef Patricia Unterman) has maintained a solid reputation among San Francisco's picky epicureans for its impeccably fresh and straightforwardly prepared fish. The concise menu offers a dozen appetizers—most of which are fresh and lively salads—a half-dozen grilled fish selections cooked to perfection and matched with your sauce of choice (Szechuan peanut, tomatillo salsa, herb-shallot butter), and a side of signature fries. Fancier seafood specials, which change with the seasons and range from mahimahi (with Vietnamese dipping sauce, baby spinach, roasted peanuts, and basmati rice) to classic paella, are balanced by a few meat-driven dishes, which may include Niman Ranch (organic and wonderful) minute steak with mustard butter and balsamic onions. Finish your meal with the outstanding crème brûlée.

320 Hayes St. (near Franklin St.). ✆ **415/863-5545.** Reservations recommended. Main courses $14–$20 lunch, $16–$23 dinner. AE, DC, DISC, MC, V. Mon–Fri 11:30am–2pm; Mon–Thurs 5–9:30pm; Fri 5–10:30pm; Sat 5:30–10:30pm; Sun 5–8:30pm. Bus: 19, 21, 31, or 38.

Zuni Café ✮✮✮ Finds MEDITERRANEAN   Zuni Café embodies the best of San Francisco dining: Its clientele spans young hipsters and gorgeous gays and lesbians as well as the everyday foodie; its cuisine is consistently outstanding; and the atmosphere is electric. Its expanse of windows overlooking Market Street gives the place a sense of space despite the fact that its always packed. For the full effect, stand at the bustling, copper-topped bar and order a glass of wine and a few oysters from the oyster menu (a dozen or so varieties are on hand at all times). Then, because *of course* you made advance reservations, take your seat in the stylish exposed-brick two-level maze of little dining rooms or on the outdoor patio. Then do what we all do: Splurge on chef Judy Rodgers's Mediterranean-influenced menu. Although the changing menu always includes meat (such as hanger steak), fish (grilled or braised in the kitchen's brick oven), and pasta (tagliatelle with nettles, applewood-smoked bacon, butter, and Parmesan), it's almost sinful not to order her brick-oven roasted chicken for two with Tuscan-style bread salad. I rarely pass up the polenta with mascarpone and a proper Caesar salad. But then again, the hamburger on grilled rosemary focaccia bread is a

Finds **Hidden Treasures**

They're on the way to nowhere, but because they're among the city's most unique, it would be a crime to leave out these destination restaurants. If you're not familiar with the streets of San Francisco, be sure to call first to get directions; otherwise, you'll spend more time driving than dining.

Thanh Long 🔥, 4101 Judah St. (at 46th Ave.; ✆ **415/665-1146**; www. anfamily.com; streetcar: N), is an out-of-the-way Sunset District Vietnamese standout that long after my mom started taking me here as a tot for excellent roasted crab and addictive garlic noodles, has remained a San Francisco secret. Since the owners, the An family, have become rather famous for their aforementioned signature dishes now that they're served in sister restaurants Crustacean in L.A., Vegas, and S.F, suffice it to say the crab's out of the bag. But this location is still far enough on the outskirts of the city to keep it from becoming too overcrowded. The restaurant is more visually pleasing than most Southeast Asian outposts (white tablecloths, tastefully exotic decor), but the extra glitz is reflected in the prices of luxury dishes (main courses run from $15–$40) such as charbroiled tiger prawns with those famed garlic noodles and steamed sea bass with scallions and ginger sauce. On the plus side, unlike the cheaper options around town, there's a full bar here, too, serving fun cocktails such as the Hanoi Sunset—an intoxicating mixture of Chambord tequila and peach schnapps. Reservations are recommended. Thanh Long is open Sunday and Tuesday through Thursday from 4:30 to 9:30pm, Friday and Saturday from 4:30 to 10:30pm, and is closed on Mondays.

The Ramp 🔥, 855 Terry François St. (at the end of Mariposa St.; ✆ **415/621-2378**; bus: 22 or 48), is an out-of-the-way mecca for seaside snacks, dancing, and drinking that's at its best when the sun is shining. If you're lucky enough to be in San Francisco on one of those rare hot days, head to this bayside hangout. The fare is of the basic pub grub variety—burgers, sandwiches, salads, and soups from $8 to $13—but the rustic boatyard environment and patio seating make this a relaxing place to dine in the sun. In summer, the place really rocks when live bands perform (4:30–7:30pm Sat–Sun Apr–Oct) and when tanned, cocktailing singles prowl the area. It's open for lunch from March to December Monday through Friday from 11am to 3:30pm, brunch Saturday and Sunday from 8:30am to 4pm. The bar is open Monday through Friday from 11am to 8pm, Friday and Saturday from 8:30am to 8pm. From May to October, outdoor barbecue is offered daily from 4 to 7:30pm; the rest of the year, appetizers are featured daily from 5:30 to 8pm.

strong contender for the city's best. Whatever you decide, be sure to order a stack of shoestring potatoes.

1658 Market St. (at Franklin St.). ✆ **415/552-2522**. Reservations recommended. Main courses $10–$19 lunch, $15–$29 dinner. AE, MC, V. Tues–Sat 11:30am–midnight; Sun 11am–11pm. Valet parking $8. Streetcar: All Market St. streetcars. Bus: 6, 7, 71, or 75.

11 Mission District

For a map of restaurants in this section, see the "Dining Around Town" map on p. 122.

MODERATE

Foreign Cinema ★★ MEDITERRANEAN This place is so chic that it's hard to believe it's a San Francisco restaurant, and it's so well hidden on Mission Street that it eludes me every time I seek the valet. An indoor seat is a lovely place to watch San Francisco's most fashionable. Outdoors (heated, partially covered, but still chilly), the enormous foreign film showing on the side of an adjoining building steals the show. (Although the actual purpose of dining here is not to watch the film, it's still a bummer for those facing away from it.) In 2001, husband-and-wife team John Clark and Gayle Pirie stepped into the kitchen and are now creating a fine Mediterranean menu. Snackers like me find solace in oysters, a devilish *brandade* (fish purée) gratin, and the cheese selections. Heartier eaters can opt for roasted half-chicken with golden chanterelle and red mustard-green risotto; or grilled Meyer Ranch natural rib-eye with Tuscan-style beans and rosemary-fried peppercorn sauce. Truth be told, even if the food weren't good, I'd come here. It's just that cool. By the way, if you have to wait for your table, consider stepping next door to the adjoining bar, Lazslo's.

2534 Mission St. (between 21st and 22nd sts.). ✆ **415/648-7600.** www.foreigncinema.com. Reservations recommended. Main courses $14–$25. AE, MC, V. Sun and Tues–Wed 5:30–10pm; Thurs–Sat 6–11pm; Sat–Sun brunch 11am–5pm. Closed Mon. Valet parking $8. Bus: 14, 14L, or 49.

Universal Café ★★ *Finds* AMERICAN/FRENCH When people ask for my list of favorite restaurants, tiny, out-of-the-way, and delicious Universal Café often comes to mind. Not only does the intimate, rather cramped place look good with its industrial-chic vibe, floor-to-ceiling windows at the front, and a row of tables running the length of the skinny restaurant and paralleling the cramped bar and open kitchen, but it also attracts a never-ending gaggle of youngish locals. I never shut up about the Universal's seasonal sautéed chicken liver with balsamic reduction, caramelized figs, and greens that graces the menu from time to time. Other superb dishes might include braised duck leg on a bed of creamy polenta; sea bass served with risotto, spinach, and caramelized onions; and hearty pot roast with lumpy mashed potatoes and fresh veggies. Granted, it's on the way to nowhere, but if you want an authentic and charming small-restaurant experience in San Francisco, the Universal is well worth the detour.

2814 19th St. (at Bryant St.). ✆ **415/821-4608.** Reservations recommended for dinner. Main courses $11–$24 dinner, $5–$12 brunch. AE, MC, V. Tues–Thurs 5:30–9:30pm; Fri 5:30–10:30pm; Sat 9am–2pm and 5:30–10:30pm; Sun 9am–2:30pm and 5:30–9:30pm. Bus: 27.

INEXPENSIVE

Delfina ★★ *Value* ITALIAN Unpretentious warehouse-chic atmosphere, reasonable prices, and chef/co-owner Craig Stoll's ultrafresh seasonal Italian cuisine have made this family-owned restaurant one of the city's most cherished. Stoll, who was one of *Food & Wine*'s Best New Chefs in 2001, changes the menu daily, while his wife Annie works the front of the house (when she's not being a mom). Standards include Niman Ranch flat-iron steak with french fries, and roasted chicken with Yukon Gold mashed potatoes and shiitake mushrooms. The winter menu might include slow-roasted pork shoulder or gnocchi with squash and chestnuts, while spring indulgences can include sand dabs with frisée, fingerling potatoes, and lemon-caper butter, or lamb with polenta and sweet peas.

Trust me—order the buttermilk *panna cotta* (custard). *A plus:* Four tables and counter seating are reserved for walk-in diners. *A downside:* It's impossible to find parking—literally—and there's no valet, so either park illegally (and perhaps get a ticket), come early to scrounge for a parking place, or take a bus or cab. Cocktail alert: Wine and beer only.

3621 18th St. (between Dolores and Guerrero sts.). ✆ **415/552-4055.** Reservations recommended. Main courses $13–$22. MC, V. Sun–Thurs 5:30–10pm; Fri–Sat 5:30–11pm. Streetcar: J. Bus: 26 or 33.

Pauline's ★★ PIZZA   Housed in a cheery yellow double-decker building that stands out like a beacon in a somewhat seedy neighborhood, Pauline's does only two things—pizzas and salads—but it does them better than most restaurants in the city. It's worth running the gauntlet of panhandlers for a slice of Italian sausage pizza on handmade thin-crust cornmeal dough. The gourmet toppings include chicken sausage, French goat cheese, roasted eggplant, Danish fontina cheese, and *tasso* (spiced pork shoulder). The salads are equally amazing: certified organic, handpicked by California growers, and topped with fresh and dried herbs (including edible flowers) from Pauline's own gardens in Berkeley. The wine list offers a smart selection of low-priced wines, where Star Canyon Vineyards, yet another of the owners' pursuits, will be showcased. Yes, prices are a bit steep (small pizzas start at $12), but what a paltry price to pay for perfection.

260 Valencia St. (between 14th St. and Duboce Ave.). ✆ **415/552-2050.** Reservations accepted for parties of 8 or more. Main courses $11–$22. MC, V. Tues–Sat 5–10pm. Bus: 14, 26, or 49.

Taquerias La Cumbre ★ MEXICAN   If San Francisco commissioned a flag honoring its favorite food, we'd probably all be waving a banner of the Golden Gate Bridge bolstering a giant burrito—that's how much we love the mammoth tortilla-wrapped meals. And while most restaurants gussy up their gastronomic goods with million-dollar decor and glamorous gimmicks, the burrito need only be craftily constructed of fresh pork, steak, chicken, or vegetables, plus cheese, beans, rice, salsa, and maybe a dash of guacamole or sour cream, and practically the whole will drive to the remotest corners to taste it. In this case, the fact that the burrito is served in a cafeteria-like brick-lined room with overly shellacked tables and chairs makes it all the better: There's no mistaking the attraction here.

515 Valencia St. (between 16th and 17th sts.). ✆ **415/863-8205.** Reservations not accepted. Tacos and burritos $3.50–$6.50; dinner plates $5–$7. No credit cards. Mon–Sat 11am–9pm; Sun noon–9pm. BART: Mission. Bus: 14, 22, 33, 49, or 53.

Ti Couz ★ CREPES   At Ti Couz (say "Tee Cooz"), one of the most architecturally stylish and popular restaurants in the Mission, the headliner is simple: the delicate, paper-thin crepe. More than 30 choices of fillings make for infinite expertly executed combinations. The menu advises you how to enjoy these wraps: Order a light crepe as an appetizer, a heftier one as a main course, and a drippingly sweet one for dessert. Recommended combinations are listed, but you can build your own from the 15 main-course selections (such as smoked salmon, mushrooms, sausage, ham, scallops, and onions) and 15 dessert options (caramel, fruit, chocolate, Nutella, and more). Soups and salads are equally stellar; the seafood salad, for example, is a delicious and generous compilation of shrimp, scallops, and ahi tuna with veggies and five kinds of lettuce. Cider, beer, and a full bar complement the cuisine.

3108 16th St. (at Valencia St.). ✆ **415/252-7373.** Reservations not accepted. Crepes $2–$11. MC, V. Mon–Fri 11am–11pm; Sat 10am–11pm; Sun 10am–10pm. BART: 16th and Mission. Bus: 14, 22, 26, 33, 49, or 53.

12 The Castro

Although you see gay and lesbian singles and couples at almost any restaurant in San Francisco, the following spots cater particularly to the gay community—but being gay is certainly not a requirement for enjoying them. For a map of restaurants in this section, see the "Dining Around Town" map on p. 122.

EXPENSIVE

Mecca ★★ *Finds* AMERICAN   In 1996, Mecca entered the scene in a decadent swirl of chocolate-brown velvet, stainless steel, cement, and brown Naugahyde. It's an industrial-chic supper club that makes you want to order a martini just so you'll match the ambience. The eclectic city clientele (with a heavy dash of same-sex couples) mingles at the oval centerpiece bar. A night here promises a live DJ spinning hot grooves and a fine American meal prepared by chef Stephen Barber and served at tables tucked into several nooks. On the menu are such classics as oysters on the half shell, seared ahi tuna, and wood-oven roasted pork tenderloin. The food is very good, but it's that only-in-San Francisco vibe that makes this place the smokin' hot spot in the Castro.

2029 Market St. (by 14th and Church sts.). ℂ 415/621-7000. www.sfmecca.com. Reservations recommended. Main courses $15–$29. AE, DC, MC, V. Tues–Thurs 5:30–10pm; Fri–Sat 6–11:30pm, bar remains open later; Sun 5–9:30pm. Valet parking $10. Streetcar: F, K, L, or M. Bus: 8, 22, 24, or 37.

MODERATE

Caffé Luna Piena ★ CALIFORNIA/MEDITERRANEAN   This is one of the Castro's warmest dining environments, complete with rich green walls adorned with local artwork. The room stretches back to the outdoor dining patio (yes, there are heat lamps and smoking is permitted) and a lush Japanese garden. The fare is contemporary California with Mediterranean influences. Lunch options include soups, salads, and sandwiches (with a choice of garlic fries or a green salad), such as grilled eggplant with roasted red pepper and smoked mozzarella on *pane integrale*. Main lunch courses might include walnut-crusted halibut with horseradish mashed potatoes. Dinner features such dishes as steak frites, New York steak, and penne pasta with house-made spicy sausage. Counter diners can watch chefs at work in the partially open kitchen. If you come for Saturday or Sunday brunch, reserve in advance or be prepared to wait in a long line. The menu includes salmon hash with poached eggs and tomato coulis, French toast with fruit compote and mascarpone cream, and other breakfast treats.

558 Castro St. (between 18th and 19th sts.). ℂ 415/621-2566. Reservations recommended. Main courses $6–$12 brunch, $9–$16 dinner. AE, MC, V. Daily 9am–10pm. Streetcar: F, K, L, or M. Bus: 24, 35, or 37.

2223 Restaurant & Bar ★★ CALIFORNIA   Surrounded by hardwood floors, candles, streamlined modern light fixtures, and loud music, festive gays and straights come here for heavy-handed specialty drinks and grilled pork chops or ever-popular roasted chicken with garlic mashed potatoes. Along with Mecca (see above), this is one of the top dining and schmoozing spots in the area—and definitely one of the better Sunday brunch spots.

2223 Market St. (between Sanchez and Noe sts.). ℂ 415/431-0692. www.2223restaurant.com. Reservations recommended. Main courses $7–$10 brunch, $13–$22 dinner. AE, DC, MC, V. Sun 10:30am–3pm and 5–10pm; Mon–Thurs 5–10pm; Fri–Sat 5–11pm. Streetcar: F, K, L, or M. Bus: 8, 22, 24, or 37.

INEXPENSIVE

Chow ★★ *Value* AMERICAN   Chow claims to serve American cuisine, but the management must be thinking of today's America, because the menu is not exactly meatloaf and apple pie. And that's just fine for eclectic and cost-conscious diners. After all, what's not to like about starting with a Cobb salad before moving on to Thai-style noodles with steak, chicken, peanuts, and spicy lime-chile garlic broth, or linguine with clams? Better yet, everything except the fish of the day costs under $15. More traditional are the budget-wise daily sandwich specials, which range from meatball with mozzarella (Sun) to baked chicken with herbed garlic mashed potatoes (Mon); both come with salad, soup, or fries. While the food and prices alone would be a good argument for coming here, beer on tap, a great inexpensive wine selection, and the fun, tavernlike environment clinch the deal. A second location, **Park Chow,** is at 1240 Ninth Ave. (© 415/665-9912). You can't make reservations unless you've got a party of eight or more, but if you're headed their way, you can call ahead to place your name on the wait list (recommended).

215 Church St. (near Market St.). © 415/552-2469. Reservations not accepted. Main courses $7–$15. MC, V. Sun–Thurs 11am–11pm; Fri–Sat 11am–midnight. Streetcar: F, J, K, L, or M. Bus: 8 or 37.

Firewood Café ★ *Value* AMERICAN/ITALIAN   One of the sharpest rooms in the neighborhood, the colorful Firewood put its money in the essentials and eliminated extra overhead. There are no waiters or waitresses; everyone orders at the counter and then relaxes at the single family-style table, at one of the small tables facing the huge street-side windows, or in the cheery back dining room. Management didn't skimp on the cozy-chic atmosphere and inspired but limited menu: The fresh salads come with a choice of three "fixin's," ranging from caramelized onions to spiced walnuts, and three gourmet dressing options. Then there are the pastas—three tortellini selections, such as roasted chicken and mortadella—and gourmet pizzas. Or how about herb-roasted half or whole chicken ($7.25 or $14, respectively) with roasted new potatoes? Wines cost $4.50 to $5.50 by the glass and a reasonable $18 to $21 per bottle. Draft and bottled beers are also available, and desserts top off at $2.95. (Thank goodness someone realized that $7 for an after-dinner treat borders on ridiculous.)

4248 18th St. (at Diamond St.). © 415/252-0999. www.firewoodcafe.com. Main courses $6.50–$14. MC, V. Mon–Thurs 11am–10:30pm; Fri–Sat 11am–11pm. Streetcar: F, K, L, or M. Bus: 8, 33, 35, or 37.

13 Haight-Ashbury

For a map of restaurants in this section, see the "Dining Around Town" map on p. 122.

MODERATE

Eos Restaurant & Wine Bar ★ EAST-WEST FUSION   Named after the Greek goddess of dawn, the modern and sleek Eos put Cole Valley on the culinary map, thanks to chef-proprietor Arnold Wong, a master of texture and taste, who perfected his craft while working at Masa's and Silks and also heads up one of the city's hottest restaurants, bacar. With a twinge of guilt, you dig in and mar the artistic presentation of each dish, such as the pan-roasted skate with roasted butternut squash, cipolini onions, and brown-butter sauce; or the braised oxtail with daikon radish, carrot, and pickled ginger. For starters, try salmon *poke* (Hawaiian style raw minced fish) rolls with chile-lime sauce. Unfortunately, the place can be downright deafening—if you want something a little more intimate, conversation-friendly, and affordable, you can always duck into their neighboring wine bar, which offers wine-friendly small-plate dishes—mostly under $10 each—along with about 40 excellent and less-common wines by the glass and 200 by the bottle.

901 Cole (at Carl St.). ℂ 415/566-3063. www.eossf.com. Reservations recommended. Main courses $10–$16. AE, MC, V. Sun–Thurs 5:30–10pm; Fri–Sat 5:30–11pm. Streetcar: N. Bus: 6, 33, or 43.

RNM ★★ AMERICAN Lower Haight is hardly known for glamour, and that's just what makes this ultraswank restaurant such a pleasant surprise. Beyond the full-length sliver mesh curtain is a deliciously glitzy diversion that looks more like it belongs in New York City rather than this funky 'hood. Warmly lit with dark-wood floors and tables, a cool full bar, and lounge mezzanine, it's the perfect setting for an equally appealing Italian- and French-inspired American tapas-style menu by chef Justine Miner who sharpened her culinary skills and knives at San Francisco's Postrio, Café Kati, and Globe. Anticipate tasty appetizers such as ahi tuna tartare with waffle chips, quail egg, and microgreens; charcuterie plate; and caramelized onion and wild-mushroom pizza with fontina cheese and truffle oil and entrees such as porcini-crusted day boat scallops on a purée of artichokes with shiitake mushroom ragout and a salad of mache greens and watermelon radishes with meyer lemon vinaigrette; and pan roasted rib-eye steak with pancetta-wrapped red Irish potatoes, wild nettles, Oakville Ranch cabernet butter, and shaved black Himalayan truffles.

598 Haight St. (at Steiner St.). ℂ 415/551-7900. www.rnmrestaurant.com. Reservations recommended. Small plates and pizza $7–$14; main courses $12–$22. MC, V. Tues–Wed 5–10pm; Thurs–Sat 5–11pm. Closed Sun–Mon. Bus: 7 or 22.

INEXPENSIVE

Cha Cha Cha ★★ Value CARIBBEAN This is one of my all-time favorite places to get festive, but it's not for everybody. Cha Cha Cha is not a meal, it's an experience. Put your name on the mile-long list, crowd into the minuscule bar, and sip sangria while you wait (try not to spill when you get bumped by all the young, attractive patrons who are also waiting). When you do finally get seated (it usually takes at least an hour), you'll dine in a loud—and I mean *loud*—dining room with Santería altars, banana trees, and plastic tropical tablecloths. The best thing to do is order from the tapas menu and share the dishes family-style. Fried calamari, fried new potatoes, Cajun shrimp, and mussels in saffron broth are all bursting with flavor and accompanied by rich, luscious sauces—whatever you choose, you can't go wrong. This is the kind of place where you take friends in a partying mood, let your hair down, and make an evening of it. If you want all the flavor without the festivities, come during lunch. Their second, larger location, in the Mission District, at 2327 Mission St., between 19th and 20th streets (ℂ 415/648-0504), is open for dinner only and has a full bar.

1801 Haight St. (at Shrader St.). ℂ 415/386-7670. Reservations not accepted. Tapas $5–$9; main courses $13–$15. MC, V. Daily 11am–4pm; Sun–Thurs 5–11pm; Fri–Sat 5–11:30pm. Streetcar: N. Bus: 6, 7, 66, 71, or 73.

Sweet Heat ★ MEXICAN If you're looking for a flavorful light lunch or a cheap, festive dinner, check out this casual place, offering "healthy Mexican food to die for." Far from traditional Mexican food, Sweet Heat has capitalized on California's love affair with old-style food prepared in new ways, and the results are addictive. Prices are low—$6.25 for a veggie burrito with grilled zucchini, red pepper, and roasted corn; and $7.25 for two grilled salmon tacos. A dining room expansion and renovation which includes a vibrant mosaic, and an expanded cocktail menu featuring a number of South American cocktails and more tequilas than you could possibly taste, add more spice to the already whimsical Haight Street haunt. There's also a happy hour from 4 to 6pm on weekdays, which features half-price nachos, $2 draft beers, and $3 house margaritas.

1725 Haight St. (between Cole and Schrader sts.). ✆ **415/387-8845.** All entrees under $10. AE, MC, V. Mon–Sat noon–11pm; Sun noon–10pm. Bus: 6, 37, or 43.

Thep Phanom ⭐⭐ THAI Thep Phanom has made the *San Francisco Chronicle's* top 100 Bay Area restaurants for 5 years running. It's the combination of super-fresh ingredients; the perfect lively balance of salty, sweet, hot, and sour flavors; and the attractive and atmospheric surroundings that usually fall short at other ethnic restaurants that make this place extra special. Those who like to play it safe will be more than happy with the likes of pad thai and coconut-lemongrass soup, but it's advisable to divert from the usual suspects for house specialties such as *Crying tiger* (beef salad with garlic dressing), prawns with eggplant and crisped basil, and *ped swan*—duck with a delicate honey sauce served over spinach. The Haight location usually attracts the young and alternative, but the restaurant's reputation brings in a truly diverse San Francisco crowd. As for the neighborhood: Don't leave anything even remotely valuable in your car.

400 Waller St. (at Fillmore St.). ✆ **415/431-2526.** Reservations recommended. Main courses $7–$12. AE, DC, DISC, MC, V. Daily 5:30–10:30pm. Bus: 6, 7, 22, 66, or 71.

14 Richmond/Sunset Districts

For a map of restaurants in this section, see the "Dining Around Town" map on p. 122.

MODERATE

Aziza ⭐⭐ MOROCCAN If you're looking for something really different—or a festive spot for a large party—head deep into the Avenues for an exotic taste of Morocco. Chef-owner Mourad Lahlou creates an excellent dining experience through colorful and distinctly Moroccan surroundings and his modern, but still authentic take on the food of his homeland. In any of the three opulently adorned dining rooms you might glimpse belly dancers gyrating (Thurs–Sun) as you indulge in the very affordable five-course tasting menu ($39) or individual treats such as kumquat-enriched lamb shank, saffron Cornish hen with preserved lemon and olives, or lavender honey-braised squab. Finish off with my favorite dessert: rhubarb galette with rose- and geranium-scented crème frâiche, vanilla aspic, and rhubarb consommé.

5800 Geary Blvd. (at 22nd Ave.). ✆ **415/752-2222.** www.aziza-sf.com. Reservations recommended. Main courses $11–$20; 5-course menu $39. AE, MC, V. Wed–Mon 5:30–10:30pm. Valet parking: $8 weekdays, $10 weekends. Bus: 29 or 38.

Beach Chalet Brewery & Restaurant ⭐ *Kids* AMERICAN While Cliff House (see below) has historic character worth exploration, this is the most modern ocean-side restaurant, with commanding views of the Pacific Ocean (fog permitting). The Chalet occupies the upper floor of a historic public lounge that originally opened in 1900, was renovated, closed, and was reopened in 1997. Today, the main floor's wonderful restored WPA frescoes and historical displays on the area are enough to lure tourists and locals, but there's nothing historic about the bright and cheery restaurant, which does the trick when you're in the 'hood, but is not a destination in itself. In fact, a great beer selection and live music have been the primary nighttime draws of late.

Dinner is pricey, and the view disappears with the sun, so come for breakfast or lunch when you can eat your hamburger, shrimp nachos, or salmon-stuffed rainbow trout with one of the best vistas around. After dinner, it's a more local thing, especially on select evenings when live bands accompany the cocktails and house-made house-brewed ales and root beer. (Call for schedules.) *Note:* Be careful getting into the parking lot (accessible only from the northbound side of the highway)—it's a quick, sandy turn.

In early 2004, owners Lara and Greg Truppelli added the adjoining **Park Chalet** restaurant. The 3,000-square-foot glass-enclosed extension behind the original landmark building offers more casual fare—with entrees ranging from $10 to $19—such as pizza with radicchio and pancetta and shepherd's pie. Retractable glass walls reveal Golden Gate Park's landmark Dutch windmill and a fireplace warms the room on chillier evenings.

1000 Great Hwy. (at west end of Golden Gate Park, near Fulton St.). ℂ **415/386-8439.** www.beachchalet. com. Main courses $9.25–$15 lunch, $10–$26 dinner. AE, MC, V. Daily 9am–midnight (however, hours change frequently based on business and seasons, so call ahead). Streetcar: N. Bus: 18, 31, or 38.

Cliff House ★ *Kids Finds* CALIFORNIA/SEAFOOD   In the old days (we're talking way back), Cliff House was *the* place to go for a romantic night on the town. Nowadays, the aging San Francisco landmark caters mostly to tourists who arrive by the busload to gander at the Sutro Baths remains next door.

But that may not be the case for long. The two restaurants in the main two-story building underwent major renovations over the past 2 years and are debuting as this book goes to press with fresh new looks and menus. (Unfortunately, details are not yet finalized, so sorry if I'm vague.) The new dining room in the Sutro Wing has panoramic views, a heavy seafood influence within its American menu, and is more formal (read: pricey). The Bistro is the more casual spot with a raw bar and takeout counter. Both spots have been refurbished to recall their glory days near the turn of the 20th century and both offer superb ocean views, particularly at sunset, when the fog lets up; unfortunately, in the past, the food has been a distant second to the scenery, but I'm hopeful the new Cliff House will give even locals a reason to head to this tourist attraction. Stay tuned. If you're headed this way, arrive before dusk, request a window seat, order a few appetizers and cocktails, and enjoy the view.

1090 Point Lobos (at Merrie Way). ℂ **415/386-3330.** www.cliffhouse.com. Reservations accepted for Sutro. Sutro main courses $9–$22 lunch, $17–$27 dinner. AE, DC, DISC, MC, V. Call for hours, which have yet to be determined. Bus: 18 or 38.

Kabuto A&S ★★ JAPANESE/SUSHI   In a town overflowing with seafood and pretentious taste buds, you'd think it would be easier to find great sushi. The truth is, finding an outstanding sushi restaurant in San Francisco is more challenging than spotting a parking space in Nob Hill. Chopsticking these fish-and-rice delicacies is one of the most joyous and adventurous ways to dine, and Kabuto is one of the best (and most expensive) places to do it. Chef Sachio Kojima, who presides over the small, crowded sushi bar (which moved into an

---

Lunching Near Golden Gate Park

Curiously (and happily), there are no restaurants other than museum cafes in Golden Gate Park, but that doesn't mean your choices are limited to the hot dog cart. The newly chic neighborhood of Inner Sunset boasts a handful of excellent, moderately priced restaurants. Try the bare-bones and traditional **Ebisu,** 1283 Ninth Ave., between Lincoln and Irving (ℂ **415/566-1770**), which has been a neighborhood favorite for nearly 20 years. It serves some of the city's best sushi, sashimi, and other Japanese fare.

even tinier space across the street from its old location in 2003), constructs each dish with smooth, lightning-fast movements known only to master chefs. If you're big on wasabi, ask for the stronger stuff Kojima serves on request.

5121 Geary Blvd. (at 16th Ave.). ✆ **415/752-5652.** Reservations not accepted. Sushi $3–$10; main courses $11–$18. MC, V. Thurs–Sat and Mon–Tues 11:30am–2:30pm and 5:30–11pm; Sun 11:30am–2:30pm and 5:30–10pm. Bus: 2, 28, or 38.

Khan Toke Thai House ⭐⭐ *Value* THAI Khan Toke Thai is so traditional, you're asked to remove your shoes before being seated. Popular for special occasions, this Richmond District fixture is easily the prettiest Thai restaurant in the city; lavishly carved teak interiors evoke the ambience of a Thai temple.

To start, order the *tom yam gong* soup of lemon grass, shrimp, mushroom, tomato, and cilantro. Follow with such well-flavored dishes as ground pork with fresh ginger, green onion, peanuts, and lemon juice; prawns with hot chiles, mint leaves, lime juice, lemon grass, and onions; or chicken with cashews, crispy chiles, and onions. For a real treat, have the deep-fried pompano topped with sautéed ginger, onions, peppers, pickled garlic, and yellow-bean sauce, or deep-fried red snapper with "three-flavors" sauce and basil leaves. A complete dinner, including appetizer, soup, salad, two main courses, dessert, and coffee, is a great value.

5937 Geary Blvd. (between 23rd and 24th aves.). ✆ **415/668-6654.** Reservations recommended Fri–Sat for parties of 3 or more. Main courses $6–$13; fixed-price dinner $19. AE, MC, V. Daily 5–10pm. Bus: 38.

Straits Café ⭐ SINGAPOREAN Straits Café is what I like to call "adventure dining," because you never quite know what kind of food you're going to get. Burlap palm trees, pastel-painted *trompe l'oeil* houses, faux balconies, and clotheslines strung across the walls evoke a surreal image of a Singaporean village in the Richmond District. The cuisine, however, is the real thing. Among chef Chris Yeo's spicy Malaysian-Indian-Chinese offerings are *murtabak* (stuffed Indian bread), chile crab, basil chicken, *nonya daging rendang* (beef simmered in lime leaves), *ikan pangang* (fish stuffed with chile paste), and, hottest of all, *sambal udang* (prawns sautéed in chile-shallot sambal sauce). For dessert, try the sago pudding.

3300 Geary Blvd. (at Parker St.). ✆ **415/668-1783.** Reservations recommended. Main courses $14–$22. AE, DC, MC, V. Mon–Thurs noon–2:30pm and 5:30–10pm; Fri–Sat noon–11pm; Sun noon–10pm. Bus: 2, 3, 4, or 38.

INEXPENSIVE

Ton Kiang ⭐⭐ *Kids* *Finds* CHINESE/DIM SUM Ton Kiang is the number one place in the city to have dim sum (served daily). Wait in line (which is out the door 11am–1:30pm), get a table on the first or second floor, and get ready to say yes to dozens of delicacies, which are brought to the table for your approval. From stuffed crab claws, roast Beijing duck, and a gazillion dumpling selections (including scallop and vegetable, shrimp, and beef) to the delicious and hard-to-find *doa miu* (snow pea sprouts flash-sautéed with garlic and peanut oil), shark-fin soup, and a mesmerizing mango pudding, every tray of morsels coming from the kitchen is an absolute delight. Though it's hard to get past the dim sum, which is served all day every day, the full menu of Hakka cuisine is worth investigation as well—fresh and flavorful soups; an array of seafood, beef, and chicken; and clay-pot specialties. This is definitely one of my favorite places to do lunch, and it happens to have an unusually friendly staff.

5821 Geary Blvd. (between 22nd and 23rd aves.). ✆ **415/387-8273.** www.tonkiang.net. Reservations accepted for parties of 8 or more. Dim sum $2–$5.50; main courses $9–$13. AE, MC, V. Daily 10am–10pm. Bus: 38.

7

Exploring San Francisco

San Francisco's parks, museums, tours, and landmarks are favorites for travelers the world over and offer an array of activities to suit every visitor. But no particular activity or place makes the city one of the most popular destinations in the world. It's San Francisco itself—its charm, its atmosphere, its perfect blend of big metropolis with small-town hospitality. No matter what you do while you're here—whether you spend all your time in central areas like Union Square or North Beach, or explore the outer neighborhoods—you're bound to discover the reason classic crooner Tony Bennett—and millions of visitors—leave their hearts in the City by the Bay.

1 Famous San Francisco Sights

Alcatraz Island ★★★ *Kids* Visible from Fisherman's Wharf, Alcatraz Island (aka "The Rock") has seen a checkered history. Juan Manuel Ayala was the first European to discover it in 1775 and named it after the many pelicans that nested on the island. From the 1850s to 1933, when the army vacated the island, it served as a military post, protecting the bay's shoreline. In 1934, the government converted the buildings of the military outpost into a maximum-security prison. Given the sheer cliffs, treacherous tides and currents, and frigid water temperatures, it was believed to be a totally escape-proof prison. Among the famous gangsters who occupied cell blocks A through D were Al Capone, Robert Stroud, the so-called Birdman of Alcatraz (because he was an expert in ornithological diseases), Machine Gun Kelly, and Alvin Karpis. It cost a fortune to keep them imprisoned here because all supplies, including water, had to be shipped in. In 1963, after an apparent escape in which no bodies were recovered, the government closed the prison. In 1969, a group of Native Americans chartered a boat to the island to symbolically reclaim the island for the Indian people. They occupied the island until 1971, the longest occupation of a federal facility by Native Americans to this day, when they were forcibly removed by the U.S. government (see www.nps.gov/alcatraz/indian.html for more information on the Native American occupation of Alcatraz). The next year the island became part of the Golden Gate National Recreation Area. The wildlife that was driven away during the military and prison years has begun to return—the black-crested night heron and other seabirds are nesting here again—and a new trail passes through the island's nature areas. Tours, including an audio tour of the prison block and a slide show, are given by the park's rangers, who entertain guests with interesting anecdotes.

Allow about 2½ hours for the round-trip boat ride and the tour. Wear comfortable shoes (the National Park Service notes that there are a lot of hills to climb on the tour) and take a heavy sweater or windbreaker, because even when the sun's out, it's cold out there. The excursion is popular and space is limited, so purchase tickets as far in advance as possible. **Blue & Gold Fleet**

Major San Francisco Attractions

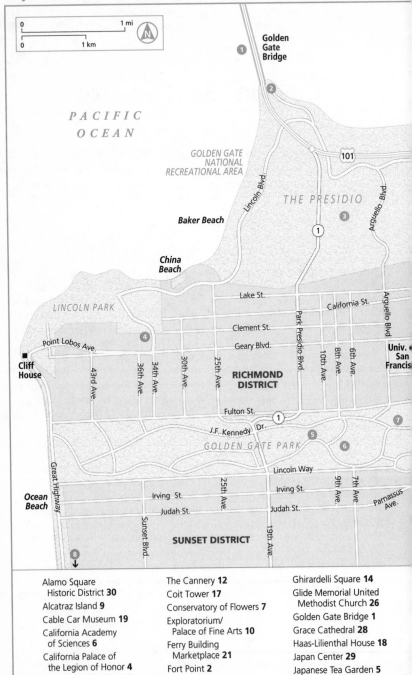

Alamo Square
  Historic District **30**
Alcatraz Island **9**
Cable Car Museum **19**
California Academy
  of Sciences **6**
California Palace of
  the Legion of Honor **4**

The Cannery **12**
Coit Tower **17**
Conservatory of Flowers **7**
Exploratorium/
  Palace of Fine Arts **10**
Ferry Building
  Marketplace **21**
Fort Point **2**

Ghirardelli Square **14**
Glide Memorial United
  Methodist Church **26**
Golden Gate Bridge **1**
Grace Cathedral **28**
Haas-Lilienthal House **18**
Japan Center **29**
Japanese Tea Garden **5**

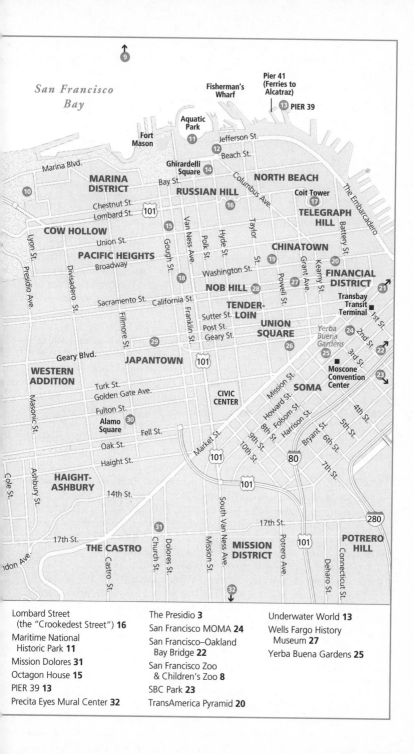

San Francisco Bay

Pier 41 (Ferries to Alcatraz)

Fisherman's Wharf

13 PIER 39

Aquatic Park

Fort Mason

11

Jefferson St.

12

Beach St.

Ghirardelli Square **14**

Columbus Ave.

NORTH BEACH

Coit Tower

17

Marina Blvd.

MARINA DISTRICT

Bay St.

RUSSIAN HILL

16

TELEGRAPH HILL

10

Chestnut St.

101

Lombard St.

Van Ness Ave.

Taylor St.

Battery St.

The Embarcadero

COW HOLLOW

Union St.

15

Polk St.

Hyde St.

CHINATOWN

19

Grant Ave.

Kearny St.

20

PACIFIC HEIGHTS

Broadway

Gough St.

18

Washington St.

FINANCIAL DISTRICT

21

Lyon St.

Presidio Ave.

Divisadero St.

Sacramento St.

California St.

NOB HILL 28

Powell St.

27

Transbay Transit Terminal

1st St.

Fillmore St.

Franklin St.

TENDER-LOIN

Sutter St.

UNION SQUARE

Yerba Buena Gardens

24

2nd St.

29

Post St.

Geary St.

26

25

3rd St.

22

Geary Blvd.

JAPANTOWN

101

Moscone Convention Center

23

WESTERN ADDITION

Turk St.

Golden Gate Ave.

CIVIC CENTER

Mission St.

SOMA

4th St.

Masonic St.

Fulton St.

Alamo Square **30**

Fell St.

Howard St.

8th St.

Folsom St.

Harrison St.

5th St.

6th St.

Oak St.

Market St.

9th St.

Bryant St.

7th St.

Haight St.

101

10th St.

80

HAIGHT-ASHBURY

14th St.

101

Ashbury St.

Cole St.

17th St.

31

Church St.

Dolores St.

Mission St.

South Van Ness Ave.

17th St.

101

280

POTRERO HILL

ndon Ave.

THE CASTRO

Castro St.

MISSION DISTRICT

Potrero Ave.

Deharo St.

Connecticut St.

32

Lombard Street (the "Crookedest Street") **16**

Maritime National Historic Park **11**

Mission Dolores **31**

Octagon House **15**

PIER 39 **13**

Precita Eyes Mural Center **32**

The Presidio **3**

San Francisco MOMA **24**

San Francisco–Oakland Bay Bridge **22**

San Francisco Zoo & Children's Zoo **8**

SBC Park **23**

TransAmerica Pyramid **20**

Underwater World **13**

Wells Fargo History Museum **27**

Yerba Buena Gardens **25**

(© **415/705-5555;** www.blueandgoldfleet.com) operates the tour; they accept American Express, MasterCard, and Visa, and there's a $2.25-per-ticket service charge for phone orders. You can also buy tickets in advance from the Blue & Gold ticket office on Pier 41 or online at www.telesales.com. Alcatraz night tours are also available and are a more intimate and wonderfully spooky experience. Check the Blue & Gold Fleet website for updated prices and departure times.

For those who want to get a closer look at Alcatraz without going ashore, two boat-tour operators offer short circumnavigations of the island (see "Self-Guided & Organized Tours," on p. 186, for complete information).

Pier 41, near Fisherman's Wharf. © **415/773-1188** (info only). Admission (includes ferry trip and audio tour) $16 adults with headset, $12 without; $15 seniors 62 and older with headset, $9.75 without; $11 children 5–11 with headset, $8.25 without. Winter daily 9:30am–2:15pm; summer daily 9:30am–4:15pm. Ferries depart 15 and 45 min. after the hour. Arrive at least 20 min. before sailing time.

Cable Cars ★★★ (Moments) (Kids)
Although they may not be San Francisco's most practical means of transportation, cable cars are certainly the best loved and are a must-experience when visiting the city. Designated official historic landmarks by the National Park Service in 1964, they clank up and down the city's steep hills like mobile museum pieces, tirelessly hauling thousands of tourists each day to nowhere in particular.

London-born engineer Andrew Hallidie invented San Francisco's cable cars in 1869. He got the idea by serendipity. As the story goes, Hallidie was watching a team of overworked horses haul a heavily laden carriage up a steep San Francisco slope. As he watched, one horse slipped and the car rolled back, dragging the other tired beasts with it. At that moment, Hallidie resolved that he would invent a mechanical contraption to replace such horses, and just 4 years later, in 1873, the first cable car made its maiden run from the top of Clay Street. Promptly ridiculed as "Hallidie's Folly," the cars were slow to gain acceptance. One early onlooker voiced the general opinion by exclaiming, "I don't believe it—the damned thing works!"

Even today, many visitors have difficulty believing that these vehicles, which have no engines, actually work. The cars, each weighing about 6 tons, run along a steel cable, enclosed under the street in a center rail. You can't see the cable unless you peer straight down into the crack, but you'll hear its characteristic clickity-clanking sound whenever you're nearby. The cars move when the gripper (not the driver) pulls back a lever that closes a pincerlike "grip" on the cable. The speed of the car, therefore, is determined by the speed of the cable, which is a constant 9½ mph—never more, never less.

The two types of cable cars in use hold a maximum of 90 and 100 passengers, and the limits are rigidly enforced. The best views are from the outer running boards, where you have to hold on tightly when taking curves.

Hallidie's cable cars have been imitated and used throughout the world, but all have been replaced by more efficient means of transportation. San Francisco planned to do so, too, but the proposal met with so much opposition that the cable cars' perpetuation was actually written into the city charter in 1955. The mandate cannot be revoked without the approval of a majority of the city's voters—a distant and doubtful prospect.

San Francisco's three existing cable car lines form the world's only surviving system of cable cars, which you can experience for yourself should you choose to wait in the endless boarding line (up to a 2-hr. wait in summer). For more information on riding them, see "Getting Around," in chapter 4, p. 54.

Fisherman's Wharf & Vicinity

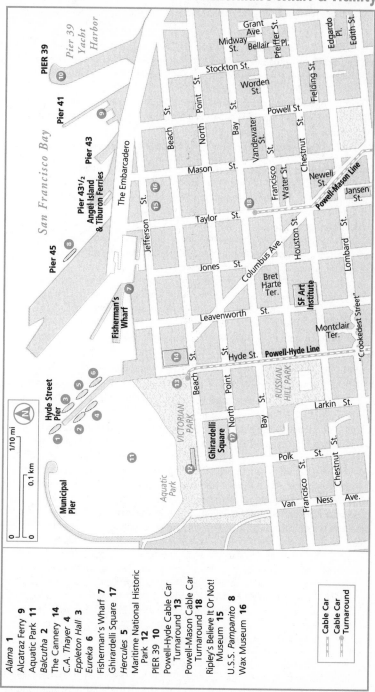

Alama 1
Alcatraz Ferry 9
Aquatic Park 11
Balcutha 2
The Cannery 14
C.A. Thayer 4
Eppleton Hall 3
Eureka 6
Fisherman's Wharf 7
Ghirardelli Square 17
Hercules 5
Maritime National Historic Park 12
PIER 39 10
Powell-Hyde Cable Car Turnaround 13
Powell-Mason Cable Car Turnaround 18
Ripley's Believe It Or Not! Museum 15
U.S.S. Pampanito 8
Wax Museum 16

Cable Car
Cable Car Turnaround

Powell-Hyde and Powell-Mason lines begin at the base of Powell and Market sts.; California St. line begins at the foot of Market St. $3 per ride.

The Cannery The Cannery was built in 1907 as a fruit-canning plant and was converted into a mall in the 1960s. It contains 30-plus shops, a ceramic studio and gallery, and several restaurants, including **Jack's Cannery Bar** (© 415/931-6400). Vendors' stalls and sidewalk cafes occupy the courtyard amid a grove of century-old olive trees and, weather permitting, street performers are usually out in force, entertaining tourists. *Note:* This is a tourist destination that many locals avoid.

2801 Leavenworth St. (between Beach and Jefferson sts.). © 415/771-3112. www.thecannery.com.

Coit Tower ★★ In a city known for its great views and vantage points, Coit Tower is one of the best. Located atop Telegraph Hill, just east of North Beach, the round, stone tower offers panoramic views of the city and the bay.

Completed in 1933, the tower is the legacy of Lillie Hitchcock Coit, a wealthy eccentric who left San Francisco a $125,000 bequest "for the purpose of adding beauty to the city I have always loved" and as a memorial to its volunteer firemen. She had been saved from a fire as a child and held the city's firefighters in particularly high esteem.

Inside the base of the tower are impressive murals titled *Life in California* and *1934,* which were completed under the WPA during the New Deal. They are the work of more than 25 artists, many of whom had studied under Mexican muralist Diego Rivera.

The only bummer: The narrow street leading to the tower is often clogged with tourist traffic. If you can, find a parking spot in North Beach and hoof it.

Telegraph Hill. © 415/362-0808. www.coittower.org. Admission to the top $3.75 adults, $2.50 seniors, $1.50 children 6–12. Daily 10am–6pm. Bus: 39 (Coit).

Ferry Building Marketplace (and Farmers' Market) ★★ *(Finds)* There's no better way to enjoy a San Francisco morning than strolling this gourmet marketplace in the newly renovated Ferry Building and snacking your way through breakfast or lunch. Tasty tenants, open daily, include many of the best of Northern California's gourmet bounty: Cowgirl Creamery's Artisan Cheese Shop, Recchiuti Confections (amazing!), Scharffen Berger Chocolate, Acme breads, Wine Country's gourmet diner Taylor's Refresher, famed Vietnamese restaurant The Slanted Door, and myriad other restaurants, eateries, and wine bars.

An added bonus and San Francisco favorite is the Farmers' Market, which is open alfresco on Saturdays from 8am to 2pm and Tuesday and Thursday from 10am to 2pm. Drop by to peruse stands hawking the finest Northern California fruits, vegetables, breads, dairy, flowers, and readymade snacks by a few local restaurants. You can also pick up locally made vinegars and oils—they make wonderful gifts. Drop in on Sunday from 8am to 2pm for the gardener's market, which focuses on plants but also has a bit of produce. Even when the market's closed, the glistening Ferry Building is now a worthy stop thanks to its new restaurants and shops.

The Embarcadero, at Market St. © 415/291-3276. Sat 8am–2pm; Tues, Thurs, and Sun 8am–2pm.

Fisherman's Wharf *(Overrated)* Few cities in America are as adept at wholesaling their historical sites as San Francisco, which has converted Fisherman's Wharf into one of the most popular tourist attractions in the world. Unless you come really early in the morning, you won't find any traces of the traditional

⟨Kids⟩ Funky Favorites at Fisherman's Wharf

The following sights clustered on or near Fisherman's Wharf are great fun for kids, adults, and kitsch-lovers of all ages. Yeah, some are kitsch, but kitsch can be fun! To reach the area by cable car, take the Powell-Mason line to the last stop and walk to the wharf; by bus, take no. 15, 30, 32, 39, 42, or 82X; by streetcar, take the F-line. If you're arriving by car, park on adjacent streets or on the wharf between Taylor and Jones streets.

The popular battle-scarred World War II fleet submarine **USS *Pampanito***, Pier 45, Fisherman's Wharf (© **415/775-1943**), saw plenty of action in the Pacific. It has been completely restored, and visitors are free to crawl around inside. Admission, which includes an audio tour, is $7 for those 13 to 61, $5 for seniors 62 and older, $4 for children 6 to 12, and free for children under 6; the family pass (two adults, up to four kids) costs $20. The *Pampanito* is open Monday through Thursday from 9am to 8pm (to 6pm in winter), Friday through Sunday from 9am to 8pm.

Also on Pier 45, the Musée Mécanique (p. 182) is worth a look.

Ripley's Believe It or Not! Museum, 175 Jefferson St. (© **415/771-6188**; www.ripleysf.com), has drawn curious spectators through its doors for over 30 years. Inside, you'll experience the extraordinary world of improbabilities: a ⅓-scale matchstick cable car, a shrunken human torso once owned by Ernest Hemingway, a dinosaur made from car bumpers, a walk through a kaleidoscope tunnel, and video displays and illusions. Robert LeRoy Ripley's infamous arsenal may lead you to ponder whether truth is, in fact, stranger than fiction. Admission is $12 for adults, $9.50 for seniors over 60, $7.95 for children 5 to 12, free for children under 5. The museum is open Sunday through Thursday from 10am to 10pm, until midnight on Friday and Saturday.

Conceived and executed in the Madame Tussaud mold, San Francisco's **Wax Museum,** 145 Jefferson St. (© **800/439-4305**), has long been a kitschy harborside tourist trap. In 1998, with the closing of the adjoining Haunted Goldmine, the museum underwent a $20-million tear-down, renovation, and expansion. It re-opened in June 2000 as a huge complex that includes the Rainforest Café, with walk-through aquariums. (Not any less of a tourist trap, mind you—only a newer, slicker one.) The overhaul spiffed up the museum's 252 lifelike figures, including Britney Spears, Marilyn Monroe, John Wayne, former President George Bush and current president George W. Bush, Giants baseball star Barry Bonds, rap singer Eminem, and "Feared Leaders" such as Fidel Castro. The Chamber of Horrors features Dracula, Frankenstein, and a werewolf, along with bloody victims hanging from meat hooks. New additions include pop icons such as Leonardo DiCaprio, Julia Roberts, and Will Smith. Admission is $13 for adults, $10 for seniors 62 and older, $6.95 for children 5 to 17, and free for children under 5. Discount group rates are available and are arranged via telephone or the website, www.waxmuseum.com, which also offers a $3 discount coupon for individual guests. The complex is open Monday through Friday from 10am to 9pm, Saturday and Sunday from 9am to 11pm.

waterfront life that once existed here; the only fishing going on around here is for tourists' dollars.

Originally called Meigg's Wharf, this bustling strip of waterfront got its present moniker from generations of fishers who used to base their boats here. Today, the bay has become so polluted with toxins that bright yellow placards warn against eating fish from the waters. A small fleet of fewer than 30 fishing boats still operates from here, but basically Fisherman's Wharf has been converted into one long shopping mall that stretches from Ghirardelli Square at the west end to PIER 39 at the east.

Accommodating a total of 350 boats, two marinas flank PIER 39 and house the Blue & Gold bay sightseeing fleet. In recent years, some 600 California sea lions have taken up residence on the adjacent floating docks. Until they abandon their new playground, which seems more and more unlikely, these playful, noisy creatures (some nights you can hear them all the way from Washington Sq.) are one of the best free attractions on the wharf. Docent-led programs, offered at PIER 39 on weekends from 11am to 5pm, teach visitors about the range, habitat, and adaptability of the California sea lion.

Some people love Fisherman's Wharf; others can't get far enough away from it. Most agree that, for better or for worse, it has to be seen at least once in your lifetime.

www.fishermanswharf.org. Take the Powell-Mason cable car to the last stop and walk to the wharf. By bus, take no. 15, 30, 32, 39, 42, or 82X. By streetcar, take the F-line. If you're arriving by car, park on adjacent streets or on the wharf between Taylor and Jones sts.

Ghirardelli Square ★ This National Historic Landmark property dates from 1864, when it served as a factory making Civil War uniforms, but it's best known as the former chocolate and spice factory of Domingo Ghirardelli (pronounced "Gear-a-deli"), who purchased it in 1984. The factory has since been converted into a three-level mall containing 50-plus stores and 11 dining establishments. Scheduled street performers entertain regularly in the West Plaza and fountain area. Incidentally, the Ghirardelli Chocolate Company still makes chocolate, but its factory is in a lower-rent district in the East Bay. Still, if you have a sweet tooth, you won't be disappointed at the mall's fantastic old-fashioned soda fountain.

900 North Point St. (between Polk and Larkin sts.). © 415/775-5500. Stores generally open 10am–8pm in summer (until 6pm in winter). Parking $4 per hour (1 hr. free with purchase and validation, max. $16).

Golden Gate Bridge ★★★ *Kids* The year 2005 marks the 68th birthday of possibly the most beautiful, and certainly the most photographed, bridge in the world. Often half-veiled by the city's trademark rolling fog, San Francisco's Golden Gate Bridge spans tidal currents, ocean waves, and battering winds to connect the City by the Bay with the Redwood Empire to the north.

With its gracefully swung single span, spidery bracing cables, and zooming twin towers, the bridge looks more like a work of abstract art than one of the 20th century's greatest practical engineering feats. Construction was completed in May 1937 at the then-colossal cost of $35 million.

The 1¼-mile-long steel link (longer if you factor in the approach), which reaches a height of 746 feet above the water, is an awesome bridge to cross. Traffic usually moves quickly, however, so crossing by car won't give you too much time to see the sights. If you drive from the city, park in the lot at the foot of the bridge on the city side and make the crossing by foot. Back in your car, continue to Marin's Vista Point, at the bridge's northern end. Look back, and you'll be rewarded with one of the greatest views of San Francisco.

Millions of pedestrians walk or bike across the bridge each year, gazing up at the tall red towers, out at the vistas of San Francisco and Marin County, and down into the stacks of oceangoing liners. You can walk out onto the span from either end, but be prepared—it's usually windy and cold, and the bridge vibrates. Still, walking even a short distance is one of the best ways to experience the immense scale of the structure.

Hwy. 101 N. www.goldengatebridge.org. $5 cash toll collected when driving south. Bridge-bound Golden Gate Transit buses (🕐 415/923-2000) depart every 30–60 min. during the day for Marin County, starting from the Transbay Terminal (Mission and First sts.) and stopping at Market and Seventh sts., at the Civic Center, and along Van Ness Ave. and Lombard St.

Lombard Street ★ *Overrated* Known (erroneously) as the "crookedest street in the world," this whimsically winding block of Lombard Street draws thousands of visitors each year (much to the chagrin of neighborhood residents, most of whom would prefer to block off the street to tourists). The angle of the street is so steep that the road has to snake back and forth to make a descent possible. The brick-lined street zigzags around the residences' bright flower gardens, which explode with color during warmer months. This short stretch of Lombard Street is one-way, downhill, and fun to drive. Take the curves slowly and in low gear, and expect a wait during the weekend. Save your film for the bottom where, if you're lucky, you can find a parking space and take a few snapshots of the silly spectacle. You can also take staircases (without curves) up or down on either side of the street. In truth, most locals don't understand what the fuss is all about. I'm guessing the draw is the combination of a classic, unusually steep San Francisco street and a great photo op. *FYI:* Vermont Street, between 20th and 22nd streets in Potrero Hill, is even more crooked, but not nearly as picturesque.

Between Hyde and Leavenworth sts.

PIER 39 *Overrated* PIER 39 is a multilevel waterfront complex a few blocks east of Fisherman's Wharf. Constructed on an abandoned cargo pier, it is, ostensibly, a re-creation of a turn-of-the-20th-century street scene, but don't expect a slice of old-time maritime life. This is the busiest mall of the lot and allegedly welcomes 11 million visitors per year. It has more than 100 stores, 11 bay-view restaurants, a two-tiered Venetian carousel, a Hard Rock Cafe, and arcade and aquarium entertainment for the kids. And everything's slated toward helping you part with your travel dollars. It's the place that locals love to hate. That said, it does have a few perks: absolutely beautiful natural surroundings of bay views, fresh sea air, and hundreds of sunbathing sea lions lounging along its neighboring dock.

On the waterfront at The Embarcadero and Beach St. 🕐 415/705-5500. www.pier39.com. Shops open daily 10:30am–8:30pm, with extended weekend hours during summer.

2 Museums

For information on museums in Golden Gate Park, see the "Golden Gate Park" section, beginning on p. 176.

Aquarium of the Bay The latest major addition to Fisherman's Wharf is Aquarium of the Bay, a $38-million, 1-million-gallon marine attraction filled with sharks, stingrays, and more. A moving footpath transports visitors through clear acrylic tunnels. The aquarium ultimately is not a destination in itself, but it's a good place to take the kids if you're in the neighborhood.

The Embarcadero at Beach St. 🕐 888/SEA-DIVE or 415/623-5301. www.aquariumofthebay.com. Aquarium admission $13 adults, $6.50 seniors and children 3–11, free for children under 3. Family (2 adults, 2 children) package $30. Behind-the-scenes tour $25 per person, including admission to the aquarium. Mon–Thurs 10am–6pm; Fri–Sun 10am–7pm.

Asian Art Museum ⭐ Reopened in its Civic Center home in March 2003, the Asian Art Museum is one of the Western world's largest museums devoted to Asian art. Its collection boasts more than 15,000 art objects, such as world-class sculptures, paintings, bronzes, ceramics, and jade items, spanning 6,000 years of history and regions of south Asia, west Asia, Southeast Asia, the Himalayas, China, Korea, and Japan. Previously in Golden Gate Park, the museum's new home in the city's Beaux Arts–style central library was renovated under Italian architect Gae Aulenti and includes 40,000 square feet of gallery space showcasing 2,500 objects at any given time. Add temporary exhibitions, live demonstrations, learning activities, cafe Asia, and a store, and you've got one very good reason to head to the Civic Center.

200 Larkin St. (between Fulton and McAllister sts.). © **415/581-3500.** www.asianart.org. Admission $10 adults, $7 seniors 65 and over, $6 youths 12–17, free for children under 12, $5 flat rate for all after 5pm Thurs. Free 1st Tues of the month. Tues–Wed and Fri–Sun 10am–5pm; Thurs 10am–9pm. Streetcar: Civic Center. Bus: All Market St. buses.

Cable Car Museum *Value* *Kids* If you've ever wondered how cable cars work, this nifty museum explains (and demonstrates) it all. Yes, this is a museum, but the Cable Car Museum is no stuffed shirt. It's the living powerhouse, repair shop, and storage place of the cable car system and is in full operation. Built for the Ferries and Cliff House Railway in 1887, the building underwent an $18-million reconstruction to restore its original gaslight-era look, install an amazing spectators' gallery, and add a museum of San Francisco transit history.

The exposed machinery, which pulls the cables under San Francisco's streets, looks like a Rube Goldberg invention. Stand in the mezzanine gallery and become mesmerized by the massive groaning and vibrating winches as they thread the cable that hauls the cars through a huge figure-eight and back into the system using slack-absorbing tension wheels. For a better view, move to the lower-level viewing room, where you can see the massive pulleys and gears operating underground.

Also on display here is one of the first grip cars developed by Andrew S. Hallidie, operated for the first time on Clay Street on August 2, 1873. Other displays include an antique grip car and trailer that operated on Pacific Avenue until 1929, and dozens of exact-scale models of cars used on the various city lines. There's also a shop where you can buy a variety of cable car gifts. You can see the whole museum in about 45 minutes.

1201 Mason St. (at Washington St.). © **415/474-1887.** www.cablecarmuseum.com. Free admission. Apr–Oct daily 10am–6pm; Nov–Mar daily 10am–5pm. Closed Thanksgiving, Christmas, and New Year's Day. Cable car: Both Powell St. lines.

California Academy of Sciences *Kids* Originally clustered around the Music Concourse in Golden Gate Park (in multiple buildings) and intending to return there around 2008 after a complete rebuild, this grouping of outstanding museums is now across from Moscone West, near the Yerba Buena Gardens and Center for the Arts. In its new location the **Steinhart Aquarium** houses some 5,400 animals, including seahorses, turtles, snakes, and poison dart frogs as well as a two-story 20,000-gallon living coral reef featuring Harlequin Tush fish, Yellow Tangs, sea stars, and a giant clam. Kids love the "touch tide pool" where they can get their mitts on live sea life.

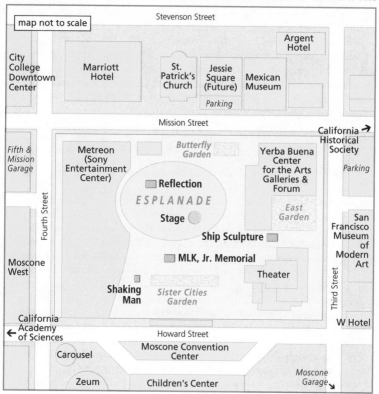

An edited version of the **Natural History Museum** has also been transplanted and hosts changing exhibits such as "Ants: Hidden Worlds Revealed," which shows the insects in action within six different live ant colonies. Some of the museum's permanent displays have moved, too, including Snake Alley, where terrestrial snakes reside; Astrobiology, an exhibit exploring life in extreme environments; and ScienceNOW, which presents a frequently changing display of Academy research, breaking science news, and expeditions around the globe. Toddlers will love the Nature Nest, an education center with hands-on learning activities.

Families should look into the Academy's calendar of events, which includes fun kid-friendly festivities such as face-painting, storytelling, animal origami, and exhibit-related stories and demonstrations.

875 Howard St. (between 4th and 5th sts.). ℂ **415/321-8000** for recorded information. www.calacademy. org. Admission $7 adults; $4.50 seniors 65 and over, students with ID, and children 12–17; $2 children 4–11; free for children under 4. Daily 10am–5pm. Streetcar: J, K, L, or M to Montgomery. Bus: 15, 30, or 45.

California Palace of the Legion of Honor ★★ Designed as a memorial to California's World War I casualties, this neoclassical structure is an exact replica of the Legion of Honor Palace in Paris, right down to the inscription HONNEUR ET PATRIE above the portal.

The Legion of Honor reopened in late 1995, after a 2-year, $35-million renovation and seismic upgrading. The exterior's grassy expanses, cliff-side paths, and incredible view of the Golden Gate and downtown make this an absolute must-visit attraction before you even get in the door. The inside is equally impressive. The museum's permanent collection covers 4,000 years of art and includes paintings, sculpture, and decorative arts from Europe, as well as international tapestries, prints, and drawings. The chronological display of 4,000 years of ancient and European art includes one of the world's finest collections of Rodin's sculptures. The sunlight Legion Café offers indoor and outdoor seating at moderate prices. Plan to spend 2 or 3 hours here.

In Lincoln Park (34th Ave. and Clement St.). ℂ **415/750-3600**, or 415/863-3330 (recorded information). www.thinker.org. Admission $8 adults, $6 seniors 65 and over, $5 youths 12–17, free for children under 12. Fees may be higher for special exhibitions. Free to all on Tues. Tues–Sun 9:30am–5pm. Bus: 18 or 38.

The Exploratorium ★★ *Kids*   *Scientific American* magazine rated the Exploratorium "the best science museum in the world"—pretty heady stuff for this exciting hands-on science fair. It contains more than 650 permanent exhibits that explore everything from giant-bubble blowing to Einstein's theory of relativity. It's like a mad scientist's penny arcade, an educational fun house, and an experimental laboratory, all rolled into one. Touch a tornado, shape a glowing electrical current, finger-paint using a computer, or take a sensory journey in total darkness in the Tactile Dome ($15 extra)—you could spend all day here and still not see everything. Every exhibit at the Exploratorium is designed to be interactive, educational, safe and, most important, fun. And don't think it's just for kids; parents inevitably end up being the most reluctant to leave. On the way out, be sure to stop in the wonderful gift store, which is chock-full of affordable brain candy.

The museum is in the Marina District at the beautiful **Palace of Fine Arts** ★, the only building left standing from the Panama-Pacific Exposition of 1915. The adjoining park and lagoon—the perfect place for an afternoon picnic—is home to ducks, swans, seagulls, and grouchy geese, so bring bread.

3601 Lyon St., in the Palace of Fine Arts (at Marina Blvd.). ℂ **415/563-7337**, or 415/561-0360 (recorded information). www.exploratorium.edu. Admission $12 adults; $9.50 seniors, youth 13–17, visitors with disabilities, and college students with ID; $8 children 4–12; free for children under 4. Free to all 1st Wed of each month. Groups of 10 or more must make advance reservations. AE, MC, V. Tues–Sun 10am–5pm. Closed Mon except MLK, Jr., Day, Presidents' Day, Memorial Day, and Labor Day. Free parking. Bus: 28, 30, or Golden Gate Transit.

Haas-Lilienthal House   Of the city's many gingerbread Victorians, this handsome Queen Anne house is one of the most flamboyant. The 1886 structure features all the architectural frills of the period, including dormer windows, flying cupolas, ornate trim, and winsome turret. The elaborately styled house is now a museum, its rooms fully furnished with period pieces. The Foundation for San Francisco's Architectural Heritage maintains the house and offers docent-led tours. The 1-hour tours (the only way to see the house) start every 20 to 30 minutes.

2007 Franklin St. (at Washington St.). ℂ **415/441-3004**. 1-hr. guided tour $8 adults, $5 seniors and children 6–12. Wed and Sat noon–3pm; Sun 11am–4pm. Cable car: California St. line. Bus: 1, 12, 19, 27, 47, 49, or 83.

Octagon House   This unusual, eight-sided, cupola-topped house of interest to architecture buffs dates from 1861 and is maintained by the National Society of Colonial Dames of America. The architectural features are extraordinary, and from the second floor it is possible to look up into the cupola, which is illuminated at night. In the small museum, you'll find Early American furniture, portraits, silver, pewter, looking glasses, and English and Chinese ceramics. There are also some historic documents, including signatures of 54 of the 56 signers of the Declaration of Independence. Even if you're not able to visit the inside, this strange structure is worth a look.

2645 Gough St. (at Union St.). 𝄐 **415/441-7512.** Free admission; donation suggested. Feb–Dec 2nd Sun and 2nd and 4th Thurs of each month noon–3pm. Closed Jan and holidays. Bus: 41 or 45.

San Francisco Maritime National Historical Park *Kids* Shaped like an Art Deco ship, the Maritime Museum is filled with sailing, whaling, and fishing lore. Remarkably good exhibits include intricate model craft and scrimshaw. The collection of shipwreck photographs and historic marine scenes includes an 1851 snapshot of hundreds of abandoned ships, deserted en masse by crews dashing off to participate in the gold rush. Beautifully carved, brightly painted wooden figureheads from old windjammers line the walls. Two blocks east, at the park's Hyde Street Pier, are several historic ships, now moored and open to the public.

The *Balclutha,* one of the last surviving square-riggers and the handsomest vessel in San Francisco Bay, was built in Glasgow, Scotland, in 1886 and carried grain from California at a near-record speed of 300 miles a day. The ship is now completely restored. Kids can climb into the bunking quarters, visit the "slop chest" ("galley" to you, matey), and read the sea chanteys (clean ones only) that decorate the walls.

The 1890 *Eureka* still carries a cargo of nostalgia for San Franciscans. It was the last of 50 paddle-wheel ferries that regularly plied the bay; it made its final trip in 1957. Restored to its original splendor at the height of the ferryboat era, the side-wheeler is loaded with deck cargo, including antique cars and trucks.

The black-hulled, three-masted *C. A. Thayer,* built in 1895, was crafted for the lumber trade and carried logs felled in the Pacific Northwest to the carpentry shops of California. Unfortunately, it's undergoing renovation and isn't slated to return until 2006.

Other historic ships docked here include the tiny two-masted *Alma,* one of the last scow schooners to bring hay to the horses of San Francisco; the *Hercules,* a huge 1907 oceangoing steam tug; and the *Eppleton Hall,* a side-wheel tugboat built in England in 1914 to operate on London's River Thames.

At the pier's small-boat shop, visitors can follow the restoration progress of historic boats from the museum's collection. It's behind the maritime bookstore on your right as you approach the ships.

At the foot of Polk St. (near Fisherman's Wharf). 𝄐 **415/561-7100.** www.nps.gov. Museum free. Tickets to board ships $5, free for children under 16. Museum daily 10am–5pm. Ships on Hyde St. Pier open Memorial Day–Oct 1 daily 9:30am–5:30pm; Oct 2 to day before Memorial Day daily 9:30am–5pm. Cable car: Powell-Hyde St. line to the last stop. Bus: 19, 30, or 47.

San Francisco Museum of Modern Art (MOMA) ★ Swiss architect Mario Botta, in association with Hellmuth, Obata, and Kassabaum, designed this $65-million museum, which has made SoMa one of the more popular areas to visit, for tourists and residents alike. The museum's permanent collection consists of more than 23,000 works, including close to 5,000 paintings and sculptures by artists such as Henri Matisse, Jackson Pollock, and Willem de Kooning. Other artists represented are Diego Rivera, Georgia O'Keeffe, Paul Klee, the Fauvists, and exceptional holdings of Richard Diebenkorn. MOMA was one of the first museums to recognize photography as a major art form; its extensive collection includes more than 12,000 photographs by such notables as Ansel Adams, Alfred Stieglitz, Edward Weston, and Henri Cartier-Bresson. Unfortunately, few works are on display at one time, and for the money the experience can be disappointing—especially compared to the finer museums of New York. Docent-led tours take place daily. Times are posted at the admission desk. Phone for current details of upcoming special events and exhibitions or check MOMA's website.

The **Caffé Museo,** to the right of the museum entrance, offers very good-quality fresh soups, sandwiches, and salads.

No matter what, don't miss the **MuseumStore,** which carries a wonderful array of architectural gifts, books, and trinkets. It's one of the best shops in town.

151 Third St. (2 blocks south of Market St., across from Yerba Buena Gardens). ✆ **415/357-4000.** www. sfmoma.org. Admission $10 adults, $7 seniors, $6 students over 12 with ID, free for children 12 and under. Half-price for all Thurs 6–8:45pm; free to all 1st Tues of each month. Thurs 11am–8:45pm; Fri–Tues 11am–5:45pm. Closed Wed and major holidays. Streetcar: J, K, L, or M to Montgomery. Bus: 15, 30, or 45.

San Francisco Zoo (& Children's Zoo) *Kids*   Located between the Pacific Ocean and Lake Merced, in the southwest corner of the city, the San Francisco Zoo is a fun place to take the kids—especially if you make it to the hands-on Children's Zoo. The zoo, which was founded at its present site adjacent to the ocean in 1929, is 125 acres, with 100 acres currently developed. Over 950,000 visitors come here annually to see the almost 950 mammals, birds, reptiles, amphibians, and invertebrates. Exhibit highlights include the new Lipman Family Lemur Forest, a forest setting for five endangered species of lemurs from Madagascar that features interactive components for the visitor; Gorilla World, a tranquil setting for a family group of western lowland gorillas; Koala Crossing, which connects to the Australian WalkAbout exhibit with its kangaroos, wallaroos, and emu; Penguin Island, home to a large breeding colony of Magellanic Penguins; the Feline Conservation Center, a wooded sanctuary and breeding facility for endangered snow leopards and other small cats; and the Primate Discovery Center, home to rare and endangered monkeys. In the South American Tropical Forest building, a large green anaconda can be found as well as other South American reptile and bird species. Puente al Sur (Bridge to the South) has a pair of giant anteaters, a rare Baird's tapir, and capybaras. The Lion House is home to rare Sumatran and Siberian tigers and African lions. You can see the big cats fed every day at 2pm (except Mon). African Savanna, the latest exhibit, which opened in mid-2004, is a 3-acre mixed-species habitat with giraffes, zebras, antelope, and birds.

The 6-acre Children's Zoo offers kids and their families opportunities for close-up encounters with domestic rare breeds of goats, sheep, ponies, and horses in the Family Farm. Touch and feel small mammals, reptiles, and amphibians along the Nature Trail (open Memorial Day to Labor Day), and gaze at eagles and hawks stationed on Hawk Hill. Visitors can see the inner-workings of the Koret Animal Resource Center, a thriving facility that houses the animals used in the educational outreach programs, and visit the incredible Insect Zoo. One of the Children's Zoo's most popular exhibits is the Meerkat and Prairie Dog exhibit, where kids can crawl through tunnels and play in sand, just like these two amazing burrowing species.

Don't miss the Little Puffer miniature steam train, which takes passengers around a ⅓-mile track, and the historic Dentzel Carousel (both $2 per ride).

Sloat Blvd. and 47th Ave. and Great Hwy. ✆ **415/753-7080.** www.sfzoo.org. Admission to main zoo and Children's Zoo $10 adults, $7 seniors and youth 12–17, $4 children 3–11, free for children under 3 accompanied by an adult; $1 discount with valid Muni transfer. Free to all 1st Wed of each month, except $2 fee for Children's Zoo. Carousel $2. Main zoo daily 10am–5pm. Children's Zoo Mon–Fri 11am–4pm, weekends and summer 10:30am–4:30pm. Streetcar: L from downtown Market St. to the end of the line.

Wells Fargo History Museum   Wells Fargo, one of California's largest banks, got its start in the Wild West. Its history museum, at the bank's head office, houses hundreds of genuine relics from the company's whip-and-six-shooter days, including pistols, photographs, early banking articles, posters, a stagecoach, and mining equipment.

420 Montgomery St. (at California St.). ℂ 415/396-2619. www.wellsfargohistory.com. Free admission. Mon–Fri 9am–5pm. Closed bank holidays. Cable car: California St. line. Streetcar: Montgomery St. Bus: Any to Market St.

Yerba Buena Center for the Arts/Yerba Buena Gardens ★★ *Finds* *Kids* The Yerba Buena Center, which opened in 1993, is the city's cultural facility, similar to New York's Lincoln Center but far more fun on the outside. It stands on top of the northern extension of the underground Moscone Convention Center. The center's two buildings present music, theater, dance, and visual arts. James Stewart Polshek designed the 755-seat theater, and Fumihiko Maki designed the Galleries and Arts Forum, which features three galleries and a space designed especially for dance. Cutting-edge computer art, multimedia shows, traditional exhibitions, and performances occupy the center's high-tech galleries.

More commonly explored is the 5-acre **Yerba Buena Gardens,** a great place to relax in the grass on a sunny day and check out several artworks. The most dramatic outdoor piece is an emotional mixed-media memorial to Martin Luther King, Jr. Created by sculptor Houston Conwill, poet Estella Majozo, and architect Joseph de Pace, it features 12 panels, each inscribed with quotations from King, sheltered behind a 50-foot-high waterfall. For most, this pastoral patch is a brief stopover to the surrounding attractions (see below). New to the gardens in 2004 are seasonal free **outdoor festivals** held on varied dates from May through October. It's definitely worth discovering whether you can catch one of these, as performances include dance, music, poetry, and more by the San Francisco Ballet, Opera, and Symphony and others; see www.ybgf.org for details.

On the periphery of Yerba Buena Gardens are a number of worthy individually operated excursions. In the Children's Center, **Zeum** (ℂ 415/777-2800) includes a cafe, interactive cultural center, bowling lanes, ice-skating rink, fabulous 1906 carousel, and interactive play and learning garden. Sony's **Metreon Entertainment Center** (ℂ 415/369-6000; www.metreon.com) is a 350,000-square-foot complex housing great movie theaters, an IMAX theater, a bountiful gourmet food court, interactive attractions (including one that features Maurice Sendak's *Where the Wild Things Are* and surprisingly exciting virtual bowling), and shops. As part of the plan to develop this area as the city's cultural hub, the **California Historical Society** opened at 678 Mission St. in 1995 and is home to a research library and a publicly accessible California photography and fine arts collection.

701 Mission St. ℂ 415/978-ARTS (box office). www.yerbabuenaarts.org. Admission $6 adults, $3 seniors and students. Free to all 1st Tues of each month. Free for seniors and students with ID every Thurs. Tues–Sun 11am–5pm; 1st Thurs of each month 11am–8pm. Streetcar: Powell or Montgomery. Bus: 5, 9, 14, 15, 30, or 45.

3 Neighborhoods Worth a Visit

To really get to know San Francisco, break out of the downtown and Fisherman's Wharf areas to explore the ethnically and culturally diverse neighborhoods. Walk the streets, browse the shops, grab a bite at a local restaurant—you'll find that San Francisco's beauty and charm are around every corner, not just at the popular tourist destinations.

Note: For information on Fisherman's Wharf, see its entry under "Famous San Francisco Sights," on p. 162. For information on San Francisco neighborhoods and districts that aren't discussed here, see "Neighborhoods in Brief," in chapter 4, beginning on p. 49.

NOB HILL

When the cable car started operating in 1873, this hill became the city's exclusive residential area. Newly wealthy residents who had struck it rich in the gold rush and were known as the "Big Four" and the "Comstock Bonanza kings" built their mansions here, but they were all destroyed by the earthquake and fire in 1906. The only two surviving buildings are the Flood Mansion, which serves today as the **Pacific Union Club,** and the **Fairmont Hotel,** which was under construction when the earthquake struck. Today, the burned-out sites of former mansions hold the city's luxury hotels—the **Mark Hopkins,** the **Stanford Court,** the **Fairmont,** and the **Huntington**—as well as spectacular **Grace Cathedral,** which stands on the Crocker mansion site. Nob Hill is worth a visit if only to stroll around **Huntington Park,** attend a Sunday service at the cathedral, or ooh and aah your way around the Fairmont's spectacular lobby.

SOUTH OF MARKET (SoMa)

From Market Street to Townsend Street and The Embarcadero to Division Street, SoMa has become the city's newest cultural and multimedia center. The process started when alternative clubs began opening in the old warehouses in the area nearly a decade ago. A wave of entrepreneurs followed, seeking to start new businesses in what was once an extremely low-rent area compared to the neighboring Financial District. Today, gentrification and high rents hold sway, spurred by a building boom that started with the **Moscone Convention Center** and continued with the **Center for the Arts at Yerba Buena Gardens,** the **San Francisco Museum of Modern Art,** the **Four Seasons Hotel,** and the **Metreon.** Other institutions, businesses, and museums move into the area on an ongoing basis. A substantial portion of the city's nightlife takes place in warehouse spaces throughout the district.

NORTH BEACH ✦✦✦

In the late 1800s, an enormous influx of Italian immigrants to North Beach firmly established this aromatic area as San Francisco's "Little Italy." Dozens of Italian restaurants and coffeehouses continue to flourish in what is still the center of the city's Italian community. Walk down **Columbus Avenue** on any given morning, and you're bound to be bombarded by the wonderful aromas of roasting coffee and savory pasta sauces. Although there are some interesting shops and bookstores in the area, it's the dozens of eclectic little cafes, delis, bakeries, and coffee shops that give North Beach its Italian-bohemian character.

For more perspective, follow the detailed walking tour in chapter 8 (beginning on p. 202) or sign up for a guided Javawalk with coffee nut Elaine Sosa (see "Walking Tours," later in this chapter).

CHINATOWN ✦✦

The first of the Chinese immigrants came to San Francisco in the early 1800s to work as servants. By 1851, 25,000 Chinese people were working in California, and most had settled in San Francisco's Chinatown. Fleeing famine and the Opium Wars, they had come seeking the good fortune promised by the "Gold Mountain" of California, and hoped to return with wealth to their families in China. For the majority, the reality of life in California did not live up to the

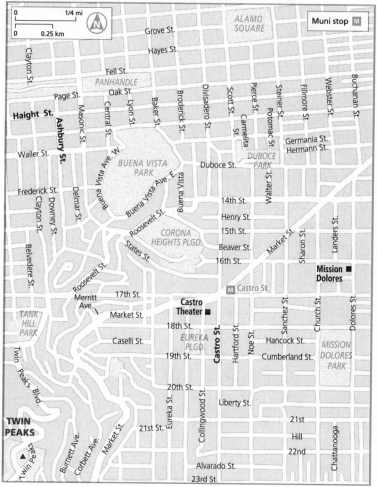

promise. First employed as workers in the gold mines during the gold rush, they later built the railroads, working as little more than slaves and facing constant prejudice. Yet the community, segregated in the Chinatown ghetto, thrived. Growing prejudice led to the Chinese Exclusion Act of 1882, which halted all Chinese immigration for 10 years and severely limited it thereafter (the Chinese Exclusion Act was not repealed until 1943). Chinese people were also denied the opportunity to buy homes outside the Chinatown ghetto until the 1950s.

Today, San Francisco has one of the largest communities of Chinese people in the United States. More than 80,000 people live in Chinatown, but the majority of Chinese people have moved out into newer areas like the Richmond and Sunset districts. Although frequented by tourists, the area continues to cater to Chinese shoppers, who crowd the vegetable and herb markets, restaurants, and shops. Tradition runs deep here, and if you're lucky, through an open window you might hear women mixing mah-jongg tiles as they play the centuries-old game. (*Be warned:* You're likely to hear lots of spitting around here, too—it seems to be part of local tradition.)

The gateway at Grant Avenue and Bush Street marks the entry to Chinatown. The heart of the neighborhood is Portsmouth Square, where you'll find locals playing board games (often gambling) or just sitting quietly.

On Waverly Place, a street where the Chinese celebratory colors of red, yellow, and green are much in evidence, you'll find three **Chinese temples:** Jeng Sen (Buddhist and Taoist) at no. 146, Tien Hou (Buddhist) at no. 125, and Norras (Buddhist) at no. 109. If you enter, do so quietly so that you do not disturb those in prayer.

A block west of Grant Avenue, **Stockton Street,** from 1000 to 1200, is the community's main shopping street, lined with grocers, fishmongers, tea sellers, herbalists, noodle parlors, and restaurants. Here, too, is the Buddhist Kong Chow Temple, at no. 855, above the Chinatown post office. Explore at your leisure. A Chinatown walking tour is outlined in chapter 8, beginning on p. 195.

JAPANTOWN

More than 12,000 citizens of Japanese descent (1.4% of the city's population) live in San Francisco, or Soko, as the Japanese who first emigrated here often called it. Initially, they settled in Chinatown and south of Market along Stevenson and Jessie streets from Fourth to Seventh streets. After the earthquake in 1906, SoMa became a light industrial and warehouse area, and the largest Japanese concentration took root in the Western Addition between Van Ness Avenue and Fillmore Street, the site of today's Japantown. By 1940, it covered 30 blocks.

In 1913, the Alien Land Law was passed, depriving Japanese Americans of the right to buy land. From 1924 to 1952, the United States banned Japanese immigration. During World War II, the U.S. government froze Japanese bank accounts, interned community leaders, and removed 112,000 Japanese Americans—two-thirds of them citizens—to camps in California, Utah, and Idaho. Japantown was emptied of Japanese people, and war workers took their place. Upon their release in 1945, the Japanese found their old neighborhood occupied. Most of them resettled in the Richmond and Sunset districts; some did return to Japantown, but it had shrunk to a mere 6 or so blocks. Among the community's notable sights are the **Buddhist Church of San Francisco,** 1881 Pine St. (at Octavia St.); the **Konko Church of San Francisco,** 1909 Bush St. (at Laguna St.); the **Sokoji-Soto Zen Buddhist Temple,** 1691 Laguna St. (at Sutter St.); **Nihonmachi Mall,** 1700 block of Buchanan Street between Sutter and Post streets, which contains two steel fountains by Ruth Asawa; and the **Japan Center,** an Asian-oriented shopping mall occupying 3 square blocks bounded by Post, Geary, Laguna, and Fillmore streets. At its center stands the five-tiered **Peace Pagoda,** designed by world-famous Japanese architect Yoshiro Taniguchi "to convey the friendship and goodwill of the Japanese to the people of the United States." Surrounding the pagoda, in a network of arcades, squares, and bridges, are dozens of shops and showrooms featuring everything from TVs and tansu chests to pearls, bonsai (dwarf trees), and kimonos. When it opened in 1968, the complex seemed as modern as a jumbo jet. Today, the concrete structure is less impressive, but it still holds some interesting surprises. **Kabuki Springs & Spa** (see the "Urban Renewal" box on p. 175) is the center's most famous tenant. The Japan Center houses numerous restaurants, teahouses, and shops, a multiplex movie theater, and the Asian-inspired 14-story **Radisson Miyako Hotel** (p. 101).

Finds **Urban Renewal**

Kabuki Springs & Spa, 1750 Geary Blvd. (© **415/922-6002**), the Japan Center's most famous tenant, was once an authentic, traditional Japanese bathhouse. The Joie de Vivre hotel group bought and renovated it, and it's now more of a pan-Asian spa with a focus on wellness. The deep ceramic communal tubs—at a very affordable $15 to $18 per person—private baths, and shiatsu massages remain and the joint stays open as late as 10pm; joining them are an array of massages and ayurvedic treatments, body scrubs, wraps, and facials, which cost from $55 to $120.

Spa Radiance, 3011 Fillmore St. (© **415/346-6281;** www.sparadiance. com), is an utterly San Francisco spa experience due to its unassuming Victorian surroundings and its wonderfully luxurious treatments such as facials (14 kinds!), body treatments, massages, manicures, pedicures, Brazilian waxing, spray-tanning, and makeup application by in-house artists.

There is often live entertainment in this neighborhood on summer weekends, including Japanese music and dance performances, tea ceremonies, flower-arranging demonstrations, martial-arts presentations, and other cultural events. The Japan Center (© **415/922-6776**) is open daily from 10am to midnight, although most shops close much earlier. To get there, take bus no. 2, 3, or 4 (exit at Buchanan and Sutter sts.) or no. 22 or 38 (exit at the northeast corner of Geary Blvd. and Fillmore St.).

HAIGHT-ASHBURY

Few of San Francisco's neighborhoods are as varied—or as famous—as Haight-Ashbury. Walk along Haight Street, and you'll encounter everything from drug-dazed drifters begging for change to an armada of the city's funky-trendy shops, clubs, and cafes. Turn anywhere off Haight, and instantly you're among the clean-cut, young urban professionals who can afford the steep rents in this hip 'hood. The result is an interesting mix of well-to-do and we'll-screw-you aging flower children, former Dead-heads, homeless people, and throngs of tourists who try not to stare as they wander through this most human of zoos. Some find it depressing, others find it fascinating, but everyone agrees that it ain't what it was in the free-lovin' psychedelic Summer of Love. Is it still worth a visit? Not if you are here for a day or two, but it's certainly worth an excursion on longer trips, if only to enjoy a cone of Cherry Garcia at the now-famous Ben & Jerry's Ice Cream Store on the corner of Haight and Ashbury streets, and then to wander and gawk at the area's intentional freaks.

THE CASTRO

Castro Street, between Market and 18th streets, is the center of the city's gay community as well as a lovely neighborhood teeming with shops, restaurants, bars, and other institutions that cater to the area's colorful residents. Among the landmarks are **Harvey Milk Plaza** and the **Castro Theatre,** a 1930s movie palace with a Wurlitzer. The gay community began to move here in the late 1960s and early 1970s from a neighborhood called Polk Gulch, which still has a number of gay-oriented bars and stores. Castro is one of the liveliest streets in the city and the perfect place to shop for gifts and revel in free-spiritedness.

THE MISSION DISTRICT

Once inhabited almost entirely by Irish immigrants, the Mission District is now the center of the city's Latino community as well as a mecca for young, hip residents. It's an oblong area stretching roughly from 14th to 30th streets between Potrero Avenue on the east and Dolores on the west. In the outer areas, many of the city's finest Victorians still stand, although many seem strangely out of place in the mostly lower-income neighborhoods. The heart of the community lies along 24th Street between Van Ness and Potrero, where dozens of excellent ethnic restaurants, bakeries, bars, and specialty stores attract people from all over the city. The area surrounding 16th Street and Valencia is a hotbed for impressive—and often impressively cheap—restaurants and bars catering to the city's hip crowd. The Mission District at night doesn't feel like the safest place (although in terms of creepiness, the Tenderloin, a few blocks off Union Square, beats the Mission by far), and walking around the area should be done with caution, but it's usually quite safe during the day and is highly recommended.

For an even better insight into the community, go to the **Precita Eyes Mural Arts Center,** 2981 24th St., between Harrison and Alabama streets (© **415/ 285-2287**), and take one of the 1½- to 2-hour tours conducted on Saturday and Sunday at 11am and 1:30pm. The 11am tour costs $10 for adults, $8 for students with ID, $5 for seniors, and $2 for children under 18; the 1:30pm tour, which is half an hour longer and includes a slide show, costs $12 for adults, $8 for students with ID, $5 for seniors, and $2 for children under 18. You'll see 60 murals in an 8-block walk. Every year during Mural Awareness Month (usually May), tours are given daily. All but the Saturday-morning tour (call for starting place) leave from the center's 24th Street location (© **415/285-2287**). Other signs of cultural life in the neighborhood are progressive theaters such as Theater Rhinoceros and Theater Artaud.

At 16th Street and Dolores is the Mission San Francisco de Assisi, better known as **Mission Dolores** (p. 183). It's the city's oldest surviving building and the district's namesake.

4 Golden Gate Park ★★★

Everybody loves **Golden Gate Park**—people, dogs, birds, frogs, turtles, bison, trees, bushes, and flowers. Literally, everything feels unified here in San Francisco's enormous arboreal front yard, but this great city landmark wasn't always a favorite place to convene. It was conceived in the 1860s and 1870s and took its current shape in the 1880s and 1890s, thanks to the skill and effort of John McLaren, a Scot who arrived in 1887 and began landscaping the park. Totaling 1,017 acres, the park is a narrow strip that stretches inland from the Pacific coast. No one had thought about the challenge the sand dunes and wind would present to any landscape artist. McLaren developed a new strain of grass called "sea bent," which he had planted to hold the sandy soil along the Firth of Forth, and he used it to anchor the soil here, too. He also built the two windmills that stand on the western edge of the park to pump water for irrigation. Every year the ocean eroded the western fringe of the park, and ultimately he solved this problem, too. It took him 40 years to build a natural wall, putting out bundles of sticks that the tides covered with sand. Under his brilliant eye, the park took shape.

Today's Golden Gate Park is a truly magical place. Spend 1 sunny day stretched out on the grass along JFK Drive, have a good read in the Shakespeare Garden,

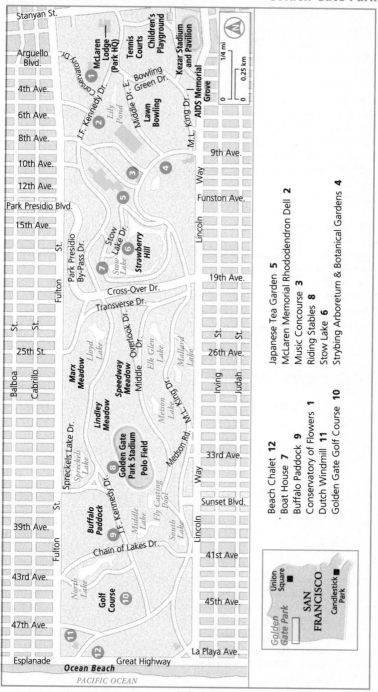

Japanese Tea Garden **5**

McLaren Memorial Rhododendron Dell **2**

Music Concourse **3**

Riding Stables **8**

Stow Lake **6**

Strybing Arboretum & Botanical Gardens **4**

Beach Chalet **12**

Boat House **7**

Buffalo Paddock **9**

Conservatory of Flowers **1**

Dutch Windmill **11**

Golden Gate Golf Course **10**

or stroll around Stow Lake, and you, too, will understand the allure. It's an interactive botanical symphony, and everyone is invited to play in the orchestra.

The park consists of hundreds of gardens and attractions connected by wooded paths and paved roads. While many worthy sites are clearly visible, there are infinite hidden treasures, so pick up information at **McLaren Lodge and Park Headquarters** (at Stanyan St. and Fell St.; © **415/831-2700**) if you want to find the more hidden spots. It's open daily and offers park maps for $3. Of the dozens of special gardens in the park, most recognized are **McLaren Memorial Rhododendron Dell, The Rose Garden, Strybing Arboretum,** and, at the western edge of the park, a springtime array of thousands of tulips and daffodils around the **Dutch windmill.**

In addition to the highlights described in this section, the park contains lots of recreational facilities: tennis courts; baseball, soccer, and polo fields; a golf course; riding stables; and fly-casting pools. The Strawberry Hill boathouse handles boat rentals. The park is also the home of two major museums: the California Academy of Sciences (currently relocated to SoMa during renovations; see listing on p. 166) and the currently closed **M. H. De Young Memorial Museum,** which is moving to 75 Tea Garden Drive (© **415/750-3600** or 415/863-3330), within the park, in late 2005 and will feature art of the Americas.

For further information, call the San Francisco Visitor Information Center at © **415/283-0177.** Enter the park at Kezar Drive, an extension of Fell Street; bus riders can take no. 5, 6, 7, 16AX, 16BX, 66, or 71.

MUSEUMS INSIDE THE PARK

In 2004, the California Academy of Sciences, which includes the Steinhart Aquarium, the Natural History Museum, and the Planetarium, moved from the park to a temporary location in downtown San Francisco to begin a 4-year renovation on its Golden Gate Park location. Limited aquarium and natural history exhibits are displayed in the temporary digs, but alas, the Planetarium did not relocate. See p. 2 for the temporary museums' details.

PARK HIGHLIGHTS

CONSERVATORY OF FLOWERS 🐾★   Built in 1879, this glorious Victorian glass structure is the oldest public conservatory in the western hemisphere. After a bad storm in 1995 and delayed renovations, the conservatory was closed and visitors were only able to imagine what wondrous displays existed within the striking glass assemblage. Thankfully, a $25-million renovation, including a $4-million exhibit upgrade, was completed in 2003, and now you can check out the rare tropical flora of the Congo, Philippines, and beyond within the stunning structure. It doesn't take long to visit, but make a point of staying a while; outside there are good sunny spots for people watching as well as paths leading to impressive gardens begging to be explored. If you're around during summer and fall, don't miss the Dahlia Garden to the right of the entrance in the center of what was once a carriage roundabout—it's an explosion of colorful Dr. Seuss–like blooms. The conservatory is open Tuesday through Sunday from 9am to 4:30pm; closed Mondays. Admission is $5 for adults; $3 for children 12 to 17 years of age, seniors, and students with ID; and free to all the first Tuesday of the month. For more information, visit www.conservatoryofflowers.org or call © **415/666-7001.**

JAPANESE TEA GARDEN   John McLaren, the man who began landscaping Golden Gate Park, hired Makoto Hagiwara, a wealthy Japanese landscape designer, to further develop this garden originally created for the 1894 Midwinter

Exposition. It's a quiet place with cherry trees, shrubs, and bonsai crisscrossed by winding paths and high-arched bridges over pools of water. Focal points and places for contemplation include the massive bronze Buddha (cast in Japan in 1790 and donated by the Gump family), the Buddhist wooden pagoda, and the Wishing Bridge, which, reflected in the water, looks as though it completes a circle. The garden is open daily November through February from 8:30am to 5pm (teahouse 10am–4:30pm), March through October from 8:30am to 6pm (teahouse 10am–5:30pm). For **information** on admission, call *C* **415/752-4227.** For the **teahouse,** call *C* **415/752-1171.**

STRAWBERRY HILL/STOW LAKE   Rent a paddleboat or rowboat and cruise around the circular lake as painters create still lifes, joggers pass along the grassy shoreline, ducks waddle around waiting to be fed, and turtles bathe on rocks and logs. Strawberry Hill, the 430-foot-high artificial island and highest point in the park that lies at the center of Stow Lake, is a perfect picnic spot; it boasts a bird's-eye view of San Francisco and the bay. It also has a waterfall and peace pagoda. For the **boathouse,** call *C* **415/752-0347.** Boat rentals are available daily from 10am to 4pm, weather permitting; four-passenger rowboats go for $13 per hour, and four-person paddleboats run $17 per hour; fees are cash-only.

STRYBING ARBORETUM & BOTANICAL GARDENS   Six thousand plant species grow here, among them some ancient plants in a special "primitive garden," rare species, and a grove of California redwoods. Docent tours begin at 1:30pm daily, with an additional 10:30am tour on weekends. Strybing is open Monday through Friday from 8am to 4:30pm, and Saturday and Sunday from 10am to 5pm. For more information, call *C* **415/661-1316** or visit www.strybing.org.

5 The Presidio & Golden Gate National Recreation Area

THE PRESIDIO

In October 1994, the Presidio passed from the U.S. Army to the National Park Service and became one of a handful of urban national parks that combines historical, architectural, and natural elements in one giant arboreal expanse. (It also contains a previously private golf course and a home for George Lucas's production company.) The 1,480-acre area incorporates a variety of terrain—coastal scrub, dunes, and prairie grasslands—that shelter many rare plants and more than 150 species of birds, some of which nest here.

This military outpost has a 220-year history, from its founding in September 1776 by the Spanish under José Joaquin Moraga to its closure in 1994. From 1822 to 1846, the property was in Mexican hands.

During the war with Mexico, U.S. forces occupied the fort, and in 1848, when California became part of the Union, it was formally transferred to the United States. When San Francisco suddenly became an important urban area during the gold rush, the U.S. government installed battalions of soldiers and built Fort Point to protect the entry to the harbor. It expanded the post during the Civil War and during the Indian Wars of the 1870s and 1880s. By the 1890s, the Presidio was no longer a frontier post but a major base for U.S. expansion into the Pacific. During the war with Spain in 1898, thousands of troops camped here in tent cities awaiting shipment to the Philippines, and the Army General Hospital treated the sick and wounded. By 1905, 12 coastal defense batteries were built along the headlands. In 1914, troops under the command of Gen. John

Golden Gate National Recreation Area

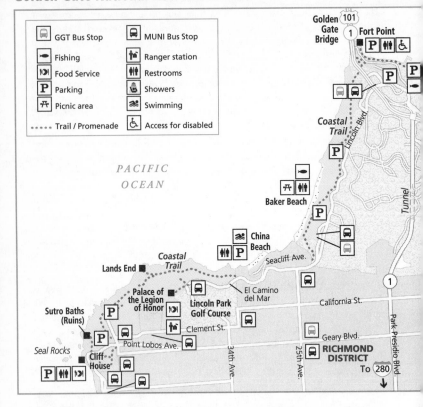

Pershing left here to pursue Pancho Villa and his men. The Presidio expanded during the 1920s, when Crissy Army Airfield (the first airfield on the West Coast) was established, but the major action was seen during World War II, after the attack on Pearl Harbor. Soldiers dug foxholes along nearby beaches, and the Presidio became the headquarters for the Western Defense Command. Some 1.75 million men were shipped out from nearby Fort Mason to fight in the Pacific; many returned to the Presidio's hospital, whose capacity peaked 1 year at 72,000 patients. In the 1950s, the Presidio served as the headquarters for the Sixth U.S. Army and a missile defense post, but its role slowly shrank. In 1972, it was included in new legislation establishing the Golden Gate National Recreation Area; in 1989, the Pentagon decided to close the post and transfer it to the National Park Service.

Today, the area encompasses more than 350 historic buildings, a scenic golf course, a national cemetery, and a variety of terrain and natural habitats. The National Park Service offers walking and biking tours around the Presidio; reservations are suggested. For more information, call the **Presidio Visitors Center** at © **415/561-4323.** Take bus no. 28, 45, 76, or 82X to get there.

GOLDEN GATE NATIONAL RECREATION AREA
The largest urban park in the world, GGNRA makes New York's Central Park look like a putting green, covering three counties along 28 miles of stunning, condo-free shoreline. Run by the National Park Service, the Recreation Area

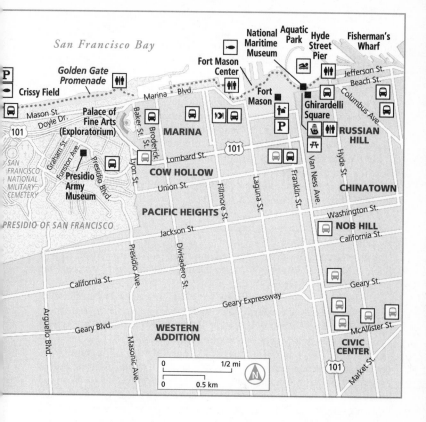

wraps around the northern and western edges of the city, and just about all of it is open to the public with no access fees. The Muni bus system provides transportation to the more popular sites, including Aquatic Park, Cliff House, Fort Mason, and Ocean Beach. For more information, contact the **National Park Service** (© 415/561-4700). For more detailed information on particular sites, see the "Getting Outside" section, later in this chapter.

Here is a brief rundown of the salient features of the park's peninsula section, starting at the northern section and moving westward around the coastline:

Aquatic Park, adjacent to the Hyde Street Pier, has a small swimming beach, although it's not that appealing (and darned cold). Far more entertaining is a visit to the ship-shaped museum across the lawn that's part of the San Francisco Maritime National Historical Park (see p. 169 for more information).

Fort Mason Center, from Bay Street to the shoreline, consists of several buildings and piers used during World War II. Today they hold a variety of museums, theaters, shops, and organizations, and Greens vegetarian restaurant (p. 143), which affords views of the Golden Gate Bridge. For information about Fort Mason events, call © 415/441-3400. The park headquarters is also at Fort Mason.

Farther west along the bay at the northern end of Laguna Street is **Marina Green,** a favorite local spot for kite-flying, jogging, and walking along the Promenade. The St. Francis Yacht Club is also here.

Next comes the 3½-mile paved **Golden Gate Promenade** ⭐, San Francisco's best and most scenic biking, jogging, and walking path. It runs along the shore past **Crissy Field** (be sure to stop and watch the gonzo windsurfers and kites surfers, who catch major wind here, and admire the newly restored marshlands) and ends at Fort Point under the Golden Gate Bridge.

Fort Point 👁 (© **415/556-1693**) was built in 1853 to 1861 to protect the narrow entrance to the harbor. It was designed to house 500 soldiers manning 126 muzzle-loading cannons. By 1900, the fort's soldiers and obsolete guns had been removed, but the formidable brick edifice remains. Fort Point is open Friday through Sunday only (temporary, due to bridge retrofit, and most likely through 2007) 10am to 5pm, and guided tours and cannon demonstrations are given at the site once or twice a day on open days, depending on the time of year.

Lincoln Boulevard sweeps around the western edge of the bay to **Baker Beach,** where the waves roll ashore—a fine spot for sunbathing, walking, or fishing. Hikers can follow the **Coastal Trail** from Fort Point along this part of the coastline all the way to Lands End.

A short distance from Baker Beach, **China Beach** is a small cove where swimming is permitted. Changing rooms, showers, a sun deck, and restrooms are available.

A little farther around the coast is **Lands End** 👁, looking out to Pyramid Rock. A lower and an upper trail offer hiking amid windswept cypresses and pines on the cliffs above the Pacific.

Still farther along the coast lie **Point Lobos,** the **Sutro Baths,** and **Cliff House** 👁. Cliff House (www.cliffhouse.com), which is completing renovations on its restaurants while still serving basic drinks and selling trinkets as this book goes to press, has been serving refreshments to visitors since 1863 and providing views of Seal Rocks, home to a colony of sea lions and many marine birds. (Alas, my favorite attraction here, the Musée Mécanique, an arcade featuring antique games, has moved to temporary digs at Pier 45; call © **415/346-2000** or visit http://museemecanique.citysearch.com for details, as nobody yet knows where its permanent home will be.) Northeast of Cliff House, only traces of the Sutro Baths remain, since the swimming facility, a major summer attraction that could accommodate up to 24,000 people, burned down in 1966.

A little farther inland at the western end of California Street is **Lincoln Park,** which contains a golf course and the spectacular California Palace of the Legion of Honor museum (p. 167).

At the southern end of Ocean Beach, 4 miles down the coast, is another area of the park around Fort Funston, where there's an easy loop trail across the cliffs (ranger office © **415/239-2366**). Here you can watch hang gliders take advantage of the high cliffs and strong winds.

Farther south along Route 280, **Sweeney Ridge,** accessible only by car, affords sweeping views of the coastline from the many trails that crisscross its 1,000 acres. From here the expedition led by Don Gaspar de Portolá first saw San Francisco Bay in 1769. It's in Pacifica; take Sneath Lane off Route 35 (Skyline Blvd.) in San Bruno.

The GGNRA extends into Marin County, where it encompasses the Marin Headlands, Muir Woods National Monument, and the Olema Valley behind the Point Reyes National Seashore. See chapter 11 for information on area highlights.

6 Religious Buildings Worth Checking Out

Glide Memorial United Methodist Church 👁 *(Moments)*   There would be nothing special about this Tenderloin-area church if it weren't for its exhilarating lively sermons and accompanying gospel choir. Reverend Cecil Williams's enthusiastic and uplifting preaching and singing with homeless and poor people of the neighborhood attracted nationwide fame over the past 30-plus years. In 1994, during the pastor's 30th-anniversary celebration, singers Angela Bofill and Bobby McFerrin joined comedian Robin Williams, author Maya Angelou, and talk-show queen Oprah Winfrey to honor him publicly. Cecil Williams now shares pastor duties with Douglas Fitch, alternating presiding over the nondogmatic, fun Sunday services in front of a diverse audience that crosses all socio-economic boundaries. Go for an uplifting experience and some hand-clapping gospel choir music.

330 Ellis St. (west of Union Square). ℂ **415/674-6000.** www.glide.org. Services Sun at 9 and 11am. Streetcar: Powell. Bus: 27. BART: Powell.

Grace Cathedral   Although this Nob Hill cathedral, designed by architect Lewis P. Hobart, appears to be made of stone, it is in fact constructed of reinforced concrete, beaten to achieve a stonelike effect. Construction began on the site of the Crocker mansion in 1928 but was not completed until 1964. Among the more interesting features of the building are its stained-glass windows, particularly those by the French Loire studios and Charles Counick, depicting such modern figures as Thurgood Marshall, Robert Frost, and Albert Einstein; the replicas of Ghiberti's bronze *Doors of Paradise* at the east end; the series of religious murals completed in the 1940s by Polish artist John de Rosen; and the 44-bell carillon. Along with its magical ambience, Grace lifts spirits with services, musical performances, and its weekly Forum (Sun 9:30–10:30am except summer and major holidays), where guests lead discussions about spirituality in modern times.

1100 California St. (between Taylor and Jones sts.). ℂ **415/749-6300.** www.gracecatherdral.org.

Mission Dolores   San Francisco's oldest standing structure, the Mission San Francisco de Assisi (aka Mission Dolores), has withstood the test of time, as well as two major earthquakes, relatively intact. In 1776, at the behest of Franciscan missionary Junípero Serra, Father Francisco Palou came to the Bay Area to found the sixth in a series of missions that dotted the California coastline. From these humble beginnings grew what was to become the city of San Francisco. The mission's small, simple chapel, built solidly by Native Americans who were converted to Christianity, is a curious mixture of native construction methods and Spanish-colonial style. A statue of Father Serra stands in the mission garden, although the portrait looks somewhat more contemplative, and less energetic, than he must have been in real life. A 45-minute audio tour costs $5; otherwise, admission is $3 for adults and $2 for children.

16th St. (at Dolores St.). ℂ **415/621-8203.** $3 adults, $2 children. May–Oct daily 9am–4:30pm; Nov–Apr daily 9am–4pm; Good Friday 9am–noon. Closed Thanksgiving and Dec 25. Streetcar: J. Bus: 14, 26, or 33 to Church and 16th sts.

7 Architectural Highlights

MUST-SEES FOR ARCHITECTURE BUFFS

ALAMO SQUARE HISTORIC DISTRICT   San Francisco's collection of Victorian houses, known as **Painted Ladies,** is one of the city's most famous assets. Most of the 14,000 extant structures date from the second half of the 19th century and are private residences. Spread throughout the city, many have been beautifully restored and ornately painted. The small area bordered by Divisadero Street on the west, Golden Gate Avenue on the north, Webster Street on the east, and Fell Street on the south—about 10 blocks west of the Civic Center—has one of the city's greatest concentrations of Painted Ladies. One of the most famous views of San Francisco—seen on postcards and posters all around the city—depicts sharp-edged Financial District skyscrapers behind a row of Victorians. This fantastic juxtaposition can be seen from Alamo Square, in the center of the historic district, at Fulton and Steiner streets.

CITY HALL & CIVIC CENTER   Built between 1913 and 1915, City Hall, located in the Civic Center District, is part of this "City Beautiful" complex done in the Beaux Arts style. The dome rises to a height of 308 feet on the exterior and is ornamented with oculi and topped by a lantern. The interior rotunda soars 112 feet and is finished in oak, marble, and limestone, with a monumental marble staircase leading to the second floor. No doubt you saw it on TV during early 2004, when much of the hoopla surrounding the short-lived and controversial gay marriage proceedings was depicted on the front steps. (Remember Rosie O'Donnell emerging from this very building after getting married to her girlfriend?)

OTHER ARCHITECTURAL HIGHLIGHTS

San Francisco is a center of many architecturally striking sights. This section concentrates on a few highlights.

The Union Square and Financial District areas have a number of buildings worth checking out. One is the former **Circle Gallery,** 140 Maiden Lane. Now a gallery housing Folk Art International, Xanadu Tribal Arts, and Boretti Amber & Design, it's the only building in the city designed by Frank Lloyd Wright (in 1948). The gallery was the prototype for the Guggenheim's seashell-shaped circular gallery space, even though it was meant to serve as a retail space for V. C. Morris, a purveyor of glass and crystal. Note the arresting exterior, a solid wall with a circular entryway to the left. Maiden Lane is just off Union Square between Geary and Post streets.

The **Hallidie Building,** 130–150 Sutter St., designed by Willis Polk in 1917, is an ideal example of a glass-curtain building. The vast glass facade is miraculously suspended between the two cast-iron cornices. The fire escapes that course down each side of the building complete the proscenium-like theatrical effect.

Two prominent pieces of San Francisco's skyline are in the Financial District. The **TransAmerica Pyramid,** 600 Montgomery St., between Clay and Washington streets, is one of the tallest structures in San Francisco. This corporate headquarters was completed in 1972, stands 48 stories tall, and is capped by a 212-foot spire. The former **Bank of America World Headquarters,** 555 California St., was designed by Wurster, Bernardi, and Emmons with Skidmore, Owings, and Merrill. This carnelian-marble-covered building dates from 1969. Its 52 stories are topped by a panoramic restaurant and bar, the Carnelian Room (p. 238). The focal point of the building's formal plaza is an abstract black granite sculpture, known locally as the "Banker's Heart," designed by Japanese architect Masayuki Nagare.

The **Medical Dental Building,** 450 Sutter St., is a steel-frame structure beautifully clad in terra cotta. It was designed by Miller and Pflueger in 1929. The entrance and the window frames are elaborately ornamented with Mayan relief work; the lobby ceiling is similarly decorated with gilding. Note the ornate elevators.

At the foot of Market Street you will find the **Ferry Building.** Built between 1895 and 1903, it served as the city's major transportation hub before the Golden Gate and Bay bridges were built; some 170 ferries docked here daily unloading Bay Area commuters until the 1930s. The tower that soars above the

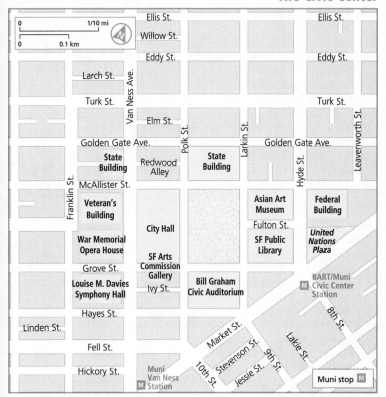

building was inspired by the Campanile of Venice and the Cathedral Tower in Seville. Plans are afoot to restore the building to its former glory by opening the soaring galleries to the sky again. If you stop by the Ferry Building, you might also want to go to **Rincon Center,** 99 Mission St., to see the WPA murals painted by the Russian artist Refregier in the post office.

Several important buildings are on or near Nob Hill. The **Flood Mansion,** 1000 California St., at Mason Street, was built between 1885 and 1886 for James Clair Flood. Thanks to the Comstock Lode, Flood rose from being bartender to one of the city's wealthiest men. He established the Nevada bank that later merged with Wells Fargo. The house cost $1.5 million to build at the time; the fence alone cost $30,000. It was designed by Augustus Laver and modified by Willis Polk after the 1906 earthquake to accommodate the Pacific Union Club.

Built by George Applegarth in 1913 for sugar magnate Adolph Spreckels, the **Spreckels Mansion,** 2080 Washington St., is currently home to romance novelist Danielle Steel (don't even try to get in to see her!). The extraordinary building has rounded-arch French doors on the first and second floors and curved balconies on the second floor. Inside, the original house featured an indoor pool in the basement, Adamesque fireplaces, and a circular Pompeian room with fountain.

Finally, one of San Francisco's most ingenious architectural accomplishments is the **San Francisco–Oakland Bay Bridge.** Although it's visually less appealing

Kids Especially for Kids

The following San Francisco attractions have major appeal to kids of all ages:

- Alcatraz Island (p. 157)
- Cable Car Museum (p. 166)
- Cable cars (p. 160)
- California Academy of Sciences, including Steinhart Aquarium (p. 166)
- The Exploratorium (p. 168)
- Golden Gate Bridge (p. 164)
- Golden Gate Park, including the Children's Playground, Bison Paddock, and Japanese Tea Garden (p. 176)
- Maritime Museum (San Francisco Maritime National Historical Park) and the historic ships anchored at Hyde Pier (p. 169)
- The Metreon Entertainment Center (p. 171)
- The San Francisco Zoo (p. 170)

In addition to the sights listed above, a number of playgrounds are of particular interest to kids. One of the most enormous, fun playgrounds for kids is in **Golden Gate Park.** Apartment buildings surround the **Cow Hollow Playground,** Baker Street between Greenwich and Filbert streets, on three of four sides. The landscaped playground features a bi-level play area fitted with well-conceived, colorful play structures, including a tunnel, slides, swings, and a miniature cable car. **Huntington Park,** Taylor Street between Sacramento and California streets, sits atop Nob Hill. This tiny play area contains several small structures particularly well suited to children under 5. **Julius Kahn Playground,** West Pacific Avenue at Spruce Street, is a popular playground inside San Francisco's great Presidio Park. Larger play structures and forested surroundings make this area attractive to children and adults alike.

than the nearby Golden Gate Bridge (except at night when it's lit up), the Bay Bridge is in many ways more spectacular. The silvery giant that links San Francisco with Oakland is one of the world's longest steel bridges (8¼ miles). It opened in 1936, 6 months before the Golden Gate. Each of its two decks contains five automobile lanes. The Bay Bridge is not a single bridge at all, but a superbly dovetailed series of spans joined mid-bay, at Yerba Buena Island, by one of the world's largest (in diameter) tunnels. To the west of Yerba Buena, the bridge is actually two separate suspension bridges, joined at a central anchorage. East of the island is a 1,400-foot cantilever span, followed by a succession of truss bridges. And it looks even more complex than it sounds. You can drive across the bridge (the toll is $2, paid westbound), or you can catch a bus at the Transbay Terminal (Mission at First St.) and ride to downtown Oakland.

8 Self-Guided & Organized Tours

THE 49-MILE SCENIC DRIVE

The self-guided, 49-mile drive is one easy way to orient yourself and to grasp the beauty of San Francisco and its extraordinary location. Beginning in the city, it follows a rough circle around the bay and passes virtually all the best-known sights, from Chinatown to the Golden Gate Bridge, Ocean Beach, Seal Rocks, Golden Gate Park, and Twin Peaks. Originally designed for the benefit of visitors to San Francisco's 1939 and 1940 Golden Gate International Exposition, the route is marked by blue-and-white seagull signs. Although it makes an excellent half-day tour, this miniexcursion can easily take longer if you decide, for example, to stop to walk across the Golden Gate Bridge or to have tea in Golden Gate Park's Japanese Tea Garden.

The San Francisco **Visitor Information Center,** at Powell and Market streets (p. 11), distributes free route maps, which are handy since a few of the Scenic Drive marker signs are missing. Try to avoid the downtown area during the weekday rush hours from 7 to 9am and 4 to 6pm.

A BART TOUR

One of the world's best commuter systems, **Bay Area Rapid Transit (BART)** runs along 104 miles of rail, linking 43 stations between San Francisco, Millbrae, and the East Bay. Under the bay, BART runs through one of the longest underwater transit tubes in the world. This link opened in September 1974, 2 years behind schedule and 6 months after the general manager resigned under fire. The train cars are 70 feet long and were designed to represent the latest word in public transport luxury. More than 3 decades later, they no longer seem futuristic, but they're still attractively modern, with carpeted floors, tinted picture windows, air-conditioning, and recessed lighting. The trains can hit a top speed of 80 mph; a computerized control system monitors and adjusts their speed.

The people who run BART think so highly of their trains and stations that they sell a $4 **"Excursion Ticket,"** which allows you, in effect, to "sightsee" the BART system, or basically ride it. "Tour" the entire system as much as you like for up to 3 hours; you must exit at the station where you entered (if you get out anywhere along the line, the gate instantly computes the normal fare). For more information, call ℂ **415/989-BART** or visit www.bart.gov.

BOAT TOURS

One of the best ways to look at San Francisco is from a boat bobbing on the bay. There are several cruises to choose from, and many of them start from Fisherman's Wharf.

Blue & Gold Fleet, PIER 39, Fisherman's Wharf (ℂ **415/773-1188;** www. blueandgoldfleet.com), tours the bay year-round in a sleek, 350-passenger sightseeing boat, complete with food and beverage facilities. The fully narrated, 1¼-hour cruise passes beneath the Golden Gate Bridge and comes within yards of Alcatraz Island. Don a jacket, bring the camera, and make sure it's a clear day for the best bay cruise. Frequent daily departures from PIER 39's West Marina begin at 10am during summer and 11am in winter. Tickets cost $20 for adults, $16 for seniors over 62 and juniors 12 to 17, and $12 for children 5 to 11; children under 5 are admitted free. There's a $2.25 charge for ordering tickets by phone; discounts are available online at www.telesails.com.

The **Red & White Fleet,** Pier 43½ (ℂ **415/447-0597;** www.redandwhite. com), offers daily "Bay Cruises" tours that leave from Pier 43½. The tour boats cruise beneath the Golden Gate Bridge and past the Marin Headlands, Sausalito, Tiburon, Angel Island, and Alcatraz and are narrated in various languages. Prices are $20 for adults, $16 for seniors and teens 12 to 18, and $12 for children 5 to 11. Discounts are available through online purchase.

BUS TOURS

Gray Line (© **888/428-6937** or 415/434-8687; www.sfsightseeing.com) is San Francisco's largest bus-tour operator. It offers several itineraries daily. Free pickup and return are available between centrally located hotels and departure locations. Reservations are required for most tours, which are available in several foreign languages, including French, German, Spanish, Italian, Japanese, and Korean.

WALKING TOURS

Javawalk is a 2-hour walking tour by self-described "coffeehouse lizard" Elaine Sosa. As the name suggests, it's loosely a coffee walking tour through North Beach, but there's a lot more going on than drinking cups of brew. Javawalk also serves up a good share of historical and architectural trivia, offering something for everyone. The best part of the tour may be the camaraderie that develops among the participants. Sosa keeps the excursion interactive and fun, and it's obvious she knows a profusion of tales and trivia about the history of coffee and its North Beach roots. It's a guaranteed good time, particularly if you're addicted to caffeine. Javawalk is offered Saturday at 10am and Tuesday through Friday for private parties of 6 or more. The price is $20 per person, $10 for kids under 13. For information and reservations, call © **415/673-WALK;** or visit www.java walk.com.

Cruisin' the Castro (© **415/550-8110;** www.webcastro.com/castrotour) is an informative historical tour of San Francisco's most famous gay quarter, which will give you new insight into the contribution of the gay community to the city's political maturity, growth, and beauty. Trevor Hailey, who was involved in the development of the Castro in the 1970s, conducts the tours. She knew Harvey Milk, the first openly gay politician elected to office in the United States: You'll learn about Milk's rise from shopkeeper to city supervisor and visit Harvey Milk Plaza, where marches, rallies, and protests begin. In addition, you'll explore the Castro Theatre, a memorial honoring gays who perished in the Holocaust, and side streets lined with beautifully restored Victorians, as well as the plethora of community-oriented stores in the Castro whose owners Hailey knows personally. Tours run Tuesday through Saturday from 10am to 2pm June through November and begin at Harvey Milk Plaza, atop the Castro Street Muni station. The cost includes lunch at a Castro area restaurant. Reservations are required. The tour, with lunch, costs $40 for adults and $35 for seniors over 62; the price for children is flexible depending on their age.

On the **Haight-Ashbury Flower Power Walking Tour** (© **415/863-1621**), you explore hippie haunts with Pam and Bruce Brennan ("the Hippy Gourmet"— see www.hippygourmet.com). You'll revisit in 2½ short hours the Grateful Dead's crash pad, Janis Joplin's house, and other reminders of the Summer of Love. Tours begin at 9:30am on Tuesdays and Saturdays. The cost is $15 per person. Reservations are required and the tour starts at the corner of Stanyan and Waller streets.

San Francisco's Chinatown is always fascinating, but for many visitors with limited time it's hard to know where to search out the "nontouristy" shops, restaurants, and historical spots in this microcosm of Chinese culture. **Wok Wiz Chinatown Walking Tours & Cooking Center,** 654 Commercial St., between Kearny and Montgomery streets (© **650/355-9657;** www.wokwiz.com), founded over 2 decades ago by author and cooking instructor Shirley Fong-Torres, is the answer. The Wok Wiz tours take you into Chinatown's nooks and crannies.

Most guides are Chinese, speak fluent Cantonese or Mandarin, and are intimately acquainted with the neighborhood's alleys and small enterprises, as well as Chinatown's history, folklore, culture, and food. Tours are conducted daily from 10am to 1:30pm and include dim sum (Chinese lunch). There's also a less expensive tour that does not include lunch. The walk is easy, as well as fun and fascinating. Groups are generally held to a maximum of 15, and reservations are essential. Prices (including lunch) are $40 for adults and $35 for children under 11; without lunch, prices are $28 and $23, respectively.

Shirley Fong-Torres also operates an **I Can't Believe I Ate My Way Through Chinatown** tour. It starts with breakfast, moves to a wok shop, and stops for nibbles at a vegetarian restaurant and dim sum, and at a marketplace before taking a break for a sumptuous authentic Cantonese luncheon. It's offered on most Saturdays and costs $75 per person, food included. The **Walk & Wok** tour includes shopping for food in Chinatown, then cooking (and eating) it together at Shirley's Cooking Center (most Sat; $75 per person). Shirley recently introduced a new $65 nighttime tour, which includes dinner.

Jay Gifford, founder of the **Victorian Homes Historical Walking Tour** (© 415/252-9485; www.victorianwalk.com) and a San Francisco resident for 2 decades, communicates his enthusiasm and love of San Francisco throughout this highly entertaining walking tour. The 2½-hour daily tour, at a very leisurely pace, starts in the lobby of the Westin St. Francis hotel and incorporates a wealth of knowledge about San Francisco's Victorian architecture and the city's history—particularly the periods before and after the great earthquake and fire of 1906. You'll stroll through Japantown, walk through the Western Addition (where you can take a break to cruise the trendy shops on Fillmore St.), and proceed to Pacific Heights and Cow Hollow. In the process, you'll see more than 200 meticulously restored Victorians, including the sites where *Mrs. Doubtfire* and *Party of Five* were filmed. Jay's guests often find that they are the only ones on the quiet neighborhood streets, where tour buses are forbidden. The tour ends with a trolley bus ride back to Union Square, passing through North Beach and Chinatown. Tours, which start at Union Square at 11am, are offered daily April through December and Thursday through Monday from January through March and cost $20 per person.

9 Getting Outside

Half the fun in San Francisco takes place outdoors. If you're not in the mood to trek it, there are other things to do that allow you to enjoy the surroundings.

BALLOONING   Although you must drive 1 hour to get to the tour site, hot-air ballooning is an ethereal and silent flight over the Wine Country. **Adventures Aloft,** P.O. Box 2500, Vintage 1870, Yountville, CA 94599 (© **800/944-4408** or 707/944-4408; www.nvaloft.com), is Napa Valley's oldest hot-air balloon company, staffed with full-time professional pilots. Groups are small, and each flight lasts about an hour. The cost of $205 per person ($170 ages 6–16) includes a postadventure champagne brunch and a framed "first-flight" certificate. Flights launch daily at sunrise (weather permitting).

BEACHES   For beach information, call the San Francisco Visitor Information Center at © **415/283-0177.** Most days it's too chilly to hang out at the beach, but when the fog evaporates and the wind dies down, one of the best ways to spend the day is ocean side in the city. On any truly hot day, thousands flock to the beach to worship the sun, build sandcastles, and throw the ball around.

Without a wet suit, swimming is a fiercely cold endeavor and is not recommended. Only two beaches are considered safe for swimming: **Aquatic Park,** adjacent to the Hyde Park Pier, and **China Beach,** a small cove on the western edge of the South Bay. But dip at your own risk—there are no lifeguards on duty. Also on the South Bay, **Baker Beach** is ideal for picnicking, sunning, walking, or fishing against the backdrop of the Golden Gate (though pollution makes your catch not necessarily worthy of eating).

Ocean Beach, at the end of Golden Gate Park, on the westernmost side of the city, is San Francisco's largest beach—4 miles long. Just offshore, at the northern end of the beach, in front of Cliff House, are the jagged Seal Rocks, inhabited by various shorebirds and a large colony of barking sea lions (bring binoculars for a close-up view). To the left, Kelly's Cove is one of the more challenging surf spots in town. Ocean Beach is ideal for strolling or sunning, but don't swim here—tides are tricky, and each year bathers drown in the rough surf.

Stop by Ocean Beach bus terminal at the corner of Cabrillo and La Playa to learn about San Francisco's playful history in local artist Ray Beldner's whimsically historical sculpture garden. Then hike up the hill to explore Cliff House and the ruins of the Sutro Baths. These baths, able to accommodate 24,000 bathers, were lost to fire in 1966.

BIKING   The San Francisco Parks and Recreation Department maintains two city-designated bike routes. One winds 7½ miles through Golden Gate Park to Lake Merced; the other traverses the city, starting in the south, and continues over the Golden Gate Bridge. These routes are not dedicated to bicyclists, who must exercise caution to avoid crashing into pedestrians. Helmets are recommended for adults and required by law for kids under 18. A bike map is available from the San Francisco Visitor Information Center, at Powell and Mason streets (see "Visitor Information," in chapter 4), and from bicycle shops all around town.

Ocean Beach has a public walk- and bikeway that stretches along 5 waterfront blocks of the Great Highway between Noriega and Santiago streets. It's an easy ride from Cliff House or Golden Gate Park.

Avenue Cyclery, 756 Stanyan St., at Waller Street, in the Haight (© **415/ 387-3155**), rents bikes for $5 per hour or $25 per day. It's open daily, April through September from 10am to 7pm and October through March from 10am to 6pm.

BOATING   At the **Golden Gate Park Boat House** (© **415/752-0347**) on Stow Lake, the park's largest body of water, you can rent a rowboat or pedal boat by the hour and steer over to Strawberry Hill, a large, round island in the middle of the lake, for lunch. There's usually a line on weekends. The boathouse is open daily from 10am to 4pm, weather permitting.

Cass Marina, 1702 Bridgeway, Sausalito (© **800/472-4595** or 415/332-6789; www.cassmarina.com), is a certified sailing school that rents sailboats measuring 22 to 101 feet. Sail to the Golden Gate Bridge on your own or with a licensed skipper. In addition, large sailing yachts leave from San Francisco and Sausalito on a regularly scheduled basis. Call or check the website for schedules, prices, and availability of sailboats. The marina is open Wednesday through Monday from 9am to sunset.

CITY STAIR CLIMBING   Many health clubs have stair-climbing machines and step classes, but in San Francisco, you need only go outside. The following city stair climbs will give you not only a good workout, but great sightseeing, too.

Filbert Street Steps, between Sansome Street and Telegraph Hill, are a particular challenge. Scaling the sheer eastern face of Telegraph Hill, this 377-step climb winds through verdant flower gardens and charming 19th-century cottages. Napier Lane, a narrow, wooden plank walkway, leads to Montgomery Street. Turn right and follow the path to the end of the cul-de-sac, where another stairway continues to Telegraph's panoramic summit.

The **Lyon Street Steps,** between Green Street and Broadway, were built in 1916. This historic stairway street contains four steep sets of stairs totaling 288 steps. Begin at Green Street and climb all the way up, past manicured hedges and flower gardens, to an iron gate that opens into the Presidio. A block east, on Baker Street, another set of 369 steps descends to Green Street.

FISHING   Berkeley Marina Sports Center, 225 University Ave., Berkeley (© **510/849-2727;** www.berkeleysportfishing.com), makes daily trips for ling cod, rock fish, and many other types of game fish year-round, and it makes trips for salmon runs April through October. Fishing equipment is available; the cost, including boat ride and bait, is $90 per person, $100 when it's a crab-and-fish combo. Reservations are required, as are licenses for adults. One-day licenses can be purchased for $11 before departure. Find out the latest on the season by contacting their hot line at © **510/486-8300.** Excursions run daily from 6am to 4pm. Fish are cleaned, filleted, and bagged on the return trip for a small fee (free for salmon fishing).

GOLF   San Francisco has a few beautiful golf courses. One of the most lavish is the **Presidio Golf Course** (© **415/561-4664;** www.presidiogolf.com). Greens fees are $42 Monday through Thursday, $52 on Friday, and $72 on Saturday and Sunday; rates decrease later in the day. Carts are $16. There are also two decent municipal courses in town.

The 9-hole **Golden Gate Park Course,** 47th Avenue and Fulton Street (© **415/751-8987;** www.goldengateparkgolf.com), charges greens fees of $13 per person Monday through Thursday, $17 Friday through Sunday. The 1,357-yard course is par 27. All holes are par 3, tightly set, and well trapped with small greens. The course is a little weathered in spots, but it's casual, fun, and inexpensive. It's open daily at 6:30am.

The 18-hole **Lincoln Park Golf Course,** 34th Avenue and Clement Street (© **415/221-9911**), charges greens fees of $31 per person Monday through Thursday, $35 Friday through Sunday, with rates decreasing after 2pm. It's San Francisco's prettiest municipal course, with terrific views and fairways lined with Monterey cypress and pine trees. The 5,181-yard layout plays to par 68, and the 17th hole has a glistening ocean view. This is the oldest course in the city and one of the oldest in the West. It's open daily at daybreak.

A good place for a tune-up is the **Mission Bay Golf Center,** Sixth Street at Channel Street (© **415/431-7888**). San Francisco's most popular driving range is an impeccably maintained 7-acre facility that consists of a double-decker steel and concrete arc containing 66 covered practice bays. The grass landing area extends 300 yards, has nine target greens, and is lit for evening use. There's a putting green and a chipping and bunker practice area. The center is open Monday from 11:30am to 11pm, Tuesday through Sunday from 7am to 11pm. A bucket of balls costs $8, and the last bucket is sold at 10pm. To get there from downtown San Francisco, take Seventh Street south to Channel Street and turn right.

HANDBALL   The city's best handball courts are in Golden Gate Park, opposite Seventh Avenue, south of Middle Drive East. Courts are available free, on a first-come, first-served basis.

PARKS   In addition to **Golden Gate Park** and the **Golden Gate National Recreation Area** (p. 176 and 180 respectively), San Francisco boasts more than 2,000 acres of parkland, most of which is perfect for picnicking or throwing around a Frisbee.

Smaller city parks include **Buena Vista Park** (Haight St. between Baker and Central sts.), which affords fine views of the Golden Gate Bridge and the area around it and is also a favored lounging ground for gay lovers; **Ina Coolbrith Park** (Taylor St. between Vallejo and Green sts.), offering views of the Bay Bridge and Alcatraz; and **Sigmund Stern Grove** (19th Ave. and Sloat Blvd.) in the Sunset District, which is the site of a famous free summer music festival.

One of my personal favorites is **Lincoln Park,** a 270-acre green on the northwestern side of the city at Clement Street and 34th Avenue. The California Palace of the Legion of Honor is here (p. 167), as is a scenic 18-hole municipal golf course (see "Golf," above). But the best things about this park are the 200-foot cliffs that overlook the Golden Gate Bridge and San Francisco Bay. To get to the park, take bus no. 38 from Union Square to 33rd and Geary streets, then walk a few blocks.

RUNNING   The **Bay to Breakers Foot Race** ✦ (© **415/359-2800; www.baytobreakers.com**) is an annual 7.5-mile run from downtown to Ocean Beach. About 80,000 entrants take part in it, one of San Francisco's trademark events. Costumed participants and hordes of spectators add to the fun. The event, sponsored by the *San Francisco Examiner* and Albertson's supermarket chain, is held on the third Sunday of May.

The *San Francisco Chronicle* **Marathon** takes place annually in the middle of July. For more information, call © **415/284-9653** or visit www.chronicle marathon.com.

Great **jogging paths** include the entire expanse of Golden Gate Park, the shoreline along the Marina, and The Embarcadero.

SKATING (CONVENTIONAL & IN-LINE)   Although people skate in Golden Gate Park all week long, Sunday is best because that's when John F. Kennedy Drive between Kezar Drive and Transverse Road is closed to automobiles. A smooth "skate pad" is on your right, just past the Conservatory. Another hot skating, biking, and walking spot is the recently renovated **Embarcadero Promenade,** which stretches from the new SBC Park (Townsend St. and The Embarcadero) to Fisherman's Wharf. **Skates on Haight,** 1818 Haight St. (© **415/752-8376**), 1 block from the park, is the best place to rent in-line or conventional skates. The cost of $6 per hour, $24 per day, includes protective wrist guards and kneepads. A major credit card and ID deposit are required. The shop is open daily from 10am to 6pm.

TENNIS   The **San Francisco Parks and Recreation Department** (© **415/ 753-7001**) maintains more than 100 courts throughout the city. Almost all are available free, on a first-come, first-served basis. The exceptions are the 21 courts in **Golden Gate Park,** which cost $4 to $8 depending on the day and whether you're a resident or visitor, and can be yours for 90 minutes max. Courts must be reserved for weekend play by calling © **415/831-6301** on Wednesday from 4 to 6pm, Thursday and Friday from 9am to 5pm. For midweek reservations, call © **415/753-7001.**

WALKING & HIKING   The **Golden Gate National Recreation Area** offers plenty of opportunities. One incredible walk (or bike ride) is along the Golden Gate Promenade, from Aquatic Park to the Golden Gate Bridge. The 3.5-mile paved trail heads along the northern edge of the Presidio out to Fort Point, passing the marina, Crissy Field's new restored wetlands, a small beach, and plenty of athletic locals. You can also hike the Coastal Trail all the way from the Fort Point area to Cliff House. The park service maintains several other trails in the city. For more information or to pick up a map of the Golden Gate National Recreation Area, stop by the park service headquarters at Fort Mason at the north end of Laguna Street (© **415/561-4700**).

Although most people drive to this spectacular vantage point, a more rejuvenating way to experience **Twin Peaks** is to walk up from the back roads of U.C. Medical Center (off Parnassus) or from either of the two roads that lead to the top (off Woodside or Clarendon aves.). The best time to trek is early morning, when the city is quiet, the air is crisp, and sightseers haven't crowded the parking lot. Keep an eye out for cars, however, because there's no real hiking trail, and be sure to walk beyond the lot and up to the highest vantage point.

10 Spectator Sports

The Bay Area's sports scene includes several major professional franchises. Check the local newspapers' sports sections for daily listings of local events.

MAJOR LEAGUE BASEBALL
The **San Francisco Giants** ✦ play at the new and absolutely stunning **SBC Park,** Third and King streets (© **415/972-2000;** www.sfgiants.com), in the China Basin section of SoMa. From April to October, 40,930 fans root for the National League Giants. The unobstructed bay vistas take in bobbing boats beyond the outfield at the recently completed $225-million "SBC Park." Tickets are hard to come by; you can try to track them down through **Tickets.com** (© **510/762-2277;** www.tickets.com). Special express bus service is available from Market Street on game days; call **Muni** (© **415/673-6864**) for pickup points and schedule information.

The American League's **Oakland Athletics** play across the bay at the Networks Associates Coliseum, at the Hegenberger Road exit from I-880, Oakland (© **510/430-8020**). The stadium holds close to 50,000 spectators and is accessible through BART's Coliseum station. Tickets are available from the Coliseum Box Office or by phone through **Tickets.com** (© **510/762-2277;** www.tickets.com).

PRO BASKETBALL
The **Golden State Warriors** of the NBA play at the Networks Associates Coliseum, at the Hegenberger Road exit from I-880, Oakland (© **510/986-2200;** www.nba.com/warriors). The Warriors play in The Arena at Oakland, a 19,200-seat facility. The season runs November through April, and most games start at 7:30pm. Tickets are available at the arena and by phone through **Tickets.com** (© **510/762-2277**).

PRO FOOTBALL
The **San Francisco 49ers** (www.sf49ers.com) play at 3Com/Candlestick Park, Giants Drive and Gilman Avenue (© **415/468-2249**), on Sundays August through December; kickoff is usually at 1pm. Tickets sell out early in the season but are available at higher prices through ticket agents beforehand and from "scalpers" (illegal ticket-sellers who are usually at the gates). Ask your hotel concierge for the best way to track down tickets. Special express bus service is available from Market Street on game days; call **Muni** (© **415/673-6864**) for pickup points and schedule information.

The 49ers' archenemies, the **Oakland Raiders** (www.ofma.com), play at the Network Associates Stadium, off the 880 freeway (Nimitz). Call © **800/949-2626** for ticket information.

COLLEGE FOOTBALL

The **University of California Golden Bears** play at California Memorial Stadium, 61 Harmon Gym, University of California, Berkeley (© **800/GO-BEARS** or 510/642-3277; wwwcalbears.com), on the university campus across the bay. Tickets are usually available at game time. Phone for schedules and information.

HORSE RACING

Ten miles northeast of San Francisco is scenic **Golden Gate Fields,** Gilman Street off I-80, Albany (© **510/559-7300;** www.goldengatefields.com). It schedules thoroughbred racing from early November through March. The track is on the seashore. Call for admission prices and post times.

Bay Meadows, 2600 S. Delaware St., off U.S. 101, San Mateo (© **650/574-7223;** www.baymeadows.com), is a thoroughbred track on the peninsula about 20 miles south of downtown San Francisco. Call for admission prices and post times.

City Strolls

Despite a handful of killer hills, San Francisco is best explored on foot. In this chapter, you'll find suggestions for introductory walks in two of the city's many great neighborhoods. For more extensive city walks, check out *Frommer's Memorable Walks in San Francisco*.

WALKING TOUR 1	CHINATOWN: HISTORY, CULTURE, DIM SUM & THEN SOME

Start:	Corner of Grant Avenue and Bush Street.
Public Transportation:	Bus no. 2, 3, 4, 9X, 15, 30, 38, 45, or 76.
Finish:	Commercial Street between Montgomery and Kearny streets.
Time:	2 hours, not including museum or shopping stops.
Best Times:	Daylight hours, when there's the most action.
Worst Times:	Too early or too late, because shops are closed and no one is milling around.
Hills That Could Kill:	None.

This tiny section of San Francisco, bounded loosely by Broadway and by Stockton, Kearny, and Bush streets, is said to harbor one of the largest Chinese populations outside Asia. Daily proof is the crowds of Chinese residents who flock to the herbal stores, vegetable markets, restaurants, and businesses. Chinatown also marks the spot where the city began its development in the mid-1800s. On this walk, you'll learn why Chinatown remains intriguing to all who wind through its narrow, crowded streets, and how its origins are responsible for the city as we know it.

To begin the tour, make your way to the corner of Bush Street and Grant Avenue, where you can't miss the Chinatown Gateway Arch.

① Chinatown Gateway Arch
Traditional Chinese villages have ceremonial gates like this one. A lot less formal than those in China, this gate was built more for the benefit of the tourist industry than anything else.

Once you cross the threshold, you'll be at the beginning of Chinatown's portion of Grant Avenue.

② Grant Avenue
This is a mecca for tourists who wander in and out of gift shops that offer a variety of unnecessary junk interspersed with quality imports. You'll also find decent restaurants and grocery stores frequented by Chinese residents, ranging from children to the oldest living people you've ever seen.

Tear yourself away from the shops and turn right at the corner of Pine Street. Cross to the other side of Pine, and on your left you'll come to St. Mary's Square.

③ St. Mary's Square

Here you'll find a huge metal-and-granite statue of Dr. Sun Yat-sen, the founder of the Republic of China. A native of Guangdong (Canton) Province, Sun Yat-sen led the rebellion that ended the reign of the Qing Dynasty.

Note also the second monument in the square, which honors Chinese-American victims of both World Wars.

Walk to the other end of the square, toward California Street, turn left, cross California Street at Grant Street, and you'll be standing in front of Old St. Mary's Cathedral.

④ Old St. Mary's Cathedral

The first Catholic cathedral in San Francisco and the site of the Chinese community's first English-language school, St. Mary's was built primarily by Chinese laborers and dedicated on Christmas Day 1854.

Step inside to find a written history of the church and turn-of-the-20th-century photos of San Francisco. Alas, the half-hour Tuesday and Thursday classical-music performances, usually held at 12:30pm, are postponed until an ongoing retrofit is completed in 2005. However, you can still check out the historical photos.

Upon leaving the church, take a right and walk to the corner of Grant Avenue and California Street, then go right on Grant. Here you'll find a shop called Canton Bazaar.

⑤ Canton Bazaar

Of the knickknack and import shops lining Grant Avenue, this is one of the most popular; it's located at 616 Grant Ave.

Continue in the same direction on Grant Avenue, and cross Sacramento Street to the northwest corner of Sacramento and Grant. You'll be at the doorstep of the Bank of America.

⑥ Bank of America

This bank is an example of traditional Chinese architectural style. Notice the dragons subtly portrayed on many parts of the building.

Head in the same direction (north) on Grant, and a few doors down is the Chinatown Kite Shop.

⑦ Chinatown Kite Shop

This store, located at 717 Grant Ave., has an assortment of flying objects, including attractive fish kites, nylon or cotton windsock kites, hand-painted Chinese paper kites, wood-and-paper biplanes, and pentagonal kites.

Cross Grant, and you'll arrive at The Wok Shop.

⑧ The Wok Shop

Here's where you can purchase just about any cleaver, wok, cookbook, or vessel you might need for Chinese-style cooking in your own kitchen. It's located at 718 Grant Ave.

When you come out of The Wok Shop, go right. Walk past Commercial Street, and you'll arrive at the corner of Grant Avenue and Clay Street; cross Clay, and you'll be standing on the original street of "American" California.

⑨ Original Street of "American" California

Here an English seaman named William Richardson set up the first tent in 1835, making it the first place that an Anglo set up base in California.

Continue north on Grant to Washington Street. Turn right, and at 743 Washington St. you will be standing in front of the Bank of Canton.

⑩ Bank of Canton

This building boasts the oldest (from 1909) Asian-style edifice in Chinatown. The three-tiered temple-style building once housed the China Telephone Exchange, known as "China-5" until 1945.

You're probably thirsty by now, so follow Washington Street a few doors down (east); on your right-hand side you will come upon Washington Bakery & Restaurant.

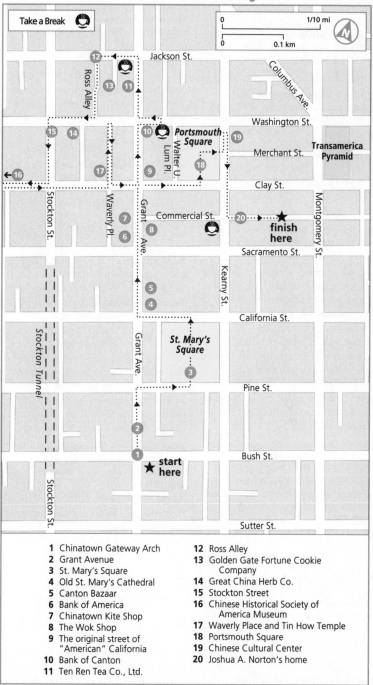

Take a Break

0   1/10 mi
0   0.1 km

Jackson St.

Columbus Ave.

Ross Alley

12
13   11

Washington St.

15   14

Portsmouth Square

Walter U. Lum Pl.

10

19

Merchant St.

Transamerica Pyramid

17

9

18

Clay St.

16

Stockton St.

Waverly Pl.

Grant Ave.

Commercial St.

20   finish here

Montgomery St.

7

8

Sacramento St.

6

Kearny St.

Stockton Tunnel

5

4

California St.

Grant Ave.

St. Mary's Square

3

Pine St.

2

start here

Bush St.

Stockton St.

Sutter St.

1 Chinatown Gateway Arch	**12** Ross Alley
2 Grant Avenue	**13** Golden Gate Fortune Cookie Company
3 St. Mary's Square	**14** Great China Herb Co.
4 Old St. Mary's Cathedral	**15** Stockton Street
5 Canton Bazaar	**16** Chinese Historical Society of America Museum
6 Bank of America	**17** Waverly Place and Tin How Temple
7 Chinatown Kite Shop	**18** Portsmouth Square
8 The Wok Shop	**19** Chinese Cultural Center
9 The original street of "American" California	**20** Joshua A. Norton's home
10 Bank of Canton	
11 Ten Ren Tea Co., Ltd.	

TAKE A BREAK
Washington Bakery & Restaurant is at 733 Washington St. No need to have a full meal here—the service can be abrupt. Do stop in, however, for a little potable adventure: snow red beans with ice cream. The sugary-sweet drink mixed with whole beans and ice cream is not something you're likely to have tried elsewhere, and it happens to be quite tasty. Whatever you do, don't fill up—a few blocks away, some wonderfully fresh dim sum awaits you.

Head back to Grant Avenue, cross Washington Street, cross Grant, and follow the west side of Grant 1 block to Ten Ren Tea Co., Ltd.

⑪ **Ten Ren Tea Co., Ltd.**

In this amazing shop at 949 Grant Ave., you can sample a freshly brewed tea variety and check out the dozens of drawers and canisters labeled with more than 40 kinds of tea. Like Washington Bakery, Ten Ren offers unusual drinks worth trying: delightful hot or iced milk teas containing giant blobs of jelly or tapioca. Try black tea or green tea and enjoy the outstanding flavors and the giant balls of tapioca slipping around in your mouth.

Leave Ten Ren, make a left, and when you reach Jackson Street, make another left. On the left side, at 735 Jackson St., through the storefront window, you'll notice stacks of steaming wooden baskets and a Chinese cook. You've reached your snacking destination.

TAKE A BREAK
It's the **House of Dim Sum**—nothing fancy, to be sure, but the dumplings are fresh, cheap, and delicious, and owners Cindy and Ben Yee are friendly, which is a plus in this sometimes abrupt community. Order at the counter: pork, chive, and shrimp dumplings; shark-fin dumplings; sweet buns; turnip cake; or sweet rice with chicken wrapped in a lotus leaf. Unless the two tables are taken, it's best to sit at one to enjoy your feast.

As you leave the House of Dim Sum, turn left so you're heading west on Jackson, and promptly make a left onto Ross Alley.

⑫ **Ross Alley**

As you walk along this narrow street, just one of the many alleyways that crisscrossed Chinatown to accommodate the many immigrants who jammed into the neighborhood, it's not difficult to recall that this block once was rife with gambling dens.

As you follow the alley south, on the left side of the street you'll encounter the Golden Gate Fortune Cookie Company.

⑬ **Golden Gate Fortune Cookie Company**

Located at 56 Ross Alley, this store is little more than a tiny place where three women sit at a conveyer belt, folding messages into warm cookies as the manager invariably calls out to tourists, beckoning them to buy a big bag of the fortune-telling treats.

You can purchase regular fortunes, unfolded flat cookies without fortunes or, if you bring your own fortunes, custom cookies (I often do this when I'm having dinner parties) at around $6 for 50 cookies—a very cheap way to impress your friends! Or, of course, you can just take a peek and move on.

As you exit the alley, cross Washington Street, take a right heading west on Washington, and you're in front of the Great China Herb Co.

⑭ **Great China Herb Co.**

For centuries, the Chinese have come to shops like this one, at 857 Washington St., which are full of exotic herbs, roots, and other natural substances. They buy what they believe will cure all types of ailments and ensure good health and long life. Thankfully, unlike owners in many similar area shops, Mr. and Mrs. Ho speak English, so you will not be met with a blank stare when you inquire what exactly is in each box, bag, or jar arranged along dozens of shelves. It is important to note that you should not use Chinese herbs without the guidance of a knowledgeable source such as an herb doctor. They may be natural, but they also can be quite powerful and are potentially harmful if misused.

Take a left upon leaving the store and walk to Stockton Street.

⓯ Stockton Street

The section of Stockton Street between Broadway and Sacramento Street is where most of the residents of Chinatown do their daily shopping.

One noteworthy part of this street's history is **Cameron House** (920 Sacramento St., at the corner of Stockton and Sacramento sts.), which was named after Donaldina Cameron (1869–1968). Called Lo Mo, or "the Mother," by the Chinese, she spent her life trying to free Chinese women who came to America in hopes of marrying well but who found themselves forced into prostitution and slavery. Today, the house still helps women free themselves from domestic violence.

A good stop if you're in the market for some jewelry is **Jade Galore** (1000 Stockton St. at Washington St.). Though the employees aren't exactly warm and fuzzy, they've got the goods. In addition to purveying jade jewelry, the store does a fair trade in diamonds.

After browsing at Jade Galore, you might want to wander up Stockton Street to absorb the atmosphere and street life of this less-tourist-oriented Chinese community before doubling back to Washington Street. At 1068 Stockton St. you'll find **AA Bakery & Café,** an extremely colorful bakery with Golden Gate Bridge–shaped cakes, bright green and pink snacks, moon cakes, and a flow of Chinese diners catching up over pastries. Another fun place at which to peek is **Gourmet Delight B.B.Q.,** at 1045 Stockton St., where barbecued duck and pork are supplemented by steamed pigs' feet and chicken feet. Everything's to go here, so if you grab a snack, don't forget napkins. Head farther north along the street and you'll see live fish and fowl awaiting their fate as the day's dinner.

Meander south on Stockton Street to Clay Street and turn west (right) onto Clay. Continue to 965 Clay St. Make sure you arrive Tuesday through Friday between 11am and 4pm or Saturday or Sunday between noon and 4pm. Also, be prepared to pay an admission fee of $3 for adults, $2 for college students (with ID) and seniors, and $1 for kids 6 to 17. You've arrived at 965 Clay St., the:

⓰ Chinese Historical Society of America Museum

Founded in 1963, this museum (ⓒ **415/391-1188**) has a small but fascinating collection that illuminates the role of Chinese immigrants in American history, particularly in San Francisco and the rest of California.

The interesting artifacts on display include a shrimp-cleaning machine; 19th-century clothing and slippers of the Chinese pioneers; Chinese herbs and scales; historic hand-carved and painted shop signs; and a series of photographs that document the development of Chinese culture in America.

The goal of this organization is not only to "study, record, acquire, and preserve all suitable artifacts and such cultural items as manuscripts, books, and works of art . . . which have a bearing on the history of the Chinese living in the United States of America," but also to "promote the contributions that Chinese Americans living in this country have made to the United States of America." It's an admirable and much-needed effort, considering what little recognition and appreciation the Chinese have received throughout American history.

The museum is open Tuesday through Friday from 11am to 4pm and Saturday and Sunday from noon to 4pm. Admission is $3 adults, $2 for college students with ID and seniors, and $1 for visitors under 18.

Retrace your steps, heading east on Clay Street back toward Grant Avenue. Turn left onto Waverly Place.

⑰ Waverly Place

Also known as "The Street of Painted Balconies," Waverly Place is probably Chinatown's most popular side street or alleyway because of its painted balconies and colorful architectural details—a sort of Chinese-style New Orleans street. You can admire the architecture only from the ground, because most of the buildings are private family associations or temples.

One temple you can visit (but make sure it's open before you climb the long, narrow stairway) is the **Tin How Temple,** at 125 Waverly Place. Accessible via the stairway three floors up, this incense-laden sanctuary, decorated in traditional black, red, and gold lacquered wood, is a house of worship for Chinese Buddhists, who come here to pray, meditate, and send offerings to their ancestors and to Tin How, the Queen of the Heavens and Goddess of the Seven Seas. There are no scheduled services, but you are welcome to visit. Just remember to quietly respect those who are here to pray, and try to be as unobtrusive as possible. It is customary to give a donation or buy a bundle of incense during your visit.

Once you've finished exploring Waverly Place, walk east on Clay Street, past Grant Avenue, and continue until you come upon the block-wide urban playground that is also the most important site in San Francisco's history:

⑱ Portsmouth Square

This very spot was the center of the region's first township, which was called Yerba Buena before it was renamed San Francisco in 1847. Around 1846, before any semblance of a city had taken shape, this plaza lay at the foot of the bay's eastern shoreline. There were fewer than 50 non–Native American residents in the settlement, there were no substantial buildings to speak of, and the few boats that pulled into the cove did so less than a block from where you're sitting.

In 1846, when California was claimed as a U.S. territory, the marines who landed here named the square after their ship, the USS *Portsmouth.* (Today, a bronze plaque marks the spot where they raised the U.S. flag.)

Yerba Buena remained a modest township until the gold rush of 1849 when, over the next 2 years, the population grew from under 1,000 to over 19,000, as gold seekers from around the world made their way here.

When the square became too crowded, long wharves were constructed to support new buildings above the bay. Eventually, the entire area became landfill. That was almost 150 years ago, but today the square still serves as an important meeting place for neighborhood Chinese—a sort of communal outdoor living room.

Throughout the day, the square is heavily trafficked by children and—in large part—by elderly men, who gamble over Chinese cards. If you arrive early in the morning, you might come across people practicing tai chi.

It is said that Robert Louis Stevenson used to love to sit on a bench here and watch life go by. (At the northeast corner of the square, you'll find a monument to his memory, consisting of a model of the *Hispañola,* the ship in Stevenson's novel *Treasure Island,* and an excerpt from his "Christmas Sermon.")

Once you've had your fill of the square, exit to the east, at Kearny Street. Directly across the street, at 750 Kearny, is the Holiday Inn. Cross the street, enter the hotel, and take the elevator to the third floor, where you'll find the Chinese Culture Center.

⑲ Chinese Culture Center

This center is oriented toward both the community and tourists, offering interesting display cases of Chinese art, and a gallery with rotating exhibits of Asian art and writings. The center is open Tuesday through Saturday from 10am to 4pm.

When you leave the Holiday Inn, take a left on Kearny and go 3 short blocks to Commercial Street. Take a left onto Commercial and note that you are standing on the street once known as the site of:

⑳ Joshua A. Norton's Home

Norton, the self-proclaimed "Emperor of the United States and Protector of Mexico," used to walk around the streets in an old brass-buttoned military uniform, sporting a hat with a "dusty plume." He lived in a fantasy world, and San Franciscans humored him at every turn.

Norton was born around 1815 in the British Isles and sailed as a young man to South Africa, where he served as a colonial rifleman. He came to San Francisco in 1849 with $40,000 and proceeded to double and triple his fortune in real estate. Unfortunately for him, he next chose to go into the rice business. While Norton was busy cornering the market and forcing prices up, several ships loaded with rice arrived unexpectedly in San Francisco's harbor. The rice market was suddenly flooded, and Norton was forced into bankruptcy. He left San Francisco for about 3 years and must have experienced a breakdown (or revelation) of some sort, for upon his return, Norton thought he was an emperor.

Instead of ostracizing him, however, San Franciscans embraced him as their own homegrown lunatic and gave him free meals.

When Emperor Norton died in 1880 (while sleeping at the corner of California St. and Grant Ave.) approximately 10,000 people passed by his coffin, which was bought with money raised at the Pacific Union Club, and more than 30,000 people participated in the funeral procession. Today you won't see a trace of his character, but it's fun to imagine him cruising the street.

From here, if you've still got an appetite, you should go directly to 631 Kearny (at Clay St.), home of the R&G Lounge.

TAKE A BREAK The R&G Lounge is a sure thing for tasty $5 rice-plate specials, deep-fried salt-and-pepper crab, chicken with black-bean sauce, and gorgeously tender and tangy R&G Special Beef.

Otherwise, you might want to backtrack on Commercial Street to Grant Avenue, take a left, and follow Grant back to Bush Street, the entrance to Chinatown. You'll be at the beginning of the Union Square area, where you can catch any number of buses (especially on Market St.) or cable cars or do a little shopping. Or you might backtrack to Grant, take a right (north), and follow Grant to the end. You'll be at Broadway and Columbus, the beginning of North Beach, where you can venture onward for our North Beach tour (see below).

⟮Finds⟯ Do-It-Yourself Excursions

The Convention & Visitors Bureau distributes a brochure detailing self-guided walking tours of North Beach, Union Square, Fisherman's Wharf, Chinatown, and Pacific Heights. Send a request plus a self-addressed business-size envelope to the San Francisco Convention & Visitors Bureau, 201 Third Street, Suite 900, San Francisco, CA 94103. You can also get the information online at **www.sfvisitor.org/visitorinfo/html/walkpdfs.html**.

Start:	Intersection of Montgomery Street, Columbus Avenue, and Washington Street.
Public Transportation:	Bus no. 10, 12, 15, 30X, or 41.
Finish:	Washington Square.
Time:	3 hours, including a stop for lunch.
Best Times:	Monday through Saturday between 11am and 4pm.
Worst Times:	Sunday, when shops are closed.
Hills That Could Kill:	The Montgomery Street hill from Broadway to Vallejo Street; otherwise, this is an easy walk.

Along with Chinatown, North Beach is one of the city's oldest neighborhoods. Originally the Latin Quarter, it became the city's Italian district when Italian immigrants moved "uphill" in the early 1870s, crossing Broadway from the Jackson Square area and settling in. They quickly established restaurants, cafes, bakeries, and other businesses familiar to them from their homeland. The "Beat Generation" helped put North Beach on the map, with the likes of Jack Kerouac and Allen Ginsberg holding court in the area's cafes during the 1950s. Although most of the original Beat poets are gone, their spirit lives on in North Beach, which is still a haven for bohemian artists and writers. The neighborhood, thankfully, retains its Italian village feel; it's a place where residents from all walks of life enjoy taking time for conversation over pastries and frothy cappuccinos.

If there's one landmark you can't miss, it's the familiar building on the corner of Montgomery Street and Columbus Avenue, the TransAmerica Pyramid.

❶ TransAmerica Pyramid

Noted for its spire (which rises 212 ft. above the top floor) and its "wings" (which begin at the 29th floor and stop at the spire), this pyramid is San Francisco's tallest building and a hallmark of the skyline. You might want to take a peek at one of the rotating art exhibits in the lobby or go around to the right and into ½-acre Redwood Park, which is part of the TransAmerica Center.

The TransAmerica Pyramid occupies part of the 600 block of Montgomery Street, which once held a historic building called the Montgomery Block.

❷ The Montgomery Block

Originally four stories high, the Montgomery Block was the tallest building in the West when it was built in 1853. San Franciscans called it "Halleck's Folly" because it was built on a raft of

redwood logs that had been bolted together and floated at the edge of the ocean (which was right at Montgomery St. at that time). The building was demolished in 1959 but is fondly remembered for its historic importance as the power center of the city. Its tenants included artists and writers of all kinds, among them Jack London, George Sterling, Ambrose Bierce, Bret Harte, and Mark Twain. This is a picturesque area, but there's no particular spot to direct you to. It's worth looking around, however, if only for the block's historical importance.

From the southeast corner of Montgomery and Washington streets, look across Washington to the corner of Columbus Avenue, and you'll see the original TransAmerica Building, located at 4 Columbus Ave.

❸ Original TransAmerica Building

The original TransAmerica Building is a Beaux Arts flatiron-shaped building covered in terra cotta; it was also the home of Sanwa Bank and Fugazi

Greenwich St.

Filbert St.

finish here ★ 20 *Washington Square*

Union St.

Greene St.

NORTH BEACH

Vallejo St.

Fresno St.

Broadway

Jack Kerouac St.

Pacific Ave.

JACKSON

SQUARE

HISTORIC

DISTRICT Gold St.

Jackson St.

CHINATOWN

Washington St.

Portsmouth Square

start here ★

Transamerica Pyramid

Clay St.

Greenwich St. · Filbert St. · Union St. · Grant Ave. · Vareness St. · Sonoma St. · Kearny St. · Margrave Pl. · Montgomery St. · Bartol St. · Sansome St. · Powell St. · Stockton St. · Columbus Ave. · Osgood Pl. · Beckett St. · Hotaling Pl. · Grant · Kearny St.

Telegraph Hill Park

0 — 1/10 mile
0 — 100 meters

☕ Take a Break
⌐⌐ Cable Car

1 Transamerica Pyramid
2 The Montgomery Block
3 Original Transamerica Building
4 Golden Era Building
5 400 block of Jackson Square
6 Columbus Tower
7 140 Columbus Avenue
8 1010 Montgomery Street
9 hungry i
10 Former site of the Condor Club
11 City Lights Bookstore
12 Vesuvio
13 Specs' Adler Museum Café and Tosca Café
14 Caffè Trieste
15 Biordi Art Imports
16 Molinari Delicatessen
17 North Beach Museum
18 Club Fugazi
19 Mario's Bohemian Cigar Store
20 Washington Square

Bank. Built for the Banco Populare Italiano Operaia Fugazi in 1909, it was originally a two-story building and gained a third floor in 1916. In 1928, Fugazi merged his bank with the Bank of America, which was started by A. P. Giannini, who also created the TransAmerica Corporation. The building now houses a Church of Scientology.

Cross Washington Street and continue north on Montgomery Street to no. 730, the Golden Era Building.

❹ Golden Era Building
Erected around 1852, this building is named after the literary magazine, *Golden Era,* which was published here. Some of the young writers who worked on the magazine were known as "The Bohemians"; they included Samuel Clemens (aka Mark Twain) and Bret Harte (who began as a typesetter here). Backtrack a few dozen feet and stop for a minute to admire the exterior of the annex, at no. 722 (marked by a faded black-and-white striped awning). The Belli Annex, as it is currently known, is registered as a historic landmark.

Continue north on Washington Street, and take the first right onto Jackson Street. Continue until you hit the 400 block of Jackson Square.

❺ 400 Block of Jackson Square
Here's where you'll find some of the only commercial buildings to survive the 1906 earthquake and fire. The building at no. 415 Jackson (ca. 1853) served as headquarters for the Ghirardelli Chocolate Company from 1855 to 1894. The Hotaling Building (no. 451) was built in 1866 and features pediments and quoins of cast iron applied over the brick walls. At no. 441 is another of the buildings that survived the disaster of 1906. Constructed between 1850 and 1852 with ship masts for interior supporting columns, it served as the French Consulate from 1865 to 1876.

Cross the street, and backtrack on Jackson Street. Continue toward the intersection of Columbus Avenue and Jackson Street. Turn right on Columbus and look across the street for the small triangular building at the junction of Kearny Street and Columbus Avenue, Columbus Tower (aka the Sentinel Building).

❻ Columbus Tower
If you walk a little farther, then turn around and look back down Columbus, you'll be able to get a better look at Columbus Tower. The flat-iron beauty—a building, shaped to a triangular site, went up between 1905 and 1907. Movie director and producer Francis Ford Coppola bought and restored it in the mid-1970s; it is now home to his film production company, American Zoetrope Studios. The building's cafe showcases all things Niebaum-Coppola (as in Coppola's winery)—including olive oil, Parmesan cheese, and wine. It's a great place to stop for a glass of wine, an espresso, or a thin-crusted pizza snack. This is one of the few pre–1906 earthquake buildings left in the city center.

Across the street from Columbus Tower on Columbus Avenue is 140 Columbus Ave.

❼ 140 Columbus Ave.
Once home to the performance venue known as the Purple Onion, this place has seen many famous headliners, often before they were famous. Phyllis Diller, who's now so big that she's famous for something as simple as her laugh, was still struggling when she played a 2-week engagement here in the late 1950s.

Continue north on Columbus, and then turn right on Pacific Avenue. After you cross Montgomery Street, you'll find brick-lined Osgood Place on the left. A registered historic landmark, it is one of the few quiet— and car-free—little alleyways left in the city. Stroll up Osgood and go left on Broadway to 1010 Montgomery St. (at Broadway).

❽ 1010 Montgomery St.
This is where Allen Ginsberg lived when he wrote his legendary poem,

"Howl," first performed on October 13, 1955, in a converted auto-repair shop at the corner of Fillmore and Union streets. By the time Ginsberg finished reading, he was crying and the audience was going wild. Jack Kerouac proclaimed, "Ginsberg, this poem will make you famous in San Francisco."

Continue along Broadway toward Columbus Avenue. This stretch of Broadway is San Francisco's answer to New York's Times Square, complete with strip clubs and peep shows that are being pushed aside by restaurants, clubs, and an endless crowd of visitors. It's among the most sought-after locations in the city as more and more profitable restaurants and clubs spring up.

Keep walking west on Broadway, and on the right side of the street, you'll come to Black Oak Books, 540 Broadway. It sells new and used discount books and is worth a quick trip inside for a good, cheap read. A few dozen yards farther up Broadway is the current location of the hungry i.

⑨ hungry i

Now a seedy strip club (at 546 Broadway), the original hungry i (at 599 Jackson St., which is under construction for senior housing) was owned and operated by the vociferous "Big Daddy" Nordstrom. If you had been here while Enrico Banducci (also of Enrico's restaurant) was in charge, you would have found only a plain room with an exposed brick wall and director's chairs around small tables. A who's who of nightclub entertainers fortified their careers at the original hungry i, including Lenny Bruce, Billie Holiday (who first sang "Strange Fruit" there), Bill Cosby, Richard Pryor, Woody Allen, and Barbra Streisand.

At the corner of Broadway and Columbus Avenue, you will see the former site of the Condor Club.

⑩ Former Site of the Condor Club

The Condor Club was located at 300 Columbus Ave.; this is where Carol Doda scandalously bared her breasts and danced topless for the first time in 1964. Note the bronze plaque claiming the Condor Club as BIRTHPLACE OF THE WORLD'S FIRST TOPLESS & BOTTOMLESS ENTERTAINMENT. Go inside what is now the Condor Sports Bar and have a look at the framed newspaper clippings that hang around the dining room. From the elevated back room, you can see Doda's old dressing room and, on the floor below, an outline of the piano that would descend from the second floor with her atop it.

When you leave the Condor Sports Bar, cross to the south side of Broadway. Note the mural of jazz musicians painted on the entire side of the building directly across Columbus Avenue. Diagonally across the intersection from the Condor Sports Bar is the City Lights bookstore.

⑪ City Lights Booksellers & Publishers

Founded in 1953 and owned by one of the first Beat poets to arrive in San Francisco, Lawrence Ferlinghetti, City Lights is now a city landmark and literary mecca. Located at 261 Columbus Ave., it's one of the last of the Beat-era hangouts in operation. An active participant in the Beat movement, Ferlinghetti established his shop as a meeting place where writers and bibliophiles could (and still do) attend poetry readings and other events. A vibrant part of the literary scene, the well-stocked bookshop prides itself on its collection of art, poetry, and political paperbacks.

Upon exiting City Lights bookstore, turn right, cross aptly named Jack Kerouac Street, and stop by Vesuvio, the bar on your right.

⑫ Vesuvio

Because of its proximity to City Lights bookstore, Vesuvio became a favorite hangout of the Beats. Dylan Thomas used to drink here, as did Jack Kerouac, Ferlinghetti, and Ginsberg. Even today, Vesuvio, which opened in 1949, maintains its original bohemian atmosphere. The bar is located at 255 Columbus Ave. (at Jack Kerouac St.) and dates from 1913. It is an excellent example of pressed-tin architecture.

Facing Vesuvio across Columbus Avenue is another favorite spot of the Beat Generation:

⓭ Spec's Adler Museum Café

Located at 12 Saroyan Place, this is one of the city's funkiest bars, a small, dimly lit watering hole with ceiling-hung maritime flags and exposed brick walls crammed with memorabilia. Within the bar is a minimuseum that consists of a few glass cases filled with mementos brought by seamen who frequented the pub from the '40s and onward.

From here, walk back up Columbus across Broadway to Grant Avenue. Turn right on Grant, and continue until you come to Vallejo Street. At 601 Vallejo St. (at Grant Ave.) is Caffè Trieste.

⓮ Caffè Trieste

Yet another favorite spot of the Beats and founded by Gianni Giotta in 1956, Caffè Trieste is still run by family members. The quintessential San Francisco coffeehouse, Trieste features opera on the jukebox, and the real thing, performed by the Giottas, on Saturday afternoons. Any day of the week is a good one to stop in for a cappuccino or espresso—the beans are roasted right next door.

Go left out of Caffè Trieste onto Vallejo Street, turn right on Columbus Avenue, and bump into the loveliest shop in all of North Beach, Biordi Art Imports, located at 412 Columbus Ave.

⓯ Biordi Art Imports

This store has carried imported hand-painted majolica pottery from the hill towns of central Italy for more than 50 years. Some of the colorful patterns

date from the 14th century. Biordi handpicks its artisans, and its catalog includes biographies of those who are currently represented.

Across Columbus Avenue, at the corner of Vallejo Street, is the Molinari Delicatessen.

⓰ Molinari Delicatessen

This deli, located at 373 Columbus Ave., has been selling its pungent, air-dried salamis since 1896. Ravioli and tortellini are made in the back of the shop, but it's the mouthwatering selection of cold salads, cheeses, and marinades up front that captures the attention of most folks. Each Italian sub is big enough for two hearty appetites.

Walk north to the lively intersection of Columbus, Green, and Stockton, and look for the U.S. Bank at 1435 Stockton St. On the second floor of the bank, you'll find the North Beach Museum.

⓱ North Beach Museum

The North Beach Museum displays historical artifacts that tell the story of North Beach, Chinatown, and Fisherman's Wharf. Just before you enter the museum, you'll find a framed, handwritten poem by Lawrence Ferlinghetti that captures his impressions of this primarily Italian neighborhood. After you pass through the glass doors, you'll see many photographs of some of the first Chinese and Italian immigrants, as well as pictures of San Francisco after the 1906 earthquake. You can visit the museum any time the bank is open (unfortunately, it's closed on weekends), and admission is free.

Now backtrack toward Columbus Avenue and go left on Green Street to Club Fugazi, at 678 Green St.

⓲ Club Fugazi

It doesn't look like much from the outside, but Fugazi Hall was donated to the city (and more important, the North Beach area) by John Fugazi, the founder of the Italian bank that was taken over by A. P. Giannini and turned into the original TransAmerica Corporation. For many years, Fugazi Hall has been staging the zany and whimsical musical revue *Beach Blanket Babylon*. The show evolved from Steve Silver's Rent-a-Freak service, which consisted of a group of partygoers who would attend parties dressed as any number of characters in outrageous costumes. The fun caught on and soon became *Beach Blanket Babylon.*

If you love comedy, you'll love this show. We don't want to spoil it for you by telling you what it's about, but if you get tickets and they're in an unreserved-seat section, you should arrive fairly early because you'll be seated around small cocktail tables on a first-come, first-served basis. (Two sections have reserved seating, four don't, and all of them frequently sell out weeks in advance; however, sometimes it is possible to get tickets at the last minute on weekdays.) You'll want to be as close to the stage as possible. This supercharged show (see p. 229 for more information) is definitely worth the price of admission.

TAKE A BREAK
Head back the way you came on Green Street. Before you get to Columbus Avenue, you'll see **O'Reilly's Irish Pub** (622 Green St.), a homey watering hole that dishes out good, hearty Irish food and a fine selection of beers (including Guinness, of course) that are best enjoyed at one of the sidewalk tables. Always a conversation piece is the mural of Irish authors peering from the back wall. (How many can you name?)

As you come out of O'Reilly's, turn left, cross Columbus Avenue, and then take a left onto Columbus. Proceed 1 block northwest to Mario's Bohemian Cigar Store.

⑲ Mario's Bohemian Cigar Store

Located at 566 Columbus Ave., across the street from Washington Square, this is one of North Beach's most popular neighborhood hangouts. No, it does not sell cigars, but the cramped and casual space overlooking Washington Square does sell killer focaccia sandwiches and coffee drinks.

Our next stop, directly across Union Street, is Washington Square.

⑳ Washington Square

This is one of the oldest parks in the city. The land was designated a public park in 1847 and has undergone many changes since then. Its current landscaping dates from 1955. You'll notice **Saints Peter and Paul Church** (the religious center for the neighborhood's Italian community) on the northwest end. Take a few moments to go inside and check out the traditional Italian interior. Note that this is the church in which baseball great Joe DiMaggio married his first wife, Dorothy Arnold. He wasn't allowed to marry Marilyn Monroe here because he had been divorced. He married Monroe at City Hall and came here for publicity photos.

Today the park is a pleasant place in which to soak up the sun, read a book, or chat with a retired Italian octogenarian who has seen the city grow and change.

From here, you can see the famous Coit Tower at the top of Telegraph Hill to the northwest.

Shopping

Like its population, San Francisco's shopping is both worldly and intimate. Every persuasion, style, era, and fetish is represented, not in big, tacky shopping malls, but in hundreds of quaint, dramatically different boutiques scattered throughout the city. Whether you're looking for Chanel or Chinese herbal medicine, San Francisco's got it. Just pick a neighborhood and break out your credit cards—you're sure to end up with at least a few take-home treasures.

1 The Shopping Scene

MAJOR SHOPPING AREAS

San Francisco has many shopping areas, but the following places are where you'll find most of the action.

UNION SQUARE & ENVIRONS   San Francisco's most congested and popular shopping mecca is centered on Union Square and bordered by Bush, Taylor, Market, and Montgomery streets. Most of the big department stores and many high-end specialty shops are here. Be sure to venture to Grant Avenue, Post and Sutter streets, and Maiden Lane. This area is a hub for public transportation; all Market Street and several other buses run here, as do the Powell-Hyde and Powell-Mason cable car lines. You can also take the Muni streetcar to the Powell Street station.

CHINATOWN   When you pass through the gate to Chinatown on Grant Avenue, say good-bye to the world of fashion and hello to a swarm of cheap tourist shops selling everything from linen and jade to plastic toys and $2 slippers. But that's not all Chinatown has to offer. The real gems are tucked away on side streets or are small, one-person shops selling Chinese herbs, original art, and jewelry. Grant Avenue is the area's main thoroughfare, and the side streets between Bush Street and Columbus Avenue are full of restaurants, markets, and eclectic shops. Stockton Street is best for grocery shopping (including live fowl and fish). Walking is best, because traffic through this area is slow at best and parking is next to impossible. Most stores in Chinatown are open daily from 10am to 10pm. Take bus no. 1, 9X, 15, 30, 41, or 45.

UNION STREET   Union Street, from Fillmore Street to Van Ness Avenue, caters to the upper-middle-class crowd. It's a great place to stroll, window-shop the plethora of boutiques, try the cafes and restaurants, and watch the beautiful people parade by. Take bus no. 22, 41, or 45.

CHESTNUT STREET   Parallel and a few blocks north, Chestnut is a younger version of Union Street. It holds endless shopping and dining choices, and an ever-tanned, superfit population of postgraduate singles who hang around cafes and scope each other out. Take bus no. 22, 28, 30, 41, 43, or 76.

Tips **Just the Facts: Hours, Taxes & Shipping**

Store hours are generally Monday through Saturday from 10am to 6pm and Sunday from noon to 5pm. Most department stores stay open later, as do shops around Fisherman's Wharf, the most heavily visited (by tourists) area.

Sales tax in San Francisco is 8.5%, which is added on at the register for all goods and services purchased. If you live out of state and buy an expensive item, you might want to have the store ship it home for you. You'll have to pay for shipping, but you'll escape paying the sales tax.

Most of the city's shops can wrap your purchase and **ship** it anywhere in the world. If they can't, you can send it yourself, either through **UPS** (© 800/742-5877), **FedEx** (© 800/463-3339), or the U.S. Postal Service (see "Fast Facts: San Francisco," in chapter 4).

FILLMORE STREET   Some of the best shopping in town is packed into 5 blocks of Fillmore Street in Pacific Heights. From Jackson to Sutter streets, Fillmore is the perfect place to grab a bite and peruse the high-priced boutiques, crafts shops, and incredible housewares stores. (Don't miss Zinc Details; p. 220.) Take bus no. 1, 2, 3, 4, 12, 22, or 24.

HAIGHT STREET   Green hair, spiked hair, no hair, or mohair—even the hippies look conservative next to Haight Street's dramatic fashion freaks. The shopping in the 6 blocks of upper Haight Street between Central Avenue and Stanyan Street reflects its clientele. It offers everything from incense and European and American street styles to furniture and antique clothing. Bus nos. 6, 7, 66, and 71 run the length of Haight Street. The Muni streetcar N line stops at Waller Street and Cole Street.

SOMA   Although this area isn't suitable for strolling, you'll find almost all the discount shopping in warehouse spaces south of Market. You can pick up a discount-shopping guide at most major hotels. Many bus lines pass through this area.

HAYES VALLEY   It's not the prettiest area in town, with some of the shadier housing projects a few blocks away. But while most neighborhoods cater to more conservative or trendy shoppers, lower Hayes Street, between Octavia and Gough streets, celebrates anything vintage, chic, artistic, or downright funky. With new shops opening frequently, it's definitely the most interesting new shopping area in town, with furniture and glass stores, thrift shops, trendy shoe stores, and men's and women's clothiers. You can find lots of great antiques shops south on Octavia and on nearby Market Street. Take bus no. 16AX, 16BX, or 21.

FISHERMAN'S WHARF & ENVIRONS *Overrated*   The tourist-oriented malls along Jefferson Street include hundreds of shops, restaurants, and attractions. Among them are Ghirardelli Square, PIER 39, The Cannery, and The Anchorage (see "Shopping Centers & Complexes," on p. 221).

2 Shopping A to Z

ANTIQUES

Jackson Square, a historic district just north of the Financial District's Embarcadero Center, is the place to go for the top names in fine furniture and fine art.

San Francisco Shopping

Aardvark's **67**
Alabaster **11**
Alessi **41**
All American Boy **18**
The Anchorage **22**
Art of China **34**
Artisan Cheese **9**
Atelier Dore **39**
Babushka **22**
Barnes & Noble **25**
Biordi Art Imports **28**
Birkenstock **54**
Bonhams & Butterfield **62**
The Booksmith **64**
Borders Books & Music **44**
Boulangerie **10**
Britex Fabrics **51**
Brooks Brothers **50**
Buffalo Exchange **67**
Bulo **13**
Cable Car Clothiers **41**
The Cannery **21**
Catharine Clark Gallery **54**
The Canton Bazaar **38**
The Chanel Boutique **48**
Chinatown **33**
The Chinatown Kite Shop **36**
Citizen Clothing **15**
City Lights Booksellers & Publishers **29**
A Clean, Well-Lighted Place for Books **58**
Cost Plus Imports **25**
Crocker Galleria **51**
Dandelion **63**
De Vera Galleries **51**
Dianne's Old & New Estates **3**
The Disney Store **40**
Distractions & Euphoria **65**
Eleonore Austerer Gallery **40**
Ferry Building Marketplace **31**
Fisherman's Wharf **23**
Flax **14**
Fraenkel Gallery **54**
Fumiki Fine Asian Arts **43**
Ghirardelli Square **20**
Gimme Shoes **8**
Golden Gate Fortune Cookies Co. **33**
Good Byes **6**
Good Vibrations **18**

Grand Women's Boutique **68**
Green Apple Books **7**
Gucci America **50**
Gump's **49**
Haight Street **68**
Hang **45**
Hayes Valley **12**
Images of the North **4**
Jackson Square **30**
Jeremys **60**
Joseph Schmidt Confections **17**
Kenneth Cole **57**
La Rosa **66**
Limn **61**
Macy's **53**
Métier **42**
Meyerovich Gallery **50**
Minis **2**
Neiman Marcus **50**
Nest **19**
The New Unique Company **35**
Niketown **47**
Nordstrom **57**
On the Road Again **24**
Pearl & Jade Empire **45**
PIER 39 **24**
Propeller **12**
Rand McNally Maps & Books **32**
Recycled Records **68**
San Francisco Shopping Centre **57**
SFMOMA MuseumStore **56**
Silkroute International **1**
Smile **40**
SoMa **56**
Streetlight Records **16**
Sue Fisher King **6**
Sur La Table **52**
Ten Ren Tea Co. **33**
Therien & Co. **62**
Three Bags Full **3**
Tiffany & Co. **46**
Union Square **53**
Union Street Goldsmith **5**
Virgin Megastore **55**
Wilkes Bashford **47**
William Stout Architectural Books **30**
Wine Club San Francisco **59**
The Wok Shop **37**
Zinc Details **10**

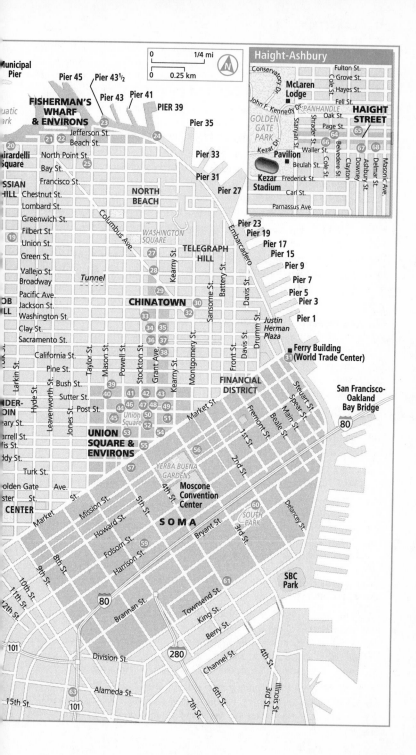

Municipal
Pier

Pier 45   Pier 43½
Pier 43   Pier 41
Pier 23   PIER 39

**FISHERMAN'S
WHARF
& ENVIRONS**   23   Pier 35
                24
Jefferson St.
21 22 Beach St.   Pier 33

uatic
ark

20   Pier 31
irardelli   North Point St.   25
quare   Bay St.   Pier 27
            Francisco St.
SSIAN   Chestnut St.   **NORTH**
HILL   Lombard St.   **BEACH**
            Greenwich St.   Pier 23
19   Filbert St.   Pier 19
            Union St.   Pier 17
            Green St.   *WASHINGTON*   Pier 15
                            SQUARE   Pier 9
            Vallejo St.   **TELEGRAPH**
            Broadway   *Tunnel* 27 **HILL**   Pier 7
OB   Pacific Ave.   28   Pier 5
ILL   Jackson St.   Pier 3
            Washington St. **CHINATOWN** 29   Pier 1
            Clay St.   30 32
            Sacramento St.   33   *Justin*
                            34 35   *Herman*
                            36 37   *Plaza*
            California St.   38   31 ■ **Ferry Building**
            Pine St.   **(World Trade Center)**
arkin St.   Bush St.
NDER-   Sutter St.   **San Francisco-**
OIN   Post St.   39   **Oakland**
eary St.   40 41 42 43   **Bay Bridge**
arrell St.   44 46 47 48 49
is St.   45 *Union* 50 51   80
ddy St.   *Square* 52
            UNION   53 54
            SQUARE &   55
            ENVIRONS
            Turk St.   57
                        YERBA BUENA
olden Gate Ave.   *GARDENS*
ster   St.   **Moscone**
CENTER   **Convention**
        Market   **Center**   *SOUTH*
                                          PARK 60
                        S O M A
                                56
            8th St. Mission St.
                    Howard St.   Bryant St.
            9th St. Folsom St. 59
                    Harrison St.   61
            10th St.
            11th St.
            80   Brannan St.   **SBC**
            12th St.   **Park**
                                    Townsend St.
101   King St.
            15th St.   280   Berry St.

            Division St.   Channel St.

63   Alameda St.
15th St.   101

Haight-Ashbury inset:

Conservatory D.   Fulton St.
                     Grove St.
McLaren   Hayes St.
Lodge   Fell St.
John F. Kennedy Dr. *PANHANDLE* **HAIGHT**
GOLDEN   Oak St.   **STREET**
GATE   Page St.   64   65
PARK Kezar *Beulah St.* 66   67 68
        Pavilion
Kezar Frederick St.
Stadium Carl St.
            Parnassus Ave.

0   1/4 mi
0   0.25 km

211

You can find a number of Asian-art dealers here. More than a dozen dealers on the 2 blocks between Columbus and Sansome streets specialize in European furnishings from the 17th to the 19th centuries. Most shops here are open Monday through Friday from 9am to 5pm and Saturday from 11am to 4pm.

Bonhams & Butterfield   This renowned auction house holds preview weekends for upcoming auctions of furnishings, silver, antiques, art, and jewelry. Call for auction schedules. 220 San Bruno Ave. (at 16th St.). *℃* **415/861-7500.**

Fumiki Fine Asian Arts   Come here for a beautiful collection of antique Japanese Imari, Korean and Japanese *tansu* (clothing chests), and Asian-style home accouterments. The extensive collection of Asian art and antiques includes Japanese baskets and Chinese artifacts and embroidery. 272 Sutter St. (at Grant St.). *℃* **415/362-6677.** A 2nd location is at 2001 Union St. (at Buchanan St.). *℃* **415/922-0573.**

Therien & Co.   For the best in Scandinavian, French, and eastern European antiques, head beyond SoMa's design center to this boutique, where you can find the real thing or antique replicas, as well as made-to-order furniture from their neighboring custom furniture shop. 411 Vermont St. (at 17th St.). *℃* **415/956-8850.** www.theiren.com.

ART

The San Francisco Gallery Guide, a comprehensive, bimonthly publication listing the city's current shows, is available free by mail. Send a self-addressed, stamped envelope to San Francisco Bay Area Gallery Guide, 1369 Fulton St., San Francisco, CA 94117 (*℃* **415/921-1600**); or pick one up at the San Francisco Visitor Information Center at 900 Market St. Most of the city's major art galleries are clustered downtown in the Union Square area.

Atelier Dore   Atelier Dore features American and European paintings from the 19th and 20th centuries. The store is open to everyone Tuesday through Saturday, but is closed on Sundays and open by appointment only on Mondays. 771 Bush St. (between Mason and Powell sts.). *℃* **415/391-2423.**

Catharine Clark Gallery *Value*   Catharine Clark's is a different kind of gallery experience. While many galleries focus on established artists and out-of-this-world prices, Catharine's exhibits works by up-and-coming contemporary as well as established artists (mainly from California). It nurtures beginning collectors by offering a purchasing plan that's almost unheard of in the art business. You can buy a piece on layaway and take up to a year to pay for it—interest free! Prices here make art a realistic purchase for almost everyone for a change, but serious collectors also frequent the shows because Clark has such a keen eye for talent. Shows change every 6 weeks. 49 Geary St. (between Kearny and Grant sts.), 2nd floor. *℃* **415/399-1439.** www.cclarkgallery.com.

Eleonore Austerer Gallery   Here you'll find limited-edition graphics by modern masters like Braque, Matisse, Miró, Picasso, Calder, Chagall, and Hockney, as well as original works by European and American contemporary artists. The gallery, in a beautiful old building near Union Square, is closed on Sunday. 565 Sutter St. (between Powell and Mason sts.). *℃* **415/986-2244.** www.austerergallery.com.

Fraenkel Gallery   This photography gallery features works by contemporary American and European artists. Excellent shows change frequently. Closed Sunday. 49 Geary St. (between Grant Ave. and Kearny St.), 4th floor. *℃* **415/981-2661.** www.fraenkelgallery.com.

Hang *(Value)*   Check out this amazingly affordable gallery for attractive pieces by yet-to-be-discovered artists. The staff is friendly and helpful, and the gallery is designed to cater to new collectors who appreciate original art at down-to-earth prices. 556 Sutter St. © 415/434-HANG. www.hangart.com.

Images of the North   The highlight here is one of the most extensive collections of Canadian and Alaskan Inuit art in the United States. There's also a small collection of Native American masks and jewelry. 2036 Union St. (at Buchanan St.). © 415/673-1273.

Meyerovich Gallery   Works on paper here are by modern and contemporary masters, including Chagall, Matisse, Miró, and Picasso. Meyerovich's new Contemporary Gallery, across the hall, features works by Lichtenstein, Motherwell, Dine, and Hockney. Closed Sunday. 251 Post St. (at Stockton St.), 4th floor. © 415/421-7171. www.meyerovich.com.

BOOKS

In addition to the listings below, there's a **Barnes & Noble** superstore at 2550 Taylor St., between Bay and North Point streets, near Fisherman's Wharf (© **415/292-6762**) and a four-storied **Borders** at 400 Post St., at Union Square (© **415/399-1633**).

Book Passage   If you're moseying through the Ferry Building Marketplace, drop into this cozy independent that emphasizes (for tourists and locals alike) local travel, boating on the Bay, food, cooking, sustainable agriculture and ecology, fiction, culinary and regional history and literature, and photo and gift books about the Bay Area. The store also hosts lots of author events. Ferry Building Marketplace (at The Embarcadero and Market St.). © 415/835-1020. www.bookpassage.com.

The Booksmith   Haight Street's best selection of new books is in this large, well-maintained shop. It carries all the top titles, along with works from smaller presses, and more than 1,000 different magazines. 1644 Haight St. (between Clayton and Cole sts.). © 800/493-7323 or 415/863-8688.

Builders Booksource San Francisco   This independently owned shop in an old factory building in Ghirardelli Square specializes in architecture, design, and construction and has a fine selection of exotic and limited-edition books on design and culture, but also offers a nicely edited selection of classic cookbooks and children's books. Ghirardelli Square, 900 North Point Ave. (at Larkin St.). © 415/440-5773. www.buildersbooksource-sf.com.

City Lights Booksellers & Publishers *(Finds)*   Brooding literary types browse this famous bookstore owned by Lawrence Ferlinghetti, the renowned Beat Generation poet. The three-level bookshop prides itself on a comprehensive collection of art, poetry, and political paperbacks, as well as more mainstream books. Open daily until midnight. 261 Columbus Ave. (at Broadway). © 415/362-8193. www.citylights.com.

A Clean, Well-Lighted Place for Books *(Finds)*   Voted best bookstore by the *San Francisco Bay Guardian,* this independent store has good new fiction and nonfiction sections, and specializes in music, art, mystery, and cookbooks. The store is well known for its author readings and events. For a calendar of events, call or check the website. 601 Van Ness Ave. (between Turk St. and Golden Gate Ave.). © 415/441-6670. www.bookstore.com.

Green Apple Books *Finds* The local favorite for used books, Green Apple is crammed with titles—more than 60,000 new and 100,000 used books. Its extended sections in psychology, cooking, art, and history; collection of modern first editions; and rare graphic comics are superseded only by the staff's superlative service. 506 Clement St. (at Sixth Ave.). ✆ 415/387-2272.

William Stout Architectural Books *Finds* Step inside this shrine to all things architectural, and even if you think you're not interested in exquisite bathrooms, Southern California's modern homes, or great gardens, you can't help but bury yourself in the thousands of design books. And if they don't have what you're looking for, it probably doesn't exist. 804 Montgomery St. (at Jackson St.). ✆ 415/391-6757. www.stoutbooks.com.

CHINA, SILVER & GLASS

Gump's *Finds* Founded over a century ago, Gump's offers gifts and treasures ranging from Asian antiquities to contemporary art glass and exquisite jade and pearl jewelry. Many items are made specifically for the store. Gump's also has one of the city's most revered holiday window displays. Closed Sunday. 135 Post St. (between Kearny St. and Grant Ave.). ✆ 415/982-1616. www.gumps.com.

CRAFTS

The Canton Bazaar Amid a wide variety of handicrafts, here you'll find an excellent selection of rosewood and carved furniture, cloisonné enamelware, rose Canton chinaware, porcelain, carved jade, embroideries, jewelry, and antiques from mainland China. Open daily until 10pm. 616 Grant Ave. (between Sacramento and California sts.). ✆ 415/362-5750.

The New Unique Company Primarily a calligraphy- and watercolor-supplies store, the shop also has a good assortment of books on these topics. In addition, there's a wide selection of carved stones for use as seals on letters and documents. Should you want a special design or group of initials, the store will carve seals to order. 838 Grant Ave. (between Clay and Washington sts.). ✆ 415/981-2036.

Silkroute International Owned and operated by an Afghan who offers fascinating wares (old and new) from his native country, the shop sells Oriental and tribal rugs, kilims, dhurries, textiles, jewelry, clothing, pillows, art, and antiques. 3119 Fillmore St. (at Filbert St.). ✆ 415/563-4936.

DEPARTMENT STORES (DOWNTOWN)

Macy's The seven-story Macy's West features contemporary fashions for women, juniors, and children, plus jewelry, fragrances, cosmetics, and accessories. The sixth floor offers a "hospitality suite" where visitors can leave their coats and packages, grab a cup of coffee, or find out more about the city from the concierge. The top floors contain home furnishings, and the Cellar sells kitchenware and gourmet foods. You'll even find a Boudin Cafe (though the food is not as good compared to their food at other locations) and a Wolfgang Puck Cafe on the premises. Across the street, Macy's East has five floors of men's fashions, the largest Men's Polo by Ralph Lauren shop in the country, and the Fresh Choice cafe. Stockton and O'Farrell sts., Union Square. ✆ 415/397-3333.

Neiman Marcus Some call this Texas-based chain "Needless Mark-ups." But those who can afford the best of everything can't deny that the men's and women's clothes, precious gems, and conservative formalwear are some of the most glamorous in town. The Rotunda Restaurant, on the top floor, is a beautiful, relaxing place for lunch and afternoon tea. 150 Stockton St. (between Geary and O'Farrell sts.), Union Square. ℂ 415/362-3900.

Nordstrom   Renowned for its personalized service, this is the largest branch of the Seattle-based fashion department-store chain. Nordstrom occupies the top five floors of the San Francisco Shopping Centre (see "Shopping Centers & Complexes," on p. 221) and is the mall's primary anchor. Equally devoted to women's and men's fashions, the store has one of the best shoe selections in the city and thousands of suits in stock. The City Centre Grill, on the fourth floor, has a panoramic view and is ideal for an inexpensive lunch or light snack. Nordstrom Spa, on the fifth floor, is the perfect place to relax after a hectic day of bargain hunting. In the San Francisco Shopping Centre, 865 Market St. (between 4th and 5th sts.). ℂ 415/243-8500.

DISCOUNT SHOPPING

Jeremy's _Value_   This boutique is a serious mecca for fashion hounds thanks to the wide array of top designer fashions, from shoes to suits, at rock-bottom prices. There are no cheap knockoffs here, just good men's and women's clothes and accessories that the owner scoops up from major retailers who are either updating their merchandise or discarding returns. 2 S. Park (between Bryant and Brannan sts. at Second St.). ℂ 415/882-4929.

FABRICS

Britex Fabrics   A San Francisco institution since 1952, Britex offers an absurd amount and variety of fabrics, not to mention a selection of more than 30,000 buttons. It's currently undergoing retrofitting, so call to be sure it's open. Closed Sunday. 117 Post St. (at Kearny St.). ℂ 415/392-2910.

FASHION

See also "Vintage Clothing," later in this section.

UNISEX

American Rag Cie _Finds_   Fashionistas flock to this find, on an unlikely stretch of busy Van Ness, for vintage and new duds sure to make you look street-swank. Check it out for everything from Juicy Couture to Paul & Joe and European vintage and modern masters such as Diesel or Marc Jacobs. 1305 Van Ness Ave. (at Sutter St.). ℂ 415/474-5214.

Gucci America   Donning Gucci's golden Gs is not a cheap endeavor. But if you've got the cash, you'll find all the latest lines of shoes, leather goods, scarves, and pricey accessories here, such as a $9,000 handmade crocodile bag. 200 Stockton St. (between Geary and Post sts.). ℂ 415/392-2808.

MAC _Finds_   No, we're not talking cosmetics. The more-modern-than-corporate stock at this hip and hidden shop just combined its men's and women's fashion meccas in a new space next door to pastry pit stop Citizen Cake. Drop in for imported tailored suits and women's separates in new and intriguing fabrics as well as gorgeous ties, vibrant sweaters, and a few choice home accouterments. Lines include London's Paul Smith, Belgium's SO, New York's John Bartlett, and local sweater sweetheart Laurie B. The best part? Prices are more reasonable than many of the trendy clothing stores in the area. 387 Grove St. (at Gough St.). ℂ 415/863-3011.

Niketown   Here it's not "I can," but "I can spend." At least that's what the kings of sportswear were banking on when they opened this megastore in 1997.

As you'd expect, inside the doors it's Nike's world, offering everything the merchandising team could create. 278 Post St. (at Stockton St.). ⓒ 415/392-6453.

Three Bags Full Snuggling up in a cozy sweater can be a fashionable event if you do your shopping at this pricey boutique, which carries the gamut in handmade and one-of-a-kind playful and extravagant knitwear. Other city locations, which are both closed on Sunday, are 500 Sutter St. and 3314 Sacramento St. (also closed Mon). 2181 Union St. (at Fillmore St.). ⓒ 415/567-5753. www.threebagsfull.com.

Wilkes Bashford *(Finds)* Wilkes Bashford is one of the most expensive and best-known clothing stores in the city. In its 3-plus decades in business, the boutique has garnered a reputation for stocking only the finest clothes in the world (which can often be seen on Mayor Willie Brown, who does his suit shopping here). Most fashions come from Italy and France; they include women's designer sportswear and couture and men's Kiton and Brioni suits (at $2,500 and up, they're considered the most expensive suits in the world). Closed Sunday. 375 Sutter St. (at Stockton St.). ⓒ 415/986-4380.

MEN'S FASHIONS

All American Boy Long known for setting the mainstream style for gay men, All American Boy is the quintessential Castro clothing shop. 463 Castro St. (between Market and 18th sts.). ⓒ 415/861-0444.

Brooks Brothers In San Francisco, this bulwark of tradition is 1 block east of Union Square. Brooks Brothers introduced the button-down collar and single-handedly changed the standard of the well-dressed businessman. The multilevel shop also sells traditional casual wear, including sportswear, sweaters, and shirts. 150 Post St. (at Grant Ave.). ⓒ 415/397-4500.

Cable Car Clothiers Dapper men head to this beautiful landmark building for traditional attire, such as three-button suits with natural shoulders, Aquascutum coats, McGeorge sweaters, and Atkinson ties. Closed Sunday. 441 Sutter St. (between Stockton and Powell sts.). ⓒ 415/397-4740.

Citizen Clothing The Castro has some of America's best men's casual clothing stores, and this is one of them. Stylish (but not faddish) pants, tops, and accessories are in stock. 536 Castro St. (between 18th and 19th sts.). ⓒ 415/558-9429.

WOMEN'S FASHIONS

Ab Fits Duck into this North Beach destination for jeans to fit all shapes, styles, and sizes as well as smart and sassy contemporary wear for gals on the go. The snuggly-fitting stock ranges from Levi's, Earl, Edwin, and Seven to chic wear from the likes of Rozae Nichols, Nanette Lepore, and James Perse. 1519 Grant Ave. (at Union and Filbert sts.). ⓒ 415/982-5726.

The Chanel Boutique Ever fashionable and expensive, Chanel is appropriately located on Maiden Lane, the quaint downtown side street where the most exclusive stores and spas cluster. You'll find here what you'd expect from Chanel: clothing, accessories, scents, cosmetics, and jewelry. 155 Maiden Lane (between Stockton St. and Grant Ave.). ⓒ 415/981-1550.

emily lee More mature fashionistas head to the quaint shopping street of Laurel Village, a block-long strip mall of shops that includes emily lee, for everything from elegant to artsy-designer garb that tends to be stylish, sensible, and loose-fitting. Designers include the likes of Eileen Fisher, Flax, Stephanie Schuster, Joan Vass, and Vivienne Tam. 3509 California St. (at Locust St.). ⓒ 415/751-3443.

Métier *(Finds)*   Some savvy shoppers consider this the best women's clothing shop in town. Within its walls you'll find classic, sophisticated, and expensive creations. Offerings include European ready-to-wear lines and designers; fashions by Italian designers Anna Molinari and Alberto Biani; and a distinguished collection of antique-style, high-end jewelry from L.A.'s Kathie Waterman as well as ultrapopular custom-designed poetry jewelry by Jeanine Payer. Closed Sunday. 355 Sutter St. (between Stockton and Grant sts.). ℰ **415/989-5395.**

CHILDREN'S FASHIONS

Minis   Christina Profili, a San Francisco native who used to design for Banana Republic, opened this children's clothing store to sell her own creations. Every piece, from shirts to pants and dresses, is made from cotton or organic cotton. Every outfit perfectly coordinates with everything else in the store. Minis also offers educational and creative toys and books with matching dolls as well as maternity wear. 2278 Union St. (between Steiner and Fillmore sts.). ℰ **415/567-9537.**

FOOD

Artisan Cheese *(Finds)*   San Francisco is fanatical about cheese, and much of the local enthusiasm can be attributed to the women behind Artisan Cheese, a simple little neighborhood shop carrying nothing other than excellent small-production local and imported cheeses. 2413 California St. (at Fillmore St.). ℰ **415/929-8610.** www.cowgirlcreamery.com.

Boulangerie *(Finds)*   A bit of Paris on Pine Street, this true-blue bakery sells authentically French creations, from delicious and slightly sour French country wheat bread to rustic-style desserts, including the locally famous *cannele de Bordeaux,* custard baked in a copper mold. 2325 Pine St. (at Fillmore St.). ℰ **415/440-0356,** ext. 204.

Golden Gate Fortune Cookies Co.   This tiny, touristy factory sells fortune cookies hot off the press. You can purchase them in small bags or in bulk, and you can even bring in your own messages and watch them fold them into fresh cookies (with a minimum order) before your eyes. Even if you're not buying, stop in to see how these sugary treats are made (although the staff can get pushy for you to buy). Open daily until 7pm. 56 Ross Alley (between Washington and Jackson sts.). ℰ **415/781-3956.**

Joseph Schmidt Confections *(Finds)*   Here, chocolate takes the shape of exquisite sculptural masterpieces—such as long-stemmed tulips and heart-shaped boxes—that are so beautiful, you'll be hesitant to bite the head off your adorable panda bear. Once you do, however, you'll know why this is the most popular—and reasonably priced—chocolatier in town. 3489 16th St. (at Sanchez St.). ℰ **800/861-8682** or 415/861-8682. www.jsc.com.

Ten Ren Tea Co. *(Finds)*   At the Ten Ren Tea Co. shop, you will be offered a steaming cup of tea when you walk in the door. In addition to a selection of almost 50 traditional and herbal teas, the company stocks related paraphernalia, such as pots, cups, and infusers. If you can't make up your mind, take home a mail-order form. The shop is open daily from 9am to 9pm. 949 Grant Ave. (between Washington and Jackson sts.). ℰ **415/362-0656.**

GIFTS

Art of China   Amid a wide variety of collectibles, this shop features exquisite, hand-carved Chinese figurines. You'll also find a lovely assortment of ivory beads, bracelets, necklaces, and earrings. Pink-quartz dogs, jade figurines, porcelain vases, cache pots, and blue-and-white barrels suitable for use as table bases are just some of the many items stocked here. 839–843 Grant Ave. (between Clay and Washington sts.). © 415/981-1602.

Babushka Located near Fisherman's Wharf, adjacent to the Anchorage mall, Babushka sells only Russian products, most of which are wooden nesting dolls. 333 Jefferson St. (at Leavenworth St.). © 415/673-6740.

Cost Plus Imports At the Fisherman's Wharf cable car turntable, Cost Plus is a vast warehouse crammed to the rafters with Chinese baskets, Indian camel bells, Malaysian batik scarves, and innumerable other items from Algeria to Zanzibar. More than 20,000 items from 40 nations, imported directly from their country of origin, pack this well-priced warehouse. There's also a decent wine shop here. It's open Monday through Saturday from 10am to 9pm and Sunday from 10am to 8pm. 2552 Taylor St. (between North Point and Bay sts.). © 415/928-6200.

Dandelion *Finds* Tucked in an out-of-the-way location in SoMa is the most wonderful collection of gifts, collectibles, and furnishings. There's something for every taste and budget here, from an excellent collection of teapots, decorative dishes, and gourmet foods to silver, books, cards, and picture frames. Don't miss the Zen-like second floor, with its peaceful furnishings in Indian, Japanese, and Western styles. The store is closed Sunday and Monday except during November and December, when it's open daily. Hours are 10am to 6pm. 55 Potrero Ave. (at Alameda St.). © 415/436-9500.

Distractions & Euphoria This is the best of the Haight Street shops selling underground-rave wear, street fashion, and electronica CDs. You'll find pipes, toys, and stickers liberally mixed with lots of cool stuff to look at. 1552 Haight St. (between Ashbury and Clayton sts.). © 415/252-8751.

Flax If you're the type of person who goes into an art store for a special pencil and comes out $300 later, don't go near this shop. Flax has everything you can think of in art and design supplies, an amazing collection of local arts and crafts, blank bound books, children's art supplies, frames, calendars—you name it. There's a gift for every type of person here, especially you. If you can't stop by, call for a mail-order catalog. 1699 Market St. (at Valencia and Gough sts.). © 415/552-2355. www.flaxart.com.

Good Vibrations A laypersons' sex-toy, book, and video emporium, Good Vibrations is specifically (but not exclusively) designed for women. Unlike most sex shops, it's not a back-alley business, but a straightforward shop with healthy, open attitudes about human sexuality. It also has a vibrator museum. 603 Valencia St. (at 17th St.). © 415/522-5460 or 800/BUY-VIBE (for mail order). www.goodvibes.com. A second location is at 1620 Polk St. (at Sacramento St.), © 415/345-0400, and a third is at 2504 San Pablo Ave., Berkeley (© 510/841-8987).

SFMOMA MuseumStore *Finds* With an array of artistic cards, books, jewelry, housewares, knickknacks, and creative tokens of San Francisco, it's virtually impossible not to find something here you'll consider a must-have. (Check out the Fog Dome!) Aside from being one of the locals' favorite shops, it offers far more tasteful mementos than most Fisherman's Wharf options. You can also check them out online at www.sfmoma.org. 151 Third St. (2 blocks south of Market St., across from Yerba Buena Gardens). © 415/357-4035.

Smile   Need a little humor in your life? Smile specializes in whimsical art, furniture, clothing, jewelry, and American crafts guaranteed to make you grin. Closed Sunday. 500 Sutter St. (between Powell and Mason sts.). ✆ 415/362-3437.

HOUSEWARES/FURNISHINGS

Alabaster *Finds*   Any interior designer who knows Biedermeier from Bauhaus knows that this Hayes Valley shop sets local home accessories trends with its predominantly off-white collection of must-haves. 597 Hayes St. (at Laguna St.). ✆ 415/558-0482.

Alessi   Italian designer Alberto Alessi, who's known for his whimsical and colorful kitchen-utensil designs, such as his ever-popular spiderlike stainless-steel lemon squeezer, opened a flagship store here. Drop by for everything from gorgeous stainless-steel double boilers to corkscrews shaped like maidens. 424 Sutter St. (at Stockton St.). ✆ 415/434-0403.

Biordi Art Imports *Finds*   Whether you want to decorate your dinner table, color your kitchen, or liven up the living room, Biordi's Italian majolica pottery is the most exquisite and unusual way to do it. The owner has been importing these hand-painted collectibles for 54 years, and every piece is a showstopper. Call for a catalog. They'll ship anywhere. Closed Sunday. 412 Columbus Ave. (at Vallejo St.). ✆ 415/392-8096. www.biordi.com.

Limn   For the latest in Europe's trendsetting and ultramodern furniture and lighting, go straight to local SoMa celebrity Limn, which also showcases artworks in its adjoining gallery. 290 Townsend St. (at Fourth St.). ✆ 415/543-5466. www.limn.com.

Nest *Finds*   Don't come into Fillmore's cutest French interiors store without your credit cards. Nest carries adorable throws, handmade quilts, vintage perfume bottles, must-have slippers and sleepwear, and a number of other things you never knew you needed until now. There's another location at 2300 Fillmore St. (✆ 415/292-6199). 2340 Polk St. (at Union St.). ✆ 415/292-6198.

Propeller   This airy skylight-lit shop is a must-stop for lovers of the latest in übermodern furniture and home accessories. Owner/designer Lorn Dittfeld handpicks pieces by emerging designers from as far away as Sweden, Italy, and Canada, as well as a plethora of national newbies. Drop in to lounge on the hippest sofas; grab pretty and practical gifts like ultracool magnetic spice racks; or adorn your home with Bev Hisey's architectural candlesticks and graphic pillows, diamond-cut wood tables by William Earle, or hand-tufted graphic rugs by Angela Adams. The shop's closed Monday except by appointment. 555 Hayes St. (between Laguna and Octavia sts.). ✆ 415/701-7767. www.propeller-sf.com.

Sue Fisher King *Finds*   For the ultimate in everything on the traditional side for the tabletop, bedroom, and beyond, head to this exclusive neighborhood boutique known by the society set as the only place to shop. Amidst the gourmet chocolates and other sweet finds, you can get your hands on exquisite table linens, cashmere blankets, towels, china, silver flatware, and more. 3067 Sacramento St. (at Baker St.). ✆ 415/922-7276. www.suefisherking.com.

Sur La Table   Cooks should bee-line it to this Union Square shop specializing in all things culinary. Its two floors are packed to the rafters with pricey but stylish high-quality pots and pans, utensils, tabletop items, books, and more. Bonuses are frequent cooking demos and an extremely helpful and knowledgeable staff. 77 Maiden Lane (at Grant St.). ✆ 415/732-7900. www.surlatable.com.

The Wok Shop   This shop has every conceivable implement for Chinese cooking, including woks, brushes, cleavers, circular chopping blocks, dishes, oyster knives, bamboo steamers, and strainers. It also sells a wide range of kitchen utensils, baskets, handmade linens from China, and aprons. 718 Grant Ave. (at Clay St.). ✆ 415/989-3797 or 888/780-7171 for mail order. www.wokshop.com.

Zinc Details *(Finds)*   One of my favorite stores in the city, Zinc Details has received accolades everywhere from *Elle Decor Japan* to *Metropolitan Home* for its amazing collection of locally handcrafted glass vases, pendant lights, ceramics, and furniture. Most pieces are true works of art created specifically for the store. 1905 Fillmore St. (between Bush and Pine sts.). ✆ 415/776-2100. www.zincdetails.com.

JEWELRY

De Vera Galleries *(Finds)*   Don't come here unless you've got money to spend. Designer Federico de Vera's unique rough-stone jewelry collection, art glass, and vintage knickknacks are too beautiful to pass up and too expensive to be a painless purchase. Still, if you're looking for a keepsake, you'll find it here. 29 Maiden Lane (at Kearny St.). ✆ 415/788-0828. www.deveraobjects.com.

Dianne's Old & New Estates   Buy yourself a bauble and treat yourself to a trinket at this shop featuring top-of-the-line antique jewelry—pendants, diamond rings, necklaces, bracelets, and natural pearls. For a special gift, check out the collection of platinum wedding and engagement rings and vintage watches. Don't worry if you can't afford it now—the shop offers 1-year interest-free layaway. Closed on Wednesday. 2181A Union St. (at Fillmore St.). ✆ 888/346-7525 or 415/346-7525.

Pearl & Jade Empire   The Pearl & Jade Empire has been importing jewelry from all over the world since 1957. It specializes in unusual pearls and jade and offers restringing on the premises as well as boasting a collection of amber from the Baltic Sea. 427 Post St. (between Powell and Mason sts.). ✆ 415/362-0606. www.pearlempire.com.

Tiffany & Co.   Even if you don't have lots of cash with which to buy an exquisite bauble that comes in Tiffany's famous light-blue box, enjoy this renowned store a la Audrey Hepburn in *Breakfast at Tiffany's*. The designer collection features Paloma Picasso, Jean Schlumberger, and Elsa Peretti in both silver and 18-karat gold, and there's an extensive gift collection in sterling, china, and crystal. 350 Post St. (at Powell St.). ✆ 415/781-7000. www.tiffany.com.

Union Street Goldsmith   A showcase for Bay Area goldsmiths, this exquisite shop sells a contemporary collection of fine custom-designed jewelry in platinum and all karats of gold. Many pieces emphasize colored stones. 1909 Union St. (at Laguna St.). ✆ 415/776-8048. www.unionstreetgoldsmith.com.

MUSIC

Recycled Records *(Finds)*   Easily one of the best used-record stores in the city, this loud shop in the Haight has a good selection of promotional CDs and cases of used "classic" rock LPs. Sheet music, tour programs, and old *TV Guides* are for sale, too. It's open late daily; hours vary, so call ahead. 1377 Haight St. (between Central and Masonic sts.). ✆ 415/626-4075.

Streetlight Records   Overstuffed with used music in all three formats, this place is best known for its records and excellent CD collection. Rock music is cheap, and the money-back guarantee guards against defects. There's a second location at 2350 Market St., between Castro and Noe streets (© **415/282-8000**). 3979 24th St. (between Noe and Sanchez sts.). © **415/282-3550**.

Virgin Megastore   With thousands of CDs, including an impressive collection of imports, videos, DVDs, a multimedia department, a cafe, and related books, this enormous Union Square store can make any music-lover blow his or her entire vacation fund. It's open Sunday through Thursday from 10am to 10pm and Friday and Saturday from 10am to midnight. 2 Stockton St. (at Market St.). © **415/397-4525**.

SHOES

Birkenstock   This relaxed store is known for its earthy form-fitting sandals, clogs, and lace-ups. 42 Stockton St. (between Market and O'Farrell sts.). © **415/989-2475**.

Bulo   If you have a fetish for foot fashions, you must check out Bulo, which carries nothing but imported Italian shoes. The selection is small but styles run the gamut, from casual to dressy, reserved to wildly funky. New shipments come in every 3 to 4 weeks, so the selection is ever-changing, eternally hip, and, unfortunately, ever-expensive, with many pairs going for close to $200. Men's store: 437A Hayes St. (at Gough St.). © **415/864-3244**. Women's store: across the street, at 418 Hayes St. (© **415/255-4939**).

Gimme Shoes   The staff is funky-fashion snobby, the prices are steep, and the European shoes and accessories are utterly chic. Additional locations are 416 Hayes St. (© **415/864-0691**) and 50 Grant Ave. (© **415/434-9242**). 2358 Fillmore St. (at Washington St.). © **415/441-3040**.

Kenneth Cole   This trendy shop carries high-fashion footwear for men and women. There is also an innovative collection of handbags and small leather goods and accessories. Other shops are at 2078 Union St., at Webster St. (© **415/346-2161**) and 166 Grant St., at Post St. (© **415/981-2653**). 865 Market St. (in the San Francisco Shopping Centre). © **415/227-4536**.

SHOPPING CENTERS & COMPLEXES

The Anchorage   This touristy waterfront mall has close to 55 stores that offer everything from music boxes to home furnishings; street performers entertain during open hours. This is not a stop for staples, but more for tourist trinkets. 2800 Leavenworth St. (between Beach and Jefferson sts. on Fisherman's Wharf). © **415/775-6000**.

The Cannery   Once a Del Monte fruit-canning plant, this attractive complex now contains a score or two of tourist-driven shops, restaurants, and nightspots. Vendors' stalls and sidewalk cafes occupy the courtyard, amid a grove of olive trees. Street performers entertain year-round, weather permitting. 2801 Leavenworth St. (at Jefferson St.). © **415/771-3112**.

Crocker Galleria   Modeled after Milan's Galleria Vittorio Emanuele, this glass-domed, three-level pavilion, about 3 blocks east of Union Square, features around 40 high-end shops with expensive and classic designer creations. Fashions include Aricie lingerie, Gianni Versace, and Polo/Ralph Lauren. Closed Sunday. 50 Post St. (at Kearny St.). © **415/393-1505**.

Ghirardelli Square   This former chocolate factory is one of the city's quaintest shopping malls and most popular landmarks. It dates from 1864, when it served as a factory making Civil War uniforms, but it's best known as the former chocolate and spice factory of Domingo Ghirardelli (say "Gear-a-deli"). A clock tower, an exact replica of the one at France's Château de Blois, crowns the complex. Inside the tower, on the mall's plaza level, is the fun Ghirardelli soda fountain. It still makes and sells small amounts of chocolate, but the big draw is the old-fashioned ice-cream parlor. (Got a late-night craving? The place stays open until midnight on Fri and Sat.) A free map and guide to the mall is available from the information booth in the center courtyard. Many national chain stores are located here. The hottest attraction, however, is restaurant Ana Mandara (p. 139). Main plaza shops' and restaurants' hours vary, with extended hours during the summer. (Incidentally, the Ghirardelli Chocolate Company still makes chocolate in the East Bay.) 900 North Point St. (at Polk St.). ✆ 415/775-5500. www.ghirardellisq.com.

PIER 39 *(Overrated)*   The automated information line reminds callers not to forget to bring your Discover credit card (their "preferred card," but not the only one accepted) to this bayside tourist trap, which also happens to have stunning views. To residents, that pretty much wraps up PIER 39—an expensive spot where out-of-towners go to waste money on worthless souvenirs and greasy fast food. For vacationers, though, PIER 39 does have some redeeming qualities— fresh crab (in season), playful sea lions, phenomenal views, and plenty of fun for the kids. If you want to get to know the real San Francisco, skip the cheesy T-shirt shops and limit your time here to one afternoon, if at all.

San Francisco Shopping Centre   Opened in 1988, this $140-million complex is one of the few vertical malls (multilevel rather than sprawling) in the United States. Its most attractive features are the four-story spiral escalators that circle up to Nordstrom (p. 215) and the nine-story atrium covered by a retractable skylight. More than 70 specialty shops include Abercrombie & Fitch, Ann Taylor, bebe, Benetton, Footlocker, J. Crew, and Victoria's Secret. In 2006, the center will expand to include a Bloomingdale's department store. If you want one-stop shopping, this is as good as it gets. 865 Market St. (at Fifth St.). ✆ 415/495-5656.

TOYS

The Chinatown Kite Shop   This shop's playful assortment of flying objects includes attractive fish kites, windsocks, hand-painted Chinese paper kites, wood-and-paper biplanes, pentagonal kites, and do-it-yourself kite kits, all of which make great souvenirs or decorations. Computer-designed stunt kites have two or four control lines to manipulate loops and dives. Open daily from 10am to 9pm. 717 Grant Ave. (between Clay and Sacramento sts.). ✆ 415/391-8217.

The Disney Store   Capitalizing on the world's love for The Mouse and his friends, this store offers everything Disney-oriented you could possibly want— from clothes and toys to high-end commissioned art from the Disney gallery. Those looking for a simple token can fork over $5 for a souvenir, while more serious collectors can throw down $4,500 for a Yamagata Disney lithograph. The store is open Monday through Friday from 10am to 7pm, Saturday from 10am to 8pm, Sunday from 11am to 7pm. Hours are extended during the holiday season; call for details. 400 Post St. (at Powell St.). ✆ 415/391-6866.

TRAVEL GOODS

Flight 001   Jetsetters zoom into this space-shuttle-like showroom for hip travel accessories. Check out the sleek luggage, "security friendly" manicure sets, and other mid-air must-haves. 525 Hayes St. (between Laguna and Octavia sts.). © 415/487-1001. www.flight001.com.

On the Road Again   This smart shop sells toiletry kits, travel bottles, travel-size items, and a good selection of related goods. It's open daily from 10am to 8pm. The Embarcadero and Beach St. (in PIER 39). © 415/434-1482.

Rand McNally Maps & Books   The best map shop in the city, Rand McNally sells street, topographic, and hiking maps depicting San Francisco, California, and the world, as well as an extensive selection of travel guides and atlases. 595 Market St. (at Second St.). © 415/777-3131 or 800/969-3072 for mail order. www.randmcnallystore.com.

VINTAGE CLOTHING

Aardvark's   One of San Francisco's largest secondhand clothing dealers, Aardvark's has seemingly endless racks of shirts, pants, dresses, skirts, and hats from the past 30 years. It's open daily from 11am to 7pm. 1501 Haight St. (at Ashbury St.). © 415/621-3141.

Buffalo Exchange   This large storefront on upper Haight Street is crammed with racks of antique and new fashions from the 1960s, 1970s, and 1980s. It stocks everything from suits and dresses to neckties, hats, handbags, and jewelry. Buffalo Exchange anticipates some of the hottest new street fashions. A second shop is at 1800 Polk St., at Washington St. (© 415/346-5726). 1555 Haight St. (between Clayton and Ashbury sts.). © 415/431-7733.

Good Byes *(Finds*   One the best new- and used-clothes stores in San Francisco, Good Byes carries only high-quality clothing and accessories, including an exceptional selection of men's fashions at unbelievably low prices (for example, $350 preowned shoes for $35). Women's wear is in a separate boutique across the street. 3464 Sacramento St. and 3483 Sacramento St. (between Laurel and Walnut sts.). © 415/346-6388.

La Rosa   On a street packed with vintage-clothing shops, this is one of the more upscale options. It features a selection of high-quality, dry-cleaned sec-ondhand goods. Formal suits and dresses are its specialty, but you'll also find sport coats, slacks, and shoes. The more moderately priced sister store, **Held Over,** is located at 1543 Haight St., near Ashbury (© 415/864-0818). 1711 Haight St. (at Cole St.). © 415/668-3744.

WINE

Wine Club San Francisco *(Value*   The Wine Club is a discount warehouse that offers bargain prices on more than 1,200 domestic and foreign wines. Bottles cost between $4 and $1,100. 953 Harrison St. (between Fifth and Sixth sts.). © 415/512-9086.

10

San Francisco After Dark

For a city with fewer than a million inhabitants, San Francisco boasts an impressive after-dark scene. Dozens of piano bars and top-notch lounges augment a lively dance-club culture, and skyscraper lounges offer dazzling city views. The city's arts scene is also extraordinary: The opera is justifiably world renowned, the ballet is on its toes, the Asian Art Museum has settled into its new Civic Center digs, and theaters are high in both quantity and quality. In short, there's always something going on, so get out there.

For up-to-date nightlife information, turn to the *San Francisco Weekly* (www.sfweekly.com) and the *San Francisco Bay Guardian* (www.sfbg.com), both of which run comprehensive listings. They are available free at bars and restaurants and from streetcorner boxes all around the city. *Where* (www.wheresf.com), a free tourist-oriented monthly, also lists programs and performance times; it's available in most of the city's finer hotels. The Sunday edition of the *San Francisco Chronicle* features a "Datebook" section, printed on pink paper, with information on and listings of the week's events. If you have Internet access, it's a good idea to check out www.citysearch.com for the latest in bars, clubs, and events. And if you want to secure seats at a hot-ticket event, either buy well in advance or contact the concierge of your hotel and see if they can't swing something for you.

Tix Bay Area (© **415/433-7827;** www.tixbayarea.org) sells half-price tickets to theater, dance, and music performances on the day of the show only; tickets for Sunday and Monday events, if available, are sold on Saturday and Sunday. Tix Bay Area also sells advance, full-price tickets for most performance halls, sporting events, concerts, and clubs. A service charge, ranging from $2 to $5, is levied on each ticket. Only cash and traveler's checks are accepted for half-price tickets; Visa and MasterCard are accepted for full-price tickets. Tix, located on Powell Street between Geary and Post streets, is open Tuesday through Thursday from 11am to 6pm, Friday and Saturday from 11am to 7pm, and Sunday from 11am to 3pm.

You can also get tickets to most theater and dance events through **City Box Office,** 180 Redwood St., Suite 100, between Golden Gate and McAllister streets off Van Ness Avenue (© **415/392-4400;** www.cityboxoffice.com). MasterCard and Visa are accepted.

Tickets.com (© **415/478-2277** or 510/762-2277; www.tickets.com) sells computer-generated tickets (with a hefty service charge of $3–$15 convenience fee per ticket!) to concerts, sporting events, plays, and special events. Call for the local office nearest you. **Ticketmaster** (© **415/421-TIXS;** www.ticketmaster.com) also offers advance ticket purchases (also with a service charge.

For information on local theater, check out www.bayareatheatre.org.

For information on major league baseball, pro basketball, pro and college football, and horse racing, see the

"Spectator Sports" section of chapter 7, beginning on p. 193.

And don't forget that this isn't New York: Bars close at 2am, so get an early start if you want a full night on the town in San Francisco.

1 The Performing Arts

Special concerts and performances take place in San Francisco year-round. **San Francisco Performances,** 500 Sutter St., Suite 710 (© **415/398-6449;** www. performances.org), has brought acclaimed artists to the Bay Area for 25 years. Shows run the gamut from chamber music to dance to jazz. Performances are in several venues, including the Performing Arts Center, Herbst Theater, and the Center for the Performing Arts at Yerba Buena Center. The season runs from late September to May. Tickets cost from $12 to $60 and are available through **City Box Office** (© **415/392-4400).**

CLASSICAL MUSIC

Philharmonia Baroque Orchestra   Acclaimed by the *New York Times* as "the country's leading early music orchestra," Philharmonia Baroque performs in San Francisco and all around the Bay Area. The season lasts September through April. Performing in Herbst Theater, 401 Van Ness Ave. © 415/392-4400 (box office) or 415/252-1288 (administrative offices). www.philharmonia.org. Tickets $28–$62.

San Francisco Symphony   Founded in 1911, the internationally respected San Francisco Symphony has long been an important part of the city's cultural life under such legendary conductors as Pierre Monteux and Seiji Ozawa. In 1995, Michael Tilson Thomas took over from Herbert Blomstedt; he has led the orchestra to new heights and crafted an exciting repertoire of classical and modern music. The season runs September through June. Summer symphony activities include a Composer Festival and a Summer in the City series. Tickets are very hard to come by, but if you're desperate, you can usually pick up a few outside the hall the night of the concert. Performing at Davies Symphony Hall, 201 Van Ness Ave. (at Grove St.). © 415/864-6000 (box office). www.sfsymphony.org. Tickets $12–$97.

OPERA

In addition to San Francisco's major opera company, you might check out the amusing **Pocket Opera,** 469 Bryant St. (© **415/972-8930;** www.pocket opera.org). From mid-February to mid-July, the comic company stages farcical performances of well-known operas in English. The staging is intimate and informal, without lavish costumes and sets. The cast ranges from 3 to 16 players, supported by a chamber orchestra. The rich repertoire includes such works as *Don Giovanni* and *The Barber of Seville.* Performances are on Saturday and Sunday. Call the box office for complete information, location (which varies), and show times. Tickets cost from $15 (students) to $30.

San Francisco Opera   The San Francisco Opera was the second municipal opera in the United States and is one of the city's cultural icons. Brilliantly balanced casts may feature celebrated stars like Frederica Von Stade and Plácido Domingo, along with promising newcomers and regular members, in productions that range from traditional to avant-garde. All productions have English supertitles. The season starts in September and lasts just 14 weeks. Performances are held most evenings, except Monday, with matinees on Sundays. Tickets go on sale as early as June for subscribers and August for the general public, and the best seats sell out quickly. Unless Domingo is in town, some less coveted seats

San Francisco After Dark

American Conservatory Theater (A.C.T.) **53**
Bambuddha Lounge **21**
Bay Area Theatresports (BATS) **1**
Beach Blanket Babylon **32**
Biscuits and Blues **54**
The Bliss Bar **12**
Blue Bar **36**
The Boom Boom Room **4**
Bottom of the Hill **74**
The Bubble Lounge **43**
Buena Vista Café **26**
The Café **11**
Cafe du Nord **8**
Caffè Greco **33**
Caffè Trieste **34**
The Carnelian Room **45**
Castro Theatre **11**
Center for the Performing Arts at Yerba Buena Center **61**
The Cinch Saloon **24**
Cityscape **52**
Club Deluxe **77**
Cobb's Comedy Club **29**
Cowell Theater **1**
Davies Symphony Hall **18**
Detour **10**
The Eagle **70**
Edinburgh Castle **22**
Empire Plush Room **49**
The Endup **63**
Eos **75**
Equinox **42**
Eureka Theater **40**
Factory 525 **59**
The Fillmore **5**
Fort Mason Center **1**
Geary Theater **53**
Gordon Biersch Brewery Restaurant **58**
Grant & Green Saloon **31**
The Great Entertainer **73**
Greens Sports Bar **25**
Harry Denton's Starlight Room **56**
Hayes and Vine **17**
Herbst Theater **20**
Jazz at Pearl's **35**
Julie's Supper Club **65**
Kimo's **23**

Li Po Cocktail Lounge **39**
London Wine Bar **44**
Lone Star Saloon **67**
Lorraine Hansberry Theatre **48**
Lou's Pier 47 Club **28**
The Magic Theatre **1**
Matrix Fillmore **2**
Metro **9**
The Mint Karaoke Lounge **15**
The Monkey Club **72**
Nickie's Bar-be-cue **6**
ODC Theatre **14**
Paradise Lounge **69**
Perry's **3**
Philharmonia Baroque Orchestra **20**
Pied Piper Bar **57**
Pier 23 **30**
Pocket Opera **16**
Punch Line **41**
Rasselas **5**
Rawhide II **64**
The Red Room **50**
Red Vic **76**
The Redwood Room **51**
Roxie **13**
Ruby Skye **55**
The Saloon **34**
San Francisco Ballet **19**
San Francisco Brewing Company **38**
San Francisco Contemporary Music Players **61**
San Francisco Opera **19**
San Francisco Symphony **18**
Slim's **68**
Spec's **37**
The Stud **66**
Ten 15 **62**
Theatre Rhinoceros **71**
Thirsty Bear Brewing Company **60**
The Tonga Room & Hurricane Bar **46**
Top of the Mark **47**
Toronado **7**
Tosca **38**
Twin Peaks Tavern **11**
Vesuvio **35**
Wish Bar **69**

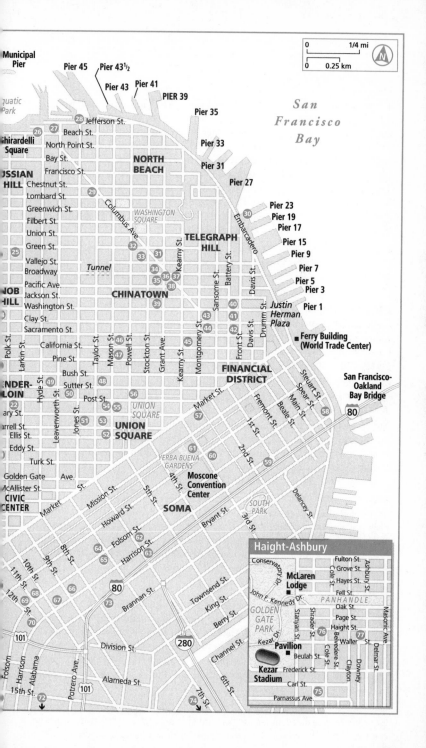

Municipal
Pier

Pier 45   Pier 43½
Pier 43   Pier 41
PIER 39

Pier 35

quatic
Park

28 Jefferson St.
27 Beach St.
26 North Point St.
hirardelli   Bay St.
Square   Francisco St.
Pier 33
Pier 31
Pier 27

JSSIAN
HILL Chestnut St.
Lombard St.
Greenwich St.
Filbert St.
Union St.
Green St.
Vallejo St.
Broadway
Pacific Ave.
Jackson St.
Washington St.
Clay St.
Sacramento St.

NORTH
BEACH

29

Columbus Ave.

WASHINGTON
SQUARE

32
33 31
34
35 36 37
38

TELEGRAPH
HILL

Pier 23
Pier 19
Pier 17
Pier 15
Pier 9
Pier 7
Pier 5
Pier 3
Pier 1

30

Sansome St.
Battery St.
Davis St.

25

Tunnel

NOB
HILL

CHINATOWN

39

San
Francisco
Bay

Justin
Herman
Plaza

40
41
43
44
42

Polk St.
Larkin St.

California St.
Pine St.
Bush St.

ENDER-
LOIN
22
ary St.
arrell St.
Ellis St.
Eddy St.

Taylor St.
Mason St.
Powell St.
Stockton St.
Grant Ave.
Kearny St.
Montgomery St.

46
47
45

Hyde St.
Leavenworth St.
Jones St.

49
50
54 55
51
53
52

Sutter St.
Post St.

56

UNION
SQUARE

FINANCIAL
DISTRICT

Market St.

57

Front St.
Davis St.
Drumm St.

Ferry Building
(World Trade Center)

San Francisco-
Oakland
Bay Bridge

80

Steuart St.
Spear St.
Main St.
Beale St.
Fremont St.
1st St.

58

59

Golden Gate   Ave.
McAllister St.
CIVIC
CENTER

Turk St.

Market

St.

Mission St.

Howard St.

YERBA BUENA
GARDENS

4th St.
5th St.

61
60

Moscone
Convention
Center

SOMA

Bryant St.

SOUTH
PARK

Delancey St.

2nd St.

3rd St.

8th St.
9th St.
10th St.
11th St.
12th St.

66
67
68
69
70

64
65

80

Folsom St.
Harrison St.

62
63

73

Brannan St.

Townsend St.

King St.

Berry St.

Haight-Ashbury

Conservatory Dr.

McLaren
Lodge

Fulton St.
Grove St.
Hayes St.
Fell St.

PANHANDLE

Oak St.

Ashbury St.
Cole St.

John F. Kennedy Dr.

GOLDEN
GATE
PARK

Page St.
Haight St.
Waller St.

Stanyan St.
Shrader St.

76

Belvedere St.
Cole St.

77

Masonic Ave.

Downey
Clayton

Delmar St.

Kezar Dr.

Pavilion

Beulah St.

Kezar
Stadium

Frederick St.

Carl St.

75

101

Division St.

Alameda St.

280

Channel St.

6th St.
7th St.

74

Folsom
Harrison
Alabama

15th St.

72

Potrero Ave.

101

are usually available until curtain time. War Memorial Opera House, 301 Van Ness Ave. (at Grove St.). © 415/864-3330 (box office). www.sfopera.com. Tickets $25–$195; standing room $15–$30.

THEATER

American Conservatory Theater (A.C.T.) *Finds*   The Tony Award–winning American Conservatory Theater made its debut in 1967 and quickly established itself as the city's premier resident theater group and one of the nation's best. The A.C.T. season runs September through July and features both classic and experimental works. A.C.T. recently returned to its home, the fabulous **Geary Theater** (1910), a national historic landmark, after the theater sustained severe damage in the 1989 earthquake and closed for renovations. Now it is fully refurbished and modernized to such an extent that it's regarded as one of America's finest performance spaces. Performing at the Geary Theater, 415 Geary St. (at Mason St.). © 415/749-2ACT. www.act-sf.org. Tickets $19–$68.

Eureka Theatre Company   Eureka produces contemporary plays September through June, and performances are usually Wednesday through Sunday. 215 Jackson St. (between Battery and Front sts.). © 415/788-7469. www.eurekatheatre.org. Tickets $16–$22, available at www.tickets.com; discounts for students and seniors.

Lorraine Hansberry Theatre   San Francisco's top African-American theater group performs in a 300-seat theater off the lobby of the Sheehan Hotel, near Mason Street. It mounts special adaptations from literature along with contemporary dramas, classics, and music. Phone for dates and programs. Performing at 620 Sutter St. (at Mason St.). © 415/474-8800. www.lhtsf.org. Tickets $25–$32.

The Magic Theatre   The highly acclaimed Magic Theatre is a major West Coast company dedicated to presenting the works of new playwrights; over the years it has nurtured the talents of such luminaries as Sam Shepard and Jon Robin Baitz. Shepard's Pulitzer Prize–winning play *Buried Child* had its premiere here, as did *Body Familiar* by Joe Goode. The season usually runs September through July; performances are held Tuesday through Sunday. Performing at Building D, Fort Mason Center, Marina Blvd. (at Buchanan St.). © 415/441-8822. www.magic theatre.org. Tickets $20–$53; discounts for students, educators, and seniors.

Theatre Rhinoceros   Founded in 1977, this was America's first (and remains its foremost) theater ensemble devoted solely to works addressing gay, lesbian, bisexual, and transgender issues. The company presents 11 main-stage shows and a dozen studio productions of new and classic works each year. The theater is 1 block east of the 16th Street/Mission BART station. 2926 16th St. © 415/861-5079. www.therhino.org. Tickets $15–$35.

DANCE

In addition to the local companies, top traveling troupes like the Joffrey Ballet and the American Ballet Theatre make regular appearances. Primary modern dance spaces include the **Cowell Theater,** at Fort Mason Center, Marina Boulevard at Buchanan Street (© 415/441-3400), and the **ODC Theatre,** 3153 17th St., at Shotwell Street in the Mission District (© 415/863-9834). Check the local papers for schedules or contact the theater box offices for more information.

San Francisco Ballet   Founded in 1933, the San Francisco Ballet is the oldest professional ballet company in the United States and is regarded as one of the country's finest. It performs an eclectic repertoire of full-length, neoclassical, and contemporary ballets. Even the *New York Times* proclaimed, "The San Francisco Ballet under Helgi Tomasson's leadership is one of the spectacular success stories of the arts in America." The 2005 Repertory Season runs February through May; the company performs *The Nutcracker* each December. The San Francisco Ballet Orchestra accompanies all performances. War Memorial Opera House, 301 Van Ness Ave. (at Grove St.). ℂ 415/865-2000 for tickets and information. www.sfballet.org. Tickets $10–$165.

2 Comedy & Cabaret

Bay Area Theatresports (BATS) *Finds*   Combining improvisation with competition, BATS operates an improvisational tournament, in which four-actor teams compete against each other, taking on hilarious challenges from the audience. Judges flash scorecards good-naturedly or honk a horn for scenes that just aren't working. Shows are on Thursday through Sunday only. Phone for reservations. Performing at Center for Improvisational Theatre at the Fort Mason Center, Building B, 3rd floor. ℂ 415/474-8935. www.improv.org. Tickets $8–$15.

Beach Blanket Babylon *Moments*   A San Francisco tradition, *Beach Blanket Babylon* evolved from Steve Silver's Rent-a-Freak service—a group of party-givers extraordinaire who hired themselves out as a "cast of characters" complete with fabulous costumes and sets, props, and gags. After their act caught on, it moved into the Savoy-Tivoli, a North Beach bar. By 1974, the audience had grown too large for the facility, and *Beach Blanket* has been at the 400-seat Club Fugazi ever since. The show is a comedic musical send-up that is best known for outrageous costumes and oversize headdresses. It's been playing for 31 years, and almost every performance sells out. The show is updated often enough that locals still attend. Those under 21 are welcome at a Sunday matinee at 3pm, when no alcohol is served; photo ID is required for evening performances. Write for weekend tickets at least 3 weeks in advance, or get them through Tix Bay Area (ℂ 415/433-7827). *Note:* There are only 44 tickets per show with assigned seating. All other tickets are within specific sections depending on price, but seating is first-come, first-seated within that section. Performances are Wednesday and Thursday at 8pm, Friday and Saturday at 7 and 10pm, and Sunday at 3 and 7pm. At Club Fugazi, Beach Blanket Babylon Blvd., 678 Green St. (between Powell St. and Columbus Ave.). ℂ 415/421-4222. www.beachblanketbabylon.com. Tickets $20–$55.

Cobb's Comedy Club   Cobb's features such national headliners as Joe Rogan, Brian Regan, and Jake Johannsen. There is comedy every night except Monday,

---

Tips Dinner Party

Hungry for dinner and a damned good time? It ain't cheap, but Teatro ZinZanni is a delightfully rollicking ride of food, whimsy, drama, and song within a stunningly elegant 1926 tent on The Embarcadero. Part musical theater and part comedy show, the 3½-hour dinner theater includes a surprisingly decent five-course meal served by dozens of performers who weave both the audience and astounding physical acts (think Cirque du Soleil) into their wacky and playful world. Anyone in need of a night of giggles should definitely book a table here. Shows are held Wednesday through Sunday and tickets are $99 to $125 including dinner. The tent is located at Pier 29 on The Embarcadero at Battery Street. Call ℂ 415/438-2668 or see www.teatrozinzanni.org for more details.

including a 15-comedian All-Pro Wednesday showcase (a 3-hr. marathon). Cobb's is open to those 18 and over, and occasionally to kids 16 and 17 when accompanied by a parent or legal guardian (call ahead). Shows are held Tuesday through Thursday and Sunday at 8pm, Friday and Saturday at 8 and 10pm. **915 Columbus Ave. (at Lombard St.).** © **415/928-4320.** www.cobbscomedyclub.com. Cover $15–$35. 2-beverage minimum.

Punch Line Comedy Club   Adjacent to The Embarcadero One office building, this is the largest comedy nightclub in the city. Three-person shows with top national and local talent are featured here Tuesday through Saturday. Showcase night is Sunday, when 15 comics take the mic. There's an all-star showcase or a special event on Monday. Shows are Tuesday through Thursday and Sunday at 9pm, Friday and Saturday at 9 and 11pm. **444 Battery St. (between Washington and Clay sts.),** plaza level. © **415/397-4337** or 415/397-7573 for recorded information. www.punchline comedyclub.com. Cover $5 Sun–Mon; $8–$15 Tues–Sat. 2-drink minimum.

3 The Club & Music Scene

The greatest legacy from the 1960s is the city's continued tradition of live entertainment and music, which explains the great variety of clubs and music enjoyed by San Francisco. The hippest dance places are South of Market Street (SoMa), in former warehouses; the artsy bohemian scene centers are in the Mission; and the most popular cafe culture is still in North Beach.

Note: The club and music scene is always changing, often outdating recommendations before the ink can dry on a page. Most of the venues below are promoted as different clubs on various nights of the week, each with its own look, sound, and style. Discount passes and club announcements are often available at clothing stores and other shops along upper Haight Street.

Drink prices at most bars, clubs, and cafes range from about $3.50 to $9, unless otherwise noted.

ROCK & BLUES CLUBS

In addition to the following listings, see "Dance Clubs," below, for (usually) live, danceable rock.

Biscuits and Blues   With a crisp, blow-your-eardrums-out sound system, New Orleans–speakeasy (albeit commercial) appeal, and a nightly lineup of live entertainment, there's no better place to muse the blues than this basement-cum-nightclub. During performances, covers range, but there's a daily happy hour from 6 to 7:30pm, when there's usually recorded music, drink specials, and inexpensive snacks—not to mention the only opportunity to socialize: Once the bands get going, it's so loud you can't even hear yourself holler. *Note:* A full din-

---

Tips **Club-Hopping Tour**

If you prefer to let someone else take the lead (and the driver's seat) for a night out, contact **3 Babes and a Bus** (© **800/414-0158;** www.three babes.com). The nightclub tour company (the head babe is a stockbroker by day) will take you and a gaggle of 20- to 40-something partyers (mostly single women) out on the town, skipping lines and cover charges, for $35 per person.

Tips Dial-a-Scene

The local newspapers won't direct you to the city's underground club scene, nor will they advise you which of the dozens of clubs are truly hot. To get dialed in, do what the locals do—turn to the **Be-At Line** (© **415/ 626-4087**) for its daily recorded update on the town's most hoppin' hip-hop, acid-jazz, and house clubs. The far more commercial **Club Line** (© **415/339-8686**; www.sfclubs.com) offers up-to-date schedules for the city's larger dance venues.

---

ner menu is available, but the only notable treat is the moist, flaky biscuits. 401 Mason (at Geary St.). © 415/292-2583. Cover (during performances) $5–$20.

The Boom Boom Room *Finds*   The late John Lee Hooker and his partner Alex Andreas bought this Western Addition club several years back and used Hooker's star power to pull in some of the best blues bands in the country (even the Stones showed up for an unannounced jam session). It's a dark and small and cramped and steamy joint—just like a blues bar should be—that hosts blues and boogie bands 7 nights a week until 2am. If you're going to The Fillmore (see below) to see a band, stop by here first for a drink and come back after your show for more great music. The neighborhood's a bit rough, so be sure to park in the underground lot across the street. 1601 Fillmore St. (at Geary Blvd.). © 415/673-8000. www.boomboomblues.com. Cover varies from free to $15.

Bottom of the Hill *Value*   Voted one of the best places to hear live rock in the city by the *San Francisco Bay Guardian,* this popular neighborhood club attracts an eclectic crowd ranging from rockers to real-estate salespeople. The main attraction is live music every night, but the club also offers pretty good burgers and a full dinner menu, outdoor seating on the back patio, and an awesome barbecue on Sunday from 4 to 7pm. Happy hour runs Fridays only from 3 to 7pm. 1233 17th St. (at Missouri St.). © 415/621-4455. www.bottomofthehill.com. Cover $6–$10.

Empire Plush Room *Finds*   San Francisco is woefully short on cabaret and jazz venues, but thanks to the Plush Room, there's still one swank little boutique establishment that lures national talent on stage. Check out their schedule and perhaps you'll get to catch a burlesque show or locals such as Paula West, Wesla Whitfield, Faith Winthrop, Jacqui Naylor, or others doing their classic and under-celebrated thing. Come thirsty: There's a two-drink minimum. In the York Hotel, 940 Sutter St. (between Hyde and Leavenworth sts.). © 415/885-2800. www.plushroom. com. Tickets $20–$55.

The Fillmore *Finds*   Reopened after years of neglect, the Fillmore, made famous by promoter Bill Graham in the 1960s, is attracting big names again. Check listings in papers, or call the theater for information on upcoming events. And if you make it to a show, check out the fabulous collection of vintage concert posters chronicling the hall's history. 1805 Geary Blvd. (at Fillmore St.). © 415/ 346-6000. www.thefillmore.com. Tickets $17–$35.

Grant & Green Saloon   The atmosphere at this historic North Beach dive bar is not that special, but the local bands (live music usually on weekends only) are pretty good and the space is an all-around good place to let your hair down. 1371 Grant Ave. (at Green St.). © 415/693-9565.

Tips   **Local Talent**

Want to see the best of local jazz, cabaret, or blues performers? Check the *San Francisco Chronicle*'s Sunday "Datebook" to see if the following artists are in the house. Better yet, buy their CDs and take San Francisco's music scene home with you:

- **Faith Winthrop,** a veteran cabaret diva with a velvet voice and heart-felt delivery.
- **Ledisi,** a young local blues singer with a penchant for scatting and smoky, deep, soulful self-written tunes.
- **Jacqui Naylor,** a seductive young talent with a love for standards and reinventing a phrase with her own modern twist.
- **Lavay Smith & Her Red Hot Skillet Lickers**—swing hasn't swung this hard since it was invented.

Lou's Pier 47 Club   You won't find many locals in the place, but Lou's happens to be good, old-fashioned fun. It's a casual spot where you can let your hair down with Cajun seafood (downstairs) and live blues bands (upstairs). A vacation attitude makes the place one of the more, um, jovial spots near the wharf. There's a $3 to $5 cover for bands that play between 4 and 7 or 8pm and a $5 to $10 cover for bands that play between 8 or 9pm and midnight or 1am. 300 Jefferson St. (at Jones St.). ✆ 415/771-5687. www.louspier47.com. Cover $5–$10.

Pier 23   If there's one good-time destination that's an anchor for San Francisco's party people, it's The Embarcadero's Pier 23. Part ramshackle patio spot and part dance floor with a heavy dash of dive bar, here it's all about fun for a startlingly diverse clientele. The well-worn box of a restaurant with tented patio is a prime sunny-day social spot for white collars, but on weekends, it's a straight-up people zoo where every age and persuasion coexist more peacefully than the cast in a McDonald's commercial. Expect to boogie down shoulder-to-shoulder to 1970s hits and leave with the contagious feel-good vibe. Pier 23, at The Embarcadero and Greenwich St. ✆ 415/362-5125. www.pier23cafe.com. Cover $5–$8 during performances.

The Saloon   An authentic gold rush survivor, this North Beach dive is the oldest bar in the city. Popular with both bikers and daytime pinstripers, it schedules live blues nightly. 1232 Grant Ave. (at Columbus St.). ✆ 415/989-7666. Cover $4–$5 Fri–Sat.

Slim's   Co-owned by musician Boz Scaggs, who sometimes takes the stage under the name "Presidio Slim," this glitzy restaurant and bar seats 430, serves California cuisine, and specializes in excellent American music—homegrown rock, jazz, blues, and alternative—almost nightly. Call for a schedule; hot bands sell out in advance. 333 11th St. (at Folsom St.). ✆ 415/522-0333. www.slims-sf.com. Cover free to $30.

JAZZ & LATIN CLUBS

Cafe du Nord *Finds*   Although it's been around since 1907, this basement supper club is rightfully self-proclaimed as the place for a "slightly lurid indie pop scene set in a beautiful old speakeasy." With a younger generation now appreciating the music—swing, jazz, alternative, pop, you name it—the place is often packed from the 40-foot mahogany bar to the back room, where the focus is on live performances. ***Note:*** If Lavay Smith and Her Red Hot Skillet Lickers or Ledici are in the house, definitely don't miss them. 2170 Market St. (at Sanchez St.). (*C*) 415/861-5016. www.cafedunord.com. Cover $5–$15.

Jazz at Pearl's   This is one of the best jazz venues in the city. The live jams last until 1:30am nightly. Ribs and chicken are served, too; they run from $5 to $20. 256 Columbus Ave. (at Broadway). (*C*) 415/291-8255. www.jazzatpearls.com. 2-drink minimum.

Rasselas   Large, casual, and comfortable in its new location, with couches and small tables, this is a favorite spot for local jazz, blues, and R&B combos. The adjacent restaurant serves Ethiopian cuisine in a Bedouin tent. Menu items range from $4 to $14. 1534 Fillmore St. (at Geary Blvd.). (*C*) 415/567-5010. www.rasselas jazzclub.com. 2-drink minimum.

DANCE CLUBS

Although a lot of clubs allow dancing, the following are the places to go if all you want to do is shake your groove thang.

The Endup   This unique party space with a huge heated outdoor deck (with waterfall and fountain), indoor fireplace, and eclectic clientele has always thrown some of the most kickin' parties in town. There's a different theme every night: Thursday sets swinging singles loose at the Kit Kat Club; Fag Friday is just what it sounds like, plus lots of throw-down dancing; and Sunday is ever-popular with the sleepless dance-all-day crowd that comes here after the other clubs close (it's open nonstop from Sat night around 10pm until Sun night/Mon morning at 4am). Call to confirm nights—offerings change from time to time. 401 Sixth St. (at Harrison St.). (*C*) 415/357-0827. www.theendup.com. Cover free to $10.

Factory 525   Late great columnist Herb Caen dubbed this disco theme park the "mother of all discos." The maze of rooms and nonstop barrage of house, funk, lounge vibes, and club classics attract swarms of young urbanites (read: college-age kids) looking to rave it up, sometimes until as late as 6am. Management tries to eliminate the riffraff by enforcing a dress code (no sneakers, hooded sweatshirts, or sports caps). 525 Harrison St. (at First St.). (*C*) 415/339- 8686. Cover $5–$20.

Nickie's Bar-be-cue   Don't show up here for dinner—the only hot thing you'll find is the small, crowded dance floor. But don't let that stop you from checking it out—Nickie's is a sure thing. Here the old-school hits are in full force, casually dressed young dancers lose all their inhibitions, and the crowd consists of all types of friendly San Franciscans. This place is perpetually hot, so dress accordingly; you can always cool down with a pint from the wine-and-beer bar. Keep in mind that lower Haight is on the periphery of a shady neighborhood, so don't make your car look tempting, and stay alert as you walk through the area. Closed on Sundays. 460 Haight St. (between Fillmore and Webster sts.). (*C*) 415/ 621-6508. www.nickies.com. Cover $3–$5.

Paradise Lounge   Labyrinthine Paradise features three dance floors simultaneously vibrating to different beats. Smaller, auxiliary spaces host different events (poetry readings are fairly common) and include a pool room with a half-dozen tables. The crowd ranges from everyday party people to grungy-alternative types. Open Friday and Saturday only. 1501 Folsom St. (at 11th St.). (*C*) 415/861-6906. www.paradiselounge.com. Cover $3–$15.

Ruby Skye Downtown's most glamorous and gigantic nightspot is all aglitter thanks to a dramatic renovation and the addition of killer light and sound systems within the 1890s Victorian playhouse previously known as The Stage Door. Inside, hundreds of partyers boogie on the ballroom floor, mingle on the mezzanine, and puff freely in the smoking room while DJs or live music bring down the dancing house Thursdays through Saturdays. Big spenders should book the VIP lounge, which offers a glitzy place to "kick it" and bird's-eye views of the whole club scene. 420 Mason St. (between Geary and Post sts.). ✆ 415/693-0777. www.rubyskye.com. Cover $10–$25.

Ten 15 Get decked out and plan on a late night if you're headed to this enormous party warehouse. Three levels, a full-color laser system, and a gigantic dance floor make for an extensive variety of dancing venues, complete with a 20- and 30-something gyrating mass who live for the DJs' pounding house, disco, and acid-jazz music. Each night is a different club that attracts its own crowd, ranging from yuppie to hip-hop. A recent $1.5-million renovation added 6,000 square feet of dance floor and a VIP area. Call ahead for a complete schedule of events. 1015 Folsom St. (at Sixth St.). ✆ 415/431-1200. www.1015.com. Cover $5–$15.

SUPPER CLUBS

If you can eat dinner, listen to live music, and dance (or at least wiggle in your chair) in the same room, it's a supper club—those are our criteria here.

Harry Denton's Starlight Room *(Moments* Come to this celestial high-rise cocktail lounge and nightclub, where tourists and locals watch the sunset at dusk and boogie down to live swing and big-band or DJs' tunes after dark. The room is classic 1930s San Francisco, with red-velvet banquettes, chandeliers, and fabulous views. But what really attracts flocks of all ages is a night of Harry Denton–style fun, which usually includes plenty of drinking and unrestrained dancing. The full bar stocks a decent collection of single-malt Scotches and champagnes, and you can snack from the pricey Starlight appetizer menu (make a reservation to guarantee a table and you'll also have a place to rest your weary dancing-dogs). Early evening is more relaxed, but come the weekend, this place gets loose. *Tip:* Come dressed for success (no jeans or sneakers), or you'll be turned away at the door. Atop the Sir Francis Drake hotel, 450 Powell St., 21st floor. ✆ 415/395-8595. www.harrydenton.com. Cover $10 Wed after 7pm; $5 Thurs after 8pm; $10 Fri after 8pm; $15 Sat after 8pm.

Julie's Supper Club Julie's is a longtime standby for cocktails and late dining in a groovy setting. The vibe in both rooms is very 1950s cartoon, with a space-age Jetsons appeal and good-looking singles on the prowl. The food is hit-or-miss, but the atmosphere is definitely a winner—casual and playful—and it comes with a little interesting history: This building is one location where the Symbionese Liberation Army held Patty Hearst hostage in the 1970s. Menu items range from $6 to $20 and happy hour, Tuesday through Friday from 5pm to 7:30pm, includes free snacks. 1123 Folsom St. (at Seventh St.). ✆ 415/861-0707. www.juliessupperclub.com.

DESTINATION BARS WITH DJ GROOVES

Bambuddha Lounge *(Finds* The hottest place for the young and the trendy to feast, flirt, or just be fabulous is this restaurant/bar adjoining the funky-cool Phoenix Hotel. With a 20-foot reclining Buddha on the roof, ultramodern San Francisco–meets–Southeast Asian decor (including waterfalls in the dining room and outdoor poolside cocktail lounge and *salas,* Balinese-style outdoor lounge areas), very affordable and above-average Pan-Asian cuisine served late into the eve and topping out at $15, and a state-of-the-art sound system streaming ambient, down-tempo, hip-hop, funk, and house music, this is the "it" joint of the moment. 601 Eddy St. (at Polk St.). ℭ 415/885-5088. www.bambuddhalounge.com.

The Bliss Bar   Surprisingly trendy for sleepy family-oriented Noe Valley, this small, stylish, and friendly bar is a great place to stop for a varied mix of locals, colorful cocktail concoctions, and a DJ spinning at the front window from 4 to 11pm 4 nights per week (call for days). If it's open, take your cocktail into the too-cool back Blue Room. And if you're on a budget, stop by from 4:30 to 7pm when martinis, lemon drops, cosmos, watermelon cosmos, and apple martinis are $3. 4026 24th St. (between Noe and Castro sts.) ℭ 415/826-6200. www.blissbar.sf.com.

The Monkey Club   Casual and tucked away in a quiet section of the Mission, this hip locals bar (think 20s through 30s) is an ever fun and rather red spot to kick it on plush and comfy couches backed by giant picture windows; nibble on decent and inexpensive appetizers; and down stiff drinks while a DJ spins grooving house, jazz, and world music Wednesday through Sunday. 2730 21st St. (at Bryant St.). ℭ 415/ 647-6546.

Wish Bar   Flirtation, fun, and a very attractive staff await at this somewhat mellow, narrow bar in the popular night crawler area around 11th and Folsom streets. Swathed in burgundy and black with exposed cinderblock walls and cement floors, all's aglow a la candlelight and red-shaded sconces. With a bar in the front, DJ spinning housey lounge music in the back, and seating—including cushy leather couches—in between, it's often packed with a surprisingly diverse (albeit youthful) crowd and ever filled with eye candy. 1539 Folsom St. (between 11th and 12th sts.). ℭ 415/278-9474.

A RETRO CLUB

Club Deluxe *Finds*   Before the recent 1940s trend hit the city, Deluxe and its fedora-wearing clientele had been celebrating the bygone era for years. Fortunately, even with all the retro hype, the vibe here hasn't changed. Expect an eclectic mix of throwbacks and generic San Franciscans in the intimate bar and adjoining lounge, and live jazz or swing most nights. Although many regulars dress the part, there's no attitude here, so come as you like. 1511 Haight St. (at Ashbury St.). ℭ 415/552-6949. Cover $3–$10.

4 The Bar Scene

Finding your idea of a comfortable bar has a lot to do with picking a neighborhood filled with your kind of people and investigating that area. There are hundreds of bars throughout San Francisco, and although many are obscurely located and can't be classified by their neighborhood, the following is a general description of what you'll find, and where:

- **Chestnut and Union Street** bars attract a postcollegiate crowd.
- Young alternatives frequent **Mission District** haunts.
- **Upper Haight** caters to eclectic neighborhood cocktailers.
- **Lower Haight** is skate- and snowboarder grungy.
- Tourists mix with theatergoers and thirsty businesspeople in **downtown** pubs.
- **North Beach** serves all types.
- **The Castro** caters to gay locals and tourists.
- **SoMa** offers an eclectic mix.

The following is a list of a few of San Francisco's most interesting bars. Unless otherwise noted, these bars do not have cover charges.

Buena Vista Café *(Moments)* "Did you have an Irish coffee at the Buena Vista?" The popular myth is that the Irish coffee was invented at the Buena Vista, but the real story is that this popular wharf cafe was the first bar in the country to serve Irish coffee after a local journalist came back from a trip and described the drink to the bartender. Since then, the bar has poured more of these pick-me-up drinks than any other bar in the world, and ordering one has become a San Francisco must-do. Fact is, it's entertaining just to watch the venerable tenders pour up to 10 whiskey-laden coffees at a time (a rather messy event). The cafe is in a prime tourist spot along the wharf, so plan on waiting for a stool or table to free up. And don't worry if you need a little snack to soak up the booze—they serve food here, too. 2765 Hyde St. (at Beach St.). ℂ **415/474-5044.** www.thebuenavista.com.

Edinburgh Castle Since 1958, this legendary Scottish pub has been known for unusual British ales on tap and the best selection of single-malt Scotches in the city. The huge pub is decorated with Royal Air Force mementos, horse brasses, steel helmets, and an authentic Ballantine caber (a long wooden pole) used in the annual Scottish games. Fish and chips and other traditional foods are available until 11pm. 950 Geary St. (between Polk and Larkin sts.). ℂ **415/885-4074.** www.castlenews.com.

The Great Entertainer This is a glorified pool hall, with 50 tables, four private billiard suites, snooker, shuffleboard, darts, table tennis, and a video arcade. Drinks, pizza, and other dishes accompany the games. Menu items run $6 to $8. 975 Bryant (at Eighth St.). ℂ **415/861-8833.**

Li Po Cocktail Lounge *(Finds)* A dim, divey, slightly spooky Chinese bar that was once an opium den, Li Po's alluring character stems from its mishmash clutter of dusty Asian furnishings and mementos, including an unbelievably huge ancient rice-paper lantern hanging from the ceiling and a glittery golden shrine to Buddha behind the bar. The bartenders love to creep out patrons with tales of opium junkies haunting the joint. 916 Grant Ave. (between Washington and Jackson sts.). ℂ **415/982-0072.**

Matrix Fillmore Closetlike booths with privacy curtains and side tables in shapes of "S," "E," and "X" spell out that this remains one of the young and yuppies' hottest singles scenes despite its dramatic detour from its previous life as the Pierce Street Annex. Those already spoken for can still appreciate the slick lounge atmosphere of candlelight, dark woods and walls, flatscreen TVs, and free-standing centerpiece fireplace with its Lincoln Log–like mantle—not to mention bar snacks like fontina and prosciutto panini and smoked duck quesadillas. Though it's a martini and mojito crowd, the bar also offers 15 wines by the glass and a large by-the-bottle selection including cult classics like Dalla Valle

---

⌐Tips **Smoke Signals**

California forbids smoking in bars, restaurants, hotel lobbies, and public areas of any kind. Some bars break the rules. Others ask their guests to step outside. Either way, don't count on lighting up inside any public place. Establishment owners are quick to enforce the rule because they can be fined if patrons disobey.

---

and Opus One. Drinks range from $7 to $10. 3138 Fillmore St. (between Greenwich and Filbert sts.). ℭ 415/563-4180. www.plumpjack.com.

Perry's   If you read *Tales of the City*, you already know that this bar and restaurant has a colorful history as a pickup place for Pacific Heights and Marina singles. Although the times are not as wild today, locals still come to casually check out the happenings at the dark mahogany bar. A separate dining room offers breakfast, lunch, dinner, and weekend brunch. It's a good place for hamburgers, simple fish dishes, and pasta. Menu items range from $6 to $22. 1944 Union St. (at Laguna St.). ℭ 415/922-9022.

Pied Piper Bar   The huge Pied Piper mural by Edwardian illustrator Maxfield Parrish steals the show at this historic mahogany bar, where high stakes were once won and lost on the roll of the dice. In the Palace Hotel, 2 New Montgomery (at Market St.). ℭ 415/512-1111.

The Red Room   Ultramodern, small, and deliciously dim, this lounge reflects no other color but ruby red. It's a sexy place to sip the latest cocktail. In the Commodore Hotel, 827 Sutter St. (at Jones St.). ℭ 415/346-7666.

The Redwood Room   This historic room flanked in redwood paneling and illuminated with beautiful sconces is still an Art Deco beauty, but the ground-floor lounge that was one of San Francisco's most comfortable and nostalgic piano bars is no longer even remotely old-school. Ian Schrager had the room revamped in 2001, and though it retains its gorgeous redwood interior made from a single 2,000-year-old tree, the vibe is now more for swinging singles, the tragically hip, and posers than for return guests who have frequented the historic room for over 50 years. Drinks go for $8 to $15. In the Clift Hotel, 495 Geary St. ℭ 415/775-4700.

Spec's *Finds*   The location of Spec's—Saroyan Place, a tiny alley at 250 Columbus Ave.—makes it less of a walk-in bar and more of a lively local hangout. Its funky decor—maritime flags hang from the ceiling; posters, photos, and oddities line the exposed-brick walls—gives it a character that intrigues every visitor. A "museum," displayed under glass, contains memorabilia and items brought back by seamen who drop in between voyages. The clientele is funky enough to keep you preoccupied while you drink a beer. 12 Saroyan Place (at 250 Columbus Ave.). ℭ 415/421-4112.

The Tonga Room & Hurricane Bar *Finds*   It's kitschy as all get out, but there's no denying the goofy Polynesian pleasures of the Fairmont Hotel's tropical oasis. Drop in and join the crowds for an umbrella drink, a simulated thunderstorm and downpour, and a heavy dose of whimsy that escapes most San Francisco establishments. If you're on a budget, you'll definitely want to stop by for the weekday happy hour from 5 to 7pm, when you can stuff your face at the all-you-can-eat bar-grub buffet (chicken wings, chow mein, pot stickers) for $6 and the cost of one drink. Settle in and you'll catch live Top-40 music after 8pm, when there's a $3 cover. In the Fairmont Hotel, 950 Mason St. (at California St.). ℭ 415/772-5278. www.tongaroom.com.

Toronado   Lower Haight isn't exactly a charming street, but there's plenty of nightlife here, catering to an artistic/grungy/skateboarding 20-something crowd. While Toronado definitely draws in the young'uns, its 40-plus microbrews on tap and 60 bottled beers also entice a more eclectic clientele in search of beer heaven. The brooding atmosphere matches the surroundings: an aluminum bar, a few tall tables, dark lighting, and a back room packed with tables and chairs.

A DJ picks up the pace on Friday and Saturday nights. 547 Haight St. (at Fillmore St.). ℭ 415/863-2276. www.toronado.com.

Tosca *Finds* Open daily from 5pm to 2am, Tosca is a low-key and large popular watering hole for local politicos, writers, media types, incognito visiting celebrities such as Johnny Depp or Nicholas Cage, and similar cognoscenti of unassuming classic characters. Equipped with dim lights, red leather booths, and high ceilings, it's everything you'd expect an old North Beach legend to be. 242 Columbus Ave. (between Broadway and Pacific Ave.). ℭ 415/986-9651.

Vesuvio Situated along Jack Kerouac Alley, across from the famed City Lights bookstore, this renowned literary beatnik hangout is packed to the second-floor rafters with neighborhood writers, artists, songsters, wannabes, and everyone else ranging from longshoremen and cab drivers to businesspeople, all of whom come for the laid-back atmosphere. The convivial space is two stories of cocktail tables, complemented by a changing exhibition of local art. In addition to drinks, Vesuvio features an espresso machine. No credit cards. 255 Columbus Ave. (at Broadway). ℭ 415/362-3370. www.vesuvio.com.

BREWPUBS

Gordon Biersch Brewery Restaurant Gordon Biersch Brewery is San Francisco's largest brew restaurant, serving decent food and tasty beer to an attractive crowd of mingling professionals. There are always several beers to choose from, ranging from light to dark. Menu items run $9.50 to $20. (See p. 125 for more information.) 2 Harrison St. (on The Embarcadero). ℭ 415/243-8246. www.gordonbiersch.com.

San Francisco Brewing Company Surprisingly low key for an alehouse, this cozy brewpub serves its creations with burgers, fries, grilled chicken breast, and the like. The bar is one of the city's few remaining old saloons (ca. 1907), aglow with stained-glass windows, tile floors, skylit ceiling, beveled glass, and mahogany bar. A massive overhead fan runs the full length of the bar—a bizarre contraption crafted from brass and palm fronds. The handmade copper brew kettle is visible from the street. Most evenings the place is packed with everyday folks enjoying music or comedy, darts, chess, backgammon, cards, dice and, of course, beer. Menu items range from $3.70—curiously, for edamame (soybeans)—to $20 for a full rack of baby back ribs with all the fixings. The happy-hour special, an 8½-ounce microbrew beer for a dollar (or a pint for $2.50), is offered daily from 4 to 6pm and midnight to 1am. 155 Columbus Ave. (at Pacific St.). ℭ 415/434-3344. www.sfbrewing.com.

ThirstyBear Brewing Company Seven superb, handcrafted varieties of brew are always on tap at this stylish high-ceilinged brick edifice. Good Spanish food is served here, too. Pool tables and dartboards are upstairs, and live flamenco can be heard on Sunday nights. 661 Howard St. (1 block east of the Moscone Center). ℭ 415/974-0905. www.thirstybear.com.

COCKTAILS WITH A VIEW

See "Supper Clubs," above, for a full review of **Harry Denton's Starlight Room.** Unless otherwise noted, these establishments have no cover charge.

Carnelian Room On the 52nd floor of the Bank of America Building, the Carnelian Room offers uninterrupted views of the city. From a window-front table you feel as though you can reach out, pluck up the TransAmerica Pyramid, and stir your martini with it. In addition to cocktails, the restaurant serves a three-course meal ($39 per person). Jackets are required and ties for men are

Finds Midnight (or Midday) Mochas

If you happen to be wandering around North Beach past your bedtime and need your caffeine fix, seek out these two cafes. They offer not only excellent espresso, but also a glimpse back at the days of the beatniks, when nothing was as crucial as a strong cup of coffee, a good smoke, and a stimulating environment.

Doing the North Beach thing is little more than hanging out in a sophisticated but relaxed atmosphere over a well-made cappuccino. You can do it at **Caffè Greco**, 423 Columbus Ave., between Green and Vallejo streets (© **415/397-6261**), and grab a bite, too—until midnight. The affordable cafe fare includes beer and wine as well as a good selection of coffees, focaccia sandwiches, and desserts (try the gelato or homemade tiramisu).

Caffè Trieste, 601 Vallejo St., at Grant Avenue (© **415/392-6739**; www.cafetriste.com), is one of San Francisco's most beloved cafes— very down-home Italian, with only espresso drinks and pastries at indoor and outdoor seating. Opera is always on the jukebox, unless it's Saturday afternoon, when the family and their friends literally break out in arias during an operatic performance from 2 to 6pm. Another perk: They offer access to free Wi-Fi with purchase, but you'll have to bring your own laptop. Check 'em out until 10:30pm Sunday through Thursday and 11:30pm on Friday and Saturday.

optional, but encouraged. *Note:* The restaurant has one of the most extensive wine lists in the city—1,600 selections, to be exact. 555 California St., in the Bank of America Building (between Kearny and Montgomery sts.). © **415/433-7500**. www.carnelian room.com.

Cityscape   When you sit under the glass roof and sip a drink here, it's as though you're sitting out under the stars and enjoying views of the bay. Dinner, focusing on steak and seafood, is available, and there's dancing to a DJ's picks nightly from 10pm. The mirrored columns and floor-to-ceiling draperies help create an elegant and romantic ambience here. *FYI:* they also offer a live champagne brunch on Sundays from 10am to 2pm. Hilton San Francisco, Tower I, 333 O'Farrell St. (at Mason St.), 46th floor. © **415/923-5002**. Cover $10 Sat night.

Equinox   Though locals don't frequent this Fi-Di (Financial District) place, it's very popular with tourists. The hook? The 17-story Hyatt's rooftop restaurant has a revolving floor that gives each table a 360-degree panoramic view of the city every 45 minutes. In addition to cocktails, the Equinox serves dinner daily. In the Hyatt Regency Hotel, 5 Embarcadero Center. © **415/788-1234**.

Top of the Mark *(Moments)*   This is one of the most famous cocktail lounges in the world, and for good reason—the spectacular glass-walled room features an unparalleled 19th-floor view. During World War II, Pacific-bound servicemen toasted their good-byes to the States here. While less dramatic today than they were back then, evenings spent here are still sentimental, thanks to the romantic atmosphere. Live entertainment (think swing band) Friday and Saturday starts at 8:30pm. Drinks range from $7 to $10. A $49 three-course fixed-price sunset dinner is served Friday and Saturday at 7:30pm. Sunday brunch, served from 10am to 2pm, costs $49 for adults and includes a glass of champagne; for children 5 to 14, the brunch is $25. In the Mark Hopkins Inter-Continental, 1 Nob Hill (California and Mason sts.). ✆ 415/616-6916. Cover $5–$10.

A SPORTS BAR

Greens Sports Bar   If you think San Francisco sports fans aren't as enthusiastic as those on the East Coast, try to get a seat at Green's during a 49ers game. It's a classic old sports bar, with lots of polished dark wood and windows that open onto Polk Street, but it's loaded with modern appliances (including two large-screen televisions and 18 smaller ones) and modern partyers (read: dot.comers and the mid-20s and -30s set). With 18 beers on tap, a pool table, and a happy hour Monday through Friday from 4pm to 7pm, there are reasons to cheer here even when the home team's got a day off. 2239 Polk St. (at Green St.). ✆ 415/775-4287.

WINE & CHAMPAGNE BARS

The Bubble Lounge   Toasting the town is a nightly event at this two-level champagne bar. With 300 champagnes, about 30 by the glass, brick walls, couches, and velvet curtains, there's plenty of pop in this fizzy lounge. 714 Montgomery St. (at Columbus Ave.). ✆ 415/434-4204. www.bubblelounge.com.

Eos   If you're downtown, head for the London Wine Bar (see below). If you're around the Civic Center, make it Hayes and Vine (see below). For anything west of these two, your top choice should be Eos, a highly successful restaurant in Cole Valley (near the Haight), with an adjoining wine bar where you can sip from the huge by-the-glass selection or choose a bottle from some 400 vintages from around the world. (See p. 152 for more information.) 901 Cole St. (at Carl St.). ✆ 415/566-3063. www.eossf.com.

Hayes and Vine   You'll find 1,200 wines (with more than 50 by the glass) from around the world at this unpretentious wine bar staffed by true cognoscenti of fine wine. (It's a good thing, too, because you have probably never heard of 90% of these wines.) Be sure to ask about taking a "flight," which allows you to try several different wines for a fixed price. Cheese, breads, antipasti, charcuterie, and desserts are also served. 377 Hayes St. (at Gough St.). ✆ 415/626-5301. www.hayesandvine.com.

London Wine Bar   This British-style wine bar and store is a popular after-work hangout for Financial District suits. It's more of a place to drink and chat, however, than one in which to admire fine wines. Usually 50 wines, mostly from California, are open at any given time and 800 are available by the bottle. It's a great venue for sampling local Napa Valley wines before you buy. 415 Sansome St. (between Sacramento and Clay sts.). ✆ 415/788-4811. www.londonwinebar.com.

5 Gay & Lesbian Bars & Clubs

Just like straight establishments, gay and lesbian bars and clubs target varied clienteles. Whether you're into leather or Lycra, business or bondage, in San Francisco, there's gay nightlife just for you.

Check the free weeklies, the *San Francisco Bay Guardian* and *San Francisco Weekly,* for listings of events and happenings around town. The *Bay Area Reporter* is a gay paper with comprehensive listings, including a weekly community calendar. All these papers are free and distributed weekly on Wednesday or Thursday. They can be found stacked at the corners of 18th and Castro streets and Ninth and Harrison streets, as well as in bars, bookshops, and other stores around town. There are also a number of gay and lesbian guides to San Francisco. See "Gay & Lesbian Travelers," in chapter 2, beginning on p. 21, for further details and helpful information. Also check out the rather homely, but very informative site titled "Queer Things to Do in the San Francisco Bay Area" at www.io.com/~larrybob/sanfran.html for a plethora of gay happenings.

Listed below are some of the city's most established mainstream gay hangouts.

The Café *Finds* When this place first got jumping, it was the only predominantly lesbian dance club on Saturday nights in the city. Once the guys found out how much fun the girls were having, however, they joined the party. Today, it's a happening mixed gay and lesbian scene with three bars, a pool table, a steamy, free-spirited dance floor, and a small, heated patio where smoking and schmoozing is allowed. A perk: They open at 3pm daily. 2367 Market St. (at Castro St.). © 415/861-3846. www.cafesf.com.

The Cinch Saloon Among the popular attributes of this cruisy neighborhood bar are the outdoor patio and progressive music by DJs (except for Tues). 49ers fans also gather here for televised games. Decorated in a Southwestern theme ("down home in Arizona"), the bar attracts a mixed crowd of gays, lesbians (now that there are almost no exclusively lesbian bars left in San Francisco), and gay-friendly straights. There is a "beer bust" (an all-you-can-drink beer party) on Sundays. 1723 Polk St. (near Washington St.). © 415/776-4162. www.thecinch.com.

Detour Right in the heart of gay San Francisco, this bar attracts a young, often hot crowd of boys, with its low lighting and throbbing house music. Chain-link fences seem to hold in the action while a live DJ spins a web of popular hits nightly. Half-price drinks are available nightly until 8pm. 2348 Market St. (near Castro St.). © 415/861-6053.

The Eagle One of the city's most traditional Levi's 'n' leather bars, The Eagle boasts a heated outdoor patio (where smoking is permitted), a happy hour (Mon–Fri 4–8pm), live bands every Thursday at 9pm ($5 cover), and a popular Sunday-afternoon beer fest from 3 to 6pm. 398 12th St. (at Harrison St.). © 415/626-0880. www.sfeagle.com.

The Endup It's a different nightclub every night of the week, but regardless of who's throwing the party, the place is always jumping to the tunes blasted by DJs. There are two pool tables, a fireplace, an outdoor patio and, on the dance floor, a mob of gyrating souls. Some nights are straight, so call ahead. (See p. 233 for more information.) 401 Sixth St. (at Harrison St.). © 415/357-0827. www.theendup.com. Cover free to $10.

Kimo's This neighborhood bar in the seedier gay section of town is a friendly oasis, decorated with plants, pictures, and "gay banners." The bar provides a relaxing venue for chatting, drinking, and quiet cruising and livens up with rock bands nightly upstairs. 1351 Polk St. (at Pine St.). © 415/885-4535. Cover $5–$10 for live music.

Lone Star Saloon Expect lesbians and a heavier, furrier motorcycle crowd (both men and women) here most every night. The Thursday-night and Saturday-afternoon beer busts on the patio are especially popular and cost $8 per person. 1354 Harrison St. (between 9th and 10th sts.). © 415/863-9999.

Metro This bar provides the gay community with high-energy dance music and the best view of the Castro District from its large balcony. The bar seems to attract people of all ages who enjoy the friendliness of the bartenders and the highly charged, cruising atmosphere. There's a Chinese restaurant on the premises if you get hungry. 3600 16th St. (at Market St.). ℂ 415/703-9750. www.metro citybarsf.com.

The Mint Karaoke Lounge   This is a gay and lesbian karaoke bar where you can sing show tunes every night. Along with song, you'll encounter a mixed 20- to 40-something crowd that combines cocktails with do-it-yourself cabaret. 1942 Market St. (at Laguna St.). ℂ 415/626-4726. 2-drink minimum. www.themint.net.

The Stud   The Stud, which has been around for more than 30 years, is one of the most successful gay establishments in town. The interior has an antiques-shop look and a miniature train circling the bar and dance floor. Music is a balanced mix of old and new, and nights vary from cabaret to oldies to disco. Call in advance for the evening's offerings. Drink prices range from $3 to $13. Happy hour runs daily until 9pm with $1 draft beers. 399 Ninth St. (at Harrison St.). ℂ 415/863-6623 or event info line ℂ 415/252-STUD. Cover $3–$10. www.studsf.com.

Twin Peaks Tavern   Right at the intersection of Castro, 17th, and Market streets is one of the Castro's most famous (at 40 years old) gay hangouts. It caters to an older crowd and claims to be the first gay bar in America. Because of its relatively small size and desirable location, the place becomes fairly crowded and convivial by 8pm, earlier than many neighboring bars. 401 Castro St. (at 17th and Market sts.). ℂ 415/864-9470.

6 Film

The **San Francisco International Film Festival** (ℂ 415/931-FILM; www.sffs. org), held in April, is one of America's oldest film festivals. Entries include new films by beginning and established directors. Call or surf ahead for a schedule or information, and check out their website for more information on purchasing tickets, which are relatively inexpensive.

If you're not here in time for the festival, don't despair. The classic, independent, and mainstream cinemas in San Francisco are every bit as good as the city's other cultural offerings.

REPERTORY CINEMAS

Castro Theatre *Finds*   Built in 1922, the beautiful Castro Theatre is known for its screenings of classics and for its Wurlitzer organ, which is played before each show. There's a different feature almost nightly, and more often than not it's a double feature. Bargain matinees are usually offered on Wednesday, Saturday, Sunday, and holidays. Phone for schedules, prices, and show times. 429 Castro St. (near Market St.). ℂ 415/621-6120. www.thecastrotheatre.com.

Red Vic   The worker-owned Red Vic movie collective originated in the neighboring Victorian building that gave it its name. The theater specializes in independent releases and contemporary cult hits and situates its patrons among an array of couches. Prices are $7 for adults ($5 for matinees) and $4 for seniors and kids 12 and under. Tickets go on sale 20 minutes before each show. Phone for schedules and show times. 1727 Haight St. (between Cole and Shrader sts.). ℂ 415/ 668-3994. www.redvicmoviehouse.com.

Roxie   The Roxie consistently screens the best new alternative films anywhere. The low-budget contemporary features are largely devoid of Hollywood candy coating; many are West Coast premieres. Films change weekly and sometimes more often. Phone for schedules, prices, and show times. 3117 16th St. (at Valencia St.). ℂ 415/863-1087. www.roxie.com.

11

Side Trips from San Francisco

The City by the Bay is, without question, captivating, but don't let it ensnare you to the point of ignoring its environs. The surrounding areas contain a multitude of natural spectacles such as Mount Tamalpais and Muir Woods; scenic communities like Tiburon and Sausalito; and great cities such as up-and-coming Oakland and its youth-oriented next-door neighbor, Berkeley.

From San Francisco, you can reach any of these points in an hour or less by car. An option is to hitch a ride with **San Francisco Sightseeing** (© 415/434-8687; www.sanfrancisco sightseeing.com), which runs regularly scheduled bus tours to neighboring towns and the countryside. Full-day trips to Muir Woods, Sausalito, Napa, and Sonoma are available, as are excursions to Yosemite and the Monterey Peninsula. Phone for prices and schedules.

1 Berkeley

10 miles NE of San Francisco

Berkeley is famous as the home of the University of California at Berkeley, which is world-renowned for its academic standards, 18 Nobel Prize winners (seven are active staff), and protests that led to the most famous student riots in U.S. history. Today, there's still hippie idealism in the air, but the radicals have aged; the 1960s are present only in tie-dye and paraphernalia shops. The biggest change the town is facing is yuppification; as San Francisco's rent and property prices soar out of the range of the average person's budget, everyone with less than a small fortune is seeking shelter elsewhere, and Berkeley is one of the top picks (although Oakland is quickly becoming a favorite, too). Berkeley is a charming town teeming with all types of people, a beautiful campus, vast parks, great shopping, and some incredible restaurants.

Pricing Categories

Note: In this chapter, hotels are organized by location, then by price range, as follows: **Very Expensive,** more than $250 per night; **Expensive,** $200 to $250 per night; **Moderate,** $150 to $200 per night; and **Inexpensive,** less than $150 per night.

Restaurants are organized by location, then by price range for a complete dinner (appetizer, entree, dessert, and glass of wine) as follows: **Expensive,** dinner from $50 per person; **Moderate,** dinner from $35 per person; and **Inexpensive,** less than $35 per person for dinner. (*Note:* The "Very Expensive" category—dinner from $75 per person—has been omitted since no restaurants in this chapter fall under its umbrella.)

ESSENTIALS

The Berkeley **Bay Area Rapid Transit (BART)** station is 2 blocks from the university. The fare from San Francisco is less than $3.

If you are coming **by car** from San Francisco, take the Bay Bridge (go during the evening commute, and you'll think Los Angeles traffic is a breeze). Follow I-80 east to the University Avenue exit, and follow University until you hit the campus. Parking is tight, so either leave your car at the Sather Gate parking lot at Telegraph Avenue and Durant Street, or expect to fight for a spot.

WHAT TO SEE & DO

Hanging out is the preferred Berkeley pastime, and the best place to do it is **Telegraph Avenue,** the street that leads to the campus's southern entrance. Most of the action lies between Bancroft Way and Dwight Way, where coffeehouses, restaurants, shops, great book and record stores, and crafts booths (vendors selling everything from T-shirts and jewelry to I Ching and tarot-card readings pack the avenue) swarm with life. Pretend you're a local: Plant yourself at a cafe, sip a latte, and ponder something intellectual, or survey the town's unique residents.

Bibliophiles must stop at **Cody's Books,** 2454 Telegraph Ave. (© **510/845-7852;** www.codysbooks.com), to peruse its gargantuan selection of titles, independent-press books, and magazines. If used and antiquarian books are your thing, stop by **Moe's Books,** 2476 Telegraph Ave. (© **510/849-2087;** www.moesbooks.com). After exploring four floors of new, used, and out-of-print books, you're unlikely to leave empty-handed.

UC BERKELEY CAMPUS

The University of California at Berkeley (www.berkeley.edu) campus is worth a stroll. It's a beautiful old place with plenty of woodsy paths, architecturally noteworthy buildings and, of course, 33,000 students, many of them scurrying to and from classes. Among the architectural highlights of the campus are a number of buildings by Bernard Maybeck, Bakewell and Brown, and John Galen Howard.

Contact the **Visitor Information Center,** 101 University Hall, 2200 University Ave., at Oxford Street (© **510/642-5215;** www.berkeley.edu/visitors), to join a free, regularly scheduled campus tour. Free tours are available March 15 through April 30, Monday through Saturday at 10am and Sunday at 1pm; $25 electric cart tours are available February through mid-May with advance reservations; no tours are given from mid-December to mid-January. Or stop by the office and pick up a self-guided walking-tour brochure.

The university's southern, main entrance is at the northern end of Telegraph Avenue, at Bancroft Way. Walk through the entrance into Sproul Plaza, and when school is in session, you'll encounter the gamut of Berkeley's inhabitants: colorful street people, rambling political zealots, chanting Hare Krishnas, and ambitious students. You'll also find the student union, complete with a bookstore, cafes, and an information desk on the second floor where you can pick up a free map of Berkeley and the student newspaper (also found in dispensers throughout campus).

You might be lucky enough to stumble upon some impromptu musicians or a heated, and possibly absurd, debate. There's always something going on here, so stretch out on the grass for a few minutes and take in the Berkeley vibe.

For viewing more traditional art forms, there are some noteworthy museums, too. The **Lawrence Hall of Science** ★ (east of campus on Centennial Dr., just above the Botanical Gardens; © **510/642-5132;** www.lawrencehallofscience.

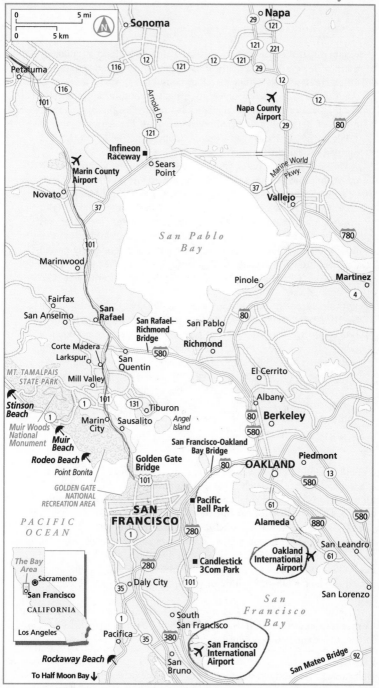

People's Park/People's Power

In late 1967, the university demolished an entire block of buildings north of Telegraph Avenue. The destruction, which forced hippies and other "undesirables" from the slum housing that stood there, was done under the guise of university expansion and urban renewal—good liberal causes. But after the lot lay vacant for almost 2 years, a group of Berkeley radicals, whose names read like a who's who of 1960s leftists, including Jerry Rubin, Bobby Seale, and Tom Hayden, decided to take the land for "the people."

On April 29, 1969, hundreds of activists invaded the vacant lot with gardening tools and tamed the muddy ground into a park. One month later, Berkeley's Republican mayor sent 250 police officers into the park, and 4,000 demonstrators materialized to challenge them. A riot ensued, and the police fired buckshot at the crowd. One rioter was killed and another blinded. Gov. Ronald Reagan sent in the National Guard, and for the next 17 days, the guardsmen repeatedly gassed innocent students, faculty, and passersby. Berkeley was a war zone, and People's Park became the decade's most important symbol of "people power."

The park again sparked controversy in 1992, when university officials decided to build volleyball courts there. In August, a park activist broke into the campus home of the university's chancellor. When a police officer arrived, the activist lunged at him with a machete and was shot dead. On the victim's body was a note with the message: "We are willing to die for this land. Are you?" On news of the contemporary radical's death, more than 150 of her supporters rioted.

Postscript: The volleyball courts didn't get much use, and now basketball courts have taken their place.

org) offers hands-on science exploration, is open daily from 10am to 5pm, and is a wonderful place to watch the sunset. Admission is $8.50 for adults; $6.50 for seniors, students, and children 7 to 18; $4 for children 3 to 6; free for kids under 3. The **UC Berkeley Art Museum** ✸ (two entrances: 2626 Bancroft Way or 2621 Durant Ave., between College and Telegraph aves.; ⓒ **510/642-0808**) is open Wednesday through Sunday from 11am to 5pm. Admission is $8 for adults; $5 for seniors, students, visitors with disabilities, and children 12 to 17; free for kids under 12 and UC students. This museum contains a substantial collection of Hans Hofmann paintings, a sculpture garden, and the Pacific Film Archive.

If you're interested in notable off-campus buildings, contact the **Berkeley Convention and Visitors Bureau** (ⓒ **510/549-7040;** www.berkeleycvb.com) for an architectural walking-tour brochure.

PARKS

Unbeknownst to many travelers, Berkeley has some of the most extensive and beautiful parks around. If you want to wear out the kids or enjoy hiking, swimming, sniffing roses, or just getting a breath of California air, jump in your car and make your way to **Tilden Park** ✸. On the way, stop at the colorful terraced

Berkeley

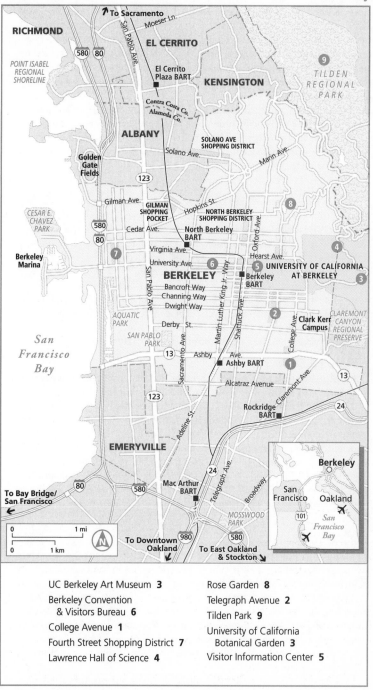

RICHMOND

To Sacramento

Moeser Ln.

EL CERRITO

POINT ISABEL
REGIONAL
SHORELINE

El Cerrito
Plaza BART

KENSINGTON

TILDEN
REGIONAL
PARK

Contra Costa Co.
Alameda Co.

ALBANY

SOLANO AVE
SHOPPING DISTRICT

Golden
Gate
Fields

Solano Ave.

Mann Ave.

CESAR E.
CHAVEZ
PARK

Gilman Ave.

GILMAN
SHOPPING
POCKET

Hopkins St.

NORTH BERKELEY
SHOPPING DISTRICT

Cedar Ave.

North Berkeley
BART

Berkeley
Marina

Virginia Ave.

University Ave.

San Pablo Ave.

BERKELEY

Bancroft Way
Channing Way
Dwight Way

Berkeley
BART

Martin Luther King Jr. Way

Shattuck Ave.

Oxford Ave.

Hearst Ave.

UNIVERSITY OF CALIFORNIA
AT BERKELEY

AQUATIC
PARK

SAN PABLO
PARK

Derby St.

Sacramento Ave.

Ashby

College Ave.

Clark Kerr
Campus

CLAREMONT
CANYON
REGIONAL
PRESERVE

San
Francisco
Bay

Ashby Ave.

Ashby BART

Alcatraz Avenue

Adeline St.

Claremont Ave.

Rockridge
BART

EMERYVILLE

Mac Arthur
BART

Telegraph Ave.

Broadway

Berkeley

San
Francisco

Oakland

To Bay Bridge/
San Francisco

San
Francisco
Bay

MOSSWOOD
PARK

0   1 mi

0   1 km

To Downtown
Oakland

To East Oakland
& Stockton

Legend

UC Berkeley Art Museum **3**	Rose Garden **8**
Berkeley Convention & Visitors Bureau **6**	Telegraph Avenue **2**
	Tilden Park **9**
College Avenue **1**	University of California Botanical Garden **3**
Fourth Street Shopping District **7**	
Lawrence Hall of Science **4**	Visitor Information Center **5**

Rose Garden ✿, in north Berkeley on Euclid Avenue between Bay View and Eunice Street. Then head high into the Berkeley hills to Tilden, where you'll find plenty of flora and fauna, hiking trails, an old steam train and merry-go-round, a farm and nature area for kids, and a chilly tree-encircled lake. By air-conditioned public transit, bus line no. 67 goes to the north end of the park, and no. 8 skirts the edge of the park. Call © **510/562-PARK** or see www.ebparks.org for further information.

Another worthy nature excursion is **The University of California Botanical Garden** (© **510/643-2755;** http://botanicalgarden.berkeley.edu), which features a vast collection of herbage ranging from cacti to redwoods. It's on campus in Strawberry Canyon on Centennial Drive; bus no. 8 from the Berkeley BART station runs there.

SHOPPING

If you're itching to exercise your credit cards, head to one of two places. **College Avenue** from Dwight Way to the Oakland border overflows with eclectic boutiques, antiques shops, and restaurants. The other option is **Fourth Street,** in west Berkeley, 2 blocks north of the University Avenue exit. This shopping strip is the perfect place to go on a sunny morning. Grab a cup of java, read the paper at a patio table, then hit the **Crate & Barrel Outlet,** 1785 Fourth St., between Hearst and Virginia (© **510/528-5500**). Prices are 30% to 70% off retail. It's open Monday through Saturday from 10am to 6pm, Sunday from 10am to 6pm. This area also boasts small, wonderful stores crammed with imported and locally made housewares. Nearby is **REI,** the Bay Area's favorite outdoors outfitter, 1338 San Pablo Ave., near Gilman Street (© **510/527-4140**).

WHERE TO STAY

Unfortunately, a little research will prove that Berkeley is not even remotely close to a good hotel town. Most accommodations are extremely basic motels and funky B&Bs. The one exception (though it's overpriced) is **The Claremont Resort & Spa,** 41 Tunnel Rd., Berkeley (© **800/551-7266** or 510/843-3000; www.claremontresort.com), a grand Victorian hotel, also on the border of Oakland, with recent building and room renovations, a fancy spa and gym, a hip bar, and grandiose surroundings. Rates range from $270 to $410 for doubles and $460 to $1,060 for suites. Or you can contact the **Berkeley & Oakland Bed and Breakfast Network** (© **510/547-6380;** www.bbonline.com/ca/berkeley-oakland), which books visitors into private homes and apartments in the East Bay area.

WHERE TO DINE

East Bay dining is a relaxed alternative to San Francisco's gourmet scene. There are plenty of ambitious Berkeley restaurants and, unlike in San Francisco, plenty of parking, provided you're not near the campus.

If you want to dine student-style, eat on campus Monday through Friday. Buy something at a sidewalk stand or in the building directly behind the Student Union. The least expensive food is available downstairs in the **Cafeteria,** on Lower Sproul Plaza. There's also the **Bear's Lair Pub and Coffee House,** the **Terrace,** and the **Golden Bear Restaurant.** All the university eateries have both indoor and outdoor seating.

Telegraph Avenue has an array of small, ethnic restaurants, cafes, and sandwich shops. Follow the students: If the place is crowded, it's good, supercheap, or both.

EXPENSIVE

Chez Panisse ★★★ CALIFORNIA   California cuisine is so much a product of Alice Waters's genius that all other restaurants following in her wake should be dated A.A.W. (After Alice Waters). Read the menus posted outside, and you'll understand why. Most of the produce and meat comes from local farms and is organically produced, and after all these years, Alice still tends her restaurant with great integrity and innovation. Chez Panisse is a delightful redwood and stucco cottage with a brick terrace filled with flowering potted plants. The two dining areas, the cafe and the restaurant, both serve Mediterranean-inspired cuisine.

In the upstairs cafe are displays of pastries and fruit and an oak bar adorned with large bouquets of fresh flowers. At lunch or dinner, the menu might feature delicately smoked gravlax or roasted eggplant soup with pesto, followed by lamb ragout garnished with apricots, onions, and spices and served with couscous.

The cozy downstairs restaurant, strewn with blossoming floral bouquets, is an appropriately warm environment in which to indulge in the $65 fixed-price four-course gourmet dinner, which is served Tuesday through Thursday. Friday and Saturday, it's $75 for four courses; and Monday is bargain night, with a three-course dinner for $50.

The restaurant posts the following week's menu, which changes daily, every Saturday. There's also an excellent wine list, with bottles ranging from $18 to $300.

1517 Shattuck Ave. (between Cedar and Vine). © **510/548-5525**, or 510/548-5049 cafe reservations. Fax 510/548-0140. www.chezpanisse.com. Reservations required. Restaurant fixed-price menu $50–$75; cafe main courses $15–$25. AE, DC, DISC, MC, V. Restaurant seatings Mon–Sat 6–6:30pm and 8:30–9:30pm. Cafe Mon–Thurs 11:30am–3pm and 5–10:30pm; Fri–Sat 11:30am–3:30pm and 5–11:30pm. BART: Berkeley. From I-80 north, take the University Ave. exit and turn left onto Shattuck Ave.

MODERATE

Cafe Rouge ★★ MEDITERRANEAN   After cooking at San Francisco's renowned Zuni Cafe for 10 years, chef-owner Marsha McBride launched her own restaurant, a sort of Zuni East. She brought former staff members and some of the restaurant's flavor with her, and now her sparse, loftlike dining room serves salads, rotisserie chicken with oil and thyme, grilled lamb chops, steaks,

---

⌜Finds **Sweet Sensations at Berkeley's Chocolate Factory**

If you haven't had chocolate nibs, you haven't lived—at least that's what chocoholics are likely to discover upon visiting **Scharffen Berger Chocolate Maker,** California's runaway-success chocolatier that opened its factory and retail-shop doors in Berkeley in mid-2001. Within the brick building, visitors can not only taste the nibs (crunchy roasted and shelled cocoa beans), but also see how the famous chocolate company uses vintage European equipment during regularly scheduled tours (call for details). And let's not forget there are plenty of tasty products, from candy bars to cocoa powder to chocolate sauce, available in the retail shop. The factory is located at 914 Heinz Ave., Berkeley (© **510/981-4050;** www.scharffenberger.com). From I-80 East take the Ashby Avenue exit, turn left on Seventh Street, and turn right on Heinz.

and homemade sausages. East Bay carnivores are especially happy with the burger; like Zuni's, it's top-notch.

1782 Fourth St. (between Delaware and Hearst). © **510/525-1440**. www.caferouge.net. Reservations recommended. Main courses $9.50–$24. MC, V. Daily 11:30am–3pm; Tues–Sat 3–5pm (interim menu); Tues–Thurs 5:30–9:30pm; Fri–Sat 5:30–10:30pm; Sun 5–9:30pm.

Rivoli ★★★ *Finds* CALIFORNIA   One of the favored dinner destinations in the East Bay, Rivoli offers top-notch food at amazingly reasonable prices. In an otherwise uninteresting space, the owners have created a warm, intimate dining room, which overlooks a sweet little garden with visiting raccoons and possums and a wine bar near the entrance. Aside from a few house favorites, the menu changes entirely every 3 weeks to feature whatever's freshest and in season; the wine list follows suit with around a dozen by-the-glass options handpicked to match the food. While many love it, I'm not a fan of the portobello-mushroom fritter, a gourmet variation of the fried zucchini stick. However, plenty of dishes shine, including chicken cooked with prosciutto di Parma, potato and scallion souffle, Marsala *jus*, snap peas, and baby carrots; artichoke lasagna with ricotta, mint salsa, and tomato sauce; and braised lamb shank with green garlic risotto, sautéed spinach, and oven-dried tomatoes. Finish the evening with an assortment of cheeses or a warm chocolate truffle torte with hazelnut ice cream, orange crème anglaise, and chocolate sauce.

1539 Solano Ave. © **510/526-2542**. www.rivolirestaurant.com. Reservations recommended. Main courses $16–$20. AE, DC, DISC, MC, V. Mon–Thurs 5:30–9:30pm; Fri 5:30–10pm; Sat 5–10pm; Sun 5–9pm.

INEXPENSIVE

O Chamé ★★ JAPANESE   Spare and plain in its decor, with ocher-colored walls etched with patterns, this spot has a meditative air to complement the traditional, experimental, and very fresh and clean Japanese-inspired cuisine. The menu, which changes daily, offers meal-in-a-bowl dishes ($9–$13) that allow a choice of soba or udon noodles in a clear soup with a variety of toppings—from shrimp and wakame seaweed to beef with burdock root and carrot. Appetizers include a flavorful melding of grilled shiitake mushrooms, as well as portobello mushrooms, watercress, and green-onion pancakes. There are also specials ($10–$18), which always include delicious roasted salmon.

1830 Fourth St. (near Hearst). © **510/841-8783**. Reservations recommended Fri–Sat dinner. Main courses lunch $9–$19, dinner $18–$24. AE, DC, MC, V. Mon–Sat 11:30am–3pm; Mon–Thurs 5:30–9pm; Fri–Sat 5:30–9:30pm.

2 Oakland

10 miles E of San Francisco

Although it's less than a dozen miles from San Francisco, Oakland is worlds apart from its sister city across the bay. Originally little more than a cluster of ranches and farms, Oakland exploded in size and stature practically overnight, when the last mile of transcontinental railroad track was laid down. Major shipping ports soon followed and, to this day, Oakland remains one of the busiest industrial ports on the West Coast.

The price for economic success, however, is Oakland's lowbrow reputation as a predominantly working-class city; it is forever in the shadow of chic San Francisco. However, as the City by the Bay has become crowded and expensive in the past few years, Oakland has experienced a rush of new residents and businesses. As a result, Oak-town is in a renaissance, and its future continues to look brighter and brighter.

Rent a sailboat on Lake Merritt, stroll along the waterfront, explore the fantastic Oakland Museum: They're all great reasons to hop the bay and spend a fog-free day exploring one of California's largest and most ethnically diverse cities.

ESSENTIALS

BART connects San Francisco and Oakland through one of the longest underwater transit tunnels in the world. Fares range from $1 to $4, depending on your station of origin; children under 5 ride free. BART trains operate Monday through Friday from 4am to midnight, Saturday from 6am to midnight, and Sunday from 8am to midnight. Exit at the 12th Street station for downtown Oakland.

By car from San Francisco, take I-80 across the San Francisco–Oakland Bay Bridge and follow signs to downtown Oakland. Exit at Grand Avenue South for the Lake Merritt area.

For a calendar of events in Oakland, contact the **Oakland Convention and Visitors Bureau,** 463 11th St., Oakland, CA 94607 (© **510/839-9000;** www. oaklandcvb.com). The city also sponsors free guided tours, including African-American Heritage and downtown tours held Wednesdays and Saturdays May through October; call © **510/238-3234** for details.

Downtown Oakland lies between Grand Avenue on the north, I-980 on the west, Inner Harbor on the south, and Lake Merritt on the east. Between these landmarks are three BART stations (12th St., 19th St., and Lake Merritt), City Hall, the Oakland Museum, Jack London Square, and several other sights.

WHAT TO SEE & DO

Lake Merritt is Oakland's primary tourist attraction, along with Jack London Square (see below). Three and a half miles in circumference, the tidal lagoon was bridged and dammed in the 1860s and is now a wildlife refuge that is home to flocks of migrating ducks, herons, and geese. The 122-acre **Lakeside Park,** a popular place to picnic, feed the ducks, and escape the fog, surrounds the lake on three sides. At the **Municipal Boathouse** ⚑ (© **510/238-2196**), in Lakeside Park along the north shore, you can rent sailboats, rowboats, pedal boats, or canoes for $6 to $12 per hour, plus a one-time $2 1-day boat permit fee. Or you can take an hour-long gondola ride with **Gondola Servizio** (© **510/663-6603;** www.gondolaservizio.com). Experienced gondoliers will serenade you as you glide across the lake; the cost ranges from $45 to $225 for two depending on the time and gondola style.

Another site worth visiting is Oakland's **Paramount Theatre** ⚑, 2025 Broadway (© **510/893-2300;** www.paramounttheatre.com), an outstanding National Historic Landmark and example of Art Deco architecture and decor. Built in 1931 and authentically restored in 1973, it's the city's main performing-arts center, hosting big-name performers like Smokey Robinson and Alicia Keys. Guided tours of the 3,000-seat theater are given the first and third Saturday morning of each month, excluding holidays. No reservations are necessary; just show up at 10am at the box office entrance on 21st Street at Broadway. Cameras are allowed, and admission is $1.

If you take pleasure in strolling sailboat-filled wharves or are a die-hard fan of Jack London, you might enjoy a visit to **Jack London Square** ⚑. Oakland's only patently tourist area, this low-key version of San Francisco's Fisherman's Wharf shamelessly plays up the fact that Jack London spent most of his youth along the waterfront. The square fronts the harbor, housing a tourist-tacky complex of

Oakland

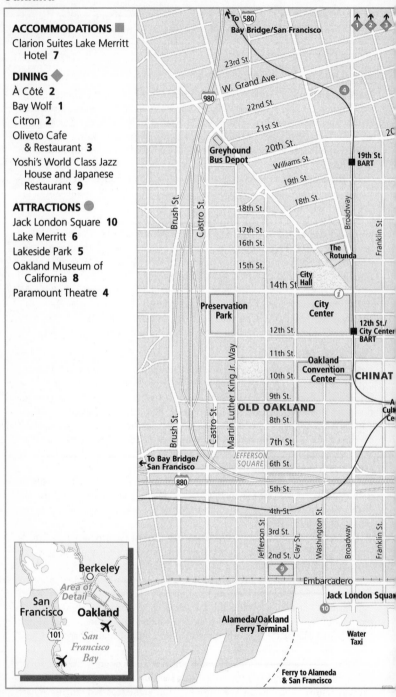

ACCOMMODATIONS ■

Clarion Suites Lake Merritt
  Hotel **7**

DINING ◆

À Côté **2**
Bay Wolf **1**
Citron **2**
Oliveto Cafe
  & Restaurant **3**
Yoshi's World Class Jazz
  House and Japanese
  Restaurant **9**

ATTRACTIONS ●

Jack London Square **10**
Lake Merritt **6**
Lakeside Park **5**
Oakland Museum of
  California **8**
Paramount Theatre **4**

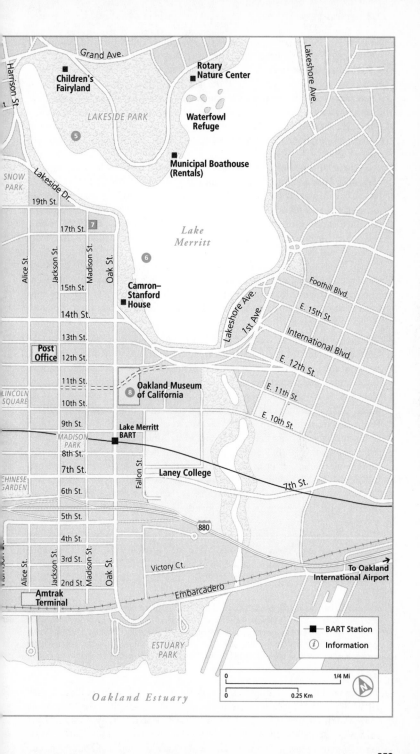

boutiques and eateries that are about as far from the "call of the wild" as you can get as well as a more locals-friendly farmers market on Sunday from 10am to 2pm. Most shops are open Monday through Saturday from 10am to 7pm (some restaurants stay open later). One of the best options is live jazz at **Yoshi's World Class Jazz House & Japanese Restaurant** ✦, 510 Embarcadero West (© **510/238-9200;** www.yoshis.com), which serves some fine sushi in its adjoining restaurant. In the center of the square is a small, reconstructed Yukon cabin in which Jack London lived while prospecting in the Klondike during the gold rush of 1897.

In the middle of Jack London Square you'll find a more authentic memorial, **Heinold's First and Last Chance Saloon** (© **510/839-6761**), a funky, friendly little bar and historic landmark that's worth a visit. This is where London did some of his writing and most of his drinking; the corner table he used has remained exactly as it was nearly a century ago. Also in the square are the mast and nameplate from USS *Oakland,* a ship that saw extensive action in the Pacific during World War II.

Jack London Square is at Broadway and Embarcadero. Take I-880 to Broadway, turn south, and drive to the end. Or you can ride BART to 12th Street station, then walk south along Broadway (about half a mile); a free shuttle runs from there Monday through Friday from 11am to 2pm. Or take bus no. 51A to the foot of Broadway.

Oakland Museum of California ✦ Two blocks south of Lake Merritt, the Oakland Museum of California incorporates just about everything you'd want to know about the state and its people, history, culture, geology, art, environment, and ecology. Inside a low, modern building set among sweeping gardens and terraces, it's actually three museums in one: exhibitions of works by California artists from Bierstadt to Diebenkorn; collections of historic artifacts, from Pomo Indian basketry to Country Joe McDonald's guitar; and re-creations of California habitats from the coast to the White Mountains. The museum holds major shows of California artists and exhibitions dedicated to major California movements. Recent exhibits included "What's Going On?," a photo and oral history exhibit of California's Vietnam-era protests and response to war and "Baseball as America," which showcases artifacts and photos of the nation's favorite sport. The museum also frequently shows photography from its huge collections.

Forty-five-minute guided tours leave from the gallery information desks on request or by appointment. There's a fine cafe, a **gallery** (© **510/834-2296**) that sells works by California artists, and a book and gift shop. The cafe is open Wednesday through Friday from 10:30am to 4:30pm, Saturday from 1:30 to 4:30pm.

1000 Oak St. (at 10th St.). © 888/625-6873, or 510/238-2200 for recorded information. www.museum ca.org. Admission $8 adults; $5 students and seniors; free for children under 6. 2nd Sun of the month is free. Wed–Sat 10am–5pm; Sun noon–5pm; open until 9pm 1st Fri of the month. Closed Jan 1, July 4, Thanksgiving, Dec 25. BART: Lake Merritt station; walk 1 block north. From I-880 north, take the Oak St. exit; the museum is 5 blocks east. Or take I-580 to I-980 and exit at the Jackson St. ramp.

WHERE TO STAY

Two fine midrange hotel options in Oakland are the **Waterfront Plaza Hotel,** 10 Washington St., Jack London Square (© **800/729-3638** or 510/836-3800; www.waterfrontplaza.com), and the **Oakland Marriott City Center,** 1001 Broadway (© **800/228-9290** or 510/451-4000; fax 510/835-3466; www. marriott.com). Most major motel chains also have locations (and budget prices) around town and near the airport. If you want to stay near the fabulous shopping and dining neighborhood of Oakland's Rockridge and pamper yourself with a killer gym, outdoor pools, and lit tennis courts, your best hotel bet (though it's undoubtedly overpriced) is **The Claremont Resort & Spa,** 41 Tunnel Rd., Berkeley (© **800/551-7266** or 510/843-3000; www.claremont resort.com), a grand Victorian hotel (with modern rooms) that borders both Berkeley and Oakland. It ain't downtown, but it's just a quick drive to all the action, and it is one of the area's prettiest options.

WHERE TO DINE
EXPENSIVE

Citron ⭐ FRENCH/CALIFORNIA   This petite, adorable French bistro was an instant smash when it opened in 1992, and it continues to earn raves for its small yet enticingly eclectic menu. Chef Chris Rossi draws the flavors of France, Italy, and Spain together with fresh California produce for results you aren't likely to have tasted elsewhere. The menu changes every few weeks; dishes range from succulent Sonoma rack of lamb, which is grilled and then baked with an aioli bread-crumb crust and served atop grilled ratatouille to spicy bayou seafood stew brimming with fried oysters, shrimp, snapper, and bell pepper and tomato sauce to rich saffron artichoke risotto. *A word of advice:* If you're into classic foods you can identify by name, head elsewhere. It's all about creative cooking here.

5484 College Ave. (north of Broadway between Taft and Lawton sts.). © **510/653-5484.** www.citron-acote.com. Reservations recommended. Main courses $20–$26; 3- to 5-course fixed-price menu (Sun–Fri only) $35–$46. AE, DC, DISC, MC, V. Mon–Tues 5:30–9pm; Wed–Thurs 5:30–9:30pm; Fri 5:30–10pm; Sat 5–10pm; Sun 5–9pm.

Oliveto Cafe & Restaurant ⭐⭐⭐ ITALIAN   Paul Bertolli, former chef at the world-renowned Chez Panisse restaurant, jumped ship to open one of the top Italian restaurants in the Bay Area (and certainly the best in Oakland). During the week it's a madhouse at lunchtime, when local workers pile in for the wood-fired pizzas and tapas served in the lower-level cafe. The upstairs restaurant—with suave neo-Florentine decor and a partially open kitchen—is slightly more civil, packed nightly with fans of Bertolli's mind-blowing housemade pastas, sausages, and prosciutto. Oliveto has a wood-burning oven, flame-broiled rotisserie, and high-end liquor cabinet (that is, hard alcohol, but no mixed drinks). An assortment of pricey grills, braises, and roasts anchor the daily changing menu, but it's the heavenly pastas, pizzetas, and awesome salads that offer the most tang for your buck. Still, the Arista (classic Italian pork with garlic and rosemary and pork *jus*) is insanely good; and no one does fried calamari, onion rings, and lemon slices better than Oliveto. *Tip:* There's free parking in the lot at the rear of the Market Hall building.

Rockridge Market Hall, 5655 College Ave. (off the northeast end of Broadway at Shafter/Keith St., across from the Rockridge BART station). © **510/547-5356.** www.oliveto.com. Reservations recommended for restaurant. Main courses $9–$15 lunch, $16–$30 dinner. AE, DC, MC, V. Tues–Fri 11:30am–2pm; Tues–Wed 5:30–9:30pm; Thurs–Sat 5:30–10pm; Sun 5–9pm.

MODERATE

À Côté ⭐⭐ FRENCH TAPAS   Christopher Rossi, who also owns neighboring Citron (see above), looks to chef Matthew Colgan to serve up killer rustic Mediterranean-inspired small plates at this loud, festive, and warmly lit joint. A "no reservations" policy means there's usually a long wait during prime dining hours, but once seated you can join locals in a nosh fest featuring the likes of

Croque monsieur; pommes frites with aioli; wood-oven cooked mussels in Pernod; grilled pork tenderloin with creamy polenta, traviso cheese, and pancetta; and cheese plates—and wash it down with excellent by-the-glass or -bottle selections from the great wine list or perky cocktails.

5478 College Ave. (at Taft Ave.). © 510/655-6469. www.citron-acote.com. Reservations not accepted. Small plates $5–$14. AE, DC, DISC, MC, V. Sun and Tues–Wed 5:30–10pm; Thurs 5:30–11pm; Fri–Sat 5:30pm– midnight. Closed Mon.

Bay Wolf ✫ CALIFORNIA The lifespan of most Bay Area restaurants is about a year; Bay Wolf, one of Oakland's most revered restaurants, has, fittingly, been going strong for nearly 3 decades. The converted brown Victorian is a comfortably familiar sight for most East Bay diners, who have come here for years to let chef-owner Michael Wilds do the cooking. Bay Wolf enjoys a reputation for simple yet sagacious preparations using only fresh ingredients. Main courses include Liberty Ranch duck breast with cassis sauce, baby onion, and potato and celery root gratin; flavorful seafood stew seasoned with saffron and brimful of cracked Dungeness crab, prawns, rockfish, and mussels; and tender braised osso buco with creamy polenta and gremolata. Informal service means you can leave the tie at home. The front deck has heat lamps, allowing for open-air evening dining—a treat that San Franciscans rarely experience.

3853 Piedmont Ave. (off Broadway between 40th St. and MacArthur Blvd.). © 510/655-6004. www. baywolf.com. Reservations recommended. Main courses $9.50–$17 lunch, $17–$22 dinner. AE, MC, V. Mon–Fri 11:30am–1:45pm; Mon–Thurs 6–9pm; Fri–Sun 5:30–9:30pm.

3 Angel Island & Tiburon

8 miles N of San Francisco

A federal and state wildlife refuge, Angel Island is the largest of San Francisco Bay's three islets (the others are Alcatraz and Yerba Buena). The island has been, at various times, a prison, a quarantine station for immigrants, a missile base, and even a favorite site for duels. Nowadays, most visitors are content with picnicking on the large green lawn that fronts the docking area; loaded with the appropriate recreational supplies, they claim a barbecue pit, plop their fannies down on the lush green grass, and while away an afternoon free of phones, televisions, and traffic. Hiking, mountain biking, and guided tram tours are other popular activities here.

Tiburon, situated on a peninsula of the same name, looks like a cross between a fishing village and a Hollywood Western set—imagine San Francisco reduced to toy dimensions. The seacoast town rambles over a series of green hills and ends up at a spindly, multicolored pier on the waterfront, like a Fisherman's Wharf in miniature. In reality, it's an extremely plush patch of yacht-club suburbia, as you'll see by the marine craft and the homes of their owners. Ramshackle, color-splashed old frame houses line Main Street, sheltering chic boutiques, souvenir stores, antiques shops, and art galleries. Other roads are narrow, winding, and hilly and lead up to dramatically situated homes. The view from here of San Francisco's skyline and the islands in the bay is a good enough reason to pay the precious price to live here.

While there is a hotel in Tiburon, I wouldn't recommend staying there: It's a 1-block town, and the hotel is very expensive. There are no hotels on Angel Island. Both destinations are better as day trips.

Marin County

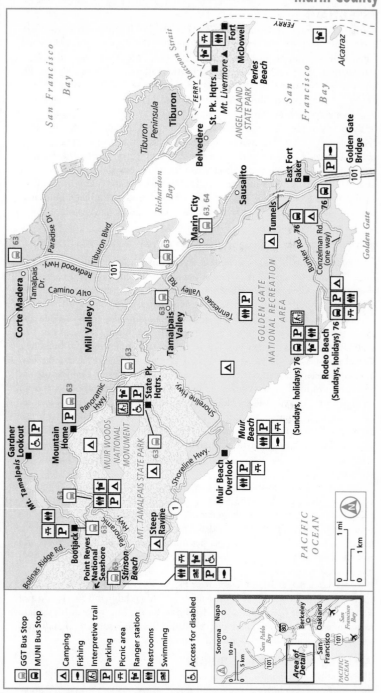

Legend:
- GGT Bus Stop
- MUNI Bus Stop
- Camping
- Fishing
- Interpretive trail
- Parking
- Picnic area
- Ranger station
- Restrooms
- Swimming
- Access for disabled

Map labels:

San Francisco Bay

Tiburon Peninsula — Tiburon

Raccoon Strait

FERRY

Fort McDowell

Mt. Livermore ▲

St. Pk. Hqtrs.

Belvedere

ANGEL ISLAND STATE PARK

Perles Beach

San Francisco Bay

Alcatraz

Golden Gate Bridge

East Fort Baker

Sausalito

101

76

Tunnels

Bunker Rd.

Conzelman Rd. (one way)

GOLDEN GATE NATIONAL RECREATION AREA

Golden Gate

Marin City 63, 64

Richardson Bay

Paradise Dr.

Tamalpais Dr.

Corte Madera

63

Redwood Hwy.

Camino Alto

Mill Valley

Tiburon Blvd.

101

63

Tennessee Valley Rd.

Tamalpais Valley

63

Shoreline Hwy.

Rodeo Beach (Sundays, holidays) 76

(Sundays, holidays) 76

Mt. Tamalpais
Gardner Lookout

Mountain Home

63

Panoramic Hwy.

State Pk. Hqtrs.

MUIR WOODS NATIONAL MONUMENT

63

Muir Beach

Muir Beach Overlook

Bootjack

63

Bolinas Ridge Rd.

Point Reyes National Seashore ←

Steep Ravine

MT. TAMALPAIS STATE PARK

Panoramic Hwy.

Shoreline Hwy.

Stinson Beach

1

PACIFIC OCEAN

N

0   1 mi

0   1 km

Inset map:

Sonoma   Napa

San Pablo Bay

Berkeley

Oakland

80

101

San Francisco

San Francisco Bay

PACIFIC OCEAN

Area of Detail

N

0   10 mi

0   5 km

ESSENTIALS

Ferries of the **Blue & Gold Fleet** (© 415/705-5555; www.blueandgoldfleet. com) from Pier 41 (Fisherman's Wharf) travel to both Angel Island and Tiburon. Boats run on a seasonal schedule; phone or look online for departure information. The round-trip fare is $12 to Angel Island, $6.50 for kids 6 to 11, and free for kids under 6. The fare includes state park fees. Tickets to Tiburon are $7.25 each way for adults, $4 for kids 6 to 11, and free for kids under 5. Tickets are available at Pier 41.

By car from San Francisco, take U.S. 101 to the Tiburon/Highway 131 exit, then follow Tiburon Boulevard all the way downtown, a 40-minute drive from San Francisco. Catch the **Tiburon–Angel Island Ferry** (© 415/435-2131; www.angelislandferry.com) to Angel Island from the dock at Tiburon Boulevard and Main Street. The 15-minute round-trip, which departs hourly from 10am to 4pm, costs $8 for adults, $6 for children 5 to 11, and $1 for bikes. One child under 4 is admitted free of charge with each paying adult. Tickets may be purchased when boarding.

WHAT TO SEE & DO ON ANGEL ISLAND

Passengers disembark from the ferry at **Ayala Cove,** a small marina abutting a huge lawn area equipped with tables, benches, barbecue pits, and restrooms. Also at Ayala Cove are a small store, gift shop, cafe (with surprisingly good grub), and an overpriced mountain-bike rental shop.

Angel Island's 12 miles of hiking and mountain-bike trails include the **Perimeter Road,** a partly paved path that circles the island. It winds past disused troop barracks, former gun emplacements, and other military buildings; several turnoffs lead to the top of Mount Livermore, 776 feet above the bay. Sometimes referred to as the "Ellis Island of the West," Angel Island was used as a holding area for detained Chinese immigrants awaiting admission papers from 1910 to 1940. You can still see faded Chinese characters on the walls of the barracks where the immigrants were held. During the warmer months you can camp at a limited number of reserved sites; call **Reserve America** at © 800/444-7275 and ask about environmental campgrounds at Angel Island. For more information about the island, call **Angel Island** at © 415/435-3522 or visit www.angelisland.org.

Guided **sea-kayak tours** ★ are also available. The all-day trips, which include a catered lunch, combine the thrill of paddling stable two- or three-person kayaks with an informative, naturalist-led tour around the island (conditions permitting). All equipment is provided, kids are welcome, and no experience is necessary. Rates run about $110 per person. A shorter trip takes 2½ hours and costs $75 per person. For more information, call **Sea Trek** (© 415/332-8494; www.seatrekkayak.com).

The 1-hour **Angel Island Tram Tour** (© 415/897-0715; www.angelisland. com) costs $13 for adults, $11 for seniors, $7.50 for children 6 to 12, and free for children under 6; schedules vary depending on the time of year. It's the lazy man's (or woman's) way to check out the island's flora and fauna, though the reason most come here is to trek around—on foot.

WHAT TO SEE & DO IN TIBURON

The main thing to do in touristy, but pretty, and very tiny Tiburon is stroll along the waterfront, pop into the stores, and spend an easy $50 on drinks and appetizers before heading back to the city. For a taste of the Wine Country, stop at **Windsor Vineyards,** 72 Main St. (© 800/214-9463 or 415/435-3113; www.

Finds The Raw Deal

If you're in the 'hood and want a taste of the latest rage in modern cooking—or rather uncooking—plan a diversion to Larkspur, home of the nation's top raw, organic, vegan restaurant, **Roxanne's** (320 Magnolia Ave., Larkspur; © **415/924-5004;** www.roxraw.com). This over-the-top natural, elegant, and very PC dining experience has L.A. models and actresses flying up for dinner. Why? Because every dish—from the lasagna terrine layered with Roma tomato sauce, mushrooms, baby spinach, corn, and cashew cheese to the spicy stuffed Anaheim chiles with *ensalada de buena noche* and *mole poblano*—is guiltlessly decadent. Every item is made from organic unprocessed ingredients that are never heated above 115°F (to preserve the living enzymes). The healthy and environmentally sensitive menu is meatless, flourless, and sugarless, but it magically amazes diners with outstanding flavor. Don't miss the pad Thai made with raw baby coconut noodles. There's an equally impressive wine list. Skip the desserts, which tend to disappoint. Book well in advance: This is one of Northern California's hottest tickets. It's open Tuesday through Sunday from 5:30 to 10pm. Two courses cost $36, three courses cost $44, and four courses cost $52. American Express, MasterCard, and Visa are accepted.

---

windsorvineyards.com)—its Victorian tasting room dates from 1888. Twenty choices are available for a free tasting. Wine accessories and gifts—glasses, cork pullers, carry packs (which hold six bottles), gourmet sauces, posters, and maps—are also available. Ask about personalized labels for your selections. The shop is open Sunday through Thursday from 10am to 6pm, Friday and Saturday from 10am to 7pm.

WHERE TO DINE IN TIBURON

Guaymas MEXICAN   Guaymas offers authentic Mexican regional cuisine and a spectacular panoramic view of San Francisco and the bay. In good weather, the two heated outdoor patios are almost always packed with diners soaking in the sun and scene. Inside, colorful Mexican artwork brightens the beige walls. Should you feel chilled, to the rear of the dining room is a beehive-shaped adobe fireplace.

Guaymas is named after a fishing village on Mexico's Sea of Cortez, and both the town and the restaurant are famous for their *camarones* (giant shrimp). The restaurant also features ceviche, handmade tamales, and charcoal-grilled beef, seafood, and fowl. In addition to a good selection of California and Central American wines, the restaurant offers an exceptional variety of tequilas and Mexican beers.

5 Main St. © 415/435-6300. www.guaymas.com. Reservations recommended. Main courses $13–$23. AE, DC, DISC, MC, V. Mon–Thurs 11:30am–10pm; Fri–Sat 11:30am–11pm; Sun 10:30am–10pm. Ferry: Walk about 10 paces from the landing. From U.S. 101, exit at Tiburon/Hwy. 131; follow Tiburon Blvd. 5 miles and turn right onto Main St. Restaurant is behind the bakery.

Sam's Anchor Café ★ *Finds* SEAFOOD   Summer Sundays are liveliest in Tiburon, when weekend boaters tie up at the docks of waterside restaurants like this one, and good-time cyclists pedal from the city to kick it here. Sam's is the kind of place where you and your cronies can take off your shoes and have a fun, relaxing time eating burgers and drinking margaritas outside on the pier. The fare is typical—sandwiches, salads, and such—but the quality and selection are inconsequential: beers, burgers, and a designated driver are all you really need.

27 Main St. © 415/435-4527. www.samscafe.com. Main courses $9–$13 brunch, $9–$21 lunch, $15–$24 dinner. AE, DC, DISC, MC, V. Mon–Fri 11am–10pm; Sat–Sun 9:30am–10pm. Ferry: Walk from the landing. From U.S. 101, exit at Tiburon/Hwy. 131; follow Tiburon Blvd. 4 miles and turn right onto Main St.

4 Sausalito

5 miles N of San Francisco

Just off the northern end of the Golden Gate Bridge is the eclectic little town of Sausalito, a slightly bohemian, nonchalant, studiedly quaint adjunct to San Francisco. With fewer than 8,000 residents, Sausalito feels rather like St. Tropez on the French Riviera—minus the starlets and the social rat race. It has its quota of paper millionaires, but they rub their permanently suntanned shoulders with a good number of hard-up artists, struggling authors, shipyard workers, and fishers. Next to the swank restaurants, plush bars, and antiques shops and galleries, you'll see hamburger joints, beer parlors, and secondhand bookstores. Sausalito's main strip is Bridgeway, which runs along the water. Those in the know make a quick detour to Caledonia Street, 1 block inland; not only is it less congested, but it also has a far better selection of cafes and shops. Since the town is all along the waterfront and only stretches a few blocks, it is easy to find your way around.

ESSENTIALS

The **Golden Gate Ferry Service** fleet, Ferry Building (© **415/923-2000;** www.goldengateferry.org), operates between the San Francisco Ferry Building, at the foot of Market Street, and downtown Sausalito. Service is frequent, running at reasonable intervals every day of the year except January 1, Thanksgiving, and December 25. Phone for an exact schedule. The ride takes a half-hour, and one-way fares are $5.60 for adults and $4.20 for kids 6 to 12. Seniors and passengers with disabilities ride for $2.80; children 5 and under ride free. Family rates are available on weekends.

Ferries of the **Blue & Gold Fleet** (© **415/705-5555;** www.blueandgold fleet.com) leave from Pier 41 (Fisherman's Wharf); the one-way cost is $6.50 for adults, $4 for kids 5 to 11. Boats run on a seasonal schedule; phone for departure information.

By car from San Francisco, take U.S. 101 north, then take the first right after the Golden Gate Bridge (Alexander exit). Alexander becomes Bridgeway in Sausalito.

WHAT TO SEE & DO

Above all else, Sausalito has scenery and sunshine, for once you cross the Golden Gate Bridge, you're out of the San Francisco fog patch and under blue California sky (we hope). Houses cover the town's steep hills, overlooking a forest of masts on the waters below. Most of the tourist action, which is almost singularly limited to window-shopping and eating, takes place at sea level on Bridgeway.

Sausalito is a mecca for shoppers seeking handmade, original, and offbeat clothes and footwear, as well as arts and crafts. Many of the town's shops are in the alleys, malls, and second-floor boutiques reached by steep, narrow staircases on and off Bridgeway. Caledonia Street, which runs parallel to Bridgeway 1 block inland, is home to more shops.

Bay Model Visitors Center *Kids*   The U.S. Army Corps of Engineers once used this high-tech, 1½-acre model of San Francisco's bay and delta to resolve problems and observe the impact of changes in water flow. Today the model is strictly for educational purposes and reproduces (in scale) the rise and fall of tides, the flows and currents of water, the mixing of freshwater and saltwater, and trends in sediment movement. There's a 10-minute film, self-guided and audio tours ($3 donation requested), and a 1-hour tour (free; book a reservation), but the most interesting time to visit is when the model is in use, so call ahead.

2100 Bridgeway. ℂ 415/332-3871. www.spn.usace.army.mil/bmvc. Free admission. Labor Day to Memorial Day Tues–Sat 9am–4pm; Memorial Day to Labor Day Tues–Fri 9am–4pm, Sat–Sun and holidays 10am–5pm.

WHERE TO STAY

Sausalito is such a desirable enclave that it offers little in the way of affordable lodging. On the bright side, it's so close to San Francisco that it takes only about 15 minutes to get here, traffic permitting. While the hotels listed below are great destinations in themselves, Sausalito itself is more of a day trip, not a destination.

VERY EXPENSIVE

The Inn Above Tide ★★   Perched directly over the bay atop well-grounded pilings, this former luxury-apartment complex underwent a $4-million transformation into one of Sausalito's—if not the Bay Area's—finest accommodations. The view clinches it: Every room affords an unparalleled panorama of the San Francisco Bay, including a postcard-quality vista of the city glimmering in the distance. Should you manage to tear yourself away from your private deck, you'll find that 23 of the sumptuously appointed rooms sport romantic little fireplaces. Some have vast oversize tubs with spa jets, remote-control air-conditioning, and wondrously comfortable queen- or king-size beds. Soothing earthtones highlight the decor, which blends in well with the bayscape outside. Be sure to request that your breakfast and newspaper be delivered to your deck, and then cancel your early appointments—on sunny mornings, nobody checks out early.

30 El Portal (next to the Sausalito Ferry Landing), Sausalito, CA 94965. ℂ 800/893-8433 or 415/332-9535. Fax 415/332-6714. www.innabovetide.com. 29 units. $255–$795 double. Rates include continental breakfast and evening wine and cheese. AE, DC, MC, V. Valet parking $12. **Amenities:** Concierge; in-room massage; same-day laundry service/dry cleaning. *In room:* A/C, TV, dataport, minibar, fridge, hair dryer, free high-speed wireless Internet access.

EXPENSIVE

Casa Madrona ★★   Sooner or later most visitors to Sausalito look up and wonder at the ornate mansion on the hill. It's part of Casa Madrona, a hideaway by the bay built in 1885 by a wealthy lumber baron. The epitome of luxury in its day, the mansion had slipped into decay when John Gallagher purchased it in 1910 and converted it into a hotel. By 1976 it was damaged and facing the threat of demolition when John Mays acquired the property and revitalized the hotel. Successive renovations and extensions have added a rambling, New England–style building to the hillside below the main house. Now a certified historic landmark, the hotel offers whimsically decorated rooms, suites, and cottages, which are accessed by steep, gorgeously landscaped pathways. The 16 free-standing units and seven cottages are gussied up with contemporary decor, four-poster beds, and marble bathrooms. Other rooms in the mansion are decorated in a variety of styles; some have claw-foot tubs and others have fireplaces. Newer rooms overlook the water, with panoramic views of the San Francisco skyline and bay. The very classy Italian Poggio restaurant (see below) has been Sausalito's hottest new thing since its late-2003 opening.

801 Bridgeway, Sausalito, CA 94965. © 800/567-9524 or 415/332-0502. Fax 415/332-2537. www.casamadrona.com. 63 units. $255–$340 double; $430 suite. AE, DC, DISC, MC, V. Valet parking $20. Ferry: Walk across the street from the landing. From U.S. 101 north, take the 1st right after the Golden Gate Bridge (Alexander exit); Alexander becomes Bridgeway. **Amenities:** Restaurant; Jacuzzi; concierge; room service (breakfast and dinner); babysitting; laundry service; dry cleaning. *In room:* TV, VCR upon availability, minibar, coffeemaker, hair dryer, robes.

WHERE TO DINE
MODERATE

Guernica ✧ FRENCH/BASQUE   Established in 1974, Guernica is one of those funky old restaurants that you'd probably pass up for something more chic and modern down the street if you didn't know better. What? You don't know about Guernica's legendary paella? Well, now you do. Be sure to share it, 'cause it's large enough to feed three. Begin with an appetizer of mussels or escargots. Other main courses include grilled lamb shank and roasted duckling with orange sauce. Rich desserts include such specialties as crème brûlée, bread pudding, and crème caramel.

2009 Bridgeway. © 415/332-1512. Reservations recommended. Main courses $12–$18. AE, DC, MC, V. Daily 5–10pm. From U.S. 101 north, take the 1st right after the Golden Gate Bridge (Alexander exit); Alexander becomes Bridgeway in Sausalito.

Poggio ✧✧ ITALIAN   Sausalito has long been low on upscale dining options, but all that changed with the late-2003 opening of elegant "Poggio," which is a loose Italian translation for "special hillside place." Adjoining the Casa Madrona hotel and across the street from the marina, everything *is* special here, from the floor-to-ceiling doors opening to the sidewalk to its interior with arches and earthen colors, mahogany accents, well-directed light, and centerpiece wood-oven manned by a cadre of chefs to the wine cellar, terra-cotta-tiled floors, comfy mohair banquettes, and white linen-draped tables. Executive chef and partner Christopher Fernandez ensures the food is equally elegant with his superb salad of endive, Gorgonzola, walnuts, figs, and honey; pizzas; addictively excellent pastas (try the garganelli with squab Bolognese or spinach ricotta gnocchi with beef ragout); and superb entrees. (Think roasted halibut with faro, snap peas, mushrooms, and spring onion *brodo* and grilled lamb chops with roasted fennel and gremolata.) With a full bar, great, well-priced wine list, and yummy desserts, this is Sausalito's premier dining destination—excluding more casual and decidedly Asian restaurant Sushi Ran (see below).

777 Bridgeway (at Bay St.). © 415/332-7771. www.casamadrona.com. Continental breakfast pastries $2.50; main courses lunch $7.50–$16, dinner $7.50–$20. AE, MC, V. Continental breakfast daily 6:30–11:30am; lunch 11:30am–5:30pm; dinner Sun–Thurs 5:30–10pm, Fri–Sat 5:30–11pm. Free valet parking.

Sushi Ran ✧✧ SUSHI/JAPANESE   San Francisco isn't exactly stellar in its Japanese-food selection, but right across from the Golden Gate Bridge is a compact, but fashionable, destination for seriously delicious sushi and cooked dishes. All walks of sushi-loving life cram into the bar, window seats, and more roomy back dining area for standard and specialty rolls. You'll also find a slew of creative dishes such as generously sized and unbelievably moist and buttery miso-glazed black cod (a must-have), oysters on the half shell with ponzu sauce and *tobiko* (fish eggs), and a Hawaiian-style ahi *poke* (Hawaiian-style minced raw fish) salad with seaweed dressing that's authentic enough to make you want to hula. Pay the extra $2.50 or so for fresh wasabi, select from the fine sake and wine list, and don't miss dessert, because here they are more creative and delicious than those served at most Japanese restaurants.

107 Caledonia St. ✆ 415/332-3620. www.sushiran.com. Reservations recommended. Sushi $5–$14; main courses $8.50–$16. AE, DC, MC, V. Mon–Fri 11:45am–2:30pm and 5:30–11pm; Sat 5:30–11:30pm; Sun 5–10:30pm. From U.S. 101 north, take the 1st right after the Golden Gate Bridge (Alexander exit); Alexander becomes Bridgeway in Sausalito. At Johnson St. turn left, then right onto Caledonia.

PICNIC, ANYONE?

Even Sausalito's naysayers have to admit that it's hard not to enjoy eating your way down Bridgeway on a warm, sunny day. If the crowds are too much or the prices too steep at the bayside restaurants, grab a bite to go for an impromptu picnic in the park fronting the marina.

Hamburgers BURGERS   Like the name says, the specialty at this tiny, narrow cafe is juicy flame-broiled hamburgers, arguably Marin County's best. Look for the rotating grill in the window off Bridgeway, then stand in line and salivate with the rest. Chicken burgers are a slightly healthier option. Order a side of fries, grab a bunch of napkins, and head to the park across the street.

737 Bridgeway. ✆ 415/332-9471. Sandwiches $4.50–$6.25. No credit cards. Daily 11am–5pm. From U.S. 101 north, take the 1st right after the Golden Gate Bridge (Alexander exit); Alexander becomes Bridgeway in Sausalito.

5 Muir Woods & Mount Tamalpais

12 miles N of the Golden Gate Bridge

While the rest of Marin County's redwood forests were being devoured to feed San Francisco's turn-of-the-20th-century building spree, Muir Woods, in a remote ravine on the flanks of Mount Tamalpais, escaped destruction in favor of easier pickings.

MUIR WOODS

Although the magnificent California redwoods have been successfully transplanted to five continents, their homeland is a 500-mile strip along the mountainous coast of southwestern Oregon and Northern California. The coast redwood, or *Sequoia sempervirens,* is the tallest tree in the immediate region; the largest known specimen in the Redwood National Forest towers 368 feet. It has an even larger relative, the *Sequoiadendron giganteum* of the California Sierra Nevada, but the coastal variety is stunning enough. Soaring toward the sky like a wooden cathedral, Muir Woods is unlike any other forest in the world and an experience you won't soon forget.

Granted, Muir Woods is tiny compared to the Redwood National Forest farther north, but you can still get a pretty good idea of what it must have been like when these giants dominated the entire coastal region. What is truly amazing is that they exist a mere 6 miles (as the crow flies) from San Francisco—close enough, unfortunately, that tour buses arrive in droves on the weekends. You can avoid the masses by hiking up the **Ocean View Trail** and returning on the **Fern Creek Trail.** The moderately challenging hike shows off the woods' best sides and leaves the lazy-butts behind.

To reach Muir Woods from San Francisco, cross the Golden Gate Bridge heading north on Highway 101, take the Stinson Beach/Highway 1 exit heading west, and follow the signs (and the traffic). The park is open daily from 8am to sunset, and the admission fee is $3 per person over 16. There's also a small gift shop, educational displays, and a ranger talk. For more information, call

the **Muir Woods information line** (© **415/388-2595**) or visit www.visitmuir
woods.com.

If you don't have a car, you can book a bus trip with the **Red & White Fleet**
(© **877/855-5506** or 415/447-0597; www.redandwhite.com), which takes you
straight to Muir Woods and makes a short stop in Sausalito on the way back.
The 3½-hour tours run several times daily and cost $56 for adults, $31 for children 5 though 11; free for kids under 5. Call for information and departure
times.

MOUNT TAMALPAIS

The birthplace of mountain biking, Mount Tam—as the locals call it—is the
Bay Area's favorite outdoor playground and the most dominant mountain in the
region. Most every local has his or her secret trail and scenic overlook, as well as
an opinion on the raging debate between mountain bikers and hikers (a touchy
subject). The main trails—mostly fire roads—see a lot of foot and bicycle traffic on weekends, particularly on clear, sunny days when you can see a hundred
miles in all directions, from the foothills of the Sierra to the western horizon. It's
a great place to escape from the city for a leisurely hike and to soak in breathtaking views of the bay.

To get to Mount Tamalpais **by car,** cross the Golden Gate Bridge heading
north on Highway 101, and take the Stinson Beach/Highway 1 exit. Follow the
shoreline highway for about 2½ miles, turn onto Pantoll Road, and continue for
about a mile to Ridgecrest Boulevard. Ridgecrest winds to a parking lot below
East Peak. From there, it's a 15-minute hike up to the top.

6 Point Reyes National Seashore

35 miles N of San Francisco

The National Seashore system was created to protect rural and undeveloped
stretches of the coast from the pressures brought by soaring real-estate values and
increasing population. Nowhere is the success of the system more evident than
at Point Reyes. Residents of the surrounding towns—Inverness, Point Reyes Station, and Olema—have steadfastly resisted runaway development. You won't
find any strip malls or fast-food joints here, just laid-back coastal towns with
cafes and country inns, where gentle living prevails.

Although the peninsula's people and wildlife live in harmony above the
ground, the situation beneath the soil is much more volatile. The infamous San
Andreas Fault separates Point Reyes—the northernmost landmass on the Pacific
Plate—from the rest of California, which rests on the North American Plate.
Point Reyes is making its way toward Alaska at a rate of about 2 inches per year,
but at times it has moved much faster. In 1906, Point Reyes jumped north
almost 20 feet in an instant, leveling San Francisco and jolting the rest of the
state. The half-mile Earthquake Trail, near the Bear Valley Visitor Center, illus-
trates this geological drama with a loop through an area torn by the slipping
fault. Shattered fences, rifts in the ground, and a barn knocked off its foundation by the quake illustrate how alive the earth is. If that doesn't convince you,
a seismograph in the visitor center will.

ESSENTIALS

Point Reyes is only 30 miles northwest of San Francisco, but it takes at least 90
minutes to reach **by car** (it's all the small towns, not the topography, that slow
you down). The easiest route is Sir Francis Drake Boulevard from Highway 101

south of San Rafael; it takes its bloody time getting to Point Reyes, but it does so without any detours. For a much longer but more scenic route, take the Stinson Beach/Highway 1 exit off Highway 101 just south of Sausalito and follow Highway 1 north.

As soon as you arrive at Point Reyes, stop at the **Bear Valley Visitor Center** (© **415/464-5100;** www.nps.gov/pore) on Bear Valley Road (look for the small sign just north of Olema on Hwy. 1) and pick up a free Point Reyes trail map. The rangers are extremely friendly and helpful and can answer any questions about the National Seashore. Be sure to check out the great natural-history and cultural displays while you're there. The center is open weekdays from 9am to 5pm, weekends from 8am to 5pm.

Entrance to the park is free. **Camping** is $12 per site per night, and permits are required. Reservations can be made up to 3 months in advance by calling © 415/663-8054 Monday through Friday from 9am to 2pm.

WHAT TO SEE & DO

When headed to any part of the Point Reyes coast, expect to spend the day surrounded by nature at its finest; however, bear in mind that as beautiful as the wilderness can be, it's also untamed. The bone-chilling waters in these areas are not only home to a vast array of sea life, including sharks, but are unpredictable and dangerous. There are no lifeguards on duty, and swimming is strongly discouraged because of the waves and rip tides. Pets are not permitted on any of the area's trails.

By far the most popular—and crowded—attraction at Point Reyes National Seashore is the venerable **Point Reyes Lighthouse** ★ (© **415/669-1534**), at the westernmost tip of Point Reyes. Even if you plan to forgo the 308 steps to the lighthouse itself (sorry—no strollers or wheelchairs), the area is still worth a visit. The dramatic scenery includes thousands of common murres and prides of sea lions that bask on the rocks far below (binoculars come in handy).

The lighthouse is also the top spot on the California coast from which to observe **gray whales** as they make their southward and northward migrations along the coast January through April. The annual round-trip is 10,000 miles— one of the longest mammal migrations known. The whales head south in December and January and return north in March. *Note:* If you plan to drive to the lighthouse to whale-watch, arrive early because parking is limited. If possible, come on a weekday. On a weekend or holiday January through March, it's wise to park at the Drake's Beach Visitor Center and take the shuttle bus (weather permitting) to the lighthouse and on to Chimney Rock to watch elephant seals; the shuttle bus runs from around New Year's Day to the beginning of April and costs $3.50 for adults, free for children under 13. Dress warmly when you come here—it's often quite cold and windy—and bring binoculars.

Whale-watching is far from the only activity at the Point Reyes National Seashore. On weekend afternoons, many different tours are offered: You can walk along the Bear Valley Trail, spotting the wildlife at the ocean's edge; see the

---

Tips Whale Sightings

Rangers suggest that during the whales' southern migration (Jan), you should go to the lighthouse for the best view. During their northern migration (Mar), you can see 'em from any of the area's beaches.

Finds **Johnson's Oyster Farm**

If you want to escape the crowds and enjoy some stinky man-made entertainment, head to **Johnson's Oyster Farm**. Located on the edge of Drakes Estero (a large saltwater lagoon on the Point Reyes peninsula that produces nearly 20% of California's commercial oyster yield), Johnson's might look and smell like a dump, but those tasty bivalves don't come any fresher or cheaper. Granted, it doesn't look like much—a cluster of trailer homes, shacks, and oyster tanks surrounded by huge piles of oyster shells—but that certainly doesn't detract from the taste of fresh-out-of-the-water oysters dipped in Johnson's special sauce. The popular modus operandi is: 1) buy a couple of dozen; 2) head for an empty campsite along the bay; 3) fire up the barbecue pit (don't forget the charcoal); 4) split and barbecue the little guys; 5) slather them in Johnson's special sauce; and 6) slurp 'em down. Johnson's (© 415/669-1149) is off Sir Francis Drake Boulevard, about 6 miles west(ish) of Inverness. It's open Tuesday through Saturday from 8am to 4:30pm and Sunday from 9am to 4:30pm.

---

waterfowl at Fivebrooks Pond; explore tide pools; view some of North America's most beautiful ducks in the wetlands of Limantour; hike to the promontory overlooking Chimney Rock to see the sea lions, harbor seals, elephant seals, and seabirds; or take a guided walk along the San Andreas Fault to observe the epicenter of the 1906 earthquake and learn about the regional geology. And this is just a sampling. Tours vary seasonally; for the most up-to-date details, call the **Bear Valley Visitors Center** (© 415/464-5100) or request a copy of *Park Paper*, which includes a schedule of activities and other useful information. You can also get the lay of the land and more details by visiting the National Park Service's website (www.nps.gov/pore/pphtml/maps.html), which also has detailed area maps. *Note:* Many tours are suitable for travelers with disabilities.

Some of the park's best—and least crowded—highlights can be approached only on foot. They include **Alamere Falls,** a freshwater stream that cascades down a 40-foot bluff onto Wildcat Beach, and **Tomales Point Trail,** which passes through the Tule Elk Reserve, a protected haven for roaming herds of tule elk that once numbered in the thousands. Hiking most of the trails usually ends up being an all-day outing, however, so it's best to split a 2-day trip into a "by car" day and a "by foot" day.

If you're into bird-watching, you'll definitely want to visit the **Point Reyes Bird Observatory** (© 415/868-1221), one of the few full-time ornithological research stations in the United States. It's at the southeast end of the park on Mesa Road. This is where ornithologists keep an eye on more than 400 feathered species. Admission to the visitor center and nature trail is free, and visitors are welcome to observe the tricky process of catching and banding the birds. The observatory is open daily from 15 minutes after sunrise to sunset. Banding hours vary; contact them (© 415/868-0655l; www.prbo.org) for exact times.

One of my favorite things to do in Point Reyes is paddle through placid Tomales Bay, a haven for migrating birds and marine mammals. **Blue Waters Kayaking** ★ (© 415/663-1743; www.bwkayak.com) organizes kayak trips, including 3-hour sunset outings, oyster tours, day trips, and longer excursions. Instruction, clinics, and boat delivery are available, and all ages and levels are welcome. Prices for tours start at $59. Rentals begin at $35 for one person, $60 for two. Don't worry—the kayaks are very stable, and there are no waves to contend with. The launching point is on Highway 1 at the Marshall Boatworks in Marshall, 8 miles north of Point Reyes Station. Blue Waters is open daily April to October from 9am to 5pm and by appointment.

WHERE TO STAY

Inns of Marin, P.O. Box 547, Point Reyes Station, CA 94956 (© **800/887-2880** or 415/663-2000), is a free service that can help you find accommodations ranging from one-room cottages to inns to complete vacation homes. Many places have a 2-night minimum, but at slow times they might make an exception. The service can also refer you to restaurants, hiking trails, and area attractions.

EXPENSIVE

Manka's Inverness Lodge & Restaurant ★★★ *(Finds)* If there was ever a reason to pack your bags and leave San Francisco for a day or two, this is it. A former hunting and fishing lodge, Manka's looks like something out of a Hans Christian Andersen fairy tale, right down to the tree-limb bed stands and the cook's roasted venison sausage in front of the hearth. It's all terribly romantic in a Jack London–ish sort of way, and tastefully done. The lodge consists of a superb restaurant on the first floor, four rooms upstairs (room nos. 1 and 2 have large private decks), and four rooms in the Redwood Annex. Two spacious one-bedroom cabins, behind the lodge and on the water, have living rooms and kitchens. For the ultimate romantic splurge, inquire about the three secluded guesthouses: Boat House, Perch, and Cabin 125. The lodge's reputation was built on its rustic and romantic restaurant, which dominates the bottom floor and continues to make visitors swoon with house specialties of game and fish on its a la carte menu (main courses $18–$25) served Monday through Wednesday and its fixed-price menu ranging from $55 to $88 the rest of the week. The limited menu might feature pheasant with Madeira *jus,* mashed potatoes, and wild-huckleberry jam; black-buck antelope chops with sweet-corn salsa; or, everybody's favorite, pan-seared elk tenderloin. It's open for dinner nightly except for the first 6 weeks of the year, when the restaurant is closed.

30 Callendar Way. (at Argyle St., off Sir Francis Drake Blvd., ¼ mile north of downtown Inverness), P.O. Box 1110, Inverness, CA 94937. © **800/58-LODGE** or 415/669-1034. Fax 415/669-1598. www.mankas.com. 14 units, including 4 cabins. $215–$365 double; $335–$565 cabin. AE, MC, V. **Amenities:** Restaurant; limited room service; in-room massage; free high-speed Internet access.

INEXPENSIVE

Motel Inverness *(Kids)* Finding an inexpensive place to stay in Point Reyes is next to impossible, because hoity-toity B&Bs reign supreme. There is, however, one exception—Motel Inverness, a homey, well-maintained lodging fronting Tomales Bay. For the outdoor adventurer who plans to spend as little time indoors as possible, it's the perfect place to hole up. (Those seeking romance should dig a little deeper into their pockets and opt for Manka's; see above.) All of the guest rooms but one twin-bed option have queen-size beds and skylights. Attached to the hotel is a giant great room, complete with fireplace and pool table to distract the kids; parents can relax and children can play on the back lawn overlooking the bay, bird sanctuary, and rolling green hills beyond. The two-bedroom suite, which has a king-size bed and a kitchenette, is ideal for families, as is the Dacha cottage, which is on the water and boasts three bedrooms. *Note:* The motel is nonsmoking.

12718 Sir Francis Drake Blvd., Inverness, CA 94937. ℰ **888/669-6909** or 415/669-1081. 8 units. $99–$175 double; $400–$500 suite. MC, V. *In room:* TV, coffeemaker.

WHERE TO DINE

See "Where to Stay," above, for details on the highly recommended **Manka's Inverness Lodge & Restaurant.**

MODERATE

Station House Café ✷ AMERICAN   For more than 2 decades, the Station House Café has been a favorite pit stop for Bay Area residents headed to and from Point Reyes. It's a friendly, low-key place with an open kitchen, an outdoor garden dining area (key on sunny days), and live music on weekend nights. Breakfast dishes include a Hangtown omelet with local oysters and bacon, and eggs with creamed spinach and mashed-potato pancakes. Lunch and dinner specials might be fettuccine with fresh local mussels steamed in white wine and butter sauce, two-cheese polenta served with fresh spinach sauté and grilled garlic-buttered tomato, or a daily fresh salmon special—all made from local produce, seafood, and organically raised Niman Ranch beef. The cafe has an extensive list of fine California wines and local imported beers.

Main St., Point Reyes Station. ℰ **415/663-1515.** Reservations recommended. Breakfast $4.50–$8.50; main courses $7–$11 lunch, $9–$25 dinner. DISC, MC, V. Sun–Tues and Thurs 8am–9pm; Fri–Sat 8am–10pm.

INEXPENSIVE

Taqueria La Quinta ✷ MEXICAN   Fresh, good, fast, and cheap: What more could you ask for in a restaurant? Taqueria La Quinta has been a favorite lunch stop in downtown Point Reyes for years and years. A huge selection of Mexican-American standards is posted above the counter, where you'll place your order, but those in the know inquire about the seafood specials. Watch out for the salsa—that sucker's hot.

11285 Hwy. 1 (at Third and Main sts.), Point Reyes Station. ℰ **415/663-8868.** Main courses $4–$9. No credit cards. Wed–Mon 11:30am–8pm.

12

The Wine Country

Even if you're having the time of your life in downtown San Francisco, I highly recommend at least a quick jaunt to the Wine Country, an hour or so north by car. Amid the mountains dipping into a grapevine-trellised valley, you'll experience an entirely different Northern California: fresh country air, mustard-flower-draped hillsides in spring, hot weather (during summer), some of the world's finest wineries, incredible restaurants, green pastures, and virtually nothing to do but overindulge. With eating, drinking, and lounging the encouraged attractions, there's virtually no better definition of a vacation than a few days here. Spend even 1 day here and you'll understand why this native San Franciscan chooses to call Wine Country home.

To decide which of the Wine Country's two distinct valleys (Napa and Sonoma) you prefer to visit, you need to consider their differences: The most obvious is size—Napa Valley dwarfs Sonoma Valley in population, number of wineries, and sheer volume of tourism (and traffic). Napa is definitely the more commercial of the two, with many more wineries to visit and spas (at far cheaper rates) to choose from, and a superior selection of fine restaurants, hotels, and quintessential Wine Country activities, like hot-air ballooning. Furthermore, if your goal is to really learn about the wonderful world of winemaking, Napa Valley should be your choice. World-class wineries such as Sterling and Robert Mondavi offer the most interesting and edifying wine tours in North America, if not the world (although Sonoma's Benziger Winery does give them a run for their money).

Meanwhile, Sonoma Valley is the answer for those who are in the less-is-more camp. Napa Valley's neighbor has fewer wineries (about 35), fewer big hotels and restaurants, and a less commercial feel. As a result, there are fewer crowds on the low-key country roads; more down-home charm in the country communities, B&Bs, and little family-run restaurants; and, in general, more opportunities for intimate pastoral experiences. For more on Sonoma Valley's offerings (as spectacular as Napa Valley's but more low-key), see the "Sonoma Valley" section.

If you're planning a more extensive trip to the area, consult *Frommer's Portable California Wine Country.*

1 Napa Valley

Just 55 miles north of San Francisco, the city of Napa and its neighboring towns have an overall tourist and big-business feel. You'll see plenty of rolling hills, flora and fauna, and vast stretches of vineyards, but they come hand-in-hand with upscale restaurants, designer discount outlets, rows of hotels and, in summer, plenty of traffic. Even with hordes of visitors year-round, Napa is still pretty sleepy, focusing on daytime attractions (wine, outdoor activities, and spas) and, of course, food. Nightlife is very limited, but after indulging all day, most visitors are ready to turn in early anyway.

Although the name "Napa Valley" seems sprawling, the actual area is relatively condensed and only 35 miles long. You can venture from the town of Napa all the way to Calistoga in half an hour (traffic permitting).

ESSENTIALS

GETTING THERE   From San Francisco, cross the Golden Gate Bridge and continue north on U.S. 101. Turn east on California Highway 37 (the fastest way is to skip the 12/121 turnoff and continue to Vallejo), then north on Highway 29, the main road through the Wine Country.

Highway 29 (the St. Helena Hwy.) runs the length of Napa Valley. You really can't get lost—there's just one north-south road, on which most of the wineries, hotels, shops, and restaurants are located.

VISITOR INFORMATION   Once you're in Napa Valley, you can stop at the **Napa Valley Conference & Visitors Bureau,** 1310 Town Center Mall, Napa, CA 94559 (© 707/226-7459; www.napavalley.org). It offers a $10 package that includes *The Napa Valley Guide,* a bunch of brochures, a map, and a "Four Perfect Days in The Wine Country" itinerary. If you don't want to pay the bucks for the official publications, point your browser to www.napavalley.org, the NVCVB's official site, which has lots of the same information for free.

TOURING THE NAPA VALLEY & WINERIES

Napa Valley claims 37,000 acres of vineyards, making it the most densely planted wine-growing region in the United States. The venture from one end to the other is easy; you can drive it in around half an hour (but expect it to take closer to 50 min. during high season, Apr–Nov). With nearly 300 wineries tucked into the nooks and crannies surrounding Highway 29 and the Silverado Trail—almost all of which offer tastings and sales—it's worthwhile to research which wineries you'd like to visit before you hit the wine trails. If you'd like a map outlining all of the region's wineries, you can grab one from the visitor center or see *Frommer's Portable California Wine Country.*

Conveniently, most of the large wineries—as well as most of the hotels, shops, and restaurants—are along a single road, Highway 29. It starts at the mouth of the Napa River, near the north end of San Francisco Bay, and continues north to Calistoga and the northern limits of the grape-growing region. When planning your tour, keep in mind that most wineries are closed on major holidays.

All of the Napa Valley establishments in this chapter—every town, winery, hotel, and restaurant—is organized below from south to north, beginning in the city of Napa, and can be reached from the main thoroughfare of Highway 29.

NAPA
55 miles N of San Francisco

The city of Napa serves as the commercial center of the Wine Country and the gateway to Napa Valley—hence the high-speed freeway that whips you right past it and on to the "tourist" towns of St. Helena and Calistoga. However, if you veer off the highway, you'll be surprised to discover a small but burgeoning community of nearly 73,000 residents with the most cosmopolitan (if you can call it that) atmosphere in the county—and some of the most affordable accommodations in the valley. It is in the process of gentrification, thanks to (relatively) affordable housing, a charming old-fashioned downtown, and new restaurants and attractions like Copia: The American Center for Wine, Food & the Arts (p. 283). Heading north on either Highway 29 or the Silverado Trail

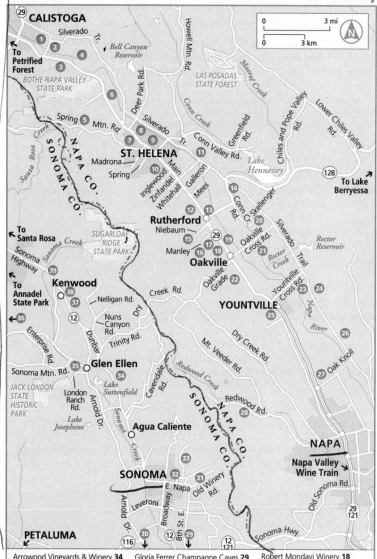

The Wine Country

0 ___ 3 mi
0 ___ 3 km

CALISTOGA (29)

Silverado Tr.

① ② ④ ③

To Petrified Forest

Bell Canyon Reservoir

BOTHE-NAPA VALLEY STATE PARK

⑥

Howell Mtn. Rd.

LAS POSADAS STATE FOREST

Moores Creek

Spring ⑤ Mtn. Rd.

Silverado Tr.

⑦ ⑧ ⑨

ST. HELENA

Madrona

Spring ⑩

Inglewood
Zinfandel
Whitehall
Main
Galleron
Mees

⑪

Conn Valley Rd.

Deer Park Rd.

Conn Creek

Greenfield Rd.

Chiles and Pope Valley Rd.

Lower Chiles Valley Rd.

Lake Hennessey

(128)

To Lake Berryessa

S O N O M A   C O.

N A P A   C O.

Santa Rosa Creek

To Santa Rosa

Sonoma Highway

SUGARLOAF RIDGE STATE PARK

Sonoma Creek

⑭ Conn Cr. Rd.

Skellenger

⑳

Rutherford

Niebaum ⑮

Manley ⑯ ⑰ ⑱ (29)

Oakville

Oakville Cross Rd.

㉑

Silverado Trail

Rector Reservoir

Rector Creek

Oakville Grade ㉒

Creek Rd.

Yountville Cross Rd.

㉓ ㉔

YOUNTVILLE

㉕

Napa River

To Annadel State Park

㉛ **Kenwood** ㊳ ㊲

Nelligan Rd.

Nuns Canyon Rd.

Dry Creek Rd.

Trinity Rd.

(12)

Dunbar

㊱

Enterprise Rd.

㉟

Glen Ellen

Sonoma Mtn. Rd.

Lake Suttonfield

㉞

London Ranch Rd.

Arnold Dr.

JACK LONDON STATE HISTORIC PARK

Lake Josephine

Sonoma Creek

Redwood Creek

Cavendale Rd.

Mt. Veeder Rd.

Dry Creek Rd.

Redwood Rd.

㉘

S O N O M A   C O.

N A P A   C O.

Oak Knoll

㉗

㉖

Agua Caliente

㉝

SONOMA

㉜

E. Napa

Old Winery Rd.

㉛

NAPA

Napa Valley Wine Train

Arnold Dr.

Leveroni

Broadway

8th St. E.

㉚ (12) ㉙

PETALUMA

(116)

Old Sonoma Rd.

(29)(121)

Sonoma Hwy.

(12)(121)

Arrowood Vineyards & Winery **34**
Beaulieu Vineyard **13**
Benziger Family Winery **35**
Beringer Vineyard **7**
Buena Vista Winery **31**
Charles Krug Winery **8**
Château St. Jean **38**
Clos Du Val **26**
Clos Pegase **1**
Cosentino **22**
Domaine Chandon **25**
Duckhorn Vineyards **6**
Frank Family Vineyards **4**

Gloria Ferrer Champagne Caves **29**
Grgich Hills Cellar **12**
The Hess Collection **28**
Joseph Phelps Vineyards **11**
Kenwood Vineyards **37**
Matanzas Creek **36**
Mumm Napa Valley **14**
Niebaum-Coppola **15**
Opus One **19**
Pine Ridge Winery **23**
PlumpJack Winery **20**
Prager Winery & Port Works **10**
Ravenswood Winery **33**
Robert Keenan Winery **5**

Robert Mondavi Winery **18**
St. Francis Winery **39**
St. Supéry Winery **17**
Sawyer Cellars **17**
Schramsberg **3**
Sebastiani Vineyards **32**
Silver Oak Cellars **21**
Stag's Leap Wine Cellars **24**
Sterling Vineyards **2**
Swanson Vineyards & Winery **16**
Trefethen Vineyards **27**
V. Sattui Winery **9**
Viansa Winery and Italian
  Marketplace **30**

271

Tips   Reservations at Wineries

Plenty of wineries' doors are open to everyone between 10am and 4:30pm. Most wineries that require reservations for visits do so because of local permits laws. It's always best to call ahead if you have your heart set on visiting a certain winery. A few wineries limit the number of guests to create a more intimate experience. In many cases, however, they'll be just as happy to see you if you arrive unannounced.

---

leads you to Napa's wineries and the more quintessential Wine Country atmosphere of vineyards and wide-open country views.

The Hess Collection ★★ *Finds*   The drive itself is quintessential country splendor. Once at Hess, tucked into the hillside of rural Mount Veeder, you'll discover one of the region's sexiest stops. This winery brings art and wine together like no other destination in the valley. In 1978, Swiss art collector Donald Hess transformed the Christian Brothers' 1903 property into a winery-cum–art gallery with gloriously lit rooms exhibiting huge, colorful works by the likes of Frank Stella and Francis Bacon. A free self-guided tour leads through Hess's collection and offers glimpses into the winemaking facilities. Equally alluring are the tranquil gardens and exceptionally tasteful gift shop. *The only downside:* Staff can be cold and stuffy. For $5, you can sample the current cabernet and chardonnay and one other featured wine. For bottles, current-release prices start at $9.95 and top off at around $35.

4411 Redwood Rd., Napa. ⓒ 707/255-1144. www.hesscollection.com. Daily 10am–4pm, except some holidays. From Hwy. 29 north, exit at Redwood Rd. west, and follow Redwood Rd. for 6½ miles.

Trefethen Vineyards   Listed on the National Register of Historic Places, the vineyard's main building was built in 1886 and is Napa's last example of 19th century wooden, gravity-flow wineries. Although Trefethen is one of the valley's oldest wineries, it didn't produce its first chardonnay until 1973—but thank goodness it did. The award-winning whites and reds are a pleasure to the palate. Tastings are $10 for four estate wines, but if you want to sample a reserve, it'll cost you $20.

1160 Oak Knoll Ave. (east of Hwy. 29), Napa. ⓒ 707/255-7700. www.trefethen.com. Daily 10am–4:30pm. From Hwy 29 north, take a right onto Oak Knoll Ave.

Clos Du Val   The beautiful, ivy-covered building and well-manicured rose garden set the scene for a romantic wine-tasting experience. Inside, the friendly, small-business atmosphere completes the all-around welcoming ambience.

Bordeaux-born founder and winemaker Bernard Portet and his newer, younger counterpart John Clews are responsible for what ends up in the glass; Portet has garnered a reputation for his cabernet (which makes up 70% of the winery's production). Other varietals include chardonnay, pinot noir, and merlot. You can try them all in the rather matter-of-fact tasting room. There's a $5 tasting charge (refunded with purchase) for about four wines, which may include a library selection or two.

Lovely picnic facilities and the lawn game *petanque* are available in grassy nooks along the grounds. A bonus is the friendly, helpful staff, which happily offers directions to other wineries, along with a small map.

5330 Silverado Trail (north of Oak Knoll Ave.), Napa. ⓒ 707/259-2200. Daily 10am–5pm. Tours by appointment only.

Stag's Leap Wine Cellars Founded in 1972, Stag's Leap shocked the oeno-logical world in 1976 when its 1973 cabernet won first place over French wines in a Parisian blind tasting. Visit the charmingly landscaped, unfussy winery and its very cramped "tasting room" where, for $10 per person, you can judge the four to six current releases; or you can fork over up to $30 for estate samples. A 1-hour tour and tasting runs through everything from the vineyard and pro-duction facilities to the ultraswank $5-million wine caves (used to store and age wine), which premiered in mid-2001.

5766 Silverado Trail, Napa. ⓒ 707/944-2020. www.cask23.com. Daily 10am–4:30pm. Tours by appointment only. From Hwy. 29, go east on Trancas St. or Oak Knoll Ave., then north to the cellars.

Pine Ridge Winery A pretty hillside location, less tourist traffic than most, good wines, and visitor-friendly touches are the reasons to pull off the Silverado Trail to Pine Ridge. Outside, vineyards surround the well-landscaped property, and a surprising number of picnic tables are perched on a knoll with grapes trel-lised along the hillside above. Across the parking lot is a demonstration vineyard, which is somewhat educational if you know something about grape growing and even more helpful if you take their tour (by appointment), which also covers the cellar and barrel tastings. Tastings, which are held inside a modest room, don't come cheaply, but they are refunded with the purchase of four bottles of wine. Current-release tastings go for $10; limited-release tastings cost $15. Private-reserve tastings, at $30, are held daily; call for times.

5901 Silverado Trail, Napa. ⓒ 800/575-9777 or 707/253-7500. www.pineridgewinery.com. Daily 10:30am–4:30pm. Tours by appointment at 10am, noon, and 2pm.

YOUNTVILLE

70 miles N of San Francisco

Yountville (pop. 2,916) was founded by the first white American to settle in the valley, George Calvert Yount. While it lacks the small-town charm of neighbor-ing St. Helena and Calistoga—primarily because its main street, though filling up with hotels, restaurants, and shops, doesn't feel like a center—it's still a great starting point for valley exploration. It's home to a handful of excellent wineries and inns and a small stretch of fab restaurants, including the world-renowned French Laundry.

Domaine Chandon ★★ *Finds* Founded in 1973 by French champagne house Moët et Chandon, the valley's most renowned sparkling winemaker rises to the grand occasion with truly elegant grounds and atmosphere. Here quintessen-tially manicured gardens showcase locally made sculpture, and guests linger—their glasses fizzing with bubbly—under the patio's umbrella shade. In the

---

Tips **Napa Valley Traffic**

Travel the Silverado Trail as often as possible to avoid California Highway 29's traffic. The Silverado Trail runs parallel to and about 2 miles east of Highway 29. You get there from the city of Napa or by taking any of the "cross roads" from Highway 29. Cross roads are not well signposted, but they're clearly defined on most maps. Avoid passing through Main Street in St. Helena during high season. While a wintertime ride from Napa to Calistoga can take 30 minutes, in summer you can expect the trek to take closer to 50 minutes.

---

restaurant, diners indulge in a formal French-inspired meal. If you can pull yourself away from the Salon's bubbly (sold in tastings for $9–$14), the comprehensive tour of the facilities is interesting, very informative, and friendly. There's also a shop, artifacts from Moët et Chandon that depict the history of champagnes, and revolving exhibits of art (available for purchase). *Note:* The restaurant, which is closed on Tuesday and Wednesday, usually requires reservations.

1 California Dr. (at Hwy. 29), Yountville. (Ⓒ) 707/944-2280. www.chandon.com. Daily 10am–6pm; hours vary by season, so call to confirm. Call for free tour schedules.

Cosentino   Known for its friendly, laid-back atmosphere and vast selection of wines, Cosentino is a great stop for anyone interested in covering a lot of wine-tasting ground under one roof. Pay $5 to taste ($10 for reserve wines) and you'll get to keep the glass, plus sample an array of wines from their portfolio, which includes the brands Cosentino, CE2V, and Crystal Valley Cellars. With jazz music playing in the background and nearly 40 different wines on sale ($12–$100), there's lots of entertainment value at the long copper-top bar. Join the wine club for free tastings and 25% off purchases, and keep an eye out for case discounts. During my last visit they were up to 30% off.

7415 St. Helena Hwy. (Hwy. 29), Yountville. (Ⓒ) 707/944-1220. www.cosentinowinery.com. Daily 10am–5pm (until 5:30pm during daylight saving time).

OAKVILLE
68 miles N of San Francisco

Driving farther north on Highway 29 brings you to Oakville, most easily recognized by Oakville Cross Road.

Silver Oak Cellars   Colorado oil man Ray Duncan and former Christian Brothers monk Justin Meyer formed a partnership and a mission to create the finest cabernet sauvignon in the world. The answer was this winery, which produces one of the valley's cabernet kings.

A narrow, tree-lined road leads to the handsome Mediterranean-style winery, where roughly 20,000 cases of 100% varietal cab are produced annually (an additional 40,000 cases are produced annually at their Alexander Valley winery in Geyserville). The elegant tasting room is refreshingly quiet and soothing, adorned with redwood panels stripped from old wine tanks and warmed by a wood fire. Tastings, which include a keepsake burgundy glass, are $10. No picnic facilities are available.

915 Oakville Cross Rd. (at Money Rd.), Oakville. (Ⓒ) 707/944-8808. www.silveroak.com. Tasting room Mon–Sat 9am–4pm. Tours Mon–Fri at 1:30pm, by appointment only.

PlumpJack Winery   If most wineries are like a Brooks Brothers suit, Plump-Jack stands out as the Todd Oldham of wine tasting: chic, colorful, a little wild, and popular with a young, hip crowd as well as a growing number of aficionados. Like the franchise's PlumpJack restaurant and wine shop in San Francisco and its resort at Lake Tahoe, this playfully medieval winery is a welcome diversion from the same old same old. With Getty bucks behind what was once Villa Mt. Eden winery, the budget covers far more than just atmosphere: There's some serious winemaking going on here, too. For $5 you can sample the cabernet, merlot, and chardonnay—each an impressive product from a winery that's only been open to the public since mid-1997. There are no tours or picnic spots, but this refreshingly stylized, friendly facility will make you want to hang out for a while nonetheless.

620 Oakville Cross Rd. (just west of the Silverado Trail), Oakville. ☎ **707/945-1220**. www.plumpjack.com. Daily 10am–4pm.

Robert Mondavi Winery ★ *Finds*   At mission-style Mondavi, computers control almost every variable in the winemaking process—it's fascinating to watch, especially since Mondavi gives the most comprehensive tours in the valley. Basic jaunts, which last about an hour, take you through the vineyards—complete with examples of varietals—and through their newest winemaking facilities. Ask the guides anything; they know a heck of a lot. After the tour, you can taste the results of all this attention to detail in selected current wines ($10). If you're really into learning more about wine, ask about in-depth tours. The "essence tasting" includes the opportunity to compare wine with the scents of fruits, spices, nuts, and more in individual glasses. An "appellation tour" includes a picnic lunch in the vineyards. You can also taste without taking a tour in the Appellation Room (an outdoor tasting area open in summer) and ToKalon Room, where a 3-ounce taste will cost you $5, a rare library wine taste $30.

The "Art of Wine and Food" program on Friday includes a slide presentation on the history of wine, a tour of the winery, and a three-course luncheon with wine pairing; the cost is around $95, and you must reserve in advance. In summer, the winery also schedules some great outdoor concerts, which sell out far in advance. Call about upcoming events.

7801 St. Helena Hwy. (Hwy. 29), Oakville. ☎ **800/MONDAVI** or 707/226-1395. www.robertmondaviwinery. com. Daily 10am–4pm. Reservations recommended for guided tour; book 1 week ahead, especially for weekend tours.

Opus One   A visit to Opus One is a serious and stately affair developed in partnership between Robert Mondavi and Baron Phillipe de Rothschild, who, after years of discussion, embarked on this state-of-the-art collaboration. Architecture buffs in particular will appreciate the tour, which takes in both the impressive Greco-Roman-meets-20th-century building and the no-holds-barred ultra-high-tech production and aging facilities.

This entire facility caters to one ultrapremium wine, which is offered here for a whopping $25 per 4-ounce taste (and a painful $150 per bottle). But wine lovers should happily fork over the cash: It's a memorable red. Grab your glass and head to the redwood rooftop deck to enjoy the view.

7900 St. Helena Hwy. (Hwy. 29), Oakville. ☎ **707/944-9442**. www.opusonewinery.com. Daily 10am–4pm. Tours by appointment only; in high season, book a month in advance.

RUTHERFORD
3 miles N of Oakville

If you so much as blink after Oakville, you're likely to overlook Rutherford, the next small town that borders on St. Helena. Each town in Napa Valley has its share of spectacular wineries, but you won't see most of them while driving along Highway 29.

Swanson Vineyards & Winery ★ *Finds*   The valley's most posh and unique wine tasting is yours with a reservation and a $25-to-$45 fee at Swanson. Here the shtick is more like a private party, which they call a "SA-lon." You and up to seven other guests sit at a centerpiece round table in a vibrant coral parlor adorned with huge paintings, seashells, and a fireplace, and take in the uncommonly refined yet whimsical atmosphere. The table's set more for a dinner party than for a tasting, with Reidel stemware, slivers of a fine cheese or two, crackers, and one superb chocolate Alexis ganache-filled bonbon, which you will be glad to know can be purchased on the premises. Over the course of the hour-or-more snack-and-sip event, a winery host will pour four to seven wines and discuss the history and fine points of each. You're likely to be in store for a bright pinot gri-gio, merlot, and hearty Alexis, their signature cab-syrah blend. Just as important to the experience are the conversation and the making of new friends (which almost invariably occurs, because the experience puts everyone in such a festive mood). Definitely a must-do for those who don't mind spending the money.

1271 Manley Lane, Rutherford. (C) 707/967-3500. www.swansonvineyards.com. Appointments available Wed–Sun 11am, 1:30pm, and 4pm.

Sawyer Cellars *Finds*   The most attractive thing about Sawyer, aside from its clean and tasty wines, is its dedication to extremely high quality while it main-tains a humble, accommodating attitude. Step into the simple restored 1920s barn to see what I mean. Whatever you ask, the tasting-room host will answer. Whatever your request, they do their best to accommodate it. Want to picnic on the back patio overlooking the vineyards? Be their guest. Like to participate in a crush? Come on over and get your hands dirty. Reserve their charming wine library for a private luncheon? Pay a minimal fee and make yourself at home. Here you can tour the property on a little tram or learn more about winemaker Brad Warner, who spent 30 years at Mondavi before embarking on this exclu-sive endeavor. Plunk down $5 to taste delicious estate-made wines: sauvignon blanc, merlot, cabernet sauvignon, and Meritage ($15–$46 for current releases), which some argue are worth twice the price. With a total production of only 4,200 cases and a friendly attitude, this winery is a rare treat.

8350 St. Helena Hwy. (Hwy. 29), Rutherford. (C) 707/963-1980. www.sawyercellars.com. Tasting by appoint-ment. Tours by appointment.

St. Supéry Winery *Kids*   The outside may look like a modern corporate office building, but inside you'll find a functional, welcoming winery that encourages first-time tasters to learn more about oenology. On the self-guided tour, you can wander through the demonstration vineyard, where you'll learn about growing techniques. Inside, kids gravitate toward coloring books and "SmellaVision," an interactive display that teaches you how to identify different wine ingredients. Adjoining it is the Atkinson House, which chronicles more than 100 years of winemaking history. For $5, you'll get lifetime tasting privileges and a tour, which includes samples of delicious sauvignon blanc, chardonnay, cab, and more. Even the prices make visitors feel at home: Many bottles go for around $22, although the tag on the 1997 Dollarhide Ranch cabernet says $70.

8440 St. Helena Hwy. (Hwy. 29), Rutherford. (C) 800/942-0809 or 707/963-4507. www.stsupery.com. Daily 10am–5pm (until 5:30pm during summer). $5 tour at 1pm and 3pm daily.

Niebaum-Coppola   Hollywood meets Napa Valley at Francis Ford Coppola's historic Inglenook Vineyards, now known as Niebaum-Coppola (*Nee*-bom *Coh*-pa-la). From the outside, the spectacular 1880s ivy-draped stone winery and grounds are historic grandeur. From the inside, it's one big retail center pro-moting Coppola's products and, more subtly, films. On display are Academy Awards and memorabilia from *The Godfather* and *Bram Stoker's Dracula;* the Centennial Museum chronicles the history of the estate and its winemaking as well as Coppola's filmmaking. Wine, food, and gift items dominate the cav-ernous tasting area, where wines such as an estate-grown blend, cabernet Franc, merlot, chardonnay, zinfandel, and others made from organically grown grapes are sampled for a steep $12 to $30 (price includes a souvenir glass). Bottles range from around $10 to more than $100. The château and garden tour is one of the most expensive in the valley at $25 a pop, though the 1½-hour journey includes a private tasting and a glass. *Tip:* Drop by, snoop around on your own, and spend the cash you save on one more bottle for your vacation collection.

1991 St. Helena Hwy. (Hwy. 29), Rutherford. © 707/968-1100. www.niebaum-coppola.com. Sept–May daily 10am–5pm; June–Aug daily 10am–6pm. Tours daily at 10:30am, 12:30pm, and 2:30pm.

Beaulieu Vineyard   Bordeaux native Georges de Latour founded the third-oldest continuously operating winery in Napa Valley in 1900. With the help of legendary oenologist André Tchelistcheff, he has produced world-class, award-winning wines that have been served by every president of the United States since Franklin D. Roosevelt. The brick-and-redwood tasting room isn't much to look at, but with Beaulieu's (*Bowl*-you) stellar reputation, it has no need to visually impress. Tastings cost $5, and a variety of bottles sell for under $20. The Private Reserve Tasting Room offers a "flight" of five reserve wines to taste for $25, but if you want to take a bottle to go, it may cost as much as $130.

1960 St. Helena Hwy. (Hwy. 29), Rutherford. © 707/967-5230. www.bvwines.com. Daily 10am–5pm.

Grgich Hills Cellar   Croatian émigré Miljenko (Mike) Grgich (*Grr*-gitch) made his presence known to the world when his 1973 Château Montelena chardonnay bested the top French white burgundies at the famous 1976 Paris tasting. Since then, the master vintner has teamed up with Austin Hills (of the Hills Brothers coffee fortune) and started this extremely successful and respected winery.

The ivy-covered stucco building isn't much to behold, and the tasting room is even less appealing, but people don't come here for the scenery: As you might expect, Grgich's chardonnays are legendary—and priced accordingly. The smart buys are the outstanding zinfandel and cabernet sauvignon, which cost around $25 and $50, respectively. The winery also produces a fantastic fumé blanc for as little as $18 a bottle. Before you leave, be sure to poke your head into the barrel-aging room and inhale the divine aroma. Tastings cost $5 (which includes the glass) on weekends. No picnic facilities are available.

1829 St. Helena Hwy. (Hwy. 29), north of Rutherford Cross Rd., Rutherford. © 707/963-2784. www.grgich. com. Daily 9:30am–4:30pm. $10 tours by appointment only, Mon–Fri 11am and 2pm; Sat–Sun 11am and 1:30pm.

Mumm Napa Valley   At first glance, Mumm, housed in a big redwood barn, looks almost humble. Once you're through the front door, however, you'll know that they mean business—big business. Just beyond the extensive gift shop (filled with all sorts of namesake mementos) is the tasting room, where you can purchase sparkling wine by the glass ($5–$8), three-wine flights ($8–$25), or the bottle ($16–$70), and appreciate breathtaking vineyard and mountain views. Unfortunately, there's no food or picnicking here, but during warm weather, out on the open patio with a glass of champagne in hand, you'll forget all about nibbling. Mumm also offers a 45-minute educational tour and is worth visiting if only to take a gander at its impressive art gallery, which features a permanent Ansel Adams collection and ever-changing photography exhibits.

8445 Silverado Trail (just south of Rutherford Cross Rd.), Rutherford. © 800/686-6272 or 707/942-3434. www.mummnapa.com. Daily 10am–5pm. Tours offered every hour daily 10am–3pm.

ST. HELENA
73 miles N of San Francisco

Located 17 miles north of Napa on Highway 29, this former Seventh-Day Adventist village maintains a pseudo–Old West feel while catering to upscale shoppers with deep pockets—hence Vanderbilt and Company, purveyor of fine housewares, at 1429 Main St. St. Helena is a quiet, attractive little town, where you'll find a slew of beautiful old homes and first-rate restaurants and accommodations.

V. Sattui Winery ★ *Kids* *Finds* So what if it's touristy and crowded? This enormous winery is also a fun picnic-party stop thanks to a huge gourmet deli and grassy expanse. It's especially great for families since you can fill up on wine, pâté, and cheese samples without ever reaching for your pocketbook, while the kids romp around the grounds. The gourmet store stocks more than 200 cheeses, sandwich meats, pâtés, breads, exotic salads, and desserts such as white-chocolate cheesecake. (It would be an easy place to graze were it not for the continuous mob scene at the counter.) Meanwhile, the wine flows at the long wine bar in the back, which offers everything from chardonnay, sauvignon blanc, Riesling, cabernet, and zinfandel to Madeira and muscat. Wines aren't distributed, so if you taste something you simply must have, buy it. (If you buy a case, ask to talk with a manager, who'll give you access to the less crowded, more exclusive private tasting room.) Wine prices start at around $9, with many in the $15 neighborhood; reserves top out at around $75. *Note:* To use the picnic area, you must buy food and wine here.

1111 White Lane (at Hwy. 29), St. Helena. ℂ **707/963-7774**. www.vsattui.com. Winter daily 9am–5pm; summer daily 9am–6pm.

Prager Winery & Port Works *Finds* If you want a real down-home, off-the-beaten-track experience, Prager's can't be beat. Turn the corner from Sutter Home winery and roll into the small gravel parking lot; you're on the right track, but when you pull open the creaky old wooden door to this shack of a wine-tasting room, you'll begin to wonder. Don't turn back! Pass the oak barrels, and you'll quickly come upon the clapboard tasting room, made homey with a big Oriental rug, and, during winter, a small space heater. Often, your host will be a Prager family member. Fork over $10 (includes a complimentary glass), and they'll pour you samples of late-harvest Johannesburg Riesling and the tawny port (which costs $45 per bottle and has won various awards). Also available is "Prager Chocolate Drizzle," a chocolate liqueur that tops ice creams and other desserts. If you're looking for a special gift, consider their bottles, which can be custom etched in the design of your choice for around $75, plus the cost of the wine.

1281 Lewelling Lane (just west of Hwy. 29, behind Sutter Home), St. Helena. ℂ **800/969-PORT** or 707/963-7678. www.pragerport.com. Daily 10:30am–4:30pm.

Joseph Phelps Vineyards ★ Visitors interested in intimate, comprehensive tours and a knockout tasting should schedule a tour at this winery. A quick turn off the Silverado Trail in Spring Valley (there's no sign—watch for Taplin Rd., or you'll blast right by), Joseph Phelps was founded in 1973 and is a major player in both the region and the worldwide wine market. Phelps himself accomplished a long list of valley firsts, including launching the syrah varietal in the valley and extending the 1970s Berkeley food revolution (led by Alice Waters) to the Wine Country by founding the Oakville Grocery Co. (p. 298).

A favorite stop for serious wine lovers, this modern, state-of-the-art winery and big-city vibe are proof that Phelps's annual 95,000 cases prove fruitful in more ways than one. When you pass the wisteria-covered trellis to the entrance of the redwood building, you'll encounter an air of seriousness that hangs heavier than harvest grapes. Fortunately, the mood lightens as the well-educated tour guide explains the details of what you're tasting while pouring samples of five to six wines, which may include Sauvignon blanc, viogner, chardonnay, syrah, merlot, cab, Rhone blends, and Bordeaux blends. (Unfortunately, some wines are so popular that they sell out quickly; come late in the season, and you may not be able to taste or buy them.) The three excellently located picnic tables, on the terrace overlooking the valley, are only available for Phelps wine club members (join and get wine shipped a certain number of times per year) by reservation.

Taplin Rd. (off the Silverado Trail), P.O. Box 1031, St. Helena. ✆ 800/707-5789. www.jpvwines.com. Mon–Sat 9am–5pm; Sun 9am–4pm. $20 seminars and tastings by appointment only; tastings $10 per person for 5 wines, $10 per person for 2-oz. pour of Insignia.

Robert Keenan Winery *Finds*   It's a winding, uphill drive to reach secluded Robert Keenan, but this far off the tourist track you're guaranteed more elbow-room at the tasting bar and a quieter, less commercial experience. When you drive in, you'll pass a few modest homes and wonder whether one of the buildings is the family winery. It's not. Keep driving (slowly—kids and dogs at play) and you'll know when you get to the main building and its redwood tasting room.

The 10,000 cases produced here per year are the result of yet another fast-paced professional who left his business behind and headed for the hills. In this case, it's native San Franciscan Robert Keenan, who ran his own insurance agency for 20 years. When his company merged with another firm and was bought out in 1981, he had already purchased his "retirement property," the winery's 176 acres (48 of which are now planted with grapes), and he soon turned his fascination with winemaking into a second career. The renovated stone building has a much older history, dating back to the old Conradi Winery, which was founded in 1890.

Today, Robert Keenan Winery is known for its big, full-bodied reds, such as the Mountain cab and merlot. Chardonnay, cabernet Franc, and zin sold exclusively at the winery range from $20 to $36 per bottle. Older vintages, which you won't find elsewhere, are for sale here as well. Take the tour to learn about the vineyards, production facilities, and winemaking in general. Those looking for a pastoral picnic spot should consider spreading your blanket out here. The three tables, situated right outside the winery and surrounded by vineyards, offer stunning views.

3660 Spring Mountain Rd. (off Hwy. 29), St. Helena. ✆ 707/963-9177. www.keenanwinery.com. Weekends 11am–4pm. Call for weekday hours. Free tours and tastings weekends 11am–4pm.

Beringer Vineyards ★ *Finds*   Follow the line of cars just north of St. Helena's business district to Beringer Vineyards, where everyone heads to taste wine and view the hand-dug tunnels in the mountainside. Founded in 1876 by brothers Jacob and Frederick, this is the oldest continuously operating winery in Napa Valley—it was open even during Prohibition, when Beringer stayed afloat by making "sacramental" wines. White zinfandel is the winery's most popular nationwide seller, but plenty of other varietals are available to enjoy. Tastings of current vintages ($5) are conducted in new facilities, where there's also a large selection of bottles for less than $20. Reserve wines are available for tasting for $3 to $12 in the remarkable Rhine House and tours range from the $5 standard or $18 historical to the $30 1½-hour vintage legacy tour.

2000 Main St. (Hwy. 29), St. Helena. ✆ 707/963-7115. www.beringervineyards.com. Off season daily 10am–5pm (last tour 4pm, last tasting 4:30pm); summer 10am–6pm (last tour 5pm, last tasting 5:30pm). $5 for 30-min. tours every 30 min. (free for anyone under 21 and accompanied by an adult).

Tips   **The Ins & Outs of Shipping Wine Home**

Perhaps the only things more complex than that $800 case of cabernet you just purchased are the rules and regulations about shipping it home. Because of absurd and forever fluctuating "reciprocity laws"—which supposedly protect the business of the country's wine distributors—wine shipping is limited by regulations that vary in each of the 50 states. Shipping rules also vary from winery to winery.

If you happen to live in a reciprocal state and the winery you're buying from offers shipping, you're in luck. You buy and pay the postage, and the winery sends your purchase for you. It's as simple as that. If that winery doesn't ship, it can most likely give you an easy solution.

If you live in a nonreciprocal state, the winery might still have shipping advice for you, so definitely ask. Some refuse to ship at all; others are more than accommodating. Be cautious of wineries that tell you they can ship to nonreciprocal states, and make sure you get a firm commitment: When one of my New York–based editors visited Napa, a winery promised to ship her purchase; when she got home, the winery reneged, leaving her with no way to get the wine and no potable memories of the trip.

You may face the challenge of finding a shipping company yourself. If that's the case, keep in mind that it's technically illegal to box your own wine and send it to a nonreciprocal state; the shipper could lose its license, and you could lose your wine. If you do get stuck shipping illegally (not that we're recommending you do that), you might want to package your wine in an unassuming box and head to a post office, UPS, or other shipping company outside the Wine Country area. It's less obvious that you're shipping wine from Vallejo or San Francisco than from Napa Valley.

Charles Krug Winery   Founded in 1861, Krug was the first winery built in the valley. The family of Peter Mondavi (yes, Robert is his brother) owns it today. It's worth paying your respects here by dropping $5 to sip current releases, $8 to sample reserves. On the grounds are picnic facilities with umbrella-shaded tables overlooking vineyards or the wine cellar.

2800 Main St. (St. Helena Hwy.; just north of the tunnel of trees at the northern end of St. Helena), St. Helena. ⓒ 707/963-5057. www.charleskrug.com. Daily 10:30am–5pm.

CALISTOGA
81 miles N of San Francisco

Calistoga, the last tourist town in Napa Valley, got its name from Sam Brannan, entrepreneur extraordinaire and California's first millionaire. After making a bundle supplying miners during the gold rush, he went on to take advantage of the natural geothermal springs at the north end of the valley by building a hotel and spa here in 1859. Flubbing up a speech, in which he compared this natural California wonder to New York State's Saratoga Springs resort town, he serendipitously coined the name "Calistoga," and it stuck. Today, this small, simple resort town, with 5,225 residents and an old-time main street (no building along the 6-block stretch is more than two stories high), is popular with city

Napa Valley Shipping Companies

The UPS Store, at 3212 Jefferson St. in the Grape Yard Shopping Center (② **707/259-1398**), claims to pack and ship anything anywhere. Rates for a case of wine were quoted at approximately $28 for ground shipping to Los Angeles and $69 to New York.

St. Helena Mailing Center, 1241 Adams St., at Highway 29, St. Helena (② **707/963-2686**), says they will pack and ship anywhere in the United States. Rates are around $30 per case for ground delivery to Los Angeles, $85 to New York. While those who live in reciprocal states get your package insured for up to $100, the Mailing Center does not insure packages shipped to nonreciprocal states. However, it's no big deal; each bottle is packed in Styrofoam and should make it home without a problem.

Sonoma Valley Shipping Companies

Mail Boxes, Etc., 19229 Sonoma Hwy., at Verano Street, Sonoma (② **707/935-3438**), has a lot of experience with shipping wine. It claims it will ship your wine to any state, via UPS (which currently ships to only a dozen states) or Federal Express. Prices vary from $22 to Los Angeles to as much as $73 to the East Coast.

The **Wine Exchange of Sonoma,** 452 First St. E., between East Napa and East Spain streets, Sonoma (② **707/938-1794**), will ship your wine, but there's a catch: You must buy an equal amount of any wine at the store (which they assured me would be in stock, and probably at a better rate). Shipping rates range from $20 to Los Angeles to $50 to the East Coast.

folk who come here to unwind. Calistoga is a great place to relax and indulge in mineral waters, mud baths, Jacuzzis, massages and, of course, wine. The vibe is more casual—and a little groovier—than you find in neighboring towns to the south.

Frank Family Vineyards ⭐ *Finds* "Wine dudes" Dennis, Tim, Jeff, Grant, and Pat will do practically anything to maintain their rightfully self-proclaimed reputation as the "friendliest winery in the valley." In recent years the name may have changed from Kornell Champagne Cellars to Frank-Rombauer to Frank Family, but the vibe's remained constant; it's all about down-home, friendly fun. No muss, no fuss, no intimidation factor. At Frank Family, you're part of their family—no joke. They'll greet you like a long-lost relative and serve you all the bubbly you want (three to four varieties: blanc de blanc, blanc de noir, and reserve rouge, at $20–$70 a bottle). Still-wine lovers can slip into the equally casual back room to sample chardonnay and a very well-received cabernet sauvignon. Behind the tasting room is a choice picnic area, situated under the oaks and overlooking the vineyards.

1091 Larkmead Lane (just off the Silverado Trail), Calistoga. ② **707/942-0859.** Daily 10am–5pm. Tours by appointment.

Schramsberg ★★ *Finds*   This 217-acre champagne estate, a landmark once frequented by Robert Louis Stevenson, has a wonderful old-world feel and is one of the valley's all-time best places to explore. Schramsberg is the label that presidents serve when toasting dignitaries from around the globe, and there's plenty of historic memorabilia in the front room to prove it. But the real mystique begins when you enter the champagne caves, which wind 2 miles (reputedly the longest in North America) and were partly hand-carved by Chinese laborers in the 1800s. The caves have an authentic Tom Sawyer ambience, complete with dangling cobwebs and seemingly endless passageways; you can't help but feel you're on an adventure. The comprehensive, unintimidating tour ends in a charming tasting room, where you'll sit around a big table and sample four surprisingly varied selections of bubbly. Tastings are a bit dear ($20 per person), but it's money well spent. Note that tastings are offered only to those who take the free tour, and you must reserve in advance.

1400 Schramsberg Rd. (off Hwy. 29), Calistoga. © **707/942-2414**. www.schramsberg.com. Daily 10am–4pm. Tours and tastings by appointment only.

Sterling Vineyards ★ *Kids* *Finds*   No, you don't need climbing shoes to reach this dazzling white Mediterranean-style winery, perched 300 feet up on a rocky knoll. Just fork over $10 and take the aerial tram, which offers stunning bucolic views along the way. If you've been here before, even before embarking, you'll notice major changes due to a complete renovation in 2001. Once you're back on land, follow the self-guided tour (one of the most comprehensive in the Wine Country) of the winemaking process. Currently owned by the Diageo company, the winery produces more than 500,000 cases per year. If you're not into taking the tram or you have kids in tow, visit anyway; there's an elevator that can take you to the tasting room, and kids get a goodie bag and a hearty welcome (a rarity at wineries). Wine tastings of four varietals in the panoramic tasting room are included in the tram fare, but more sophisticated sips—a la limited releases or reserve flights—will set you back $10 and $25 respectively. Expect to pay anywhere from $14 to $75 for a souvenir bottle ($20 is the average).

1111 Dunaweal Lane (off Hwy. 29, just south of downtown Calistoga), Calistoga. © **707/942-3344**. www.sterlingvineyards.com. Daily 10:30am–4:30pm.

Clos Pegase ★ *Finds*   What happens when a man falls in love with art and winemaking, purchases more than 450 acres of prime grape-growing property, and sponsors a competition commissioned by the San Francisco Museum of Modern Art to create a "temple to wine"? You'll find out when you visit this magnificent winery. Renowned architect Michael Graves designed this incredible oasis, which integrates art, 20,000 square feet of aging caves, and a luxurious hilltop private home. Viewing the art is as much the point as tasting the wines—which, by the way, don't come cheap: Prices range from $13 for the 2000 Vin Gris merlot to as much as $80 for the 1998 Hommage Artist Series Reserve, an extremely limited blend of the winery's finest lots of cabernet sauvignon and merlot. Tasting current releases costs $7.50 for samples of three premium wines. The grounds at Clos Pegase (Clo Pey-*goss*) feature an impressive sculpture garden as well as scenic picnic spots.

1060 Dunaweal Lane (off Hwy. 29 or the Silverado Trail), Calistoga. © **707/942-4981**. www.clospegase.com. Daily 10:30am–5pm. Tours daily at 11am and 2pm.

Duckhorn Vineyards   With quintessential pastoral surroundings and a unique wine-tasting program, Duckhorn Vineyards has much to offer for visitors interested in spending a little money and time to relax and taste. Here the airy Victorian farmhouse is very welcoming, not only because you can stand on the veranda and look out on the surrounding meadow, but also because the interior affords equally bucolic views. If you're going to taste wine in their surprisingly modern tasting room, complete with cafe tables and a centerpiece bar, you'll pay $10 for a tasting or $25 for an estate-wine tasting, the latter of which you can book in advance. The fee may sound steep, but this is not your run-of-the-mill drink and dash. You'll get plenty of attention and information on their current releases of sauvignon blanc, merlot, and cabernet sauvignon.

1000 Lodi Lane (at the Silverado Trail), St. Helena. (✆ **707/963-7108**. www.duckhorn.com. Daily 10am–4pm. Tastings by appointment only.

BEYOND THE WINERIES: WHAT TO SEE & DO IN NAPA VALLEY
NAPA/ST. HELENA

If you have plenty of time and a penchant for Victorian architecture, seek out the **Napa Valley Conference & Visitors Bureau**, 1310 Napa Town Center Mall, off First Street (✆ **707/226-7459**; www.napavalley.com), which offers self-guided walking tours of the town's historic buildings.

A MUSEUM The biggest new attraction in Napa Valley, **Copia: The American Center for Wine, Food & the Arts** ✦, at 500 First St. (✆ **707/259-1600**; www.copia.org), opened at the end of 2001 with a mission to explore how wine and food influence our culture. This $50-million multifaceted facility, which was spearheaded by Robert Mondavi, tackles the topic in a myriad of ways, including visual arts a la rotating exhibits, vast vegetable and herb gardens, culinary demonstrations, basic wine classes, concerts, and opportunities to dine and drink on the premises. Fortunately, programs are geared toward all types of visitors. Kids will get a kick out of identifying candy bars through pictures, while connoisseurs might slip into a class on lemon meringue pie by the likes of Julia Child or other famous chefs. Day passes include entrance into the building and gardens, exhibitions, tours, and free 30-minute introductory classes. More advanced food, wine, and garden classes cost extra. If all the food exploration

---

Finds Enjoying Art & Nature

Anyone with an appreciation for art absolutely must visit the **di Rosa Preserve**. Rene and Veronica di Rosa collected contemporary American art for more than 40 years and then converted their 215 acres of prime property into a monument to Northern California's regional art and nature. Veronica has passed on, but Rene still carries the torch through his world-renowned collection featuring 2,000 works in all media, by more than 800 Greater Bay Area artists. The di Rosas' treasures are on display practically everywhere—along the shores of the property's 30-acre lake and in each nook and cranny of their 145-year-old winery-turned-residence, adjoining building, two newer galleries, and gardens. With hundreds of surrounding acres of rolling hills (protected under the Napa County Land Trust), this place is a must-see for both art and nature lovers. It's at 5200 Carneros Hwy. (Hwy. 121/12); look for the gate. Tours are by appointment only. Each tour lasts 2 to 2½ hours, has a maximum of 25 guests, and costs $12 per person (free the 1st and 3rd Wed of each month). Call ✆ **707/226-5991** to make reservations.

gets you hankering for a snack, the cafe offers gourmet picnic items, while the adjoining restaurant, Julia's Kitchen, which is named after chef Child, is a more formal and delicious French-California affair. Do make reservations for the restaurant, as it's bound to be busy.

If you're around in the summer, definitely check out the Monday-night outdoor concert series. I often grab a lawn chair and head to the amphitheater for spectacular vocal and dance performances under Napa's soothing night sky— it's Napa at its best.

Admission costs $12.50 for adults, $10 for students and seniors 62 and over, and $7.50 for children ages 6 to 12. The center is open Wednesday through Monday from 10am to 5pm. The restaurant stays open until 9:30pm Thursday through Sunday. Wednesday admissions are half-price.

SHOPPING   Shopaholics should make a beeline to the **Napa Premium Outlets** (© **707/226-9876**; www.premiumoutlets.com), where Barneys New York can inspire even a jaded local to take the First Street exit off Highway 29 and brave the crowds. (Unfortunately, Barneys has only carried cheap outlet-store stuff lately, but on occasion I scoop up Prada shoes at a third of the price.) Along with the aforementioned Barneys, you'll find multiple places to part with your money, including TSE (killer cashmere at basement prices), Nine West, Benetton, Jones New York, BCBG, a few kitchenware shops, a food court, and a decent (but expensive) sushi restaurant. The shops are open Monday through Saturday from 10am to 8pm and Sunday from 10am to 6pm.

Farther north on Highway 29, plan to spend at least an hour if you visit **Red Hen's** co-op collection of antiques, which is open daily from 10am to 5:30pm. You'll find everything from baseball cards to living-room sets, and prices are remarkably affordable. You can't miss the enormous red barn–style building at 5091 St. Helena Hwy. (Hwy. 29) at Oak Knoll Avenue West (© **707/257-0822**).

St. Helena's Main Street is the best place to go if you're suffering serious retail withdrawal. Take, for example, **Vanderbilt and Company** ☆, 1429 Main St., between Adams and Pine streets (© **707/963-1010**). It offers the crème de la crème of cookware, hand-painted Italian dishes, and everything else you could possibly convince yourself you need for your gourmet kitchen and dining room. It's open daily from 9:30am to 5:30pm.

Shopaholics won't be able to avoid at least one sharp turn off Highway 29 for a stop at the **St. Helena Premier Outlets,** 2 miles north of downtown St. Helena (© **707/963-7282**; www.sthelenapremieroutlets.com). Featured designers include Escada, Coach, and Movado. The stores are open daily from 10am to 6pm.

One last favorite stop: **Napa Valley Olive Oil Manufacturing Company,** 835 Charter Oak Rd., at the end of the road behind Tra Vigne restaurant (© **707/963-4173**). The tiny market presses and bottles its own oils and sells them at a fraction of the price you'll pay elsewhere. In addition, it has an extensive selection of Italian cooking ingredients, imported snacks, and the best deals on exotic mushrooms. You'll love the age-old method for totaling the bill, which you simply must find out for yourself.

HORSEBACK RIDING   If you like horses and venturing through cool, misty forests, then $75 will seem like a bargain for a 1¾-hour ride with a friendly tour guide from the **Sonoma Cattle Company and Napa Valley Trailrides,** P.O. Box 5808, Napa, CA 94581 (© **707/255-2900**; www.napasonomatrailrides. com). After a lesson in the basics of horse handling at the stable, you'll be led on a leisurely stroll, with the occasional trot thrown in for excitement. The ride goes through beautiful Skyline Park in Napa.

SPA-ING IT If the Wine Country's slow pace and tranquil vistas aren't soothing enough for you, the region's diverse selection of spas can massage, bathe, wrap, and steam you into an overly pampered pulp. Should you choose to indulge, do so toward the end of your stay—when you've wined and dined to the point where you have only enough energy left to make it to and from the spa.

Compared to the cosmopolitan-chic day spas of Sonoma Mission Inn (Sonoma; see "The Super Spa" box on p. 312) and Health Spa Napa Valley (St. Helena), which isn't much more than a gym and a spa, **White Sulphur Springs Retreat & Spa** ⭑, 3100 White Sulphur Springs Rd. (© **707/963-4361;** www.whitesulphursprings.com), offers a more spiritual day of cleansing and pampering. Yes, you will encounter massages, aromatherapy treatments, seaweed or mineral mud wraps, and a pool and Jacuzzi for guests' use. But the most blissful benefits are not the product of some well-known architect or a fancy new massage oil. Mother Nature takes the credit for the magic here: acres of redwoods, streams, grassy fields, and wooded groves. The spa treatments in the newly renovated spa make the experience that much more relaxing. The resident spotted owls, woodpeckers, raccoon, deer, and fox don't take advantage of the natural outdoor sulfur spring, pool, or Jacuzzi, but you might catch a glimpse of them as you bathe. Massages ($80–$95 per hour) are given in the homey spa building or outside, amid the redwoods. A day of peaceful pampering doesn't come any cheaper. *Take note:* This is a casual place, rather than an upscale resort with a formal atmosphere.

BIKING The quieter northern end of the valley is an ideal place to rent a bicycle and ride the Silverado Trail. **St. Helena Cyclery,** 1156 Main St. (© **707/ 963-7736**), rents bikes for $7 per hour or $30 a day, including rear rack, helmet, lock, and bag in which you can pack a picnic.

NIGHTLIFE The whole valley has little in the way of after-dinner entertainment, which leaves revelers with little choice but to turn to **1351 Lounge,** 1351 Main St. (© **707/963-1969**), a renovated stone-walled former bank complete with a shiny vault. Here locals and visitors settle around cocktail tables or at the old mahogany bar for cocktails and entertainment ranging from open-mic night to a DJ to live rock, blues, or funk.

CALISTOGA

BICYCLING Cycling enthusiasts can rent bikes from **Getaway Adventures BHK,** 1522 Lincoln Ave. (© **800/499-BIKE** or 707/763-3040; www.getaway adventures.com). Full-day group tours cost $115, include lunch and a visit to four or five wineries, and require six participants; downhill cruises are available for people who hate to pedal. Bike rental without a tour costs $9 an hour, $20 per half-day, or $28 per day. You can also inquire about the company's kayaking and hiking tours.

MUD BATHS The one thing you should do while you're in Calistoga is what people have been doing here for the past 150 years: Take a mud bath. The natural baths contain local volcanic ash, imported peat, and naturally boiling mineral hot-springs water, mulled together to produce a thick mud that simmers at a temperature of about 104°F (40°C).

Indulge yourself at any of these Calistoga spas: **Dr. Wilkinson's Hot Springs,** 1507 Lincoln Ave. (© 707/942-4102); **Golden Haven Hot Springs Spa,** 1713

Lake St. (© 707/942-6793); **Calistoga Spa Hot Springs,** 1006 Washington St. (© 707/942-6269); **Calistoga Village Inn & Spa,** 1880 Lincoln Ave. (© 707/ 942-0991); **Indian Springs Resort,** 1712 Lincoln Ave. (© 707/942-4913); **Nance's Hot Springs,** 1614 Lincoln Ave. (© 707/942-6211); or **Roman Spa Motel,** 1300 Washington St. (© 707/942-4441).

NATURAL WONDERS   Old Faithful Geyser of California, 1299 Tubbs Lane (© **707/942-6463;** www.oldfaithfulgeyser.com), is one of only three "old faithful" geysers in the world. It's been blowing off steam at regular intervals for as long as anyone can remember. The 350°F (176°C) water spews at a height of about 60 feet every 40 minutes, day and night. The performance lasts about 3 minutes, and you can bring a picnic lunch to munch on between spews. An exhibit hall, gift shop, and snack bar are open every day. Admission is $8 for adults, $7 for seniors, $3 for children 6 to 12, free for children under 6. The geyser is open daily from 9am to 6pm (to 5pm in winter). To get there, follow the signs from downtown Calistoga; it's between Highway 29 and Calif. 128.

You won't see thousands of trees turned into stone, but you'll still find many interesting petrified specimens at the **Petrified Forest,** 4100 Petrified Forest Rd. (© **707/942-6667;** www.petrifiedforest.org). Volcanic ash blanketed this area after an eruption near Mount St. Helena 3 million years ago. You'll find red-woods that have turned to rock through the slow infiltration of silicas and other minerals, as well as petrified seashells, clams, and marine life indicating that water covered this area before the redwood forest appeared. Admission is $5 for adults, $4 for seniors and youths 12 to 17, $3 for children 5 to 11, free for chil-dren under 4. The forest is open daily from 9am to 6pm (to 5pm in winter). Heading north from Calistoga on Calif. 128, turn left onto Petrified Forest Road, just past Lincoln Street.

WHERE TO STAY IN NAPA VALLEY

Accommodations in Napa Valley run the gamut—from motels and B&Bs to world-class luxury retreats—and all are easily accessible from the main highway. While I recommend shacking up in the more romantically pastoral areas such as St. Helena, there's no question you're going to find better deals in the towns of Napa or laid-back Calistoga.

When planning your trip, keep in mind that during the high season— April to November—most hotels charge peak rates and sell out completely on weekends; many also have a 2-night minimum. If you need help organizing your Wine Country vacation, contact an agency. **Accommodation Referral Bed & Breakfast Exchange** (© **800/240-8466** or 707/965-3400; www. accommodationsreferral.com), which also represents hotels and inns, will ask for dates, price range, and accommodations type before coming up with recom-mendations. **Bed & Breakfast Inns of Napa Valley** (© **707/944-4444**), an association of B&Bs, provides descriptions and makes reservations. **Napa Valley Reservations Unlimited** (© **800/251-NAPA** or 707/252-1985; www.napa valleyreservations.com) is also a source for booking everything from hot-air bal-loon to wine-tasting tours by limousine.

NAPA

Wherever tourist dollars are to be had, you're sure to find big hotels with famil-iar names, catering to independent vacationers, business travelers, and groups. **Embassy Suites,** 1075 California Blvd., Napa, CA 94559 (© **800/362-2779** or 707/253-9540; www.embassynapa.com), offers 205 of its usual two-room suites. Each has a kitchenette, a coffeemaker, modem capability, and two TVs;

Pricing Categories

The listings below are arranged first by area, then by price, using the following categories: **Very Expensive,** more than $250 per night; **Expensive,** $200 to $250 per night; **Moderate,** $150 to $200 per night; and **Inexpensive,** less than $150 per night.

---

there are indoor and outdoor pools and a restaurant. Rates range from $169 to $280 and include cooked-to-order breakfast. The 272-room **Napa Valley Marriott,** 3425 Solano Ave., Napa, CA 94558 (© **800/228-9290** or 707/253-8600; www.napavalleymarriott.com), has an exercise room, a heated outdoor pool and spa, and two restaurants; rates range from $154 to $320 for rooms, $300 to $500 for suites.

Very Expensive

Milliken Creek Inn ★★   This riverfront retreat, just north of downtown Napa, captures the essence of upscale boutique hotel accommodations and country living. Part of its allure is due to a change of hands and a $1-million renovation in 2001. The rest is due to the inn's great taste and location. Right off the Silverado Trail and surrounded by tranquil gardens, oaks, and redwoods, the 12 spacious and refined rooms are located in three neighboring buildings (including the restored 1857 Coach House) and are luxuriously appointed. Soothing shades of brown and beige, greens, and yellows become even warmer and more welcoming when the fireplace is in action. King-size beds are firm and draped in Frette linens, tubs are the whirlpool variety, and fluffy robes await you. Delicious perks include a picnic breakfast delivered to your door and a wine-and-cheese tasting nightly in the equally sophisticated parlor. Often live jazz piano accompanies the affair. No doubt this hotel is one of Napa's finest choices.

1815 Silverado Trail, Napa, CA 94558. © **888/622-5775** or 707/255-1197. Fax 707/255-3112. www.milliken creekinn.com. 12 units. $295–$625 double. AE, DC, DISC, MC, V. **Amenities:** Yoga gazebo; in-room massage. *In room:* A/C, TV/DVD, dataport, minibar, hair dryer, iron on request, wireless Internet access, CD player.

Moderate

Cedar Gables Inn ★★ *(Finds*   This grand, romantic B&B in Old Town Napa is in a stunning Victorian built in 1892. Rooms reflect that era, with rich tapestries and stunning gilded antiques. Four rooms have fireplaces, five have whirlpool tubs, and all feature queen-size brass, wood, or iron beds. Guests meet each evening in front of the roaring fireplace in the lower parlor for wine and cheese. At other times, the family room is a perfect place to cuddle up and watch the large-screen TV. Bonuses include a full breakfast each morning, port in every room, and VIP treatment at many local wineries.

486 Coombs St., Napa, CA 94559. © **800/309-7969** or 707/224-7969. Fax 707/224-4838. www.cedar gablesinn.com. 9 units. $189–$309 double; winter specials available. Rates include full breakfast, evening wine and cheese, and port. AE, DISC, MC, V. From Hwy. 29 north, exit onto First St. and follow signs to downtown; turn right onto Coombs St.; the house is at the corner of Oak St. **Amenities:** Dataport (in the shared living room). *In room:* A/C, hair dryer, iron.

Napa River Inn ★★   Downtown Napa's most luxurious hotel manages an old-world boutique feel throughout most of its three buildings, which house 66 rooms. The main building, part of the recently renovated Historic Napa Mill and Hatt Market Building, is an 1884 historic landmark. Each of the fantastically appointed rooms is exceedingly romantic, with burgundy-colored walls, original brick, wood furnishings, plush fabrics, and seats in front of the gas fireplace. A gilded claw-foot tub beckons in each luxurious bathroom. The newest addition is a 2001 building with bright and airy accommodations overlooking the Napa River. In another building are the less luxurious, but equally well appointed, mustard-and-brown rooms that also overlook the riverfront, but have a nautical theme and less daylight. Perks abound and include complimentary vouchers to breakfast at adorable Sweetie Pie's bakery and wine at nearby very swank wine bar The Bounty Hunter. A small but excellent spa is located in the hotel's parking lot.

500 Main St., Napa, CA 94559. © **877/251-8500** or 707/251-8500. Fax 707/251-8504. www.napariver inn.com. 66 units. $179–$499 double. Rates include vouchers to a full breakfast and evening cocktails at one of the adjoining restaurants. AE, DC, DISC, MC, V. **Amenities:** Restaurant; concierge; business services; same-day laundry service/dry cleaning. *In room:* A/C, TV, dataport, fridge, coffeemaker, hair dryer, iron, safe, CD clock radio.

Inexpensive

Chablis Inn ⭐ There's no way around it: If you want to sleep cheaply in a town where the *average* room rate tops $200 per night in high season, you're destined for a motel. Look on the bright side: Because your room is likely to be little more than a crash pad after a day of eating and drinking, a clean bed and a remote control are all you'll really need anyway. And Chablis offers much more than that. All of the motel-style rooms are superclean, and some even boast kitchenettes or whirlpool tubs. Guests have access to an outdoor heated pool and hot tub.

3360 Solano Ave., Napa, CA 94558. © **707/257-1944.** Fax 707/226-6862. www.chablisinn.com. 34 units. May to mid-Nov $125–$235 double; mid-Nov to Apr $70–$120 double. AE, DC, DISC, MC, V. **Amenities:** Heated outdoor pool; Jacuzzi. *In room:* A/C, TV, dataport in some rooms, kitchenette in some rooms, fridge, coffeemaker, hair dryer.

Wine Valley Lodge ⭐ *Value* Dollar for dollar, the Wine Valley Lodge offers a great deal. At the south end of town in a quiet residential neighborhood, the mission-style motel is extremely well kept and accessible, just a short drive from Highway 29 and the wineries to the north. The reasonably priced deluxe units, which are two bedrooms connected by a bathroom, are great for families.

200 S. Coombs St. (between First and Imola sts.), Napa, CA 94559. © **800/696-7911** or 707/224-7911. www.winevalleylodge.com. 54 units. $79–$135 double; $150–$165 deluxe. AE, DC, DISC, MC, V. **Amenities:** Heated outdoor pool. *In room:* A/C, TV.

YOUNTVILLE
Very Expensive

Napa Valley Lodge ⭐⭐ *Finds* Many frequent visitors compare this contemporary hotel to the nearby, upscale Vintage Inn (see below), noting that it's even more personable and accommodating. The lodge is just off Highway 29, beyond a wall that does a good job of disguising the road. Guest rooms, which were upgraded in 2001, are large, ultraclean, and better appointed than many in the area. Many have vaulted ceilings, and 39 have fireplaces. Each comes with a king- or queen-size bed, wicker furnishings, robes, and a private balcony or a patio. The least expensive units, at ground level, are smaller and get less sunlight than those on the second floor. Extras are a concierge, afternoon tea and cookies in the lobby, Friday-evening wine tasting in the library, and a full champagne breakfast—with all this, it's no wonder AAA gave the Napa Valley Lodge the four-diamond award for excellence. Ask about winter discounts, which can be as high as 30%.

2230 Madison St., Yountville, CA 94599. © **800/368-2468** or 707/944-2468. Fax 707/944-9362. www.napavalleylodge.com. 55 units. $252–$445 double. Rates include champagne breakfast buffet, afternoon tea and cookies, and Fri-evening wine tasting. AE, DC, DISC, MC, V. **Amenities:** Heated outdoor pool; small exercise room; Jacuzzi; redwood sauna; concierge; free high-speed Internet access. *In room:* A/C, TV w/pay movies, dataport, minibar, coffeemaker, hair dryer, iron.

Vintage Inn ★★   This contemporary, French-country hotel is situated on an old 23-acre winery estate in the heart of Yountville. The complex feels far more corporate than "inn" would suggest, but its big-business appearance does have its perks, like a very professional staff for one. Rooms are bright and cozy, each with fireplace and private veranda, oversize bed, Jacuzzi tub, plush bathrobes, and welcoming bottle of wine. If you're looking for a workout, you may rent a bike, reserve one of the two tennis courts, or take a dip in the 60-foot swimming pool or outdoor whirlpool, both heated year-round. A champagne breakfast buffet and afternoon tea are served daily in the lobby. If they're booked, ask about their sister property, the spa-centric Villagio Inn & Spa, a Tuscan-style hotel complex just down the road.

6541 Washington St. (between Humboldt St. and Webber Ave.), Yountville, CA 94599. © **800/351-1133** or 707/944-1112. Fax 707/944-1617. www.vintageinn.com. 80 units. $215–$400 double; $300–$630 minisuites and villas. Rates include champagne breakfast buffet, complimentary wine upon arrival, and afternoon tea. AE, DC, MC, V. Free parking. From Hwy. 29 north, take the Yountville exit and turn left onto Washington St. Pets $30. **Amenities:** Concierge; business center; secretarial services; room service; in-room massage; laundry service; dry cleaning. *In room:* A/C, TV/VCR w/movie library, fridge, coffeemaker, hair dryer, iron, $10-per-day high-speed Internet access.

Inexpensive

Maison Fleurie ★★   Maison Fleurie, one of the prettiest hotels in the Wine Country, is a trio of beautiful 1873 brick-and-fieldstone buildings overlaid with ivy. The main house—a charming Provençal replica with thick brick walls, terracotta tile, and paned windows—holds seven rooms; the rest are in the old bakery building and the carriage house. Some feature private balconies, patios, sitting areas, Jacuzzi tubs, and fireplaces. Breakfast is served in the quaint little dining room; afterward, you're welcome to wander the landscaped grounds or hit the wine-tasting trail, returning in time for afternoon hors d'oeuvres and wine. It's impossible not to enjoy your stay at Maison Fleurie.

6529 Yount St. (between Washington St. and Yountville Cross Rd.), Yountville, CA 94599. © **800/788-0369** or 707/944-2056. Fax 707/944-9342. www.foursisters.com. 13 units. $120–$275 double. Rates include full breakfast and afternoon hors d'oeuvres. AE, DC, MC, V. **Amenities:** Heated outdoor pool; Jacuzzi; free use of bikes. *In room:* A/C, TV, dataport, hair dryer, iron.

Napa Valley Railway Inn ★   This is a favorite place to stay in the Wine Country. Why? Because it's inexpensive and it's cute as all get-out. Looking hokey as heck from the outside, the Railway Inn consists of two rows of sun-bleached cabooses and rail cars sitting on a stretch of Yountville's original track and connected by a covered wooden walkway. Things get considerably better when you enter your private caboose or car. Each is sumptuously appointed, with comfy love seat, king-size brass bed, and tiled bathroom. The coups de grâce are the bay windows and skylights, which let in plenty of California sunshine. The cars are all suites, so if you're looking to save your pennies, opt for a caboose. Adjacent to the inn is Yountville's main shopping complex.

6503 Washington St., Yountville, CA 94599. © **707/944-2000.** 9 units. $90–$170 double. AE, MC, V. *In room:* A/C, TV, coffeemaker, hair dryer upon request.

OAKVILLE & RUTHERFORD
Very Expensive

Auberge du Soleil ★★★ *Moments*   This spectacular Relais & Châteaux member is the kind of place you'd imagine movie stars frequenting for clandestine affairs or weekend retreats. Set high above Napa Valley in a 33-acre olive grove, it's quiet, indulgent, and luxuriously romantic. The Mediterranean-style rooms are large enough to get lost in, and you might want to once you discover all the amenities. The bathtub alone—an enormous hot tub with a skylight overhead—will entice you to grab a glass of California red and settle in for a while. Oversize, cushy furniture surrounds a wood-burning fireplace—the ideal place to relax and listen to CDs (the stereo comes with a few selections). Fresh flowers, original art, terra-cotta floors, and wood and leather furnishings whisk you out of the Wine Country and into the Southwest. Each sun-washed private deck has views of the valley that are nothing less than spectacular. Those with money to burn should opt for the $2,250-per-night cottage suite; the 1,800-square-foot hideaway has two fireplaces, two full bathrooms, a den, and a patio Jacuzzi. Now, that's living. All guests have access to a celestial swimming pool, exercise room, and the Wine Country's most fabulous spa, which opened in 2001. Only guests can use the spa, but if you want to get all the romantic grandeur of Auberge without staying overnight, have lunch on the patio at the wonderful restaurant overlooking the valley (see p. 295 for more information). Overall, this is one of my favorite Wine Country places. *Parents take note:* This is not the kind of place you take the kids.

180 Rutherford Hill Rd., Rutherford, CA 94573. (**800/348-5406** or 707/963-1211. Fax 707/963-8764. www.aubergedusoleil.com. 50 units. $400–$750 double; $675-$1,275 suite. AE, DC, DISC, MC, V. From Hwy. 29 in Rutherford, turn right on Calif. 128 and go 3 miles to the Silverado Trail; turn left and head north about 600 ft. to Rutherford Hill Rd.; turn right. **Amenities:** Restaurant; 3 outdoor pools ranging from hot to cold; 3 tennis courts; health club and full-service spa; sauna; steam; bikes; concierge; secretarial services; salon; 24-hr. room service; massage; same-day laundry service/dry cleaning; free Internet access. *In room:* A/C, TV/DVD w/pay movies, dataport, kitchenette, minibar, fridge, coffeemaker, hair dryer, iron.

Moderate

Rancho Caymus Inn ★   This Spanish-style hacienda, with two floors opening onto wisteria-covered balconies, was the creation of sculptor Mary Tilden Morton (of Morton Salt). Morton wanted each room in the hacienda to be a work of art, so she hired the most skilled craftspeople she could find. She designed the adobe fireplaces herself, and she wandered through Mexico and South America purchasing artifacts for the property, which was completed in 1985.

Guest rooms surround a whimsical garden courtyard with an enormous outdoor fireplace. The mix-and-match decor is on the funky side, with overly varnished dark-wood furnishings and braided rugs. The inn is cozy, however, and units are decent-size, split-level suites with queen-size beds, wet bars, sofa beds in the sitting areas, and small private patios. Most of the suites have fireplaces, one has a kitchenette, and five have whirlpool tubs. Breakfast, which includes fresh fruit, granola, orange juice, and pastries, is served in the inn's dining room. Since chef Ken Frank's La Toque opened here, this funky inn has also become a dining destination (see p. 300 for complete details).

1140 Rutherford Rd., P.O. Box 78, Rutherford, CA 94573. (**800/845-1777** or 707/963-1777. Fax 707/963-5387. www.ranchocaymus.com. 26 suites. $195–$390 double; $255–$430 master suite; $385 2-bedroom suite. Rates include continental breakfast. AE, MC, V. From Hwy. 29 north, turn right onto Rutherford Rd./Calif. 128 east; the hotel is on your left. **Amenities:** Restaurant. *In room:* A/C, TV, dataport, kitchenette in some rooms, minibar, fridge, hair dryer, iron in some rooms.

ST. HELENA
Very Expensive

The Inn at Southbridge ★★   Eschewing the lace-and-latticework theme that plagues most Wine Country inns, the Inn at Southbridge takes an unswervingly modern, pragmatic approach. Instead of stuffed teddy bears, you'll find terry robes, fireplaces, bathroom skylights, down comforters, private balconies, and a host of other luxuries. The decor is upscale Pottery Barn trendy, and for some it's a welcome departure from quaintly traditional hotel-style stuff. Functional touches include voice mail and fax modems. One notable bummer: The inn is along the highway, so it lacks that reclusive feel offered by many other upscale hotels. The hotel is not ideal for families (especially considering the high price tag), but the adjoining casual and cheap Italian restaurant with games, TV, and pizzas is ideal for kids.

1020 Main St., St. Helena, CA 94574. © 800/520-6800 or 707/967-9400. Fax 707/967-9486. 21 units. $235–$590 double. AE, DC, MC, V. **Amenities:** Restaurant; large heated outdoor pool; excellent health club and full-service spa; Jacuzzi; concierge; limited room service; massage; same-day laundry service/dry cleaning. *In room:* A/C, TV, dataport, minibar, coffeemaker, hair dryer, iron.

Meadowood Napa Valley ★★★ *Finds*   This ultraluxurious resort, tucked away on 250 acres of pristine mountainside in a forest of madrone and oak trees, is quiet and secluded enough to make you forget that the busy wineries are just 10 minutes away. Originally a private country club for Napa's well-to-do families, Meadowood is one of California's top-ranked privately owned resorts, a favorite retreat for celebrities, CEOs, and, well, me. Units, which vary in size tremendously depending on the price, are furnished with American country classics and have beamed ceilings, private patios, stone fireplaces, and views of the forest. Many are individual suite-lodges so far removed from the common areas that you must drive to get to them. Lazier folks can opt for more centrally located accommodations.

The resort offers a wealth of activities: golf on a challenging 9-hole course, tennis on seven championship courts, and croquet (yes, croquet) on two international regulation lawns. There are private hiking trails, a health spa, heated pools, and a whirlpool. Those who might actually want to leave and do some wine tasting can check in with the hotel's wine tutor whose sole purpose as an employee is to help guests better understand and enjoy Napa Valley wines.

900 Meadowood Lane, St. Helena, CA 94574. © 800/458-8080 or 707/963-3646. Fax 707/963-3532. www.meadowood.com. 85 units. $375–$790 double; 1-bedroom suite from $865; 2-bedroom from $1,500; 3-bedroom from $2,000; 4-bedroom from $3,585. Ask about promotional offers and off-season rates. 2-night minimum stay on weekends. AE, DC, DISC, MC, V. **Amenities:** 2 restaurants; 2 large heated outdoor pools; golf course; 7 tennis courts; health club and full-service spa; Jacuzzi; sauna; concierge; secretarial services; complimentary Internet access in business center; 24-hr. room service; same-day laundry service/dry cleaning; 2 croquet lawns. *In room:* A/C, TV, dataport, kitchenette in some rooms, minibar, coffeemaker, hair dryer, iron.

Moderate

Deer Run Inn ★   If romantic solitude is a big part of your vacation plan, Deer Run should be on your itinerary. Situated 4½ miles (10 min. by car) from downtown St. Helena along a winding mountain road, this four-room B&B is a heavenly hideaway. All of the wood-paneled rooms look onto owners Tom and Carol Wilson's 4 acres of forest, and each features gorgeous antiques, a feather bed, a private entrance, a deck, a decanter of brandy, a fridge, coffee and tea, robes, and access to hiking trails. One unit adjoins the cedar-shingled main house and boasts a king-size bed, Ralph Lauren textiles, a wood-burning fireplace, and an open-beam ceiling. The Carriage House Suite offers an antique queen-size bed,

Spanish tile floors, a gas stove, and a huge bathroom. The Studio Bungalow is fashioned after Ralph Lauren, with Spanish tile, a cathedral ceiling, and white-washed cedar walls. Outside, there's a very small pool.

3995 Spring Mountain Rd., P.O. Box 311, St. Helena, CA 94574. ② **707/963-3794.** Fax 707/963-9026. 3 units, all with bathroom (shower only). $160–$175 double. Rates include full breakfast. AE, MC, V. **Amenities:** Outdoor unheated pool. *In room:* A/C, TV, fridge, hair dryer.

Wine Country Inn ★★ Just off the highway behind Freemark Abbey vine-yard, this attractive wood-and-stone inn, complete with a French-style mansard roof and turret, overlooks a pastoral landscape of vineyards. The individually decorated rooms contain iron or brass beds, antique furnishings, and handmade quilts; most have fireplaces and private terraces overlooking the valley, and oth-ers have private hot tubs. One of the inn's best features (besides the absence of TVs) is the heated outdoor pool, which is attractively landscaped into the hill-side. Another favorite feature is the selection of suites, which come with stereos, plenty of space, and lots of privacy. The family that runs this place puts personal touches everywhere and makes every guest feel welcome. They serve wine and plenty of appetizers nightly, along with a big dash of hotel-staff hospitality in the inviting living room. A full buffet breakfast is served there, too. Five luxury cot-tages opened in mid-2003.

1152 Lodi Lane, St. Helena, CA 94574. ② **888/465-4608** or 707/963-7077. Fax 707/963-9018. www.wine-country-inn.com. 24 units, 12 with shower only. $185–$595 double. Rates include breakfast and appetizers. MC, V. **Amenities:** Heated outdoor pool; Jacuzzi; concierge; free Internet access. *In room:* A/C, hair dryer.

Inexpensive

El Bonita Motel ★ *Kids* *Value* This 1930s Art Deco motel is a bit too close to Highway 29 for comfort, but the 2½ acres of beautifully landscaped gardens behind the building (away from the road) help even the score. The rooms, while small and nothing fancy, are spotlessly clean (and sometimes smell strongly of air freshener). They are decorated with newer furnishings and kitchenettes, and some have a whirlpool bathtub. Many families consider El Bonita one of the best values in Napa Valley—especially considering the pool, Jacuzzi, and sauna.

195 Main St. (at El Bonita Ave.), St. Helena, CA 94574. ② **800/541-3284** or 707/963-3216. Fax 707/963-8838. www.elbonita.com. 41 units. $89–$259 double. Rates include continental breakfast. AE, DC, DISC, MC, V. **Amenities:** Heated outdoor pool; spa; Jacuzzi; free Internet access. *In room:* A/C, TV, fridge, coffeemaker, hair dryer, iron, microwave.

White Sulphur Springs Retreat & Spa ★ If your idea of the ultimate vaca-tion is a cozy cabin on 45 acres, paradise is a short, winding drive away from downtown St. Helena. Established in 1852, Sulphur Springs claims to be the oldest resort in California. The property holds creeks, waterfalls, a naturally heated sulfur hot spring, and redwood, madrone, and fir trees. Guests stay in different-size creek-side cabins (which were renovated in 1998 and 1999), the inn, or the Carriage House. The cabins are decorated with simple but homey furnishings; cabin no. 9 has two queen-size beds and a kitchenette. From here you can take a dip in the natural hot sulfur spring; lounge by the large outdoor unheated pool; sit under a tree and watch for deer, fox, raccoon, spotted owl, or woodpecker; or schedule a day of massage (fantastic massage!), aromatherapy, and other spa treatments in their spa, which was completed in early 2001. *Note:* No RVs are allowed without advance notice. All rooms are nonsmoking. Call well in advance; the resort is often rented by large groups.

3100 White Sulphur Springs Rd., St. Helena, CA 94574. ② **800/593-8873** in California, or 707/963-8588. Fax 707/963-2890. www.whitesulphursprings.com. 37 units, 14 with shared bathroom; 9 cottages. Carriage

House (shared bathroom) $100–$200 double; inn $115–$140 double; creek-side cottages $175–$200. Rates include continental breakfast. Off-season and midweek discounts available. 2-night minimum stay on weekends Apr–Oct and all holidays. AE, DC, DISC, MC, V. **Amenities:** Heated outdoor pool; soaking pool; full-service spa; Jacuzzi; free Internet hook-up in hospitality room. *In room:* A/C in some rooms, hair dryer on request.

CALISTOGA
Expensive

Cottage Grove Inn 🏆🏆 Standing in two parallel rows at the end of the main strip in Calistoga is the perfect retreat—adorable cottages that, though on a residential street (with a paved road running between two rows of accommodations), seem removed from the action once you've stepped across the threshold. Each compact guesthouse has a wood-burning fireplace, homey furnishings, cozy quilts, and an enormous bathroom with a skylight and a deep, two-person Jacuzzi tub. Guests enjoy such niceties as gourmet coffee, a stereo with CD player, a VCR (the inn has a video library), and a wet bar. Several major spas are within walking distance. This is a top pick if you want to do the Calistoga spa scene in comfort and style. Smoking is allowed only in the gazebos.

1711 Lincoln Ave., Calistoga, CA 94515. ⓒ **800/799-2284** or 707/942-8400. Fax 707/942-2653. www.cottagegrove.com. 16 cottages. $250–$325 double. Rates include continental breakfast and evening wine and cheese. AE, DC, DISC, MC, V. *In room:* A/C, TV/VCR, dataport, fridge, coffeemaker, hair dryer.

Moderate

Christopher's Inn 🏆 *Kids* A cluster of five buildings makes up one of Calistoga's more attractive accommodations options. Ten years of renovations and expansions by architect-owner Christopher Layton have turned sweet old homes at the entrance to downtown into hotel rooms with a little pizzazz. Options range from somewhat simple but tasteful rooms with colorful and impressive antiques and small bathrooms to huge lavish abodes with four-poster beds, rich fabrics and brocades, and sunken Jacuzzi tubs facing a gas fireplace. Room no. 3 impresses you with its commanding 9-foot-tall black-wood carved Asian panels. Most rooms have gas fireplaces, and some have quirks like small, older TVs (with cable). Outstanding bouquets attest that the management goes the distance on the details. Those who prefer homey accommodations will feel comfortable here, since the property doesn't have corporate polish or big-business blandness. The two rather plain but very functional two-bedroom units are ideal for families, provided you're not expecting the Ritz. An extended continental breakfast is delivered to your room daily.

1010 Foothill Blvd., Calistoga, CA 94515. ⓒ **866/876-5755** or 707/942-5755. Fax 707/942-6895. www.christophersinn.com. 22 units. $175–$425 double; $330–$350 house sleeping 5. Rates include continental breakfast. AE, V. *In room:* TV, dataport.

Euro Spa & Inn 🏆🏆 In a quiet residential section of Calistoga, this small European-style inn and spa provides a level of solitude and privacy that few other spas can match. The horseshoe-shaped inn consists of 13 stucco bungalows, a spa center, and an outdoor patio, where a light breakfast and snacks are served. The rooms, although small, are pleasantly decorated in Pottery Barn decor that was implemented in 2000, whirlpool tubs, decks, wood stoves, and kitchenettes. Spa treatments range from clay baths and foot reflexology to minifacials.

1202 Pine St. (at Myrtle), Calistoga, CA 94515. ⓒ **707/942-6829.** Fax 707/942-1138. 13 units. $119–$229 double. Rates include continental breakfast. Off-season and midweek package discounts available. AE, DC, DISC, MC, V. **Amenities:** Outdoor heated pool; Jacuzzi. *In room:* A/C, TV, kitchenette, hair dryer, iron.

Silver Rose Inn & Spa ⭐ If you'd like a big, ranch-style spread complete with a large wine bottle–shaped heated pool, a smaller unheated pool, two hot tubs, dual tennis courts, and even a chipping and putting green, then you'll love the Silver Rose Inn & Spa. Situated on a small oak-covered knoll overlooking the upper Napa Valley, the inn, which is known for its polished hospitality, offers so many amenities that you'll have a tough time searching for reasons to leave (other than to eat dinner, which is not yet available). Each of the spacious guest rooms, which surround a centerpiece two-story atrium living room, is individually—and whimsically—decorated in themes ranging from the peach-colored Peach Delight to the Oriental room, complete with shoji screens and Oriental rugs, to the Mardi Gras room, which is adorned with colorful masks. Several rooms come with fireplaces, whirlpool baths, and private balconies or terraces. Guests can partake of the exclusive full-service spa as well as an after-noon "hospitality hour" of wine, cheese, and crackers. Also, the winery is open and offers free samples ($5 for outside guests) as well as daily 11am barrel tastings.

351 Rosedale Rd. (off the Silverado Trail), Calistoga, CA 94515. ☎ **800/995-9381** or 707/942-9581. www. silverrose.com. 20 units. $165–$255 double weekdays; $195–$300 double weekends. Rates include continental breakfast. AE, DISC, MC, V. **Amenities:** 2 pools; spa; 2 Jacuzzis. *In room:* A/C, dataport, hair dryer, iron upon request.

Inexpensive

Calistoga Spa Hot Springs ⭐ *Kids* *Value* Very few hotels in the Wine Coun-try cater specifically to families with children, which is why I recommend Calistoga Spa Hot Springs if you're bringing the little ones: They classify them-selves as a family resort and are very accommodating to visitors of all ages. In any case, it's a great bargain, offering unpretentious yet comfortable rooms, as well as a plethora of spa facilities. All of Calistoga's best shops and restaurants are within easy walking distance, and you can even whip up your own grub at the barbecue grills near the large pool and patio area.

1006 Washington St. (at Gerrard St.), Calistoga, CA 94515. ☎ **866/822-5772** or 707/942-6269. www. calistogaspa.com. 58 units. Winter $99 double, $154 family unit; summer $121 double, $176 suite. MC, V. **Amenities:** 3 heated outdoor pools; kids' wading pool; exercise room; spa. *In room:* A/C, TV, kitchenette, fridge, coffeemaker, hair dryer on request, iron.

Dr. Wilkinson's Hot Springs Resort ⭐ This spa/"resort," located in the heart of Calistoga, is one of the best deals in Napa Valley. The rooms range from attractive Victorian-style accommodations with sun decks and garden patios to modern, cozy, recently renovated guest rooms in the main 1950s-style motel. All rooms are spiffier than most in the area's other hotels, with surprisingly tasteful textiles and basic motel-style accouterments. Larger rooms have refrigerators and/or kitchens. Facilities, which are the highlight of a Calistoga visit, include three mineral-water pools (two outdoor and one indoor), a Jacuzzi, a steam room, and mud baths. Facials and all kinds of body treatments are available in the salon, and spa service is excellent. Be sure to inquire about their excellent midweek packages.

1507 Lincoln Ave. (Calif. 29, between Fairway and Stevenson aves.), Calistoga, CA 94515. ☎ **707/942-4102.** www.drwilkinson.com. 42 units. Winter $109–$139 double; summer $149–$189 double. Weekly discounts and packages available. AE, MC, V. *In room:* A/C, TV, dataport, coffeemaker, hair dryer, iron on request.

WHERE TO DINE IN NAPA VALLEY

Napa Valley's restaurants draw as much attention to the valley as its award-winning wineries. Nowhere else in the state are kitchens as deft at mixing fresh seasonal, local, organic produce into edible magic, which means that menus change constantly to reflect the best available ingredients. Add that to a great

Pricing Categories

The restaurants listed below are classified first by town, then by price, using the following categories: **Expensive,** dinner from $50 per person; **Moderate,** dinner from $35 per person; and **Inexpensive,** less than $35 per person for dinner. (*Note:* The "Very Expensive" category—dinner from $75 per person—has been omitted since no restaurants in this chapter fall under its umbrella.) These categories reflect prices for an appetizer, a main course, a dessert, and a glass of wine.

bottle of wine and stunning views, and you have one heck of an eating experience. To best enjoy Napa's restaurant scene, keep one thing in mind: Reserve in advance—especially for a seat in a famous room.

NAPA
Moderate

Angèle ⭐ COUNTRY FRENCH   A family affair by Claude Rouas (Auberge du Soleil; p. 290) and daughters Bettina and Claudia, this riverside spot incited a stampede of restaurateurs and winemakers when it opened at the end of 2002. The draw? Its cozy combo of raw wood beams, taupe-tinted concrete-block walls, concrete slab floors, bright yellow leather bar stools, candlelight, and a menu that tips its toque to country French classics. Sure things include rich oxtail-and-lentil salad perked with elegantly acidic "ravigote" dressing ($10), giant white bowls of steamed mussels in a light braised fennel broth ($12), and braised chicken with chestnuts, celery root, and foie gras butter ($18). Perks include a citrus-tree-flanked, heater-warmed patio above the Napa River (weather permitting), a festive full bar, and hobnobbing with restaurateurs and winemakers.

540 Main St. (In the Hatt Building), Napa. ℂ **707/252-8115.** www.angele.us. Reservations recommended. Most main courses $16–$22. AE, MC, V. Daily 11:30am–10pm.

Bistro Don Giovanni ⭐⭐⭐ (Value REGIONAL ITALIAN   Donna and Giovanni Scala—who launched Scala's Bistro in San Francisco—own this bright, bustling, and cheery Italian restaurant, which also happens to be one of my favorite restaurants in Napa Valley. Fare prepared by chef/partner Scott Warner highlights quality ingredients and California flair and never disappoints, especially when it comes to the thin-crusted pizzas and house-made pastas. Every time I grab a menu, I can't get past the salad of beets and *haricots verts* or the pasta with duck Bolognese. On the rare occasion that I do, I am equally smitten with outstanding classic pizza Margherita fresh from the wood-burning oven, seared wild salmon filet perched atop a tower of buttermilk mashed potatoes, and steak frites. Even though portions are generous, there's always room for tiramisu! Alfresco dining in the vineyards is available—and highly recommended on a warm, sunny day. Midwinter, I'm a fan of ordering a bottle of wine and dining at the bar.

4110 Howard Lane (at St. Helena Hwy.), Napa. ℂ **707/224-3300.** Reservations recommended. Main courses $12–$24. AE, DC, DISC, MC, V. Sun–Thurs 11:30am–10pm; Fri–Sat 11:30am–11pm.

Inexpensive

Alexis Baking Company ⭐⭐ BAKERY/CAFE   Alexis (aka ABC) is a quaint, casual stop for residents and in-the-know tourists. On weekend mornings—especially Sunday, which is the only time you can get their out-of-this-world huevos rancheros—the line stretches out the door. Once you order (from the counter during the week and at the table on weekends) and find a seat in the sunny room, you can relax and enjoy the coffeehouse atmosphere. Start your day with spectacular pastries, coffee drinks, and breakfast goodies like pumpkin pancakes with sautéed pears. Lunch also bustles with locals who come for simple, fresh fare like grilled hamburgers with Gorgonzola; grilled-chicken Caesar salad; roast lamb sandwich with minted mayo and roasted shallots on rosemary bread; and lentil bulgur orzo salad. Desserts run the gamut; during the holidays, they include a moist and magical steamed persimmon pudding. Oh, and the pastry counter's cookies and cakes beg you to take something for the road.

1517 Third St. (between Main and Jefferson sts.), Napa. ℂ 707/258-1827. Main courses $5–$10 breakfast, $7–$10 lunch. MC, V. Mon–Fri 6:30am–4pm; Sat 7:30am–3pm; Sun 8am–2pm.

Villa Corona ☆ MEXICAN   The best Mexican food in town is served in this bright, funky, and colorful restaurant hidden in the southwest corner of a strip mall behind an unmemorable sports bar and restaurant. The winning plan here is simple: Order and pay at the counter, sit at either a plastic-covered table or at one of the few sidewalk seats, and wait for the huge burritos, enchiladas, and chimichangas to be delivered to your table. Those with pork preferences shouldn't miss the carnitas, which are abundantly flavorful and juicy. My personal favorites are hard-shell tacos or chicken enchiladas with light savory red sauce, a generous side of beans, and rice. Don't expect to wash down your menudo, or anything else for that matter, with a margarita. The place serves only beer and wine. Don't hesitate to come for a hearty breakfast, too. Excellent *chilaquiles* (eggs scrambled with salsa and tortilla) and huevos rancheros are part of the package.

3614 Bel Aire Plaza, on Trancas St., Napa. ℂ 707/257-8685. Breakfast $4.55–$6.75; lunch and dinner $3.75–$9.75. MC, V. Tues–Fri 9am–9pm; Sat 8am–9pm; Sun 8am–8pm.

ZuZu ☆☆ TAPAS   The most exciting Napa restaurant opening in 2002 wasn't a big fancy dining room, but rather this tiny downtown spot serving delicious affordable small plates of Spanish fare ($2–$11). A local place to the core, ZuZu takes no reservations, and diners crowd into the cramped wine-and-beer bar until they can be seated. The comfortable, warm, and not remotely corporate atmosphere extends from the environment to the food, which is seriously good. Chef Charles Weber presides over the tiny kitchen cranking out sizzling skillets of tangy and fantastic paella, fresh and clean corn soup, addictive sizzling prawns with requisite bread-dipping sauce, light and delicate sea scallop ceviche salad, and Moroccan barbecued lamb chops with a sweet-and-spicy sauce guaranteed to make you swoon. Desserts aren't as fab, but with a bottle of wine and more tasty plates than you can possibly devour, who cares? Stop here and I promise that you'll wish there was a ZuZu in your neighborhood.

829 Main St., Napa. ℂ 707/224-8555. Reservations not accepted. Tapas $2–$11. AE, MC, V. Mon–Thurs 11:30am–10pm; Fri 11:30am–midnight; Sat 4pm–midnight; Sun 4–9pm.

YOUNTVILLE
Expensive

The French Laundry ☆☆☆ CLASSIC AMERICAN/FRENCH   It's almost futile to include this restaurant, because you're about as likely to secure a reservation—or get through on the reservation line, for that matter—as you are to drive Highway 29 without passing a winery. Several years after renowned chef-owner Thomas Keller bought the place and caught the attention of epicureans worldwide (including the judges of the James Beard Awards, who named him

"Chef of the Nation" in 1997), this discreet restaurant is the hottest dinner ticket *in the world*. At least you can read about it.

Plainly put, The French Laundry is unlike any other dining experience, period. Part of it has to do with the intricate preparations, often finished table side and always presented with uncommon artistry and detail, from the food itself to the surface it's delivered on. Other factors are the service (superfluous, formal, and attentive) and the sheer length of time it takes to ride chef Keller's culinary magic carpet. The atmosphere is as serious as the diners who quietly swoon over the ongoing parade of bite-size delights. Seating ranges from downstairs to upstairs to seasonal garden tables. Technically, the prix-fixe menu offers a choice of five or nine courses (including a vegetarian menu), but after a slew of cameo appearances from the kitchen, everyone starts to lose count. Signature dishes include Keller's "tongue in cheek" (a marinated and braised round of sliced lamb tongue and tender beef cheeks) and "macaroni and cheese" (sweet butter-poached Maine lobster with creamy lobster broth and orzo with mascarpone cheese). The truth is, the experience defies description, so if you absolutely love food, you'll simply have to try it for yourself. Portions are small, but only because Keller wants his guests to taste as many things as possible. Trust me, nobody leaves hungry.

The staff is well acquainted with the wide selection of regional wines; there's a $50 corkage fee if you bring your own bottle. On warm summer nights, request a table in the flower-filled garden. *Hint:* If you can't get a reservation, try walking in—on occasion folks don't keep their reservation and tables open up, especially during lunch on rainy days. Also, Auberge du Soleil (p. 290) reserves two tables nightly which are doled out on a first-come, first-served basis. Reservations are accepted 2 months in advance of the date, starting at 10am. Anticipate hitting redial many times for the best chance. Also, insiders tell me that fewer people call on weekends, so you have a better chance at getting through the busy signal.

6640 Washington St. (at Creek St.), Yountville. © **707/944-2380.** Reservations required. Vegetarian menu $80; 5-course menu $105; chef's 9-course tasting menu $120. AE, MC, V. Fri–Sun 11am–1pm; daily 5:30–9:30pm.

Moderate

Bistro Jeanty ★★ FRENCH BISTRO This casual, warm bistro, with muted buttercup walls, two dining rooms divided by the bar, and patio seats, is where chef Phillipe Jeanty creates outstanding French comfort food for legions of fans. A few years back, the highly regarded chef left his 20-year post at Domaine Chandon (p. 273) to open this well-known and affordably priced gem. Jeanty was previously known for formal French cooking, but his cheery bistro is far more laid-back—and equally outstanding. The all-day menu includes legendary tomato soup in puff pastry; foie gras pâté; steak tartare; and house-smoked trout with potato slices. No meal should start without a paper cone filled with fried smelt, and none should end without the most insanely good crème brûlée, made with a thin layer of chocolate cream between classic vanilla custard and a caramelized sugar top. In between, I vote for decadent, fall-off-the-bone coq au vin with earthy, smoky red-wine sauce; or a juicy, thick-cut pork chop with *jus,* spinach, and mashed potatoes. I'm not as excited by the cassoulet of white beans, fennel sausage, pork, and duck leg, which tends to be overwhelming, with an overly dry breadcrumb crust. My only complaint: The menu tends to be very rich and heavy, which is great in winter but a little bit much in midsummer. That said, it's hard not to love this place.

6510 Washington St., Yountville. ① **707/944-0103**. www.bistrojeanty.com. Reservations recommended. Appetizers $6.50–$11; most main courses $14–$23. AE, MC, V. Daily 11:30am–10:30pm.

Bouchon ★★ FRENCH BISTRO   Perhaps to appease the crowds who never get a reservation at French Laundry, Thomas Keller opened this far more casual, but still delicious, French brasserie. Adam Tihany, who also conceptualized New York's Le Cirque 2000, designed the friendly and chic dining room here. Along with a raw bar, expect superb renditions of steak frites, mussels meunière, grilled-cheese sandwiches, and other heavenly French classics (try the expensive and rich foie gras pâté, which is made at French Laundry). My all-time favorite

---

⸝Tips Where to Stock Up for a Gourmet Picnic

You can easily plan your whole trip around restaurant reservations, but gather one of the world's best gourmet picnics, and the valley's your oyster.

One of the finest gourmet-food stores in the Wine Country, if not all of California, is the **Oakville Grocery Co.,** 7856 St. Helena Hwy., at Oakville Cross Road, Oakville (① **707/944-8802**). You can put together the provisions for a memorable picnic or, with at least 24 hours' notice, the staff can prepare a picnic basket for you. The store, with its small-town vibe and claustrophobia-inducing crowds, can be quite an experience. You'll find shelves crammed with the best breads and choicest cheeses in the northern Bay Area, as well as pâtés, cold cuts, crackers, top-quality olive oils, fresh foie gras (domestic and French, seasonal), smoked Norwegian salmon, fresh caviar (Beluga, Sevruga, Osetra) and, of course, an exceptional selection of California wines. The store is open daily from 9am to 6pm. There's also an espresso bar tucked in the corner (open daily 7am–6pm), offering breakfast and lunch items, and house-baked pastries.

Another of my favorite places to fill a picnic basket is New York's version of a swank European marketplace, **Dean & DeLuca,** 607 S. Main St. (Hwy. 29), north of Zinfandel Lane and south of Sulphur Springs Road, St. Helena (① **707/967-9980**; www.deananddeluca.com). The ultimate in gourmet grocery stores is more like a world's fair of foods, where everything is beautifully displayed and often painfully pricey. As you pace the barn-wood plank floors, you'll stumble upon more high-end edibles than you've probably ever seen under one roof. They include local organic produce (delivered daily); 200 domestic and imported cheeses (with an on-site aging room to ensure proper ripeness); shelves and shelves of tapenades, pastas, oils, hand-packed dried herbs and spices, chocolates, sauces, cookware, and housewares; an espresso bar; one hell of a bakery section; and more. Along the back wall, you can watch the professional chefs prepare gourmet take-out. Try fresh seared salmon with chanterelle mushrooms ($7.50 for a 6-oz. serving), rotisserie meats, salads, and sautéed vegetables. Wine master Didier Loustau presides over the 1,200-label collection. The store is open daily from 9am to 7pm (the espresso bar is open Mon–Sat at 7:30am and Sun at 9am).

must-orders: the bibb lettuce salad (seriously, trust me on this), french fries (perhaps the best in the valley), and roasted chicken bathed in wild mushroom ragout. Prices and atmosphere are far more down-to-earth than those at French Laundry. A bonus, especially for restless residents and off-duty restaurant staff, is the late hours, although they offer a more limited menu when the crowds dwindle. Another plus: Sunday brunch featuring Granny Smith apple beignets, cold-poached salmon, and fresh squeezed juices.

6534 Washington St. (at Humbolt), Yountville. ✆ **707/944-8037.** Reservations recommended. Main courses $14–$23. AE, MC, V. Mon–Sat 11:30am–1am; Sun 11am–1am.

Mustards Grill ★★ CALIFORNIA   Mustards is one of those standby restaurants that everyone seems to love because it's dependable and its menu has something that suits any food craving. Housed in a convivial, barn-style space, it offers an 11-page wine list and an ambitious chalkboard list of specials. My party started out with wonderfully light seared ahi tuna that melted in the mouth the way ahi should. Although the tea-smoked Peking duck with almond onion sauce and grilled rabbit with potatoes, fennel, and saffron broth were tempting, we opted for a moist, perfectly flavored grilled lemon-garlic chicken breast with mashed potatoes and fresh herbs. The menu includes something for everyone, from vegetarians to good old burger lovers, and the wine list features nothing but "New World" wines.

7399 St. Helena Hwy. (Hwy. 29), Yountville. ✆ **707/944-2424.** Reservations recommended. Main courses $11–$27. AE, DC, DISC, MC, V. Mon–Thurs 11:30am–9pm; Fri 11:30am–10pm; Sat 11am–10pm; Sun 11am–9pm.

Inexpensive
Bouchon Bakery ★ FRENCH BAKERY   In the summer of 2003, famed French Laundry chef Thomas Keller opened this adorable and extremely authentic French bakery next door to his restaurant Bouchon (see above). It ain't cheap, but that doesn't stop locals and visitors from lining up amid the pretty green-mosaic-tiled storefront for the outstanding bread baked twice daily, paper-wrapped panini, killer treats (think éclairs, cookies, tarts, and more), coffee drinks, classic sandwiches, and near-perfect pastry. Grab it to go or snack at one of the garden tables, which overlook Yountville's main drag.

6534 Washington St. (between Jefferson and Yount sts.). ✆ **707/944-2253.** Pastries and sandwiches 75¢–$7. MC, V. Daily 7am–6pm.

RUTHERFORD
Expensive
Auberge du Soleil ★★ *Finds* WINE COUNTRY CUISINE   There is no better restaurant view than the one at Auberge du Soleil, perched on a hillside overlooking the valley. Alfresco dining rises to an entirely new level here, particularly on warm summer afternoons at sunset. In fact, I recommend coming during the day (request terrace seating) to join the wealthy patrons, many of whom have emerged from their überluxury guest rooms and are slinking to a table to dine above the vines. The kitchen, previously overseen by the very talented chef Richard Reddington, is awaiting a replacement, since he began working at **Masa's** (p. 112) in San Francisco in July of 2004. We hope that whoever it is will continue to turn out superb seasonal dishes such as well-prepared sautéed sweetbreads, venison loin with butternut squash, stuffed squab, and roasted saddle of lamb. The interior is warm, bustling, and formal enough that some folks wear ties. The only drawback: Service is unsteady. *Tip:* If you didn't make

reservations, know that the restaurant reserves two tables nightly that are doled out on a first-come, first-served basis.

180 Rutherford Hill Rd., Rutherford. ℂ 707/963-1211. Reservations recommended. Main courses $19–$23 lunch, $28–$34 dinner; 4-course fixed-price dinner $79. AE, DISC, MC, V. Daily 7–11am and 11:30am–2:30pm; Sun–Thurs 6–9:30pm; Fri–Sat 5:30–9:30pm.

La Toque ★★ FRENCH   Renowned chef Ken Frank left Los Angeles's fenix at the Argyle Hotel to open one of the Wine Country's most formal dining rooms, which features a beautifully presented five-course extravaganza. Each table at the elegant restaurant adjoining Rancho Caymus Inn (p. 290) is well spaced, creating plenty of room to showcase the chef-owner's memorable and innovative French-inspired cuisine. Service is almost too laid-back with conversational attitude, but simultaneously it is very professional, ensuring that you'll never want for anything. If you're lucky, the menu will feature an incredible Indian spice–rubbed foie gras with Madras carrot purée (one of the best I've had); melt-in-your-mouth yellowfin tuna with braised daikon, red wine, and sautéed pea sprouts; knockout Maine lobster with creamy orzo and lobster cabernet sauce; or Niman Ranch rib roast with roasted root vegetables and red wine. However, the menu changes weekly, so you're likely to find a completely different, but equally delicious, menu when you get there. (Check the website for menus and a wine list!) Should you find room and the extra few bucks for the cheese course, try a few delicious selections, served with walnut bread. For an additional $56 per person you can also drink well-paired wines with each course.

1140 Rutherford Rd., Rutherford. ℂ 707/963-9770. www.latoque.com. Reservations recommended. Fixed-price menu $92. Wed–Sun 5:30–10pm. Closed Mon–Tues.

ST. HELENA
Expensive

Terra ★★★ CONTEMPORARY AMERICAN   Terra is one of my favorite restaurants, because it manages to be humble even though it serves some of the most extraordinary food in Northern California. The creation of Lissa Doumani and her husband, Hiro Sone, a master chef who hails from Japan, is a culmination of talents brought together nearly 15 years ago, after the duo worked at L.A.'s Spago. Today, the menu reflects Sone's full use of the region's bounty and his formal training in classic European and Japanese cuisine. Dishes—all of which are incredible and are served in the rustic-romantic dining room—range from understated and refined (broiled sake-marinated cod with shrimp dumplings and shiso broth) to rock-your-world flavorful (petit ragout of sweetbreads, prosciutto, mushroom, and white truffle oil; or grilled squab with leek and bacon bread pudding and roasted garlic foie gras sauce). I cannot express the importance of saving room for dessert (or forcing it even if you didn't). Doumani's recipes, which include tiramisu and an out-of-this-world heavenly orange risotto in a brandy snap cookie with passion fruit sauce, are some of the best I've ever tasted.

1345 Railroad Ave. (between Adams and Hunt sts.), St. Helena. ℂ 707/963-8931. www.terrarestaurant. com. Reservations recommended. Main courses $19–$29. AE, DC, MC, V. Sun–Mon and Wed–Thurs 6–9:30pm; Fri–Sat 6–10pm. Closed for 2 weeks in early Jan.

Moderate

Tra Vigne Restaurant ★★ ITALIAN   Tra Vigne's combination of good ultrafresh food, high-energy atmosphere, gorgeous patio seating, and "reasonable" prices makes this restaurant a long-standing favorite among visitors and locals. Add to that plenty of seating and service running from lunch through dinner, and it's no wonder the enormous dining room packs 'em in. Whether guests are in the Tuscany-evoking courtyard, terrace (heated on cold nights), or in the center of the bustling scene, they're usually thrilled just to have a seat. Even though the wonderful bread (served with house-made flavored olive oils) is tempting, save room for the robust California dishes, cooked Italian-style. The menu features about one daily oven-roasted pizza special; tried-and-true stand-bys like short ribs; fritto misto; and irresistible whole roasted fish. Equally tempting are the fresh pastas—such as spaghettini with cuttlefish Bolognese and spring onions—and delicious desserts.

1050 Charter Oak Ave., St. Helena. ⓒ **707/963-4444.** Reservations recommended. Main courses $13–$22. DC, DISC, MC, V. Daily 11:30am–10pm.

Wine Spectator Greystone Restaurant ⍟ CALIFORNIA This place offers a visual and culinary feast that's unparalleled in the area, if not the state. The room is an enormous stone-walled former Christian Bros. winery, warmed by the festive decor and heavenly aromas. Cooking islands—complete with scur-rying chefs, steaming pots, and rotating chickens—provide entertainment. The tastings (appetizer) menu features dishes inspired by fresh, seasonal ingredients such as grilled mahimahi with asparagus salad, oven-roasted chicken breast with mashed potatoes, and Dungeness crab salad with avocado and grapefruit sauce.

I recommend that you opt for a barrage of appetizers for your table to share. You should also order the "Flights of Fancy"—$14 to $34 allows you to sample three 3-ounce pours of local wines such as white rhone, pinot, or zinfandel. While the food is serious, the atmosphere is playful—casual enough that you'll feel comfortable in jeans or shorts. If you want to ensure a meal here, reserve far in advance. I prefer to stop by, have a snack at the bar, and eat big meals elsewhere.

At the Culinary Institute of America at Greystone, 2555 Main St., St. Helena. ⓒ **707/967-1010.** Reservations recommended. Tastings $9; main courses $17–$27. AE, DC, MC, V. Daily 11:15am–10pm.

Inexpensive

Market ⍟⍟ AMERICAN San Francisco veterans Nick Peyton (of Restaurant Gary Danko; p. 138) and Douglas Keane (chef at Jardinière; p. 146) aim to fill a much-needed niche of affordable St. Helena dining with this upscale but cheap ode to American comfort food. Mimicking its wealthy farming environs, it's a marriage of contradictions, where fancy stone-wall and Brunswick bar surroundings are paired with clunky steak knives and simple white-plate presentations. Try meaty Dungeness crab cakes with avocado coulis; barbe-cue sauce–glazed meatloaf over gravy, mashed potatoes, and carrots; or toast-it-yourself s'mores with crisp homemade graham crackers. Trust me: This is the ultimate find for anyone who wants great atmosphere and a nice meal at an absurdly low price—especially if you drop by for their obscenely cheap (around $13) three-course lunch.

1347 Main St., St. Helena. ⓒ **707/963-3799.** Most main courses $7–$15. AE, MC, V. Wed–Mon lunch 11:30am–2pm, bar menu 2–4:30pm; dinner 5:30–9pm, bar menu 9–11pm. Closed Tues.

Pizzeria Tra Vigne ⍟ *Kids* *Value* ITALIAN After spending a week in Wine Country, I usually can't stand the thought of another decadent wine and foie gras meal. That's when I race here for a $5.95 chopped salad, a welcome respite from gluttonous excess. Families and locals come here for another reason: Although the menu is limited, it's a total winner for anyone in search of freshly prepared, wholesome food at atypically cheap Wine Country prices. A Caesar salad, for example, costs a mere $5.95. "Piadine"—pizzas folded like a soft taco—are the house specialty and come filled with such delights as fresh Maine clams and oregano. Pizzas are of the build-your-own variety, with gourmet toppings like sautéed mushrooms, fennel sausage, baby spinach, sun-dried tomatoes, and homemade pepperoni. The 13 respectable local wines come by the glass starting at a toast-worthy $4.50, or $15 per bottle. Dessert, at less than $4 a pop for gelato, biscotti, or pound cake, is an overall sweet deal. Kids especially like the pool table and big-screen TV.

At the Inn at Southbridge, 1016 Main St., St. Helena. ℂ **707/967-9999.** Pastas $6–$8; pizzas $8–$19. DC, DISC, MC, V. Daily 11:30am–9pm (Fri–Sat until 9:30pm).

Taylor's Automatic Refresher ★★ DINER   It isn't every day that a roadside burger shack gets a huge spread in *Food & Wine* magazine, but then again, Taylor's Automatic Refresher isn't your average fast-food stop. At this completely outdoor diner built in 1949, you order at the counter, settle at a picnic table in the front facing Highway 29 or in the more pastoral back, and wait for your name to be called. When it is, you'll receive totally gourmet versions of classic diner food—burgers on surprisingly soft but sturdy buns, fries, and creamy shakes. Those who are less carnivorous can opt for an ahi tuna burger or various tacos and salads.

933 Main St., St Helena. ℂ **707/963-3486.** www.taylorsrefresher.com. Main courses $4–$13. AE, MC, V. Daily 11am–8pm, 9pm in summer.

CALISTOGA
Moderate
All Seasons Café ★★ CALIFORNIA   Wine Country devotees wend their way to the All Seasons Café in downtown Calistoga because of its extensive wine list and knowledgeable staff. The trick is to buy a bottle of wine from the cafe's wine shop, then bring it to your table; the cafe adds a corkage fee of around $15 instead of tripling the price of the bottle (as most restaurants do). The diverse menu dances with decadences such as seared Maine scallops with truffle-scented risotto, or red-wine-braised short ribs. Culinary Director Sonja Murphy saves guests from any major faux pas by matching wines to dishes on the menu, so you know just what's right for smoked salmon and Crescenza cheese pizza.

1400 Lincoln Ave. (at Washington St.), Calistoga. ℂ **707/942-9111.** Reservations recommended on weekends. Main courses $10–$14 lunch, $16–$26 dinner. DISC, MC, V. Lunch Wed–Sun 11am–3pm; dinner nightly 6–9pm.

Inexpensive
Palisades Market ★★ DELI/MARKET   Trust me, sandwiches as delicious as those served at this adorable, old-fashioned gourmet market are an absolute rarity and a sure-fire addiction. Drop in for wine, juice, soda, cheese, tamales, green salads, lasagna, soup, picnic items, and every kind of treat you can think of, but under no circumstances should you skip the sandwiches. If they have chicken and Swiss cheese and almond butter on a toasted bun, don't hesitate! Order it heated and devour immediately. I promise you'll remember it for days. Other favorites: ham, Gruyère cheese, onions, lettuce, mayo, and Dijon mustard on a baguette; or roast beef, cheddar cheese, grilled onions, lettuce, and roasted-garlic mayo on a soft French roll. Call 2 days in advance and Palisades will box a lunch for you; $16 will get you a sandwich, salad, fruit, cookie, and utensils.

1506 Lincoln Ave., Calistoga. ℂ **707/942-9549.** Sandwiches $4.95–$7.95. AE, MC, V. Sun–Wed 7:30am–6pm; Thurs–Sat 7:30am–7pm.

Wappo Bar & Bistro GLOBAL   One of the best alfresco dining venues in the Wine Country is under Wappo's jasmine-and-grapevine–covered arbor. Unfortunately, food and service are a very distant second. But much can be forgiven when the wine's flowing and you're surrounded by pastoral splendor. The menu offers a global selection, from tandoori chicken to roast rabbit with oven tomato tagliarini. Desserts of choice are black-bottom coconut cream pie and strawberry rhubarb pie.

1226B Washington St. (off Lincoln Ave.), Calistoga. © **707/942-4712**. www.wappobar.com. Main courses $14–$22. AE, MC, V. Wed–Mon 11:30am–2:30pm and 6–9:30pm.

2 Sonoma Valley

A pastoral contrast to Napa, Sonoma manages to maintain a backcountry ambience, thanks to its far lower density of wineries, restaurants, and hotels. Small, family-owned wineries are Sonoma's mainstay; tastings are low-key and come with plenty of friendly banter with the winemakers. Basically, this is the valley to target if your ideal vacation includes visiting a handful of wineries along quiet woodsy roads, avoiding shopping outlets and Napa's high-end glitz, and simply enjoying the laid-back country atmosphere.

The valley is some 17 miles long and 7 miles wide, and it's bordered by two mountain ranges: the Mayacamas to the east and the Sonomas to the west. Unlike in Napa Valley, you won't find palatial wineries with million-dollar art collections, aerial trams, and Hollywood ego trips (*read:* Niebaum-Coppola). Rather, the Sonoma Valley offers a refreshing dose of reality, where modestly sized wineries are integrated into the community. If Napa Valley feels like a fantasyland, where everything exists to service the almighty grape and the visitors it attracts, then the Sonoma Valley is its antithesis, an unpretentious gaggle of ordinary towns, ranches, and wineries that welcome tourists but don't necessarily rely on them. The result is a chance to experience what Napa Valley must have been like long before the Seagrams and Moët et Chandons of the world turned the Wine Country into a major tourist destination.

As in Napa, you can pick up *Wine Country Review* throughout Sonoma. It gives you the most up-to-date information on wineries and related area events.

ESSENTIALS
GETTING THERE   From San Francisco, cross the Golden Gate Bridge and stay on U.S. 101 north. Exit at Highway 37; after 10 miles, turn north onto Highway 121. After another 10 miles, turn north onto Highway 12 (Broadway), which takes you directly into the town of Sonoma.

VISITOR INFORMATION   While you're in Sonoma, stop by the **Sonoma Valley Visitors Bureau,** 453 First St. E. (© **707/996-1090;** www.sonomavalley. com). It's open daily from 9am to 7pm in summer and from 9am to 5pm in winter. An additional **Visitors Bureau** is a few miles south of the square at 25200 Arnold Dr. (Hwy. 121), at the entrance to Viansa Winery (© **707/935-4747**); it's open daily from 9am to 4pm, to 5pm in summer.

If you prefer advance information from the bureau, you can contact the Sonoma Valley Visitors Bureau to order the free *Sonoma Valley Visitors Guide,* which lists almost every lodge, winery, and restaurant in the valley.

TOURING THE SONOMA VALLEY & WINERIES
Sonoma Valley is currently home to about 35 wineries (including California's first winery, Buena Vista, founded in 1857) and 13,000 acres of vineyards. It

produces roughly 25 types of wines, totaling more than five million cases a year. Unlike the rigidly structured tours at many of Napa Valley's corporate-owned wineries, tastings and tours on the Sonoma side of the Mayacamas Mountains are usually free and low-key.

The towns and wineries covered below are organized geographically from south to north, starting at the intersection of Highway 37 and Highway 121 in the Carneros District and ending in Kenwood. The wineries tend to be a little more spread out here than they are in Napa Valley, but they're easy to find. Still, it's best to decide which wineries you're most interested in and devise a touring strategy before you set out, so you don't do too much backtracking.

I've reviewed some of my favorite Sonoma Valley wineries here—more than enough to keep you busy tasting wine for a long weekend. If you'd like a complete list of local wineries, be sure to pick up one of the free guides available at the Sonoma Valley Visitors Bureau (see "Visitor Information," above).

For a map of the below wineries, please see "The Wine Country" map on p. 271.

THE CARNEROS DISTRICT

As you approach the Wine Country from the south, you must first pass through the Carneros District, a cool, windswept region that borders the San Pablo Bay and marks the entrance to both the Napa and Sonoma valleys. Until the latter part of the 20th century, this mixture of marsh, sloughs, and rolling hills was mainly used as sheep pasture (*carneros* means "sheep" in Spanish). However, after experimental plantings yielded slow-growing, high-quality grapes—particularly chardonnay and pinot noir—several Napa and Sonoma wineries expanded their plantings here. They eventually established the Carneros District as an American Viticultural Appellation, a legally defined wine-grape growing area. Although about a dozen wineries are spread throughout the region, there are no major towns or attractions—just plenty of gorgeous scenery as you cruise along Highway 121, the major junction between Napa and Sonoma.

Viansa Winery and Italian Marketplace ✸ *Finds* The first major winery you'll encounter as you enter Sonoma Valley from the south, this sprawling Tuscan-style villa perches atop a knoll overlooking the entire lower valley. Viansa is the brainchild of Sam and Vicki Sebastiani, who left the family dynasty to create their own temple to food and wine. (*Viansa* is a contraction of "Vicki and Sam.") While Sam, a third-generation winemaker, runs the winery, Vicki manages the marketplace, a large room crammed with a cornucopia of high-quality preserves, mustards, olive oils, pastas, salads, breads, desserts, Italian tableware, cookbooks, and wine-related gifts.

The winery, which does an extensive mail-order business through The Tuscan Club, has established a favorable reputation for its cabernet, sauvignon blanc, and chardonnay. Blended from premium Napa and Sonoma grapes, they're sold in the sexiest-shaped bottles in Sonoma. Sam is also experimenting with Italian grape varieties such as vernaccia, sangiovese, and nebbiolo, most of which are sold exclusively at the winery. Free tastings are poured at the east end of the marketplace, and the self-guided tour includes a trip through the underground barrel-aging cellar adorned with colorful hand-painted murals. Guided tours, held at 11am and 2pm, will set you back $5.

Viansa is also one of the few wineries in Sonoma Valley that sells deli items— the focaccia sandwiches are delicious. You can dine alfresco under the grape trellis while you admire the bucolic view.

25200 Arnold Dr. (Calif. 121), Sonoma. (C) **800/995-4740** or 707/935-4700. www.viansa.com. Daily 10am–5pm. Daily self-guided tours.

Gloria Ferrer Champagne Caves ⭐ *(Finds)*   When you have had it up to here with chardonnays and pinots, it's time to pay a visit to Gloria Ferrer, the grande dame of the Wine Country's sparkling-wine producers. Who's Gloria? She's the wife of José Ferrer, whose family has made sparkling wine for 5 centuries. The family business, Freixenet, is the largest producer of sparkling wine in the world; Cordon Negro is its most popular brand. That equals big bucks, and certainly a good chunk went into building this palatial estate. Glimmering like Oz high atop a gently sloping hill, it overlooks the verdant Carneros District. On a sunny day, enjoying a glass of dry brut while soaking in the magnificent views is a must.

If you're unfamiliar with the term *méthode champenoise,* be sure to take the free 30-minute tour of the fermenting tanks, bottling line, and caves brimming with racks of yeast-laden bottles. Afterward, retire to the elegant tasting room for a flute of brut or cuvée ($5–$9 a glass, $20 and up per bottle), find an empty chair on the veranda, and say, "Ahhh. *This* is the life." There are picnic tables, but it's usually too windy for comfort, and you must buy a bottle of sparkling wine to reserve a table.

23555 Carneros Hwy. (Calif. 121), Sonoma. (C) **707/996-7256**. www.gloriaferrer.com. Daily 10am–5:30pm. Tours daily 11am–4pm.

SONOMA

At the northern boundary of the Carneros District along Highway 12 is the centerpiece of Sonoma Valley. The midsize town of Sonoma owes much of its appeal to Mexican general Mariano Guadalupe Vallejo, who fashioned this pleasant, slow-paced community after a typical Mexican village—right down to its central plaza, Sonoma's geographical and commercial center. The plaza sits at the top of a T formed by Broadway (Hwy. 12) and Napa Street. Most of the surrounding streets form a grid pattern around this axis, making Sonoma easy to negotiate. The plaza's Bear Flag Monument marks the spot where the crude Bear Flag was raised in 1846, signaling the end of Mexican rule; the symbol was later adopted by the state of California and placed on its flag. The 8-acre park at the center of the plaza, complete with two ponds populated by ducks and geese, is perfect for an afternoon siesta in the cool shade.

Buena Vista Winery   Count Agoston Haraszthy, the Hungarian émigré who is universally regarded as the father of California's wine industry, founded this historic winery in 1857. A close friend of General Vallejo, Haraszthy returned from Europe in 1861 with 100,000 of the finest vine cuttings, which he made available to all growers. Although Buena Vista's winemaking now takes place at an ultramodern facility in the Carneros District, the winery maintains a tasting room inside the restored 1862 Press House. The beautiful stone-crafted room brims with wines, wine-related gifts, and accessories.

Tastings are $5 for four wines with complimentary glass, $10 for a flight of three of the really good stuff. You can take the self-guided tour any time during operating hours; a "Historical Tour and Tasting," offered daily at 11am and 2pm, details the life and times of Count Haraszthy. After tasting, grab your favorite bottle, a selection of cheeses from the Sonoma Cheese Factory, salami, bread, and pâté (all available in the tasting room), and plant yourself at one of the many picnic tables in the lush, verdant setting.

18000 Old Winery Rd. (off E. Napa St., slightly northeast of downtown), Sonoma. ℂ **800/926-1266** or 707/938-1266. www.buenavistawinery.com. Daily 10am–5pm. Self-guided tours only.

Sebastiani Vineyards & Winery The name Sebastiani is practically synonymous with Sonoma. What started in 1904, when Samuele Sebastiani began producing his first wines, has in three generations grown into a small empire, producing some 300,000 cases a year. After a few years of seismic retrofitting, a face-lift, and a temporary tasting room, the original 1904 winery is now open to the public with more extensive educational tours, an 80-foot S-shaped tasting bar, and lots of shopping opportunities in the gift shop. In the contemporary tasting room's minimuseum area you can see the winery's original turn-of-the-20th-century crusher and press, as well as the world's largest collection of oak-barrel carvings, crafted by local artist Earle Brown. If it's merely wine that interests you, you can sample an extensive selection of wines for $6 to $15, the latter of which includes a keepsake glass. Bottle prices are reasonable, ranging from $8 to $90. A picnic area adjoins the cellars; a far more scenic spot is across the parking lot in Sebastiani's Cherryblock Vineyards.

389 Fourth St. E., Sonoma. ℂ **800/888-5532** or 707/938-5532. www.sebastiani.com. Daily 10am–5pm. Tours Mon–Fri 11am and 3pm, Sat–Sun 11am, 1pm, and 3pm.

Ravenswood Winery Compared to old heavies like Sebastiani and Buena Vista, Ravenswood is a relative newcomer to the Sonoma wine scene. Nevertheless, it has quickly established itself as the sine qua non of zinfandel, the versatile grape that's quickly gaining ground on the rapacious cabernet sauvignon. In fact, Ravenswood is the first winery in the United States to focus primarily on zins, which make up about three-quarters of its 500,000-case production; it also produces merlot, cabernet sauvignon, and a small amount of chardonnay.

Moments **Touring the Sonoma Valley by Bike**

Sonoma and its neighboring towns are so small, close together, and relatively flat that it's not difficult to get around on two wheels. In fact, if you're in no great hurry, there's no better way to tour the Sonoma Valley than by bicycle, even though there are no great bike routes (it's all along the road for the most part). You can rent a bike from the **Goodtime Bicycle Company** ✦ (ℂ **888/525-0453** or 707/938-0453; www.goodtimetouring.com). The staff will happily point you to easy bike trails, or you can take an organized excursion to Kenwood-area wineries or south Sonoma wineries. Goodtime also provides a gourmet lunch featuring local Sonoma products. If you purchase wine along the way, Goodtime will carry it for you and help with shipping arrangements. Lunch rides start at 10:30am and end around 3:30pm. The cost, including food and equipment, is $99 per person (that's a darn good deal). Rentals cost $25 a day, and include helmets, locks, everything else you'll need, and delivery and pick-up to and from local hotels.

Mountain bikes, helmets, and locks are also available for rent from **Sonoma Valley Cyclery**, 20093 Broadway, Sonoma (ℂ **707/935-3377**), for $35 a day.

The winery is smartly designed—recessed into the hillside to protect its treasures from the simmering summers. Tours follow the winemaking process from grape to glass, and include a visit to the aromatic oak-barrel aging rooms. You're welcome to bring your own picnic basket to any of the tables. Tastings are $5 for four wines, which is refundable with purchase.

18701 Gehricke Rd. (off Lovall Valley Rd.), Sonoma. ✆ **888/NO-WIMPY** or 707/938-1960. www.ravenswood-wine.com. Daily 10am–4:30pm. Tours by reservation only at 10:30am.

GLEN ELLEN

About 7 miles north of Sonoma on Highway 12 is the town of Glen Ellen. Although just a fraction of the size of Sonoma, Glen Ellen is home to several of the valley's finest wineries, restaurants, and inns. Aside from the addition of a few new restaurants, this charming town hasn't changed much since the days when Jack London settled on his Beauty Ranch, about a mile west. Other than the wineries, you'll find few real signs of commercialism; the shops and restaurants, along one main winding lane, cater to a small, local clientele—that is, until the summer tourist season begins and traffic nearly triples on the weekends. If you haven't decided where you want to set up camp during your visit to the Wine Country, I highly recommend this lovable little town.

Arrowood Vineyards & Winery   Richard Arrowood had already established a reputation as a master winemaker at Château St. Jean when he and his wife, Alis Demers Arrowood, set out on their own in 1986. Their picturesque winery stands on a gently rising hillside lined with perfectly manicured vineyards. Tastings take place in the Hospitality House, the newer of Arrowood's two stately gray-and-white buildings. They're fashioned after New England farmhouses, complete with wraparound porches. Richard's focus is on making world-class wine with minimal intervention, and his results are impressive: More than one of his current releases has scored over 90 points in *Wine Spectator*. Mind you, excellence doesn't come cheap: a taste here is $5 or $10 for limited-production wines, but if you're curious about what near-perfection tastes like, it's well worth it. ***Note:*** No picnic facilities are available here.

14347 Sonoma Hwy. (Calif. 12), Glen Ellen. ✆ **707/935-2600**. www.arrowoodvineyards.com. Daily 10am–4:30pm. Tours by appointment only, daily at 10:30am and 2:30pm.

Benziger Family Winery ⭐ *Finds*   A visit here confirms that this is indeed a family winery. At any given time, two generations of Benzigers (*Ben*-zigger) may be running around tending to chores, and they instantly make you feel as if you're part of the clan. The pastoral, user-friendly property features an exceptional self-guided tour ("The most comprehensive tour in the wine industry," according to *Wine Spectator*), gardens, a spacious tasting room staffed by amiable folks, and an art gallery. The 40-minute tram tour, pulled by a beefy tractor, is both informative and fun. It winds through the estate vineyards and into caves, and ends with a tasting of one estate wine. ***Tip:*** Tram tickets—a hot item in the summer—are available on a first-come, first-served basis, so either arrive early or stop by in the morning to pick up afternoon tickets.

Tastings of the standard-release wines are $5. Tastes of several limited-production wines or reserve or estate wines cost $10. The winery offers several scenic picnic spots.

1883 London Ranch Rd. (off Arnold Dr., on the way to Jack London State Historic Park), Glen Ellen. ✆ **800/989-8890** or 707/935-3000. www.benziger.com. Tasting room daily 10am–5pm. Tram tours daily (weather permitting) $10 adults and $5 children at 11:30am and at 12:30, 1:30, 2:30, and 3:30pm.

KENWOOD

A few miles north of Glen Ellen along Highway 12 is the tiny town of Kenwood, the valley's northernmost outpost. Although Kenwood Vineyards' wines are well known throughout the United States, the town itself consists of little more than a few restaurants, wineries, and modest homes on the wooded hillsides. The nearest lodging, the luxurious Kenwood Inn & Spa (p. 314), is about a mile south of the vineyards. Kenwood makes for a pleasant day trip—a tour of Château St. Jean (see below), dinner at Kenwood Restaurant (p. 319)—from Glen Ellen or Sonoma.

Kenwood Vineyards   Kenwood's history dates from 1906, when the Pagani brothers made their living selling wine straight from the barrel and into the jug. In 1970 the Lee family bought the property and dumped a ton of money into converting the aging winery into a modern, high-production facility (most of it cleverly concealed in the original barnlike buildings). Since then, Kenwood has earned a solid reputation for consistent quality with each of its varietals: cabernet sauvignon, chardonnay, zinfandel, pinot noir, merlot and, most popular, sauvignon blanc—a crisp, light wine with hints of melon.

Although the winery looks rather modest in size, its output is staggering: nearly 500,000 cases of ultrapremium wines fermented in steel tanks and French and American oak barrels. Popular with collectors is winemaker Michael Lee's Artist Series cabernet sauvignon, a limited production from the winery's best vineyards, featuring labels with original artwork by renowned artists. The tasting room, housed in one of the old barns, offers $2 to $5 tastings of most varieties and sells gift items. *FYI:* The Lees no longer own the winery.

9592 Sonoma Hwy. (Calif. 12), Kenwood. © 707/833-5891. www.kenwoodvineyards.com. Daily 10am–4:30pm.

Château St. Jean ★ *Finds*   Château St. Jean is notable for its exceptionally beautiful buildings, expansive landscaped grounds, and gourmet marketlike tasting room. Among California wineries, it's a pioneer in vineyard designation—the procedure of making wine from, and naming it for, a single vineyard. A private drive takes you to what was once a 250-acre country retreat built in 1920; a well-manicured lawn overlooking the meticulously maintained vineyards is now a picnic area, complete with a fountain and umbrella-shaded picnic tables.

In the huge tasting room—where there's also a charcuterie shop and plenty of housewares for sale—you can sample Château St. Jean's wide array of wines. They range from chardonnays and cabernet sauvignon to fumé blanc, merlot, Johannesburg Riesling, and Gewürztraminer. Tastings are $5 per person; $10 per person for reserve wines.

8555 Sonoma Hwy. (Calif. 12), Kenwood. © 800/543-7572 or 707/833-4134. www.chateaustjean.com. Tasting daily 10am–5pm. Tours 11am and 3pm. At the foot of Sugarloaf Ridge, just north of Kenwood and east of Hwy. 12.

St. Francis Winery   Although St. Francis Winery makes a commendable chardonnay, zinfandel, and cabernet sauvignon, it's their highly coveted merlot that they're best known for. Winemaker Tom Mackey, a former high-school English teacher from San Francisco, has been hailed as the "Master of Merlot" by *Wine Spectator* for his uncanny ability to craft the finest merlot in California.

If you've visited this winery and haven't been here in a while, don't follow your memory to the front door. In 2001, St. Francis moved a little farther north to digs bordering on the Santa Rosa County line. The original property was planted in 1910 as part of a wedding gift to Alice Kunde (scion of the local Kunde family) and christened St. Francis of Assisi in 1971 when Joe Martin and Lloyd Canton—two white-collar executives turned vintners—completed their long-awaited dream winery. Today the winery still owns the property, but there's new history in the making at their much larger facilities, which include two tasting rooms and an upscale gift shop. Tastings are $10 for four current releases. The $20 for reserve tasting is paired with food, served in the private reserve tasting room, and requires an appointment. Now that St. Francis is planning more special activities, it's worthwhile to call or check their website for their calendar of events.

100 Pythian Rd. (Calif.12/Sonoma Hwy.), Santa Rosa (at the Kenwood border). (C) 800/543-7713 or 707/833-4666. www.stfranciswine.com. Daily 10am–5pm.

JUST UP FROM THE SONOMA VALLEY: SANTA ROSA

Matanzas Creek (★) *Finds* It's not technically in Sonoma Valley, but if there's one winery that's worth a detour, it's Matanzas (Mah-*tan*-zas) Creek. After a scenic 20-minute drive, you'll arrive at one of the prettiest wineries in California, blanketed by fields of lavender (usually in bloom near the end of June) and surrounded by rolling hills of well-tended vineyards.

The winery has a rather unorthodox history. In 1978, Sandra and Bill MacIver, neither of whom had any previous experience in winemaking or business, set out with one goal in mind: to create the finest wines in the country. Actually, they overshot the mark. With the release of their Journey 1990 chardonnay, they were hailed by wine critics as the proud parents of the finest chardonnay ever produced in the United States, comparable to the finest white wines in the world. Though they no longer own the property, their heritage of excellence lives on.

This state-of-the-art, environmentally conscious winery produces chardonnay, sauvignon blanc, merlot, syrah, and cabernet, all of which are available for tasting for $5, which is applied toward purchase. Prices for current releases are, as you would imagine, at the higher end. Also available for purchase are culinary lavender and handmade lavender products from Matanzas Creek's own 1-acre lavender field. Purchase a full glass of wine and bring it outside to savor as you wander through these wonderfully aromatic gardens. Picnic tables hidden under groves of oak have pleasant views of the surrounding vineyards. On the return trip, be sure to take the Sonoma Mountain Road detour for a real backcountry experience.

6097 Bennett Valley Rd. (off Warm Springs Rd.), Santa Rosa. (C) 800/590-6464 or 707/528-6464. www.matanzascreek.com. Daily 10am–4:30pm. Tours daily, by appointment only, at 10:30am (and 3pm Mon–Fri). From Hwy. 12 in Kenwood or Glen Ellen, take Warm Springs Rd. turnoff to Bennett Valley Rd.; the drive takes 15–20 min.

WHERE TO STAY IN SONOMA VALLEY

Keep in mind that during the peak season and on weekends, most B&Bs and hotels require a minimum 2-night stay. Of course, that's assuming you can find a vacancy; make reservations as far in advance as possible. If you are having trouble finding a room, call the **Sonoma Valley Visitors Bureau** ((C) **707/996-1090;** www.sonomavalley.com). The staff will try to refer you to a lodging that has a room to spare but won't make reservations for you. Another option is the **Bed and Breakfast Association of Sonoma Valley** ((C) **800/969-4667**), which can refer you to a B&B that belongs to the association and make reservations for you, too.

Pricing Categories

Hotel listings are arranged below first by area, then by price, using the following categories: **Very Expensive,** more than $250 per night; **Expensive,** $200 to $250 per night; **Moderate,** $150 to $200 per night; and **Inexpensive,** less than $150 per night.

SONOMA
Very Expensive

Fairmont Sonoma Mission Inn & Spa ★★★   As you drive through Boyes Hot Springs, you may wonder why someone decided to build a multimillion-dollar spa resort in this ordinary little town. There's no view to speak of, and it certainly isn't within walking distance of any wineries or fancy restaurants. So what's the deal? It's the naturally heated artesian mineral water, piped from directly underneath the spa into the temperature-controlled pools and whirlpools. Set on 12 meticulously groomed acres, the Sonoma Mission Inn consists of a massive three-story replica of a Spanish mission (well, aside from the pink paint job) built in 1927, an array of satellite wings housing numerous superluxury suites and, of course, world-class spa facilities. It's a popular retreat for the wealthy and well known, so don't be surprised if you see Barbra Streisand or Harrison Ford. Big changes have occurred here since the resort changed ownership in 2000. It has gained 60 suites, a $20-million spa facility (you won't even recognize the old one), and the Sonoma Golf Club.

The modern rooms have plantation-style shutters, ceiling fans, down comforters, and oversize bath towels. The Wine Country rooms feature king-size beds, desks, refrigerators, and huge limestone and marble bathrooms; some offer wood-burning fireplaces, too, and many have balconies. The older, slightly smaller Historic Inn rooms were newly appointed in 2004. For the ultimate in luxury, the opulently appointed Mission Suites are the way to go.

Corner of Boyes Blvd. and Calif. 12, P.O. Box 1447, Sonoma, CA 95476. © **800/441-1414** or 707/938-9000. Fax 707/938-4250. www.fairmont.com/sonoma. 228 units. $199–$1,000 double. AE, DC, MC, V. Valet parking is free for day use (spa goers) and $12 for overnight guests. From central Sonoma, drive 3 miles north on Hwy. 12 and turn left on Boyes Blvd. **Amenities:** 2 restaurants; 2 large heated outdoor pools; golf course; health club and spa (see box, "The Super Spa," on p. 312 for the complete rundown); Jacuzzi; sauna; bike rental; concierge; business center; salon; room service (6am–11pm); babysitting; same-day laundry service/dry cleaning. *In room:* A/C, TV, dataport, minibar, hair dryer, iron, safe, high-speed Internet access ($13 per day) in most rooms, complimentary bottle of wine upon arrival.

MacArthur Place ★★   A highly recommended alternative to the Fairmont Sonoma Mission Inn & Spa (see above) is this much smaller and more intimate luxury property and spa located 4 blocks south of Sonoma's plaza. Once a 300-acre vineyard and ranch, MacArthur Place has since been whittled down to a 5½-acre "country estate" replete with landscaped gardens and tree-lined pathways, various free-standing accommodations, and a spa and heated swimming pool and whirlpool. Most of the individually decorated guest rooms are Victorian-modern cottages scattered throughout the resort; all are exceedingly well stocked with custom linens, oversize comforters, and original artwork. The newer suites come with fireplaces, porches, wet bars, six-speaker surround sound, and whirlpool tubs that often have shutters opening to the bedroom. Everyone has access to complimentary wine and cheese in the evening and the DVD library anytime. The full-service spa offers a fitness center, body treatments, skin care, and massages. Within the resort's restored century-old barn is Saddles, Sonoma's only steakhouse specializing in grass-fed beef, organic and sustainably farmed produce, and whimsically classy Western decor. An array of other excellent restaurants—as well as shops, wineries, and bars—is a short walk away. In fact, that's where MacArthur Place has Sonoma Mission Inn beat: Once you park your car here, you can *leave* it parked during a good part of your stay.

29 E. MacArthur St., Sonoma, CA 95476. ℂ 800/722-1866 or 707/938-2929. www.macarthurplace.com. 64 units. Sun–Thurs $169–$425 double; Fri–Sat $299–$525 double. Rates include continental breakfast. AE, DC, MC, V. Free parking. **Amenities:** Restaurant and bar specializing in martinis; outdoor heated pool; exercise room; full-service spa; outdoor Jacuzzi; steam; rental bikes; concierge; limited room service; massage; laundry service; same-day dry cleaning. *In room:* A/C, TV/DVD, dataport, hair dryer, iron, wireless Internet access ($10 per day), wet bar and coffeemaker in suites.

Expensive

Best Western Sonoma Valley Inn *(Kids)*   There are just two reasons to stay here: 1) It's the only place left with a vacancy or 2) you're bringing the kids along. Otherwise, unless you don't mind staying in a rather drab room with thin walls and small bathrooms, you're probably going to be a little disappointed. Kids, on the other hand, will love this place: There's plenty of room to run around, plus a large heated outdoor pool, gazebo-covered spa, and sauna to play in. The rooms *do* come with a lot of perks, such as continental breakfast delivered to your room each morning, a gift bottle of white table wine (chilling in the fridge), and satellite TV with HBO. Most rooms have either a balcony or a deck overlooking the inner courtyard. The inn is also in a good location, just a block from Sonoma's plaza.

550 Second St. W. (1 block from the plaza), Sonoma, CA 95476. ℂ 800/334-5784 or 707/938-9200. Fax 707/938-0935. www.sonomavalleyinn.com. 80 units. $109–$349 double. Rates include continental breakfast. AE, DC, MC, V. **Amenities:** Heated outdoor pool; exercise room; Jacuzzi; sauna; steam room. *In room:* A/C, TV, dataport, fridge, coffeemaker, hair dryer, iron.

Moderate

El Dorado Hotel *(★★)*   This 1843 mission revival building may look like a 19th-century Wild West relic from the outside, but inside it's all 21st-century deluxe. Each modern, handsomely appointed guest room—designed by the same folks who put together the ultraexclusive Auberge du Soleil (p. 290) resort in Rutherford—has French windows and tiny balconies. Some rooms offer lovely views of the plaza; others overlook the private courtyard and heated lap pool. All rooms (except those for guests with disabilities) are on the second floor and were upgraded in 2004. The four rooms on the ground floor are off the private courtyard, and each has a partially enclosed patio. Though prices reflect its prime location on Sonoma Square, this is still one of the more charming options within its price range.

405 First St. W., Sonoma, CA 95476. ℂ 800/289-3031 or 707/996-3030. Fax 707/996-3148. www.hotel eldorado.com. 27 units. Summer $170–$190 double; winter $135–$155 double. AE, MC, V. **Amenities:** Restaurant; heated outdoor pool; free access to nearby health club; concierge; room service (11:30am–10pm); laundry service; dry cleaning. *In room:* A/C, TV/DVD, dataport, fridge, hair dryer, iron, CD player.

Inexpensive

Sonoma Hotel *(★★)*   This cute little historic hotel on Sonoma's tree-lined town plaza emphasizes 19th-century elegance and comfort. Built in 1880 by German immigrant Henry Weyl, it has attractive guest rooms decorated in early California style, with French country furnishings, antique beds, and period decorations. In a bow to modern luxuries, recent additions include private bathrooms, cable TV, phones with dataports, and (this is crucial) air-conditioning.

Finds **The Super Spa**

The **Sonoma Mission Inn, Spa & Country Club,** 18140 Sonoma Hwy. (ⓒ **800/862-4945** or 707/938-9000; www.fairmont.com), has always been the most complete—and the most luxurious—spa in the entire Wine Country. With its recent $20-million, 43,000-square-foot facility, this super spa is now one of the best in the country. The Spanish mission–style retreat offers more than 50 spa treatments, ever-popular natural mineral baths, and virtually every facility and activity imaginable. You can pamper yourself silly: Take a sauna or herbal steam, have a facial set to music, indulge in a grape-seed body wrap, relax with a massage, go for a dip in the outdoor pool, or soak away your worries in the celestial indoor mineral pool area—the list goes on and on (and, alas, so will the bill). You can also work off those wicked Wine Country meals with aerobics, weights, and cardio machines; get loose in a yoga class; or just lounge and lunch by the pool. There is a catch, however: Since the renovations, the spa has become "private," which means you must be a guest to reap the relaxation rewards. However, they do offer a day package, which includes use of the pool, classes, and hot tub for $85—treatments cost extra. If you don't mind splurging and are a fan of luxury living, you'll agree that the Sonoma Mission Inn Spa is one of the best ways to unwind in the Wine Country.

Perks include fresh coffee and pastries in the morning and wine in the evening. The lovely restaurant, The Girl & the Fig (p. 315) serves California-French cuisine.

110 W. Spain St., Sonoma, CA 95476. ⓒ **800/468-6016** or 707/996-2996. Fax 707/996-7014. www.sonoma hotel.com. 16 units. Summer $110–$245 double; winter $95–$195 double. 2-night minimum required for summer weekends. Rates include continental breakfast and evening wine. AE, DC, MC, V. *In room:* A/C, TV, dataport.

Victorian Garden Inn 🏵🏵 Here, proprietor Donna Lewis runs what is easily the cutest B&B in Sonoma Valley. A small picket fence, a wall of trees, and an acre of gardens enclose an adorable Victorian garden brimming with violets, roses, camellias, and peonies, all shaded under flowering fruit trees. It's truly a marvelous sight in the springtime. The guest units—three in the century-old water tower and one in the main building (an 1870s Greek Revival farmhouse), as well as a cottage—continue the Victorian theme, with white wicker furniture, floral prints, padded armchairs, and claw-foot tubs. The most popular units are the Top o' the Tower and the Woodcutter's Cottage. Each has its own entrance and a garden view; the cottage boasts a sofa and armchairs set in front of the fireplace. After a hard day of wine tasting, spend the afternoon cooling off in the pool or on the shaded wraparound porch, enjoying a mellow merlot while soaking in the sweet garden smells. *New parents, take note:* The property recommends you leave young tots behind.

316 E. Napa St., Sonoma, CA 95476. ⓒ **800/543-5339** or 707/996-5339. Fax 707/996-1689. www.victorian gardeninn.com. 3 units, 1 cottage. $139–$259 double. Rates include continental breakfast. AE, DC, MC, V. **Amenities:** Outdoor pool; hot tub; concierge; business center; room service (8am–5pm); laundry service; dry cleaning. *In room:* A/C, fireplaces in some rooms.

GLEN ELLEN
Expensive

Gaige House Inn ★★★ *Finds*   Owners Ken Burnet, Jr., and Greg Nemrow have managed to turn what was already a fine B&B into *the* finest in the Wine Country. They've done it by offering a level of service, amenities, and decor normally associated with outrageously expensive resorts—but without the snobbery. Every nook and cranny of the 1890 Queen Anne–Italianate building and Garden Annex is swathed with fashionable articles found during the owners' world travels. Spacious rooms offer everything you could want—firm mattresses, wondrously silky-soft Frette linens, and premium comforters gracing the beds; even the furniture and artwork are the kind you'd like to take home with you. All 15 rooms, artistically decorated in a plantation theme with Asian and Indonesian influences (trust me, they're beautiful), have king- or queen-size beds; four rooms have Jacuzzi tubs, one has a Japanese soaking tub, and several have fireplaces. Bathrooms are equally luxe, range in size, and are stocked with Aveda products and slippers. Attention to detail means you'll be treated to the best robe you've ever worn. For the ultimate retreat, reserve one of the suites, which have patios overlooking a stream.

But wait, it gets better. Behind the inn is a 1½-acre oasis with perfectly manicured lawns, a 40-foot-long heated pool, and an achingly inviting creek-side hammock shaded by a majestic Heritage oak. Evenings are best spent in the reading parlor, sipping premium wines. Appetizers at wine hour might include freshly shucked oysters or a sautéed scallop served ready-to-slurp on a Chinese soup spoon. Breakfast is a momentous event, accented with herbs from the inn's garden and prepared by a chef who cooked at the James Beard House in 2001. On sunny days, the meal can be served at individual tables on the large terrace.

Greg and Ken also manage four long-term rentals (private guesthouses on private estates) for those who want more privacy and fewer services and are adding eight new deluxe spa garden suites in late 2004.

13540 Arnold Dr., Glen Ellen, CA 95442. ℂ **800/935-0237** or 707/935-0237. Fax 707/935-6411. www.gaige.com. 15 units. Summer $275–$525 double, $475–$575 suite; winter $175–$325 double, $325–$525 suite. Rates include full breakfast and evening wines. AE, DC, DISC, MC, V. **Amenities:** Large heated pool; in-room massage; free Internet access. *In room:* A/C, TV, fax, dataport, hair dryer, iron, safe.

Inexpensive

Beltane Ranch ★ *Finds*   The word *ranch* conjures up a big ol' two-story house in the middle of hundreds of rolling acres, the kind of place where you laze away the day in a hammock watching the grass grow or pitching horseshoes in the garden. Well, friend, you can have all that and more at the well-located Beltane Ranch, a century-old buttercup-yellow manor that's been everything from a bunkhouse to a brothel to a turkey farm. You simply can't help but feel your tensions ease away as you prop your feet up on the shady wraparound porch overlooking the quiet vineyards, sipping a cool, fruity chardonnay while reading *Lonesome Dove* for the third time. Each room is uniquely decorated with American and European antiques; all have sitting areas and separate entrances. A big and creative country breakfast is served in the garden or on the porch overlooking the vineyards. For exercise, you can play tennis on the private court or hike the trails meandering through the 400-acre estate. The staff here is knowledgeable and helpful. *Tip:* Request one of the upstairs rooms, which have the best views.

11775 Sonoma Hwy. (Hwy. 12), Glen Ellen, CA 95442. ℂ **707/996-6501.** www.beltaneranch.com. 5 units, 1 cottage. $130–$180 double; $220 cottage. Rates include full breakfast. No credit cards; personal checks accepted. **Amenities:** Outdoor, unlit tennis court. *In room:* No phone.

Glenelly Inn ★★ The Glenelly Inn is a great place to stay in the Wine Country. First off, the rates are reasonable, particularly when you factor in the included breakfast and afternoon snacks. More important, this former railroad inn, built in 1916, is positively drenched in serenity. Located well off the main highway on an oak-studded hillside, the peach-and-cream inn comes with everything you would expect from a country retreat. Long verandas offer comfy wicker chairs and views of the verdant Sonoma hillsides; a hearty country breakfast is served beside a large cobblestone fireplace; and bright, immaculate units contain old-fashioned claw-foot tubs, Scandinavian down comforters, and ceiling fans. The staff understands that it's the little things that make the difference; hence the firm mattresses, good reading lights, and a simmering hot tub in a grapevine- and rose-covered arbor. All rooms, decorated with antiques and country furnishings, have queen-size beds, terry robes, and private entrances. Top picks are the Vallejo and Jack London family suites, both with large private patios, although I also like the rooms on the upper veranda—particularly in the spring, when the terraced gardens below are in full bloom. The new freestanding garden cottages are for those who want to splurge and come with fireplaces, TV/VCRs, CD players, coffeemakers, and fridges.

5131 Warm Springs Rd. (off Arnold Dr.), Glen Ellen, CA 95442. ℂ 707/996-6720. Fax 707/996-5227. www.glenelly.com. 10 units. $150–$185 double/suite; $250 cottage. Rates include full breakfast. AE, DISC, MC, V. **Amenities:** Free Internet access.

KENWOOD
Very Expensive

Kenwood Inn & Spa ★★ Inspired by the villas of Tuscany, the Kenwood Inn's honey-colored Italian-style buildings, flower-filled flagstone courtyard, and pastoral views of vineyard-covered hills are enough to make any northern Italian homesick. The friendly staff and luxuriously restful surroundings made this California girl feel right at home. What's not to like about a spacious room lavishly and exquisitely decorated with imported tapestries, velvets, and antiques, plus a fireplace, balcony (except on the ground floor), feather bed, CD player, and down comforter? With no TV in the rooms, relaxation is inevitable—especially if you book treatments at the spa, which gets creative with its rejuvenating program. A minor caveat is road noise, which you're unlikely to hear from your room but can be slightly audible over the tranquil pumped-in music around the courtyard and decent-size pool. Longtime guests will be surprised to find more bodies around the pool—18 guest rooms and an adjoining building joined this slice of pastoral heaven in June 2003. Anyone with a hefty credit card limit can buy complete seclusion by renting the inn's new nearby and very private two-bedroom villa.

An impressive three-course gourmet breakfast is served poolside or in the Mediterranean-style dining room. Mine consisted of a poached egg accompanied by light flavorful potatoes, red bell peppers, and other roasted vegetables, all artfully arranged, followed by a delicious homemade scone with fresh berries, and a small lemon tart.

10400 Sonoma Hwy., Kenwood, CA 95452. ℂ 800/353-6966 or 707/833-1293. Fax 707/833-1247. www.kenwoodinn.com. 30 units. Apr–Oct $400–$725 double; Nov–Mar $375–$675 double, $800–$1,000 villa. Rates include gourmet breakfast and bottle of wine. 2-night minimum on weekends. AE, MC, V. **Amenities:** Heated outdoor pool; full-service spa; concierge; free Internet access. *In room:* Hair dryer, iron, CD player.

Pricing Categories

The restaurants listed below are classified first by town, then by price, using the following categories: **Expensive,** dinner from $50 per person; **Moderate,** dinner from $35 per person; and **Inexpensive,** dinner less than $35 per person. (*Note:* The "Very Expensive" category—dinner from $75 per person—has been omitted since no restaurants in this chapter fall under its umbrella.) These categories reflect prices for an appetizer, a main course, a dessert, and a glass of wine.

WHERE TO DINE IN SONOMA VALLEY
SONOMA
Moderate

Cafe La Haye ★★ ECLECTIC   Well-prepared and wholesome food, an experienced waitstaff, friendly owners, a soothing atmosphere, and reasonable prices—including a modestly priced wine list—make La Haye a favorite. In truth, everything about this cafelike restaurant is charming. The atmosphere within the small split-level dining room, pleasantly decorated with hardwood floors, an exposed-beam ceiling, and revolving contemporary artwork, is smart and intimate. The vibe is small business—a welcome departure from Napa Valley's big-business restaurants. The straightforward, seasonally inspired cuisine, which chefs bring forth from the tiny open kitchen, is delicious and wonderfully well priced. Although the menu is small, it offers just enough options. Expect a risotto special; pasta such as fresh tagliarini with butternut squash, prosciutto, sage, and garlic cream; and pan-roasted chicken breast, perhaps with goat cheese–herb stuffing, caramelized shallot *jus,* and fennel mashed potatoes. Meat eaters are sure to be pleased with filet of beef seared with black pepper–lavender sauce and served with Gorgonzola-potato gratin; and no one can resist the creative salads.

140 E. Napa St., Sonoma. © **707/935-5994.** Reservations recommended. Main courses $14–$24. MC, V. Tues–Sat 5:30–9pm.

The Girl & The Fig ★★ COUNTRY FRENCH   Well established in its downtown Sonoma digs (it used to be in Glen Ellen), this modern, attractive, and cozy eatery, with lovely patio seating, is the home for Sondra Bernstein's (The Girl) beloved restaurant. Here the cuisine, orchestrated by chef de cuisine Matt Murray, is nouveau country with French nuances, and yes, figs are sure to be on the menu in one form or another. The wonderful winter fig salad contains arugula, pecans, dried figs, Laura Chenel goat cheese, and fig-and-port vinaigrette. Toulze uses garden-fresh produce and local meats, poultry, and fish whenever possible, in dishes such as pork tenderloin with a potato-leek pancake and roasted beets, and sea scallops with lobster-scented risotto. For dessert, try the warm pear galette topped with gingered crème fraîche, a glass of Jaboulet muscat, and a sliver of raclette from the cheese list. Sondra knows her wines and will be happy to choose the best accompaniment for your meal.

110 W. Spain St., Sonoma. © **707/938-3634.** www.thegirlandthefig.com. Reservations recommended. Main courses $18–$23. AE, MC, V. Daily 11:30am–11pm.

Harmony Club ★★ *Finds* CONTINENTAL   The most welcome addition to Sonoma's dining scene in 2003, the Harmony Club is not only a looker with its elegant Italianate dining room with dark woods, high ceilings, marble flooring, and a wall of giant doors opening to sidewalk seating and Sonoma's plaza. It also delivers in great food and live entertainment. Drop in anytime after their gourmet breakfast for fantastic "small plates" such as tender Moroccan spiced lamb loin with saffron couscous, grapes, and mint; french fries with tarragon aioli; seared scallops with vegetable ragout and truffle beurre blanc; and Scharffen Berger chocolate and orange Muscat tort. Go for sidewalk seating during warmer weather (they also have heat lamps), sit inside, or hang at the carved wood bar. Either way you'll want to face the piano when the nightly performer is tinkling the keys and singing jazz standards. Alas, the only letdown is the wine list, which leaves little in the way of options since this spot, owned by Steve Ledson of Ledson Winery, naturally features only Ledson wines.

480 First St. E. (at the plaza), Sonoma. ℂ 707/996-9779. Reservations not accepted. Small plates $6–$14. AE, MC, V. Sun–Thurs 11:30am–10pm; Fri–Sat 11:30am–11:30pm.

La Poste ⭐ FRENCH BISTRO   It's a gastronome's game of sardines at this shoebox-size French bistro. The original Williams-Sonoma storefront is now downtown Sonoma's tiniest dining room with 26 chairs and maple banquettes strategically squeezed amid brass sconces, mahogany wainscoting, a whitewashed press tin ceiling, and just enough space on the concrete-tiled floor for staff to refill wineglasses. The ever-changing chalkboard menu announces chef Rob Larman's generously portioned offerings, which change faster than you can say "Pass the profiteroles," but recent winners included seared scallops seasoned with tomato-herb vinaigrette over truffled mashed potatoes; braised veal cheeks with cream, Calvados, English peas, and chanterelles; and quail stuffed with foie gras and sweetbreads on a warm salad of fingerling potatoes. Desserts, such as chocolate mousse, aren't as fab as what proceeds it, but it will placate any chocoholic. Oh, and when weather permits, you'll find 14 more seats on the sidewalk.

599 Broadway (just south of the plaza), Sonoma. ℂ 707/939-3663. Reservations recommended. Main courses $16–$25. AE, MC, V. Sun and Wed–Thurs 5:30–9pm; Fri–Sat 5:30–10pm.

Meritage ⭐⭐ SOUTHERN FRENCH/NORTHERN ITALIAN   Learning from the previous occupants' mistakes—that Sonoma ain't New York and shouldn't treat its customers that way—chef-owner Carlo Cavallo eliminated the big-city attitude and prices at his restaurant without diminishing style, service, or quality. The former executive chef for Giorgio Armani, Cavallo combines the best of southern French and northern Italian cuisines (hence "Meritage," after a blend made with traditional Bordeaux varieties), giving Sonomans yet another reason to eat out. The menu, which changes twice daily, is a good read: handmade roasted pumpkin tortellini in Parmesan cheese sauce; napoleon of escargot in champagne and wild thyme sauce; organic greens, strawberries, corn, and French feta salad; and wild boar chops in white truffle sauce with mashed potatoes. Shellfish fans can't help but love the oyster raw bar and options of fresh crab and lobster. A lovely garden patio is prime positioning for sunny breakfasts and lunches and summer dinners. Such edible enticement—combined with reasonable prices, excellent service, a stellar wine list, cozy booth seating, a handsome dining room, and Carlo's practiced charm—make Meritage a trustworthy option.

522 Broadway, Sonoma. ℂ 707/938-9430. www.sonomameritage.com. Reservations recommended. Main courses $13–$30. AE, MC, V. Wed–Sun 8am–9pm; Mon 11:30am–9pm.

Sonoma Saveurs ⭐ MEDITERRANEAN BISTRO/WINE BAR   Anyone who appreciates foie gras (duck liver) should look no further than this restaurant. Housed in a historic adobe, this small wine bar/bistro swathed in warm earth tones feels unfinished, while the back garden is pleasant enough. But Executive Chef Mary Dumont's limited yet inspired menu of charcuterie, two soups, a few salads and sandwiches, and grilled items (squab, chicken, hanger steak, fish) is a true find for any gourmand. Dumont cooked under famed San Francisco chefs Laurent Manrique and Daniel Patterson and her pedigree shows in everything from sexy salads—like baby greens with seared foie gras, roasted apples, chestnuts, and apple cider vinaigrette—to the charcuterie plate, which includes to-die-for foie gras mousse and perfectly prepared grilled duck breast. The menu offers color-coded wine pairings, which would be even cooler if the by-the-glass wine selection were better, more expansive, and less expensive. Unfortunately, during my visit our waiter was clueless about wine and sloppy in service, and dessert wasn't worth the calories (except for the moist Gâteau Basque—or custard tort), but I'm betting this new place will get itself in gear soon enough. *Tip:* If you're picnicking, you'll be hard-pressed to find better offerings than those at the charcuterie counter here.

487 First St. (at the plaza). © 707/996-7007. www.sonomasaveurs.com. Reservations not accepted. Main courses $9–$15. MC, V. Tues–Sun 11:30am–7:30pm.

Swiss Hotel ♠ CONTINENTAL/NORTHERN ITALIAN With its slanting floors and beamed ceilings, the historic Swiss Hotel, located right in the town center, is a Sonoma landmark and very much the local favorite for fine food served at reasonable prices. The turn-of-the-20th-century oak bar at the left of the entrance is adorned with black-and-white photos of pioneering Sonomans. The bright white dining room and sidewalk patio seats are pleasant spots to enjoy lunch specials such as penne with chicken, mushrooms, and tomato cream; hot sandwiches; and California-style pizzas fired in a wood-burning oven. But the secret spot is the very atmospheric back garden patio, a secluded oasis shaded by a wisteria-covered trellis and adorned with plants, a fountain, gingham tablecloths, and a fireplace. Dinner might start with a warm winter salad of radicchio and frisée with pears, walnuts, and bleu cheese. Main courses run the gamut; I like the linguine and prawns with garlic, hot pepper, and tomatoes; the filet mignon wrapped in bleu-cheese crust; and roasted rosemary chicken. The food may not knock your socks off, but it's all very simply satisfying.

18 W. Spain St (at First St. W.), Sonoma. © 707/938-2884. Reservations recommended. Main courses lunch $8.50–$16, dinner $10–$24. AE, MC, V. Daily 11:30am–2:30pm and 5–9:30pm. (Bar daily 11:30am–2am.)

Inexpensive

Black Bear Diner (Kids) DINER When you're craving a classic Americana breakfast with all the cholesterol and the fixin's (perhaps to counterbalance that wine hangover), make a beeline for this old-fashioned diner. First, it's fun with its over-the-top bear paraphernalia, gazette-style menu listing local news from 1961 and every possible diner favorite, and absurdly friendly waitstaff. Second, it's darned cheap. Third, helpings are huge. What more could you want? Kids get a kick out of coloring books, old-timers reminisce over Sinatra playing on the jukebox, and everyone leaves stuffed on omelets, scrambles, and pancakes. Lunch and dinner feature steak sandwiches, salads, and comfort food faves like barbecued pork ribs, roast beef, fish and chips, and spaghetti and meat sauce. But unless you like old-school run-of-the-mill diner fare, your best bet is to dine elsewhere. That said, you can load up here on the cheap, especially since dinners come with salad or soup, bread, and two sides and seniors can order from a specially priced menu.

201 West Napa St. (at Second St.), Sonoma. © 707/935-6800. Main courses breakfast $5–$8.50, lunch and dinner $5.50–$17. AE, DISC, MC, V. Sun–Thurs 6am–10pm; Fri–Sat 6am–midnight.

Della Santina's ★★ TUSCAN   For those of you who just can't swallow another expensive, chichi California meal, follow the locals to this friendly, traditional Italian restaurant. How traditional? Ask father-and-son team Dan and Robert: When I last dined here, they pointed out Signora Santina's hand-embroidered linen doilies as they proudly told me about her Tuscan recipes. (Heck, even the dining room looks like an old-fashioned, elegant Italian living room.) And their pride is merited: Every dish my party tried was refreshingly authentic and well flavored, without overbearing sauces or one *hint* of California pretentiousness. Be sure to start with traditional antipasti, especially sliced mozzarella and tomatoes, or delicious white beans. The nine pasta dishes are, again, wonderfully authentic (gnocchi lovers, rejoice!). The spit-roasted meat dishes are a local favorite (although I found them a bit overcooked); for those who can't choose between chicken, pork, turkey, rabbit, or duck, there's a selection that offers a choice of three. Don't worry about breaking your bank on a bottle of wine, because many choices here go for under $40. Portions are huge, but be sure to save room for a wonderful dessert.

133 E. Napa St. (just east of the square), Sonoma. ✆ 707/935-0576. Reservations recommended. Main courses $9–$18. AE, DISC, MC, V. Daily 11:30am–3pm and 5–9:30pm.

Rin's Thai ★ THAI   When valley residents or visitors get a hankering for Pad Thai, curry chicken, or *tom yam* (classic spicy soup), they head to this adorable little restaurant just off Sonoma Plaza. The atmosphere itself—contemporary, sparse yet warm environs within an old house—is tasty and the staff is extremely accommodating. After you settle into one of the well-spaced tables within or on the outside patio (weather permitting), go for your favorites—from satay with peanut sauce and cucumber salad or salmon with grilled veggies to yummy *gai kraprao* (minced chicken, chiles, basil, and garlic sauce) or char-broiled ribs with chile-garlic dipping sauce. They've got it all covered, including that oh-so-sweet Thai iced tea, fried bananas with coconut ice cream, and fresh mango with sticky rice (seasonal).

139 E. Napa St. (just east of the plaza), Sonoma. ✆ 707/938-1462. Reservations recommended. Main courses lunch $7.50–$9.25, dinner $8.25–$11. MC, V. Daily 11:30am–9:30pm.

GLEN ELLEN
Moderate

the fig café & wine bar ★★ NEW AMERICAN   The Girl & the Fig's (p. 315) sister restaurant is more casual than its downtown Sonoma sibling. But don't let the bucolic neighborhood vibe fool you. Surrounded by an open kitchen, soothing colors of sage and mustard, and airy environs, here you'll be able to savor the kind of rustic sophistication more commonly associated with urban restaurants. Start with *pissaladieres* (thin-crust pizzas), mussels in a fennel broth, a cheese plate, or killer chopped salad, move on to duck confit with white-bean-and-mushroom ragout or braised short ribs, and finish with fantastic butterscotch pot de crème. A perk: the "Rhone Alone" wine selections are available by the flight, glass, or bottle.

13690 Arnold Dr. (at Madrone Rd). ✆ 707/938-2130. www.thefigcafe.com. Reservations not accepted. Main courses $11–$21. AE, DISC, MC, V. Thurs and Sun–Mon 5:30–9pm; Fri–Sat 5:30–9:30pm.

Glen Ellen Inn Restaurant ★ CALIFORNIA   Christian and Karen Bertrand have made this place so quaint and cozy that you feel as if you're dining in their home, and that's exactly the place's charm. Garden seating is the favored choice on sunny days, but the covered, heated patio is also always welcoming. The first course from Christian's open kitchen might be a wild-mushroom-and-sausage purse served in brandy cream sauce or warm goat-cheese croquettes. Main courses, which change with the seasons, range from linguine with artichoke hearts and feta to stellar late-harvest ravioli stuffed with pumpkin, walnuts, and sun-dried cranberries on a bed of butternut squash. Other favorites include marinated pork tenderloin on smoked mozzarella polenta, topped with roasted pepper–onion compote; and utterly tender Nebraska corn-fed filet mignon in a foie gras–brandy reduction sauce. On my last visit, the Sonoma Valley mixed-green salad, seared ahi tuna, and homemade French vanilla ice cream floating in bittersweet caramel sauce made a lovely meal. The 550-selection wine list offers numerous bottles from Sonoma, as well as more than a dozen wines by the glass. *Tip:* There's a small parking lot behind the restaurant.

13670 Arnold Dr. (at O'Donnell Lane), Glen Ellen. ✆ 707/996-6409. www.glenelleninn.com. Reservations recommended. Main courses $18–$25. AE, MC, V. Mon–Thurs 11:30am–2:30pm and 5:30–9:30pm; Fri–Sun 11:30am–9:30pm. Closed 1 week in Jan.

Wolf House ✿ ECLECTIC   The most polished-looking dining room in Glen Ellen is elegant yet relaxed whether you're seated in the handsome dining room—smartly adorned with maple floors, gold walls, dark-wood wainscoting, and a corner fireplace—or outside on the multilevel terrace under the canopy of trees with serene views of the adjacent Sonoma Creek. The lunch menu adds fancy finishes to old favorites such as the excellent chicken Caesar salad, fresh grilled ahi tuna niçoise sandwich, or a juicy half-pound burger with Point Reyes Original Blue cheese. During dinner, skip the soggy sparkling-wine battered prawns with upland cress salad and head straight for seared Sonoma lamb sirloin with roasted eggplant, chickpea ragout, and tomato confit; or pan-seared day boat scallops with heirloom tomatoes and avocado-cucumber emulsion. The reasonably priced wine list offers many by-the-glass options as well as a fine selection of Sonoma wines. Locals love the brunch, complete with huevos rancheros, steak and eggs, omelets, and brioche French toast. During my visits, service was rather languid, but well meaning.

13740 Arnold Dr. (at London Ranch Rd.), Glen Ellen. ✆ 707/996-4401. Reservations recommended. Main courses brunch and lunch $8–$12, dinner $18–$20. AE, DISC, MC, V. Brunch Sat–Sun 10:30am–3pm; lunch Mon–Fri 11am–3pm; dinner nightly 5:30–9:30pm.

KENWOOD
Moderate

Kenwood Restaurant & Bar ✿✿ CALIFORNIA/CONTINENTAL   This is what Wine Country dining should be—but often, disappointingly, is not. From the terrace of the Kenwood Restaurant, diners enjoy a view of the vineyards set against Sugarloaf Ridge as they imbibe Sonoma's finest at umbrella-covered tables. On nippy days, you can retreat inside to the Sonoma-style roadhouse, with its shiny wood floors, pine ceiling, vibrant artwork, and cushioned rattan chairs at white cloth–covered tables. Regardless of where you pull up a chair, expect first-rate cuisine, perfectly balanced between tradition and innovation, complemented by a reasonably priced wine list. Great starters are Dungeness crab cake with herb mayonnaise; superfresh sashimi with ginger, soy, and wasabi; and a wonderful Caesar salad. The main dish might be poached salmon in creamy caper sauce or prawns with saffron Pernod sauce. But the Kenwood doesn't take itself too seriously: Great sandwiches and burgers are also available.

9900 Sonoma Hwy. (just north of Slattery Rd.), Kenwood. ✆ 707/833-6326. www.kenwoodrestaurant.com. Reservations recommended. Main courses $13–$26. MC, V. Wed–Sun 11:30am–9pm.

Appendix:
San Francisco in Depth

Born as an out-of-the-way backwater of colonial Spain and blessed with a harbor that would have been the envy of any of the great cities of Europe, San Francisco boasts a story as varied as the millions of people who have passed through its "Golden Gate," a strait linking the San Francisco Bay to the Pacific Ocean. It was not named for the gold rush; rather, Col. John C. Fremont named it in 1848 after "Chrysoceras" or "Golden Horn," in Constantinople.

THE AGE OF DISCOVERY

After Columbus "discovered" the New World in 1492, legends of the fertile land of California were discussed in the universities and taverns of Europe, even though no one really understood where the mythical land was. (Some evidence of arrivals in California by Chinese merchants hundreds of years before Columbus's landing has been unearthed, although few scholars are willing to draw definite conclusions.) The first documented visit by a European to Northern California was by the Portuguese explorer Juan Rodriguez Cabrillo, who circumnavigated the southern tip of South America as far north as the Russian River in 1542. Nearly 40 years later, in 1579, Sir Francis Drake landed on the Northern California coast, stopping for a time to repair his ships and to claim the territory for Queen Elizabeth of England. Another Portuguese, Sebastian Cermeño, "discovered" Punta de los Reyes (King's Point) in the mid-1590s. All three adventurers completely missed the narrow entrance to San Francisco Bay, either because it was enshrouded in fog or, more likely,

Dateline

- **1542** Juan Rodriguez Cabrillo sails up the California coast.
- **1579** Sir Francis Drake lands near San Francisco, missing the entrance to the bay.
- **1769** Members of the Spanish expedition led by Gaspar de Portolá become the first Europeans to see San Francisco Bay.
- **1775** The *San Carlos* is the first European ship to sail into San Francisco Bay.
- **1776** Captain Juan Bautista de Anza establishes a presidio (military fort); San Francisco de Asis Mission opens.
- **1821** Mexico wins independence from Spain and annexes California.
- **1835** The town of Yerba Buena develops around the port; the United States tries unsuccessfully to purchase San Francisco Bay from Mexico.
- **1846–48** War between the United States and Mexico.
- **1848** Americans annex Yerba Buena and rename it San Francisco. Also, gold is discovered in Coloma, near Sacramento. San Francisco's population swells from about 900 to 26,000.
- **1851** Lawlessness becomes acute before attempts to curb it.
- **1869** The transcontinental railroad reaches San Francisco.
- **1873** Andrew S. Hallidie invents the cable car.
- **1906** The Great Earthquake strikes, and the resulting fire levels the city.
- **1915** The Panama-Pacific International Exposition celebrates San Francisco's restoration and the completion of the Panama Canal.
- **1936** The Bay Bridge is completed.
- **1937** The Golden Gate Bridge is completed.
- **1945** The United Nations Charter is drafted in San Francisco and adopted by the representatives of 50 countries.

because they simply weren't looking for it. Believe it or not, the bay's entrance is nearly impossible to see from the open ocean.

Two more centuries passed before a European actually saw the bay that would later extend Spain's influence over much of the American West. Gaspar de Portolá, a soldier sent from Spain to meddle in a rather ugly conflict between the Jesuits and the Franciscans, accidentally stumbled upon the bay in 1769, en route to somewhere else. However, he stoically plodded on to his original destination, Monterey Bay, more than 100 miles to the south. Six years later, Juan Ayala actually sailed into San Francisco Bay while on a mapping expedition for the Spanish and immediately realized the enormous strategic importance of his find.

Colonization quickly followed. Juan Bautista de Anza and around 30 Spanish-speaking families marched through the deserts from Sonora, Mexico, arriving after many hardships at the northern tip of modern-day San Francisco in June 1776. They immediately claimed the peninsula for Spain. (Their claim of allegiance to Spain occurred only about a week before the 13 English-speaking colonies of North America's Eastern seaboard, a continent away, declared their independence from Britain.) Their headquarters was an adobe fortress, the Presidio, built on the site of today's park with the same name. The settlers' church, a mile to the

- 1950 The Beat Generation moves into the bars and cafes of North Beach.
- 1967 A free concert in Golden Gate Park attracts 20,000 people, ushering in the Summer of Love and the hippie era.
- 1974 BART's high-speed transit system opens the tunnel linking San Francisco with the East Bay.
- 1978 Harvey Milk, a city supervisor and America's first openly gay politician, is assassinated, along with Mayor George Moscone, by political rival Dan White.
- 1989 An earthquake registering 7.1 on the Richter scale hits San Francisco just before a World Series baseball game, as 100 million watch on TV; the city quickly rebuilds.
- 1991 Fire rages through the Berkeley and Oakland hills, destroying 2,800 homes.
- 1993 Yerba Buena Center for the Arts opens.
- 1995 The new San Francisco MOMA opens.
- 1996 Former Assembly Speaker Willie Brown is elected mayor of San Francisco.
- 1998 El Niño deluges San Francisco with its second-highest rainfall in history.
- 2000 Pacific Bell Park (later renamed SBC Park) opens as the new home of the San Francisco Giants baseball team with an exhibition game against the Milwaukee Brewers.
- 2003 Debonair Gavin Newsome is elected mayor of San Francisco.
- 2004 Mayor Newsome's permission of gay marriages garners national attention before it's stopped by governmental higher-ups.

south, was the first of five Spanish missions later developed around the edges of San Francisco Bay. Although the name of the church was officially *Nuestra Señora de Dolores,* it was dedicated to St. Francis of Assisi and nicknamed San Francisco by the Franciscan priests. Later, the name applied to the entire bay.

In 1821, Mexico broke away from Spain, secularized the Spanish missions, and abandoned all interest in the natives. Freed of Spanish restrictions, California's ports suddenly opened to trade. The region around San Francisco Bay supplied large amounts of hides and tallow for transport around Cape Horn to the tanneries and factories of New England and New York. The prospect of prosperity persuaded an English-born sailor, William Richardson, to jump ship in

1822 and settle on the site of what is now San Francisco. To impress the commandant of the Presidio, whose daughter he loved, Richardson converted to Catholicism and established the beginnings of what would soon become a thriving trading post and colony. Richardson named his trading post Yerba Buena (or "good herb") because of a species of wild mint that grew there, near the site of today's Montgomery Street. (The city's original name was recalled with endless mirth 120 years later, during San Francisco's hippie era.) He conducted a profitable hide-trading business and eventually became harbormaster and the city's first merchant prince. By 1839, the place was a veritable town, with a mostly English-speaking populace and a saloon of dubious virtue.

Throughout the 19th century, armed hostilities between English-speaking settlers from the Eastern seaboard and the Spanish-speaking colonies of Spain and Mexico erupted in places as widely scattered as Texas, Puerto Rico, and along the frequently shifting U.S.-Mexico border. In 1846, a group of U.S. marines from the warship *Portsmouth* seized the sleepy main plaza of Yerba Buena, ran the U.S. flag up a pole, and declared California an American territory. The Presidio (occupied by about a dozen unmotivated Mexican soldiers) surrendered without a fuss. The first move made by the new, mostly Yankee citizenry was to officially adopt the name of the bay as the name of their town.

THE GOLD RUSH

The year 1848 was one of the most pivotal in European history, with unrest sweeping through Europe, horrendous poverty in Ireland, and widespread disillusionment about hopes for prosperity throughout Europe and the East Coast of the United States. Stories about the golden port of San Francisco and the agrarian wealth of the American West filtered slowly east, attracting slow-moving groups of settlers. Ex-sailor Richard Henry Dana extolled the virtues of California in his best-selling novel, *Two Years Before the Mast,* and helped fire the public's imagination about the territory's bounty, particularly that of the Bay Area.

The first overland party crossed the Sierra and arrived in California in 1841. San Francisco grew steadily, reaching a population of approximately 900 by April 1848, but nothing hinted at the population explosion that was to follow. Historian Barry Parr has referred to the California gold rush as the most extraordinary event to ever befall an American city in peacetime. Even without the lure of gold, San Francisco's winning combination of raw materials, healthful climate, and freedom would eventually have attracted thousands of settlers. But the gleam of the soft metal is said to have compressed 50 years of normal growth into less than 6 months. In 1848, the year gold was discovered, the population of San Francisco jumped from under 1,000 to 26,000. As many as 100,000 more passed through San Francisco in the space of less than a year on their way to the rocky hinterlands where the gold was rumored to be.

If not for the discovery of some small particles of gold at a sawmill that he owned, Swiss-born John Augustus Sutter would have left a far less flamboyant legacy. Despite Sutter's wish to keep the discovery quiet, his employee, John Marshall, leaked word of the discovery to friends. It eventually appeared in local papers, and smart investors on the East Coast took immediate heed. The rush did not start, however, until Sam Brannan, a Mormon preacher and famous charlatan, ran through the streets of San Francisco shouting, "Gold! Gold in the American River!" (Brannan, incidentally, bought up all the harborfront real estate he could and cornered the market on shovels, pickaxes, and canned food just before making the announcement that was heard around the world.)

A world on the brink of change responded almost frantically. The gold rush was on. Shop owners hung GONE TO THE DIGGINGS signs in their windows. Flotillas of ships set sail from ports throughout Europe, South America, Australia, and the East Coast, sometimes nearly sinking with the weight of mining equipment. Townspeople from the Midwest headed overland, and the social structure of a nation was transformed almost overnight. Not since the Crusades of the Middle Ages had so many people mobilized in so short a time. Daily business stopped; ships arrived in San Francisco, and their crews almost immediately deserted. News of the gold strike spread like a plague through every discontented hamlet in the known world.

Although other settlements were closer to the gold strike, San Francisco was the famous name and, therefore, was where the gold-diggers disembarked. Tent cities sprang up, and demand for virtually everything skyrocketed. Although some miners actually found gold, smart merchants quickly discovered more enduring business in servicing the needs of the thousands of miners who arrived ill-equipped and ignorant of the lay of the land. Prices soared. Miners, faced with staggeringly inflated prices for goods and services, barely turned a profit after expenses. Most prospectors failed, many died of hardship, and others committed suicide at the alarming rate of 1,000 a year. Yet despite the tragedies, graft, and vice associated with the gold rush, within mere months San Francisco had been forever transformed from a tranquil Spanish settlement into a roaring, boisterous boomtown.

BOOMTOWN FEVER

By 1855, most of California's surface gold had already been panned out, leaving only the richer but deeper veins of ore, which individual miners couldn't retrieve without massive capital investments. Despite that, San Francisco had evolved into a vast commercial magnet, sucking into its warehouses and banks the staggering riches that overworked newcomers had dragged, ripped, and distilled from the rocks, fields, and forests of western North America.

Investment funds poured into more than mining, however. Speculation on the newly established San Francisco stock exchange could make or destroy an investor in a single day, and several noteworthy writers (including Mark Twain) were among the young men forever influenced by the boomtown spirit. The American Civil War left California firmly in the Union camp, ready, willing, and able to receive hordes of disillusioned soldiers fed up with the internecine warmongering of the Eastern seaboard. In 1869, the transcontinental railway linked the Eastern and Western seaboards of the United States, ensuring the fortunes of the barons who controlled it. The railways shifted economic power bases, however, as cheap manufactured goods from the East undercut the costly articles brought on ships that sailed or steamed around the tip of South America. The "Big Four"—iron-willed capitalists Leland Stanford, Mark Hopkins, Collis P. Huntington, and Charles Crocker—almost completely controlled ownership of the newly formed Central Pacific and Southern Pacific railroads, and their ruthlessness was legendary. (Much of the bone-crushing railway labor was done by low-paid Chinese newcomers, most of whom arrived in overcrowded ships at San Francisco ports.) As the 19th century came to a close, civil unrest became more frequent as the monopolistic grip of the railways and robber barons became more obvious. Adding to the discontent were the uncounted thousands of Chinese immigrants who fled starvation and unrest in Asia at rates rivaling those of the Italians, Poles, Irish, and British.

During the 1870s, the flood of profits from the Comstock Lode in western Nevada diminished to a trickle, a cycle of droughts wiped out part of California's agricultural bounty, and local industry struggled to survive the flood of manufactured goods coming by rail from well-established East Coast and Midwestern factories. Often, discontented workers blamed their woes on the now-unwanted hordes of Chinese workers who, by preference and for mutual protection, had congregated in teeming all-Asian communities.

Despite these downward cycles, the city enjoyed other bouts of prosperity around the turn of the 20th century, thanks to the Klondike gold rush in Alaska and the Spanish-American War. Long accustomed to making a buck off gold fever, San Francisco managed to position itself as a point of embarkation for supplies bound for Alaska. Also during this time, the Bank of America emerged; it eventually grew into the largest bank in the world. Founded in North Beach in 1904, the bank was the brainchild of Italian-born A. P. Giannini, who later funded part of the construction for a bridge that many critics said was preposterous: the Golden Gate.

THE GREAT FIRE

On the morning of April 18, 1906, San Francisco changed for all time. The city has never experienced an earthquake as destructive as the one that hit at 5:13am; scientists estimate its strength at 8.1 on the Richter scale. All but a handful of the city's 400,000 inhabitants lay fast asleep when the ground went into a series of convulsions. As one eyewitness put it, "The earth was shaking . . . it was undulating, rolling like an ocean breaker." The quake ruptured every water main in the city and simultaneously started a chain of fires that rapidly fused into one gigantic conflagration. The fire brigades were helpless, and for 3 days San Francisco burned.

Militia troops finally stopped the flames from advancing by dynamiting entire city blocks, but not before more than 28,000 buildings lay in ruins. Minor tremors lasted another 3 days. The final damage stretched across a path of destruction 450 miles long and 50 miles wide. In all, 497 city blocks, or about one-third of the city, were razed. As Jack London wrote in a heartrending newspaper dispatch, "The city of San Francisco is no more." The earthquake and subsequent fire so decisively changed the city that post-1906 San Francisco bears little resemblance to the town before the quake. Out of the ashes rose a bigger, healthier, and more beautiful town, although latter-day urbanologists regret that the rebuilding that followed the San Francisco earthquake did not have a more enlightened plan. So eager was the city to rebuild that the old, somewhat unimaginative gridiron plan was reinstated, despite the opportunities for more daring visions afforded by the quake's aftermath.

In 1915, in celebration of the opening of the Panama Canal and to prove to the world that San Francisco was restored to its full glory, the city was host to the Panama-Pacific International Exhibition, a world's fair that introduced hundreds of thousands of visitors to the city's unique charms. The frenzy of boosterism, however, reached its peak during the years just before World War I, when investments and civic pride might have reached an all-time high. Despite Prohibition, speakeasies in and around the city did a thriving business, and building sprees were as high-blown and lavish as the profits on the San Francisco stock exchange.

THE 1950S: THE BEATS

San Francisco's reputation as a rollicking place where anything goes dates from the Barbary Coast days when gang warfare, prostitution, gambling, and drinking were major pursuits, and citizens took law and order into their own hands. Its more modern role as a catalyst for social change and the avant-garde began in the 1950s. A group of young writers, philosophers, and poets challenged the materialism and conformity of American society by embracing anarchy and Eastern philosophy, expressing their notions in poetry. They adopted a uniform of jeans, sweaters, sandals, and berets, called themselves "Beats," and hung out in North Beach, where rents were low and cheap wine was plentiful. *San Francisco Chronicle* columnist Herb Caen, to whom they were totally alien, dubbed them "beatniks" in his column.

Allen Ginsberg, Gregory Corso, and Jack Kerouac had begun writing at Columbia University in New York, but it wasn't until they came West and hooked up with Lawrence Ferlinghetti, Kenneth Rexroth, Gary Snyder, and others that the movement gained national attention. The bible of the Beats was Ginsberg's "Howl," which he first read at the Six Gallery on October 13, 1955. By the time he finished reading, Ginsberg was crying, the audience was chanting, and his fellow poets were announcing the arrival of an epic bard. Ferlinghetti published "Howl," which was deemed obscene, in 1956. A trial followed, but the court found that the poem had redeeming social value, reaffirming the right of free expression. Another major Beat work, Kerouac's *On the Road,* was published in 1957 and instantly became a bestseller. (He had written it as one long paragraph in 20 days in 1951.) The freedom and sense of possibility the book conveyed became the bellwether for a generation.

While the Beats gave poetry readings and generated controversy, two clubs in North Beach were also making waves, notably the hungry i and the Purple Onion, where everyone who was anyone or became anyone on the entertainment scene appeared. Mort Sahl, Dick Gregory, Lenny Bruce, Barbra Streisand, and Woody Allen all worked there. Maya Angelou appeared as a singer and dancer at the Purple Onion. The cafes of North Beach—Vesuvio, Caffè Trieste, Caffè Tosca, and Enrico's Sidewalk Cafe—were the center of bohemian life in the '50s. When the tour buses started rolling in, rents went up, and Broadway became a sex-club strip in the early 1960s. Thus ended an era, and the Beats moved on—the alternative scene eventually shifting to Berkeley and the Haight.

THE 1960S: THE HAIGHT

The torch of freedom passed from the Beats and North Beach to the hippies and Haight-Ashbury, but it was a radically different torch. The hippies replaced the Beats' angst, anarchy, negativism, nihilism, alcohol, and poetry with love, communalism, openness, drugs, rock music, and a back-to-nature philosophy. Although the scent of marijuana wafted everywhere—on the streets, in the cafes, in Golden Gate Park—the real drugs of choice were LSD (a tab of good acid cost $5) and other hallucinogenics. Timothy Leary experimented with its effects and exhorted youth to "turn on, tune in, and drop out." Instead of hanging out in coffeehouses, the hippies went to concerts at the Fillmore or the Avalon Ballroom to dance. The first Family Dog Rock 'n' Roll Dance and Concert, "A Tribute to Dr. Strange," was at the Longshoremen's Hall in 1965. It featured Jefferson Airplane, the Marbles, the Great Society, and the Charlatans. At the event, the first major happening of the 1960s, Ginsberg led a snake dance through the crowd. In January 1966, Longshoremen's Hall was the site of the 3-day Trips Festival, organized by rock promoter Bill Graham. The climax was the Ken Kesey and the Merry Pranksters Acid Test show, which used five movie screens, psychedelic visions, and the sounds of the Grateful Dead and Big Brother and the Holding Company. The "be-in" followed in the summer of 1966 at the polo grounds in Golden Gate Park, when an estimated 20,000 heard Jefferson Airplane perform and Ginsberg chant, while the Hell's Angels acted as unofficial police. During the Summer of Love, in 1967, thousands of young people streamed into the city in search of drugs and sex.

One way that the '60s Haight scene was very different from the '50s Beat scene was that the hippies were much younger than the Beats had been, constituting the first youth movement to take over the nation. (They also became the first generation of young, independent, and moneyed consumers to be courted by corporations.)

Ultimately, the Haight and the hippie movement deteriorated from love and flowers into drugs and crime, drawing a fringe of crazies like Charles Manson and leaving a legacy of sex, drugs, violence, and consumerism. As early as October 1967, the "Diggers," who had opened a free shop and soup kitchen in the Haight, symbolically buried the dream in a clay casket in Buena Vista Park.

The end of the Vietnam War and the resignation of President Richard Nixon took the edge off politics. The last fling of the mentality that had driven the 1960s occurred in 1974, when the Symbionese Liberation Army kidnapped newspaper heiress Patty Hearst from her Berkeley apartment and took her on a bank-robbing spree before surrendering in San Francisco.

THE 1970S & 1980S: GAY RIGHTS

The homosexual community in San Francisco developed at the end of World War II, when thousands of military personnel returned to the United States via San Francisco. A substantial number of those men were homosexual and decided to stay in the city. A gay community grew up along Polk Street between Sutter and California. Later, the larger community moved into the Castro District, where it remains today.

The gay political-protest movement is usually dated from the 1969 Stonewall raid in Greenwich Village. Although the political movement started in New York, California had already given birth to two major organizations for gay rights: the Mattachine Society, founded in 1951 by Henry Hay in Los Angeles; and the Daughters of Bilitis, a lesbian organization founded in 1955 in San Francisco.

After Stonewall, the Committee for Homosexual Freedom was created in the spring of 1969 in San Francisco and a Gay Liberation Front chapter was organized at Berkeley. In the fall of 1969, Robert Patterson, a columnist for the *San Francisco Examiner,* referred to homosexuals as "semi males," "drag darlings," and "women who aren't exactly women." On October 31 at noon, a group began a peaceful picket of the *Examiner.* Peace reigned until someone threw a bag of printer's ink from an *Examiner* window. Things got violent and, eventually, the police moved in to clear the crowd, clubbing people as they went. The remaining picketers retreated to Glide Methodist Church, then marched on city hall. Unfortunately, the mayor was away. Unable to air their grievances, the picketers started a sit-in that lasted until 5pm, when they were ordered to leave. Most did, but three remained and were arrested.

Later that year, at an anti-Thanksgiving rally, gays protested against several national and local businesses: Western and Delta airlines (the former for firing lesbian stewardesses, the latter for refusing to sell a ticket to a young man wearing a Gay Power button); radio station KFOG, for its antihomosexual broadcasting; and some local gay bars for exploitation. On May 14, 1970, a group of gay and women's liberationists invaded the convention of the American Psychiatric Association in San Francisco to protest the reading of a paper on aversion therapy for homosexuals, forcing the meeting to adjourn.

The rage against intolerance was appearing on all fronts. At the National Gay Liberation conference in August 1970 in the city, Charles Thorp, chairman of the San Francisco State Liberation Front, called for militancy and issued a challenge to come out with a rallying cry of "Blatant is beautiful." He also argued for the use of what he felt was the more positive, celebratory term *gay* instead of *homosexual,* and decried the fact that homosexuals were kept in their place at the three Bs: the bars, the beaches, and the baths. As the movement grew in size and power, debates on strategy and tactics occurred, most dramatically between those gays who wanted to withdraw into separate ghettos, and those who wanted to enter mainstream society. The most extreme proposal was made in California by Don Jackson, who suggested establishing a gay territory in California's Alpine County, about 10 miles south of Lake Tahoe. It would have had a totally gay administration, civil service, university, museum—everything. The residents of Alpine County were not pleased with the proposal. But before the situation turned really ugly, Jackson's idea was abandoned because of lack of support in the gay community. In the end, the movement concentrated on integration and civil rights, not separatism. Gays elected politicians who were sympathetic to their cause and celebrated their new identity by establishing National Gay Celebration Day and Gay Pride Week, the first of which was celebrated in June 1970, when 1,000 to 2,000 marched in New York, 1,000 in Los Angeles, and a few hundred in San Francisco.

By the mid-1970s, the gay community craved a more central role in city politics. Harvey Milk, owner of a camera store in the Castro, decided to run for the board of supervisors. He won, becoming the first openly gay person to hold a major public office. He and liberal mayor George Moscone developed a gay rights agenda, but in 1978 they were both shot and killed by former supervisor Dan White, after Moscone refused White's request for reinstatement. White, a former police officer, had consistently opposed Milk's and Moscone's more liberal policies. At his trial, White successfully pleaded temporary insanity caused by additives in his fast-food diet. The media dubbed it the "Twinkie defense," but the murder charges against White were reduced to manslaughter. On that day, angry and grieving, the gay community rioted, overturning and burning police cars in a night of rage. To this day, a candlelight memorial parade is held on November 27. Milk's martyrdom was both a political and a practical inspiration for gay candidates across the country.

The emphasis in the gay movement shifted abruptly in the 1980s, when the AIDS epidemic struck the community. AIDS has had a dramatic impact on the Castro: While it's still a thriving and lively community, it's no longer the constant party it once was. The hedonistic lifestyle that had played out in the discos, bars, baths, and streets changed as the seriousness of the epidemic sank in and the number of deaths increased. Political efforts by gays have shifted away from enfranchisement and toward demands for social services and research money to deal with the AIDS crisis. Despite its difficulties, the gay community in San Francisco is still thriving. And let's not forget the hullabaloo around gay marriage, which Mayor Gavin Newsome legalized for a moment in early 2004 until higher-ranking governmental officials put a stop to them.

THE BIG ONE, PART TWO

Compared to previous decades, the 1980s may have arrived in San Francisco with a whimper, but they went out with quite a bang. At 5:04pm on Tuesday, October 17, 1989, as more than 62,000 baseball fans filled Candlestick Park for the third game of the World Series—and the Bay Area commute moved into its heaviest flow—an earthquake of magnitude 7.1 struck. Within the next 20 seconds, 63 lives were lost, $10 billion in damage occurred, and the entire Bay Area community was reminded of its humble insignificance. Centered about 60 miles south of San Francisco in the Forest of Nisene Marks, the deadly temblor was felt as far away as San Diego and Nevada.

Although scientists had predicted an earthquake on this section of the San Andreas Fault, certain structures built to withstand such an earthquake failed miserably. The most catastrophic event was the collapse of the elevated Cypress Street section of Interstate 880 in Oakland; the upper level of the freeway pancaked onto the lower level, crushing everything between them with such force that cars were reduced to inches. Other heavily damaged structures included the San Francisco–Oakland Bay Bridge, shut down for months when a section of the roadbed collapsed; San Francisco's Marina District, where several multimillion-dollar homes collapsed on their weak, shifting bases of landfill and sand; and the Pacific Garden Mall in Santa Cruz, which was devastated.

President George Bush declared the seven hardest-hit counties a disaster area; at least 3,700 people were reported injured and more than 12,000 were displaced. More than 18,000 homes were damaged and 963 others destroyed. Although fire raged in the city and water supply systems were damaged, the major fires in the Marina District were brought under control within 3 hours.

After the rubble finally settled, it was unanimously agreed that San Francisco and the Bay Area had pulled through miraculously well—particularly when the quake was compared with the recent earthquake in Kobe, Japan, which had killed thousands and displaced an entire city. After the quake, a feeling of esprit de corps swept the city as neighbors helped each other rebuild and donations poured in from all over the world. Although over a decade has passed, San Francisco is still feeling the effects of the quake, most noticeably during rush hour as commuters take a variety of detours to circumvent freeways that were damaged or destroyed and are still under construction.

THE 1990S: THE NEW GOLD RUSH

During the early 1990s, nothing earth-shattering took place. The nationwide recession influenced the beginning of the decade, and the quiet rumblings of the new frontier in Silicon Valley escaped much notice. By the middle of the decade, however, San Francisco and the surrounding areas had discovered a new kind of gold rush—the Internet industry.

Not unlike the gold fever of the 1800s, people flocked to the Western shores to strike it rich—and they did. In 1999, local media reported that every day 64 Bay Area residents were gaining millionaire status. Real estate prices went into the stratosphere, and the city's gentrification financially squeezed out many of those residents who didn't mean big business (read: many of the alternative types, the elderly, and minorities who made the city colorful). New businesses popped up everywhere—especially in the SoMa area, where startup companies jammed warehouse spaces to the rafters. As the most popular posteducation destination for, San Francisco no longer opened its Golden Gate to everyone looking for the legendary alternative lifestyle—unless they could afford a $1,000 studio apartment and $20-per-day fees to park their cars.

The new millennium was christened with bubbly in hand, foie gras and caviar in mouth, and seemingly everyone in the money. New restaurants charging $35 per entree were all the rage, hotels were renovated, the new bayfront ballpark was packed, and stock market tips were as plentiful as million-dollar SoMa condos and high-rises. San Franciscans were too busy raking in the dough and working and playing hard to heed the writing on the wall.

THE NEW MILLENNIUM: A REALITY CHECK

The new millennium started off well enough. The initial fallout in the market and the stability of previously well-funded companies was expected; everyone cashing in on the new economy knew the situation was too good to be true. Venture capitalists began holding onto their funding with both hands, rather than doling it out freely to anyone with an idea and a ".com" suffix. The business community figured the scale was finally balancing, with sound companies outweighing the less-concrete ideas on the bandwidth bandwagon.

By mid-2000, investors began to shy away from companies with high valuations and no profits. The billions of dollars of funding that poured into the Bay Area had dried up. Dot.com obituaries and layoff notifications grew longer and grimmer, until finally, by early 2001, it seemed the entire industry had collapsed. Fancier dining rooms braced themselves, while on the bright side, there was finally no shortage of restaurant staff. Whereas apartments had been scarce for the past 5 years, they were more available, while those who were paying absurd rents negotiated reasonable decreases with landlords. SoMa became SloMa with perhaps more commercial FOR RENT signs than surviving dot.coms. And many of those newly arrived gold-diggers returned from whence they came.

The events of the September 11, 2001, terrorist attacks coupled with the recent war as well as economic uncertainty made matters that much worse. The tourist industry disappeared for a while, business travel dropped off, hotels were nearly empty, and restaurant closings were announced almost daily. It's gotten much better as of late, but the tourist industry, business travel, and hotel, restaurant, and retail businesses are still in recovery mode and exhibit cautious optimism.

Today the City by the Bay may be perched on prime coastal real estate, but by no means is it out of the financial woods. Hotels and restaurants have actually decreased their rates to attract customers, and all things small, authentic, and family owned are leading today's trends. But that's not to say that San Francisco isn't in fine shape. Just a short while ago, the city was too crowded, too successful, too rich, and becoming too ruthless. Today we're more humble, more appreciative and supportive, even more in love with our comfortable, friendly, and provincial city. Tough times have given us a chance to look at where we've come from and to move forward at a more thoughtful and reasonable speed to where we'd like to go. And even during the darkest days we needed only to look at our stunning surroundings to know we are truly blessed.

Index

See also Accommodations and Restaurant indexes, below.

GENERAL INDEX

A
AAA (American Automobile Association), 31, 42–43
Aardvark's, 223
Ab Fits, 216
Accommodations, 64–105.
    See also Accommodations Index
    Berkeley, 248
    best bets, 5–8
    family-friendly, 93
    with free parking, 87
    Napa Valley, 286–294
        Calistoga, 293–294
        Napa, 286–288
        Oakville and
            Rutherford, 290
        St. Helena, 291–293
        Yountville, 288–289
    Oakland, 254–255
    Point Reyes National
        Seashore, 267–268
    pricing categories, 64
    reservations, 65
    Sausalito, 261–262
    Sonoma Valley, 309–314
        Glen Ellen, 313–314
        Kenwood, 314
        Sonoma, 310–312
    surfing for, 24–26
    tipping, 46–47
    what's new in, 1
A Clean, Well-Lighted Place
    for Books, 213
A.C.T. (American Conservatory Theater), 228
Addresses, finding, 49
Adventures Aloft, 189
Airfares
    discounts for international
        visitors, 40
    getting the best, 29–31
    surfing for, 23–24
Airlines, 28
    international, 40–41
Airports, 26–28
Airport security, 28–29
Air travel, 26–31
    around the U.S., 41

Alabaster, 219
A La Carte, A La Park, 16–17
Alamere Falls, 266
Alamo Square Historic
    District, 183–184
Alcatraz Island, 3, 157, 160
Alessi, 219
All American Boy, 216
Alma, 169
American Automobile Association (AAA), 31, 42–43
"American" California, original street of, 196
American Conservatory
    Theater (A.C.T.), 228
American Express, 61
American Rag Cie, 215
The Anchorage, 221
Angel Island, 256–260
Antiques, 209–212
    Napa Valley, 284
Aquarium, Steinhart, 166
Aquarium of the Bay,
    165–166
Aquatic Park, 181, 190
Architectural highlights,
    183–186
Area codes, 61
Arrowood Vineyards & Winery (Glen Ellen), 307
Art galleries, 212–213
Artisan Cheese, 217
Art of China, 217–218
Artspan Open Studios, 17
Asian Art Museum, 166
Atelier Dore, 212
ATMs (automated teller
    machines), 11, 39
Ayala Cove, 258

B
Babes and a Bus, 230
Babushka, 218
Baker Beach, 182, 190
Balclutha, 169
Ballet, 228–229
Ballooning, 189
Bambuddha Lounge,
    234–235
Bank of America, 196

Bank of America World
    Headquarters, 184
Bank of Canton, 196
Barnes & Noble, 213
Bars, 235–240
    destination bars with DJ
        grooves, 234–235
    gay and lesbian, 240–242
    wine and champagne, 240
BART (Bay Area Rapid
    Transit), 58
    to Berkeley, 244
    Excursion Ticket, 187
    to Oakland, 251
Baseball, 193
Basketball, 193
Bay Area Theatresports
    (BATS), 229
Bay Meadows, 194
Bay Model Visitors Center
    (Sausalito), 261
Bay to Breakers Foot Race,
    15, 192
Beach Blanket Babylon,
    207, 229
Beaches, 189–190
Be-At Line, 231
The Beats, 325–326
Beaulieu Vineyard
    (Rutherford), 277
Bed and Breakfast Association of Sonoma Valley, 309
Belden Place, restaurants on,
    119
Benziger Family Winery
    (Glen Ellen), 307
Beringer Vineyards
    (St. Helena), 279
Berkeley, 243–250
    accommodations, 248
    restaurants, 248–250
    sights and attractions,
        244–248
    shopping, 248
    traveling to, 244
Berkeley & Oakland Bed and
    Breakfast Network, 248
Berkeley Convention and
    Visitors Bureau, 246
Berkeley Marina Sports
    Center, 191

Bicycling, 190
    Mount Tamalpais, 264
    Napa Valley, 285
    Sonoma Valley, 306
Biordi Art Imports, 206, 219
Bird-watching, Point Reyes
    Bird Observatory, 266
Birkenstock, 221
Biscuits and Blues, 230–231
The Bliss Bar, 235
Blue & Gold Fleet, 17, 60,
    157, 187, 258, 260
Boathouse, Golden Gate
    Park, 179
Boating, 190. See also
    Kayaking
Boat tours and cruises, 187
    Alcatraz Island, 157, 160
    Oakland, 251
Bonhams & Butterfield, 212
Book Passage, 213
Books, recommended, 32–33
The Booksmith, 213
Bookstores, 213–214
    Berkeley, 244
The Boom Boom Room, 231
Borders, 213
Bottom of the Hill, 231
Boulangerie, 217
Brewpubs, 238
Britex Fabrics, 215
Brooks Brothers, 216
The Bubble Lounge, 240
Bucket shops, 29–30
Buddhist Church of San
    Francisco, 174
Buena Vista Café, 236
Buena Vista Park, 192
Buena Vista Winery
    (Sonoma), 305–306
Buffalo Exchange, 223
Builders Booksource San
    Francisco, 213
Bulo, 221
Business hours, 61
Bus tours, 188
Bus travel, 55
    around the U.S., 42

Cable Car Clothiers, 216
Cable Car Museum, 166
Cable cars, 3, 54–55, 160,
    162
Cabs, 58
The Café, 241
Cafe du Nord, 232–233
Caffè Trieste, 10, 206
California Academy of
    Sciences, 2, 166
California Historical Society,
    171

California Palace of the
    Legion of Honor, 167–168
Calistoga
    accommodations, 293–294
    mud baths and spas,
        285–286
    restaurants, 302–303
    wineries, 280–283
Calistoga Spa Hot Springs,
    286
Calistoga Village Inn & Spa,
    286
Cameron House, 199
The Cannery, 162, 221
Canton Bazaar, 196
The Canton Bazaar, 214
Carnelian Room, 238–239
The Carneros District,
    wineries, 304–305
Carnival, 15
Car rentals, 42, 58–60
Car travel, 31, 58
    around the U.S., 42
Cass Marina, 190
The Castro, 4, 54
    accommodations, 103–104
    restaurants, 151–152
    sights and attractions, 175
Castro Street Fair, 17
Castro Theatre, 175, 242
Catharine Clark Gallery, 212
C. A. Thayer, 169
The Chanel Boutique, 216
Charles Krug Winery
    (St. Helena), 280
Château St. Jean (Kenwood),
    308
Cherry Blossom Festival, 15
Chestnut Street, shopping
    on, 208
Children, families with
    accommodations, 93
    fashions, 217
    information and resources,
        22–23
    sights and attractions, 186
    toys, 222
China Beach, 182, 190
Chinatown, 4, 52
    restaurants, 129–132
    shopping, 208
    sights and attractions,
        172–174
    walking tours
        guided, 188–189
        self-guided, 195–201
Chinatown Gateway Arch,
    195
The Chinatown Kite Shop,
    196, 222
Chinese Culture Center,
    200–201

Chinese Historical Society of
    America Museum, 199
Chinese New Year, 14
Chinese temples, 174
The Cinch Saloon, 241
Cinco de Mayo
    Celebration, 15
Cinemas, 242
Circle Gallery, 184
Citizen Clothing, 216
City Box Office, 224
City Hall, 184
City Lights Booksellers &
    Publishers, 205, 213
Cityscape, 239
City stair climbing, 190–191
Civic Center, 53, 184
    accommodations, 102
    restaurants, 146–148
Classical music, 225
Cliff House, 182
Climate, 13–14
Clos Du Val (Napa), 272
Clos Pegase (Calistoga), 282
Club and music scene,
    230–235
    gay and lesbian, 240–242
Club Deluxe, 235
Club Fugazi, 206–207
Club Line, 231
Coastal Trail, 4, 182
Cobb's Comedy Club, 230
Cody's Books (Berkeley),
    244
Coit Tower, 162
Columbus Ave., No. 140, 204
Columbus Tower, 204
Condor Club, former site of
    the, 205
Consolidators, 29–30
Consulates, 43–44
Copia: The American Center
    for Wine, Food & the Arts
    (Napa), 283–284
Cosentino (Yountville), 274
Cost Plus Imports, 218
Cowell Theater, 228
Cow Hollow, 53
    accommodations, 98–100
    restaurants, 140–146
Crafts, 214
Crate & Barrel Outlet
    (Berkeley), 248
Credit cards, 12, 39
Crissy Field, 4, 182
Crocker Galleria, 221
Cruisin' the Castro, 188
Currency and currency
    exchange, 43
Customs regulations, 36–37

Dance clubs, 233–234
Dance companies, 228–229
Dandelion, 218
Dean & DeLuca (St. Helena), 298
Dentists, 61
Department stores, 214–215
Detour, 241
De Vera Galleries, 220
Dianne's Old & New Estates, 220
Dining, 106–156. *See also* Restaurant Index
    Berkeley, 248–250
    best bets, 9–10
    by cuisine, 107–110
    family-friendly, 130
    multicourse menus, 110
    Napa Valley, 294–303
        Calistoga, 302–303
        Napa, 295–296
        Rutherford, 299–300
        St. Helena, 300–302
        Yountville, 296–299
    Oakland, 255–256
    Point Reyes National Seashore, 268
    pricing categories, 106
    reservations, 107
    Sausalito, 262–263
    Sonoma Valley, 315–319
    Tiburon, 259–260
    tipping, 47
    what's new in, 1–2
Di Rosa Preserve (Napa), 283
Disabilities, travelers with, 20–21
The Disney Store, 222
Distractions & Euphoria, 218
Doctors, 61
Domaine Chandon (Yountville), 273–274
Drinking laws, 43
Driver's licenses, foreign, 35
Driving safety, 40
Drugstores, 61–62
Dr. Wilkinson's Hot Springs (Calistoga), 285
Duckhorn Vineyards (Calistoga), 282–283

Eagle, The, 241
Earthquakes, 62
Edinburgh Castle, 236
Electricity, 43
Eleonore Austerer Gallery, 212
The Embarcadero, 49
Embarcadero Promenade, 192

Embassies and consulates, 43–44
Emergencies, 44, 62
Emily lee, 216
Empire Plush Room, 231
The Endup, 233, 241
Entry requirements, 34–36
Eos, 240
Eppleton Hall, 169
Equinox, 239
Eureka, 169
Eureka Theatre Company, 228
Exotic Erotic Halloween Ball, 18
The Exploratorium, 168

Factory 525, 233
Families with children
    accommodations, 93
    fashions, 217
    information and resources, 22–23
    sights and attractions, 186
    toys, 222
Farmers' Market, 162
Fashions (clothing), 215–217
    vintage, 223
Fax machines, 46
Fern Creek Trail, 263
Ferries, 60–61
    Sausalito, 260
    Tiburon—Angel Island, 258
Ferry Building, 4, 184–185
Ferry Building Marketplace (and Farmers' Market), 2, 162
Filbert Street Steps, 191
The Fillmore, 231
Fillmore Street, shopping on, 209
Fillmore Street Jazz Festival, 16
Film, flying with, 30
Film Festival, San Francisco International, 15, 242
The Financial District, 49, 52
    accommodations, 94–95
    restaurants, 117–121
Fisherman's Wharf, 52
    accommodations, 95–98
    restaurants, 137–140
    shopping, 209
    sights and attractions, 162–165
Fishing, 191
Flax, 218
Fleet Week, 17
Flight 001, 222–223
Flood Mansion, 185

Folsom Street Fair, 17
Food stores and markets, 217
Football, 193–194
Foreign visitors, 34–47
    customs regulations, 36–37
    entry requirements, 34–36
    immigration and customs clearance, 41
    money matters, 38–39
    safety, 39–40
    traveling around the U.S., 41–42
    traveling to the U.S., 40–41
Fort Mason Center, 181
Fort Point, 182
49-mile scenic drive, 186–187
Fourth of July Celebration & Fireworks, 16
Fraenkel Gallery, 212
Frank Family Vineyards (Calistoga), 281
Frequent-flier clubs, 31
Frommers.com, 24
Fumiki Fine Asian Arts, 212

Gardens
    Strybing Arboretum & Botanical Gardens, 179
    The University of California Botanical Garden (Berkeley), 248
Gasoline, 44
Gay and lesbian travelers
    in 1970s and 1980s, 326–328
    bars and clubs, 240–242
    information and resources, 21–22
    special events, 16–18
Geary Theater, 228
Ghirardelli Square, 164, 221–222
Gifts, 217–219
Gimme Shoes, 221
Ginsberg, Allen, 204–205, 325, 326
Glen Ellen
    accommodations, 313–314
    restaurants, 318–319
    wineries, 307
Glide Memorial United Methodist Church, 5, 182–183
Gloria Ferrer Champagne Caves (Sonoma), 305
Golden Era Building, 204
Golden Gate Bridge, 3, 164–165
Golden Gate Fields, 194
Golden Gate Fortune Cookie Company, 198

Golden Gate Fortune Cookies Co., 217
Golden Gate National Recreation Area, 180–182
 walking and hiking, 192–193
Golden Gate Park, 4–5, 176–179
 highlights of, 178–179
 museums inside, 178
 tennis courts, 192
Golden Gate Park Boat House, 190
Golden Gate Park Course, 191
Golden Gate Promenade, 3–4, 181
Golden Haven Hot Springs Spa (Calistoga), 285–286
Golden State Warriors, 193
Golf, 191
Gondola Servizio (Oakland), 251
Good Byes, 223
Good Vibrations, 218
Gordon Biersch Brewery Restaurant, 238
Grace Cathedral, 183
Grant & Green Saloon, 231
Grant Avenue, 195
Gray Line, 188
Great China Herb Co., 198–199
The Great Entertainer, 236
Green Apple Books, 214
Greens Sports Bar, 240
Grgich Hills Cellar (Rutherford), 277
Gucci America, 215
Gump's, 214

Haas-Lilienthal House, 168
Haight-Ashbury, 54, 326
 accommodations, 104
 restaurants, 152–154
 sights and attractions, 175
Haight-Ashbury Flower Power Walking Tour, 188
Haight Street, shopping on, 209
Haight Street Fair, 15–16
Hallidie Building, 184
Halloween, 18
Handball, 191
Hang, 213
Harry Denton's Starlight Room, 234
Harvey Milk Plaza, 175
Hayes and Vine, 240
Hayes Valley, shopping on, 209

Health concerns, 19–20
Health insurance, 19, 38
Heinold's First and Last Chance Saloon (Oakland), 254
Held Over, 223
Hercules, 169
The Hess Collection (Napa), 272
Hiking, in Muir Woods, 263
Holidays, 44
Horseback riding, Napa Valley, 284–285
Horse racing, 194
Hot-air ballooning, 189
Hotels, 64–105. *See also* Accommodations Index
 Berkeley, 248
 best bets, 5–8
 family-friendly, 93
 with free parking, 87
 Napa Valley, 286–294
  Calistoga, 293–294
  Napa, 286–288
  Oakville and Rutherford, 290
  St. Helena, 291–293
  Yountville, 288–289
 Oakland, 254–255
 Point Reyes National Seashore, 267–268
 pricing categories, 64
 reservations, 65
 Sausalito, 261–262
 Sonoma Valley, 309–314
 surfing for, 24–26
 tipping, 46–47
 what's new in, 1
Hot springs, Calistoga, 285–286
Housewares and furnishings, 219–220
hungry i, 205

I Can't Believe I Ate My Way Through Chinatown, 189
Images of the North, 213
Immigration and customs clearance, 41
Ina Coolbrith Park, 192
Indian Springs Resort (Calistoga), 286
Insurance, 18–19
International visitors, 34–47
 customs regulations, 36–37
 entry requirements, 34–36
 immigration and customs clearance, 41
 money matters, 38–39

 safety, 39–40
 traveling around the U.S., 41–42
 traveling to the U.S., 40–41
Internet access, 62
Italian Heritage Parade, 18

Jack London Square (Oakland), 251
Jack's Cannery Bar, 162
Jackson Square
 400 block of, 204
 shopping on, 209, 212
Jade Galore, 199
Japan Center, 174
Japanese Tea Garden, 178–179
Japantown, 53
 accommodations, 100–102
 sights and attractions, 174–175
Javawalk, 188
Jazz
 clubs, 232–233
 Fillmore Street Jazz Festival, 16
 San Francisco Jazz Festival, 18
Jazz at Pearl's, 233
Jeremy's, 215
Jewelry, 220
Jogging paths, 192
Johnson's Oyster Farm, 266
Joseph Phelps Vineyards (St. Helena), 278–279
Joseph Schmidt Confections, 217
Joshua A. Norton's Home, 201
Julie's Supper Club, 234

Kabuki Springs & Spa, 174, 175
Kayaking
 Angel Island, 258
 Point Reyes National Seashore, 266–267
Kenneth Cole, 221
Kenwood
 accommodations, 314
 restaurant, 319
 wineries, 308–309
Kenwood Vineyards, 308
Kids
 accommodations, 93
 fashions, 217
 information and resources, 22–23
 sights and attractions, 186
 toys, 222

Kimo's, 241
Konko Church of San Francisco, 174

Lakeside Park, 251
Lands End, 182
Larkspur, ferries, 60
La Rosa, 223
Lawrence Hall of Science (Berkeley), 244
Layout of San Francisco, 48–49
Legal aid, 44
Limn, 219
Lincoln Park, 182, 192
Lincoln Park Golf Course, 191
Li Po Cocktail Lounge, 236
Liquor laws, 62
Lombard Street, 165
London Wine Bar, 240
Lone Star Saloon, 241
Lorraine Hansberry Theatre, 228
Lost-luggage insurance, 19
Lou's Pier 47 Club, 232
Lyon Street Steps, 191

MAC, 215
McLaren Lodge and Park Headquarters, 178
Macy's, 214
The Magic Theatre, 228
Mail, 44–45
Mail Boxes, Etc. (Sonoma), 281
Main arteries and streets, 49
Marathon, San Francisco, 16
The Marina District, 52–53
  accommodations, 98–100
  restaurants, 140–146
Marina Green, 181
Market Street, 49
Matanzas Creek (Santa Rosa), 309
Matrix Fillmore, 236–237
Medical Dental Building, 184
MedicAlert identification tag, 20
Medical insurance, 19, 38
Medical requirements for entry, 35
Merritt, Lake, 251
Métier, 217
Metreon Entertainment Center, 171
Metro, 241–242
Meyerovich Gallery, 213
M. H. De Young Memorial Museum, 178
Minis, 217

The Mint Karaoke Lounge, 242
Mission Bay Golf Center, 191
Mission District, 53–54
  restaurants, 149–150
  sights and attractions, 176
Mission Dolores, 183
Moe's Books (Berkeley), 244
Molinari Delicatessen, 206
MOMA (San Francisco Museum of Modern Art), 5, 169–170
Money matters, 11–12
  for international visitors, 38–39
The Monkey Club, 235
The Montgomery Block, 202
Montgomery St., No. 1010, 204–205
Movies, 242
Mud baths, 285–286
Muir Woods, 5, 263–264
Mumm Napa Valley (Rutherford), 277
Municipal Boathouse (Oakland), 251
Museum of Modern Art (MOMA), 5, 169–170
Museums, 165–171
  inside Golden Gate Park, 178
MuseumStore, SFMOMA, 170, 218
Music
  classical, 225
  jazz
    clubs, 232–233
    Fillmore Street Jazz Festival, 16
    San Francisco Jazz Festival, 18
  opera, 225, 228
Music stores, 220–221

Nance's Hot Springs (Calistoga), 286
Napa
  accommodations, 286–288
  restaurants, 295–296
  sights and attractions, 283–284
  wineries, 270–273
Napa Premium Outlets, 284
Napa Valley, 269–303
  accommodations, 286–294
    Calistoga, 293–294
    Napa, 286–288
    Oakville and Rutherford, 290
    St. Helena, 291–293
    Yountville, 288–289

restaurants, 294–303
  Calistoga, 302–303
  Napa, 295–296
  Rutherford, 299–300
  St. Helena, 300–302
  Yountville, 296–299
sights and attractions, 283–286
touring the wineries, 270–283
  Calistoga, 280–283
  Napa, 270–273
  Oakville, 274–275
  reservations at, 272
  Rutherford, 275–277
  St. Helena, 277–280
  Yountville, 273–274
traveling to, 270
visitor information, 270
Napa Valley Olive Oil Manufacturing Company (Napa), 284
Natural History Museum, 167
Neighborhoods, 49, 52–54
  sights and attractions in, 171–176
Neiman Marcus, 214–215
Nest, 219
Newspapers and magazines, 62
The New Unique Company, 214
Nickie's Bar-be-cue, 233
Niebaum-Coppola (Rutherford), 276–277
Nightlife and entertainment, 224–242
  bar scene, 235–240
    destination bars with DJ grooves, 234–235
    gay and lesbian, 240–242
    wine and champagne, 240
  club and music scene, 230–235
  comedy and cabaret, 229–230
  current listings, 224
  Napa Valley, 285
  performing arts, 225–229
Nihonmachi Mall, 174
Niketown, 215–216
Nob Hill, 52
  accommodations, 83–87
  restaurants, 127–129
  sights and attractions, 172
Nordstrom, 215
North Beach, 52
  accommodations, 95–98
  cafes, 4

restaurants, 132–137
sights and attractions, 172
walking tour, 202–207
North Beach Festival, 16
North Beach Museum, 206
Norton, Joshua A., Home,
201
The Nutcracker, 18, 229

Oakland, 250–256
Oakland Athletics, 193
Oakland Convention and
Visitors Bureau, 251
Oakland International
Airport, 27–28
Oakland Museum of
California, 254
Oakland Raiders, 194
Oakville Grocery Co., 298
Oakville
accommodations, 290
wineries, 274–275
Ocean Beach, 190
Ocean View Trail, 263
Octagon House, 168–169
ODC Theatre, 228
Old Faithful Geyser of Cali-
fornia, 286
Old St. Mary's Cathedral, 196
On the Road Again, 223
Opera, 225, 228
Opera in the Park, 17
Opus One (Oakville), 275
Original TransAmerica
Building, 202, 204
Outdoor activities, 189–193

Pacific Heights, 53
accommodations, 98–100
restaurants, 140–146
Package tours, 31–32
Painted Ladies, 183–184
Palace of Fine Arts, 168
Pampanito, USS, 163
Paradise Lounge, 233
Paramount Theatre
(Oakland), 251
Parking, 60
Parks, 192
Berkeley, 246, 248
Passport information, 35–36
Peace Pagoda, 174
Pearl & Jade Empire, 220
People's Park (Berkeley), 246
Performing arts, 225–229
Perimeter Road (Angel
Island), 258
Perry's, 237
Petrified Forest, 286
Petrol, 44

Philharmonia Baroque
Orchestra, 225
Picnic fare, Napa Valley, 298
Pied Piper Bar, 237
PIER 39, 165, 222
Pier 23, 232
Pine Ridge Winery (Napa),
273
PlumpJack Winery (Oakville),
274–275
Pocket Opera, 225
Point Lobos, 182
Point Reyes, 5
Point Reyes Bird
Observatory, 266
Point Reyes Lighthouse, 265
Point Reyes National
Seashore, 264–268
Police, 62
Portsmouth Square, 200
Post offices, 63
Prager Winery & Port Works
(St. Helena), 278
Precita Eyes Mural Arts
Center, 176
Prescription medications, 20
The Presidio, 179–180
Presidio Golf Course, 191
Propeller, 219
Punch Line Comedy Club, 230

Rainfall, average, 14
Rand McNally Maps &
Books, 223
Rasselas, 233
Ravenswood Winery
(Sonoma), 306–307
Recycled Records, 220
Red & White Fleet, 187, 264
Red Hen Antiques (Napa),
284
The Red Room, 237
Red Vic, 242
The Redwood Room, 237
Reggae in the Park, 17–18
Religious buildings, 182–183
Renaissance Pleasure
Faire, 17
Restaurants, 106–156. *See
also* Restaurant Index
Berkeley, 248–250
best bets, 9–10
by cuisine, 107–110
family-friendly, 130
multicourse menus, 110
Napa Valley, 294–303
Calistoga, 302–303
Napa, 295–296
Rutherford, 299–300
St. Helena, 300–302
Yountville, 296–299

Oakland, 255–256
Point Reyes National
Seashore, 268
pricing categories, 106
reservations, 107
Sausalito, 262–263
Sonoma Valley, 315–319
Tiburon, 259–260
tipping, 47
what's new in, 1–2
Restrooms, 47
Richmond and Sunset
districts, 54
Richmond/Sunset Districts,
restaurants, 154–156
Rincon Center, 185
Ripley's Believe It or Not!
Museum, 163
Robert Keenan Winery
(St. Helena), 279
Robert Mondavi Winery
(Oakville), 275
Rock and blues clubs,
230–232
Roman Spa Motel
(Calistoga), 286
Rose Garden (Berkeley), 248
Ross Alley, 198
Roxie, 242
Ruby Skye, 234
Running, 192
Russian Hill, 52
restaurants, 127–129
Rutherford
accommodations, 290
restaurants, 299–300
wineries, 275–277

Safety, 20, 39–40
for foreign visitors, 63
St. Francis Winery (Kenwood),
308–309
St. Helena
accommodations, 291–293
restaurants, 300–302
shopping, 284
wineries, 277–280
St. Helena Mailing Center,
281
St. Helena Premier Outlets,
284
St. Mary's Square, 196
St. Patrick's Day Parade, 14
Saints Peter and Paul
Church, 207
St. Supéry Winery
(Rutherford), 276
The Saloon, 232
San Francisco 49ers, 193
San Francisco Ballet,
18, 228–229

San Francisco Blues Festival, 17
San Francisco Brewing Company, 238
San Francisco Chronicle, 224, 232
San Francisco Convention and Visitors Bureau, 11
The San Francisco Gallery Guide, 212
San Francisco Giants, 193
San Francisco International Airport, 26–27
    accommodations near, 105
San Francisco International Film Festival, 15, 242
San Francisco Jazz Festival, 18
San Francisco Lesbian, Gay, Bisexual, Transgender Pride Parade & Celebration, 16
San Francisco Marathon, 16
San Francisco Maritime National Historical Park, 169
San Francisco Municipal Railway (Muni), 54
San Francisco Museum of Modern Art (MOMA), 5, 169–170
San Francisco—Oakland Bay Bridge, 185–186
San Francisco Opera, 225, 228
San Francisco Performances, 225
San Francisco Reservations, 65
San Francisco Shopping Centre, 222
San Francisco Sightseeing, 243
San Francisco Symphony, 225
San Francisco Visitor Information Center, 48
San Francisco Weekly, 224
San Francisco Zoo (& Children's Zoo), 2, 170
Santa Rosa, 309
Sausalito, 2, 260–263
    ferries, 60
Sausalito Art Festival, 17
Sawyer Cellars (Rutherford), 276
SBC Park, 193
Scharffen Berger Chocolate Maker (Berkeley), 249
Schramsberg (Calistoga), 282

Sea kayaking
    Angel Island, 258
    Point Reyes National Seashore, 266–267
Seasons, 12–13
Sebastiani Vineyards & Winery (Sonoma), 306
Senior travel, 22
SFMOMA MuseumStore, 170, 218
Shipping purchases, 209
    wines, 280–281
Shoes, 221
Shopping, 5, 208–223
    Berkeley, 248
    major shopping areas, 208–209
    Napa Valley, 284
    sales tax, 209
    shipping purchases, 209
    store hours, 209
Shopping centers and complexes, 221–222
Sights and attractions, 157–189
    architectural highlights, 183–186
    for kids, 186
    museums, 165–171
    Napa Valley, 283–286
    in neighborhoods, 171–176
    religious buildings, 182–183
    self-guided and organized tours, 186–189
    what's new in, 2
Sigmund Stern Grove, 192
Silkroute International, 214
Silverado Trail, 273
Silver Oak Cellars (Oakville), 274
Skates on Haight, 192
Skating, 192
Slim's, 232
Smile, 219
Smoking, 63
Sokoji-Soto Zen Buddhist Temple, 174
SoMA (South of Market), 53
    accommodations, 87–94
    restaurants, 121–127
    shopping on, 209
    sights and attractions, 172
Sonoma
    accommodations, 310–312
    restaurants, 315–318
    wineries, 305–307
Sonoma Mission Inn, Spa & Country Club, 312

Sonoma Valley, 303–319
    accommodations, 309–314
        Glen Ellen, 313–314
        Kenwood, 314
        Sonoma, 310–312
    restaurants, 315–319
    touring the wineries, 303–309
    traveling to, 303
    visitor information, 303
Sonoma Valley Visitors Bureau, 309
Spa Radiance, 175
Spas, 175
    Napa Valley, 285–286
    Sonoma, 312
Spec's, 237
Spec's Adler Museum Café, 206
Spectator sports, 193–194
Spreckels Mansion, 185
Stag's Leap Wine Cellars (Napa), 273
Stair climbing, 190–191
STA Travel, 30
Steinhart Aquarium, 166
Sterling Vineyards (Calistoga), 282
Stern Grove Midsummer Music Festival, 16
Stinson Beach, 5
Stockton Street, 174, 199
Stow Lake, 179, 190
Strawberry Hill, 179
Streetcars, 55, 58
Streetlight Records, 220–221
Strybing Arboretum & Botanical Gardens, 179
The Stud, 242
Sue Fisher King, 219
Supper clubs, 234
Sur La Table, 219
Sutro Baths, 182
Swanson Vineyards & Winery (Rutherford), 275–276
Sweeney Ridge, 182

Tamalpais, Mount, 264
Taxes, 45, 63
Taxis, 58
Teatro ZinZanni, 229
Telegraph and telex services, 46
Telegraph Avenue (Berkeley), 244
Telegraph Hill restaurants, 132–137
Telephone, 45–46
Telephone directories, 46
Temperatures, average, 14

Ten 15, 234
Tennis, 192
Ten Ren Tea Co., Ltd., 198, 217
Theater, 228
Theatre Rhinoceros, 228
Therien & Co., 212
ThirstyBear Brewing Company, 238
Three Bags Full, 216
Tiburon, 256, 258, 259
Ticketmaster, 224
Tickets.com, 224
Tiffany & Co., 220
Tilden Park (Berkeley), 246
Time zones, 46, 63
Tin How Temple, 200
Tipping, 46–47
Tix Bay Area, 224
Toilets, 47
Tomales Point Trail, 266
The Tonga Room & Hurricane Bar, 237
Top of the Mark, 239–240
Toronado, 237–238
Tosca, 238
Tours, 186–189. See also Boat tours and cruises
    Angel Island, 258
    bus, 188
    package, 31–32
    walking
        guided, 188–189
        self-guided, 195–207
Toys, 222
Train travel, 31
    around the U.S., 41–42
TransAmerica Building, Original, 202, 204
TransAmerica Pyramid, 184, 202
Transit information, 63
Transportation, 54–61
    BART (Bay Area Rapid Transit), 58
    bus, 55
    cable cars, 54–55
    discount passes, 55
    ferries, 60–61
    streetcars, 55, 58
    taxis, 58
Traveler's checks, 11–12, 38–39
Travel goods, 222–223
Travel insurance, 18–19
Trefethen Vineyards (Napa), 272
Trip-cancellation insurance, 18–19
Twin Peaks, 193
Twin Peaks Tavern, 242

UC Berkeley Art Museum, 246
Union Square, 49
    accommodations, 65–83
    restaurants, 111–117
    shopping, 208
Union Street, shopping on, 208
Union Street Art Festival, 15
Union Street Goldsmith, 220
University of California at Berkeley, 244, 246
The University of California Botanical Garden (Berkeley), 248
University of California Golden Bears, 194
The UPS Store (Napa Valley), 281

Vanderbilt and Company (St. Helena), 284
Van Ness Avenue, 49
Vesuvio, 205–206, 238
Viansa Winery and Italian Marketplace (Sonoma), 304–305
Victorian Homes Historical Walking Tour, 189
Video, flying with, 30
Vintage clothing, 223
Virgin Megastore, 221
Visitor information, 11, 48
Visitor Information Center (Berkeley), 244
V. Sattui Winery (St. Helena), 278

Walk & Wok tour, 189
Walking and hiking, 192–193
Walking tours
    guided, 188–189
    self-guided, 195–207
        Chinatown, 195–201
        Napa, 283
        North Beach, 202–207
Washington Square, 207
Waverly Place, 200
Wax Museum, 163
Weather, 12–14
Websites, 11
    traveler's toolbox, 25
    travel-planning and booking, 23–26
Wells Fargo History Museum, 171
Whale-watching, 265

Where, 224
Wilkes Bashford, 216
William Stout Architectural Books, 214
Windsor Vineyards (Tiburon), 258–259
Wine Club San Francisco, 223
Wine Country, 269–319. See also Napa Valley; Sonoma Valley
    what's new in, 2
Wine Exchange of Sonoma, 281
Wineries
    Napa Valley, 270–283
        Calistoga, 280–283
        Napa, 270–273
        Oakville, 274–275
        reservations at, 272
        Rutherford, 275–277
        St. Helena, 277–280
        Yountville, 273–274
    Sonoma Valley, 303–309
Wines, shipping, 280
Wine stores, 223
Wish Bar, 235
The Wok Shop, 196, 220
Wok Wiz Chinatown Walking Tours & Cooking Center, 188–189

Yerba Buena Center for the Arts/Yerba Buena Gardens, 171
Yountville
    accommodations, 288–289
    restaurants, 296–299
    wineries, 273–274

Zeum, 171
Zinc Details, 220

ACCOMMODATIONS

Alisa Hotel, 78
The Andrews Hotel, 78
The Archbishop's Mansion, 5, 100–101
The Argent Hotel, 87
Argonaut Hotel, 93, 96
Auberge du Soleil (Rutherford), 290
Beck's Motor Lodge, 87, 103
Beltane Ranch (Glen Ellen), 313
Best Western Sonoma Valley Inn (Sonoma), 311
Best Western Tuscan Inn at Fisherman's Wharf, 95–96

Bistro Jeanty (Yountville), 297–298

Black Bear Diner (Sonoma), 317

Bouchon (Yountville), 298–299

Calistoga Spa Hot Springs, 294

Campton Place Hotel, 8, 65–66

The Cartwright Hotel, 78–79

Casa Madrona (Sausalito), 261–262

The Castillo Inn, 103

Cedar Gables Inn (Napa), 287

Chablis Inn (Napa), 288

Christopher's Inn (Calistoga), 293

The Claremont Resort & Spa (Berkeley), 248, 255

Clift Hotel, 8, 66

Comfort Suites, 93, 105

The Commodore Hotel, 73

The Cornell Hotel de France, 79

Cottage Grove Inn (Calistoga), 293

Cow Hollow Motor Inn & Suites, 87, 93, 99–100

Deer Run Inn (St. Helena), 291–292

Della Santina's (Sonoma), 318

The Donatello, 66, 68

Dr. Wilkinson's Hot Springs Resort (Calistoga), 294

Edward II Inn & Suites, 100

El Bonita Motel (St. Helena), 292

El Dorado Hotel (Sonoma), 311

Embassy Suites (Napa), 286–287

Embassy Suites (San Francisco), 105

Euro Spa & Inn (Calistoga), 293

The Fairmont Hotel & Tower, 6, 83–84

Fairmont Sonoma Mission Inn & Spa, 310

The Fitzgerald, 79

Four Seasons Hotel San Francisco, 6–8, 87, 90

The French Laundry (Yountville), 296–297

Gaige House Inn (Glen Ellen), 313

The Girl & The Fig (Sonoma), 315

Glenelly Inn (Glen Ellen), 314

The Golden Gate Hotel, 79–80

Grand Hyatt San Francisco, 68

Grant Plaza Hotel, 80

Handlery Union Square Hotel, 70, 93

The Harbor Court, 90

Harmony Club (Sonoma), 315–316

Hilton San Francisco, 70–71

Holiday Inn, 73

Hostelling International San Francisco—Downtown, 80

Hostelling International San Francisco—Fisherman's Wharf, 87, 100

Hotel Adagio, 73–74

Hotel Beresford, 80–81

Hotel Beresford Arms, 81

Hotel Bijou, 81

The Hotel Bohème, 5, 96–97

Hotel Del Sol, 93, 98–99

Hotel Diva, 74

Hotel Drisco, 98

The Hotel Griffon, 90–91

Hotel Halcyon, 82

The Hotel Majestic, 5, 102

Hotel Milano, 71

Hotel Monaco, 68

Hotel Palomar, 91

Hotel Rex, 71

Hotel Triton, 74

Hotel Vintage Court, 75

The Huntington Hotel, 6, 84

Hyatt Regency San Francisco, 95

The Inn Above Tide (Sausalito), 261

The Inn at Southbridge (St. Helena), 291

The Inn at Union Square, 75

Inn on Castro, 103–104

Inns of Marin (Point Reyes Station), 267

InterContinental Mark Hopkins, 84–85

Jackson Court, 99

Joie de Vivre, 73

The Juliana Hotel, 75–76

The Kensington Park Hotel, 76

Kenwood Inn & Spa, 314

King George Hotel, 82

La Poste (Sonoma), 316

Laurel Inn, 7, 87, 99

MacArthur Place (Sonoma), 310–311

Maison Fleurie (Yountville), 289

The Mandarin Oriental, 8, 94

Manka's Inverness Lodge & Restaurant, 267

Marina Inn, 7, 100

The Maxwell Hotel, 71–72, 93

Meadowood Napa Valley (St. Helena), 291

Meritage (Sonoma), 316

Milliken Creek Inn (Napa), 287

The Monticello Inn, 76

The Mosser, 92–94

Motel Inverness, 267–268

Mustards Grill (Yountville), 299

Napa River Inn (Napa), 287–288

Napa Valley Lodge (Yountville), 288–289

Napa Valley Marriott (Napa), 287

Napa Valley Railway Inn (Yountville), 289

The Nob Hill Inn, 86

Nob Hill Lambourne, 86

Oakland Marriott City Center, 254–255

The Palace Hotel, 5, 91

Pan Pacific San Francisco, 1, 68–69

The Parker Guest House, 103

The Park Hyatt San Francisco, 94–95

Personality Hotels, 73

Petite Auberge, 76–77

The Phoenix Hotel, 8, 87, 93, 102

Prescott Hotel, 69

The Queen Anne Hotel, 101–102

Radisson Miyako Hotel, 101

Rancho Caymus Inn (Rutherford), 290

Renoir Hotel, 82–83

Rin's Thai (Sonoma), 318

The Ritz-Carlton, 6, 8, 85

San Francisco Airport North Travelodge, 93, 105

San Francisco Marriott, 1, 92

The San Remo Hotel, 7, 97–98

The Savoy Hotel, 8, 83

Seal Rock Inn, 94

Serrano Hotel, 77

The Sheehan Hotel, 83

Sheraton Fisherman's Wharf Hotel, 96

Silver Rose Inn & Spa (Calistoga), 294

Sir Francis Drake, 72

Sonoma Hotel, 311–312

Sonoma Saveurs, 316–317
Stanford Court, A Renaissance Hotel, 85–86
Stanyan Park Hotel, 93, 104
Swiss Hotel (Sonoma), 317
24 Henry, 104
Union Street Inn, 8, 98
Victorian Garden Inn (Sonoma), 312
Villa Florence, 77
Vintage Inn (Yountville), 289
The Warwick Regis, 8, 77–78
The Washington Square Inn, 97
Waterfront Plaza Hotel (Oakland), 254
Westin St. Francis, 5, 69–70, 93
The Wharf Inn, 87, 97
White Sulphur Springs Retreat & Spa (St. Helena), 285, 292–293
White Swan Inn, 7, 73
The Willows Inn, 104
Wine Country Inn (St. Helena), 292
Wine Valley Lodge (Napa), 288
W San Francisco Hotel, 8, 92
York Hotel, 83

RESTAURANTS

AA Bakery & Café, 199
Absinthe, 9, 147
Ace Wasabi's Rock 'n' Roll Sushi, 142
Alexis Baking Company (Napa), 295–296
Alioto's, 138–139
All Seasons Café (Calistoga), 302
Ana Mandara, 139
Andalé Taqueria, 130, 144
Angèle (Napa), 295
Aqua, 9, 117
A. Sabella's, 137
AsiaSF, 126
A16, 1, 141–142
Auberge du Soleil (Rutherford), 299–300
Aziza, 154
bacar, 121, 124
Bay Wolf (Oakland), 256
Beach Chalet Brewery & Restaurant, 130, 154–155
B44, 119
Bistro Don Giovanni (Napa), 295
Bix, 132
Bouchon Bakery, 2, 299

Boulevard, 9, 124
Brandy Ho's Hunan Food, 129, 130
Cafe Bastille, 119
Café Claude, 115
Cafe Kati, 141
Cafe La Haye (Sonoma), 315
Cafe Pescatore, 139–140
Cafe Rouge (Berkeley), 249–250
Cafe Tiramisu, 119
Caffè Greco, 239
Caffé Luna Piena, 151
Caffè Macaroni, 134
Caffé Museo, 170
Caffè Sport, 132
Caffè Trieste, 239
Capp's Corner, 134–135
Cha Cha Cha, 9, 153
Charles Nob Hill, 9, 127
Chez Nous, 144–145
Chez Panisse (Berkeley), 249
Chow, 151–152
Citron (Oakland), 255
Cliff House, 130, 155
A Côté (Oakland), 255–256
Delfina, 10, 149–150
Dining Room, 2
Dottie's True Blue Café, 115–116, 130
E'Angelo Restaurant, 145
Ebisu, 155
The Elite Café, 142
Eliza's, 130, 145
Ella's, 10, 130, 142
Emporio Armani Cafe, 116
Enrico's, 133
Eos Restaurant & Wine Bar, 152–153
Farallon, 9, 111
Fifth Floor Restaurant, 124
the fig café & wine bar (Glen Ellen), 318
Firewood Café, 152
Fleur de Lys, 9, 111
Florio, 142
Fog City Diner, 133
Forbes Island, 137–138
Foreign Cinema, 149
Frjtz Fries, 140
Glen Ellen Inn Restaurant, 318–319
The Golden Turtle, 128–129
The Gold Spike, 135
Gordon Biersch Brewery Restaurant, 125
Gourmet Delight B.B.Q., 199
Grand Café, 9, 112, 114
Greens Restaurant, 10, 143
Guaymas (Tiburon), 259
Guernica (Sausalito), 262

Hamburgers (Sausalito), 263
Harbor Village, 117–118
Hard Rock Cafe, 130, 140
Harris', 140
Hayes Street Grill, 147
House of Dim Sum, 198
House of Nanking, 129
House of Prime Rib, 128
Il Pollaio, 135
Isa, 143
Jardinière, 146
Kabuto A&S, 155–156
Kenwood Restaurant & Bar, 319
Khan Toke Thai House, 156
Kokkari, 120
Kuleto's, 114
Kyo-Ya, 118
La Folie, 127–128
La Méditerranée, 145
La Toque (Rutherford), 300
Le Colonial, 114
Long Life Noodle Company & Jook Joint, 126
L'Osteria del Forno, 135
The Mandarin, 139
Manora's, 126
Mario's Bohemian Cigar Store, 10, 135–136, 207
Market (St. Helena), 301
Masa's, 112
Maykedah, 133
Mecca, 151
Mel's Diner, 130, 145–146
Millennium, 114–115
Mocca, 116
MoMo's, 125
Moose's, 132–133
Mo's Gourmet Burgers, 130, 136
O Chamé (Berkeley), 250
Oliveto Cafe & Restaurant (Oakland), 255
One Market, 118
O'Reilly's Irish Pub, 207
Palisades Market (Calistoga), 302
Pane e Vino, 130, 143–144
Park Chalet, 155
Park Chow, 152
Pasta Pomodoro, 9–10, 130, 136
Pauline's, 150
Pho Hoa, 116
Piperade, 9, 133–134
Pizzeria Tra Vigne (St. Helena), 301–302
Plouf, 119
PlumpJack Café, 144
Pluto's, 146
Poggio (Sausalito), 262

Postrio, 112
Quince, 1, 141
The Ramp, 148
R&G Lounge, 129, 132
Restaurant Gary Danko, 138
Rivoli (Berkeley), 250
RNM, 153
Roxanne's (Larkspur), 259
Rubicon, 9, 117
Sam's Anchor Café (Tiburon), 259–260
Sam's Grill & Seafood Restaurant, 120
San Francisco Art Institute Café, 136–137
Sanraku Japanese Restaurant, 116–117
Scala's Bistro, 115
Scoma's, 138
The Slanted Door, 1, 118–119
Station House Café (Point Reyes Station), 268
The Stinking Rose, 134

Straits Café, 156
Sushi Ran (Sausalito), 262–263
Swan Oyster Depot, 128
Sweet Heat, 153–154
Tablespoon, 1, 128
Tadich Grill, 121
Taqueria La Quinta (Point Reyes Station), 268
Taquerias La Cumbre, 150
Taylor's Automatic Refresher (St. Helena), 302
Terra (St. Helena), 300
Terrace Restaurant, 10, 85
Thanh Long, 148
Thep Phanom, 154
Ti Couz, 150
Tomasso's, 130
Tommaso's, 9, 137
Tommy Toy's, 119
Ton Kiang, 10, 130, 156
Town Hall, 1, 125

Tra Vigne Restaurant (St. Helena), 300–301
Tú Lan, 126–127
2223 Restaurant & Bar, 151
Universal Café, 149
Villa Corona (Napa), 296
Wappo Bar & Bistro (Calistoga), 303
Washington Bakery & Restaurant, 198
The Waterfront Restaurant, 120
Wine Spectator Greystone Restaurant (St. Helena), 301
Wolf House (Glen Ellen), 319
Yank Sing, 121
Yoshi's World Class Jazz House & Japanese Restaurant (Oakland), 254
Zuni Café, 147–148
ZuZu (Napa), 296

Preserve and share your travel memories — FREE!

One vacation, multiple destinations and hundreds of photos…You've captured the moments, but now what? Upload your digital photos or get your film developed and scanned into an online account at Snapfish. It's the easy way to print, store and share your photos with friends and family all over the world. And, your satisfaction is 110% guaranteed!

Great Trips Like Great Days Begin with a Plan

FranklinCovey and Frommer's Bring You *Frommer's Favorite Places*® Planner

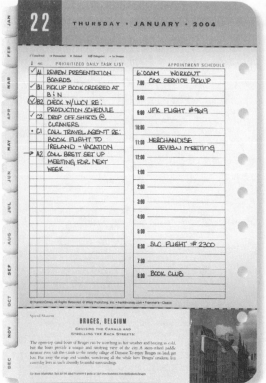

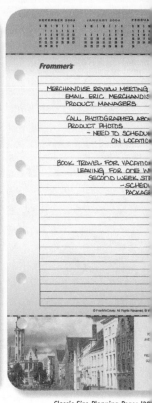

JAN | FEB | MAR | APR | MAY | JUN | JUL | AUG | SEP | OCT | NOV | DEC

22 THURSDAY · JANUARY · 2004

PRIORITIZED DAILY TASK LIST

APPOINTMENT SCHEDULE

✓ A1 REVIEW PRESENTATION BOARDS
✓ B1 PICK UP BOOK ORDERED AT B & N
✓ B2 CHECK W/LUCY RE: PRODUCTION SCHEDULE
✓ C2 DROP OFF SHIRTS @ CLEANERS
• C1 CALL TRAVEL AGENT RE: BOOK FLIGHT TO IRELAND - VACATION
→ A2 CALL BRETT SET UP MEETING FOR NEXT WEEK

6:00AM WORKOUT
7:00 CAR SERVICE PICKUP
8:00
9:00 JFK FLIGHT #9619
10:00
11:00 MERCHANDISE REVIEW MEETING
12:00
1:00
2:00
3:00
4:00
5:00
6:00 SLC FLIGHT #2300
7:00
8:00 BOOK CLUB

Frommer's

MERCHANDISE REVIEW MEETING
EMAIL ERIC MERCHANDISE PRODUCT MANAGERS

CALL PHOTOGRAPHER ABO
PRODUCT PHOTOS
— NEED TO SCHEDU
ON LOCATION

BOOK TRAVEL FOR VACATION
LEAVING FOR ONE W
SECOND WEEK STI
— SCHEDU
PACKAG

BRUGES, BELGIUM
CRUISING THE CANALS AND
STROLLING THE BACK STREETS:

The open-top canal boats of Bruges can be scorching in hot weather and bracing in cold, but the boats provide a unique and unifying view of the city. A stern-wheel paddle steamer even sails the canals to the nearby village of Damme. To enjoy Bruges on land, get lost. Far away the map and wander, wondering all the while how Bruges' residents live everyday lives in such a beautiful surrounding.

Classic Size Planning Pages $39

The planning experts at FranklinCovey have teamed up with the travel experts at Frommer's. The result is a full-year travel-themed planner filled with rich images and travel tips covering fifty-two of Frommer's Favorite Places.

- Each week will make you an expert about an intriguing corner of the world
- New facts and tips every day
- Beautiful, full-color photos of some of the most beautiful places on earth
- Proven planning tools from FranklinCovey for keeping track of tasks, appointments, notes, address/phone numbers, and more

Save 15%

when you purchase Frommer's Favor Places travel-themed planner and a binder.

Order today before yo next big trip.

www.franklincovey.com/frommers
Enter promo code 12252 at checkout for discount. Offer expires June 1, 2005

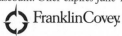

FranklinCovey.

Frommer's is a trademark of Arthur Frommer.

avel Tip: He who finds the best hotel deal has more to spend on facials involving knobbly vegetables.

Hello, the Roaming Gnome here. I've been nabbed from the garden and taken round the world. The people who took me are so terribly clever. They find the best offerings on Travelocity. For very little cha-ching. And that means I get to be pampered and exfoliated till I'm pink as a bunny's doodah.

travelocity

88-TRAVELOCITY / travelocity.com / America Online Keyword: Travel

Travel Tip: Make sure there's customer service
for any change of plans – involving
friendly natives, for example.

One can plan and plan, but if you don't book with the
right people you can't seize le moment and canoodle
with the poodle named Pansy. I, for one, am all for
fraternizing with the locals. Better yet, if I need to
extend my stay and my gnome nappers are willing, it
can all be arranged through the 800 number at, oh look,
how convenient, the lovely company coat of arms.

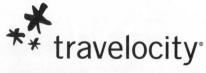

Travel Tip: He who finds the best hotel deal has more to spend on facials involving knobbly vegetables.

Hello, the Roaming Gnome here. I've been nabbed from the garden and taken round the world. The people who took me are so terribly clever. They find the best offerings on Travelocity. For very little cha-ching. And that means I get to be pampered and exfoliated till I'm pink as a bunny's doodah.

travelocity®

-888-TRAVELOCITY / travelocity.com / America Online Keyword: Travel